Additional Books by the Editor

The First Session in Brief Therapy, 1992,
with S. H. Budman and S. Friedman

Constructive Therapies, 1994

Brief Therapy and Managed Care:
Readings for Contemporary Practice, 1995

Constructive Therapies, Volume 2, 1996

The Handbook of Constructive Therapies

Innovative Approaches from Leading Practitioners

Michael F. Hoyt, Editor

Foreword by Kenneth J. Gergen

Jossey-Bass Publishers
San Francisco

Jossey-Bass books and products are available through most
bookstores. To contact Jossey-Bass directly, call (888)378–2537,
fax to (800)605–2665, or visit our website at
www.josseybass.com.

Substantial discounts on bulk quantities of Jossey-Bass books
are available to corporations, professional associations, and
other organizations. For details and discount information,
contact the special sales department at Jossey-Bass.

For sales outside the United States, please contact your local
Simon & Schuster International Office.

TCF Manufactured in the United States of America
on Lyons Falls Turin Book. This paper is acid-free
and 100 percent totally chlorine-free.

Library of Congress Cataloging-in-Publication Data
The handbook of constructive therapies : innovative approaches
from leading practitioners / Michael F. Hoyt, editor : foreword by
Kenneth J. Gergen. — 1st ed.
p.   cm.
Includes bibliographical references and index.
ISBN 0-7879-4044-5
1. Psychotherapy.   2. Constructivism (Psychology)
3. Postmodernism—Psychological aspects.   I. Hoyt, Michael F.
RC480.5.H2755   1998
616.89'14—dc21   98-6859

FIRST EDITION
HC Printing
10 9 8 7 6 5 4 3 2 1

I am the poet of the Body and I am the poet of the Soul,
The pleasures of heaven are with me and the pains of hell are with me,
The first I graft and increase upon myself, the latter I translate into a new tongue.

—WALT WHITMAN

Among the truths you will do well to contemplate most frequently
are these two: First, that things can never touch the soul, but stand inert
outside it, so that disquiet can arise only from fancies within; and secondly,
that all visible objects change in a moment, and will be no more. Think of
the countless changes in which you yourself have had a part. The whole universe
is change, and life itself is but what you deem it.

—MARCUS AURELIUS

A theory is not built on observation. In fact, the opposite is true.
What we observe follows from our theory.

—ALBERT EINSTEIN

A life is not important except in the impact it has on others' lives.

—JACKIE ROBINSON

All the world's a stage,
And all the men and women merely players.

—WILLIAM SHAKESPEARE

O chestnut-tree, great-rooted blossomer
Are you the leaf, the blossom or the bole?
O body swayed to music, O brightening glance,
How can we know the dancer from the dance?

—W. B. YEATS

We must rapidly begin to shift from a thing-oriented society to a
person-oriented society. When machinery and computers, profit motives
and property rights are considered more important than people, the giant triplets
of racism, materialism, and militarism are incapable of being conquered.

—MARTIN LUTHER KING JR.

To my next client

CONTENTS

FOREWORD

It is a singular pleasure to welcome the first *Handbook of Constructive Therapies* into existence. A volume on the construction of meaning, its very existence is itself a vital entry into our contemporary dialogues. These are dialogues on contemporary culture, on the character of therapy, and ultimately on what it is to be a human being. Because they are too often overlooked in our professional deliberations, I wish first to comment on the cultural implications of the present work. The therapeutic movement has been, and continues to be, a vital force within the culture. For almost a century it has played a pivotal role in determining how and what it is we define as problematic in our lives, and how it is we might respond to these determinations. And from Freud to the present the mental health profession has been a continuous source of challenge to the culture, questioning the conventions, fashioning catalytic metaphors of understanding, and generating encampments for alternatives. In this respect, I see the present volume as signifying a shift of profound significance, for it is the first handbook to mark the passing of cultural modernism in the domain of the therapeutic. Or to put it otherwise, it substantially restores the vitality of the therapeutic profession in its role as cultural catalyst.

To take but one illustration, the present volume forms an implicit commentary on the waning of concepts pivotal to the age of modernism: truth, objectivity, rationality, and moral principle. All too often we have found that such concepts have functioned to impede the flow of cultural conversation. Too often they have been used to delimit the nature of our expressions, to separate those allowed to participate in determining our collective future from those who are silenced, and ultimately to create self-rationalizing hierarchies of privilege. In contrast, the pages of the present volume are teeming with practices and examples that demonstrate the possibility of bracketing these traditional concepts in the service of achieving dialogue without division. For most of these authors there is no word, no image, or metaphor that should command another's silence, nor conversely, be placed out of conversational bounds. As amplified in these offerings, we must recognize and grapple with intelligibilities of all forms and varieties, for it is in the to and fro of the ensuing interchange that our best hopes for the future may be located. Thus, with the waning of the modernist faith in a "single great ordering" we find here the emergence of an alternative vision, one emphasizing at once the value of diversity and the simultaneous need for coordinating forms of communication. Whether on the level of individual life, the family, the community, or global relationships, our hope lies in the "con-joint" construction of the real and the good.

In similar respects, the present volume functions as a significant marker in contemporary dialogues on therapeutic process. For until recently, the therapeutic community itself has largely played the game of cultural modernism; such concepts as truth, objectivity, and rationality have long been central to its intelligibility. It is also owing to its alliance with cultural modernism that the profession's conceptions of *mental health* have subtly defined the nature of moral being within the culture more generally. Thus we have created a professional tradition in which claims are made to objective and value-free knowledge of minds, relationships, disease and dysfunction, and in which there is a continuing race to establish the most efficacious treatment. However, as Michael Hoyt effectively elaborates in his Introduction, recent decades of constructive inquiry have raised serious question with the modernist legacy. What one calls knowledge is inevitably wedded to a particular framework of understanding or forestructure of meaning. And these forms of meaning are inevitably embedded within relationships in which certain ends are valued over others, in which values, ideology, and politics are inherent. It is we in the professions who have created these realities, just as it is in the therapeutic relationship that we work with clients to fashion life-determining realities.

The fruits of this radical re-visioning are everywhere apparent in the present work. While these chapters will largely speak for themselves in this regard, I wish to comment on several significant but otherwise undiscussed features of these offerings, and then to suggest several directions for future deliberation. In my view the present chapters are marked by a refreshing *spirit of cooperation*. On the modernist account, there is only one truth and it is typically realized in the mind of the most discerning, astute, or otherwise brilliant scientist. This view has led to a virtual cacophony of competing schools of therapy, each making clamorous claims on its own behalf at the expense of all competitors. Yet, with the realization of the constructed character of our realities, antagonism, competition, and hierarchy are slowly obviated. To develop an aggressive encampment of the *really real* is gradually to withdraw from the infinite process of meaning making within the profession and culture alike; it is the beginning of an ending. Rather, with a general aversion to banner waving, these chapters begin to demonstrate the strength apparent in communal inquiry, in the continuous cross-fertilization of languages and practice.

Similarly, we find in these chapters a robust *blurring of boundaries,* between what falls within the domain of professional sophistication (the "sacred") and what lies outside (the "irrelevant" or the "profane"). There is first the attempt to remove the artificial boundaries between individual, family, community, and nation in considerations of the therapeutic. Interestingly, with increasing consciousness of therapy as co-construction, so do clients become relevant participants in creating the logic of therapy. The boundary between professional and client is thus subverted. We also find here a congenial openness to ongoing discussions in otherwise alien domains—for example, communication theory, philosophy, culture critique, literary theory, and semiotics. I would like to think that with the removal of hierarchies of knowledge, the therapeutic community recognizes itself as vitally interdependent with others in the creation of the larger society.

There is a third feature of these chapters that bears special note, what might essentially be termed the *inspiration of the incomplete.* The reader will notice from a cursory glance at the Table of Contents that there is little here in the way of canonized subject matter. There are no treatments of "the nature of family structure," "principles of meaning making," or "foundations of family relations." Rather, the titles are typically more casual and more local; they don't attempt to supply the last word, but rather, some useful words in a conversation that is not yet complete. And, in my view, the energy and enthusiasm evidenced in so many of these chapters essentially tells us that this incompletion is a vital catalyst. By avoiding foundations and principles, we remain engaged. The drama is not yet at an end; there are new and unanticipated turns forthcoming. And what is perhaps most important, it is through our continuing and creative participation that the drama will thus unfold.

It is in this spirit of incompletion that I also wish to point in several directions that, for me, seem especially ripe for future discussion. First, with consciousness of construction we become acutely aware of the historical, cultural, and political lodgement of our concepts of "illness," "disorder," and "dysfunction." There is ample critique now extant in the constructionist literature, critique that points to ways in which, for example, these categories villainize persons and families, drive wedges between persons, foster what we take to be illness, and create a dependence on mental health professionals. However, in spite of these concerns there is little in the way of concerted action. If these issues are significant, the conversation must move outward into the society, alternatives to diagnosis must be developed, and new mental health policies hammered out. Similarly, engagement in constructive therapies sensitizes us to the problematics of measurement, and particularly the presumption that the efficacy of therapy is subject to empirical—perspective-free, value-neutral—evaluation. Again, although the presumption is manifestly flawed, there has been little in the way of concerted effort to broaden the discussion and actively transform mental health practices.

Finally, in the interest of pressing forward the present discussions, there is much now to be gained by further extending the perimeters of dialogue. While moves toward inclusion are everywhere apparent in the present work, important voices yet remain absent. Most notably, the time is ripe for a resuscitation of therapies typically identified as modernist. Regardless of the problematic grounds on which they were rationalized, the therapeutic practices of psychoanalysis, behavior modification, Rogerian therapy, cognitive therapy, and the like can be viewed as contexts for the generation of meaning. While for the most part these practices are far different from those represented in the present work, they remain intelligible for significant segments of the culture more generally. If the challenge of constructive therapies is to broaden the pragmatic means by which transformation in meaning and action is achieved, then there is no principled reason for excluding more traditional therapies. This expanded dialogue should also include voices otherwise marginalized by the therapeutic establishment. I think here especially of the teeming number of therapists whose practices are nourished by the discourse of spirit, love, and God, and yet who are unable to gain legitimacy in speaking of these matters. These therapists represent rich and significant traditions within the culture, and if constructive therapies do indeed emphasize the value of co-construction, then room must be made for constructive dialogue. In effect, there are new conversations to be invited, and my hope is that the next edition of the *Handbook* will welcome them into the arena.

We have now glimpsed the significance of the present volume for ongoing deliberations on cultural life, and on the process of therapy. I wish at last to point to a way in which this work raises questions of the most profound variety, a way in which it subtly begins to shift our very conceptions of who we are as human selves. Central to the modernist tradition is the presumption of the individual mind as the fundamental atom of society. It is the individual's capacity for independent thought upon which our democratic institutions are based; it is on the basis of the individual's capacity to love that we trust our institutions of intimacy; and it is the individual's capacity for free agency that forms the foundation for our conceptions of moral responsibility. Yet as the dialogues on constructive therapy unfold, we find the presumption of independent, self-contained individuals increasingly problematic. To construct an intelligible world essentially requires relationship; indeed, out of relationship emerges the very intelligibility of the individual self. In effect, the fundamental material out of which society emerges, from which institutions of democracy, intimacy, and moral responsibility derive, is that of relational process. We are scarcely ready to take on all that is implied by the present conversations. However, the shift in sensibility represented within these pages is bracing and dramatic. The broadest participation is needed in the forthcoming drama of exploration.

April 1998   Kenneth J. Gergen
Swarthmore, Pennsylvania

Introduction

Michael F. Hoyt

Constructive therapies are approaches that begin with the recognition that humans are meaning-makers who construct, not simply uncover, their psychological realities. They are based on "the construction that we are constructive" (Hoyt, 1996a, p. 8), that we are actively building a worldview that influences our actions. Clinicians who draw from some of the theoretical models that can be gathered under the *constructive therapies* umbrella—such as solution-focused, narrative, collaborative language systems, reflecting team, interactional, and neo-Ericksonian[1]—especially appreciate the therapeutic possibilities that open when there is an emphasis on the enhancement of choice through respectful collaboration and the fuller utilization of clients' competencies and resources.[2] The goal of constructive therapies is to bring about positive consequences in clients' lives via attention to the social construction of preferred ("clinical" or "therapeutic") realities (see Freedman & Combs, 1996; Watzlawick, 1976, 1984, 1992). We help clients "make a difference" that "makes a difference" (Bateson, 1972, 1988; de Shazer, 1991).[3]

The Handbook of Constructive Therapies is a rich compendium of expert practitioners' and theoreticians' offerings of creative concepts, specific techniques, and fascinating case examples that illustrate ways this can be achieved. It is my hope and intention that this volume will serve as a "user's guide," providing a wide range of practical how-to skills based on fuller recognition of the powers of language and imagination plus the principles of caring, collaboration, and respect for clients' competencies.

1

WHAT ARE THE KEY ELEMENTS OR DISTINGUISHING CHARACTERISTICS OF CONSTRUCTIVE THERAPIES?

There is a movement in the psychotherapy field toward a "new direction" (O'Hanlon & Weiner-Davis, 1989), one that invites a fuller appreciation of human agency and potential. There is more focus on the strengths and resources that patients or clients bring to the enterprise than on their weaknesses or limitations. Greater emphasis is being put on where people want to go rather than on where they have been. While not ignoring the painfulness and seriousness of some situations, the shift has been away from conventional psychiatric pathologizing and toward a more optimistic view of people as unique and resourceful creators—for better or worse—of their own realities.[4]

While the therapist is still recognized as bringing certain skills and expertise to the clinical moment, there is a profound shift away from the objectivist notion that it is the therapist who knows what is "right" and will thus "intervene" or "treat" the "patient" (or "client")[5] to bring about what is "best" (and thus "fix" the "problem"). Rather, the therapist and client are seen as coparticipants in a meaning-generating process that constructs a more hopeful, empowering, and ultimately more salutary sense of self-in-the-world. As Hoffman (1997, p. 337) explains, "As a result, the field is on the cusp of a philosophical divide. On the one hand you have the traditional or 'modern' stance, which is based on the claims to objectivity of modern science. On the other, you have a 'postmodern' stance, which is that reality in any complex human sense is never immutably out there, independent of our languaged ways of knowing it."[6]

This shift is part of the social constructionist movement in psychology (Gergen, 1985). The constructive therapist recognizes that we are looking through "lenses" (Hoffman, 1990; Zeig & Munion, 1990) into a "mirrored room" (Hare-Mustin, 1992, 1994; Rorty, 1979); that knowledge is "perspectival" (Smith, 1997); that "how we look determines what we see, and what we see determines what we do" (Hoyt & Berg, Chapter Sixteen of this volume); that we are, wittingly or not, engaged in self-recursive autopoiesis (Maturana & Varela, 1980); that we are "making history" and not just "taking history" (Hoyt, 1996a; White, 1993). The constructive therapist gives up "temptations of power and certainty" (Amundson, Stewart, & Valentine, 1993); maintains "curiosity" (Cecchin, 1987) and a "healthy irreverence" (Keeney, 1990; Cecchin, Lane, & Ray, 1992); and is "suspicious of great subjects and all encompassing theories . . . because no social theory can make claims to validity outside a particular context and value system" (Doherty, 1991, p. 40). The constructive therapist recognizes that psychotherapy is an exercise in "clinical epistemology" (O'Hanlon & Wilk, 1987), a "process of semiosis" (Gergen & Kaye, 1992, p. 182); that it is hermeneutics rather than engineering, and poetics rather than physics, that are the fields of study that examine the warp and weft of human life (Hoyt, 1996a).[7] The constructive therapist forgoes the dryness of the positivist shore, joining the collaborative flow of "the third wave" (O'Hanlon, 1994) as an intersubjective coparticipant or coauthor.

The constructive therapist recognizes, as Gergen (1985, p. 267; see also Gergen, 1994, and Gergen, in Hoyt, 1996c) has put it, that "the terms in which the world is understood are social artifacts, products of historically situated interchanges among people. From the constructionist position the process of understanding is not automatically driven by the forces of nature, but is the result of an active, cooperative enterprise of persons, in relationship." Similarly, Hoffman (1990, pp. 89–90) echos and expands the theme:

> In contrast, social construction theory posits an evolving set of meanings that emerge unendingly from the interactions between people. These meanings are not skull-bound and may not exist inside what we think of as individual "mind." They are part of a general flow of constantly changing narratives. Thus, the theory bypasses the fixity of the model of biologically based cognition, claiming instead that the development of concepts is a fluid process, socially derived. It is particularly helpful for the therapist to think of problems as stories that people have agreed to tell themselves. . . . Many styles of doing therapy that would otherwise compete can crowd together under its broad rim, as long as their practitioners agree that all therapy takes the form of conversations between people and that the findings of these conversations have no other "reality" than that bestowed by mutual consent.[8]

Hence, as Friedman (1996, pp. 450–451) has described it, the constructive therapist:[9]

- Believes in a socially constructed reality.
- Emphasizes the reflexive nature of therapeutic relationships in which client and therapist co-construct meanings in dialogue or conversation.
- Moves away from hierarchical distinctions toward a more egalitarian offering of ideas and respect for differences.
- Maintains empathy and respect for the client's predicament and a belief in the power of the therapeutic conversation to liberate suppressed, ignored, or previously unacknowledged voices or stories.
- Co-constructs goals and negotiates direction in therapy, placing the client back in the driver's seat, as an expert on his or her own predicaments and dilemmas.
- Searches for and amplifies client competencies, strengths, and resources and avoids being a detective of pathology or reifying rigid diagnostic distinctions.
- Avoids a vocabulary of deficit and dysfunction, replacing the jargon of pathology (and distance) with the language of the everyday.[10]
- Is oriented toward the future and optimistic about change.
- Is sensitive to the methods and processes used in the therapeutic conversation.

LANGUAGE AND LANGUAGING

We "know" and "understand" through our linguistic systems (Anderson, 1997; de Shazer, 1994; Efran, Lukens, & Lukens, 1990; Furman & Ahola, 1992; Gilligan & Price, 1993; Miller, 1997; Watzlawick, 1978; Watzlawick, Beavin, & Jackson, 1967). *Language* and *languaging* are the ways we make meaning and exchange information.[11] Language is inherently and intrinsically interpersonal. What we call "reality" is socially constructed; hence, Hoffman (1993) refers to "collaborative knowing" and de Shazer (1991, p. 50) succinctly states, "Between, not inside."[12]

Language is a medium, and more. How we punctuate organizes us, formatting our consciousness and structuring our reality. As Hillman (1995, p. 20) notes, "The Greek word for 'idea,' *eidos*, comes from *idein*, 'to see,' and is related to the noun, which means two things: (a) something seen like a form and (b) a way of seeing like a perspective. We both see ideas and see by means of them. They are both the forms our minds take and what allows our minds to form events into shaped experiences." Language is not just a "conduit" (Lakoff, 1995; Reddy, 1993). Highlighting the verbal channel, Rybczynski (1986, pp. 20–21) observes, "Words are important. Language is not just a medium, like a water pipe, it is a reflection of how we think. We use words not only to describe objects but also to express ideas, and the introduction of words into the language marks the simultaneous introduction of ideas into the consciousness. As Jean-Paul Sartre wrote, 'Giving names to objects consists in moving immediate, unreflected, perhaps ignored events on to the plane of reflection and of the objective mind.'"

Constructive therapists focus on how language builds our worldview and the practical consequences (utility) of these constructions. Watzlawick, Weakland, and Fisch (1974, p. 86) make this clear in their seminal work, *Change: Principles of Problem Formation and Problem Resolution:*

> But since past events are obviously unchangeable, either we are forced to abandon all hope that change is possible, or we must assume that—at least in some significant respects—the past has influence over the present only by way of a person's *present* interpretation of *past* experience. If so, then the significance of the past becomes a matter not of "truth" and "reality," but of looking at it here and now in one way rather than another.[13] Consequently, there is no compelling reason to assign to the past primacy or causality in relation to the present, and this means that the re-interpretation of the past is simply one of many ways of possibly influencing present behavior. In this case, then, we are back at the only meaningful question, i.e., the pragmatic one: How can desirable change of present behavior be produced most efficiently?

How one "looks at it" occurs through language. Gergen (1993, p. x) explains:

> The various accounts brought to therapy by the client—tales of misery, oppression, failures, and the like—serve not as approximations to the truth, perhaps biased by desires or cognitive incapacities, but as life constructions, made up of narratives, metaphors, cultural logics, and the like. They are more like musical or poetic accompaniments than mirrors or maps. And their major significance lies not in their relative validity, but in their social utility. In this context a major aim of therapy becomes one of freeing the client from a particular kind of account and opening the way to alternatives of greater promise.

Roth and Chasin (1994, p. 189; see also Atwood, 1993) also emphasize the many ways language constricts and/or liberates: "Our many life stories are both our creations and our creators. They are the principal way that each of us participates with others in the making and remaking of ourselves as social beings. When the relationships we count on to sustain and invigorate us are in trouble, however, we often feel ourselves to be less agents in creating our own stories than actors playing roles shaped, if not scripted, by others, in dramas that consign us to unsatisfying repetitions or direct us toward some painful end."

Within this view, *therapy* is seen therefore as a special kind of *conversation:*

> Meaning and understanding are socially and intersubjectively constructed. By intersubjective, we refer to an evolving state of affairs in which two or more people agree (understand) that they are experiencing the same event in the same way. . . . Therapy is a linguistic event that takes place in what we call a therapeutic conversation. The therapeutic conversation is a mutual search and exploration through dialogue, a two-way exchange, a criss-crossing of ideas in which new meanings are continually evolving toward the "dis-solving" of problems and, thus, the dissolving of the therapy system and, hence, the *problem-organizing, problem dis-solving system. Change is the evolution of new meaning through dialogue* [Anderson & Goolishian, 1988, p. 372, emphasis in original; see also Anderson, 1997, and Chapter Two of this volume].

Anderson and Goolishian (1988, pp. 382–383) go on to highlight some of the therapist's choices in cocreating such a "therapeutic conversation":

- The therapist keeps inquiry within the parameters of the problem as described by the clients.
- The therapist entertains multiple and contradictory ideas simultaneously.
- The therapist chooses cooperative rather than uncooperative language.
- The therapist learns, understands, and converses in the client's language.
- The therapist is a respectful listener who does not understand too quickly (if ever).

- The therapists asks questions, the answers to which require new questions.
- The therapist takes the responsibility for the creation of a conversational context that allows for mutual collaboration in the problem-defining process.
- The therapist maintains a dialogical conversation with himself or herself.

It is important to keep in mind that *language* and *languaging* need to be conceived more broadly than mere *talk* and *talking*. Terms like *conversation* and *dialogue* seem to focus on the exchange of words and may gloss over various social complexities. As Coale (1992) notes, there is much that goes on in therapy that is not verbal per se. Along similar lines, Wick (1996, p. 74) comments that "Constructionists have a language myopia." Goldner (1993, pp. 159–160) explains her preference for the term *discourse:* "I think 'discourse' is our best description of therapeutic dialogue because, as [Michel] Foucault has demonstrated, discourse brings together language, meaning, knowledge, and power. It insists that we see psychotherapy as a social practice shaped by, and embedded in, an elaborate professional culture that inevitably constrains what can be seen and named, and that, like any 'knowledge/power discourse,' necessarily elevates those who produce and manage it over those for whom it is intended."

Tom Andersen (1992, p. 64–65; see also Eron & Lund, 1996, Chapter Eighteen of this volume) also emphasizes the constructive use of "therapeutic talk" in the development of a new story or *narrative:* "Talking with oneself and/or others is a way of defining oneself. In this sense the language we use makes us who we are in the moment we use it. . . . One might say that the search for new meanings, which often comprises searching for new language, is a search for us to be the selves with which we feel most comfortable. So-called 'therapeutic' talk might be regarded as a form of search; a search for new descriptions, new understandings, new meanings, new nuances of the words, and ultimately for new definitions of oneself."

This is part of "retelling a life" (Schafer, 1992), continuing "the rest of the story" (Meichenbaum, in Hoyt, 1996e), the creation of "narrative truth" (Spence, 1982), the development of a "helpful conversation" (Eron & Lund, 1996).[14] The narrative metaphor entails a shift in interactional viewing:

> A focus on interactional pattern continues to be an essential aspect of a narrative approach although it is understood quite differently than other interactional models of therapy (e.g., Watzlawick, Weakland, & Fisch, 1974). . . . Within narrative therapy "interactional patterns" can be thought of as the specific contexts in which stories evolve across time and in which the experience of the interaction provides the "stuff" that constitutes stories (Zimmerman & Dickerson, 1994). This represents a change from cybernetic metaphors. A person creates an account to make sense of their experience that emerges in the context of specific interactions; it is an *effect* of the experience of interactional pattern. . . . Stories also can be experienced as reciprocally influencing each

other within the context of a relationship. Thus, the reciprocal quality of an interactional perspective remains while a richness is gained through metaphors that capture a sense of experience over time [Neal, 1996, p. 75].

Narrative therapists commonly invite "family members to participate in the construction of new descriptions of the problem itself—an externalized description" (White, 1988/1989, p. 37).[15] This is part of the "restorying" or "re-authoring of lives" (White & Epston, 1990; White, 1995): "Stories are full of gaps which persons must fill in order for the stories to be performed. These gaps recruit the lived experience and the imagination of persons. With every performance, persons are reauthoring their lives. The evolution of lives is akin to their process of reauthoring, the process of persons' entering stories, taking them over and making them their own" (White & Epston, p. 13).

As is their wont, Berg and de Shazer (1993, p. 7) put it simply: "Change is seen to happen within language. What we talk about and how we talk about it makes a difference and it is these differences that can be used to make a difference (to the client)."

In this regard, narrative therapists and solution-focused therapists (or at least two of the originators) clearly agree (quoted in Duvall and Beier, 1995, p. 65):

Michael White:. . . . this is only one interpretation about what Insoo's doing and I wouldn't want to impose this, but, my guess is that Insoo makes it possible for people to talk differently about their lives, differently about themselves. It perhaps makes it possible for people to relate to themselves with compassionate ways. Would that fit for you, Insoo, that in some way people come along to see you and do wind up talking a bit differently about who they are and about other people?

Insoo Kim Berg: Differently than, than what?

Michael White: Than the ways that have them judging themselves harshly and measuring themselves against some way they should be.

Insoo Kim Berg: I should hope so. Isn't that what we all try to do?

Michael White: Yes.

CHANGE

As Miller (1997, pp. 213–214) has written:

We construct our social worlds, selves, and others by attending to and interpreting our life experiences in particular ways. Further, our ongoing story construction is not so much about describing the "objective facts" that shape our lives as it is about testing—and usually confirming—our assumptions about social reality. The facts of life change when we construct new life stories that recast what once was taken as immutable truth and objective reality. Put differently, the stories we tell about our lives, and the meanings that we draw from the stories, often operate as self-fulfilling prophecies. We use stories to teach ourselves lessons that we already know. Brief therapists use their clients' skills in and proclivity for developing self-fulfilling prophecies by encouraging the clients to construct new stories about themselves and their lives.

The constructive therapist knows that what counts are the *real effects* of how persons construe their reality. Gergen (in Hoyt, 1996c, p. 351) emphasizes both the cardinal significance of context in making information *meaningful* and the importance of *real consequences:*

> It is not so much "how things are" as how we interpret them that will typically bring us into therapy. A physical touch may itself be unremarkable; however, in different frames of meaning it may spark a sense of friendly support, move one to ecstasy, or incite litigation for harassment. A blow to the chin will send a family member in search of a therapist, but will move a boxer to change his tactics. With this emphasis in place, we are invited to see effective therapy as a transformation of meaning. However, as you can see from the preceding remarks, I don't see this transformation principally as a cognitive event. Rather, it is an alteration in actions—relying importantly on language but not at all limited to language.[16]

Even if we cannot know it except through the knower,[17] there is a *there* there, not to be ignored except at considerable peril (see Coyne, 1985; Fish, 1993; Held, 1995; Hoyt, 1996a; Speed, 1984, 1991). As Coale (1992), among others, has argued, "talking about it" may not fit for some clients and may be used as an excuse for not doing anything to change. As they say, "Actions sometimes speak louder than words" and "You've got to walk the walk, not just talk the talk." Pittman (1992) rails against anyone who would sophistically change words rather than right wrongs. Coale (1992, p. 19) says a lot when she says, "Reframing hunger has no usefulness to poor families."[18] She then goes on to quote Minuchin (1991, p. 49): "Families of poverty have been stripped of much of the power to write their own stories. Their narratives of hopelessness, helplessness and dependency have been cowritten, if not dictated, by social institutions. When the institutional and societal coauthors of these stories are made invisible, when the family narratives are presented as if constructed by the families alone, family members become even more depressed, potential helpers are confused, and everybody becomes less effectual."

WHOSE THERAPY IS IT? WHOSE STORY IS IT? WHOSE LIFE IS IT?

While strategic therapists, such as Haley (1977), have been explicit in assigning to the therapist responsibility for making something happen, in practice *all* clinicians wield considerable power. As Weakland (1993, p. 143) has written:

Just as one cannot *not* communicate, one cannot *not* influence. Influence is inherent in all human communication. We are bound to influence our clients, and they are bound to influence us. The only choice is between doing so without reflection, or even with attempted denial, and doing so deliberately and responsibly. Clients come seeking change which they could not achieve on their own; expertise in influencing them to change usefully seems to us the essence of the therapist's job. Therefore, we give much thought—guided, of course, by what the client does and says—to almost every aspect of treatment: To whom we will see in any given session, to the timing of sessions, to what suggestions we will offer as to new thoughts and actions, to responses we make to clients' reports of progress or difficulties encountered, and especially not just to the content of what we say, but to how we will phrase it. This strategic emphasis, however, does not mean that we propose or favor any arrangement in which a therapist has all the power, knowledge, control, and activity, while the patient is just a passive object of therapeutic actions—if indeed this were possible, which is very doubtful.

Writing from a solution-focused perspective, Weiner-Davis (1993, p. 156) comes right to the point: "Since we cannot avoid leading, the question becomes, 'Where shall we lead our clients?'" Miller (1997, p. 183) elaborates: "Solution-focused therapists . . . use their questions to construct mutually satisfactory conversations with clients. The questions are not designed to elicit information about worlds outside ongoing therapy conversations, but to elicit information in building new stories about clients' lives. Within solution-focused brief therapy discourse, then, all questions are constructive. They are designed to define goals and to construct solutions that solution-focused therapists assume are already present in clients' lives."[19]

Similarly, in *Narrative Solutions in Brief Therapy*, Eron and Lund (1996, p. 34) highlight the intentionality of narrative therapists:

Michael White and David Epston provide a map for the therapist to navigate an effective conversation. There's purpose to the therapist's comments and questions, and a direction to the search for alternative stories. White and Epston view therapists as accountable for what they do. Although the client is seen as the expert and primary author, and the therapist as the secondary author in the restorying process, it's the therapist who assumes primary responsibility for change. Therapists restory with the specific aim of deconstructing the problem, changing its meaning, and loosening its hold over people's lives. . . . [White and Epston have] brought the person back into the system—by affirming that an individual's preferences, intentions, stories, and experiences are relevant to the process of change. Like strategic family therapists of the 1970s and 1980s, however, these postmodern therapists have a plan for changing problems.

White (in Hoyt & Combs, 1996, pp. 38–40) also agrees that we are "influential" and that there is a "power differential" and suggests the following:

We can't pretend that we are not somehow contributing to the process. We can't pretend that we are not influential in the therapeutic interaction. There is no neutral position in which therapists can stand. I can embrace this fact by joining with people to address all of those things that they find traumatizing and limiting of their lives. . . . And, because the impossibility of neutrality means that I cannot avoid being "for" something, I take the responsibility to distrust what I am for—that is, my ways of life and my ways of thought—and I can do this in many ways. For example, I can distrust what I am for with regard to the appropriateness of this to the lives of others. I can distrust what I am for in the sense that what I am for has the potential to reproduce the very things that I oppose in my relations with others. I can distrust what I am for to the extent that what I am for has a distinct location in the worlds of gender, class, race, culture, sexual preference, etc. And so on.

Constructive therapists—who frame their practices in terms such as *collaboration, coparticipation, intersubjectivity,* and *cocreation*—pay special attention to issues of causation, control, power, and direction. Unless cognizance is truly given to honoring "narrative intentions" (Combs & Freedman, 1994) and client self-determination, "inviting," "wondering," and "questioning" could be used disingenuously to offer indirect hypnotic suggestions (see Freedman & Combs, 1996, p. 6; Schmidt & Trenkle, 1985)—manipulation could be "cloaked in transparency," so to speak.[20]

In contradistinction, as part of their commitment to respectful collaboration, constructive therapists avoid usurping power. Extra care is taken to include multiple points of view, to hear (and sometimes evoke) the "voice" of the marginalized, to create space for the recognition and expression of oppressed, sometimes inchoate experience. As the playwright Tony Kushner (1995, pp. 7–9) has said: "The truest characteristic of freedom is generosity, the basic gesture of freedom is to include, not to exclude. . . . Listing the full catalogue of the complaints of the disenfranchised is sure to raise howls decrying 'victimology' and 'political correctness' from those who need desperately to believe that democracy is a simple thing. Democracy isn't simple and it doesn't mean that majorities tyrannize minorities."

Thus, for some constructive therapists, therapy is an explicitly political act, a place for exposing the trappings of power and for giving privilege to the special knowledges of the subjugated or disenfranchised (often persons of color, women, children, elders, gays and lesbians, the poor and homeless, people who are physically or mentally different, and so on). Personal problems are often seen as resulting from pernicious cultural practices, both blatant social injustices and the subsequent (and perhaps more subtle) internalization of deleterious institutionalized attitudes (Albee, 1997; Brown, 1997; Markowitz, 1997; Waldegrave, 1990). For others, the clinical situation is not construed in conventional political terms, but there is still keen concern for who determines how we talk and what we talk about, for what Laing (1967) called "the politics of experience." As Efran, Lukens, and Lukens (1988, p. 32) have articulated:

> Because constructivists regard the language community as all important, therapists working from this point of view must get used to the idea that they are engaged in an essentially political endeavor. Like other human pursuits, therapy fosters the establishment, exchange, and maintenance of particular traditions and language formulations. Issues of personal responsibility and ethics can neither be ducked nor masked by objective-sounding terms like "treatment," "mental health," "the normal family," "family loyalties," and so on. . . . For constructivists, the *entire therapeutic venture* is fundamentally an exercise in ethics—it involves the inventing, shaping, and reformulating of codes for living together. In other words, from this point of view, therapy is a dialogue about the interlocking wants, desires, and expectations of all the participants, including the therapist.

Constructive therapists meet their clients somewhere in the middle. Clients may seek the therapist's assistance, but one side is not superior or the arbiter of what is valid, legitimate, or right. (Or one is—but ultimately it's not the therapist.) The approach is "mutualistic" (Griffith, 1997); the therapist is a "true participant" (Cantwell & Holmes, 1994). Drengenberg (1996, p. 52) describes an encounter evocative of both Buber's (1958) "I-Thou" and Gergen's (in Hoyt, 1996c) "relational sublime":

> . . . We meet in a shared space . . . non-hierarchically . . .
> respectfully . . . afloat in a sea of recursivity . . . seeing more
> clearly who we are and what we do and need . . .
> our encounter of exchange . . . activating innate potentials
> for growth . . . each never again to be the same . . .

Scrupulous attention must be paid to identifying and serving *clients'* goals. Clients who in conventional terms may be described as noncompliant or resistant may be in a power-politics struggle (see Albee, 1997; Tomm, 1993), engaged in counter-oppressive practices to refuse being psychologically colonized or bent in directions they don't wish to go. Hence, White (1995; see also White, cited in Hoyt & Combs, 1996) calls for "accountability structures" to help keep us keenly alert to the politics of the therapeutic situation; T. Andersen (1991, 1992) invites families to hear "reflecting teams," and Madigan (1993) "situates" the therapist's curiosity and motivation before the family; de Shazer (1984, 1985, 1988; see also de Shazer, in Hoyt, 1994b, and de Shazer and Weakland, in Hoyt, 1996d) and Berg (1989) assert that "resistance" can be "dissolved" if we form relationships that honor what the client is a "customer" for; Anderson and Goolishian (1992) suggest that "the client is the expert"; Rosenbaum (Rosenbaum & Dyckman, 1996) silently bows to his clients as they enter his office to help orient himself to the upcoming encounter; and Tomm (1991;

see also Tomm, Hoyt, & Madigan, Chapter Ten, this volume; Bernstein, 1990; Freedman & Combs, 1996, pp. 269–272) calls for greater awareness of "ethical postures" that "open space" without imposing upon clients. In the chapters that follow, the reader is encouraged to note the many ways these intentions are promulgated, nuanced, and often achieved.

HOW THIS BOOK CAME TO BE AND HOW TO USE IT

In the past few years there has been a burgeoning interest in different models of therapy that offer a more optimistic and user-friendly approach toward helping those that seek mental health services. This movement has been fueled by some combination of desire for more humanistic ways of thinking about human change processes, various theoretical and clinical developments paralleling broader social forces (e.g., computers and the information-processing explosion, eco-systemic environmental awareness, greater recognition of cultural diversity), and—to some extent—the efficacy-driven pressures of managed care (Hoyt, 1995) to think about new ways to deliver services (rather than simply doing less of the same).[21] Popular response to different publications, conferences, and workshops attests to these interests.

This handbook was undertaken to extend and greatly expand the scope of its two predecessor volumes (Hoyt, 1994a, 1996b), to provide in one place a resource for both tyros and seasoned practitioners. A wide range of leading experts were invited to participate. The basic request was as follows:

> I envision a comprehensive volume that will contain some interesting interviews plus chapters describing various "constructivist" approaches to treatment. We want each chapter to present briefly the theory/rationale of a given approach, and then to present transcripts and related case material to illustrate how the work is actually done. No single chapter (or book) can teach fully a method of psychotherapy, of course, but we hope that readers will, through transcripts and commentaries, get a sense of what actually happens and what characterizes a particular approach. The goal is a stimulating book, both readable and useful.

Contributors also received a further instruction:

> Suppose tonight, while you are sleeping, a miracle occurs, and the chapter you are doing is written! Tomorrow, when you awaken, what will you find in the manuscript? What basic, fundamental ideas will there be? What more advanced, clinically sophisticated suggestions will aid therapists as they go beyond initial interventions? What bright ideas, new methods, and interesting discussions will you—as well as other readers—be delighted to find? How will your thinking get stretched? What will be the tastiest part of the chapter, what spices will you add to the rest, etc., etc.?

I am delighted by the extraordinarily thoughtful, highly creative, and wonderfully variegated ways contributors responded. One reader might prefer first to explore some of the discussions in Part One, "Theoretical Perspectives," such as James and Barbara Allen on redecision therapy (Chapter One), Harlene Anderson and Susan Levin on their collaborative language systems approach (Chapter Two), Jon Carlson and Len Sperry on Adlerian therapy (Chapter Three), Albert Ellis on Rational Emotive Behavior Therapy (Chapter Four), Lynn Hoffman on the uses and limits of models (Chapter Five), Stephen and Carol Lankton on Ericksonian therapy (Chapter Six), Bill O'Hanlon on possibility therapy (Chapter Seven), and Carlos Sluzki on family therapy (Chapter Eight).

Another reader might turn directly to Part Two, "Conversations and Songs," to study the multifaceted interviews conducted with Paul Watzlawick, on constructivism and the MRI strategic interactional approach (Chapter Nine), and with Karl Tomm, for a highly personal look into the development and application of his ideas about ethics and the "internalized other" (Chapter Ten). In Chapter Eleven, Rob Doan interviews Fear and Love directly, portraying some of the powers of these two forces within the context of narrative therapy. In Chapter Twelve, one can find the witty and highly perceptive song lyrics about the work of Michael White and Steve de Shazer that were first presented live by Joseph Goldfield at the Narrative Solutions/Solution Narratives conference featuring the two leaders, held in Milwaukee during October 1996.

Another reader might delve immediately into Part Three, "Specific Clinical Applications," for discussion of a particularly perplexing clinical situation such as therapy with troubled children and families (Chapter Thirteen, by Jeff Chang; and Chapter Eighteen, by Thomas Lund and Joseph Eron), the use of reflecting teams to minimize hierarchy in therapeutic relationships (Chapter Fourteen, by Michele Cohen, Gene Combs, Bill DeLaurenti, Pat DeLaurenti, Jill Freedman, David Larimer, and Dina Shulman), therapy with traditionally longer-term clients (Chapter Fifteen, by Barry Duncan, Mark Hubble, Scott Miller, and Suzanne Coleman; and Chapter Seventeen, by James Kreider), couples in conflict (Chapter Sixteen, by Michael Hoyt and Insoo Kim Berg), people in the grip of eating disorders (Chapter Nineteen, by Stephen Madigan and Elliot Goldner), violent men (Chapter Twenty, by David Nylund and Victor Corsiglia, with commentary by Alan Jenkins), the use of "therapeutic splits" to construct more empathic narratives (Chapter Twenty-One, by Haim Omer), and collaborative work with abuse victims (Chapter Twenty-Two, by Robert Schwarz).

Some readers might prefer to work through the book from front to back. Each chapter has its value and, read like a reflecting team (see Andersen, 1991; Friedman, 1995), the whole is intended to be greater than the sum of its parts.

We don't want to suggest that there is one way to approach *The Handbook of Constructive Therapies*. There is not a single best or right reading. Paralleling the processes of constructive therapies, each person takes his or her own (multiple) meanings (see de Shazer, 1993). This is not a new idea: As Zen Master Rinzai warned his students several centuries ago: "All I am talking about is only medicine appropriate for curing specific ailments. In my talks there is nothing absolutely real" (quoted in Schloegl, 1975, p. 48).[22] The Native American teacher Rolling Thunder also advises, "I want to warn you not to copy me, but to work out your own method. Our people tell us to be original. If you can watch the method, though, and the way I go about it, maybe that would give you some thoughts about what to follow, what it's all about. Then you work out your own substance, your own songs, your own prayers and things to go with it" (quoted in Boyd, 1974, p. 92).

I encourage readers to be receptive and generative, to apply their own insights and experience, to learn more than is printed, and to find ways to help clients make changes that bring them more of what the clients prefer.

ACKNOWLEDGMENTS

¡Muchas gracias! Kamsa hamnida! Danke schön! Todah rabah! and *Thank you!* to my fine colleagues whose words grace the pages of this handbook. Their expertise, generosity, and diligence have made it a great pleasure to work with them.

I am also grateful to the (anonymous) clients and patients who permitted reports of their experiences to help inform the ideas contained herein, and to various authors and publishers who kindly permitted quotation from their works.

Additional appreciation goes to Jossey-Bass Publishers (especially to Alan Rinzler and Katie Levine) and to Kaiser Permanente for their continuing support.

To my dear wife, Jennifer, and to my beloved son, Alex, I am grateful for everything . . . past, present, and future, the ground and the sky, the words and the music.

Endnotes

1. This list, of course, is not exhaustive. As will be seen in the discussion that follows and in the chapters contained in this volume, other theoretical schools—including those that go under such rubrics as strategic, cognitive-behavioral, personal construct, transactional analytic, Gestalt, Adlerian, Jungian, and some of the newer developments in the psychoanalytic realm—are also more actively recognizing the constructive nature of psychotherapeutic work. As Sluzki (1988, pp. 80–81) has noted: "Constructivism is a way of *talking about* therapy, rather than of *doing* it. Being a theory of knowledge rather than a set of techniques, constructivism offers us not a particular way of helping clients, but a way of understanding how we use our clinical tools and the interplay between practitioners' beliefs and their practice."

2. While usually referring especially to trance phenomena when discussing *utilization* (see de Shazer, cited in Short, 1997, p. 19; Gilligan, 1987; Goldfield, 1994), Milton Erickson prefigured much when he recommended "the fullest possible utilization of the functional capacities and abilities and the experiential and acquisitional learnings of the patient. These should take precedence over the teaching of new ways in living which are developed from the therapist's possibly incomplete understanding of what may be right and serviceable to the individual concerned" (Erickson, 1980, p. 540).

3. According to Luepnitz (1988, p. 73), the phrase "the difference that makes a difference," of which Bateson was so fond, was coined by William James.

4. *Constructive Therapies* (Hoyt, 1994a) and *Constructive Therapies, Volume 2* (Hoyt, 1996b) were the immediate predecessors of the handbook in hand. Readers are encouraged to consult them for further theoretical disquisition and a range of clinical applications. Additional useful resources include the following: *The Invented Reality: How Do We Know What We Believe We Know? (Contributions to Constructivism)* (Watzlawick, 1984); "Constructivism: What's in It for You?" (Efran, Lukens, & Lukens, 1988); *Narrative Means to Therapeutic Ends* (White & Epston, 1990); *Therapy as Social Construction* (McNamee & Gergen, 1992); *The New Language of Change* (Friedman, 1993); *Therapeutic Conversations* (Gilligan & Price, 1993); *The Stories We Live by* (McAdams, 1993); *Story Re-Visions: Narrative Therapy in the Postmodern World* (Parry & Doan, 1994); *Constructivism in Psychotherapy* (Neimeyer & Mahoney, 1995); *Depth-Oriented Brief Therapy* (Ecker & Hulley, 1996); *Constructing Realities* (Rosen & Kuelhwein, 1996); *Narrative Solutions in Brief Therapy* (Eron & Lund, 1996); *Narrative Therapy: The Social Construction of Preferred Realities* (Freedman & Combs, 1996); *If Problems Talked* (Zimmerman & Dickerson, 1996); *Narrative Therapy in Practice* (Monk, Winslade, Crocket, & Epston, 1997); *Narrative Therapy with Children and Adolescents* (Smith & Nylund, 1997); *Playful Approaches to Serious Problems* (Freeman, Epston, & Lobovits, 1997); *Becoming Miracle Workers* (Miller, 1997); and *Narratives of Therapists' Lives* (White, 1997).

5. Deconstruction of the very terms *patient, client, doctor, therapist, clinician* (and such related terms as *therapy, treatment, intervention, consultation, conversation*) reveals implicit and powerful assumptions about the process, its purposes, and the role of the participants (see Hoyt, 1979, 1985; Hoyt & Friedman, in press). Most of the contributors to this handbook seem to prefer the term *client* to emphasize the egalitarian and minimize the medical connotation of sickness or pathology.

6. For an interesting discussion of how scientists grapple with subjectivity and the limits of knowledge, see Horgan (1996).

7. Following the poem "Thirteen Ways of Looking at a Blackbird" by Wallace Stevens, Shafarman (1996, p. 25) describes "Thirteen Ways of Looking at How a Poet and a Therapist Are One": "1. The ability to sustain accurate attention. 2. The power to use language and the silences that surround language as the medium of change. 3. The vision to perceive the possibility of transformation that

rests within the next moment. 4. Experience with subtle transitions that guide one towards skillful beginnings and appropriate endings. 5. The development of a skilled intelligence that can shape what is emerging into a communicable form. 6. The ability to speak, act, and witness truth with compassion. 7. An appreciation of the power of pacing, time, and rhythm in choreographing change. 8. A respect for the capacity of form to contain and transmute suffering into wisdom. 9. A regard for lineages and the power of our ancestors. 10. Skills that inspire humor, growth, and play. 11. A recognition of the beauty of form—and the need to judiciously break form. 12. The creation of something that endures over time. 13. A sense of the mystery that exists within the ordinary acts of everyday life."

8. Hoffman (1990, pp. 90–91) goes on: "I rely on three powerful new lenses. One is social construction theory. The next is what I call a second-order view. The third is gender. Social construction theory is really a lens about lenses. The other two are only handmaidens in that they dramatize and shake up world views in their respective areas. All three can be metaphorically applied to psychotherapy. All three represent sets of lenses that enforce an awareness that what you thought looked one way, immutably and forever, can be seen in another way. You don't realize that a 'fact' is merely an 'opinion' until you are shocked by the discovery of another 'fact,' equally persuasive and exactly contradictory to the first one. The pair of facts then presents you with a larger frame that allows you to alternate or choose. At the cost of giving up moral and scientific absolutes, your social constructionist does get an enlarged sense of choice." A related view is expressed by W. T. Anderson in his succinctly named book, *Reality Isn't What It Used to Be* (1990, p. 3): "If there is anything we have plenty of, it is belief systems. But we also have something else: a growing suspicion that all belief systems—all ideas about human reality—are social constructions. This is a story about stories, a belief about beliefs."

9. Various terms mark the map to the gates of the virtual territory of *Terra Constructiva: constructivist, constructionist, deconstructionist, solution-focused, solution-oriented, possibility, cooperative, dialogic, conversational, collaborative, competency, reflective, postmodern, narrative, poststructural, intersubjective.* . . .

10. Hence, with twisted tongue in cheek, Berger and Kellner (1979, p. 308) wrote: "Not being convinced, however, that theoretical lucidity is necessarily enhanced by terminological ponderosity, we shall avoid as much as possible the use of the sort of jargon for which both sociologists and phenomenologists have acquired dubious notoriety."

11. The use of the term *languaging* as a gerund (as in Anderson & Goolishian, 1988; Maturana, 1988) emphasizes both the activity of language and the power of The Word to give shape to being. Thus, in the Bible story of *Genesis* 1, 3: "God said, 'Let there be light,' and there was light." Being as a process more than an event, an activity more than an entity, is highlighted in book titles such as Buckminster Fuller's (1970) *I Seem to Be a Verb* and O'Hanlon and Hudson's (1995) *Love Is a Verb.* If René Descartes wrote "I think, therefore I am" and Professor Higgins's motto (in G. B. Shaw's *Pygmalion*) was "Speak that I may know you," the social constructionist might say, "Speak that we may be."

12. To cite one example, the *customer, complainant,* and *visitor* distinctions made in solution-focused therapy (see de Shazer, 1988, pp. 85–90; Berg, 1989) refer more to therapist-client *relationship* patterns than to individuals. The use of terms like *cooperation* and *fit* imply that *system, connection,* and *context* are the unit of analysis.

13. The present-centered construction of all time may have inspired the famous opening lines of T. S. Eliot's (1943, p. 13) *Burnt Norton:*

Time present and time past

Are both perhaps present in time future

And time future contained in time past.

A similar observation was made long ago by St. Augustine in his *Confessions* (quoted in Boscolo & Bertrando, 1993, p. 34): "What is by now evident and clear is that neither future nor past exists, and it is inexact language to speak of three times—past, present, and future. Perhaps it would be exact to say: there are three times, a present of things past, a present of things present, a present of things to come. In the soul there are these three aspects of time, and I do not see them anywhere else. The present considering the past is the memory, the present considering the future is expectation."

14. Recognition of the power of language is not new in the psychotherapy field. Thus de Shazer (1994) borrowed a phrase from Sigmund Freud for the title of his book, *Words Were Originally Magic.* Freud's words (1915/1961, p. 17): "Nothing takes place in a psycho-analytic treatment but an exchange of words. . . . The patient talks. . . . The doctor listens. . . . Words were originally magic and to this day words have retained much of their ancient magical power. By words one person can make another blissfully happy or drive him to despair. . . . Words provoke affects and are in general the means of mutual influence among men. Thus we shall not depreciate the use of words in psychotherapy and we shall be pleased if we can listen to the words that pass between the analyst and his patient." Constructivist trends can also be seen in the work of Alfred Adler (1931/1958; see also Carlson & Sperry in Chapter Three of this volume) and Carl Jung (Young-Eisendrath & Hall, 1991), among others.

15. Elsewhere, White (1989, p. 5; see also Roth & Epston, 1996) describes the value of *externalizing the problem:* "'Externalizing' is an approach to therapy that encourages persons to objectify, and at times, to personify, the problems that they experience as oppressive. In this process, the problem becomes a separate entity and thus external to the person who was, or the relationship that was, ascribed the problem. Those problems that are considered to be inherent, and thus relatively fixed qualities that are attributed to persons and to relationships, are rendered less fixed and less restricting."

16. Later in the same conversation, he remarked: "As we move in this constructionist and narrational direction, we sometimes fix on the words as ends in themselves. We try as therapists to generate a new sense of meaning, new narratives, new

constructions, as if a new set of words would 'do the trick.' In fact, I tend to talk that way myself at times. However, this is to miss the ultimate concern, which is relatedness itself—out of which meanings are generated. In effect, relations precede meaning. . . . We might develop a sense of ourselves as fully immersed in relatedness—with all humanity, all that is given—and that we might conceive of this awesome sensibility of pure relatedness (itself born of relationship) as approaching what we might mean by the domain of the spiritual" (Hoyt, 1996c, pp. 364–365).

17. So-called "radical constructivists" such as von Glaserfeld (1984) and von Foerster (1984; also described in Segal, 1986) have made the philosophically impeccable argument that all knowledge is bound by the perceiver. As Watzlawick (1984, p. 9) has put it: *"How do we know what we believe we know?. . . . What* we know is generally considered to be the result of our exploration and understanding of the real world, of the way things *really* are. . . . *How* we know is a far more vexing problem. To solve it, the mind needs to step outside itself, so to speak, and observe itself at work; for at this point we are no longer faced with facts that apparently exist independently of us in the outside world, but with mental processes whose nature is not at all self-evident. In this respect the title of this book *[The Invented Reality]* is somewhat less nonsensical, for if *what* we know depends on *how* we came to know it, then our view of reality is no longer a true image of what is the case outside ourselves, but is inevitably determined also by the processes through which we arrived at this view." We are meaning-makers, always part of the equation, "natural ontologists but reluctant epistemologists" (Bruner, 1986, p. 155). This awareness only heightens our personal responsibility. Neutral objectivity is a myth. To borrow McBride's phrase (1996), only God is "the color of water."

18. This is an apparent allusion to Gandhi's famous statement, "God comes to the hungry in the form of food."

19. Haiku (see also Hoyt, 1996f):

Focusing language

On solutions, not problems

Miracles happen

20. Constructive therapies can also extend to the use of psychopharmacological intervention. *Restoring restorying* is the term I prefer for the appropriate use of medication to support clients' self-empowerment. While there is great room for abuse (mind control), there are also patients for whom medication may allow thinking to focus and mood to abate enough for them to get on with the "reauthoring" and living of their lives. I am not in agreement with those who would not offer or suggest medication if the client had not first brought it up, any more than I would ignore or abstain from mentioning alternatives to oppressive social circumstances if these situations were apparent. This may be part of our expertise that we can bring to the clients' service. People sometimes need input (information). What

will be most important, of course, is full respect for informed consent, with invitation, not imposition, being the key.

21. While various constructive therapy approaches may be attractive to those interested in efficacy and efficiency, such approaches long antedated the drive for cost containment that is now dominating so much of therapeutic practice. Steve de Shazer, the prime originator of solution-focused therapy, has made his view very clear: "We are *not* a response to managed care. We've been doing brief therapy for 30 years. We developed this a long time before managed care was even somebody's bad idea" (Short, 1997, p. 18). O'Hanlon (1991), Lipchik (1994), and Nylund and Corsiglia (1994)—all brief therapy advocates—have also written against the use of rigid time limits as a method for "forcing" or curtailing treatment; elsewhere (Hoyt, 1995, 1997; Hoyt & Friedman, in press) I have also indicated my opposition to such practices and discussed some of the therapeutic dilemmas imposed by managed care.

22. In *Constructing the Self, Constructing America,* Cushman (1995, p. 3) sets this in modern context: "Each era has a predominant configuration of the self, a particular foundational set of beliefs about what it means to be human. Each particular configuration of the self brings with it characteristic illnesses, local healers, and local healing technologies. These selves and roles are not interchangeable or equivalent. Each embodies a kind of unique and local truth that should not be reduced to a universal law, because such reductions inevitably depend on a particular cultural frame of reference, which in turn inevitably involves an ideological agenda."

References

Adler, A. (1958). *What life should mean to you.* New York: Capricorn Books. (Original work published 1931)

Albee, G. W. (1997). Speak no evil? *American Psychologist, 52*(10), 1143–1144.

Amundson, J., Stewart, K., & Valentine, L. (1993). Temptations of power and certainty. *Journal of Marital and Family Therapy, 19,* 111–123.

Andersen, T. (Ed.). (1991). *The reflecting team: Dialogues and dialogues about the dialogues.* New York: Norton.

Andersen, T. (1992). Reflections on reflecting with families. In S. McNamee & K. J. Gergen (Eds.), *Therapy as social construction* (pp. 54–68). Newbury Park, CA: Sage.

Anderson, H. (1997). *Conversation, language, and possibilities: A postmodern approach to therapy.* New York: Basic Books.

Anderson, H., & Goolishian, H. A. (1988). Human systems as linguistic systems: Evolving ideas about the implications of theory and practice. *Family Process, 27,* 371–393.

Anderson, H., & Goolishian, H. A. (1992). The client is the expert: A not-knowing approach to therapy. In S. McNamee & K. J. Gergen (Eds.), *Therapy as social construction* (pp. 25–39). Newbury Park, CA: Sage.

Anderson, W. T. (1990). *Reality isn't what it used to be: Theatrical politics, ready-to-wear religion, global myths, primitive chic, and other wonders of the postmodern world.* San Francisco: Harper San Francisco.

Atwood, J. D. (1993). Social constructionist couple therapy. *Family Journal: Counseling and Therapy for Couples and Families, 1*(2), 116–130.

Bateson, G. (1972). *Steps to an ecology of mind.* New York: Ballantine.

Bateson, G. (1979). *Mind and nature: A necessary unity.* New York: Dutton.

Berg, I. K. (1989). Of visitors, complainants and customers. *Family Therapy Networker, 13*(1), 27.

Berg, I. K., & de Shazer, S. (1993). Making numbers talk: Language in therapy. In S. Friedman (Ed.), *The new language of change: Constructive collaboration in psychotherapy* (pp. 5–24). New York: Guilford Press.

Berger, P. L., & Kellner, H. (1979). Marriage and the social construction of reality. In H. Bobboy, S. Greenblatt, & C. Clark (Eds.), *Social interaction: Introductory readings in sociology* (pp. 308–322). New York: St. Martin's Press.

Bernstein, A. (1990). Ethical postures that orient one's clinical decision making. *AFTA Newsletter, 41*, 13–15.

Boscolo, L., & Bertrando, P. (1993). *The times of time.* New York: Norton.

Boyd, D. (1974). *Rolling Thunder.* New York: Delta.

Brown, L. (1997). The private practice of subversion: Psychotherapy as Tikkun Olam. *American Psychologist, 52* (4), 449–462.

Bruner, J. (1986). *Actual minds, possible worlds.* Cambridge, MA: Harvard University Press.

Buber, M. (1958). *I and thou.* New York: Scribner.

Cantwell, P., & Holmes, S. (1994). Social construction: A paradigm shift for systemic therapy and training. *Australian and New Zealand Journal of Family Therapy, 15*(1), 17–26.

Cecchin, G. (1987). Hypothesizing, circularity, and neutrality revisited: An invitation to curiosity. *Family Process, 26*, 405–413.

Cecchin, G., Lane, G., & Ray, W. A. (1992). *Irreverence: A strategy for therapists' survival.* London: Karnac Books.

Coale, H. W. (1992). The constructivist emphasis on language: A critical conversation. *Journal of Strategic and Systemic Therapies, 11*(1), 12–26.

Combs, G., & Freedman, J. (1994). Narrative intentions. In M. F. Hoyt (Ed.), *Constructive therapies* (pp. 67–91). New York: Guilford Press.

Coyne, J. C. (1985). Toward a theory of frames and reframing. *Journal of Marital and Family Therapy, 11*, 337–344.

Cushman, P. (1995). *Constructing the self, constructing America: A cultural history of psychotherapy.* Reading, MA: Addison-Wesley.

de Shazer, S. (1984). The death of resistance. *Family Process, 23*, 79–93.

de Shazer, S. (1985). *Keys to solution in brief therapy.* New York: Norton.

de Shazer, S. (1988). *Clues: Investigating solutions in brief therapy.* New York: Norton.

de Shazer, S. (1991). *Putting difference to work.* New York: Norton.

de Shazer, S. (1993). Creative misunderstanding: There is no escape from language. In S. G. Gilligan & R. Price (Eds.), *Therapeutic conversations* (pp. 81–90). New York: Norton.

de Shazer, S. (1994). *Words were originally magic.* New York: Norton.

Doherty, W. J. (1991). Family therapy goes postmodern. *Family Therapy Networker, 15*(5), 36–42.

Drengenberg, C. (1996). Cyber-cyber!!! *Journal of Systemic Therapies, 15*(3), 52.

Duvall, J. D., & Beier, J. M. (1995). Passion, commitment, and common sense: A unique discussion with Insoo Kim Berg and Michael White. *Journal of Systemic Therapies, 14*(3), 57–80.

Ecker, B., & Hulley, L. (1996). *Depth-oriented brief therapy: How to be brief when you were trained to be deep—and vice versa.* San Francisco: Jossey-Bass.

Efran, J. S., Lukens, M. D., & Lukens, R. J. (1990). *Language, structure, and change: Frameworks of meaning in psychotherapy.* New York: Norton.

Efran, J. S., Lukens, R. J., & Lukens, M. D. (1988). Constructivism: What's in it for you? *Family Therapy Networker, 12*(5), 26–36.

Eliot, T. S. (1943). *Four quartets.* Orlando: Harcourt Brace.

Erickson, M. H. (1980). *The collected papers of Milton H. Erickson on hypnosis* (Vol. 1–4, E. L. Rossi, Ed.). New York: Irvington.

Eron, J. B., & Lund, T. W. (1996). *Narrative solutions in brief therapy.* New York: Guilford Press.

Fish, V. (1993). Poststructuralism in family therapy: Interrogating the narrative/ conversational mode. *Journal of Marital and Family Therapy, 19*(3), 221–232.

Freedman, J., & Combs, G. (1996). *Narrative therapy: The social construction of preferred realities.* New York: Norton.

Freeman, J., Epston, D., & Lobovits, D. (1997). *Playful approaches to serious problems: Narrative therapy with children and their families.* New York: Norton.

Freud, S. (1961). Introductory lectures on psycho-analysis. In *The standard edition of the complete psychological works of Sigmund Freud.* Vol. 15 (J. Strachey, Ed. & Trans.). London: Hogarth Press. (Original work published 1915)

Friedman, S. (Ed.). (1993). *The new language of change: Constructive collaboration in psychotherapy.* New York: Guilford Press.

Friedman, S. (Ed.). (1995). *The reflecting team in action: Collaborative practice in family therapy.* New York: Guilford Press..

Friedman, S. (1996). Couples therapy: Changing conversations. In H. Rosen & K. T. Kuehlwein (Eds.), *Constructing realities: Meaning-making perspectives for psychotherapists* (pp. 413–453). San Francisco: Jossey-Bass.

Fuller, B. (1970). *I seem to be a verb.* New York: Bantam Books.

Furman, B., & Ahola, T. (1992). *Solution talk: Hosting therapeutic conversations.* New York: Norton.

Gergen, K. J. (1985). The social constructionist movement in modern psychology. *American Psychologist, 40,* 266–275.

Gergen, K. J. (1993). Foreword. In S. Friedman (Ed.), *The new language of change: Constructive collaboration in psychotherapy* (pp. ix–xi). New York: Guilford Press.

Gergen, K. J. (1994). *Realities and relationships.* Cambridge, MA: Harvard University Press.

Gergen, K. J. (1992). Beyond narrative in the negotiation of therapeutic meaning. In S. McNamee & K. J. Gergen (Eds.), *Therapy as social construction* (pp. 166–185). Newbury Park, CA: Sage.

Gergen, K. J., & Kaye, J. (1992). Beyond narrative in the negotiation of therapeutic meaning. In S. McNamee & K. J. Gergen (Eds.), *Therapy as social construction* (pp. 166–185). Newbury Park, CA: Sage.

Gilligan, S. G. (1987). *Therapeutic trances: The cooperation principle in Ericksonian hypnotherapy.* New York: Brunner/Mazel.

Gilligan, S. G., & Price, R. (Eds.). (1993). *Therapeutic conversations.* New York: Norton.

Goldfield, J. (1994, December). *A utilization approach for working with adolescents and their families.* Workshop held at the Sixth International Congress on Ericksonian Approaches to Hypnosis and Psychotherapy, Los Angeles.

Goldner, V. (1993). Power and hierarchy: Let's talk about it! *Family Process, 32*(2), 157–162.

Griffith, M. E. (1997). Foreword. In C. Smith & D. Nylund (Eds.), *Narrative therapies with children and adolescents* (pp. xvii–xix). New York: Guilford Press.

Haley, J. (1987). *Problem-solving therapy* (2nd ed.). San Francisco: Jossey-Bass.

Hare-Mustin, R. T. (1992). Meanings in the mirrored room: On cats and dogs. *Journal of Marital and Family Therapy, 18,* 309–310.

Hare-Mustin, R. T. (1994). Discourses in the mirrored room: A postmodern analysis of therapy. *Family Process, 33,* 19–35.

Held, B. S. (1995). *Back to reality: A critique of postmodern theory in psychotherapy.* New York: Norton.

Hillman, J. (1995). *Kinds of power: A guide to its intelligent uses.* New York: Doubleday.

Hoffman, L. (1990). Constructing realities: An art of lenses. *Family Process, 29,* 1–12.

Hoffman, L. (1993). *Exchanging voices: A collaborative approach to family therapy.* London: Karnac Books.

Hoffman, L. (1997). Postmodernism and family therapy. In J. K. Zeig (Ed.), *The evolution of psychotherapy: The third conference* (pp. 337–348). New York: Brunner/Mazel.

Horgan, J. (1996). *The end of science: Facing the limits of knowledge in the twilight of the scientific age.* Reading, MA: Addison-Wesley.

Hoyt, M. F. (1979). "Patient" or "client": What's in a name? *Psychotherapy: Theory, Research and Practice, 16,* 46–47. Reprinted in M. F. Hoyt, *Brief therapy and managed care: Readings for contemporary practice* (pp. 205–207). San Francisco: Jossey-Bass, 1995.

Hoyt, M. F. (1985). "Shrink" or "expander": An issue in forming a therapeutic alliance. *Psychotherapy, 22,* 813–814. Reprinted in M. F. Hoyt, *Brief therapy and managed care: Readings for contemporary practice* (pp. 209–211). San Francisco: Jossey-Bass.

Hoyt, M. F. (1994a). Introduction: Competency-based future-oriented therapy. In M. F. Hoyt (Ed.), *Constructive therapies* (pp. 1–10). New York: Guilford Press.

Hoyt, M. F. (1994b). On the importance of keeping it simple and taking the patient seriously: A conversation with Steve de Shazer and John Weakland. In M. F. Hoyt (Ed.), *Constructive therapies* (pp. 11–40). New York: Guilford Press.

Hoyt, M. F. (1995). *Brief therapy and managed care: Readings for contemporary practice.* San Francisco: Jossey-Bass.

Hoyt, M. F. (1996a). Introduction: Some stories are better than others. In M. F. Hoyt (Ed.), *Constructive therapies* (Vol. 2, pp. 1–32). New York: Guilford Press.

Hoyt, M. F. (Ed.). (1996b). *Constructive therapies* (Vol. 2). New York: Guilford Press.

Hoyt, M. F. (1996c). Postmodernism, the relational self, constructive therapies, and beyond: A conversation with Kenneth Gergen. In M. F. Hoyt (Ed.), *Constructive therapies* (Vol. 2, pp. 347–368). New York: Guilford Press.

Hoyt, M. F. (1996d). Solution building and language games: A conversation with Steve de Shazer. In M. F. Hoyt (Ed.), *Constructive therapies* (Vol. 2, pp. 60–86). New York: Guilford Press.

Hoyt, M. F. (1996e). Cognitive-behavioral treatment of posttraumatic stress disorder from a narrative constructivist perspective: A conversation with Donald Meichenbaum. In M. F. Hoyt (Ed.), *Constructive therapies* (Vol. 2, pp. 124–147). New York: Guilford Press.

Hoyt, M. F. (1996f). Haiku. In M. F. Hoyt (Ed.), *Constructive therapies* (Vol. 2, p. 375). New York: Guilford Press.

Hoyt, M. F. (1997, August). *Brief therapy and managed care: Prospects for the future.* Distinguished Speaker, Continuing Education Seminar, American Psychological Association Convention, Chicago.

Hoyt, M. F., & Combs, G. (1996). On ethics and the spiritualities of the surface: A conversation with Michael White. In M. F. Hoyt (Ed.), *Constructive therapies* (Vol. 2, pp. 33–59). New York: Guilford Press.

Hoyt, M. F., & Friedman, S. (in press). Dilemmas of postmodern practice under managed care and some pragmatics for increasing the likelihood of treatment authorization. *Journal of Systemic Therapies.*

Keeney, B. P. (1990). *Improvisational therapy.* St. Paul, MN: Systemic Therapy Press.

Kushner, T. (1995). American things. In *Thinking about the longstanding problems of virtue and happiness* (pp. 3–11). New York: Theatre Communications Group.

Laing, R. D. (1967). *The politics of experience.* New York: Pantheon.

Lakoff, G. (1995). Body, brain, and communication. In J. Brook & I. A. Boal (Eds.), *Resisting the virtual life: The culture and politics of information* (pp. 115–129). San Francisco: City Lights Books.

Lipchik, E. (1994). The rush to be brief. *Family Therapy Networker, 18*(2), 34–39.

Luepnitz, D. A. (1988). Bateson's heritage: Bitter fruit. *Family Therapy Networker, 12*(5), 48–50, 52–53, 73.

Madigan, S. P. (1993). Questions about questions: Situating the therapist's curiosity in front of the family. In S. Gilligan & R. Price (Eds.), *Therapeutic conversations* (pp. 219–230; with commentary by D. Epston, pp. 231–236). New York: Norton.

Markowitz, L. (1997). The cultural context of intimacy. *Family Therapy Networker, 21*(5), 51–58.

Maturana, H. R. (1988). Reality: The search for objectivity or the quest for a compelling argument. *Irish Journal of Psychology, 9,* 46–48.

Maturana, H. R., & Varela, F. J. (1980). *Autopoiesis and Cognition.* Dordrecht, Holland: Reidel.

McAdams, D. P. (1993). *The stories we live by: Personal myths and the making of the self.* New York: Guilford Press.

McBride, J. (1996). *The color of water: A black man's tribute to his white mother.* New York: Riverhead Books.

McNamee, S., & Gergen, K. J. (Eds.). (1992). *Therapy as social construction.* Newbury Park, CA: Sage.

Miller, G. (1997). *Becoming miracle workers: Language and meaning in brief therapy.* Hawthorne, NY: Aldine de Gruyter.

Minuchin, S. (1991). The seductions of constructivism. *Family Therapy Networker, 9*(5), 47–50.

Monk G., Winslade, J., Crocket, K., & Epston, D. (Eds.). (1997). *Narrative therapy in practice: The archaeology of hope.* San Francisco: Jossey-Bass.

Neal, J. H. (1996). Narrative training therapy and supervision. *Journal of Systemic Therapies, 15*(1), 63–78.

Neimeyer, R. A., & Mahoney, M. J. (Eds.). (1995). *Constructivism in psychotherapy.* Washington, DC: American Psychological Association.

Nylund, D., & Corsiglia, V. (1994). Becoming solution-focused forced in brief therapy: Remembering something important we already knew. *Journal of Systemic Therapies, 13*(1), 5–12.

O'Hanlon, W. H. (1991). Not strategic, not systemic: Still clueless after all these years. *Journal of Strategic and Systemic Therapies, 10,* 105, 109.

O'Hanlon, W. H. (1994). The third wave. *Family Therapy Networker, 18*(6), 18–26, 28–29.

O'Hanlon, W. H., & Hudson, P. O. (1995). *Love is a verb.* New York: Norton.

O'Hanlon, W. H., & Weiner-Davis, M. (1989). *In search of solutions: A new direction in psychotherapy.* New York: Norton.

O'Hanlon, W. H., & Wilk, J. (1987). *Shifting contexts.* New York: Guilford.

Parry, A., & Doan, R. E. (1994). *Story re-visions: Narrative therapy in the postmodern world.* New York: Guilford Press.

Pittman, F. (1992). It's not my fault. *Family Therapy Networker, 16*(1), 56–63.

Reddy, M. (1993). The conduit metaphor. In A. Ortony (Ed.), *Metaphor and thought* (2nd ed.). Cambridge: Cambridge University Press.

Rorty, R. (1979). *Philosophy and the mirror of nature.* Princeton, NJ: Princeton University Press.

Rosen, H., & Kuelhwein, K. (Eds.). (1996). *Constructing realities: Meaning-making perspectives for psychotherapists.* San Francisco: Jossey-Bass.

Rosenbaum, R., & Dyckman, J. (1996). No self? No problem! Actualizing empty self in psychotherapy. In M. F. Hoyt (Ed.), *Constructive therapies* (Vol. 2, pp. 238–274). New York: Guilford Press.

Roth, S., & Chasin, R. (1994). Entering one another's worlds of meaning and imagination: Dramatic enactment and narrative couple therapy. In M. F. Hoyt (Ed.), *Constructive therapies* (pp. 189–216). New York: Guilford Press.

Roth, S., & Epston, D. (1996). Consulting the problem about the problematic relationship: An exercise for experiencing a relationship with an externalized problem. In M. F. Hoyt (Ed.), *Constructive therapies* (Vol. 2, pp. 148–162). New York: Guilford Press.

Rybczynski, W. (1986). *Home: A short history of an idea.* New York: Penguin.

Schafer, R. (1992). *Retelling a life: Narration and dialogue in psychoanalysis.* New York: Basic Books.

Schloegl, I. (1975). *The wisdom of the Zen masters.* New York: New Directions.

Schmidt, G., & Trenkle, B. (1985). An integration of Ericksonian techniques with concepts of family therapy. In J. K. Zeig (Ed.), *Ericksonian psychotherapy: Vol. II. Clinical applications* (pp. 132–154). New York: Brunner/Mazel.

Segal, L. (1986). *The dream of reality: Heinz von Foerster's constructivism.* New York: Norton.

Shafarman, G. (1996). Thirteen ways of looking at how a poet and a therapist are one. *Poetry Flash,* June-July, p. 25.

Short, D. (1997). Interview: Steve de Shazer and Insoo Kim Berg. *The Milton H. Erickson Foundation Newsletter, 17*(2), 1, 18–20.

Sluzki, C. (1988). Case commentary II. *Family Therapy Networker, 12*(5), 77–79.

Smith, C. (1997). Introduction: Comparing traditional therapies with narrative approaches. In C. Smith & D. Nylund (Eds.), *Narrative therapy with children and adolescents.* New York: Guilford Press.

Smith, C., & Nylund, D. (Eds.). (1997). *Narrative therapy with children and adolescents.* New York: Guilford Press.

Speed, B. (1984). How really real is real? *Family Process, 23,* 511–517.

Speed, B. (1991). Reality exists, OK? An argument against constructivism and social constructivism. *Family Therapy, 13,* 395–409.

Spence, D. P. (1982). *Narrative truth and historical truth: Meaning and interpretation in psychoanalysis.* New York: Norton.

Tomm, K. (1991). The ethics of dual relationships. *Calgary Participator, 1*(Winter), 11–15.

Tomm, K. (1993). The courage to protest: A commentary on Michael White's work. In S. G. Gilligan & R. Price (Eds.), *Therapeutic conversations* (pp. 62–80). New York: Norton.

von Foerster, H. (1984). On constructing a reality. In P. Watzlawick (Ed.), *The invented reality* (pp. 41–61). New York: Norton.

von Glaserfeld, E. (1984). An introduction to radical constructivism. In P. Watzlawick (Ed.), *The invented reality* (pp. 17–40). New York: Norton.

Waldegrave, C. (1990). Just Therapy. *Dulwich Centre Newsletter,* no. 1, pp. 1–47.

Watzlawick, P. (1976). *How real is real? Communication, disinformation, confusion.* New York: Vintage.

Watzlawick, P. (1978). *The language of change: Elements of therapeutic communication.* New York: Norton.

Watzlawick, P. (Ed.). (1984). *The invented reality: How do we know what we believe we know? (Contributions to constructivism).* New York: Norton.

Watzlawick, P. (1992). The construction of clinical "realities." In J. K. Zeig (Ed.), *The evolution of psychotherapy: The second conference* (pp. 55–62). New York: Brunner/Mazel.

Watzlawick, P., Beavin, J. B., & Jackson, D. D. (1967). *Pragmatics of human communication: A study of interactional patterns, pathologies, and paradoxes.* New York: Norton.

Watzlawick, P., Weakland, J. H., & Fisch, R. (1974). *Change: Principles of problem formation and problem resolution.* New York: Norton.

Weakland, J. H. (1993). Conversation—but what kind? In S. G. Gilligan & R. Price (Eds.), *Therapeutic conversations* (pp. 136–145). New York: Norton.

Weiner-Davis, M. (1993). Pro-constructed realities. In S. G. Gilligan & R. Price (Eds.), *Therapeutic conversations* (pp. 149–157). New York: Norton.

White, M. (1988). The process of questioning: A therapy of literary merit? *Dulwich Centre Newsletter,* Winter, pp. 8–14. Reprinted in M. White, *Selected papers* (pp. 37–46). Adelaide, South Australia: Dulwich Centre Publications, 1989.

White, M. (1989). The externalizing of the problem and the reauthoring of lives and relationships. *Dulwich Centre Newsletter,* Summer. Reprinted in M. White, *Selected papers* (pp. 5–28). Adelaide, South Australia: Dulwich Centre Publications, 1989.

White, M. (1993). Commentary: The histories of the present. In S. G. Gilligan & R. Price (Eds.), *Therapeutic conversations* (pp. 121–135). New York: Norton.

White, M. (1995). *Re-authoring lives: Interviews and essays.* Adelaide, South Australia: Dulwich Centre Publications.

White, M. (1997). *Narratives of therapists' lives.* Adelaide, South Australia: Dulwich Centre Publications.

White, M., & Epston, D. (1990). *Narrative means to therapeutic ends.* New York: Norton.

Wick, D. T. (1996). Social constructionism: Groping toward this something. *Journal of Systemic Therapies, 15*(3), 65–81.

Young-Eisendrath, P., & Hall, J. A. (1991). *Jung's self psychology: A constructivist perspective.* New York: Guilford Press.

Zeig, J. K., & Munion, W. M. (1990). What is psychotherapy? In J. K. Zeig & W. M. Munion (Eds.), *What is psychotherapy? Contemporary perspectives* (pp. 1–14). San Francisco: Jossey-Bass.

Zimmerman, J. L., & Dickerson, V. C. (1994). Using a narrative metaphor: Implications for theory and clinical practice. *Family Process, 33,* 233–246.

Zimmerman, J. L., & Dickerson, V. C. (1996). *If problems talked: Narrative therapy in action.* New York: Guilford Press.

PART ONE

THEORETICAL PERSPECTIVES

CHAPTER ONE

Redecision Therapy

Through a Narrative Lens

James R. Allen, Barbara A. Allen

D uring the 1960s and 1970s, Bob and Mary Goulding developed redecision therapy in that coastal area of California between Big Sur and San Francisco that has been so fertile in psychotherapeutic innovation. At that time, the Esalen Institute was encouraging humanistic and growth therapies of various types, and Fritz Perls, Virginia Satir, and Eric Berne were local celebrities and friends (Anderson, 1983; Hoyt, 1995). Working primarily in Carmel and later on Mt. Madonna near Watsonville, the Gouldings combined the script theory of Berne (1972) with some of the Gestalt techniques of Perls (Goulding, 1976; Perls, 1969). The result was a potent, new, brief narrative therapy that can be employed both in groups and with individuals alone (Goulding & Goulding, 1978, 1979).

THE REDECISION PROCESS

Redecision therapy proceeds through the following stages:

1. Development of a therapeutic contract.

2. Reexperiencing of a key early scene related to the contract. This includes early decisions about oneself, other people, and life.

3. Introduction of new information, experience, or affect into this scene.

4. A redecision.

5. Anchoring and reaffirmation of the new decision.

6. Reintegration of the patient back into the community.

John: "The Boy Who Shouldn't Have Been"

In describing his unruly children, two of whom had become drug addicts, John added, "Well, when things get bad enough, I can always kill myself"—and laughed.

THERAPIST: It's not funny for you.

JOHN: *[eyes filling with tears]* No.

THERAPIST: When you were young, who might have been pleased in some way by your killing yourself?

JOHN: Me. I don't know of anybody else. I've always felt this way, like I was a nuisance.

THERAPIST: Stay with that sense of being a nuisance and go back in time— as early as possible—to another time when you felt this way.

JOHN: *[shuts his eyes, pauses a few moments]* Yes, I'm about five and lying down on the grass in our backyard. My parents are fighting about me again. I put my hands over my ears. I feel that I can't take it anymore. I eat some dirt to kill myself, but it doesn't.

THERAPIST: Go more fully into the scene. Put your hands over your eyes. Taste the dirt.

JOHN: *[after a few minutes]* I'm lying on the ground crying and all alone. Then my dog, Cuddles, comes over and licks my face.

THERAPIST: OK, now imagine you have Cuddles in your arms. Feel your love for the dog and the dog's love for you.

JOHN: I can feel her licking my face. I feel loved. She and Big Mama *[his maternal grandmother]* were the only ones who cared about me.

THERAPIST: Is there a part of you that doesn't feel like killing yourself?

JOHN: Yes. That part appreciates Cuddles' kisses and her warm softness and that she is glad to be with me.

THERAPIST: OK, John. Imagine the part of you that wants to die in this chair over here. *[brings up a chair]* Now be the part of you that wants to live. Talk to the part that wants to die. *[John leans forward]*

THERAPIST: What do you have to say to the suicidal part?

JOHN: Don't! It's not OK. Your parents don't care about you, but Cuddles does—and so does Big Mama.

THERAPIST: How old are you?

JOHN: About four or five. The same as the other part.

THERAPIST: Now sit in this other chair and be Big Mama.

JOHN: *[as Big Mama]* John, I love you and always have. You deserve
to have been born into a family where you were wanted. It's too bad
your parents weren't grown up when they had you.

THERAPIST: OK, switch chairs again. Now John, what do you reply?

JOHN: Big Mama, all my life I have wanted to feel loved and that I
belonged—but never did except for you.

THERAPIST: *[brings up two chairs]* Say that to your parents.

JOHN: Damn you! *[shouting]* I wanted to feel loved and that I belonged.
Why did you have me if you didn't want me? It's not my fault you
couldn't love me. *[begins sobbing, and holds breath]*

THERAPIST: Keep breathing. You are blocking your sadness.

JOHN: *[utters a long wail, then shouts]* It's not my fault you couldn't love
me. At least you could have given me up for adoption, so someone else
could have.

THERAPIST: Yes. Imagine you grew up in a family where you were wanted,
as you were by Big Mama and Cuddles. What do you say to your parents?

JOHN: Damn you to Hell! I'm not going to kill myself just because you didn't
want me. I'm going to live—and find love from people who can give it.

THERAPIST: Say that again.

JOHN: I'm going to look for love from people who can be loving. And I'm
going to accept it.

THERAPIST: Experiment, repeating that to various people here in the group
and see how you feel.

John does so, experimenting with various tones of voice and postures. Finally,
he speaks.

JOHN: I feel good. I feel strong.

THERAPIST: Sit down again. Imagine that you, as an adult, are holding that
little five-year-old boy in your arms.

JOHN: *[shutting his eyes]* Yes, I have him in my arms and he is leaning into
my chest and neck.

THERAPIST: Good. Now tell him that you are proud that he is a survivor,
and add "I will take care of you and keep you safe"—or something
similar that would fit better for you.

JOHN: *[gentle smile coming across his face]* Yes. And it's not OK to kill yourself.

THERAPIST: Right. Now John, one final thing. Will you make a contract with yourself—not with me, but with yourself—that you will not hurt or kill yourself accidentally or on purpose, now or in the future?

JOHN: Yes. Now I can.

In transactional analysis terminology as used in redecision therapy, we speak of *injunctions, decisions,* and *redecisions.* Injunctions are early messages, often preverbal, that encourage destructive life themes (e.g., Don't think, Don't feel, Don't be a child, Don't grow up, Don't trust people, Don't!, Don't be). They may be given by parents, other family members, society, or even by accidents of fate. We would say John received an injunction "Don't be" arising from the fact his birth was inopportune and from his experiences of not being loved by his parents, and also the injunction "Don't belong." Childhood decisions are made in response to such injunctions, and form the basis of a person's future life narrative. It is sobering to think that many people are leading lives (scripts) that they decided when they were not yet in grade school. In John's case, the decision was "When things are bad enough, I can always kill myself." A redecision, as here, is a new decision that changes or supplants the early childhood one. It is a reauthoring of one's life.

This example demonstrates several useful techniques: following a feeling back to an early key scene, two-chair Gestalt work that permits intensification of feeling and externalization of a problem in the present, and the use of a no-suicide contract. It demonstrates work with early interactions between John and his parents as well as work with the conflict between the part of John that wanted to die and the part that didn't. This is similar to the evocation and amplification of exceptions to a problem pattern (de Shazer, 1985) or the evocation of a suppressed narrative (Foucault, 1980).

John's initial sentence—"I can always kill myself, ha ha"—is known as a *gallows transaction,* a transaction that invites others to laugh and thereby indirectly to approve of the person's doing something self-destructive (Berne, 1972). Had the therapist laughed with him, John might have taken this as permission to kill himself. This remark also was an invitation for the therapist to not notice that John was discounting therapy. These are the reasons the therapist dove right in, even to the extent of not first getting a clear, formal contract for this specific piece of work, although John had made an earlier contract to stop depressing himself. The therapist's intention was to show John that what he said was taken seriously, and that it definitely was not OK for him to kill himself; that is, to offer immediate protection, as well as permission to live.

A few months after this intervention, John and his wife visited his parents, who live in another state. During that visit, John's mother revealed a family secret to his wife. She and John's father had been planning to divorce when she had found herself pregnant with John. She had attempted to abort him with potassium permanganate and a coat hanger. She had failed and, overcome with guilt at what she had done, decided to have him. However, shortly after his birth she gave him to some cousins to raise. He stayed with them for over a year. Then she and her husband got back together and took John back—and the whole matter was never talked about again. This story, which had been suppressed or at least made unavailable to him, did not really surprise John. Rather, he took it as confirmation of what he had always known at some level. It was useful, however, in helping him appreciate that his early decision had made good sense, given the world as he knew it at age four or five, but that he no longer needed to live life based on it.

Muriel: "The Big, Amorphous Blob"

THERAPIST: What do you want to change?

MURIEL: I want to stop being a big, amorphous blob.

THERAPIST: What exactly do you mean?

MURIEL: I am a hundred pounds overweight. I don't know how to use makeup or do my hair. What's worse, I'm getting heavier and heavier. Now I even hide chocolate bars so I don't have to share them with my children.

THERAPIST: [getting up and gesturing as if heaving a large weight from her and placing it on a nearby chair] OK, pretend that this is the big, amorphous blob. What do you want to say to it?

MURIEL: I don't want you. I hate you! I hate you because you are ruining my life! [crying]

THERAPIST: Now come over here and be the blob.

MURIEL: [switches chairs] Muriel, I'm your blob. You're lucky to have me. Otherwise, you wouldn't be anything at all.

THERAPIST: Muriel, who wouldn't have wanted you to be anything at all? Who might have said or felt this?

MURIEL: My father. [crying]

THERAPIST: [bringing up a new chair] OK, sit in this chair and be your father. Tell Muriel she's lucky to be anything at all.

MURIEL: [as father] You were supposed to be a boy. I sure didn't want a girl. Better for you to be an amorphous blob than a girl.

THERAPIST: [to Muriel as her father] Father, tell Muriel how come you didn't want a girl.

MURIEL: [as father] Girls make me uncomfortable. They are a different species. I never had any sisters and after my mother died, we were all males. The only girl I ever really knew was your mother and she was more like a boy, a real tomboy.

THERAPIST: So, father, it was your discomfort around females that led you to not want Muriel to be a girl?

MURIEL: *[as father]* Yes. I feared it. I feared her.

THERAPIST: Since you are now dead, would it be OK if Muriel gets in touch with her feminine side and feels like a real woman rather than an amorphous blob?

MURIEL: *[as father]* Yes.

THERAPIST: Tell her.

MURIEL: *[as father]* Muriel, it's OK with me if you become a real woman and feel like a woman. I never intended to make you unhappy. I only knew I was scared of girls and more comfortable around boys. After all, I was a coach and was used to boys. You have the right to be you.

THERAPIST: *[pointing to other chair]* Now, as Muriel, respond to him.

MURIEL: *[switches chairs]* Yes, Dad. I do have that right and I am going to take it. I'm going to stop overeating and I'm going to learn how to dress and put on makeup and do my hair—and I'm going to enjoy it! I'm not going to waste my life just to show you up.

THERAPIST: Say that again.

MURIEL: *[louder]* I'm not going to waste my life just to show you up. I am going to find people who can teach me what mother could not. I'm going to learn how to dress and how to look like a woman. *[excited laugh]* And I'm going to enjoy myself.

Because of his discomfort with women, we would say Muriel's father gave her an injunction such as "You can be only if you are not a girl" or "Don't be you" (a girl). In addition, he married a woman who was a tomboy and not able to teach Muriel how to be feminine in a way that was important to her. Muriel's early decision seems to have been something like, "OK, I won't be a girl—but I'll be something. You'll have to acknowledge me because I'll be a big blob."

This vignette demonstrates externalization (the blob) that is then transformed into the person who gave the restricting messages (the father), an interview with the patient's internalized parent, a redecision and child delight in the redecision.

Three months later Muriel had stopped eating sweets, had begun to walk three miles a day, and had lost twenty-five pounds. She had found some women to help her dress better, put on makeup, and fix her hair.

ELEMENTS OF PRACTICE

Let us now look at some key aspects of redecision therapy more closely.

Contract

A therapeutic contract sets the stage for and is the focus of treatment. The therapist makes sure that the contract is for change, and that the goals are meaningful, measurable, and achievable. The goal should be phrased in such a way that both the therapist and the patient will know when it is achieved. "I want to get rid of this depression" is very different from "I want to stop telling myself I am no good" or "I don't want to spend all day yearning for my dead mother." The contract should also be legal. Finally, it should be acceptable to all parts of the patient and the therapist. "I should lose weight (or stop smoking, or whatever) is a New Year's resolution type of contract and won't, by itself, last long. The redecision therapist would try to expand it to include reasons based on current facts (Adult thinking, in transactional analytic terminology) and what the patient would gain—such as becoming more sexy (if that is not frightening)—or lose, such as feeling tired (Child). During this process, the therapist acts as a careful travel guide and offers protection so that patients do not choose goals that are not in their best interests. Consequently, no-suicide and no-homicide contracts take precedence over others (Allen & Allen, 1984).

A therapeutic contract needs to be distinguished from an administrative one. A patient can promise to come in once a week, pay the bills, and make other arrangements—but not make any contract for change. A therapeutic contract is for change—not for explanation, education, companionship, or self-harassment with "shoulds." A good therapeutic contract allows redecision therapy to be brief, for it circumscribes the problem and limits exploration to a specific goal. The process fits for people who have decided to change something specific. If, however, they are contemplating changing sometime but not just yet, or if they believe they have no need to change, this approach is not for them. However, even these people may still find participation in a group useful, for the work of other patients may stir up issues that they have not resolved. Alternatively, they might wish to enter a specific exploratory contract.

Developing a Key Scene

In redecision work, patients are asked to find some key scene in their life wherein they made a decision related to their current contract. The scene may be a current or recent incident, an early scene, a fantasy scene, a dream, something that develops from the exaggeration of a gesture or movement, a laugh (as in John's gallows transaction), or something that evolves from the externalization of a problem (as in Mary's amorphous blob).

For most patients, redecision is done most easily if they involve scenes from early in their lives because they are children in such scenes. The redecision is experienced most fully when the featured protagonists are the people who gave the original messages.

Using a Dream. A depressed young woman came to a weekend marathon. She was an unwanted child. She developed an imaginary scene of a time her mother was trying to abort her, screaming, "Die! Die!" With great difficulty, we were able to get a no-suicide contract—but then only until the end of the workshop. We gave clear negative and positive permissions to live: that she didn't have to please her mother by killing herself now, and that she had a right to live. On going to her room after the session, she passed a statue of the Virgin Mary. That night she dreamed that the Blessed Virgin told her that, as a child, it was her birthright to be born into a loving family. By role-playing both herself and the Virgin Mary in a two-chair dialogue the next morning, she was able to give herself permission to live—and to accept it.

Many years later, she revealed that she had come to the workshop to get us to say she was too sick to stay and that she had intended to use our rejection to justify killing herself. Instead, she gave herself permission to live. To her surprise, her lifelong depression disappeared.

Tracking a Feeling or a Phrase. To help a patient recall an early scene, we might say, "Be a little girl and hear the words . . . " or "Who told you not to . . . ?"— repeating words the patient just said. We might say, "Shut your eyes and go back in time to when you were feeling this same way or having the same problem," as we did with John.

Externalizing. In cases of pain, anger, or sorrow we might ask the patient to talk to this problem as if it were a person, and then, as the problem, to reply, developing a two-chair Gestalt dialogue. Sometimes it is then useful to have the patient imagine some person sitting in the chair where the problem sat—as we did in the case of Muriel's blob and father. This is an externalization of an introject (Hoyt, 1994) or of a problem and its underlying object representation. Patients may treat such an externalization as something foreign and fight against it, as is encouraged by White and Epston (1990), but more likely they will be helped to come to some new understanding of it, to change it or to resolve it in some new way.

Utilization of Body Movement. Key scenes can also be developed out of some body movement or gesture to which the patient is asked to give a voice.

For example, Diane came to therapy because she was afraid she could no longer control her rage at her husband.

THERAPIST: What do you want to change?

DIANE: I want to stop what I'm doing with my husband. I either say nothing although I am absolutely enraged with him, or I blow up. I have no medium. It's like I paint with red paint or with white paint, but never with pink.

While giving this description, she was tapping the arm of her chair.

THERAPIST: Give a voice to your hand. What is it saying?

DIANE: I don't know.

THERAPIST: Intensify what you are doing. [demonstrating]

DIANE: I'm pushing you down. Then I let you go. [pauses] Oh, my God, that's just what my father always did. I wasn't supposed to feel—or at least I wasn't supposed to express my feelings. I could have them, but I wasn't supposed to show them. Every once in a while I'd have a big temper tantrum, and then we would make up and he'd be real nice to me.

Supplementation. One of our functions as therapists is to listen and watch for something missing from patients' accounts. Life is rich and our stories do not tell all that happened. Some details are left out, others highlighted. If the therapist pays attention to this, the patient may be able to develop some new understanding of the key scene. This supplementation procedure has similarities to White and Epston's (1990) practice of developing an alternative narrative and de Shazer's (1985, 1988) work with exceptions, but each has developed within a different tradition (de Shazer, 1993).

FURTHER ELEMENTS OF PRACTICE

Let us now consider in more detail the process of making decisions and redecisions.

Changing the Early Scene and Redecision

Many key scenes involve a two-chair conversation between the patient and one or both parents as the client reexperiences some childhood event. Sometimes, we interview the patient as if he or she were the mother or father and, as in Muriel's therapy, explore how it happened that they gave the messages they did. This usually introduces a whole new way for the patient to see his or her parents and why they behaved as they did. Thus, the patient experiences something new, and gains some new information. All this is done in the present. Experiencing in the now (not talking about the past) is the key.

It should be noted that decisions are usually made when a child is quite young, at a time when the belief in magic is still strong. Given the world as the child knew it, these decisions had survival value, and adults experience them as still having this quality. After all, they are still alive!

In ferreting out these decisions, the Gouldings (1978, 1979) looked for *injunctions*—early messages or life themes that patients use to decide their life stories. These are primarily preverbal or nonverbal and may come from the child's early milieu rather than from any one person. The most common are Don't be, Don't be you, Don't be close, Don't belong, Don't feel, Don't be a child, Don't think, Don't make it, Don't grow up, Don't, Don't be important, and Don't be OK. We have found it useful to look at the flip side, the *permissions* that the patient needed and still needs—such as Be, Be yourself, Be close, Be a child, and so on (Allen & Allen, 1996, 1997a, 1997b, 1997c; Allen et al., 1997). A large body of current research confirms that these permissions are the basis of childhood and adult resilience, the ability to bounce back after misfortune and catastrophe or to deal effectively with internal weaknesses (Allen, 1998).

Some redecision therapists conceptualize injunctions as real. However, the therapist can do this work without assuming privileged access to ultimate objective truth or to what "really" happened. Rather, we help the patient move from a narrative that is restricting to one that leaves more options available. Perhaps the mother never really did give the apparent injunctions. However, assuming she did and talking to her in fantasy usually gives the patient a sense of conviction. He is left with a sense that he has chosen a new life: "The power is in the patient" as the Gouldings put it (Goulding & Goulding, 1978). In addition, the experience can serve as a marker—an event that explains whatever changes the patient later makes.

Whatever the chosen scene or the therapist's belief system about injunctions, the purpose of redecision work is to help the patient reject messages that were previously accepted and to decide something new. As Mary Goulding (1997, p. 87) has written:

> Clients make redecisions when they are stuck in childhood decisions that are hurtful or impede growth in their current lives. Their redecisions are often made in the context of an early childhood scene.
>
> Sometimes their scenes actually occurred, and sometimes they are the client's beliefs about what occurred. In the field of psychotherapy, the controversies about real and fake memory syndrome arise because therapists think they must judge the validity of each scene a client reports. Therapists are not detectives, judges, or members of juries. Their job has never been to discover truth. Their function is to help clients deal as well as possible with their own present lives. Past scenes are helpful in this task.

In general, I believe my clients, and I know that my belief is not an issue. What is important is that the client recovers from the past, real and imagined, and goes on to a fulfilling life.

The therapist has a responsibility to make sure the patient makes a redecision that is beneficial, and that does not just repeat some past unhappiness. Strengths can be forged in the smithy of adversity. Life experiences can be treated as resources, and hopes can become treatment goals.

In the redecision process the patient has both an emotional experience (Child ego state in transactional terminology) and a new cognitive framework for understanding the experience (Adult ego state). In the terms of transactional analysis, the redecision is made from the Free Child ego state.

Anchoring and Reintegration

Redecision is a beginning rather than an end. The patient begins to think, feel, and act in new ways. We prefer that patients practice their redecision without additional immediate therapy, then return later if they encounter difficulties or have something new they wish to change.

After the patient has made a redecision, however, an important therapeutic task is to help him or her translate it into concrete action in daily life. We generally ask patients to close their eyes and to pretend they are at home, with their family or at work: "Notice the change you are making in the way you feel, the way you think, the way you behave. How are you and the others interacting? Do they notice changes in you? Who do you imagine is pleased? Who is displeased?"

If the patient experiences difficulties, we recontract and work on solving these new problems. This process roots the new life-plan in real life. It is also useful in helping patients delineate clearly exactly what they will need to keep their redecision and to support their new pro-solution story line. Impulsive patients, for example, frequently need practice in changing destructive behavior and finding appropriate substitutes for the excitement they had been receiving through pathological activities.

Although a redecision may be made quite rapidly—in a session or two— many patients need reinforcement of it over a longer period of time. Most will experiment with playing their old games and experiencing stereotyped emotions, but at a reduced level of intensity. They then can either engage in self-harassing internal dialogue or congratulate themselves for recognizing what they are doing and then do something else. The second option is preferable.

REDECISION THERAPY AS A NARRATIVE THERAPY

Appreciation of the importance of narrative and of simultaneous and coexisting interpretations of the world seems a hallmark of postmodernity. In the family therapy area, White and Epston (1990) have elaborated approaches that bring hitherto suppressed stories into the foreground of a person's life. By exploring what the patient would be doing if his or her problem were already resolved and looking at exceptions, de Shazer's solution-focused therapy (1985, 1988) does something similar, and highlights a future problem-free narrative. Redecision therapy, we believe, does much the same. Injunctions are narrative themes and redecisions are a way of reauthoring one's life.

By reenacting a key scene and then introducing something different into it, the patient is freed to conceptualize the situation anew and feel differently about it. As a result, the patient can make a different decision than the one he or she originally made. In this way, the process of redecision therapy provides a context in which the patient can decide a new life story. The therapist guides the process, and helps modify the patient's understanding by asking questions that supplement what the patient previously believed. However, it is the patient who, in consultation, sets the goals of therapy (contract) and actually makes the new decision. In so doing, he or she has the sense of having chosen a new life narrative.

The redecision itself is followed by planning for the future. How will the patient get future support for the new story and obtain positive "strokes" for the new course of action? In many ways this appears similar to de Shazer's "Miracle Question" (1985). The emphasis is not, however, on what the patient would do if change miraculously appeared. Rather, the emphasis is on what the patient will do differently now, having made a new decision—one that frees the life narrative from old restraints.

When looking at different therapies, or the use of one therapeutic framework by different therapists, it is informative to consider the four-stage progression Baudrillard (1984) suggested in an essay on the postmodern loss of reality. The first of these stages is characterized by the assumption that an image (read: narrative) reflects basic reality. In the second stage, the image (read: narrative), is assumed to hide a basic reality with which we humans cannot have contact. In the third phase, the narrative only plays at being an appearance, while actually masking the absence of a basic reality. In the fourth and final stage, the narrative becomes transparently fictional. This is the stage of the *simulacra*, of images without originals. Depending on the therapist and the patient, redecision therapy can, we believe, be practiced on any of these levels.

Redecision therapy helps patients reauthor their narratives, rather than just correct their accounts. If psychotherapy is understood in this way, it is a process of *semiosis*—the forging of meaning in the context of collaborative discourse. The patient-therapist interaction is where the patient's story (or "text") unfolds. It is a co-construction by the two. The therapeutic goal is facilitating, coauthoring, cocreating—not imposing some new narrative.

A REDECISION VIEW OF OTHER NARRATIVE THERAPIES

White and his colleagues (White & Epston, 1990) try to find an alternative story in the patient's history by focusing on alternative outcomes. This seems similar to redecision therapy, but the redecision therapist puts more emphasis on the patient's reexperiencing the past in the present and on active decision making. The redecision therapist does encourage the creation of an externalization narrative, and in the course of Gestalt dialogue may have the patient confront a problem such as pain or sorrow. Usually, however, this is a preliminary step in understanding the problem better and learning something new that will lead to the redecision. Redecision therapists would not be likely to develop an Anti-anorexic League; this implies the problem is contained but not resolved (de Shazer, 1993).

The redecision therapist takes charge of the therapeutic process by seeking a clear contract and by establishing clear goals. This limits the area of exploration and is quite different from the style of Goolishian and Anderson (1988), for example, who engage in therapeutic conversation from a stance of "not knowing," and who espouse a multiperspective conversation of ambiguity and mutual reflexivity. It should be noted, however, that while the collaboratively negotiated goal (contract) portion of the redecision process is influenced by the therapist, the power to make the redecision is the patient's. In White's work, by contrast, the power often seems more in the therapist. Like the work of solution-focused therapists, the redecision process is quite goal directed. However, the redecision therapist seeks emotional reexperiencing in the present and leaves future choices for the patient to decide. The patient is "stroked" for coming up with his or her own personal solutions. Focus is on the patient's ability and choice in making a redecision, and on the patient's modifying the environment to support a new way of life, not on solutions per se. Through the use of transactional analysis, redecision therapy offers the patient both a way of "restorying" and a way of understanding the experience. Hoyt (1997, p. xvii) has written: "Solution-focused therapists such as de Shazer (1985, 1988) may appreciate the redecision therapist stroking the Natural Child . . . as the evocation and amplification of exceptions to the problem pattern, and may see the use of anchoring, changes in the stroke economy, and Adult planning as ways to further structure and support the emergence of a pro-solution worldview and storyline."

Our stories are constrained by our ideas of what makes a good story—a beginning, middle, and end; organization of events relevant to an end point; logical connection of incidents, and some form such as progression, regression, and stability; or mystery, comedy, and tragedy. Redecision therapy shares with other constructive therapies the belief that the stories in which we situate our experiences determine the aspects of experience to which we give later attention, the meanings we give them, and ultimately the direction of and the relationships in our lives. However, life is not synonymous with story. It is the performance of a story.

In a defense he made of literature, Oscar Wilde made a statement that seems appropriate to end this discussion: "As life has no shape and literature has, literature is throwing away its one distinctive quality when it tries to imitate life" (Graff, 1979, p. 52). In redecision therapy we do the opposite, conceptualizing life as literature or at least as narrative, and helping patients to create a new, less problem-saturated narrative.

References

Allen, J. R. (1998, in press). Of resilience and vulnerability—and a woman who never existed. In B. Pfefferbaum (Ed.), *Child-adolescent psychiatric clinics of North America.* Philadelphia: Saunders.

Allen, J. R., & Allen, B. A. (1984). *Psychiatry: A guide* (2nd ed.). New York: Medical Examination.

Allen, J. R., & Allen, B. A. (1991). Towards a constructivist TA. In B. R. Loria (Ed.), *The Stamford papers: Selections from the 29th annual ITAA conference* (pp. 1–22). Madison, WI: Omnipress.

Allen, J. R., & Allen, B. A. (1996). Narrative theory, redecision therapy and postmodernism. *Transactional Analysis Journal, 25*(4), 327–334.

Allen, J. R., & Allen, B. A. (1997a). A new version of transactional analysis and script work, with a constructionist sensitivity. *Transactional Analysis Journal, 27*(2), 1–11.

Allen, J. R., & Allen, B. A. (1997b). Of constructivism, constructionism, postmodernism and psychotherapy. *Journal of Transactional Social Psychology.* Internet. http://www.bravenewweb.com/idea/. Editor, Alan Jacobs.

Allen, J. R., & Allen B. A. (1997c). Redecision therapy with children and adolescents. In C. Lennox (Ed.), *Redecision therapy: A brief action-oriented approach* (pp. 227–253). Northvale, NJ: Aronson.

Allen, J. R., Allen, B. A., Barnes, G., Hibner, B., Krausz, R., Moiso, C., Welch, S., & Welch, C. (1997). Permission: Two decades later. *Transactional Analysis Journal, 26*(3), 196–205.

Anderson, W. T. (1983). *The upstart spring: Esalen and the American awakening.* Reading, MA: Addison-Wesley.

Baudrillard, J. (1984). The progression of simulacra. In B. Wallis (Ed.), *Art after modernism* (pp. 253–281). New York: New York Museum of Contemporary Art.

Berne, E. (1972). *What do you say after you say hello?* New York: Grove Press.

de Shazer, S. (1985). *Keys to solution in brief therapy.* New York: Norton.

de Shazer, S. (1988). *Clues: Investigating solutions in brief therapy.* New York: Norton.

de Shazer, S. (1993). Commentary: de Shazer and White—Vive la différence. In S. Gilligan and R. Price (Eds.), *Therapeutic conversations* (pp. 112–120). New York: Norton.

Foucault, M. (1980). *Power/knowledge: Selected interviews and other writings 1972–1977* (C. Gordon, Ed.). New York: Pantheon.

Goolishian, H. A., & Anderson H. (1988). Human systems as linguistic systems. *Family Process, 27,* 371–393.

Goulding, M. M. (1997). Childhood scenes in redecision therapy. In C. Lennox (Ed.), *Redecision therapy: A brief action-oriented approach* (pp. 87–94). Northvale, NJ: Aronson.

Goulding, R. L. (1976). Gestalt therapy and transactional analysis. In C. Hatcher & P. Himelstein (Eds.), *Handbook of Gestalt therapy* (pp. 615–634). New York: Aronson.

Goulding, R. L., & Goulding, M. M. (1978). *The power is in the patient.* San Francisco: TA Press.

Goulding, R. L., & Goulding, M. M. (1979). *Changing lives through redecision therapy.* New York: Brunner/Mazel.

Graff, C. (1979). *Literature against itself.* Chicago: University of Chicago Press.

Hoyt, M. F. (1994). Single session solutions. In M. F. Hoyt (Ed.), *Constructive therapies* (pp. 140–159). New York: Guilford Press. Reprinted in M. F. Hoyt, *Brief therapy and managed care: Readings for contemporary practice* (pp. 141–162). San Francisco, Jossey-Bass, 1995.

Hoyt, M. F. (1995). Contact, contract, change, encore: A conversation with Bob Goulding. *Transactional Analysis Journal, 25*(4), 300–311.

Hoyt, M. F. (1997). Foreword. In C. Lennox (Ed.), *Redecision therapy: A brief action-oriented approach* (pp. xiii–xix). Northvale, NJ: Aronson.

Perls, F. (1969). *Gestalt therapy verbatim.* Lafayette, CA: Real People Press.

White, M., & Epston, D. (1990). *Narrative means to therapeutic ends.* New York: Norton.

CHAPTER TWO

Generative Conversations

A Postmodern Approach to Conceptualizing and Working with Human Systems

Harlene Anderson, Susan B. Levin

Our postmodern approach draws upon social constructionism, narrative theory, and contemporary hermeneutics as explanatory concepts (see Anderson, 1995, 1997).[1] These concepts challenge the culture, tradition, and relevance of familiar psychotherapy premises—including individual, marital, and family therapy—and the practices, research, and education based on them.[2] They challenge the expert/nonexpert dichotomy and the hierarchical structures that flow from it as out of step with our fast-changing contemporary world. Our approach has evolved over the years and is based on clinical experiences and discussions with clients, colleagues, and students about successful and unsuccessful therapy conversations.[3] Acknowledging the relational and generative nature of language and knowledge, the essence of our postmodern practice is *conversation*. Human life and relationships, knowledge and expertise, are shaped and reshaped in and through conversation, and thus the potential for transformation and change is as infinite in variety and expression as the individuals who realize them. The goal of our postmodern approach becomes accessing and expanding the unknown, yet-to-be-created possibilities through conversation instead of discovering and predicting the already known. We value "not-knowing" (Anderson & Goolishian, 1988, 1992). Not-knowing does not mean that we think we do not know anything. Rather, it refers to how therapists position themselves in relation to what they know or think they know. The therapist's knowing does not lead, is always tentatively held, and is always open to challenge and change.

The core premise of our approach is that the natural consequence of conversation is transformation. We call these kinds of transformative therapy conversations *dialogic conversations*. These are the kinds of conversations that German author and historian Friedrich Paff refers to when he writes, "If all conversations were successful, there would be no need for therapists" (1996). Given this premise, the important question becomes, *How can therapists create the kinds of conversations with their clients that allow both parties to access their creativities and develop possibilities where none seemed to exist before?* (Anderson, 1997). The aim, therefore, of our practice, whether in the psychotherapy, teaching, consultation, or research domain, is to provide a space and facilitate a process for these kinds of conversations. In partial response to this question and to illustrate our practice, this chapter highlights our philosophical premises and then narrates a clinical story from Sue's experience.

CONTRASTING CULTURES OF THERAPY

Modern and *postmodern* are umbrella epistemological and philosophical positions that inform the culture of therapy. Each umbrella includes common unifying and distinguishing characteristics, although there is diversity among their champions. Two essential characteristics of each position that can be compared are the concepts of *knowledge* and *language*. In general, modernism posits the objective reality of an out-there-waiting-to-be-discovered world and human nature as a universal phenomenon. From this viewpoint, knowledge is independent of the knower, cumulative, and static. Knowledge legitimizes; it privileges the knower and creates social structures that grant authority and power. The knowing subject is central and the subject or *self* is knowable. Knowledge collects into grand overarching narratives that, in turn, gain currency as univocal metadiscourses, becoming more important than the personal experiences, narratives, and everyday knowledge of the individual person. A therapist is a metaknower of normality and pathology, an authority on how people *ought* to live their lives, on what is the *better* life to live, and on how to repair defective human lives. Preferably, therapy outcomes are known within this certainty and therefore decided ahead of time. As therapists draw from professionally and culturally legitimized psychotherapy knowledge or narratives, their voices are privileged over their clients'.

For modernists, language (spoken and unspoken, verbal and nonverbal) is representational; it reflects reality, given facts, and the natural order of things—things that already are—rather than things as they might be. Social systems (for example, political, economic, governmental, community, and family systems) within this top-down tradition are hierarchically and dualistically structured and organized. Professional descriptors (e.g., *borderline, codependency,* and *family patterns of denial*) are predetermined and fixed.

Postmodernism offers a broad philosophical and pragmatic challenge to these enshrined traditions and values. Long identified with art and literary critique, postmodernism is increasingly found in social theory. Postmodernism radically questions what modernism stands for: legitimizing authoritative and universal social and cultural narratives. What is postmodern is not an extension of or what comes beyond modernity; rather, it is a distinct philosophical tradition. Reality—and thus *knowledge*—in this view becomes relational—socially created and influenced by people's coordinated language and actions. Reality becomes dynamic, continuously created, and therefore fluid and ever-changing. The central concept that language is creative and generative both limits and provides opportunities for the ways in which we experience and make sense of our world and our life events.

Narrative and storytelling metaphors are often central organizing descriptors in both modern and postmodern therapy theories and practices. In any therapy theory or practice, the metaphor is distinguished by the *intent* with which a therapist uses it and the position the therapist takes vis-à-vis a client's narrative. From a modernist perspective, a therapist is a master storyteller, a narrative editor. Therapists have an idea of what a client's retold or new story should look like. They would select out known story parts to highlight or new ones to add. In other words, therapists would be actively involved in guiding and crafting the outcome of therapy based on their narrative expertise.

From a postmodern perspective, we live, organize, and make sense of our living through socially constructed narratives. Our stories do not form in isolation or in the mind of a single person; they are relational. The meanings and understandings that we attribute to the events and experiences of our lives—including our self-identities—are created, experienced, and shared by individuals in relationship and conversation with each other.

Each person is the narrator of his or her own story, the expert on his or her life, and the knower of his or her narrative experience. At the same time a story is used to convey an experience, in its telling it simultaneously creates and potentially transforms that experience—all depending on the context and purpose of the storytelling. A client's narrative is not an object of change and a therapist is not an expert on other people's narratives. Our goal is not to construct a particular kind of narrative, for instance, a positive or preferred one. In our experience the natural consequence of dialogic conversation is transformation.

Critics of postmodern therapy charge that it includes an "anything goes" attitude. This is not our intent. What postmodernism submits is that there is not one correct or more correct association between what we believe to be the out-there objective truth and our social world. As Kenneth Gergen (1994a, 1994b) suggests, *truths* are socially constructed through—and transformed through—discourse. Postmodernism does not claim to be the truth about truths. Instead, embedded within postmodern thought and critique is the important insight that postmodernism itself is open to analysis, and inevitably to its own transformation.

IMPLICATIONS FOR THERAPY

These premises have implications for how a therapist conceptualizes a therapy system, a therapy process, and a therapy relationship whether the designation is individual, marital, or family therapy. They raise a number of important questions.

Therapy Systems

• *Who is in the conversation? How is the membership of a therapy system envisioned? Who decides who should be talking, and as Tom Andersen has said, "With whom, when, where, and about what?"* (1991).

Thinking about human systems and relationships in terms of language moves us to conceptualize human systems as language systems (Anderson, 1995, 1997; Anderson & Goolishian, 1988; Goolishian & Anderson, 1987, 1992). A therapy system is simply one kind of language or conversation system in which people coalesce with each other around a *relevance*. The relevance is usually thought of as a "problem" in search of a "solution." In this conceptualization, the problem determines the system that coalesces in therapy; the system does not determine the problem. Any system, any single person or combination of persons, is conceptualized as a language/conversation system. A significant implication is that because a therapy system is not distinguished by social roles such as individual, couple, or family, the usual distinctions between individual, couple, and family therapy are, therefore, dissolved.

Who a therapist meets with at the beginning and at any one time and what is talked about in therapy is mutually determined by the conversation's members on a meeting-to-meeting basis. The structure of the system and content of the conversation are not determined ahead of time, but by moment-to-moment exchanges. Likewise, the outcome cannot be determined or predicted ahead of time.

Each therapy system, each therapy conversation, is viewed as a unique event. Each so-called problem is conceptualized as a unique version of a unique life situation and has meaning only within the context of the social exchanges, relationships, and circumstances in which it is embedded. This does not mean that if we look for commonalities (for instance, across problems and dilemmas or across individuals and human groups) that we cannot find them. We can. The focus here, however, is on the uncommon, the differences between and among people and the problems and dilemmas, or *life situations* as we prefer to call them, they present.

Two Swedish therapists who visited the Houston Galveston Institute for two months, Britta Lodgo and Gunilla Strom, described their experiences of this conceptualization of a therapy system as "to see the flow and flexibility and constant movement of people coming and going. . . . That's how ideas are created; not in order or within regulations or strict structure but in constant movement, meeting, and crossbreeding" (quoted in Anderson, 1996, p. 3).

Therapy Process

• *What occurs in the conversation process? How is change or transformation conceptualized?*

Therapy is viewed as a linguistic activity characterized by a dialogic conversation—a process in which client and therapist become *conversational partners* who mutually explore familiar narratives and develop new ones. The mutuality involves an in-here-together, back-and-forth, give-and-take, talking-with process. This kind of mutuality spontaneously effects a collaborative inquiry and relationship where people connect, collaborate, and construct (Anderson & Goolishian, 1992).

We want to create a space and process that helps people, as Tom Andersen has said, "talk with each other in a way that they have not talked with themselves or with each other before" (1991). They talk in ways we describe as leading to self-agency, possibilities, and continuing conversations. Our clients describe it as leading to "freedom" and "hope." To invite and sustain dialogue, a therapist's actions and words must be coherent with a person's story. We want to learn more about what each person is saying and has not yet said. We want to listen and hear what each person wants us to hear. We want to ask questions and make comments that are coherent with and in sync with the conversation. Questions and comments are not known ahead of time; they are not categorized. They come from and are unique to the conversation at the moment—engendering expansion, clarification, preservation, and transformation of narrative.

We also want to be tentative. We want to leave space for the other person to participate in the conversation that he or she wants to participate in, not in the one we choose. This means always being poised to change as the conversation changes, being willing to have our own strong opinions, biases, and values challenged, and being willing to be open to what evolves—as the clinical situation presented later in this chapter will illustrate.

Being in dialogue requires that each person be able to tell his or her personal story and express his or her personal views. It requires room for familiar views, confusing ambiguities, and vigorous attitudes to exist side by side. Dialogue invites opportunity for exploration, expansion, clarification, erasure, and newness. Dialogue invites opportunity to listen and hear differently. For instance, we have found that when we focus on one person's story at a time, others in our presence listen to and hear the story differently. As we demonstrate our interest in each person's story, the listeners are less likely to interrupt or feel that they need to correct an incorrect version. They know or sense that we also will hear their story.

Dialogic or two-way conversation differs from monologic or one-way conversation (Anderson, 1995, 1997; Anderson & Goolishian, 1988; Goolishian & Anderson, 1987). Dialogue is talking *with*. Monologue is talking *to*. When dialogue collapses into monologue, access to creativity and newness are limited as one or several ideas monopolize or take up all the room.

Therapy Relationships

• *How is a therapist positioned in relationship with other people? What is the therapist's expertise and responsibility?*

A therapist's expertise lies in the ability to create and facilitate a conversational space and process. The focus of responsibility is on developing the kinds of relationships that invite and enhance that process. The focus is not on content.

Critical to this expertise is the way that a therapist positions himself or herself to relate—the therapist's way of being with, thinking about, and talking with the people with whom he or she works. It is an authentic, spontaneous, natural way of being, characterized by an attitude, posture, and tone that communicates to the other, "I respect you," "You have something worthy of saying," and "I want to hear it." Put simply, we relate to individual *human beings* and not to categories of people.

The *not-knowing* position invites the client to teach the therapist. Not-knowing is a natural invitation to dialogue, a natural invitation to join a conversation in which "people feel they belong" (Shotter, 1993). That is, people feel that they can or have contributed and that they will or have been heard. We are often asked, "But don't people expect you to be, pay you to be, an expert?" Yes, of course they do. Not-knowing does not mean a passive stance. If someone asks us a question, we will respond. If we have an opinion, we will offer it. Important, however, is that these kinds of questions dissolve in the kind of system, process, and relationship that we develop. Our Swedish colleagues Britta and Gunilla mentioned how they would frequently leave the Institute at the end of the day with "many questions and confusions" that they hoped to talk about and have answered when they returned the next day: "Most of the time we spent the evenings discussing with each other, considering different possibilities. What often happened was that the following morning when you asked if there was anything special on our minds, we frequently found that the confusions we had the day before had more or less vanished. We had not 'solved' any problem but our reflections with each other had made the answer we were sure that we needed the day before unnecessary. The openings and possibilities we saw [in their conversations with each other] were enough for the moment. The present problem had *dissolved.*"

In summary, conventional psychotherapy premises and practices have lost their relevance in our world of rapid social and technological transformation. This phenomenon is accompanied by a growing skepticism of the modern empiricist-scientific discourse. Postmodern ideologies including social constructionism—emphasizing the relationally dependent and generative nature of knowledge and language—challenge the culture and traditions of psychotherapy. Alternatively, they permit a philosophy of therapy, a conceptualization of human beings and their behaviors, and a client-therapist relationship that invite collaboration. Therapy becomes a partnership endeavor. For illustration, we now turn to a clinical story from Sue's practice.

"LIKE IT OR NOT, LIFE IS FULL OF THESE REQUIREMENTS"

To help make our approach come alive on these pages, we offer our narratives of a course of therapy, summarizing it and selecting segments of a transcribed videotaped therapy meeting for more detailed illustration.[4] Our story unfolds in chronological order, beginning with Sue's first contact with the family members and ending with her telephone follow-up a year after therapy ended.

We jointly tell the story, narrating it from the perspective and position from which we participated in the therapy. Sue begins with a past-tense, first-person narrative summary of her contacts with the family members prior to the first meeting. To help the reader form another picture of the family, Harlene describes and summarizes the videotaped meeting as she watches it for the first time. She uses a present-tense, third-person narrative, beginning with what she "sees" as the family members are walking into the room and continuing as the meeting unfolds. She inserts the family members' own words, using quotation marks and segments of the transcript. Sue's voice returns, offering a follow-up. For readers who have an idea about how a story should be told, the shift from first-person to third-person and back again may be jarring. We hope not.

Beginning a Conversation

I (Sue) first met Michael and his daughter Linda when a therapist who knew that I have a compelling interest in working with clients who are described as violent or battered (Levin, 1992) called to ask if I would see Michael, who was distressed over the deterioration in his relationship with his daughter, thirteen-year-old Linda. Linda was the second of his three children from a former marriage. Linda had stopped visiting Michael, claiming that he physically abused her. Michael had consulted his attorney to try to enforce the visitation schedule. The attorney negotiated with Michael's ex-wife Debbie to try to resolve the father-daughter conflicts through therapy.

As I am with all the people I work with, I was curiously challenged to find a way to talk with this family and its members that could be useful to each and all. My usual first step is to hear their stories. I first talked with Michael, as he was the one who called requesting consultation. As Michael had seemingly had a "bad" experience with prior therapy, I was curious about his interests in trying therapy again. I learned that despite his experience, he would not give up trying to regain visitation with his daughter. I asked what other avenues he thought might work. He believed that Linda's mother, his ex-wife Debbie, was "behind" the problem. He thought that if Debbie would force Linda to visit, and would talk about him more positively, that things would be fine. He did not have much hope for therapy because everyone took Linda's side. But since the attorney made the therapy agreement with Debbie, he would try it. I suggested that he and I meet so that I could learn more about the situation. He agreed, but stated his concern that we not spend too much time together individually, because he strongly felt that nothing would happen until he could talk to Linda directly (in therapy).

I then called Debbie to introduce myself and to hear her ideas about how I might be helpful to her daughter. Debbie reiterated what Michael had told me, that Linda was determined not to be in the same room with her dad, and that she was confused about how to deal with Linda about this. She expressed a dilemma: Although she believed that it was her job to support her daughter's decision not to visit her father, she had agreed with the attorney to try therapy because she wanted to avoid further conflict with Michael and additional court proceedings. I suggested that Debbie and Linda come in for an appointment, and that I might spend a few minutes with Debbie alone to discuss her dilemma. Debbie readily agreed that this was the way to proceed.

The initial meetings with Michael, and with Debbie and Linda, reinforced some of the ideas I was beginning to form about them and their situation. The situation had indeed escalated. There was the potential to see Michael as intimidating and threatening, and his commitment and passion about his role as a father could seem secondary; to see Linda and Debbie as victimized by Michael; and to see Debbie as sabotaging Linda and Michael's relationship.

Michael was intense, expressing his need for a therapist who would be "honest" with him and not just feel sorry for his daughter without understanding his side of the story. He wanted a therapist who would recognize that his court-mandated visitation rights were being violated. We explored how he would know I was being honest, fair, and supportive. I learned more about Michael's view of Linda's determination not to see him, and his story of their relationship in the past. He described a tender father-daughter relationship, talking about Linda in her "early years." She was his first daughter, and in his words, a "classic Daddy's little girl" until he separated from Debbie when Linda was about ten years old. He said he made a "big mistake" by leaving Debbie and his family for Karen (his second wife, who was divorcing him). He believed that Debbie leaned on Linda during their divorce and still blamed Michael for leaving the family, even though Debbie had "moved on" and had remarried about a year ago. Michael repeated his belief that unless he could meet with Linda in therapy, there would be no progress with the visitation problem.

Linda was quiet at first when I met with her and her mother, letting her mother tell the story, but jumped in quickly to say that she had seen another therapist at one time—and that therapist saw her dad for what he was and was not going to force her to see him. Linda blamed her father for the termination with her prior therapist, complaining that "he always has to mess up everything; he always has to have things his way." Debbie said that the therapist had suggested that Linda and Michael write to each other about the issues between them. Michael had written one letter, but Linda had not yet replied. I inquired about Linda's reaction to his letter and she stated that she did not care what he had to say and could not remember the letter's contents. Linda adamantly reiterated that she did not want any contact with her father. She had only come to therapy because otherwise her father was going to sue her mother. She was concerned that her mother "did not have the money" to go back to court, and believed that at her age she should be able to decide whether she wanted to see her father or not.[5] I requested a few minutes with Debbie to discuss the court concerns, and Linda politely stepped out to the waiting room.

My conversation with Debbie included questions about how determined she thought Michael was in trying to restart visitation, what she believed his motives were, how she understood Linda's refusal to visit, and how she was handling the dual pressure of a threatened lawsuit and a determined daughter. Debbie's view was consistent with Michael's description of Linda as an independent child and with a strong will, much like her father. She said that Linda and her father used to spend a lot of time together, and that she sometimes worried that her brother and sister were somewhat slighted by their father. Debbie also pinpointed Michael's leaving as a turning point where Linda, "a mature ten-year-old," would ask her questions about the separation. Linda consequently became Mom's confidante during that "hard and lonely" process. Debbie described their current relationship as "more like friends than mother and daughter." She added that this was sometimes a strain because Linda did not listen to her (that is, obey her), and that verbal battles ensued when she set limits that Linda did not like. Debbie said that her current husband often complained that Linda did not respect her mother. Debbie agreed with him to some extent, but also felt loved, supported, and understood by Linda.

Debbie described ongoing struggles with Michael about visitation with their two other children. For instance, Michael often refused to allow the children to attend extracurricular activities during his visitation time, saying that he had such a limited amount of time. The children complained to her that not only did they miss these activities, but that Dad did not do anything with them during these visits except watch television. Debbie also reported ongoing disputes over child support, claiming that Michael accused her of spending the child support money on herself and not the children. He frequently demanded an accounting from her for the money, and quizzed the children about what their mother had bought them.

We concluded our conversation by discussing what would help to settle things down between her, Michael, and Linda. Debbie said she now believed that the only thing that might help would be Linda's "giving in." I asked if that meant she supported the idea that Linda should start seeing her dad, and if so, under what conditions. "Yes," she had been trying to encourage Linda to discuss the anger and fear directly with her father. She added, however, that Linda was so adamantly opposed to seeing her father that she did not think she could force it. We decided to talk with Linda to discuss the possibility of a conjoint meeting with her father, and to hear her concerns and objections.

Continuing the Conversation

Meanwhile, I met with Michael again, and further explored the complaints that he knew Linda, Debbie, and Karen (now his second ex-wife) had about him, and how he felt misunderstood by them. He said that they said he was controlling, violent, intimidating, and manipulative. He felt their descriptions were very unfair, exaggerated, and untrue. He said that the "physical events" that had occurred with Linda were his attempts to discipline a "very rebellious" and "disrespectful young lady." He described other avenues that he had pursued with Linda prior to the physical discipline to try to change her attitude. Michael also voluntarily described a one-time physical incident with Karen, in which, as a response to her attacking him, he had grabbed her and pushed her away, leaving marks that led to his arrest. He said he knew that "everyone thinks I'm lying" because "people don't usually believe that women are violent."

We also discussed the possibility of a conjoint meeting with Linda, and what he hoped would happen. Michael's immediate response was that he just wanted to see his daughter as it had been almost four months since he had seen her. He hoped that if he could talk to her that he could "get through to her," describing a metaphorical barrier that he felt she had constructed to keep him out of her life. He seemed to believe that he might be able to find a way to "break through" this barrier, but had no plans for how. I wondered if there were things he knew to avoid to keep from strengthening this barrier, and he became interested in talking about what not to do if we had this meeting. I also wondered what he thought Linda would respond to, and added that her determination to avoid interacting with her father seemed as strong as his determination to reconnect with her. I let him know that I would talk with Linda about a conjoint meeting.

Because "She Did Not Care" and "He Had To"

In the discussion that Linda and I had about the possibility of a conjoint meeting, while Debbie listened, Linda was immediately tearful and disappointed when the idea was presented to her. She protested, "You aren't listening. I don't want to do this." I told her that I had heard that she did not want to do this, but at the same time, I did not know any other way to proceed that could keep them from court. I then asked her and Debbie if court would be a better option. Debbie expressed her preference for avoiding court, and for Linda to try a conjoint meeting. I asked Linda about her worst-case and best-case scenarios for a meeting with her father. Though Linda offered a few explanations about her fears ("that he'll act nice and pretend that he cares about me, just to impress you"), she repeatedly said "I just don't want to do this."

An interesting conversation evolved about how she handles things that she does not want to do. Debbie joined in to talk again about how difficult it is when Linda makes up her mind not to do something. We talked about discipline at home, and what happens if Linda does not listen to her Mom. The discussion broadened to how and why people do things they do not want to do. Eventually, it became clear that Linda would come to a meeting with her Dad, if everyone understood that she did not want to, but was only doing it because she "had" to. We also discussed her right to not talk, and the possibility that she could stop the meeting at any time, as could her father or I. I asked Linda what she thought her father might want to say to her, but she did "not care" what he had to say.

Comment: As with all therapy conversations, my hope for this one was that the possibilities for dialogue, whether in or outside of therapy, would open up. As with all therapy conversations, I did not have an expectation for the content outcome. Modestly, I hoped that it would be a step toward their beginning to talk with each other and with themselves in a way that they had not done before. Where that would lead was unknown. My thoughts at this point were simply that a conjoint meeting would give Linda and Michael the opportunity to express and show their determinations. The unpredictable possibilities might include Linda's (lack of) participation might produce some new understanding on Michael's part; Michael's determination to connect with Linda might meet with some success; Michael might develop some understanding of her refusal. My (tentatively held) ideas of a successful outcome for the meeting were that we would not have to terminate it prematurely, and that possibly we might schedule a follow-up meeting.

As mentioned earlier, this does not imply an anything-goes attitude, but simply that the outcome of the kinds of conversations that we talk about and participate in cannot be predicted ahead of time. We do not want to guide the content of the conversation. We simply want to provide a space and facilitate a process where people can talk about what is important to them and what needs to be talked about. In our experience, when given this space, they do.

The Next Conversation: Tensions and Protests

A very nervous father and daughter arrived at my office, and a nervous mother waited alone in the reception area. I started by asking each how nervous they were, and we had a few chuckles about our mutual nervousness. I then asked what Linda was most worried about. She said she was afraid her Dad would try to hug her or make her talk to him. I asked him if he was planning to try to hug her or make her talk to him. He said that he was so glad to see her and that was enough for now even though he wished for more. He expressed worry about doing something that would make things worse. Linda jumped in to complain that just having to be here was making it worse. She made it clear to both her father and me that even her mother was not supporting her by forcing her to be at this meeting. In response to my asking, Linda again explained why she did not want to be here. I asked Michael if he understood that Linda was here under protest, and he again reiterated how happy he was just to get a chance to see her.

Michael then talked about how she looked to him, about how pretty she was and how old she was getting. This led to a discussion of Linda's upcoming fourteenth birthday, and Michael's expressed disappointment that he had been missing important events in her life. Linda angrily interrupted that he never did anything special with them during visits, and accused him of lying about his interest in seeing her and her siblings. She believed that the only reason he wanted them to visit was to make them miserable and that he kept them from their regular activities and friends because he was selfish and unhappy himself. She accused him of not wanting them to be happy since he was not happy. She complained that he would only let them watch TV and that he would not let them talk on the phone or buy foods that they liked.

The tension and protests rose as Michael interrupted to explain himself to Linda and me, describing how hard it was just to see the kids twice a month, and sometimes less when their mother disregarded the visitation schedule. He said he "had to fight" for his time with his children and felt it was perfectly reasonable to try to limit their outside activities. Michael gave several instances of when Linda's brother attended soccer events during his visitation. Linda argued that those were few and far between, and that Michael forced her brother to "make up" for the time he missed. Linda and Michael continued to differ about the how and why of things. I asked them if they felt like they were getting anywhere in this discussion. Michael replied by stating his frustration of being misunderstood and maligned, while Linda said that she did not see how things would ever change if her father continued to lie.

I wondered aloud what would be, or could be different, if we tried it again. Linda again protested seeing her father under any conditions and Michael said that he had no intention of "giving up." Linda asked him why it was so important to him, that he "had to force her" to see him when she did not want to. He said that he loved her and that he was always going to be her father whether she wanted him to or not. Linda sharply responded that even if he could force her to see him now, that someday it would be up to her and then she would never see him again.

We soon ended the meeting. Michael left first, as Linda seemed reluctant to leave at the same time. I walked to the waiting room with Linda and watched as she fell crying into her mother's arms. I told Debbie I would call her, and they left. Later that day, I called Debbie to ask how bad Linda had said the meeting was, and she described a "quick recovery." She said that Linda seemed to have to let out a lot of emotion, but did not have much to say. I told her that Linda and her father disagreed on just about everything and wondered whether it might end up helping Linda to get to tell her Dad how she's felt about these issues. Debbie let the question hang.

Comment: Whether to schedule another meeting with Linda and her father was an open question. Each conversation determines the next. That is, the members of each conversation participate in deciding whether there should be another therapy conversation, and if so, who should be included. On this occasion, Debbie wanted to set up another appointment for Linda and her father and Linda protested but reluctantly agreed again. Michael had already expressed interest in another meeting. We now turn to Harlene's narration of the videotaped next meeting.

The Conversation Continues: The Music Box

As the videotape starts, Dad is walking into the room and loudly saying "Hello." He seats himself on the sofa, leans back in a relaxed position, props his elbow on the arm of the sofa, and places a shopping bag on the cushion beside him. He maintains this posture throughout the meeting except when he occasionally talks with his hands and sits on the edge of the sofa as the conversation intensifies. Linda is already seated in a chair to the left of the sofa, looking straight ahead and not acknowledging Dad's entrance. Her hands are folded on her lap and she fiddles with her fingers and slightly bounces her heels on the floor. During the meeting she oscillates between a monotone and a raised voice when she disagrees with or challenges Dad. She wears jeans, a knit pullover, and running shoes, and her straight below-the-shoulders brown hair is pulled behind her ears on one side and tossed forward on the other.

Dad is medium height, thinnish, and has a close-cropped beard and mustache; his hair is receding on the sides. He is dressed casually, wearing khaki pants and a plaid shirt with pencils in his pocket and looking as if he has just come from work. Father and daughter have a family resemblance.

Sue moves from adjusting the camera and takes a chair to Linda's left. Sue's manner and voice throughout the conversation are composed and friendly. She looks relaxed and often smiles. As she sits down, she comments on Dad's "loud hello." He responds, "I wanted to make sure she heard me." Sue, addressing Dad and referring to a previous conversation between herself, Dad, and Linda, asks him: "How nervous are you today?" He quickly answers, "Not too bad." Sue turns to Linda, who laughs and says she is "nervous." Dad comments on Linda's "nervous laugh" and tells how he tries to get her to laugh because he thinks "laughing is good." Confused about a remark that Sue makes, Dad says, "Maybe I'm missing the point here but when I see her laugh it's an indication that she is a little more at ease, a little less uncomfortable."

The conversation shifts as Sue asks Linda and Dad, "Any goals today or things that you would want not to happen?" Dad responds immediately that he "certainly wouldn't want any troubles or problems . . . hope we could have some fun . . . take another step toward normalized relations." Sue learns that "normalized relations" refers to the "visitation problems." Linda continues to face straight ahead, shifting her eyes back and forth between Sue and Dad. As Dad elaborates on the visitation issue, the first of many dueling realities begins as Linda interrupts and disagrees. Sue asks Linda, "So, you have a different memory about that?" Sue learns about each of their perspectives as Linda and Dad correct each other's versions of past visitations. Sue continually checks to make sure that she has heard what each wanted her to hear, giving each a chance to verify, correct, and expand. For instance, in response to Dad, she asks: "But you can be flexible enough to see her less often than you would wish. Is that what you're saying?" Dad explains, "I will accept it. I wouldn't be satisfied with it, but I will accept it."

Comment: Throughout the meeting the conversation takes many shifts. We find that when we try to learn more about what each person is saying that a conversation will twist and turn, often touching back on something that was said earlier and then moving on again. Here the conversation shifts again as Linda shares her belief that Dad is trying to put on a good show to impress Sue.

As Linda continues she challenges Dad that he does not spend money on her brother and sister when they come to visit. Linda and Dad debate how much he pays for child support compared to what her friends' parents pay. Sue wonders, "How come the two of you would argue over something like that?" Dad believes that her mother is trying to minimize the value of what he contributes. He leans forward to protest to Sue that Linda does not appreciate his contribution and the sacrifices he makes to give it, Linda interrupts, and off they go again. Sue, reduced to being a referee, whistles and calmly says: "Time out. Are we getting anywhere with this conversation?"

Sue wonders about Dad's persistence in explaining his views and actions to Linda. It worked with his other two children, he explains. Sue replies, "This is the one you're trying to get somewhere with today. What's going to work with her?" He leans back and directs his comments to Sue: "[My] repetitive nature . . . I go out of my way to explain because I want other people to understand me."

Linda interrupts to give further evidence of Dad's poor fathering. Sue breaks in: "That's getting on another topic. Can we save that one for just a minute?" Returning to what's happening between Linda and her Dad at the moment, Sue asks curiously if perhaps there are some other ways Dad could try to relate to Linda. She wonders, addressing Linda, if perhaps Dad could try to learn what "other things bother you . . . [turning to Dad] rather than getting into a position of defending or explaining maybe what you could do is start trying to find out from her what things bother her?" Dad turns to Linda: "What's the problem?" He is baited by Linda's response and Sue comments using the word "explaining." "Defending," Dad corrects her. He again asks Linda, "What's the problem?" They tensely discuss Linda's brother's and sister's weekend visits with Dad. Dad threatens that he can resort to legal action if necessary to make sure that the visits with Linda happen. Although Linda escalates in response to this threat, Dad says that he feels that at this point he has nothing to lose. Linda reiterates that everything that Dad does bothers her.

Comment: Any conversation consists of bits and pieces, of talking about one thing and then another, and returning back again. It is often difficult to keep up with fast-moving conversations like this one. When Sue suspended Linda's interruption with "That's getting on another topic. Can we save that one for just a minute?" it was an attempt to try to hear both voices. She wanted to stick with Dad's talk of his repetitive nature and wanted to know his thoughts about alternative ways of relating to Linda other than through his repetitive nature. Sue, however, respected Linda's preoccupation with her father's "poor fathering" and indicated to her that they would return to Linda. But the conversation again took another shift when Linda reiterated that everything that Dad does bothers her. Sue remembered something that Linda had said about her Dad in a previous conversation that really bothered her that she had not mentioned in this meeting. Sue had no intent other than to say aloud what she was remembering and give Linda an opportunity to talk about it if she wanted to at that time.

Sue turns to Linda and refers to this previous conversation asking, "Is it all right if I tell him that"? Linda nods affirmatively. Sue tells Dad that Linda thinks he is "going out of [his] way to impress [her]." Linda referred to this earlier in the conversation but left unsaid her fear that outside of therapy he will remain the "same old Dad." Linda then begins to talk about how "mean" her father is, that he calls her names and gets "physical." She gives examples: "pulling my hair, pulling my ears, and slapping me." Dad refutes that he is any different in therapy than he is at home.

SUE: Would you get physical in this room?

DAD: I'd try not to. There are times that I have grabbed her . . . slapped her . . . grabbed her ear. I expect her to be well behaved. I expect discipline from her. I expect her to respect my authority and she's been trained to disrespect my authority. And I don't like that.

LINDA: No, I haven't been trained.

SUE: And so your way of handling disrespect would be to get physical?

DAD: There have been times when I have done that. There have been times when I've held her down and whipped her with a belt, too, because of her disrespect. All of the things she mentioned about physical things were a result of her disrespect. And it is not out of line, in my opinion, to expect a daughter to treat a father with respect. . . . What did I do to make you disrespect me so much?

Comment: This last question indicates a shift for Dad as he briefly moves from defending to being curious and trying to understand his daughter's perspective. Linda questions his "demand" for all three children to say "Yes, sir" and "No, sir."

DAD: That's a way of making you understand who's boss. Whether you like it or not, life is full of these requirements to show respect for other people—the requirements to observe discipline—it's everywhere, Linda, not just in the home. But it starts in the home and I as a good parent am obligated to teach that to you, whether you like it or not.

LINDA: You don't have to teach me by yelling and hitting.

DAD: I don't like hitting you or anybody.

LINDA: Yes, you do.

DAD: I won't answer to that.

Linda continues, and Sue interrupts, "Let me talk to your Dad about that a minute, because I think that's an important issue." Sue summarizes some of what has just been said between Dad and Linda. She comments on how far they are from having a good relationship.

SUE: I guess in general the question would be, "Are you open to reconsidering that approach?" *[to discipline]* That may be real important for her to know if she's going to be coming to visit, "What I am going to be up against?"

Linda protests Sue's "coming to visit" words: "I don't really want to." This time Dad responds to Sue's question instead of Linda's protest. Linda jumps in, returning the conversation to the "hitting." Dad asks, "Did I ball up my fist and do that to you?" *(swiftly and forcefully smacking his fist in his hand).* "No," says Linda. Dad then recounts the last time that he disciplined Linda physically, telling about an incident where Linda, "on purpose," threw a rock at her sister, cutting her ear. For the first time, Linda bodily turns toward Dad, tears up, and pointedly protests, "I didn't." Sue expresses curiosity about the words "on purpose," "punishment," and "logical" that arise in their stories about the rock incident. Sue addresses the challenge that Dad faces because, in his description, Linda is different from his other two children. Hearing Sue's words as a challenge to him, he leans forward and points to himself:

DAD: I have a right to decide how to raise my children.

SUE: All I said was that you might want to think about it differently because I don't think you're going to have the same relationship with her as the other two. You haven't and I don't know how you could.

DAD: You're right and I know that. And I've chosen a different path with this child than the other two because they are different. I have that right, I have that obligation, and I have the responsibility of deciding how to pursue it. That's what led us here [referring to therapy].

SUE: Exactly.

DAD: It is my opinion that this child needs other things than the other two and I have tried to do those things . . . I have been prevented . . . because other people [seemingly referring to Linda's mother] don't agree or see them differently. I don't care what other people see or think. My obligation and my responsibility is still the same. I have to pursue what I think it does to my child. This child does not have any respect for authority.

LINDA: Yes, I do, Dad, just not for you.

After a brief further exchange between Linda and Dad, Dad turns back to Sue:

DAD: You were trying to make a point . . . I've got your point. . . . [however] I don't have a good enough feel for where you're coming from. I haven't talked with you enough to know what goals you may want to create. I'm open to what you might suggest but I don't know what you're suggesting.

SUE: Finding . . . a different approach, getting out of this position . . . that's not working. And I don't know what that different approach would be.

DAD: Why isn't it working?

Dad returns to the issue of respect: "I would like that to change. [referring to his description of Linda's lack of respect for him] . . . In a typical family . . . how do parents work on it?" The conversation continues as Sue and Dad puzzle over who wants change and what kind of change. Linda is listening attentively, not interrupting. Dad circles back to the physical discipline issue, asking:

DAD: Why is physical discipline such an unacceptable thing in modern society when it's been around for *[years]* for all of society. I think in the Bible it says, "Spare the rod and spoil the child," right? Did we suddenly throw that out? Is physical punishment no longer an acceptable form of parental guidance?

SUE: Do you want me to answer that?

DAD: I want you to answer for society.

After a brief exchange about discipline the conversation shifts again as Sue proposes that Dad cannot change what has happened in the past but that "[you] can change what you do today . . . tomorrow . . . next week . . . the rest of your life." Dad then turns to Linda and asks her to "go over" her complaints. She readily lists them and returns to the issue of respect. As the time to end the meeting draws near, Sue asks Dad, "Should I tell her what you asked me about?" referring to a birthday present in the shopping bag that Dad had placed on the sofa when he sat down. Linda says, "I don't want it." Sue wonders with Linda if there are any other ways that she and her Dad could handle this situation rather than the usual standoff. Sue wonders aloud about imagined possibilities. Nothing is decided. Dad slowly pulls out the present, a box wrapped in aqua-blue paper tied with ribbons, and offers it to Linda. She takes it, lingeringly unwraps it, smiles, and softly laughs as she sees a label. Dad gently asks, "Is that a nervous laugh? . . . I'll be watching for that." Linda pulls out a music box, opens the lid, and then closes it after the first few notes of the song play.

SUE: Oh, what music is that?

DAD: It's a special song.

SUE: *[to Linda]* Do you know what it is?

LINDA: Yes. I used to like this song in the second grade.

SUE: Really, wow! What is the name of it?

Linda says that she heard the song at a concert that her father took her to but does not remember its name. Dad tells Sue that the song is *Unchained Melody* by the Righteous Brothers. Linda repeats that she does not want the gift, places the music box in its box, and hands it to Dad. Without commenting, Dad takes it, pauses momentarily, then puts it back in the shopping bag.

As they talk about scheduling the next appointment, Sue mentions that Debbie (Linda's mother) has said that she would like to come to "talk about some things that concern her." Dad asks, "In this meeting?" Sue says that no decision has been made and invites his thoughts. He indicates that he would like to talk with Sue "privately" about it. "OK," Sue responds and the meeting ends.

Comment: Sue did not have an investment in whether Linda accepted the present or not. Nor was she steering them toward visits, reconciliations, or more meetings. She was not trying to negotiate a particular outcome. Her actions and words here, as throughout the meeting, were attempts to facilitate a space and process where Linda and her father could talk and act with each other and with themselves differently. And in doing so, in her experience, new meanings, new options would emerge—ones that were not predictable. The newness would come from the conversation, each person would contribute to it, and it would be specific to each person and their circumstances. We now turn to the next meeting.

"I Will Always Love You"

To my (Sue) surprise the next meeting with Michael turned out to be the next-to-last one. Michael described having a hard week and thinking a lot. He said that Linda's reaction to her birthday present caught him by surprise and that he now realized how serious she was about not having anything to do with him. He asked, with quiet desperation in his voice, whether there was anything I thought he could do that would change her mind. I responded that I thought there were things he could do to show her how much he cared about her, but that I thought she seemed firm in her position. Michael seemed sincere and open as he asked what things I thought he should do to show his caring with respect for her and without imposition.

We discussed ways that he could be in contact with Linda that would be the least (or less) intrusive, without demanding or expecting something from her in return. Michael wondered aloud what would happen if he "gave her what she wanted" and dropped the therapy and visitation for a while. Michael seemed down and different from the past, lacking the animation and drive that he often exuded. I asked about this and he responded that reality had "hit" him, and that he was trying to figure out the best way to handle it. I asked him that if he decided to drop therapy and visits, if there was anything he wanted to say to Linda about that, if he wanted to have a meeting to let her know what he was thinking. He agreed and we spent the rest of the meeting discussing his plans for the conversation with Linda if she would come.

Linda agreed to come. The meeting was brief. Michael expressed his sadness and fear about stopping therapy and visits, while telling Linda that he was not giving up on her. "I will always love you, Linda, and I will always be your father. I will always hope that we can have a good relationship." Michael added that he was sorry for hurting her and for leaving her when he divorced her mother. I asked Linda if her Dad had ever talked to her about this before, and she said no. I asked if she wanted to reply to anything that her Dad had said.

Her reply was a quick smile, and a "Thanks, Dad," but nothing further. After a few more questions to see if there was more they wanted to say, we ended the meeting. Linda left the room with a smile on her face and a bounce in her step, while Michael sat for a short time as if he could not move. I spent a few minutes with him, remarking on how touching his words were, and how "tough" Linda was. I offered to be available to Michael, as needed, in the future, and wished him all the best as he waited and hoped for Linda to "come around." We now turn to Sue's follow-up.

Follow-Up

So what happened? Did any of these conversations make a difference, "create possibilities where none seemed to exist before?" (Anderson, 1997). Did alternative ways of narrating events, generating new meanings for them and new stances toward self and others, evolve? Were the therapy conversations carried into the relationships outside the therapy room? (Gergen, 1994a, 1994b).

A year and a few months have gone by since I (Sue) last saw Michael and Linda. Two phone calls from Michael in the first four months related that Linda was still not responding to him, and he wondered whether he should continue waiting, try more therapy, or go to court. Our conversations were brief, with decisions and options for future appointments left open. My next contact with Michael was a year later when I called him to follow up on his story for this chapter. Michael shared the "success story" of our work together. He and Linda, he said, had been visiting again for several months, and she had just finished a two-week summer visit. Their relationship was going well. I asked how he understood the change, and he described that she had needed "time" and "space" to be ready to see him. His tone was optimistic. He only mentioned positive changes; he did not mention the problematic past events: discipline, respect, or the music box.

RETURNING TO THE PHILOSOPHICAL STANCE

Sue's work with these family members represents our philosophy of therapy that informs the way that we think about, talk with, and act with the people we meet in therapy. It illustrates how we conceptualize a therapy system, a therapy process, and client-therapist relationships. It represents one illustration of how to create a space for and facilitate conversations that allow all parties to access their creativity and develop possibilities. There is no one way to operationalize our philosophy. Each clinical circumstance is different, each problem is different, and each person (or group of persons) is different. Each expression of the philosophical stance depends on these differences and the personhood and style of the therapists.

Endnotes

1. We distinguish between *social constructionism* and *constructivism:* The former emphasizes the communal, relational aspect of constructing meaning and reality (see Gergen, 1994a, 1994b), whereas the latter emphasizes the individual construction (see Kelly, 1955; von Glaserfeld, 1987). In our view, when thinking about "constructive therapies" it is important to distinguish how the client and the therapist participate in co-constructing. In this regard, our philosophy and practice of therapy more closely resemble the work of Andersen (1987, 1995), Hoffman (1993), and Penn and Frankfurt (1994) than the other authors in this book.

2. We use the word *therapy* hesitantly because we think a major implication of a postmodern perspective is the extinction of therapy as it has come to be defined and known.

3. *Client* is another uncomfortable word. In our everyday work we tend to simply refer to "the people we talk with." We use *client* in this paper because of the awkwardness of the longer phrase. By *conversation* or *talking* we include inner and outer talk—silent thoughts and spoken words.

4. We selected this session for the detailed illustration because it was videotaped and transcribed. We thank Bernadette Williams, University of Houston Clear Lake family therapy student, for the transcription.

5. In Texas (where we practice), children who are twelve years old have the right to have their interests heard in custody and visitation decisions. This does not require the judge to act on their requests, but rather to take them into consideration. At the age of fifteen, children have the right to decide custody and visitation for themselves.

References

Andersen, T. (1987). The reflecting team: Dialogue and meta-dialogue in clinical work. *Family Process, 26,* 415–428.

Andersen, T. (1991). *Relationship, language, and pre-understanding in the reflecting process.* Paper presented at the Houston Galveston Narrative and Psychotherapy Conference, New Directions in Psychotherapy, Houston, TX.

Andersen, T. (1995). Reflecting processes, acts of informing and forming: You can borrow my eyes, but you must not take them away from me! In S. Friedman (Ed.), *The reflecting team in action: Collaborative practice in family therapy* (pp. 11–37). New York: Guilford Press.

Anderson, H. (1995). Collaborative language systems: Towards a postmodern therapy. In R. Mikesell, D. D. Lusterman, & S. McDaniel (Eds.), *Integrating family therapy: Family psychology and systems theory.* Washington, DC: American Psychological Association.

Anderson, H. (1996, Fall). Chocolate cake and coke. *Houston Galveston Institute Newsletter.*

Anderson, H. (1997). *Conversation, language, and possibilities: A postmodern approach to therapy.* New York: Basic Books.

Anderson, H., & Goolishian, H. A. (1988). Human systems as linguistic systems: Evolving ideas about the implications of theory and practice. *Family Process, 27,* 371–393.

Anderson, H., & Goolishian, H. A. (1992). The client is the expert: A not-knowing approach to therapy. In S. McNamee & K. J. Gergen (Eds.), *Therapy as social construction* (pp. 25–39). Newbury Park, CA: Sage.

Gergen, K. J. (1994a). *Realities and relationships: Soundings in social construction.* Cambridge, MA: Harvard University Press.

Gergen, K. J. (1994b). *Toward transformation in social knowledge* (2nd ed.). London: Sage.

Goolishian, H. A., & Anderson, H. (1987). Language systems and therapy: An evolving idea. *Psychotherapy, 24,* 529–538.

Goolishian, H. A., & Anderson, H. (1992). Strategies and interventions versus non-intervention: A matter of theory. *Journal of Marital and Family Therapy, 18,* 51–55.

Hoffman, L. (1993). *Exchanging voices: A collaborative approach to family therapy.* London: Karnac Books.

Kelly, G. (1955). *The psychology of personal constructs* (Vols. 1–2). New York: Norton.

Levin, S. B. (1992). *Hearing the unheard: Stories of women who have been battered.* Unpublished doctoral dissertation, The Union Institute, Cincinnati, OH.

Paff, F. (1996). *Poetry in crisis: Conversations and stories in Marburg.* Paper presented at conference titled The Social Poetics of Therapy: Systemic Therapy and Beyond, Marburg, Germany.

Penn, P., & Frankfurt, M. (1994). Creating a participant text: Writing, multiple voices, narrative multiplicity. *Family Process, 33,* 217–231.

Shotter, J. (1993). *Conversational realities: Constructing life through language.* London: Sage.

von Glaserfeld, E. (1987). The control of perception and the construction of reality. *Dialectica,* pp. 3337–3350.

CHAPTER THREE

Adlerian Psychotherapy as a Constructivist Psychotherapy

Jon Carlson, Len Sperry

There is increasing awareness that *reality* is more a construction of what an individual perceives, thinks, and believes than what it actually and objectively is. Alfred Adler, a contemporary of Sigmund Freud and Carl Jung, was one of the first psychological thinkers to assert that individuals play an active role in creating a view of self and the world on which they then base their subsequent perceptions and interpretations (Dinkmeyer, Dinkmeyer, & Sperry, 1987). For example, in *What Life Should Mean to You*, Adler wrote, "Human beings live in the realm of meanings. We do not experience pure circumstances; we always experience circumstances in their significance for men. Even at its source our experience is qualified by our human purposes. . . . We experience reality always through the meanings we give it; not in itself, but as something interpreted. It will be natural to suppose, therefore, that this meaning is always more or less unfinished, incomplete; and even that is never altogether right. The realm of meaning is the realm of mistakes" (1931/1958, p. 4).

This realization that individuals participate in the origination and maintenance of these constructions—but can also question, deconstruct, or reconstruct reality for themselves—is the basis not only of Adlerian psychotherapy but also of other constructivist psychotherapies. Mahoney (1991) describes two rival camps of constructivism: *radical constructivism,* which has been articulated by such family therapists and theorists as Maturana, Varela, and Watzlawick, and *critical constructivism,* which is based on the critical or hypothetical realism of Popper (1983) and espoused by such theorists as Guidano, Liotti, Kelly,

Mahoney, Piaget, and Weimer. Many constructivists credit Adler as a forerunner to constructivism (Mahoney, 1984, 1991), and an increasing number now contend that Adlerian psychotherapy is a full-fledged constructivist psychotherapy (Masters, 1991; Shulman & Watts, 1997; Watts & Critelli, 1997). It has even been suggested that Adlerian psychotherapy may function as an integrative bridge between the radical and critical constructivist camps (R. Watts, personal communication, April 12, 1997).

This chapter will briefly describe some of the philosophical and theoretical underpinnings of constructivist psychotherapies and Adlerian psychotherapy. It will then focus in greater detail on a number of therapeutic strategies and interventions common to both. Extensive case material that illustrates these commonalties will also be presented.

PHILOSOPHICAL UNDERPINNINGS

Adlerians and constructivists share a similar philosophical heritage. Both espouse *phenomenological, holistic,* and *teleological* principles. Phenomenologically, Adlerians and constructivists—particularly the critical constructivists—are rooted in Kant's critical philosophy and Hans Vaihinger's (1924) philosophy of "as if." Adler (1956) insisted that a clinician must approach a client by seeing life from the client's phenomenal field, which can be likened to Kant's categorical spectacles. Adler also incorporated Vaihinger's "as if" philosophy into his concept of *fictional goals.* The fictions that a client constructs are interpretations of the world as experienced by the individual. Although these fictions do not exactly correspond with objective or external reality, they enable the client to move purposely (that is, teleologically) toward selected goals. Because the individual moves toward fictions that are more imagined (or psychologically constructed) than "real," Adlerians view clients not as static beings, but as ones who are always "becoming" (Adler, 1956). While Vaihinger serves as a common source for both Adlerian and other constructivist views of purposive action,[1] most constructivists prefer the word *teleonomy* to teleology (Mahoney, 1991) because constructivists do not view such actions as seeking a specific final form or destination. *Viability,* in the sense of evolution and adaptation, is more important to constructivists; they describe it as teleonomic rather than teleological. Similar to the Adlerian concept of *becoming,* constructivists view the person as a *self-in-process* (Guidano, 1987, 1991; Mahoney, 1991).

Holism characterizes both Adlerian psychotherapy and other constructivist psychotherapies. Holism represents a rejection of reductionism and the dissection of the human personality into parts or polarities. Rather, all components that make up personality or contribute to it are seen to function holistically; polarities such as mind-body and conscious-unconscious are viewed as false dichotomies (Jones, 1995). Instead of emphasizing the components of personality, Adlerians emphasize how clients put these components to use—what Adler (1956) called the *psychology of use.*

Furthermore, Adlerian psychotherapy and other constructivist psychotherapies agree that because there is no meaning intrinsic to life, clients create their own construct of reality, meaning takes on personal significance in the form of *personal meanings,* and these personal meanings—and changes in them—are key to psychological well-being (Mahoney, 1991). Here there is some difference between the two constructivist camps. The radical or social constructionists do not believe there is a knowable reality beyond the individual's construction, while the critical constructionists—including Adlerians—recognize a reality beyond the individual. In this regard, Adler distinguished between *personal logic* and *common sense* (Adler, 1956).

Theoretical Considerations

Both Adlerians and constructivists focus on cognitive organization as a central tenet (Jones, 1995). Adler was probably the first cognitive therapist as well as being an early constructivist (Forgus & Shulman, 1979; Shulman, 1985). The concept of cognitive organization in Adlerian psychotherapy centers on what Adlerians call *life-style.* The life-style or cognitive organization comprises a client's basic convictions, by which he or she moves through life toward selected goals. These convictions are based on the client's interpretations of subjective experience, called a *schema of apperception* (Adler, 1956), a term akin to what modern cognitive behaviorists sometimes call a *cognitive schema* and what transactional analysts might call *scripts.* Life-style remains relatively constant throughout life, whereas behaviors to fulfill the goals inherent in the life-style can vary. Life-style change occurs only when (second order) changes in basic convictions occur. Essentially, Adlerian psychotherapy endeavors to assist clients in understanding and modifying their life-style.

Constructivists, especially critical constructivists, describe cognitive organization in terms of *core* and *peripheral constructs,* or *superordinate* and *subordinate constructs* (Kelly, 1955; Mahoney, 1991; Safran & Segal, 1990). While Adlerians focus on the content and process, constructivists often add structure to the description of cognitive organization. Similar to the Adlerian view of conscious and nonconscious is the constructivistic concept of *explicit* and *implicit* or *tacit knowledge.* Tacit knowledge is the unconscious or out-of-awareness framework for explicit knowledge (Polanyi, 1967).

Adlerians recognize that behavior occurs in a social context the result of person-environment interaction. There is an emphasis on the interpersonal nature of goals and behavior. Accordingly, *social embeddedness, community feeling,* and *social interest* are key concepts, and social interest is the criterion for assessing one's life-style as useful or useless (Dinkmeyer, Dinkmeyer, & Sperry, 1987).

Generally speaking, constructivists agree with Adler on the importance of social context (Safran & Segal, 1990).

Because Adlerians view the social context as critical in understanding a client's basic convictions, early experiences are important considerations. Adlerians use *life-style analysis,* including *early recollections, birth-order,* and *family constellation* explorations, to assess the client's phenomenological interpretation of life. Typically, the life-style is derived from an analysis of data gathered from a semi-structured interview. This interview format may take one or more sessions during which several early recollections are elicited and an intensive inquiry of family and sibling influences is conducted (Dinkmeyer, Dinkmeyer, & Sperry, 1987). Many other constructivists also hold a high regard for the contributions of early experiences to the construction of core processes (Guidano & Liotti, 1983; Mahoney, 1991). The *life-themes* described by Guidano and Liotti are similar to the *life-style.* Constructivists have also integrated attachment theory (Bowlby, 1988) into their theoretic framework and relate attachment patterns to certain pathologies (Jones, 1995). While *early recollections* help Adlerians understand client interpretations of the world, attachment theory helps constructivists arrive at core constructs or core beliefs (Guidano & Liotti, 1983).

Furthermore, constructivists have also appropriated Bandura's (1977, 1986) concept of *triadic reciprocality.* They view the relation among cognition, emotion, and behavior as reciprocal rather than linear (Mahoney, 1991). Emotion and action are viewed as *ways of knowing.* Therapeutically, emotion has often been viewed as "the problem." However, constructivists note that emotion, rather than being the problem, is often a path to the solution (Jones, 1995).

The concept of *resistance* is our last theoretical consideration. Adlerians view resistance as a coping mechanism for *inferiority feelings* or as a device for solving problems. It functions to protect or safeguard the client's self-esteem (Mosak, 1989). Generally, Adlerians prefer the term *safeguarding* over the term *resistance. Safeguarding* is the Adlerian analogue for *defense mechanisms.* As the individual strives to move from inferiority to superiority, safeguarding protects against feelings of inferiority and lack of courage. Adler (1929/1964) notes that "The so-called 'resistance' is only lack of courage to return to the useful side of life: which causes the patient to put up a defense against treatment, for fear that his relations with the psychologist should force him into some useful activity in which he will be defeated. For this reason we must never force a patient, but guide him very gently toward his easiest approach to usefulness" (p. 73). Mahoney's (1991) description of the constructivistic view of resistance is similar to the Adlerian concept of safeguarding. Adlerians view resistance as one of the many neurotic strategies an individual employs to safeguard or protect against loss of self-esteem. Thus, safeguarding behaviors are a reflection of the client's life-style. Accordingly, resistance is not something to work against but rather a phenomenon to work with (Jones, 1995).

Treatment Considerations

Because of their common phenomenological heritage, it should not be too surprising that Adlerian psychotherapy and constructivist psychotherapies tend to approach the therapy process in similar ways. Both have a similar view of the therapeutic relationship. Because they view the client as self-in-process, both view assessment as dynamic rather than static. And because constructive therapies favor technical eclecticism, they utilize a variety of techniques.

Therapeutic Relationship. "Collaborative empiricism" is how some describe an effective therapeutic relationship (Beck, 1976; Guidano & Liotti, 1983). Adlerians hold that the therapeutic relationship is optimal when equality and mutuality between clinician and client are achieved (Dinkmeyer, Dinkmeyer, & Sperry, 1987). Encouragement and empowerment are both values and strategies for bringing about change. Establishing a mutual and collaborative relationship is the first important task in therapy. Achieving such a relationship means that clinician and client align—or realign—their goals for the outcome of the treatment process. The Adlerian clinician seeks to understand the client's life-style since it is through the life-style that the client will relate to and safeguard against the clinician and the therapeutic context (Dinkmeyer, Dinkmeyer, & Sperry, 1987).

Offering a therapeutic alliance that creates a secure base is an early consideration in treatment. Adlerians and other constructivists believe that how the client relates to others will eventually surface in the therapeutic relationship. What transpires in therapy is an important process for understanding the client. Accordingly, the use of immediacy of thoughts, feelings, and intuitions become important in early sessions (Jones, 1995).

Assessment. Since Adlerians and other constructivists emphasize process, they tend to approach assessment similarly. Assessment is viewed as a dynamic process, rather than as a static event with the endpoint of establishing a clinical diagnosis and a diagnostic code. Assessment begins immediately and is always in process. Adlerians perform a life-style analysis, exploring family-of-origin issues, early recollections, and the influence of birth-order rank (Dinkmeyer, Dinkmeyer, & Sperry, 1987). Constructivists tend to assess core processes, including identification of the client's dominant attachment figures (Guidano & Liotti, 1983). Furthermore, both approaches emphasize the importance of articulating the client's expectations about the methods and outcomes of treatment.

An interesting and effective assessment strategy popularized by constructivist family therapists is the use of *therapeutic questions*. Although popularized by Selvini-Palazzoli, Boscolo, Cecchin, and Prata (1980) and elaborated by others (e.g., Tomm, 1987), Sperry (1992) notes that it appears that Adler first described this strategy over seventy years ago! Therapeutic questioning is used to understand relationships among family members and difference among relationships. Besides a method of gathering information, this strategy is also a powerful intervention for provoking change in the identified client as well as in the family. Perhaps the most well-known Adlerian example of therapeutic questioning is "The Question" first described by Adler (1956) in the 1920s and popularized by Rudolf Dreikurs in the 1950s and 1960s. For example, Dreikurs (1954) would ask a patient: "'Let us imagine I gave you a pill and you would be completely well as soon as you left this office. What would be different in your life, what would you do differently than before?' . . . The answer to 'The Question' indicates against whom or against what condition the symptom is directed. If he were well the patient might look for another job, do better on his present job, get along better with his wife. . . . They indicate why the patient is sick, if the illness is entirely neurotic, or what use the patient may make of an actual physical ailment" (p. 132). A highly similar question, called the "Miracle Question" (de Shazer, 1988, p. 5), has become commonplace among solution-focused constructivist psychotherapists in the last few years.

Treatment Interventions and Strategies. A basic treatment goal of Adlerian and constructivist approaches is a reconstruction of the client's cognitive organization. For Adlerians, this process of reconstruction is referred to as *reorientation*. Accordingly, treatment planning is directed at reorienting the client's life-style pattern (Sperry & Carlson, 1996).

Both Adlerian psychotherapy and constructivist psychotherapies are characterized as technically eclectic systems. That means each approach places a premium on tailoring treatment and employing a variety of interventions—irrespective of their theoretical origins—to meet and fit client needs (Jones, 1995). For example, the Adlerian technique, *acting 'as if,'* reflects the constructivist perspective. When someone has difficulty acting prosocially, that is, speaking assertively or responding with some measure of empathy, the clinician might encourage them to act 'as if' they were assertive or empathic several times a day until the next session. The rationale for this reconstruction strategy is that as someone begins to act differently and to feel differently, they become a different person (Mosak, 1989, p. 91). Carlson and Slavik (1998) describe and illustrate other Adlerian reconstruction strategies.

Whereas Adlerians have developed specific techniques that stem from their theory, they also employ a variety of cognitive, behavioral, and experiential techniques from other therapy systems. Narrative and narrative reconstruction techniques have recently garnered considerable interest among both Adlerians and many other constructivist psychotherapists. Narratives or stories are understood to be coauthored by clients and the cultures in which they live; and presumably clients seek psychotherapy when their life stories become ineffectual. From this perspective, the therapeutic process attempts to assist clients to develop "alternative stories" as part of "narrative means to therapeutic ends" (White & Epston, 1990). A critical therapeutic strategy is *externalization of the problem,* in which a client or family is assisted in defining the problem as external to the person of the identified client. Another strategy is the *objectification of the problem* by viewing the problem as a self-defeating script that can then be challenged by the client. Like White and Epston (1990), some Adlerians have advocated, when appropriate, the *sharing of client progress notes* in the form of inquiries about how they were able to begin to refuse to conform to the requirements of the problem (Neimeyer, 1993). Other variants of narrative reconstruction involve the novel use of personal journal work to deepen and broaden the client's self-transformation (Mahoney, 1991). Along related lines, Neimeyer's (1992) casebook describes a variety of narrative reconstruction techniques used for constructivistic assessment and therapy, while Mahoney (1991) describes the use of experiential techniques from a constructivistic perspective.

A somewhat different reconstruction strategy is the *prescription of therapeutic rituals.* This strategy was developed by and is employed by constructivist family therapists for the purpose of reconstructing a family problem. This ritual prescription is particularly cogent when two differing interpretations of a symptomatic behavior prevail within a family. For example, when family members are divided over whether a parent's depression is biological or psychological in origin, the clinician might prescribe that the biological interpretation be honored on even days of the week, while the psychological interpretation is honored on the odd days of the week (Neimeyer, 1993). This ritual strategy conveys the notion that it is possible to have more than one interpretation of a difficulty and that each carries distinct implications for behavior. Adler described a similar intervention, which he termed *prescribing the symptom,* while Dreikurs called it *antisuggestion* (Sherman & Dinkmeyer, 1987, p. 52). For instance, a client who engaged in compulsive housecleaning was prescribed scrubbing the floors between 1 and 3 A.M. daily for two weeks. She was to awaken, get dressed, do the prescribed housecleaning, and then return to bed. Usually, after a few days of complying with such a prescription, the client gives up the symptom, in this case the compulsion.

Adlerian psychotherapy appears to have influenced—albeit indirectly—many constructivist systems, just as it is being influenced by these same systems. Furthermore, Adlerian clinicians are very comfortable in using a variety of techniques developed or refined by different constructivist camps—as will be seen in the following report. Indeed, features of Adlerian psychotherapy can serve as an integrative bridge between the different camps (Watts, 1997).

CLINICAL EXAMPLE: THE CASE OF SANDRA

Sandra was a twenty-five-year-old female who was brought to treatment by her mother. She was in the process of finishing the final two classes for a Master of Arts degree in music at a university in a nearby state when problems began to surface. Sandra drove her car off the road at seventy-five miles per hour. Fortunately, she was not hurt and only minor damage occurred. She was, however, placed involuntarily in a local psychiatric hospital and her parents were summoned. Her hospital treatment was largely pharmacological and she was discharged taking antipsychotic, antidepressant, and anti-anxiety medication. Her parents forced her to withdraw from school and to move home for her own safety. Sandra agreed to move home but was disappointed as this required her to end her relationship with a man whom she had been seeing. The man (who was twenty-two years her senior) had his own psychological problems and was also unemployed.

First Session

Sandra appeared to be in good physical health. She did not make eye contact and spent the first meeting looking around the room or at the floor. Her mother, a very large and elegantly dressed woman, accompanied her. She indicated that she owned a local women's clothing store. Mother allowed Sandra to talk, only to interrupt and discount Sandra's observations and opinions. Sandra readily accepted the criticism and deferred to her mother. The therapist continued to focus on Sandra and encouraged her to tell her own stories. Sandra described a long history of social problems and rejection by her peer group. She reported having no friends and only a few acquaintances. Her youth was spent perfecting her musical abilities. Although attractive, she had very few dates. It seemed likely that her peer group had viewed her as being very odd and kept their distance.

She had one sister who was three years younger. Sandra believed that her sister "has it all." Mother described each of her daughters being "different." The younger sister was completing her college degree in education and hoped to teach. She was also engaged to a man that the family liked very much.

Sandra reported a family history in which her paternal aunt was also "very strange" and was still being supported by her parents. On the maternal side of the family there was an uncle who had not been able to get his life going. Sandra was often compared to these two by her parents. They would say, "You don't want to be like Aunt Millie or Uncle Clark."

The therapist asked many questions about how she could possibly be compared to them.

THERAPIST: Do you look like your aunt or uncle?

SANDRA: I don't think so. Do I, Mom?

MOTHER: Not really.

THERAPIST: Were your aunt and uncle musical?

SANDRA: No.

THERAPIST: Did they go to college or graduate school?

SANDRA: No, actually they both dropped out of high school.

THERAPIST: What do they do for a living?

SANDRA: Nothing. My grandparents take care of them.

THERAPIST: You have a job, college degree, musical ability. . . .
How are you really like them?

SANDRA: I'm not exactly sure.

Questions such as these allowed Sandra to begin to look at her life from a different (and more positive) viewpoint. Sandra had never had a job outside the family until two weeks prior to the first therapy session, when she began cleaning houses for a family friend's business. Although she liked it a lot and thought that she was doing fine, she was let go after eight days on the job. Sandra applied for a job at a local fast food restaurant and was hired and began a training program immediately. Although this is not much of an accomplishment for someone two classes shy of a master's degree, Sandra was thrilled. She saw this as the place to start on the road to being independent and to not being like her aunt or uncle. The therapist helped empower Sandra to consider that she was beginning to see herself accurately. Her long-range goal was to be a professional musician, but she believed that this would take time and in the interim she needed to be able to take care of herself until her big break came. Her mother believed that being a professional musician was an attainable goal.

Sandra was very critical of herself. She used the word *should* frequently, highlighting her levels of discouragement with "I should be further along with my career," "I should be the one with the boyfriend that everyone likes because I am the oldest," "I should have more friends," and similar remarks.

THERAPIST: I notice that you keep saying that you should do this or should have done that. Who says?

SANDRA: I don't know what you mean.

THERAPIST: Who says that you should have done these other things?

SANDRA: I don't know. I guess I have never thought about it before.

THERAPIST: When you do that you put yourself down and act as if you are not OK.

Sandra was willing to admit that her mind had been "playing tricks" on her. Recently she had been "hearing voices" that told her to harm herself. She listened to the voices and swallowed some straight pins while doing a sewing project. The voices had also been telling her to inhale a pen cap in order to asphyxiate herself, but so far she had not been compliant. She reported that when she masturbated and reached orgasm the voices quieted and she was able to return to constructive activities. The therapist gave her positive feedback about the fact that she was able to find a solution to her problem and how capable she was.

Sandra clearly described being less than her sister in her parents' eyes. She reported that her father took a superior position to Aunt Millie and Mom did the same with her brother Clark. Sandra was able to see the pattern extending down to her and her sister. The question was, why is this happening? The therapist continued to help Sandra to look at some of her assets and to help her to question why she would let people treat her this way. She was in her own right a pretty impressive person. She had good educational credentials and exceptional musical ability, and was attractive. With this input, she began to construct a new view of reality. She eventually said, "It isn't really necessary for there to be one good sibling and one that isn't good. We can both be successful in our own way."

In the initial session, the therapist focused on understanding how Sandra viewed her world and the systemic factors that were keeping her stuck. The therapist was very positive and encouraging, attempting to give Sandra power.

Second Session

The therapist began this session by conducting a brief lifestyle assessment. This procedure allowed both the therapist and client to gain insight into her thoughts, feelings, and behaviors. The therapist asked Sandra to compare herself to her sister on a number of characteristics. Sandra saw herself as someone who found her place through intelligence, hard work, good grades, helping around the house, having a temper, having high aspirations, being materialistic, and getting punished the most. She described her sister as being the opposite of her in many ways.

The therapist then asked Sandra to recall some early recollections. She was asked to remember as far back as she could to a specific memory that she could actually see. Two of her recollections are as follows:

Age 4: I was riding a Ferris wheel with my aunt. I was on the top of the world. I was waving my arms and she thought she had to restrain me for fear I would fall out. The most vivid part was how high I was and how ecstatic I felt.
Age 6: I remember getting spanked in first grade because I had a messy art drawer. I didn't know why I was being paddled in front of the class. I felt so

embarrassed and confused. The most vivid part was that I had no idea why
I was in trouble. Later on the teacher told me what the problem was.

In both of these recollections Sandra reported needing to be managed by
someone else. This seems to be an important part of her worldview: "I can't
take care of myself and I need others to look after me." She also reported feelings of being kept down when she was at the top. In her life she depended on
her parents and on the much older boyfriend who took care of her when she
was at school. She reported that people treated her like a baby. On one hand
she resented this, while on the other she expected it and found great comfort
in it. Additional early recollections showed patterns of someone who created a
new problem with her solution to the old problem, leaving her in a perpetual
state of discouragement.

The therapist asked her to talk about what it was like for her growing up.
She reported a lot of abuse in her early childhood, especially being picked on
at school. Sandra had no clue as to why these things happened to her. She was
not a "cool kid" in school and was generally treated cruelly. Her first boyfriend
would verbally abuse her and sodomize her.

Further assessment was provided when a Millon Clinical Multiaxial Inventory-
III (MCMI-III) (Millon, Davis, & Millon, 1994) was administered at the end of
the second session. Sandra's profile of scores supported a diagnosis of Avoidant
and Dependent Personality Disorder. Her scores also supported the likelihood
that she had psychotic thinking and could benefit from medication. The Lifestyle
Scale (Kern, 1990) showed Sandra to have a lifestyle priority of being a victim.
It is therefore very likely that she will think in ways that will keep her being victimized through the self-defeating of her stated goals.

Through the use of the lifestyle assessment Sandra felt more comfortable
with the therapist. Questions were asked that she could answer and the results
helped her to develop new insights into her life. A collaborative relationship
was established, one in which Sandra felt like an equal in the exploration
process. This was an unfamiliar position for her—she was not used to being a
person who was being treated with respect.

Third Through Sixth Sessions

From the brief assessment it became clear that Sandra had constructed a world
where everything was in balance. Her parents, family, and friends would treat
her badly (either through abuse or by infantilizing her) and she would live
down to this by acting immature, weird, and at times outright crazy. The challenge became one of helping her understand and construct a new worldview.
In Adlerian terms this meant rewriting the life-style. The formula for the life-
style is: "I am. . . . Life is. . . . Therefore. . . ." In Sandra's case, the formula was

"I am weak and not capable. The world is dangerous and confusing. Therefore I need help from others to make it."

The therapist endeavored to help her redefine her lifestyle. This involved the use of the Miracle Question (de Shazer, 1988) to help her develop some meaningful solutions to her problems.

THERAPIST: If you were to have a miracle happen tonight and your problems were to be gone, how would you know?

SANDRA: I don't know.

THERAPIST: Think about it, how would you know?

SANDRA: I guess I'd have somewhere to go and someone to be with.

This gave the therapist some clues as to what might be important components of her treatment plan. The therapist began to work with Sandra on making friends of both sexes. She found a local musician and invited her out for coffee after a community band practice. She found another person at her work and they went to a movie together. She got a pocket calendar and activities were planned for each day that placed her in situations where she might meet other people. Due to her avoidant and dependent personality, it was necessary to pick places where there were not large crowds. She began to go to the local library, record store, and coffee shop each day. She began an exercise program that took her to the local fitness center five days each week. Therapy sessions focused on helping her to behave successfully in these situations. This involved social skills training, including helping her to learn how to maintain eye contact, initiate conversations, and to have a number of possible topics for discussion.

Sandra was also told the Hans Christian Anderson tale "The Ugly Duckling"—and she beamed at the possibility that maybe she was a swan who had been living with ducks.

Seventh Through Tenth Sessions

The supportive nature of the therapy was very helpful for Sandra. She reported infrequent thoughts of self-harm and quieted voices. The use of circular questions allowed her to look more at her relationships and to become more psychologically minded. Examples are as follows: "When you approached Jim at the church coffee hour and stood next to him, saying nothing and looking at your feet, I wonder what he thought?" "I wonder what went on inside your Mom when she discovered you were not telling the truth?" "How did your swallowing a quarter affect your sister and her interest in doing things with you?"

She responded well to regular task setting as part of the treatment. Initially, the ideas for homework tasks came from the therapist but in sessions seven through ten Sandra created her own assignments.

Additional Sessions

This is a highly compressed description of a severely disturbed person who was able to benefit from a reconstruction of her world. She began to construct a new view of herself and the world: "I am capable. The world is challenging. Therefore, I must work harder and more deliberately." The use of Adlerian treatment formulation and interventions helped her to make good progress over a short time span. The focus on the goals and purposes of her behavior, as well as her style of connection to the social community, proved very useful to her. Sandra continued in therapy for two years, with visits moving from weekly to monthly. Sandra needed guidance as she developed social maturity and worked at rewriting the transgenerational patterns of over-and underfunctioning siblings.

○

It appears that Adler was a constructivist long before the term was coined. As we have demonstrated, there are considerable similarities with contemporary constructivism, particularly with the *critical constructivists,* and many of their clinical techniques can be incorporated or integrated into an Adlerian framework.

Unfortunately, survey textbooks tend to frame Adler as merely a dissident psychoanalyst and his approach, Individual Psychology, as a historical footnote. Constructivist clinicians who read any of Adler's original books may find a treasure trove of clinical insights and techniques in these pages. They are likely to reconstruct their view of Adlerian psychotherapy!

Endnote

1. *Editor's note:* In the conversation reported in Chapter Nine of this volume, Paul Watzlawick also pays tribute to the influence of Vaihinger's "as if" philosophy on his ideas about constructivism.

References

Adler, A. (1956). *The individual psychology of Alfred Adler: A systematic presentation in selections from his writings.* (H. L. Ansbacher & R. R. Ansbacher, Trans.). New York: Basic Books.

Adler, A. (1958). *What life should mean to you.* New York: Capricorn Books. (Original work published 1931)

Adler, A. (1964). *Problems of neurosis: A book of case histories.* (P. Mairet, Ed.). New York: HarperCollins. (Original work published 1929)

Bandura, A. (1977). *Social learning theory.* Upper Saddle River, NJ: Prentice Hall.

Bandura, A. (1986). *Social foundations of thought and action: A social cognitive theory.* Upper Saddle River, NJ: Prentice Hall.

Beck, A. T. (1976). *Cognitive therapy and emotional disorders.* New York: International Universities Press.

Bowlby, J. (1988). *A secure base.* New York: Basic Books.

Carlson, J., & Slavik, S. (Eds.). (1998). *Techniques of Adlerian psychotherapy.* Philadelphia: Taylor & Francis.

de Shazer, S. (1988). *Clues: Investigating solutions in brief therapy.* New York: Norton.

Dinkmeyer, D., Dinkmeyer, D., & Sperry, L. (1987). *Adlerian counseling and psychotherapy* (2nd ed.). Columbus, OH: Merrill.

Dreikurs, R. (1954). The psychological interview in medicine. *American Journal of Individual Psychology, 10,* 99–122.

Forgus, R., & Shulman, B. H. (1979). *Personality: A cognitive view.* Upper Saddle River, NJ: Prentice Hall.

Guidano, V. F. (1987). *Complexity of the self: A developmental approach to psychopathology and therapy.* New York: Guilford Press.

Guidano, V. F. (1991). *The self in process: Toward a postrationalist cognitive therapy.* New York: Guilford Press.

Guidano, V. F., & Liotti, G. (1983). *Cognitive processes and the emotional disorders.* New York: Guilford Press.

Jones, J. V. (1995). Constructivism and individual psychology: Common ground for dialogue. *Individual Psychology, 51,* 3, 231–243.

Kelly, G. (1955). A *theory of personality: The psychology of personal constructs (Vols. 1–2).* New York: Norton.

Kern, R. (1990). *Lifestyle Scale.* Coral Springs, FL: CMTI Press.

Mahoney, M. J. (1984). Behaviorism and individual psychology: Contacts, conflicts, and future directions. In T. Reinelt, Z. Otalora, & H. Kappus (Eds.), *Contacts of individual psychology with other forms of therapy* (pp. 70–82). Munich: Ernst Reinhardt Verlag.

Mahoney, M. J. (1991). *Human change processes.* New York: Basic Books.

Masters, S. (1991). Constructivism and the creative power of the self. *Individual Psychology, 47*(4), 447–455.

Millon, T., Davis, R., & Millon, C. (1994). *Millon Clinical Multiaxial Inventory-III.* Minneapolis, MN: National Computer Systems.

Mosak, H. (1989). Individual psychology. In R. J. Corsini & D. Wedding (Eds.), *Current psychotherapies* (pp. 65–116). Itasca, IL: Peacock.

Neimeyer, G. J. (Ed.). (1992). *A casebook of constructivist assessment.* Newbury Park, CA: Sage.

Neimeyer, G. J. (1993). An appraisal of constructivist psychotherapies. *Journal of Consulting and Clinical Psychology, 61,* 2, 221–234.

Polanyi, M. (1967). *The tacit dimension.* Garden City, NY: Anchor.

Popper, K. (1983). *Realism and the aim of science.* Totowa, NJ: Rowman & Littlefield.

Safran, J. D., & Segal, Z. V. (1990). *Interpersonal process in cognitive therapy.* New York: Basic Books.

Safran, J. D., Vallis, T. M., Segal, Z. V., & Shaw, B. F. (1986). Assessment of core cognitive processes in cognitive therapy. *Cognitive Therapy & Research, 10*(5), 509–526.

Selvini-Palazzoli, M., Boscolo, L., Cecchin, G., & Prata, G. (1981). Hypothesizing-circularity-neutrality. *Family Process, 19,* 3–12.

Sherman, R., & Dinkmeyer, D. (1987). *Systems of family therapy: An Adlerian integration.* New York: Brunner/Mazel.

Shulman, B. H. (1985). Cognitive therapy and the individual psychology of Alfred Adler. In M. Mahoney & A. Freeman (Eds.), *Cognition in psychotherapy* (pp. 46–62). New York: Plenum.

Shulman, B., & Watts, R. (1997). Adlerian and constructivist theories: An Adlerian perspective. *Journal of Cognitive Psychotherapy, 11*(3), 181–194.

Sperry, L. (1992). The "rediscovery" of interventive interviewing. *North American Society of Adlerian Psychology Newsletter, 25*(1), 3–4.

Sperry, L., & Carlson, J. (Eds.). (1996). *Psychopathology and psychotherapy: From DSM-IV diagnosis to treatment* (2nd ed.). Washington, DC: Accelerated Development.

Tomm, K. (1987). Interventive interviewing: Part II. Reflexive questioning as a means to enable self-healing. *Family Process, 26*(2), 167–183.

Vaihinger, H. (1924). *The philosophy of "as if"* (C. K. Ogden, Trans.). Orlando: Harcourt Brace.

Watts, R., & Critelli, J. (1997). Roots of cognitive theories in the individual psychology of Alfred Adler. *Journal of Cognitive Psychotherapy, 11*(3), 147–156.

White, M., & Epston, D. (1990). *Narrative means to therapeutic ends.* New York: Norton.

CHAPTER FOUR

How Rational Emotive Behavior Therapy Belongs in the Constructivist Camp

Albert Ellis

lthough I was formerly in the logical positivist camp, I now consider myself largely a postmodernist and constructivist. Rational Emotive Behavior Therapy, which I originated as the first modern Cognitive Behavior Therapy, was always constructivist in that it holds, with Kelly (1955), that people have strong innate tendencies to solve their life problems and to actualize themselves. They also have inborn as well as acquired powerful tendencies to defeat themselves and the social groups to which they belong, but they can use their constructive proclivities to defeat their defeatism and to make themselves and their social group healthier and happier (Ellis, 1962, 1990, 1994, 1996a; Ellis & Dryden, 1997; Ellis & Harper, 1997; Ellis, Gordon, Neenan, & Palmer, 1997; Ellis & Tafrate, 1997). Some of the main constructivist and postmodern views include these:

• *Perhaps some kind of indubitable objective reality or thing in itself exists, but we only seem to apprehend or know it through our fallible, personal-social, different, and changing human perceptions.* We do not have any absolute certainty about what reality is or what it will be—in spite of our often being strongly convinced that we do.

• *Our views of what is good or bad, what is right and wrong, what is moral and immoral are, as George Kelly (1955) pointed out, largely personal-social constructions.* Kelly held that the identification of universal truths is an impossible task and that all ethical beliefs have a constructionist nature. I agree.

• *Although human personality has some important innate and fairly fixed elements it also largely arises from relational and social influences.* It is much less individualistic than it is commonly thought to be.

• *People are importantly influenced or conditioned by their cultural rearing.* Their behaviors are amazingly multicultural and there is no conclusive evidence that their diverse cultures are *right* or *wrong, better* or *worse* (Ivey & Rigazio-DiGilio, 1991; Sampson, 1989).

• *Either/or concepts of goodness and badness often exist and are rigidly held, but they tend to be inaccurate, limited, and prejudiced.* More open-minded apperceptions of human and nonhuman reality tend to show that things and processes exist on a both/and and an and/also basis. Thus almost every human act or condition has its advantages *and* disadvantages. Even *helpful* acts have their *bad* aspects. Giving a person money, approval, or therapy may encourage him or her to be weaker, more dependent, and less self-helping. Berating a person may encourage her or him to become stronger, less dependent, and more self-helping. Because monolithic either/or solutions to problems have their limitations, we had better consider the range of alternate and/also solutions and test them out to see how well—and badly—they work.

• *Unfortunately—or fortunately—all the solutions we strive to achieve for our problems depend on our choosing goals and purposes from which to work.* Such goals and purposes are just about always arguable, never absolute. Even the near-universal human goal of survival is debatable, for some of us stress individual and others stress group or social survival. And at least a few people choose suicide, and a few think that the annihilation of the whole human race—and perhaps of the entire universe—is preferable. So we can arrive here at a consensus but not any absolute agreement of what goals and purposes are *better* and *worse.*

These postmodernist views have recently been promulgated by a host of writers (Bartley, 1984; Feyerband, 1975; Gergen, 1995; Hoshmand & Polkinghorne, 1992; Popper, 1985; Simms, 1994). They have also been applied to the field of mental health counseling and psychotherapy by a number of other writers (Ellis, 1994, 1996a, 1996b, 1996c; Gergen, 1991; Guterman, 1994; Ivey & Goncalves, 1988; Ivey & Rigazio-DiGilio, 1991; Kelly, 1955; Mahoney, 1991; Neimeyer & Mahoney, 1995). Postmodernism is an important—and growing—aspect of today's psychotherapy.

HOW RATIONAL EMOTIVE BEHAVIOR THERAPY IS CONSTRUCTIVIST

Rational Emotive Behavior Therapy (REBT), along with other cognitive-behavior therapies—such as those of Beck (1976), Maultsby (1984), and Meichenbaum (1977)—has been criticized as being rationalist and sensationalist by a number of critics (Guidano, 1991; Guterman, 1994, 1996; Mahoney, 1991; Neimeyer & Mahoney, 1995). I have refuted this charge and tried to show that REBT is quite constructivist, and in some ways is actually more so than many of the other constructionist therapies (Ellis, 1991, 1994, 1996a, 1996b, 1996c). The following paragraphs discuss a number of factors that make it particularly constructivist.

• Kelly (1955), Guidano (1991), Mahoney (1991), and other constructivist therapists show that disturbed people generate deep cognitive structures and had better be helped to adopt alternative models of the self and the world so that their deep structures can work in a more flexible and adaptive manner. REBT more specifically holds that the rigid, absolutistic musts and necessities by which people usually upset themselves are not merely learned from their parents and culture but are also created by their own constructivist, and partly biological, tendencies.

• REBT therefore holds that both clients and their therapists had better work hard, preferably in a highly active-directive and persistent manner, to help bring about profound philosophic, highly emotive, and strongly behavioral changes. Discovering and disputing their automatic self-defeating thoughts, as most cognitive-behavioral therapies do, is not enough. In addition, they had better be helped to see that they create core dysfunctional philosophies and that they can constructively change by thinking, by thinking about their thinking, and by thinking about thinking about their thinking (Dryden, 1995; Ellis, 1990, 1994, 1996a; Ellis & Dryden, 1997).

• In dealing with people's basic problems about self-worth, REBT agrees with the constructivist and existentialist position of Heidegger (1962), Tillich (1953), and Rogers (1961) that humans can define themselves as good or worthy just because they choose to do so. But it also shows them how to construct a philosophically unfalsifiable position of choosing life goals and purposes and then only rating and evaluating their thoughts, feelings, and actions as good when they fulfill and as bad when they fail to fulfill their chosen purposes. In this REBT solution to the problem of unconditional self-acceptance (USA), people can choose to view their self or essence as too complex and multifaceted to be given *any* global rating. It exists and can be enjoyed without the rigidities and dangers of either/or evaluation (Ellis, 1994, 1996a; Ellis & Dryden, 1997; Ellis & Harper, 1997; Ellis & Tafrate, 1997).

• Constructivists like Guidano (1991) and Hayek (1978) emphasize people's tacit observations and reactions to life problems, and REBT has always agreed that unconscious and tacit processes create both disturbance and problem solving (Ellis, 1962; Goleman, 1995). But REBT also particularly emphasizes and abets people's innate and acquired constructive abilities to design, plan, invent, and carry through better solutions to life's problems and to self-actualization. It shows clients how to make themselves aware of their unconscious constructivist self-defeating tendencies—and also how to use their conscious intentions and plans to lead a happier—more constructivist—life.

• Mahoney (1991), Guidano (1991), Robert and Greg Neimeyer (Neimeyer & Mahoney, 1995), and other constructivists often hold that because people are natural constructivists—with which I agree—active-directive cognitive-behavior therapy may interfere with their natural ability to change. But this is like saying that because children (and adults) have natural abilities to solve problems and help themselves, their parents and teachers should give them little if any instruction! REBT takes a both/and instead of an either/or position here, holding that clients do have considerable natural ability to make themselves *both* disturbed and less disturbed, and teaches them how to help themselves minimize their disturbances. Moreover, while encouraging them to use their self-aiding tendencies—which obviously they are usually doing badly when they come to therapy—it tries to give them greater understanding—and determination—to collaborate with the therapist to help themselves more. It also stresses therapist and client efficiency in their choice and practice of the multitude of therapeutic techniques now available.

• Constructionist approaches often put down science—especially rational science—and in some ways they make good points. Science has many advantages but is hardly sacrosanct. REBT holds, with postmodernists, that science has its limitations, especially because the objective truths that it often claims to reveal are at bottom person-centered and include important subjective aspects. Science, however, is important for psychotherapy. For if we can agree on what the main goals of counseling and therapy are—which is not as easy as it may at first seem!—scientifically oriented observation, case history, and experimentation may check our theory and show us how accurately our goals are achieved. Not certainly—but at least approximately. So science has its usefulness, and REBT—along with other cognitive-behavior therapies—uses science and rationality and also other criteria to check its theories and to change them and its practices. Healthy constructivism includes rational scientific method while abjuring dogmatic scientism.

My personal change from logical positivism to postmodernism began in 1976 when Michael Mahoney sent me a copy of his book *Scientist as Subject,* and I saw that Bartley (1984), Popper (1985), and other philosophers rightly showed that logical positivism was not consistent with some of its own postulates. Even before that, however, I was beginning to get uncomfortable with it.

I had determined, on the basis of clinical experience, that people's basic problems usually arose when they raised their preferences for success, love, and comfort into rigid, absolutistic musts and demands (Ellis, 1962, 1972). But the so-called truths of logical positivism seemed a little too rigid and absolutistic; and the postmodernists were more in tune with the flexible thinking that REBT was recommending for clients and other people. The main backing for some of its ideas seemed to come from the postmodernist idea that there were no eternal verities and that no matter how true a hypothesis appeared to be it could always be supplanted by later evidence and by the slant humans gave to this evidence.

I particularly saw that "proper" behavior related to one's basic choices and desires. Thus one of my clients wanted the certainty that his wife "truly" loved him and I showed him that he could only get a high degree of probability that she did. Certainty did not seem to exist; and if it did, it might not last. Moreover, even if he had it, it would depend upon his *definition* of "true love." Did he mean passionate love, sexy love, companionate love, or all of the above? Did he mean long-lasting intense love, long-lasting moderate love, short-lasting intense love, or what? "True love" had any number of definitions—depending on the lover.

The kind and degrees of love he wished for were largely a matter of his choice; and if he achieved this choice, it might later change, and it had advantages and disadvantages, depending on the conditions of his life. The best I could do for this client was to help him define more clearly (not perfectly) what he wanted and help him achieve it at that time—without the certainty that he would gain it and that it would last!

The client was helped to be less rigid about his demands and all was well. But I saw that not only had human desires better be less imperative but also that there were a myriad of them, and that they could change. One woman's meat was another woman's poison. Therefore, general and universal rules for human conduct did not seem to exist. REBT could, with some degree of probability, tell people that if they hold rules of living rigidly and absolutely they are likely to get into trouble. But it could not tell them what to prefer or desire.

REBT, moreover, has always been somewhat postmodern and constructivist in that it largely follows Epictetus' two-thousand-year-old idea, "People are disturbed not by the things that happen to them but by their views of these things." It therefore takes a phenomenological stand rather than an objectivist position. And its unabsolutistic view—that it is healthy to have strong wants and preferences but unhealthy to raise them to grandiose commands—is particularly consonant with the postmodern position that desires are not sacrosanct.

For these reasons—and more that could be presented—REBT tries to be as constructivist as, and in some ways more constructivist than, other therapies. Whether it actually succeeds in this respect only further study, including scientific and experimental study, will show.

The foregoing positions sound, to my prejudiced ears, like open-minded, flexible, and postmodern views. I favor them and try to follow them in my life and in my theory and practice of therapy. With some difficulty! For although I am willing to live with answers and rules that I realize are not final, utterly consistent, and indubitably correct, I would like to have some degree of probability that the ethics I choose for my life and my therapy relationships are reasonably correct and beneficial. Kelly (1955) thought that although we cannot be certain about the goodness or rightness of our morals, we can still have probabilistic faith that they are workable. I tend to agree with him.

The trouble with postmodern ethics, as a number of critics have pointed out, is that they can easily be taken to relativist and even anarchic extremes (Fuchs & Ward, 1994; Ginter, 1996; Haughness, 1993; Raskin, 1995). Humans seem to require fairly clear-cut social rules when they live and work together; and counselors and therapists especially had better adopt and follow fairly strict ethical standards. Active-directive therapists like me are particularly vulnerable in this respect, because we tend to be more authoritative, more didactic, and more forceful than passive, quiescent therapists are. Therefore, we are often accused of being more authoritarian, self-centered, and harmful than passive therapists. I don't quite agree with this allegation and could write a book on the enormous harm that is often done by passive therapists, who often keep clients in needless pain and solidly block what they can do to change themselves. But let me fully admit that directive therapy has its distinct dangers and show how I, partly from taking a postmodernist outlook, ethically deal with these dangers.

AN ACTIVE-DIRECTIVE APPROACH

Let us take one of the very important problems of therapy, and one that has distinct ethical considerations, to see how I use postmodern views to handle it. As a therapist, shall I mainly be a fairly passive listener, hear all sides of my clients' problems, explore with them the advantages of their doing this and not doing that, have faith in their own ability to make presumably good decisions for themselves, and patiently wait for them to do so? Or should I instead more active-directively zero in on what I think are my clients' core disturbances, show them what they are specifically thinking, feeling, and doing to needlessly upset themselves, and directly challenge them and teach them how to think, feel, and behave more effectively?

A number of schools of therapy—especially classical psychoanalysis, Rogerian person-centered, and cognitive-experiential therapy—largely favor the more passive approach, while a number of other schools—especially behavior therapy, cognitive-behavior therapy, problem-solving, and Gestalt therapy—largely favor the more active-directive approach. Which one is more ethical and which shall I use?

As almost everyone in the field of therapy already knows, I—and REBT, the special form of therapy that I use—favor active-directive methods. I consider these to be ethical and efficient for several reasons.

• *Most clients—especially those with severe personality disorders—are disturbed for both biological and environmental reasons.* They are innately prone to anxiety, depression, and rage and they also learn dysfunctional thoughts, feelings, and behaviors. They practice them so often that they have great difficulty changing even when they gain considerable insight into their origin and development. Therefore, they had better be taught how they are probably upsetting themselves and taught specific and general methods to change themselves (Ellis, 1994; Ellis & Dryden, 1997; Ellis, Gordon, Neenan, & Palmer, 1997).

• *Clients are usually in pain when they come to therapy.* Active-directive methods, as research has shown, tend to be more effective in a brief period of time than more passive methods are (Elkin, 1994; Hollon & Beck, 1994; Lyons & Woods, 1991; Silverman, McCarthy, & McGovern, 1992). There is also some evidence that the active-directive methods of cognitive-behavior therapy may lead to a more lasting change than some of the more passive techniques tend to produce (Hollon & Beck, 1994; Weishar, 1993).

• *Therapy is often expensive.* It seems ethical to help clients benefit from it as quickly as feasible—which is what active-directive methods tend to do (Ellis, 1996a).

• *More passive therapists—such as classical analysts and Rogerian person-centered practitioners—have often appeared to be passive while actually sneaking in more active methods.* They may therefore not be as honest compared to more active therapists who fully acknowledge their directiveness.

• *In REBT terms, passive techniques such as relating warmly to clients instead of focusing on their specific dysfunctioning may help them* feel *better but not get better.* Clients often enjoy being endlessly listened to rather than urged to change, and feel conditionally better because their therapist approves of them rather than being *un*conditionally self-accepting, *whether or not* their therapist likes them (Ellis, 1972, 1990, 1991, 1994, 1996a).

• *Actively showing clients how to function better often helps them achieve a sense of self-efficacy.* This may not amount to unconditional self-acceptance, but nonetheless may be quite therapeutic (Bandura, 1986).

• *Active therapy may push clients to do difficult beneficial tasks—such as in vivo desensitization—that are quite beneficial but that they would rarely do on their own.* Clients often change more when they first make themselves uncomfortable and then later become comfortable with their new behaviors. Active-directive therapy is likely to do more than passive therapy to encourage them to *un*comfortably change (Ellis, 1994, 1996a; Ellis & Dryden, 1997).

For all these advantages of active-directive therapy, I had better acknowledge its possible disadvantages, including these:

- It may be too directive and interrupt clients' innate proactive propensities to work on their own problems and to actualize themselves.

- It may induce clients to use methods that the therapist strongly believes in but that have little efficacy or that may even be iatrogenic.

- It may encourage clients to try suggested methods too quickly without giving them proper thought and preparation.

- It may lead clients to adopt goals and values that the therapist sells them on and therefore not really to fulfill *themselves.*

- It may tempt directive therapists to go to authoritarian, one-sided, and even righteous extremes and to neglect important individual differences, multicultural influences, and other aspects of individual and group diversity.

- It may put too much power and responsibility on the therapist, disrupt a potentially collaborative and cooperative client-therapist relationship, and detract from the humanistic aspects of counseling.

Even though much published evidence shows that active-directive therapy is often quite advantageous and effective, we can postmodernistically question whether at bottom, these results are *really* effective, good, deep, or lasting. These terms have multiple meanings, some of which directly contradict other meanings of the same term. Which of these meanings shall we accept as true?

My personal solution to this issue is to take an and/also rather than an either/or approach. Thus, in accordance with REBT theory, I usually zero in quite quickly on my clients' basic or core philosophies—especially on their dysfunctional or irrational beliefs—and show them how to differentiate these from their rational and functional preferences, as well as how to use several cognitive, emotive, and behavioral methods to dispute and act against these beliefs.

But I also show them some important other sides of their dysfunctional thinking, feeling, and behaving. Even their highly irrational ideas—their absolutistic shoulds, oughts, or musts—have advantages and virtues. "I must perform well or I am worthless!" produces anxiety and avoidance, but it is also motivating, energizing, and brings some good results. Likewise, even questionable ideas—such as the Pollyannaish beliefs, "Day by day in every way I'm getting better and better" or "No matter what I do kind Fate will take care of me"—may jolt one out of a depressed state and help one function better.

Strong negative feelings can be good *and* bad, helpful and unhelpful. When you do poorly, your strong feelings of disappointment and regret may push you to do better next time. But your strong feelings of horror and self-hatred may harm you immensely. Yes, and even your feelings of horror and self-hatred may *sometimes* help you give up damaging behavior patterns such as compulsive smoking or drinking!

Rational ideas and behaviors are not always really *rational*—certainly not always sensible and effective. Rationally and empirically believing that the universe is senseless and uncaring will help some people to be self-reliant and energized—and help others to be depressed and hopeless. Accurately believing that no one in the world really cares for you will motivate some people to work at being more social and others to withdraw socially.

CAUTIONS AND LIMITATIONS

In spite of the disadvantages of active-directive therapy, I strongly favor it over passive therapy. But to make reasonably sure that I do not take it to extremes I try to keep in mind several safeguards. Here are some of my main—and I think postmodernistically oriented—cautions.

Awareness of My Technique's Limitations

I do therapy on the basis of my sincere and strong faith in REBT—meaning, my belief that it most probably works well with most of my clients much of the time but that it also has its distinct limitations. I *tentatively* endorse and follow it but keep looking for its flaws and its shortcomings. I keep checking my own results, those of my colleagues and trainees, and those reported in the literature. I try to keep especially aware of its dangers and its inefficiencies. Thus, I keep looking for the limitations of my active-directiveness, pointing them out to my clients and encouraging them to be more active-directive in their own right (Ellis, 1996a; Ellis & Dryden, 1997).

Awareness of Clients' Differing Reactions

I assume that REBT methods help most of my clients much of the time—but hardly *all* of them all of the time. Although I often see clients as having disturbances stemming from similar dysfunctional or irrational beliefs, I also keep reminding myself that even people with the same problems—for example, severe states of depression—have vastly different biochemical reactions, temperaments, histories, family and cultural influences, socioeconomic conditions, therapeutic experiences, and so on. Moreover, they react differently to me and my personality and preferences. Although I still start out with what I think are the best REBT methods for each of them—which usually means the ones I have successfully used with somewhat similar clients in the past—I remain quite ready to vary my methods considerably with each individual client. I even consider, when REBT doesn't seem to be working, using methods that REBT theory and practice usually opposes (Ellis, 1996a). Thus I am uncharacteristically passive with a few clients who would resist more active methods, and I am superoptimistic with some clients who do not take well to the hard-headed realism I use with most of my clients.

Experimenting with Various Techniques

Aubrey Yates (1975), a behavior therapist, once said that each session of therapy had better be an experiment—and one that leads the therapist to change tactics as the results of that experiment are observed. I add: I had better observe and review each *series* of sessions, and the length of therapy as a whole, as an experiment. As I note the good and bad results—or what I *think* are the good and bad results—of my sessions with each individual client, I try to repeat successful REBT methods and modify unsuccessful ones with this particular client. If my REBT methods do not appear to be working, I experiment with some non-REBT—or even anti-REBT—methods. If these do not seem to be effective, I refer the client to another REBT or non-REBT therapist. As usual, I keep experimenting with a number of active-directive methods—and with some more passive ones as well.

Using Multimodal Methods

From the start, REBT has always used a number of cognitive, emotive, and behavioral methods with most clients, and over the years it has added a number of additional methods that appear to be effective (Ellis, 1957, 1962, 1988, 1994, 1996a; Kwee & Ellis, 1997). All these methods have their disadvantages and limitations, particularly with some clients some of the time. I therefore try to keep these limitations in mind and to have available for regular or occasional use literally scores of REBT techniques—as well as, as noted earlier, a number of non-REBT techniques. I thereby remain open-minded and alternative-seeking in my therapy. Most methods of REBT are active-directive. But some—like the Socratic method of discovering and questioning irrational beliefs—are more passive. When directiveness fails, more passive methods are borrowed from psychoanalytic, person-centered, and other therapies.

Using Therapeutic Creativity

I originally used or adopted several REBT methods from other theorists and therapists, believing them to be effective implementers of REBT theory—which tentatively but still strongly holds several major propositions. I soon found that I could better adapt many of these methods to REBT—and to therapy in general—by slightly or considerably modifying them. And I also devised new methods—such as REBT's shame-attacking exercises and its very forceful and vigorous disputing of clients' irrational beliefs—that seem to add to and improve upon my original ones (Bernard, 1993; Dryden, 1995; Ellis, 1988, 1994; Ellis & Dryden, 1997; Walen, DiGiuseppe, & Dryden, 1992). I—and hopefully other REBT practitioners—remain open to using our therapeutic creativity to adapt and devise new methods with special clients and with regular ones. I mostly have created new active-directive methods. But I also designed the more passive method of exploring clients' early irrational beliefs, as well as the dysfunctional beliefs of others, to prime them indirectly to note and deal with their own self-defeating ideas. I have also for many years encouraged clients to teach REBT to their friends and relatives and thereby indirectly learn it better themselves (Ellis, 1996a). I use a number of paradoxical methods with my clients—such as encouraging them to get at least three rejections a week—so that they see and believe that being rejected is not horrible or shameful.

Varying Relationship Methods

REBT theory holds that the majority of therapy clients can benefit from achieving unconditional self-acceptance (USA)—that is, fully accepting themselves as good or deserving persons *whether or not* they perform well and *whether or not* significant other people approve of them (Ellis, 1972, 1988; Ellis & Harper, 1997; Hauck, 1991; Mills, 1994). Consequently, I try to give all my clients what Rogers (1961) called *unconditional positive regard;* and I go beyond this and do my best to teach them how to give it to themselves. I recognize, however, that even USA has its limitations—because some people only change their self-defeating and antisocial behavior by damning *themselves* as well as their *actions.* I especially recognize that methods of showing clients unconditional acceptance range from warmly loving or approving them to unemotionally accepting them with their revealed failings and hostilities. All these methods have their advantages and disadvantages, and all of them work well and badly with different clients. So I vary the specific ways I relate to clients and cautiously observe the results of my interactions with them. Occasionally, I even go along with their self-damning when, oddly enough, it seems to help them. So I generally give clients unconditional acceptance and actively teach them how to give it to themselves. But I work in many different individual and specific ways, including indirect and passive ones.

Varying Interpersonal Methods

REBT, again on theoretical grounds, teaches clients the advantages of unconditional other acceptance (UOA)—or the Christian philosophy of accepting the sinner but not the sin (Ellis, 1994, 1996a; Ellis & Dryden, 1997). I do this with my clients because I believe that their anger, rage, and fighting are frequently self-destructive and also ruin relationships with others. A good case can be made that rage and noncooperativeness seriously sabotage human survival and happiness, and that the essence of psychotherapy, therefore, is helping people achieve both USA and UOA (Gergen, 1991; Sampson, 1985).

Nonetheless, clients' achieving unconditional self-and other-acceptance may well have some drawbacks—such as helping people to justify their own and other people's immoral behavior and thereby encouraging it. So I try to realize it is not exactly a panacea.

Moreover, therapists' ways of giving and teaching USA and UOA can easily be interpreted wrongly by their clients. Thus, when Carl Rogers (1961) showed clients unconditional positive regard, they often wrongly concluded that they were good persons because of his approval of them. But this is highly conditional self-acceptance! Similarly, if I accept my clients unconditionally when, say, they have stolen or cheated, they may wrongly conclude that I don't really think that their behavior is evil, and may therefore excuse their doing it.

So although I do my best to give my clients unconditional acceptance and encourage them to give it to others, I closely watch their reception and interpretation of what I am doing. I solicit their feedback, watch their reactions with themselves, with me, and with others—and once again use a variety of relationship and interpersonal relating approaches to determine which ones actually seem to work. I actively give and teach self-acceptance and forgiveness of others. But I also actively watch and try to counter its potential dangers.

Once again, REBT has always actively used the therapeutic relationship to help clients become aware of their interpersonal cognitive, emotional, and behavioral deficiencies. But I keep reminding myself that if my clients involve themselves too closely with me that may increase their neurotic neediness and interfere with their outside relations with others. I am also skeptical of my assumption that the main ways my clients react to me—who may be a uniquely accepting person in their life—are the same ways that they react to others. So I often tone down their involvement with me, encourage their participation in one of my therapy groups, recommend suitable workshops, talks, and books, and teach them interpersonal skills specifically designed to help them in their outside life. I do not assume that their relationships with me are clearly transferred from their feelings and prejudices about their early family members—though occasionally that is so. I assume, rather, that they often have an idiosyncratic and personal relationship with me and I watch closely to see if it is over- or underinvolved and how it can be constructively used despite its possible dangers. When my actively relating to my clients seems to be iatrogenic, I try to deliberately ameliorate it with a more passive kind of interaction with them.

Skepticism About the Infallibility of the Therapist and the Main Therapeutic Methods Employed

REBT encourages clients to have two almost contradictory beliefs: First, that they are able to understand how they largely disturb themselves, how they can reduce their disturbances and increase their individual and social fulfillment, and how they can use several REBT cognitive, emotive, and behavioral methods to try to actively work at doing what they theoretically can do. REBT thus tries to help clients have an active, strong feeling of self-efficacy about changing themselves. Second, it keeps encouraging them to see and accept their human fallibility and imperfection realistically—to acknowledge that they now are, and in all probability will continue to be, highly error-prone, inconsistent, unreasonable, inefficacious individuals. Always? Yes. To a high degree? Yes.

Can clients, then, have confidence in their ability to grow and change—have a sense of self-efficacy in this regard—*and* still acknowledge and accept their quite human fallibility? Why not? People are fallible at all sports—and also have real confidence that they can usually play one of them well, and actually do so. They are highly fallible students—but feel efficacious, say, at test taking and usually get decent marks. So it is almost certain that they are generally fallible. But at the same time, they are highly proficient in certain tasks, know they are proficient, and help themselves remain proficient by having a sense of self-efficacy about these tasks.

So I can safely active-directively show my clients that they are generally fallible, and even often fallible about changing themselves. Nonetheless, if they are willing to work at changing themselves, they can have what I call *achievement-confidence* and what Albert Bandura (1986) calls *self-efficacy*. Believing that *highly probably*—not *certainly*—they can change, they often do.

Therapists, too, can feel confident that they are effective—in spite of their fully acknowledging their therapeutic (and general) fallibility. This is what happens as I do active-directive REBT. I am quite confident that I will often significantly help my clients, and usually help them more than if I used another main form of therapy. But I also know full well that I am a fallible human—quite fallible. I recognize that with each client I can and at times easily do REBT inefficiently—yes, even though I created it, have used it with many thousands of clients, and am the world's leading authority on it. Nonetheless, with this particular client, I may well have my prejudices, weaknesses, hostilities, frustration intolerances, ignorances, rigidities, stupidities, and so on and on. Indeed I may!

While seeing a client, I therefore often do several things:

- Acknowledge my prejudices and weaknesses.

- Accept myself unconditionally with them.

- Try to ameliorate and compensate for them.

- Decide whether, in spite of my failings, I am still probably able to help this client. If I decide that I am able, I push myself on with a good degree of confidence or self-efficacy.

- Do my best to use REBT (and possibly other) methods with each client. Sometimes discuss my weaknesses with the client, to see if he or she is willing to continue to see me. If so, I proceed actively, energetically with the therapy—mainly with a high degree of confidence but also with some doubts.

- Keep checking on my doubts and often change my tactics with this (and other) clients and/or refer some to another therapist.

O

Postmodern philosophy, when not taken to relativist extremes, has a great deal to offer to the field of psychotherapy, particularly in the area of psychotherapy ethics. Rational Emotive Behavior Therapy (REBT) is active-directive but is also unusually postmodernistic and constructivist in that it specializes in showing clients how their conscious and unconscious absolutistic philosophies lead to much of their dysfunctional feelings and behaviors, and what they can do to make themselves more open-minded and flexible in their intrapersonal and interpersonal relationships.

Active-directive therapies, however, may dangerously neglect some aspects of constructivist therapy, such as ignoring less intrusive and more passive ways of collaboration between therapists and their clients. This chapter shows how I, as an active-directive practitioner of REBT, address some of its potential dangers and use postmodernist ethics and safeguards to retain its efficiency and reduce its risks. In particular, it stresses therapists' becoming aware of REBT's limitations and of clients' different reactions to its techniques; experimenting with various multimodal methods of REBT and non-REBT therapy in response to client feedback, both solicited and observed, using therapeutic activity; varying relationship and interpersonal approaches; and remaining highly skeptical about the therapist's and the therapeutic method's infallibility. These caveats and cautions will not make active-directive REBT—nor any other form of therapy—entirely flexible and safe. But they may considerably help.

I have tried, in this chapter, to show how Rational Emotive Behavior Therapy definitely belongs in the constructivist camp. Definitely—but not absolutistically!

References

Bandura, A. (1986). *Social foundations of thought and action: A social cognitive theory.* Upper Saddle River, NJ: Prentice Hall.

Bartley, W. W., III. (1984). *The retreat to commitment.* (Rev. ed.). Peru, IL: Open Court.

Beck, A. T. (1976). *Cognitive therapy and the emotional disorders.* New York: International Universities Press.

Bernard, M. E. (1993). *Staying rational in an irrational world.* New York: Carol Publishing.

Dryden, W. (1995). *Brief rational emotive behavior therapy.* London: Wiley.

Elkin, I. (1994). The NIMH treatment of depression collaborative research program: Where we began and where we are. In A. E. Bergin & S. L. Garfield (Eds.), *Handbook of psychotherapy and behavior change* (pp. 114–139). New York: Wiley.

Ellis, A. (1962). *Reason and emotion in psychotherapy.* Secaucus, NJ: Citadel.

Ellis, A. (1975). *How to live with a neurotic: At home and at work* (Rev. ed.). Hollywood, CA: Wilshire Books.

Ellis, A. (1988). *How to stubbornly refuse to make yourself miserable about anything— yes, anything!* Secaucus, NJ: Lyle Stuart.

Ellis, A. (1990a). Is rational-emotive therapy (RET) "rationalist" or "constructivist"? In W. Dryden & A. Ellis (Eds.), *The essential Albert Ellis* (pp. 114–141). New York: Springer.

Ellis, A. (1990b). *Psychotherapy and the value of a human being.* In A. Ellis & W. Dryden, *The essential Albert Ellis.* New York: Springer. (Original work published 1972)

Ellis, A. (1991). Using RET effectively: Reflections and interview. In M. E. Bernard (Ed.), *Using rational-emotive therapy effectively* (pp. 1–33). New York: Plenum.

Ellis, A. (1994). *Reason and emotion in psychotherapy.* (Rev. ed.). New York: Birch Lane Press.

Ellis, A. (1996a). *Better, deeper and more enduring brief therapy.* New York: Brunner/Mazel.

Ellis, A. (1996b). Postmodernity or reality? A response to Allen E. Ivey, Don C. Locke, and Sandra Rigazio-DiGilio. *Counseling Today, 39*(2), 26–27.

Ellis, A. (1996c). A social constructionist position for mental health counseling: A response to Jeffrey T. Guterman. *Journal of Mental Health Counseling, 18,* 16–28.

Ellis, A., & Dryden, W. (1997). *The practice of rational emotive behavior therapy.* (Rev. ed.). New York: Springer.

Ellis, A., Gordon, J., Neenan, M., & Palmer, S. (1997). *Stress counseling: The rational emotive behavior therapy approach.* London: Cassell.

Ellis, A., & Harper, R. A. (1997). *A guide to rational living* (Rev. ed.). North Hollywood, CA: Powers.

Ellis, A., & Tafrate, R. C. (1997). *How to control your anger—and not let it control you.* Secaucus, NJ: Birch Lane Press.

Feyerband, P. (1975). *Against method.* New York: Humanities Press.

Fuchs, S., & Ward, S. (1994). What is deconstruction and where and when does it take place? *American Sociological Review, 59,* 481–500.

Gergen, K. J. (1991). *The saturated self: Dilemmas of identity in contemporary life.* New York: Basic Books.

Gergen, K. J. (1995). Postmodernism as humanism. *Humanistic Psychologist, 23,* 71–82.

Ginter, E. J. (1996). *Ethical issues in the postmodern era* [Cassette recording]. Alexandria, VA: American Counseling Association.

Goleman, D. (1995). *Emotional intelligence.* New York: Bantam.

Guidano, V. F. (1991). *The self in process: Toward a postrationalist cognitive therapy.* New York: Guilford Press.

Guterman, J. T. (1994). A social constructionist position for mental health counseling. *Journal of Mental Health Counseling, 16,* 226–244.

Guterman, J. T. (1996). Reconstructing social construction: A response to Albert Ellis. *Journal of Mental Health Counseling, 18,* 29–40.

Hauck, P. A. (1991). *Overcoming the rating game.* Louisville, KY: Westminster.

Haughness, N. (1993). Postmodern anti-foundationalism examined. *Humanist, 53*(4), 19–20.

Hayek, F. A. (1978). *New studies in philosophy, politics, economics, and the history of ideas.* Chicago: University of Chicago Press.

Heidegger, M. (1962). *Being and time.* New York: HarperCollins.

Hollon, S. D., & Beck, A. T. (1994). Cognitive and cognitive-behavioral therapies. In A. E. Bergin & S. L. Garfield (Eds.), *Handbook of psychotherapy and behavior change* (pp. 428–466). New York: Wiley.

Hoshmand, L. T., & Polkinghorne, D. E. (1992). Redefining the science-practice relationship and professional training. *American Psychologist, 47,* 55–66.

Ivey, A. E., & Goncalves, D. (1988). Developmental therapy: Integrating developmental process into the clinical practice. *Journal of Counseling and Development, 66,* 406–413.

Ivey A. E., & Rigazio-DiGilio, S. A. (1991). Toward a developmental practice of mental health counseling: Strategies for training practice, and political unity. *Journal of Mental Health Counseling, 13,* 21–26.

Kelly, G. (1955). *The psychology of personal constructs (Vols. 1–2).* New York: Norton.

Kwee, M. G. T., & Ellis, A. (1997). Can multimodal and rational emotive behavior therapy be reconciled? *Journal of Rational-Emotive & Cognitive-Behavior Therapy.*

Lyons, L. C., & Woods, P. J. (1991). The efficacy of rational-emotive therapy: A quantitative review of the outcome research. *Clinical Psychology Review, 11,* 357–369.

Mahoney, M. (1976). *Scientist as subject.* Cambridge, MA: Ballinger.

Mahoney, M. J. (1991). *Human change processes.* New York: Basic Books.

Maultsby, M. C., Jr. (1984). *Rational behavior therapy.* Upper Saddle River, NJ: Prentice Hall.

Meichenbaum, D. (1977). *Cognitive-behavior modification.* New York: Plenum.

Mills, D. (1994). *Overcoming self-esteem.* New York: Institute for Rational-Emotive Therapy.

Neimeyer, R. A., & Mahoney, M. J. (Eds.). (1995). *Constructivism in psychotherapy.* Washington, DC: American Psychological Association.

Popper, K. R. (1985). *Popper selections* (D. Miller, Ed.). Princeton, NJ: Princeton University Press.

Raskin, J. D. (1995). On ethics in personal construct theory. *Humanistic Psychologist, 23,* 97–114.

Rogers, C. R. (1961). *On becoming a person: A therapist's view of psychotherapy.* Boston: Houghton Mifflin.

Sampson, E. E. (1989). The challenge of social change in psychology: Globalization and psychology's theory of the person. *American Psychologist, 44,* 914–921.

Silverman, M. S., McCarthy, M., & McGovern, T. (1992). A review of outcome studies of rational-emotive therapy from 1982–1989. *Journal of Rational-Emotive and Cognitive-Behavior Therapy, 10,* 111–186.

Simms, E. (1994). Phenomenology of child development and the postmodern self: Contriving the dialogue with Johnson. *Humanistic Psychologist, 22,* 228–235.

Tillich, P. (1953). *The courage to be.* New York: Oxford.

Walen, S., DiGiuseppe, R., & Dryden, W. (1992). *A practitioner's guide to rational-emotive therapy.* New York: Oxford University Press.

Weishar, M. (1993). *Aaron T. Beck.* London: Sage.

Yates, A. (1975). *Theory and practice of behavior therapy.* New York: Wiley.

CHAPTER FIVE

Setting Aside the Model in Family Therapy

Lynn Hoffman

Ever since I began to watch and do family therapy, I had been looking for what I called "the thing in the bushes" (Hoffman, 1981). I believed that someday we family therapists would find the cause of emotional suffering in family communication. So I went searching from model to model, looking for the key to my Rosetta Stone. Luckily, a shift in the zeitgeist rescued me from what was beginning to seem a hopeless quest. Aided by two movements, feminism and postmodernism, many of us began to question the objectivist belief systems on which the early approaches to family therapy had been based. The idea that a person called a professional "changed" some unit or behavior that was other and outside of herself seemed less and less sure. Familiar landmarks like assessment and intervention began to look shaky. The causal models we had relied on, in particular, were losing their distinctness and dissolving into some kind of theoretical mist.

In this respect, I found a recent article by psychologist Margaret Singer (1996) very helpful. In "From Rehabilitation to Etiology" she states that there has been a shift in psychotherapy during this century from a rehabilitation template to an etiological one. According to Singer, the first person to apply the word *therapy* to psychological problems was the psychologist Adolf Meyer, whose notion of psychobiology gave rise to a rehabilitative approach to psychiatric disorders.

Note: A version of this chapter appeared in the *Journal of Marital and Family Therapy*, 1998, 24(2), 145–146. Reprinted with permission.

Not much was known about the causes of emotional problems or medications to relieve them, so Meyer emphasized a supportive, educational type of treatment, geared to immediate relief rather than fundamental change. This rehabilitation approach was influential in the United States during the first part of the century.

What Singer calls an etiological approach, mainly influenced by psychoanalysis, became popular after World War II. Although Freud initially used hypnosis for symptom alleviation, his later theories fostered a deeper type of therapy tied to recovery of unconscious material. Singer describes how variations on this formula proliferated after the end of the war, most of them based on the assumption that getting to the early life sources of people's distress and helping them to reexperience and work through the attached memories and emotions has a curative effect.

Singer states that this etiological view, over time, turned into what some of her colleagues have called a "blame and change" approach. The idea is that if people can find the cause for their distress in something or somebody outside themselves, then they can change. This belief has led to therapies where cure depends on uncovering and confronting malign influences such as toxic parents, abusing therapists, dysfunctional families, and—at the extreme edge—satanic cults, abduction by aliens, and persons from past lives. Some of the therapists who take this position are recovered memory specialists who use hypnosis-like methods similar to those of cults to help their clients "remember." Singer, who has looked closely at these practices in her studies of cults (Singer & Lalich, 1997), feels that they have offered many opportunities for error, fingering the innocent and guilty alike.

Singer's article gave voice to some of my own thinking. Family therapy's contribution to the "blame and change" template is often based on what I think of as family therapy's version of repression theory. Throughout the development of the field, much has been written about covert coalitions, family secrets, unconscious myths, and unacknowleged grief. Items like these are said to be responsible for emotional problems and must be uncovered and worked through for healing to take place. The belief that the symptomatic child masks the dysfunctional relationship between the parents offers another hidden cause and another opportunity for blame.

As a result, a who-done-it question has been built into the family therapy movement, with a chilling effect on families and practitioners alike. During its early years, it seemed that mothers were at fault. Then whole families came under the gun. With the advent of feminist therapies, the onus shifted to fathers and husbands. Caught in the turbulence were other professionals, who often felt accused of complicity if they did not join the fight against women's oppression.

But the moving finger moved on, to distinctions based on ethnicity, class, and race. Ideas about the etiology of emotional problems have been extended to the larger cultural discourses that entangle us all. This pressure has spurred long-overdue efforts to open doors to groups that have not always felt welcome in a field dominated by middle-class whites. The profession of mental health itself has been held up as an oppressive discourse and, as a result, a much-needed consciousness-raising is taking place. This is one cause I am very glad to join.

The danger is that it could turn into another blame-and-change game. As if in answer to these concerns, a shift in the tectonic plates of the family therapy field is moving it in a less pejorative direction. The managed care revolution, with its interest in short-term results, has given a new vote of confidence to the Brief Therapy approach of the Mental Research Institute of Palo Alto (Watzlawick, Weakland, & Fisch, 1974), a group that has always refused to acknowledge an etiological base. The Solution-Focused approach of Steve de Shazer and Insoo Berg (de Shazer, 1991) is another example of a move away from a blame-evoking framework. So is the growing emphasis on resilience and strength of practitioners like Bill O'Hanlon (O'Hanlon & Weiner-Davis, 1989; Chapter Seven of this book) and Steve and Sybil Wolin (1993).

Singer's recovery of psychotherapy's rehabilitative past sends a similar signal. I had always assumed that the term *therapy* had its origin in something like physiotherapy—a humble, sensible field. *Psychotherapy* has seemed to me like a pretentious relative and *family therapy* is similarly suspect. Singer's work has encouraged me to think of myself as a kind of general practice counselor and to wonder whether we might not be moving back toward a rehabilitative point of view.

However, I am also noticing something new. A practice style is evolving that is in sharp contrast to the strategized interviewing in which I was trained. This style is quite free-floating. It shows a high degree of earnestness and concern, attends to suffering, is often personal, is patient to the point of being boring, and has ragged edges and an uneven pace. It is attentive to signs of goodness or hope, but it is not concerned with "fixing" or "healing." In some ways, it hardly seems professional. Can it even be called "therapy"?

THE REFLECTIVE CONVERSATION

Let me start to answer this by talking about the ideas of management consultant Donald Schön (1983) and his rationale for a more subjective way of working. Schön's thinking has functioned for me like a high-powered flashlight on a dark road. Trying to figure out how therapy would look if I no longer used the objective reality map made me feel as if I had stepped off the world. Psychologists Harlene Anderson and Harry Goolishian (1992) might talk about taking a position of "not-knowing," and I would agree, but in my heart I would hear Lily

Tomlin saying, "I always wanted to be somebody but now I feel I should have been more explicit."

I owe my knowledge of Schön's work to Argentinean psychiatrist Marcelo Pakman (1996), whose interest in therapy as a critical social practice brought him to Schön's attention. Pakman told me that Schön had been involved in an unusual research in which he would ask a variety of professionals about their practice rationales while watching them teach or work. Some of the time they seemed to know where they were going but at other times, they stopped short or suddenly changed direction. When asked why, they would give pat, unconvincing answers or say "I don't know."

Schön called these explanations "espoused theories" because they were so thin and flat compared to what seemed to be going on. If he asked more closely about the shift in question, the person often unearthed a rule that seemed to be pulled from the depths of the activity itself. These ideas Schön called "theories-in-use." They operated on a totally different level from the formulaic ones and they were not accessible to ordinary consciousness except when the creative process went wrong.

In his classic book *The Reflective Practitioner* (1983), Schön offers some reasons for these findings. He says that most professions follow the implicit hierarchy of Western science. According to the positivist elevation of the scientific framework, the principles of basic science are primary and the tenets of applied science derive from them. Schön calls this the "Technical Rational" view. The success of medicine and engineering in using this framework has captivated the less exact disciplines like urban planning or social work. As a result, Schön says, technical rationality is "the preferred epistemology of current professional practice."

But is it the best epistemology for all fields? In many domains, Schön finds a mismatch between the high ground of theory and the "swampy lowland" of practice. The Technical Rational view does not do well in fields like divinity and social work. In these cases, Schön suggests that we stand the positivist hierarchy on its head and build inductively from practice to theory. This means engaging in a process that Schön calls "Reflection-in-Action," which operates in a moment-to-moment, highly reflexive way. In comparing the two, Schön says that the Technical Rational view assumes "an objectively knowable world, independent of the practitioner's values and views. The practitioner must keep a boundary between himself and his object of inquiry. In order to exert technical control over it, he must observe it and keep his distance from it. His stance toward inquiry is that of spectator/manipulator" (1983, p. 163).

In the Reflection-in-Action mode, in contrast, the practitioner and student base their understandings on what they experience *from within* the process. There is a premium on metaphoric frameworks: what Schön calls "seeing as" and "doing as." All parties get involved in testing out many possibilities, derived from "on-the-spot experiments" and "virtual worlds like sketch pads and stories." This activity is not like ordinary research because these inquirers have no objective quarry in mind but are looking for something more elusive, which he calls "the situation's potential for transformation."

Schön says that Reflection-in-Action requires a type of practice where each move or exchange informs the next one. I was reminded here of a passage from Robert Pirsig's *Zen and The Art of Motorcycle Maintenance:* "The [good] craftsman isn't ever following a single line of instruction. He's making decisions as he goes along. For that reason he'll be absorbed and attentive to what he's doing even though he doesn't deliberately contrive this. He isn't following any set of written instructions because the nature of the material at hand determines his thoughts and motions, which simultaneously change the nature of the material at hand" (1974, p. 148).

Schön calls this type of activity "reflective conversation." Whatever the discipline—organizational consulting, architecture, psychotherapy, urban planning, medicine, even engineering—there is a continuous back and forth between the professional and the medium. The same is true when Schön watches professionals work with their trainees. In most cases, he finds that the teacher not only gives feedback about the student's process but also about his own. If this does not happen, a breakdown may occur.

A reflective conversation demands a high tolerance for vulnerability because it means exposing one's own process. At the same time, it puts the consulting persons into a partnership very different from the usual client-professional relationship based on the assumption that the professional has the knowledge that the client needs and lacks. Let me turn now to the work of Harlene Anderson (1997; see also Chapter Two, this volume), who was among the first persons to take this idea seriously. For her, therapy is not a treatment but a mutual conversation through which a new reality may be born.

THE CLOUD OF PERCEPTIONS

Drawing on the Collaborative Language Systems approach developed by Harry Goolishian and herself, Anderson proposes that therapy is a process in which a problem is not so much solved as dis-solved. For her, a problem is defined by the conversation that forms on behalf of an "alarmed objection" and what dissolves it is another conversation, but one that contradicts the etiological premise of traditional family therapy.

Influenced by social construction theory (Gergen, 1994), Anderson believes that what we experience as real is not already out there, waiting to be confirmed by our senses, but is constantly being woven and rewoven on social and linguistic looms. Even our ideas about how to do therapy depend on this sort of web. For instance, cognitive researcher George Lakoff (Lakoff and Johnson, 1980) says that the metaphor of problem solving suggests a puzzle or a test. It also implies that there is a right answer and the problem specialist will know it. Lakoff then tells the story of a student from Iran who thought the phrase "the solution to my problems" meant a *chemical* solution. He had an image in his mind of beakers bubbling away in which problems kept being precipitated out and then dissolved. Applying this story to therapy, if you think "problem solving," your approach will follow a causal idea of change, where if you think "chemical solution" you assume something closer to alchemy.

Anderson may not have an alchemical analogy in mind, but the phrase aptly describes her way of working. One day, a couple of years ago, I observed Anderson listening to a young woman speak at length while the rest of the family just sat back. Jay Haley used to criticize practitioners who did that, saying that all they were doing was individual therapy in the setting of the family. So I came right out and asked her what she thought she was up to. She said, "I think that when I listen that attentively, the other family members listen in a less judgmental way."

A light went off in my head. Harlene was not concentrating so much on the act of speaking but on the act of hearing. By offering an experience of indirect listening, she gave those present a chance to overhear the speaker's story without having to be defensive or to respond immediately. I saw that the context of listening could act as a solvent that altered the feelings and attitudes—or what I began to call the "cloud of perceptions"—that had come in the door.

This notion of a cloud of perceptions takes us back to social constructionism. One of the concerns of the social construction movement is to find a relational language to replace unit language. We have many words for items like the self or the family, but very few ways to describe what philosopher Ludwig Wittgenstein (1963) called the "language games" of social life. In this vein, sociolinguist Jean-Paul Lyotard (1993) suggests replacing "Newtonian anthropologies" like the ones based on structuralism or systems theory with "a pragmatics of language particles." And social theorist Edward Sampson (1990) observes that in place of the freestanding individual of modern psychology, postmodern psychology sees an "embedded individual" who is inseparable from "communities of belonging" or "ensembles of relationship."

Why is this turn away from the Newtonian unit important? Mostly because we may have gone too far in trying to "change" a behavior, "restructure" a family, or "intervene" in a system. What if a problem consists of a "swarm of participations" like a cloud of gnats? What if we decide that our task is to influence that cloud but that we have to do so from the position of *one of the gnats!*

My point is that influencing a process of which one is a living part is a different operation from fixing a problem seen from the outside. If this is true, we need an alternative to instrumental language. I now think of the therapeutic conversation as a kind of filter, much like those used in the process of dialysis. If we are doing our job, people who come in the door angry, anxious, or sad should go out feeling a larger sense of hope. The emphasis on the positive that keeps coming up in family therapy can be seen in this light. If one can influence a cloud of perceptions so that the persons involved feel more positive about each other, the chances of other things getting ironed out will be better. At the same time, we have to start off where people are, so it is not just a question of playing Pollyanna or handing out solutions on a silver tray.

In support of Anderson and Goolishian's idea of therapy as a conversation, I would like to mention Conversation Theory, since it really does exist and really does apply. Its inventor, the late cybernetician Gordon Pask, coined the term when he was building a "smart" computer that could respond in its user's own conversational style. Pask warned against thinking that communication, which he defined as exchanging messages about what is already known, is the same as conversation, which he called "a generative activity that gives identity to participants and leads to what is new" (Pangaro, 1996).

FOLDING OVER

Tom Andersen's (1990) reflecting team also acts like a filter. By continually folding over the personal thoughts and feelings of those present in the meeting, alternating who speaks and who listens, Andersen creates a remarkably benevolent environment. As in Harlene Anderson's work, there is an absence of the usual strategizing features. A therapist and family will talk, the reflecting team will make some comments, then therapist and family will comment on the comments, without any final message or prescription. Andersen explains that his only goal is to "continue the conversation." Despite this cavalier attitude toward intervention, changes do take place, but since the reflecting team interview is the antithesis of a causal operation, it is hard to explain to others how it works.

I find myself as usual turning to an analogy. When I was a faculty wife in the early 1950s, living in the country, an older neighbor taught me how to bake bread. The most memorable lesson she gave me was on kneading the dough. You put these inert elements—flour, water, yeast, salt—into a bowl and mixed them into a sticky ball. Then, with the help of more flour, you began to turn the edges over toward the center. After a while, my teacher told me, the dough would come alive. "How will I know that?" I asked, slightly unnerved. She said that it would begin to resist my hands. She was right. The process of folding, cherished by the heat of my hands, created a loaf ready to rise.

A "folding over" format can be used in many kinds of meetings, simply by thinking of the group as a collection of smaller units and asking them to comment one upon another in a cumulative way. But there is one element, symbolized in my analogy by the warmth of the hand, that is crucial. I am talking about something like Virginia Satir's relentless optimism. People who believe that this means leaving their critical faculties at the door are appalled, but if they wish to influence a conversation *from within,* their offerings must come from an empathic place—meaning a place of understanding from behind each person.

Drawing on my own experience of the reflecting team, I was amazed by its ability to generate images. My colleagues and I found ourselves moving away from analyzing family dynamics or making interpretations. More and more these practices seemed to objectify people and to feel offensive. Instead, we expressed ourselves by using metaphors, legends, poetry, and stories—including our own. It seemed appropriate to share personal experiences that mirrored the difficulties of those who consulted with us.

We also felt freer to show feelings. I recall a colleague consulting with a family in which a suicide had occurred. Right at the beginning, he shared the fact that he had recently watched his own wife die. Despite the private nature of this remark, it felt exactly right. My colleague Mary Olson (1995) once remarked that social construction theory had no theory of suffering. At the time I thought "How true," and decided later that family systems theory didn't either. The reflecting stance gave us permission to acknowledge suffering. I felt exonerated, because this practice had long been a part of my work. I called it "corny therapy" for years and kept it secret.

What then happened was that the sacred icon of the therapeutic boundary began to erode. For some reason, our increased openness did not seem to have the bad effects predicted by the prescription against self-disclosure. I have wondered about this. Perhaps it was because the therapeutic relationship was no longer rooted in a preferred picture that saw the client as a vulnerable child and the therapist as a powerful parent. In becoming more equal, therapy started to become more open. Or was it the other way round?

THE ATTENDING COMMUNITY

To address this question, let me make some observations. about the innovations of Narrative Therapy (White & Epston, 1990; White, 1995). In this chapter I will mainly refer to White's recent interviews. They seem to exist on an unusually subjective wavelength, and to fit with the different way of working I have been describing here.

White's contribution has many sides. One is his ability to use a conversation to reinvent itself (see Kogan & Gale, 1997). He directs himself against the enfolding cultural discourses that mold our ideas about ourselves, including those opinions that come from the field of mental health. By targeting the "discourse," he avoids blaming the person. On a practice level, his "externalizing" techniques separate the difficulties people are caught in from the people themselves. I approve of this. It is like reweaving the carpet while standing on it instead of calling it ugly and throwing it away.

What White has done in general is to naturalize therapy. If the therapeutic boundary was shaky before, it has now collapsed. White goes directly into the lives of the persons consulting with him, ignoring the caste lines of traditional mental health. An early idea, which he developed with David Epston (1989), was to send people letters appreciating their strengths, or to give them "documents of identity" that testified to ways in which they were worthwhile. Rituals of celebration or remembrance, attended by people both within and outside the therapy world, became part of this work too.

White's use of reflecting groups as witnesses is in my mind an unforeseen legacy of Tom Andersen's invention. More than any other practitioner, White tries to create for people what he calls a "community of concern" and I call an "attending community." In this category is White's practice of "re-membering." He goes to great lengths to recruit supportive individuals to what he calls "The Club of Your Life". Of course, one of the most important members he recruits is himself. Others could be anybody, dead or alive, imaginary or real, who might be perceived as playing an inspiring role. They could also be total strangers. Some of us who went to a recent workshop were charmed by the story of a little boy who had overcome a soiling problem and came to an interview wearing a fireman's uniform. White suggested that his father take him to visit the local firehouse and talk with the firemen about controlling "messy" situations.

White might also recruit as reflecting witnesses the audiences that attend his workshops. Although people are encouraged to speak from a personal rather than a professional standpoint, those defined by the context as helpers must think of their reflections as gifts to be "taken back" to the persons who inspired them. White has developed a treasure trove of such practices that add layer upon layer to "thicker descriptions" of a person's life.

It is that patient layering that is at the heart of White's interviewing, too. In a taped session I saw at a workshop, he threaded himself bit by bit to a small boy who was famous for tantrums and never talking to therapists. White got the boy to agree that although he wanted to keep his tantrums, he didn't like the aggression they provoked because he might get hurt. This was the point of entry, White said, for reauthoring his story. White inquired into the skills the boy had already used at school to fight the aggression, and a new story was built upon how he could apply them at home. The family commented on his usual volubility, and he put himself at the top of a ten-to-one scale for speaking up. After this session, White said, things at home improved impressively. But it would be hard to say what was of more consequence, the change in the child's behavior, or the change in the perceptions of those who witnessed it.

Finally, I want to mention a less tangible element of White's style that I call "withness." He is careful not to engage in any move or reaction without checking it out. "Is this all right with you?" is a frequent question. If he intrudes with his own agenda too quickly, he reminds himself to step back. This gives his more recent interviews the same reflexive, groping quality as those of Harlene Anderson, Harry Goolishian, or Tom Andersen. When I first began to see him working this way I felt a rush of recognition. He dedicates himself to never being more than an inch away from the experience of the persons he is with.

In this short piece, I can't cover all the ways in which White has undermined psychotherapy's most cherished assumptions. He helps bereaved people "say hello" to their loved ones instead of working through their grief. He suggests to people who hear voices that they recruit the friendly ones as allies in the fight against those that are hostile. To persons undergoing traditional forms of treatment, he offers nonconfronting ways to question professional authority. The man is a fountain of subversive ideas. Many people admire him for the way he stands up against discourses that promote injustice and abuse. But what I admire most is something on a smaller scale: the way he weaves together the tiniest tendrils of connection or amplifies the most reclusive voice.

SETTING ASIDE MODELS

These innovations in the style of relationship therapy have caused me to ask myself what would happen if we set aside the model. Models in family therapy, as I have said, have generally been attached to an etiological and prescriptive point of view: "This is what is wrong, so this is what you do." Even though each new model brought forth a different field of operations, each one more inclusive than the last, they were always within the nine-dot square. My new inspiration allowed me to see outside the square. As it dissolved, I became aware of a tapestry of practice that lay beneath, brilliant as an oriental rug and stretching out in all directions.

The only analogy I can think of for this experience is the story of my mother's ashes. My mother, Ruth Reeves, was a pioneering textile designer who studied the design vocabularies of countries with rich folk traditions. For the last ten years of her life, she catalogued village textiles for the Indian government. At age seventy-five, having been diagnosed with cancer, she was sent back to the States. Her young Indian assistants, who adored her, thought they would never see her again, but after three months of treatment she came back, eager to complete her work. When she did die a year later of a heart stoppage, her Indian friends took half her ashes and sprinkled them where the Ganges and the Jumna meet, a spot reserved for highly evolved persons. The other half was sent back in care of my sister.

Shortly thereafter I was cleaning out Ruth's studio with a friend, and came upon some metal canisters containing powdered colors: blue, red, white, yellow, gray. I checked each one, then set it aside to throw out. My friend was struck by the intricate design chased into the surface of one of the cans. Looking inside, she said, "I don't think this is powdered paint." I looked too. It was my mother! Thus began a family quandary. We knew she wanted to be buried on the land where she had built her house, but I was afraid that some future developer might come and bulldoze it up.

After talking to a number of people, an anthropologist friend came to my rescue. He said, "Look, your problem is not the ashes but the urn. All you have to do is take the ashes out and you can do what you like with them." This idea brought immediate relief. Once her ashes were out of the container, it seemed no problem to bury them in her favorite spot: a mossy place where two streams flowed together, surrounded by ferns and presided over by a tall tulip tree.

Getting rid of models felt exactly like throwing away the urn. As I did this, I experienced a new sense of space. Instead of having to integrate the various approaches, I felt free to take a new look at the practice ideas I had most valued, ignoring their rationale. Why couldn't one base a set of guidelines on a study of practice? "Of course," people could say, "such a framework is a model too." Perhaps, but in a different sense. The word *model,* by setting up an objective methodology, stays within the Western science paradigm. For this reason, the job ahead means looking behind or beyond the formalized approaches to family therapy (or relational practice, as I sometimes call it) to see what else appears.

Does this mean that I am throwing out larger theories of knowledge along with models? No, I am only reconstituting them for their own good. As long as they are *paradigms,* which means useful pots to put things in, they are necessary. A scientific framework needs a Newtonian pot and a sociolinguistic framework needs a postmodern one. It is not that one is better than the other, but they have to be congruent with the domains they address. "Soft" areas like psychotherapy need a philosophy that can explain the nonlinear complexity of human events and suggest nonobjectivist ways to influence them.

As for models, they create brand names and become competitive and exclusionary. It is better to think of them in Schön's sense as metaphors or as-if renderings. Again, the question of fit is important. The central metaphor of a Narrative approach, which is "stories," matches the description of the work, which is "re-authoring lives." The metaphor of the "conversation" is congruent with the concept of the socially languaged nature of reality. And the "reflecting team" is itself an embodied metaphor for a reflexive style.

Models are heuristic fairy tales, holders of complex realities, and one wouldn't want to lose the ideas that they contain. To this end, I have proposed a category called Biggest Hits of Family Therapy. Our field is full of wondrous things that we can use even if we do not accept the theories that produced them. A *genogram* is such an idea—did you ever try doing a reflecting genogram or one based on themes like courage? Other hits include *paradoxical tasks*—I sometimes offer them but explain what they are all about and never worry about whether people try them or not. Or *triangles*—people are fascinated by triangles, and know about them intuitively. You can make your own list of favorites.

I also like to think back over all the family therapists whose work I have loved. I realize now how often the model obscured the practice. Salvador Minuchin sometimes used what seemed to me paradoxical moves but wouldn't acknowledge them because they didn't fit his structural approach. Braulio Montalvo once told me about analyzing an interview by Carl Whitaker, who was nothing if not experiential, and being amazed by its structural implications. I myself have been resisting the takeover of Milton Erickson's oeuvre by the strategic wing because I find it contains so many examples of my "different voice" (Hoffman, 1993, 1997; Hoffman & Wheat, 1997).

If you look at common elements of practice across models, the most pervasive element is the "emphasis on the positive," as Haley called it. In the work of Erickson and Virginia Satir (1964), this emphasis has been seen as a way of "dealing with resistance." For Carl Whitaker (1989), it was the "anesthetic for the surgery." For the Milan group (Boscolo, Cecchin, Hoffman, & Penn, 1987), the positive connotation coated the bitter pill of the interpretation. In the name of widely different rationales, this use of the positive erupts again and again. What interests me is that now, in the new work I have been describing, it seems to have evolved beyond a strategy to something more like an entire stance.

THERAPEUTIC OPTIMISM

When you come to think of it, Satir (1964) was the pioneer of this stance par excellence. Dismissed as a guru from the human potential movement, she had a voice so ahead of its time that only now can it be heard. But you have to go directly to what she did. A month ago, I thought to look up a long, tortuous (and unpublished) article I wrote thirty-five years ago called "Another Version of Virginia Satir." On rereading it, I had a kind of epiphany. The writer of that article was an uninformed outsider trying to understand a process she had never heard of. And here she was, thirty-five years later, still trying. I could not resist including some material from that attempt. It shows Virginia applying the same hopeful attributions that I believe characterizes the best work in our field today.

The following excerpts are from an interview Satir did with the family of a policeman whose son had stolen a car. The boy was on probation and living with a foster family. He had just told Satir that he knew he was doing wrong when he stole the car.

Satir answered: "I don't believe that. I think you had a different purpose in mind, that you saw it fitting you in some way that was good." The boy agreed, saying: "Well, my friend's relatives had this ranch up near Sonoma, and he told me a lot about the town; it sounded real nice, with all those hick policemen and women and all. We were going to saw wood and make money that way, and I wasn't ever going to come back."

The boy had broken probation by seeing some members of his old gang. He explained that they had been meeting and getting away with it so he thought he could, too. So Satir said to him: "You, of all those boys, must be careful about getting caught because you are marked out, made special, by your talent, your intelligence, your good looks. The people who are trying to help you, myself included, will be angry if you disappoint them to the same degree that they are attracted by your potential."

As I sat there watching, I saw the boy's head shoot up and the depressed-looking policeman father straighten his back, as if to look the world in the eye. In retrospect, I believe that Satir was always working with the attending community and its "cloud of perceptions" in mind.

MY OWN PRACTICE

Before ending, I should say something about how the shift away from an objectivist stance has influenced what I do. When I am consulting privately with people, I pretend that I am a big bowl into which illuminating ideas or bits of information may fall. I will occasionally reflect back some of those bits, to confirm or disconfirm them, or I will follow hopeful openings. I try as much as possible to make public the background for what I do or say. I also try to find places where I can connect by offering experiences from my own life. But mainly I sit and listen in a very free-form fashion.

However, there is one thing I always look for. Within a person's story I try to find evidence for what family therapist Chris Kinman (1995), calls "gifts and potentials," and reflect that back. In other words, I look for some sign that the person is already embarked upon an important voyage. This may sound like an Ericksonian utilization move or a solution-focused technique, but for me it is more serendipitous than that, arising not from me but from the ongoing tapestry of the exchange.

As an example, here is an anecdote about a recent and very ordinary consultation. I don't want to analyze it here but will just set it forth as I experienced it. Helen, a college professor in her fifties whom I had seen in family therapy some years before, came in because of a pervasive fear that there was something wrong with her children. They were grown up and doing well in their lives but to Helen they seemed "not normal." Neither James nor Molly was married.

Helen wondered if Molly could be a lesbian. She said that Molly tried to find men to go out with, but the most recent eligible male dropped her because she "fell asleep on a date."

As more evidence of her fears, Helen said that her children's features looked "blunted." She used to drink socially when she was pregnant—could they be suffering from fetal alcohol syndrome? She said she was also disappointed because neither of them looked like her and they didn't seem to move in the same intellectual and cultural world as she and their father. She had an extremely close relationship with her mother and she has an equally close relationship with her husband, and she longed to have the same connection with her children.

I said that for some years my own children weren't talking to me. As a result, I made "spirit daughters" out of younger colleagues. Helen, who directs her own department at a small college, said she was very proud of two of her students but had not considered a more personal relationship. In the category of useless suggestions, I asked her if she had ever thought of giving her children a collage of family pictures. She said she didn't think they would be very interested in that kind of thing. However, she mentioned finding some comfort in going back to her cradle religion, Catholicism. Even though she didn't take part socially, she said, going to Mass offered her spiritual sustenance.

Next week, Helen told me, she would be going to visit both children in the city where James has gone back to school and Molly works. She described to me how she used to love it when her mother came to visit the city she was living in and she would stay over in her mother's hotel room. Molly would never dream of doing such a thing. I asked if Molly had ever been particularly affectionate. Helen said that four years ago, Molly put her arms around her mother and thanked her for giving her so much love as a child. This demonstration had not been repeated.

So Helen dreaded this visit with her daughter, afraid of being disappointing and disappointed both. I asked how Molly disappointed her. She replied that her daughter was on the heavy side, didn't try to be "feminine," and might be jealous of her mother's looks. I then asked what Molly shared with her. Helen said Molly liked to go shopping with her mother, get makeovers in the department stores. But these, Helen said, were just cheap material things, not anything of value.

I said to Helen that I could see that she was suffering from a broken heart. To myself, I wondered how I could give her some useful thought to take with her. So I asked whether she would be shopping with her daughter. She said yes. I said that because Molly so obviously valued her mother's taste and looks, what Helen thought of as "only things" were important. In fact, they were like blessings. Helen was struck by the idea. "Oh," she said, "I never thought of it that way." She teared up. She kept weeping while repeating, "Just like blessings, yes, like benedictions." I was very moved. I thought of my own children, too.

Three weeks later, Helen called me. The trip to Washington was a huge success. Molly and she had enjoyed shopping together. James was happy with his courses. What surprised us both, however, was that Molly and James had put together a gift for Helen: a framed display of childhood pictures.

References

Andersen, T. (Ed.). (1990). *The reflecting team: Dialogues and dialogues about the dialogues.* Broadstairs, Kent: Borgmann.

Anderson, H. (1997). *Conversation, language, and possibilities: A postmodern approach to therapy.* New York: Basic Books.

Anderson, H., & Goolishian, H. A. (1992). The client is the expert: A not-knowing approach to therapy. In S. McNamee & K. J. Gergen (Eds.), *Therapy as social construction* (pp. 25–39). Newbury Park, CA: Sage.

Boscolo, L., Cecchin, G., Hoffman, L., & Penn, P. (1987). *Milan Systemic Family Therapy.* New York: Basic Books.

de Shazer, S. (1991). *Putting difference to work.* New York: Norton.

Epston, D. (1989). *Collected papers.* Adelaide, South Australia: Dulwich Centre Publications.

Gergen, K. J. (1994). *Realities and relationships: Soundings in social construction.* Cambridge, MA: Harvard University Press.

Hoffman, L. (1981). *Foundations of family therapy.* New York: Basic Books.

Hoffman, L. (1993). *Exchanging voices: A collaborative approach to family therapy.* London: Karnac Books.

Hoffman, L. (1997). Postmodern and family therapy. In J. K. Zeig (Ed.), *The evolution of psychotherapy: The third conference* (pp. 337–348). New York: Brunner/Mazel.

Hoffman, L., & Wheat, D. (1997). The evolution of a different voice in family therapy. *Journal of Systemic Techniques, 18,* 101–112.

Kinman, C. (1995). *Honouring community.* Abbotsford, BC, Canada: Fraser Valley Education & Therapy Services.

Kogan, S. M., & Gale, J. E. (1997). Decentering therapy: Textual analysis of a narrative therapy session. *Family Process, 36,* 101–126.

Lakoff, G., & Johnson, M. (1980). *Metaphors we live by.* Chicago: University of Chicago Press.

Lyotard, J. P. (1993). *The postmodern condition* (G. Bennington & B. Massumi, Trans.). Minneapolis, MN: University of Minnesota Press.

O'Hanlon, W. H., & Weiner-Davis, M. (1989). *In search of solutions: A new direction in psychotherapy.* New York: Norton.

Olson, M. (1995). Conversation and writing: A collaborative approach to bulimia. *Journal of Feminist Family Therapy, 6,* 21–44.

Pakman, M. (1996). Therapy in contexts of ethnic dissonance. *Journal of Systemic Therapies, 14,* 64–71.

Pangaro, P. (1996). Biography of Gordon Pask. Eulogy delivered at the Department of Management Science, American Society for Cybernetics, George Washington University, Washington, DC.

Pirsig, R. (1974). *Zen and the art of motorcycle maintenance.* New York: Bantam Books.

Sampson, E. (1990). Social psychology and social control. In I. Parker and J. Shotter (Eds.), *Deconstructing social psychology.* London: Routledge.

Satir, V. (1964). *Conjoint family therapy.* Palo Alto: Science and Behavior Books.

Schön, D. (1983). *The reflective practitioner.* New York: Basic Books.

Singer, M. (1996). From rehabilitation to etiology: Progress and pitfalls. In J. K. Zeig (Ed.), *The evolution of psychotherapy: The third conference.* New York: Brunner/Mazel.

Singer, M., & Lalich, J. (1997). *"Crazy" therapies.* San Francisco: Jossey-Bass.

Watzlawick, P., Weakland, J. H., & Fisch, R. (1974). *Change: Principles of problem formation and problem resolution.* New York: Norton.

Whitaker, C. (1989). *Midnight musings of a family therapist* (M. O. Ryan, Ed.). New York: Norton.

White, M. (1995). *Re-authoring lives: Interviews and essays.* Adelaide, South Australia: Dulwich Centre Publications.

White, M., & Epston, D. (1990). *Narrative means to therapeutic ends.* New York: Norton.

Wittgenstein, L. (1963). *Philosophical investigations* (G. Anscombe, Trans.). New York: Macmillan.

Wolin, S., & Wolin, S. (1993). *The resilient self.* New York: Villard Books.

CHAPTER SIX

Ericksonian Emergent Epistemologies

Embracing a New Paradigm

Stephen Lankton, Carol Lankton

The epistemology of modern therapy can be illustrated with two worldviews: one that describes how people don't change and another that guides actions to create change. This chapter compares and contrasts the central foundation evident in traditional approaches and emergent-constructive approaches to modern therapy. It examines the rationale and interventions unique to these approaches. An Ericksonian framework is used to illustrate the emergent epistemological and ontological position for therapists and change-agents. Holding this framework or worldview facilitates congruence about therapeutic change and allows practitioners to move beyond reliance on mere intuition about how to change.

HISTORY OF THE TRADITIONAL WORLDVIEW

Tracing the historical development of thought in psychology, psychoanalysis, and psychotherapy demonstrates the flawed (limiting) logic that has shaped the traditional worldview. Significant developments that will be discussed are listed in Table 6.1. The left column summarizes Western thought beginning with ancient history and spanning centuries. In so doing, it describes both the birth of psychology and the epistemology from which it is being weaned. The right column contains parallel emergent thought.

Table 6.1. Comparison of Epistemologies

Traditional Worldview	Emergent Worldview
Truth exists and can be known	Cocreation of what is considered true
Observing carefully will reveal the truth	Participation is all that is possible—observation is participation
Adversarial position is taken toward nature	Cooperative position is taken toward nature
Observers are separate from the observed	Observers are in the system they observe
Reduction of larger parts will get closer to the truth	Punctuation of experience is basically arbitrary
Labeling of parts is a banal event	Pattern identification is limited by the labeler's experience and choices
Problem-oriented—identifies causes	Goal-oriented—solves the task
Pathology-uncovering—disease can be uncovered	Health-discovering—helps build desired resources
Past-oriented—causes lie in past	Future-oriented—purpose lies in present and immediate future
Individuals operate independent of environment	Individuals and environments form an ecosystem
Causes are inside the individual	Problems are reciprocally and cyclically between and among parts of the system
Experts "give" treatment	Change agents help create a context for problem solving

The first assumption from ancient thinking regards the existence of an independent truth that can be known. Beginning in the fourth century B.C., Plato's contribution of *a priori deductive idealism* insisted that there exists, a priori, a truth of the universe that in some manner can come to be known by us. "On the Heavens" was written by his student, Aristotle, and introduced the world to *induction* and empirical observation. But of equal importance, Aristotle introduced the early syllogisms of logic by means of which a person, with very little sensory investigation, might reason the way to the truth. For example, for spiritual reasons he argued that Earth was the center of the Universe. Within just 140 years, an elaboration of this was accomplished by Ptolemy (known as the Ptolemaic model of the Universe) and became widely accepted. It is astounding that this idea, built upon the premise of a knowable truth outside of ourselves, went unquestioned for almost two thousand years. In fact, the methodology still influences the reasoning of our most mundane routines even today. For example, the media will earnestly question the cause of drug abuse or why children commit suicide as if we can isolate some explanatory truth that will eliminate the problems. A better question would concern how we can help our children become happy. Just as the old methodology biased those who looked into the skies, it still biases many of us as we look into the lives of our clients, children, and mates.

Traditional epistemology is also based on an assumption of our separateness from nature and an adversarial posture toward nature. We might also trace this to Plato, but the principle of mind-body dualism (found in Plato) was greatly magnified by the Latin church and Saint Augustine (354–430 A.D.), who wrote with authority the *City of God*. Already biased in their worldview, people had come to seek the truth by rising above the adversarial human body, which seemed to tether them to what they regarded as the less-worthy world of the senses. This atmosphere makes it easy to understand how members of an entire civilization could delude their senses for fourteen centuries. We developed layer upon layer of presuppositions that we were separate from nature and able to seek an independent truth.

The change in worldview began when the Pole Nicholas Copernicus anonymously circulated his model of the Universe in 1514 A.D. It was nearly a hundred years before the heretical idea that Earth was not the center of the Universe could take root, in 1609. This came only after the invention of the telescope—when Galileo, using the Kepler telescope, discovered the moons in orbit around Jupiter. This was at last evidence that not everything in the heavens orbited the Earth. Finally people began to have the data and the courage to reason from more careful observations.

However, the stroke of brilliance known as the Enlightenment proved to be only a mixed blessing for psychology. This was due primarily to the slightly misguided notion that we could observe linear causality in the universe without affecting it—but perhaps this is getting ahead of the story. Let's continue to examine the growing traditional epistemology so as to better appreciate the climate in which therapists now reach for an alternative.

The Age of Reason was born and with it the enormous scientific and intellectual advancements of the seventeenth century. But it further alienated us from a sense of cooperation and participation in nature. For instance, in 1620, the empiricist Francis Bacon wrote *Novum Organum* and put forth the idea that we must "torture" nature and make her give up her secrets. (This, by the way, may have been the same year that the first ships carrying slaves landed on American shores.) These are the intellectual influences into which modern psychology was born. In the Age of Enlightenment, the truth existed in nature independent of the observer, who was separate from and at times extremely adversarial toward it. We came to accept as fact that we were impartial observers—and that if nature or even some race of people did not seem to conform to our conception, we could torture them and make them give up their secrets. This has far-reaching ramifications for our culture, one of which is that it is easy to see how we could come to label people as resistive and pathological, and treat them with suspicion even in this so-called Postmodern Age of therapy.

Referring again to Table 6.1, the left column describes traditional epistemology embodying the concepts of *truth, observing, separateness,* and an *adversarial position.* The next two items are *reduction* and *labeling.* These are part of the traditional epistemology rising from the ideas that emerged during the next 150 years. To illustrate briefly, Ole Rømer in 1676 determined the speed of light fairly closely, especially for his time. This sort of knowledge was an advancement of significant dimension. It must have seemed that there was nothing civilization could not reduce, label, and measure! Very few of us could come anywhere close to such a feat today, even with all of our desktop computing power. What a reinforcement this accomplishment must have been for relying upon the traditional epistemology that was developing! To add further reinforcement, René Descartes's student Isaac Newton, in 1687, developed the laws of motion, calculus, and the principles of gravity, space, and time.

This worldview was quickly developing a forceful momentum as all sorts of learning and knowledge advanced. Within less than two hundred years James Clark Maxwell had developed the wave theory. Twenty years later Michelson and Morley performed their famous experiments with light that were later reexamined by Einstein. The changes brought by observation and reductionism were so remarkable that they gave the world enormously moving details about the nature of *things.* At this point the tools of mathematics and technology had taken man from the heavens all the way to the inside of the atom. All the while it taught us to reduce and label, to observe and feel separate from, and to seek the truth as if we did not influence that which we sought.

Sigmund Freud entered the scene with his *Studies on Hysteria* in 1896 and launched the ship of psychology, with concepts such as the *unconscious mind* (see Freud, 1938). He was hugely influenced by the science of his day and the belief in natural law and universal order. It was in these waters that his ship set sail. He could be expected to invent an approach that searched for problems with linear causes rooted in the past. By reduction, he would look inside the individual and consider himself capable of finding the truth by observation. That is exactly what he did and what he suggested.

The scientist and the psychiatrist were experts who would gather the facts and provide the passive patient with a "treatment" leading to a "cure," just as a physician would provide surgery or medication. Therapists would reduce and label reified parts of individuals as they looked for the cunningly hidden causes within. Any subject who did not respond as the expert desired was labeled "resistant"—or worse.

It would be awhile before the notion of a participatory universe found acceptance in physics. However, there was a rising problem in the developing epistemology. Hume had mentioned aspects of it, as Kant did later, in 1781. In the natural sciences several experiments were leading thinkers to the conclusion that we impose order on the universe by our attempts to observe it. One could see this in the "wave-particle" theory (eleven years before Kant), in the Michelson-Morley problem with light, in the conceptualization of the quantum principle in 1920 by Max Plank, and of course in the "Indeterminacy Principle," better known as the "Uncertainty Principle" of Heisenberg, in 1926 (Hawking, 1988).

But none of this did much to dismantle the traditional worldview at the time. It was felt by most that further scientific work would resolve any anomalies or paradoxes present in these new conceptions of reality. In fact, Freud seems to have aggressively dismissed Kant's ideas (Freud, 1923/1966, p. 538). Although particle physics and quantum mathematics helped theorists come to grips with the anomalies of this epistemology and begin to understand a participatory universe, these understandings were vague to those outside the advanced science laboratories; so psychology continued to travel in the direction in which it was launched. Nonetheless, physics had demonstrated the inability to observe without participating and to know an independent truth without cocreating it.

RECENT HISTORY AND THE DEVELOPMENT OF EMERGENT EPISTEMOLOGIES

A different epistemology also began to emerge in the social sciences. Perhaps the most articulate and capable of the thinkers grappling with this was Gregory Bateson, who was originally a biologist. In the early 1950s, he was instrumental (along with Norbert Weiner, Heinz von Foerster, and others) in the development of the field of cybernetics. After this work on self-governing mechanisms and cybernetics, which drew on his knowledge of natural systems, he turned to human systems and created a study team known as the "Palo Alto Communication Project."

In 1952, Bateson's research project on communication elected to investigate the transactional nature of information flow between family members. They recorded some important findings about healthy and unhealthy communication in the important 1956 paper "Toward a Theory of Schizophrenia," wherein Bateson, Jackson, Haley, and Weakland discussed the interpersonal genesis of schizophrenia. Subsequently, this team developed a systems and communications approach to family therapy (see Jackson, 1968a, 1968b; Satir, 1964), especially as related to change in human systems and brief strategic therapy. These developments—which may be seen as one of the three major approaches to family therapy (with the human potential movement and the psychoanalytic approach being the other two)—were extremely influenced by the work of Milton Erickson (Haley, 1963, 1985), which we discuss later in this chapter.

Bateson frequently attempted to clarify the difference between the traditional and emerging approach, as seen in this statement from *Steps to an Ecology of Mind:* "The difference between the Newtonian world and the world of communication is simply this: that the Newtonian world ascribes reality to objects and achieves its simplicity by excluding the context. In contrast, the theorist of communication insists upon examining the metarelationships while achieving its simplicity by excluding all objects" (1972, p. 250). Bateson saw that with little exception, the entire profession of therapy had been influenced by the erroneous belief that we could know the truth of a separate reality and the fallacy that acts of observation did not alter this external reality. Psychology's posture toward reality was separation from it. The simple act of reducing and labeling seems innocent enough, but it does not credit the so-called observer with the action of inventing the label that is applied, then punctuating the stream of experience and ordering the events. Consequently, Bateson felt that traditional therapy, in its attempts to search for problems rooted in the past, developed a rich, pathologically oriented language to describe the intrapsychic domain of the single individual, typically excluding or diminishing his or her present life context.

The subsequent language of therapy reflects this adversarial position with metaphors of resistance, conflict, defense, hidden motive, suppression, power, and so on. Szasz (1961) and Laing (1967, 1972), among others, have spoken eloquently about the individual and social injuries that are the by-product of attempting to help within such a framework. Placed in an adversarial position, purposefully or inadvertently, labeled individuals will easily demonstrate more behaviors that will reinforce a therapist's conviction about the independent existence of an internal pathology.

These features of emergent approaches to therapy are summarized in the right column of Table 6.1. Instead of believing in an observable truth, we might better say that we cocreate the truth with our participation. In reframing and retrieving experiential potentials, therapists offer views that are attempts to express clients' unique desires in a way that they had not previously been able to do. In this simple act, we clearly see the importance of the therapist's and client's negotiated way of viewing the situation. This is not the way of an expert passively viewing the truth linked to the past in a causal and linear manner. Instead, it is that of an active coparticipant, helping create a context for change, discovering health as it unfolds, punctuating it, and orienting both therapist and client toward the current and future goal by retrieving and organizing personal and experiential resources.

INDICATIONS OF THE NEW EPISTEMOLOGY

A participatory and cocreative worldview lies at the heart of many active interventions and emergent approaches of constructive therapy. Newtonian laws of nature, as the traditional paradigm is often called, work well for a limited range of events in the universe. They do not work well for garnering information from very tiny masses at the subatomic level, nor for very large masses at the macro astronomy level. And—most noteworthy in the therapy context—they do not work well for producing usable knowledge of how change occurs in the domain of complex and nonlinear systems, living things, and especially people. The traditional paradigm, when applied beyond its usable range, works best at explaining why things can not be changed—and the emerging paradigm is a worldview for *creating* change.

The ramifications of this paradigm shift are tremendously widespread and important. It is not limited to therapy alone, but useful in any area dealing with human behavior. For instance, media news reporters are not passive observers of violence—they are participators, and they can cocreate a kind and supportive world or a paranoid and violent one. The same is true in public schools. Educators do not rightly discover "learning disabilities"—they discover a need for their methods of teaching to improve. But their worldview allows educators to believe they passively observe the truth and are simply choosing the proper label for that truth. The "disabled" child is seen to have a *problem* "in his head" and is then turned over for medical, psychological, and usually pharmaceutical intervention. So many experts treat the child in a manner consistent with the antiquated worldview that change becomes nearly impossible. It becomes difficult for therapists to instead teach the child and his or her family how to notice differently, articulate differently, communicate differently, and use themselves more effectively.

Society as a whole is still largely applying rudimentary and sloppy methods from the traditional epistemology in a vague mix with some of the emerging epistemology. In such a hybrid mix, some change does eventually occur. Many people intuitively sense that the traditional epistemology lacks a certain "goodness of fit" and that somehow it fails to account for what they understand about our participatory world. However, the vocabulary for the new model and the elaboration of its principles in action has not penetrated into the daily life of society. These paradigms are also in flux at the household level. Spouses get more of what they punctuate and label. Hostility or love in a couple is not the objective truth for that couple, it is the cocreated truth. Analyzing the history and nuance of a problem will never lead to a novel solution—analyzing the desired goal and available resources will.

Many therapies make use of only portions of the modern epistemology. Many therapists rely upon the habits of the old traditional paradigm. They do this because of the training that they have experienced—as in the case of the practitioner who is happy to medicate a person diagnosed with "anxiety attacks." Once labeled, the patient turns attention away from the very phenomenological knowledge that could lead to a rapid resolution. After the label is firmly affixed, questions of how the person creates the world to generate or recall anxiety—and who helps create it and how—are not asked and are not answered. Therapists who label in that manner limit the ability of clients to change. They do this not out of malice but out of training in an antiquated paradigm.

For each of us, it takes an intense personal effort to check our use of the traditional paradigm and implement action according to the emerging paradigm. Society will probably require more experience before shifting to the emerging paradigm for problem solving at a personal and household level of awareness. In the meanwhile, and in recent history, we find it among many of our modern therapists, most notably, Milton Erickson, whose work demonstrated these principles.

ERICKSON'S CONTRIBUTION TO EMERGENT EPISTEMOLOGIES

Where Freud made his contribution in terms of theory, Erickson made an equal impact in terms of intervention. Many professionals feel that Erickson's significant contribution was the advancement of the use of hypnosis. Others feel it was his use of language in one way or another: indirect suggestion, metaphor, anecdotes, confusion, and therapeutic binds. Others would argue that his contribution was the development of concepts known as utilization, indirection, speaking the client's language, and so on.

Although the merits of each of these aspects of intervention are numerous, the more crucial contribution common to all these interventions is his *approach* to people and problems, that is, the epistemological and ontological position they embody. Just as Bateson discussed Erickson's thoughts and perceptions and practices as the best example of the emergent epistemology based on observations of his work, we also credit Erickson's work as the best available model of these ideas in action.

An emergent epistemology operationalizes how people change. It does not attempt to explain truth or causation. It is an active approach to therapy that builds on resources leading to desired goals. Therapists and clients cooperate in building an awareness of the experiences and an understanding of their meaning.

These characteristics are certainly typical of Ericksonian interventions such as *reframing* and *retrieving experiential potentials,* as seen in the case of the newlyweds who came to Erickson for counsel due to a lack of sexual intercourse

(Haley, 1973). Erickson did not opine that the husband did not have love for his bride (which might have seemed true to some observers). Furthermore, it was not formulated, a la Freud's Oedipus, that the man had erotic desires for his mother but experienced internal conflicts due to his fear of retribution from his father. Rather, Erickson offered the view that the husband was attempting to express his unique and profound desire for his wife in a way he had not previously been able to do and he needed to develop some special manner to make his superlative expression now known. Erickson's way of viewing the situation was to help create a context for change, discovering health as it unfolds, and orienting the couple toward the current and future goal by retrieving resources. Some of the essences of an Ericksonian approach are summarized in Table 6.2.

Looking at Therapy in Action

To reflect the difference between traditional and emergent epistemologies, we will look at four issues of therapy from the Ericksonian perspective. These issues, seen in Table 6.3, are the *purpose and use of suggestion, metaphor as indirect intervention, the meaning of a symptom,* and *what constitutes a cure.* Some of the distinctive features of therapy and interventions associated with Erickson's work are important, not for being "uncommon" (see Haley, 1973) but for their function as a vehicle to connect the therapist and client in the process of cocreating a context for change. Consider *indirection* and its use as one example. The traditional epistemology favors the use of direct suggestion,

Table 6.2. Elements of an Ericksonian Approach

Nonpathology-based model	Problems are best available attempts at problem solving
Utilization	Whatever the patient brings to the session is used toward treatment goals
Indirection	The act of stimulating thinking and avoiding giving orders
Action	Getting the client to start taking actions related to desired goals
Strategic	Therapist actively sets goals, initiates interventions, and evaluates feedback
Future orientation	Focusing on current and future goals rather than analyzing past problems
Enchantment	Facilitating a pleasant mental arousal associated with therapy challenges

which could be used by experts to tell observed subjects just what they should do to resolve the problems they bring to the office. Indirect suggestion, on the other hand, is presented so that a client will apprehend that portion that is of subjective value and apply it to the process of retrieving and associating experiences needed to reach the current goals. Indirect suggestion assumes an active and participating client with a certain innate wisdom. The therapist learns from the response of the client when to elaborate the presented ambiguity in even more helpful ways.

The conceptualization of a problem or symptom as a sign or communication is another facet of the emerging epistemology. The existence and continuance of the symptom can be seen as many things: It may be feedback the client cannot associate to the needed resources; it may be a probe by the client to stimulate the environment; it may be a communication, and so on. These views are part of an interactive, goal-oriented, future-oriented perspective. Contrast this to the perspective that a symptom is a sign of an internal conflict within an individual. People are indeed conflicted when they are not solving problems in an adaptive and creative manner. The decisive difference between the old and new epistemologies may lie in the conception of priority as it pertains to the idea of a symptom. Is this strip of experiences that we call a *symptom* due to the conflict within—or is the symptom a sign of the person's attempts to solve a relational problem? We would suggest that if we say a symptom is the former, we operate from the old tradition; if we say the latter is more accurate, we operate from the emergent view.

The idea of *cure* can also be seen to reflect the differences in approaches. The traditional view of cure is related to the resolution of an internal conflict,

Table 6.3. Comparing Four Elements

Item	Traditional	Emergent
Use of suggestion	Direct, authoritarian	Indirect, permissive
Indirection, metaphor	If done by client, indicates primary process, a sign of client regression	Resource retrieval, allowing client to create a unique response, an experiential context that helps build a bridge for learning
Meaning of symptom	Internal conflict, not well defended	A communication about developmental needs
Cure	Due to insight, ego strengthening, internal conflict resolution	Due to development of new relational pattern and creative response to environment

building of ego strength in the individual, removal of resistance, removal of symptoms, and finally the capacity for work and love. The emphasis in this scenario is on an individual who has somehow "worked through" events from the past about which he or she was conflicted, lacked ego strength, and from which he or she developed "parataxic" distortions. Of course, this often involved "insight" and sometimes "corrective emotional experiences." This concept of cure is based on a past-orientation. From a future-oriented perspective, a cure would involve development of adaptive relationships with those persons in the current social environment and the acquisition of new skills for handling developmental demands.

Erickson's Changing Views

Many students of Erickson's work have encountered difficulty finding the "real" Erickson. Some may have read articles that portrayed Erickson as very directive and not indirect, as others have claimed. Some contend that he was very authoritarian and others claim he was permissive. From our reading and time spent with him, we believe Erickson's views changed and developed over time. There was a different awareness in his work in 1945 than in his work in 1975. To demonstrate how his view of clients and problems reflected this emerging epistemology, we can chronicle this change in the four issues just charted: purpose and use of suggestion, use of metaphor as indirection, meaning of symptoms, and concept of cure.

Direct Suggestions and Redundant Suggestions. Erickson's early explanations of hypnosis suggest that he moved from the position of an authoritarian expert who did something to a client, to a position of cocreator of a context for change who offered stimuli to subjects who put ideas together for themselves. In a 1945 published transcript, he used "deeper" redundantly in the following sentence: "Now I want you to go deeper and deeper asleep" (p. 54). The statement "I can put you in any level of trance" (Erickson, with Haley & Weakland, 1967, p. 64) indicates his directive stance at the time, which was still strongly influenced by the traditional epistemology of his training.

By 1976, Erickson had fully reversed this method of redundant suggestion and wrote that indirect suggestion was a "significant factor" in his work (Erickson, Rossi, & Rossi, 1976, p. 452). But more interesting still is the growth evident at the end of his life, published after his death in 1980. Here he took the position not of an authoritative expert who makes someone go into trance, but of someone who will "offer" ideas and suggestions (pp. 1–2). Contrary to his earlier conduct, he stated, "I don't like this matter of telling a patient I want you to get tired and sleepy" (Erickson & Rossi, 1981, p. 4). This is the exact opposite position and represents a departure from the traditional to the emerging epistemology!

Metaphor as Indirect Intervention. Erickson was comfortable with the role of ambiguity in therapy. In 1944, Erickson used a complex story to help stimulate and resolve a client's neurotic mechanisms (Erickson, 1967). In 1954, Erickson was delivering what he called "fabricated case histories" to help a client be relieved of fleeting symptomatology (Erickson, 1954/1980c, p. 152). And of course by the early 1970s there are several examples of case stories used for illustrating points in therapy and normal communication (Haley, 1973). Finally, in a 1979 publication, there are section headings on "metaphor" as intervention (Erickson & Rossi, 1979). It would be most correct to conclude from this evidence that Erickson's use of ambiguity, permissiveness, and indirection in therapy was present from the beginning of his work and progressed with increasing frequency.

The Meaning of a Symptom. Regarding the meaning that Erickson attributed to symptoms, there is a pattern of change from the traditional analytic view in his early career to that of the systemic and interpersonal view by the time of his death. His medical degree was obtained in 1928 and he then went to Colorado General Hospital for his internship and was there until 1938 or 1939. As late as 1954 he wrote, "The development of neurotic symptoms constitutes behavior of a defensive, protective character" (Erickson, 1954/1980c, p. 149). This is a traditional analytic view with concepts like *defense* and *attack.*

Again, we see movement to an emergent epistemology by 1966, when he wrote, "Mental disease is the breaking down of communication between people" (Erickson, 1966/1980a, p. 75). Finally, in 1979, he had arrived at the fully formed idea: "Symptoms are forms of communication" and "cues of developmental problems that are in the process of becoming conscious" (Erickson & Rossi, 1979, p. 143). This view is much more in keeping with the ideas expressed verbally by Erickson on repeated occasions, that he did not have a theory of personality and invented a new theory with each unique client: "Each person is a unique individual. Hence, psychotherapy should be formulated to meet the uniqueness of the individual's needs, rather than tailoring the person to fit the Procrustean bed of a hypothetical theory of human behavior" (Zeig & Lankton, 1988).

Cure Seen as Reassociation of Experience, Not Direct Suggestion. Erickson's ideas of cure remained essentially the same from 1948 to the end of his work. In 1948 he recognized that cure was not the result of suggestion but rather developed from reassociation of experience (Erickson, 1948/1980b, p. 38). (In this work, we also can see that Erickson did not wish to use direct suggestion in treatment, preferring to use indirect suggestion, although, as in the 1954 statement quoted earlier, he still used direct suggestion for induction.) We see essentially the same view in Erickson's writing at the end of his career (Erickson, 1979; Erickson & Rossi, 1980, p. 464; Erickson & Rossi, 1981).

Honoring the Spirit

It is curious that Ericksonian interventions can be used in the spirit of either the traditional or the modern epistemologies. If a therapist were to so choose, he or she could use an intervention such as metaphor and deliver it in a manner similar to giving a patient Prozac. Indeed, there are books that prescribe telling this or that metaphor to a client with a particular diagnostic label. Such interventions, delivered by therapists who are still dominated by the antiquated epistemology, will get success now and again. Those therapists will not find much of interest about Erickson's approach—at least not for long. Soon enough, many of them will be searching for some new techniques that promise to deliver terrific therapeutic results.

Erickson's greatest contribution was not his remarkable interventions. In fact, therapists bound in the traditional epistemology can use his interventions and they may "work," so to speak—but they will be no more useful, exciting, or dramatic than the conventional interventions on most occasions. Furthermore, it will be a chore to conceive of them from that framework.

On the contrary, Erickson's *approach* to clients and problems predicts novel interventions with little effort. Assuming an emergent epistemology will result in an abundance of new interventions for each client. That is, the use of Ericksonian interventions will not create an awareness of the new epistemology but the emergent goal-oriented epistemology will generate interventions. Interventions flow from the posture created with the new epistemology. The combination of Ericksonian interventions and the posture of an emerging epistemology creates a package for powerful change—even, at times, in a small number of sessions.

REASSOCIATING EXPERIENTIAL LIFE—EPISTEMOLOGY IN USE

When Erickson described *cure* in terms of facilitating a reassociation of experiential life, he did not specify a time frame. Theoretically, it need only take a moment, not even an entire session, to retrieve a needed resource experience and build an associative link to the context in which the client desires it be available. For extra measure, the therapist might help the client confuse the sequence or pattern of events that had been described as a problem or symptom, and shape perception to notice the first signal of that problem as a reminder of the newly associated option. The complexity of the symptom, availability of experiential resources, client motivation, and therapist skill will all contribute to the length of this process. However, it is often possible to resolve even major therapy goals in a satisfactory way in far less time and with far less angst than anyone would have thought possible (when thinking from the traditional epistemology).

For example, there is a conventional consensus that problems stemming from severe abuse and trauma will necessarily require a long and grueling therapy. It may involve recovering memories of and reliving the trauma, having a catharsis for the horror and rage, perhaps taking medication for the expected depression or anxiety, and slowly healing from the wounds of abuse. While such a course of therapy might actually be the best choice for a particular client, it seems to have become, for some therapists, a blueprint or "treatment plan" for almost every client presenting certain symptoms or sharing a similar history of abuse.

The new epistemology emphasizes taking a new and fresh look at each client to determine the specific treatment that will best fit that client. We do not treat diagnostic categories or symptom labels with a uniform therapy similarly applied to all clients. Even though they may share a similar symptom, such as an eating disorder, panic disorder, or depression, every client comes to that symptom through a highly idiosyncratic and unique history and consequently will have different needs and goals in order to accomplish a "cure."

To illustrate with a brief case example, an overweight fifty-four-year-old schoolteacher, Joan, was referred to us for therapy due to problems with physical pain and growing limitations of agoraphobia and depression thought to be resulting from sexual abuse in her childhood. The referring therapist had suggested that she might benefit from hypnotherapy for pain management and "to get in touch with feelings from the past" so that she might have a catharsis, which would result in a "corrective emotional experience" and "sharing" that presumably would improve her psychological condition.

Joan impressed us as a pleasant, hardworking woman who was dedicated to her job. Her physical problems included Barrett's esophagus, stomach ulcers, spastic colitis, pain in her shoulder, knee, and ankle joints, and pain most overwhelmingly in her left hip. This hip pain was reduced in her first session, providing her hope that therapy could make a difference and establishing her as a client able to take relevant suggestions and apply them to her goals quickly. She very much wanted to reduce the several medications she was taking.

In the next session she was comfortable enough to describe the events of her sexual abuse background, which included repeated forced fellatio with her older brother, from whom she was estranged. She also revealed suicidal ideation and her inability to consume any liquids except water for her entire teenage years and adult life due to her associations to the fellatio incidents of her childhood. She had no relationships with men, outside of work, and she had been sexually inactive all of her life. She was decidedly sad about the absence of such contact but considered herself basically a bad package due to her psychological and physical difficulties.

Hypnosis was first introduced to her by utilizing her religious orientation. She felt that she could get in touch with peaceful feelings through praying and she was encouraged to develop these during the session by the use of prayer. Together with the therapist, she was able to develop a strong sense of comfort and safety, with some additional aspects of what the therapist labeled and she accepted as joy. In the next few sessions, these feelings of comfort and joy were expanded to overcome all the physical pain she had in her hip and leg and finally her shoulder. The symptom of being unable to drink liquids was reduced by having her imagine herself drinking desired liquids while keeping constant her experiences of safety and comfort and joy. Somewhat coura- geously and reluctantly, she was willing to attempt to drink orange juice, apple juice, and thicker liquids such as malted milk. She now regularly drinks all liquids of her choosing.

Expanding her social contacts was accomplished by further use of visual self- rehearsal and posthypnotic suggestion, repeated attention to hypnosis via prayer, and the feelings of comfort and joy she was able to develop during the session. She found that she could conceptualize and rehearse in fantasy the possibility of taking vacations and retreats. Subsequently, and for the first time in her life, she took a major vacation to Alaska with boat and glacier tours and proudly reported how she had even stood bravely on the pontoon of a sea plane in the glacier lake.

Whenever she spoke of suicidal ideation, her experience was discussed and, over time, she came to a new conclusion. The conversation is more important than the technique, even though the name of turning her experience from neg- ative to positive would be considered a *reframing* intervention. Reframing needs to be considered a successful transaction when the therapist offers a way of con- ceptualizing experience that is acceptable to the client. It is not simply the use of an "intervention." Specifically, in this case, her suicidal ideation and memo- ries became reframed as awareness of her own courage and strength to attempt to build feelings of comfort and support and joy despite the fact that her pain and sorrow was so great that she would wish to end it immediately. Therefore, her past memories of suicide attempts became memories of courage that meant she had some deep conviction of hope that she could improve her life. Com- bining that with her perception and awareness that she was improving her life led her to apply through association and further posthypnotic suggestion those experiences to her overeating, which she had previously used to reduce stress and increase her sense of love and acceptance. As a result, within two months, she was noticeably losing weight and was happy and satisfied that she was now progressing in a reduction of weight, depression, social isolation, and pain. She began to reduce her medication, keeping her physician informed as she did so. At the end of three months, she had reduced her large amount of medication by more than half and was still reducing it, was experiencing no pain, was increasing her social contacts, was eating in a healthy manner, and had even changed her wardrobe to match her improving self-image.

All this therapy was goal directed as opposed to analyzing difficulties of the past or expecting her to make an announcement of her pain. Instead, she was helped to build experiences she never actually had in the past, such as joy and comfort and satisfaction and pride, and helped to find ways of associating those into new social interfaces that were being built. These were applied, also, through the concentrated attention of hypnosis, to help her alter her eating behavior and her general sense of confidence about approaching people and work. The emphasis then changed to her cognitive framework of the abuse. Several sessions were devoted to a complex association/dissociation exercise so that she could explain her memories and experiences of the sexual abuse of the past and make it possible for her occasionally to remember or be reminded of those without their forcing automatic bad experiences on her in current daily life. This led to focusing on her self-talk and helping her develop conscious and unconscious tools for inhibiting negative self-talk. She accomplished this over several sessions by means of establishing a comfortable trance and, holding on to the feelings of comfort and safety, dissociating from pictures of her younger self. In that state, she would practice nurturing self-talk repeatedly until it became a learned habit. Her new habit started the nurturing self-talk in the very same second she noticed the beginning of any negative self-talk, as well as at those times when she could see that nurturing talk would be useful. This process was most evident as she grappled with spiritual beliefs and made some landmark decisions that would become more lasting in her overall development. Chief among these were whether or not she really was a worthy person who could be entitled to an ongoing experience of comfort and joy outside the office. This was manifested in her daily life in her ability to monitor her self-talk and to supply to herself a new self-talk that was more in keeping with generating a positive experience. This conscious tool was built upon training and education in the session, using hypnosis for practice, and rehearsal to be certain that she knew how to do these things successfully.

At one point well into the therapy, she remarked that she had seen her referring therapist, who commented how well she looked and figured that must be because she had "gotten her anger out." Joan responded, "What anger? I don't feel any anger." The client realized that the conventional approach of the other therapist had been built on the assumption that she needed to dwell upon her negative experiences and share them with the therapist. Instead, she had experienced therapy that focused on working in a goal-directed fashion with hypnosis, indirect suggestion, and metaphor to help her locate positive resources in her own experience. With posthypnotic suggestion, behavioral rehearsal, and actual assignments, she had applied those experiential resources to areas of her life including eating, work, physical comfort, and socialization.

CHOOSING INTERVENTIONS: IN THE BEGINNING . . .

A mindful attention to the client guides the therapist at every juncture in the Ericksonian approach. As mentioned before, the techniques that bear Erickson's thumbprint (hypnosis, paradoxical prescription, indirect suggestion, metaphor, ambiguous assignments, and so on) have too often been taken out of context of the approach and considered to *be* the approach. This is akin to thinking that the ingredients of a recipe actually are the meal. The art of preparing the meal is where the attention must be. In psychotherapy, the interventions themselves will best be discovered *after* they have been used rather than the other way around. And because of this hierarchy of importance, and in the context of this chapter focused on epistemology, we have chosen not to detail the how-to of specific interventions. Certainly, being skillful at using interventions is important, and we have written extensively about this (Lankton, 1980; Lankton & Lankton, 1983, 1986, 1989). The interventions are more tangible and easily taught than the essence of the approach. In this section, we will metadiscuss selection of interventions by looking at the chronological flow of meeting the client, understanding problems, creating rapport, determining the goal of the treatment, and arriving at some contractual arrangement. These activities occur in the first moments of therapy and literally set the pace and style for all that follows, determining whether the subsequent encounter is a child of the traditional or the emerging epistemology.

Much is determined in the opening moments of the first session. Patients usually come to specialists expecting them to be experts who will behave in a manner similar to physicians or dentists. That is, the patient will say, "My third tooth on the lower left hurts" and expect that this is all the information that needs to be given for the expert to investigate, determine what needs to be done, and do it to the passive patient, who sits anesthetized in the chair. This approach— based on a traditional epistemology—works sufficiently when operating upon teeth, although in that area, too, there are often more productive ways to handle expectations. In therapy, the extent to which the client is allowed to place the therapist in the role of the traditional expert will be the degree to which the Ericksonian approach and all its interventions will fail. The extent to which the therapist initially explains an ability and willingness to help the client but avoids the expert role will be the degree to which this constructive therapy will emerge and be helpful.

The most blatant example of this sort of dilemma occurs when, in the initial telephone call, a potential client says—as one recently said to us—"Do you think that if I come to Florida [where we practice] you have the skills to take away this eating disorder?" My (S.R.L.) response was, "I absolutely don't have the skill to take away this eating disorder and you shouldn't come to Florida in order to have me accomplish that." I expect that this was the first time anyone had talked that way to this client. It was absolutely true to me. I went on to explain that I expected *he* had the capability of overcoming his eating disorder and that I might have the skills to help him do that, but I never hypnotized anybody and I never took away anybody's pain, or symptom, or whatever. I simply am frequently capable of creating a context where people were able to do that for themselves, sometimes with good ideas from me and sometimes *despite* my ideas. The initial approach to the client determines how therapy will unfold, whether successfully cocreated or with the therapist struggling to proceed on a foundation of the traditional epistemology and attempting to borrow isolated techniques from the Ericksonian bag of tricks.

Another aspect in the chronology of clients coming to therapy that determines choice of intervention is how the problem is presented and framed. Traditionally, we are trained to believe that we must spend one to three or more sessions gathering a detailed history of the problems. If a therapist operates in this manner in the first three sessions, he or she will be stuck in the role of the expert from the client's perspective. The therapist will be unable to operate with the degree of flexibility necessary to work efficiently from the new epistemology. Instead, history needs to be gathered only so much as it is required to understand why the client, at the current moment, is not succeeding at being healthy in the way he or she would consider a successful state of health. Here are some useful questions to consider at this point:

- What is on their mind, or in their memory, or in some other way inhibiting them from being in sensory contact or emotionally tender with their spouse right at this moment?

- Are they remembering something?

- What prevents them from not remembering what they wish?

- What would happen if they operated in this possible manner instead of that manner?

If they use the experimental improvisations that result from their answers to such questions to move forward, it may be entirely appropriate to avoid any further history. It would be appropriate to continue doing so until such time that the forward movement is blocked by some intrusive habit or cognition that the client finds beyond his or her capability to overcome without more guidance and help from the therapist.

A third angle in which intervention selection can be crucial in the chronology of meeting the client and getting the contract arranged has to do with how rapport is established. Much has already been written about speaking the client's language and matching the client's body posture, tone, breathing, and so on. However, the mood of the therapist in performing these behaviors will radically influence the outcome of success or failure. The behaviors of matching the client and speaking the client's language need to be done from an attitude of trying to get inside the client's experiential world, feeling, and point of view, and not from trying to use certain techniques. This is not merely a semantic trick but a distinctive and serious difference with regard to whether or not the client is more important than the interventions or the interventions are more important than the client. People occasionally facilitate trust and rapport via such subtle behaviors. This should happen in therapy.

Finally, what the goals are and how contracts are negotiated will significantly influence choice of interventions. In this era of growing emphasis on accountability, behavioral health care, and HMOs, many therapists must rapidly specify, verbalize, and get signatures from clients about what their goals are and how therapy will unfold to reach those goals. This incessant pressure is unfortunate in that interventions to help people change must unfold in almost every sentence spoken by the therapist. This takes place in the form of numerous presuppositions, using ongoing moment-to-moment resources, laughter, hesitations, doubts, curiosities that arise in clients as they speak, and so on. All this is instrumental to continuing the ongoing flow of building resources, framing problems in ways that lead to a realization that they can be overcome, and helping clients apply the resources quickly. This dynamic and subtle process is not easily constrained to an insurance approval form. While the emphasis on goal orientation can sharpen strategic concentration and sometimes be chunked as evolving smaller component goals, such procedures seem too often to aim at locking the therapy session into the old epistemology (see Hoyt & Friedman, in press).

FORWARD TOGETHER

Fundamental to successful therapy is that the therapist be instructed by feedback from the client that helpfully corrects any deviance from the desired course with new information. Interventions become more valuable because of the new information they yield about how the client grows and changes. In this view of the world, there are no mistakes (from the experts), simply outcomes (cocreated). If we are prepared to experience therapy as a way of helping clients construct the realities they desire, we are operating within the emerging epistemology.

References

Bateson, G. (1972). *Steps to an ecology of mind.* New York: Ballantine.

Erickson, M. H. (1967). The method employed to formulate a complex story for the induction of the experimental neurosis. In J. Haley (Ed.), *Advanced techniques of hypnosis and therapy: Selected papers of Milton H. Erickson, M.D.* (pp. 312–325). New York: Irvington.

Erickson, M. H. (1980a). Hypnosis: Its renascence as a treatment modality. In E. L. Rossi (Ed.), *The collected papers of Milton H. Erickson on hypnosis: Vol. 4. Innovative hypnotherapy* (pp. 52–75). New York: Irvington. (Original work published 1966)

Erickson, M. H. (1980b). Hypnotic psychotherapy. In E. L. Rossi (Ed.), *The collected papers of Milton H. Erickson on hypnosis: Vol. 4. Innovative hypnotherapy* (pp. 35–51). New York: Irvington. (Original work published 1948)

Erickson, M. H. (1980c). Special techniques of brief hypnotherapy. In E. L. Rossi (Ed.), *The collected papers of Milton H. Erickson on hypnosis: Vol. 4. Innovative hypnotherapy* (pp. 149–173). New York: Irvington. (Original work published 1954)

Erickson, M. H., with Haley, J., & Weakland, J. H. (1967). A transcript of a trance induction with commentary. In J. Haley (Ed.), *Advanced techniques of hypnosis and therapy: Selected papers of Milton H. Erickson, M.D.* New York: Irvington.

Erickson, M. H., & Rossi, E. L. (1979). *Hypnotherapy: An exploratory casebook.* New York: Irvington.

Erickson, M. H., & Rossi, E. L. (1980). The indirect forms of suggestion. In E. L. Rossi (Ed.), *The collected papers of Milton H. Erickson on hypnosis: Vol. 1. The nature of hypnosis and suggestion* (pp. 452–477). New York: Irvington.

Erickson, M. H., & Rossi, E. L. (1981). *Experiencing hypnosis: Therapeutic approaches to altered state.* New York: Irvington.

Erickson, M. H., Rossi, E. L., & Rossi, S. I. (1976). *Hypnotic realities: The induction of clinical hypnosis and forms of indirect suggestion.* New York: Irvington.

Freud, S. (1938). *The basic writings of Sigmund Freud.* New York: Random House, Modern Library.

Freud, S. (1966). *The complete introductory lectures on psychoanalysis* (J. Strachey, Trans.). New York: Norton. (Original work published 1923)

Haley, J. (1963). *Strategies of psychotherapy.* New York: Grune & Stratton.

Haley, J. (1973). *Uncommon therapy: The psychiatric techniques of Milton H. Erickson, M.D.* New York: Norton.

Haley, J. (1985). *Conversations with Milton H. Erickson, M.D.: Vol. 1. Changing individuals.* New York: Norton.

Hawking, S. (1988). *A brief history of time: From the big bang to the black holes.* New York: Bantam Books.

Hoyt, M. F., & Friedman, S. (in press). Dilemmas of postmodern practice under managed care and some pragmatics for increasing the likelihood of treatment authorization. *Journal of Systemic Therapies.*

Jackson, D. (Ed.). (1968a). *Communication, family, and marriage* (Vol 1). Palo Alto: Science and Behavior Books.

Jackson, D. (Ed.). (1968b). *Therapy, communication, and change* (Vol. 2). Palo Alto, CA: Science and Behavior Books.

Laing, R. D. (1967). *The politics of experience.* New York: Pantheon.

Laing, R. D. (1972). *The politics of the family.* New York: Ballantine Books.

Lankton, S. R. (1980). *Practical magic: A translation of basic neuro-linguistic programming into clinical psychotherapy.* Cupertino, CA: Metapubs.

Lankton, S. R., & Lankton, C. (1983). *The answer within: A clinical framework of Ericksonian hypnotherapy.* New York: Brunner/Mazel.

Lankton, S. R., & Lankton, C. (1986). *Enchantment and intervention in family therapy.* New York: Brunner/Mazel.

Lankton, S. R., & Lankton, C. (1989). *Tales of enchantment: Goal-directed metaphors for adults and children in therapy.* New York: Brunner/Mazel.

Satir, V. (1964). *Conjoint family therapy.* Palo Alto, CA: Science and Behavior Books.

Szasz, T. (1961). *The myth of mental illness: Foundations of a theory of personal conduct.* New York: HarperCollins.

Zeig, J. K., & Lankton, S. R. (Eds.). (1988). *Developing Ericksonian therapy: State of the art.* New York: Brunner/Mazel.

CHAPTER SEVEN

Possibility Therapy

An Inclusive, Collaborative, Solution-Based Model of Psychotherapy

William (Bill) O'Hanlon

Possibility therapy derived in large part from the work of Milton Erickson, with whom I studied in the late 1970s and about whose work I wrote my first published book (O'Hanlon, 1987). He usually saw people as very skilled, even when they were having symptoms. He had a competence view of people. Erickson found a way to utilize people's symptoms, their family backgrounds, their hobbies and interests, and their social network to help them resolve their concerns.

In the early 1980s, I began a correspondence with Steve de Shazer, who had moved from California, where he had written a number of papers on Erickson's work (see de Shazer, 1982), to Milwaukee, Wisconsin, where he and some colleagues had begun what came to be called the Brief Family Therapy Center (BFTC). De Shazer and I shared a common view that mainstream therapies that saw clients as pathological and resistant were all wrong. People were naturally cooperative if approached in the right way and treated as resourceful and competent. De Shazer's work began to take shape and has turned into "solution-focused therapy" (de Shazer, 1985, 1988). My work took shape and I began to call it "solution-oriented therapy" (O'Hanlon, 1988; O'Hanlon & Weiner-Davis, 1989). Because the two were often confused and I have some major differences with the Milwaukee approach, I began to speak of my approach as "possibility therapy" (e.g., O'Hanlon, 1993a, 1993b; O'Hanlon & Beadle, 1994). While I see much of value in the BFTC emphasis on client strengths and solutions, there are some areas of clear difference. In this chapter, I will first distinguish my approach from solution-focused therapy and then put forth some of the basic principles and working methods of possibility therapy.

DISTINGUISHING POSSIBILITY THERAPY FROM SOLUTION-FOCUSED THERAPY

It became clear to me that because the Milwaukee approach put such a value on minimalism, it left out several elements that I found crucial in my therapeutic work. The first was that there is no significant discussion of the importance of the validation of emotions in the Milwaukee approach. Because the emphasis is so much on "solution talk," sometimes clients have the sense that the therapist is minimizing or not attending to the problem. This has led some students of the Milwaukee approach to find that some clients get angry and frustrated when they feel "forced" or "rushed" by the solution-focused approach (Lipchik, 1994; Nylund & Corsiglia, 1994). In contrast, hearing, acknowledging, and validating the client's experience is a major first step in possibility therapy, laying the foundation for subsequent work. I learned this long ago from Carl Rogers's work (see O'Hanlon, in Hoyt, 1996a), and will discuss it more later in this chapter.

Another difficulty I see with the Milwaukee approach is its tendency to be formulaic. One invariably asks certain questions (like the "Miracle Question") and follows certain sequences. There are flow charts (de Shazer, 1985) giving directions for response to various client responses. While this may be a fine way to learn a new approach (see Walter & Peller, 1992), the ultimate effect is often one of dogma and orthodoxy coming to the fore. Even though the principal proponents of the Milwaukee approach may protest that this is merely evidence of the approach being done wrong, I frequently encounter these reports from both beginning and advanced students of the approach.

Another concern I have about the Milwaukee approach is that it studiously ignores political, historical, and gender influences on the problem (as well as the inner worlds of physiology and biochemistry) as being irrelevant to the process of therapy, since all one has to do is develop solutions and solution-focused conversations. Because of its minimalist approach, in its strictest version, one gets the sense that if a couple came in for therapy and the man was drunk or the woman had a black eye, the solution-focused therapist would be constrained from mentioning or inquiring about the potential evidence of alcohol problems or domestic abuse unless the couple mentioned it themselves or violence was what they were referred for. In contrast, in possibility therapy, while I take care not to bring in extraneous material and inquiries, at times these areas are crucial for both the therapist's understanding of the issues and felt experience of the client and for the development of solutions. Possibility therapy maintains that it is inappropriate for the therapist to impose ideas about the problem or to push topics for discussion unless there is a suspicion of danger-ousness (such as suicidality, homicidality, sexual abuse of children, or seriously self-harming behaviors) of if blatantly socially oppressive issues (such as racism, sexism, ideals of gender or weight, sexual orientation biases) are present. In these situations, it is then incumbent on the therapist, regardless of whether the clients think it is relevant or whether or not they brought up the topic, to pursue these lines of inquiry and to do his or her best to ensure physical safety or to explore the social context of the problem. It gave me more than pause when, in an interview (quoted in Hoyt, 1994, p. 18), de Shazer answered, "I don't think so" when asked if he had ever tried to get clients to expand their options if a solution they were taking was extremely limiting or even hurtful to them.[1]

SOME FEATURES AND TYPICAL METHODS IN POSSIBILITY THERAPY

What follows are some suggestions and guidelines. Consistent with the spirit of possibility therapy, they are intended to open doors, increase respectful coop-eration, and empower clients and therapists. They are not directive or defini-tive. During my time living in the colder Northern parts of the United States, I learned about the winter game called *curling*, in which the players use brooms to sweep the ice in front of the moving stone. I liken this image to what possi-bility therapists do: we metaphorically sweep a path in front of our clients to facilitate their movement to where they want to go.

Collaborative Shaping of the Therapy Process

Clients are not merely experts in solutions and goals for therapy, but also quite capable of helping ensure the success of therapy by giving their reactions and preferences as to therapy process, methods, and styles. Therefore, I regularly make clients part of the treatment planning process: they are consulted about goals, directions, and their responses to the process and methods of therapy. I also make myself and the treatment process as transparent as possible: diag-nostic procedures, conclusions, and case notes are available and understand-able to clients. I am careful to ask questions and make speculations in a nonauthoritarian way, giving the client ample room and permission to disagree or correct me.

- Diagnostic procedures can also be done in a collaborative, transparent manner. Sometimes I haul out the *DSM* and read aloud the category (or cate-gories) I think most likely fit with the client's situation. "Do you have at least three of these five symptoms? If you do, you have this diagnosis." I do not do this with all clients, but some of them really appreciate knowing the diagnosis and the criteria for making the diagnosis. I also tell them that by the end of treatment, I should be able to read the list of symptoms, and if we are successful they will no longer have those three symptoms, and therefore no longer have the diagnosis.

• In a similar vein, I had a psychiatrist friend who was remiss at doing his case notes and charting, and he cleverly devised a collaborative case notes process. At the end of a session, he would, after explaining to his clients what he was doing, dictate a case note about the session into his Dictaphone. The clients had the opportunity to hear what he was putting in the chart as well as to correct anything he got wrong or about which they had thought differently. One could use the same procedure with written notes and treatment plans to make the therapy process more collaborative.

• I typically give clients many options and let them coach me on the next step or the right direction. Sometimes this applies to something as simple as the time lapse between sessions: "Would you like to come back? If so, would a week be the right time or too soon to tell if what we talked about is helpful? How about two weeks or a month?" Other times, I give multiple-choice options for the directions for treatment or the therapy discussion: "Is what we are talking about helpful to you? Is this a good direction to be pursuing? Would you like us to talk more about the right place for your son to live or should we be focusing more on the hallucinations?"

• If I have an idea and realize that I have been keeping it as a hidden agenda, I make it public, including it in the conversation not as the truth or the right direction, but as an idea, a personal perception, or an impression. I want to let clients know that I have ideas and opinions, some of them informed by my professional training and experience, but that I do not have the Truth or the Ten Commandments for how to live correctly, how to be mentally healthy, how to have a great relationship (I guarantee I don't know this one). I don't want to have to keep my opinions to myself; they leak out in my questions and nonverbals anyway, so I take care to say them in a more tentative way, giving ample room for disagreement.

For example, once I was working with a family in which the son was regularly violent in the home. After trying many solutions and directions, the violence was continuing. I then told a story about how my father had told me that he had learned one thing from raising eight children: that kids have to hit brick walls to learn about limits. I explained that my father had said that he had tried to warn each of his children when he saw that they were acting in a way that would potentially harm their futures. But it was as if the kids were riding a motorcycle toward a brick wall. Early on, he said, before he'd learned better, he had even stood in front of the brick wall, trying to shield the child from the consequences of his or her actions. After several children, though, he had finally realized that all kids learn this way. Was this family standing in front of the brick wall, providing soft love for their son, and would a harder kind of love, one in which he would receive consequences for being violent, be better for all concerned? The parents—and amazingly even the son—agreed. We began to work on setting limits and providing consequences for violence (calling the police, living in another place for a time after the violence, and so on).

Where Do Clients Want to Go?

In the beginning of therapy there are two things I want to find out. First, what is the person complaining about? I need to ascertain why the person is in therapy, since this will give me a hint as to what we need to focus on resolving. Second, I want to find out how the person will know when the therapy is done. From these two pieces of information, I can gain a sense of where someone wants to go and what it may look like when they get there.

Therapists' knowing what they are being asked to accomplish and clarifying the goal of the person or people who are asking for help is what I call *developing a focus*. As Hoyt (1996b) has said, using a golf metaphor, "It's a long day on the course if you don't know where the hole is." This focus takes into account the multiple customers with different agendas. If it is not mutual and all parties do not agree on what constitutes a successful outcome, there may be trouble. Here are some questions and guidelines to help clarify this crucial issue in therapy.

Determining the Complaint(s)

- What is bothering someone enough to get them to seek or get sent to treatment?
- Who is complaining?
- Who is alarmed about something?
- What are they complaining or alarmed about?
- What action descriptions *(videotalk)* correspond to the vague and blaming words that open the discussion?
- When has the complaint typically occurred?
- Where has the complaint typically occurred?
- What are the patterns surrounding or involved in the complaint?
- How does the person, the customer, or others involved in the situation explain the complaint?

Ascertaining the Customer(s)

- Who is willing to pay for therapy and/or do something to effect change?
- Whose concerns will constrain or affect therapy?
- Who is pushing for change?

- Who is paying you?
- Who is complaining the most?
- Who will be able to terminate therapy?
- What are the legal and ethical restraints or considerations (suicidal plans or attempts, homicidal and violence plans or history, court or legal involvement, and so on)?

Clarifying the Goal(s)

- How will the client(s) or customer(s) know when therapy has been helpful enough to terminate or when the agreed-upon results have been achieved?
- What are the first signs that will indicate (or already have indicated) progress toward the goal(s)?
- What are the final actions or results (again in *videotalk*—seeable, hearable, checkable if possible) that will indicate that this is no longer a problem? (See O'Hanlon & Wilk, 1987.) Translate labels or theoretical concepts into action descriptions if possible. If not, get the client to rate the subjective experience of the problem on a scale and select a target number for success on that scale.
- How will we know when therapy is done, when it has been successful?

INTERVENING: ACKNOWLEDGING EXPERIENCE AND CHANGING VIEWS, ACTIONS, AND CONTEXTS

I conceptualize four areas for intervention in therapy. These are: *Experience, Actions, Views,* and *Context.* Table 7.1 summarizes these areas.

Within *experience* lie all the inner aspects of people's lives, their feelings, fantasies, sensations, and their sense of themselves. All these could be placed in the realm of being—they are subjective and interior, unavailable to others unless we somehow—through words, art, or gestures—communicate them. What possibility therapy suggests for therapists to do with this area is to just acknowledge, value, and validate it. Let people know their experience has been heard and not judged as wrong or invalid. Let them know that they are valued as people and they have valid experiences. This is the realm of acceptance, not change (although communicating that acceptance may, of course, lead to change).

I start by acknowledging what clients indicate they are experiencing. Clients need to know that you, the therapist, get not only the content of the problem but also understand the emotional weight or resonance it has for them. This is fundamental for the rest of the treatment process and for some clients this *is* the treatment. Most clients, however, need more than acknowledgment. They

Table 7.1. Realms of Intervention

Experience	Views	Actions	Context
Feelings	Points of views	Action patterns	Time patterns
Sense of self	Attentional patterns	Interactional patterns	Spatial patterns
Bodily sensations			Cultural background and propensities
Sensory experience	Interpretations	Language patterns	
Automatic fantasies and thoughts	Explanations	Nonverbal patterns	Family/historical background and propensities
	Evaluations		
	Assumptions		Biochemical/genetic background and propensities
	Beliefs		
	Identity stories		Gender training and propensities

not only need to be heard and validated but then given help to begin actively making changes to solve the problem. Acknowledgment may last anywhere from minutes to many sessions. If clients don't feel heard and understood, you will not be able to move on to the other stages in therapy. If acknowledgment is all you offer, it won't be enough for most clients. If, as a therapist, I feel that I am starting to experience lack of cooperation or hostility in the treatment, I stop and move back into acknowledgment.

The next three columns in Table 7.1 define the realms in which change occurs. The focus is on three areas: *changing the viewing of the problem, changing the doing of the problem,* and *changing the context surrounding the problem.* In these three areas, I search for both the *problem* and *solution patterns.* What are the problematic views that clients hold about themselves? What are more helpful, supportive, change-enhancing or change-inviting views? What are the problematic action or interaction patterns that occur around the problem, between family members or with others? What are more helpful action and interaction patterns? And finally, what are the aspects of the context that are conducive to change and results and what are the aspects of the context that hold people back or keep them having problems?

I try to help clients change the habitual ways they think about, attend to, or see the problem (the *viewing* of the problem) and to change the habitual ways they have been acting and interacting in the problem situation (the *doing* of the problem). Some years ago the brief therapist John Weakland told me, "Life is just one damn thing after another. Therapy can't change that. But people who seek therapy are no longer experiencing that—life for them has become the same damn thing *over and over and over.*" Our task as possibility therapists, then, is to help people get from a situation in which life has become "the same damn thing over and over" back to a life where it's "one damn thing after another." People will always have some problems, but what discourages and disempowers them so is struggling unsuccessfully with the same damn problem over and over.

To the ideas of assessing and changing the "doing" and the "viewing" I have added changing the *context* of the problem. As a therapist, I have become much more aware of the influence of culture, gender, biochemistry, and other contextual aspects on people's problems. Problems do not occur in a vacuum. I believe that contextual aspects are influences (not causes) and that there are both problematic and helpful contextual influences. A client may have a biochemical context that suggests a predisposition toward obsessiveness or schizophrenia, but that does not *cause* him or her to act in a particular way. For example, one may be subject to hallucinations, but that does not *cause* one to run down the street naked or hit someone. Or just because a man is from a cultural tradition where males are trained not to express feelings doesn't mean he is or will always be unable to express his feelings.

I search for helpful contextual patterns as well as attempt to identify problematic contextual patterns. For example, I might say, "So there has been quite a history of alcohol abuse and dependency in your family. Dad, three of your uncles died from drinking in their thirties. Mom, your mother was a secret drinker until a few years ago. Tell me this: How did your mother stop drinking, Mom? And Dad, who in your family didn't succumb to the invitations of alcohol?" Or, "Since I don't know much about Pakistani culture, perhaps you can help me with this. When there has been violence between a couple, how does it typically stop, if it does, in Pakistani culture? What aspects of the culture support violence within couples and what aspects of the culture challenge or restrain violence in those situations?"

CHANGING THE VIEWING OF THE PROBLEM

When clients enter therapy, they often have stories (ideas, beliefs, hypotheses) about each other or the problem. These stories tend to be rigid and divisive. Stories are unhelpful when they get in the way of change, and I typically find that clients come to therapy with unhelpful stories that have become part and parcel of the problem. Table 7.2 outlines these four areas.

I have identified four typical problematic stories. These beliefs may be held by anyone interacting about the problem—the family, the therapist, and/or the referral source.

Table 7.2. How to Intervene in the Four Areas

Experience	Views	Actions	Context
Give messages of acceptance, validation, and acknowledgment. There is no need to change or analyze experience as it is not inherently a problem.	Identify and challenge views that are: Impossibility Blaming Invalidating No accountability or determinism Also offer new possibilities for attention.	Find action and interaction patterns that are part of the problem and that are the "same damn thing over and over." Then suggest disrupting the problematic patterns or find and use solution patterns.	Identify unhelpful and helpful aspects of the context and then suggest shifts in the context around the problem (for example, changes in biochemistry, time, space, cultural habits and influences).

Impossibility Stories

In impossibility stories, clients, therapists, or others in their lives often hold beliefs that suggest that change is impossible.

- He has ADHD and can't control his behavior.
- She'll never change.
- She is just like my mother.

Blaming Stories

Stories of blame assume or view oneself or others as having bad intentions or bad traits.

- He's just trying to get attention.
- It's all my fault.
- They are trying to drive me crazy.

Invalidating Stories

Ideas of invalidation lead to clients' personal experience or knowledge being undermined by others.

- He needs to express his anger about his father's death.
- He's too sensitive.
- You're too emotional.

Deterministic Stories

Stories of nonchoice—deterministic stories—suggest that people have no choices about what they do with their bodies (voluntary actions) or have no ability to make any difference in what happens in their lives.

- If that teacher knew how to handle a classroom,
  Kate wouldn't have these problems at school.
- I was raised in a home where silence was the way to express anger,
  so when I get angry, I stop talking and go my own way.
- If she didn't nag me, I wouldn't hit her.

Dealing with Problematic Stories

I challenge or cast doubt on problematic stories in three ways:

• *Transform the story by acknowledging and softening or by adding possibility.* Validate the current or past problematic points of view but add a twist that softens a bit or adds a sense of possibility. For example, a parent may say of a son, "He doesn't care about our family. He just wants to do anything he feels like doing, regardless of the pain it causes us." One could respond by acknowledging the feelings and point of view of the parent, but reflect it back with a softer, less globalized sense to it. "So a lot of the things he's been doing have given you the sense he cares more for himself than for you or the family." Or another reflection could add a sense of the possibility that things could change in the future: "So you'd like to see him doing more things that show that he can put the family above his own interests at times."

• *Find counterevidence.* Get clients or others who know them to tell you something that doesn't fit with the problematic story. For example, "Gee, you tell me that he's out of control, but now you're telling me that his teacher said he kept his cool when another boy taunted him in class." Or, "So, you tell me that you were raised in a family in which the only way to express anger was violence. But I'm curious: When you get angry, you typically hit your wife and your son, but when you get mad at work, do you hit your boss or the customers?"

• *Find alternative stories or frames to fit the same evidence or facts.* Give the facts a more benevolent interpretation. For example, "You get the sense he just wants to do anything he wants when he wants to do it, but my sense is that he's trying to find a way to be independent and make his own decisions. When you come down hard on him, the only way he can see to show he's independent is to rebel and resist you, even if it gets him in trouble." Or, "You think your father hates you because he grounds you, but I wonder whether you've thought that if he didn't care for you, he'd just let you do what you want as long as it wasn't a hassle for him."

TYPES OF INTERVENTIONS IN POSSIBILITY THERAPY

Two types of interventions are made in the three areas of change (the doing, the viewing, and the context):

- *Ascertain the repetitive sequences that surround and are involved in the problem and suggest changes in the problem pattern.*

- *Discover, highlight, and encourage more use of solution patterns instead of problem patterns.*

After getting an initial sense of what is bothering the person, I begin to elicit more detailed information. What I am seeking is patterns. To find the patterns, I must get descriptions of what the person is doing that constitutes or accompanies the problem. Descriptions are different from theories or conclusions. I have referred to this process as getting people to use *videotalk* (O'Hanlon & Wilk, 1987), that is, getting people to describe their problem so it can be seen and heard as if on a videotape. Videotalk replays the doing of the problem.

For example, I might ask a person to describe to me the doing of self-mutilation. "When do you typically hurt yourself? How do you start to hurt yourself? What kinds of implements do you use to hurt yourself, if any? What parts of your body do you typically hurt? What parts do you never hurt?" Even if the complaint is about something internal, the therapist can still elicit a description of the doing that accompanies it. For example, one could ask, "When you are having your flashbacks, what would someone who is watching you at that moment see as different from other moments when there are no flashbacks?" Or, "What do you typically do when you get depressed?" Focusing on the doing helps isolate the problem.

From this perspective, a therapeutically addressable problem:

- Must occur repetitively.

- Must be distinguished and attended to.

- Must be valued negatively (as bad, wrong, sick, crazy, evil, shameful, unacceptable, intolerable).

- Must be considered to be involuntary in at least some aspect, that is, the person feels unable to solve it or stop it from happening.

Milton Erickson was fascinated with clients' problems and symptoms and the way they did them. Essentially, he wanted to map out the details of the problem. Erickson would focus on the problem so intently it was almost like he was studying someone in order to play them in a movie. He would ask clients to describe in minute detail the particulars of their problem. He would ask questions about:

- How the problem occurred
- Where the problem occurred
- With whom the problem occurred
- How often the problem occurred (frequency)
- How long the problem occurred (duration).

I was infected by Erickson's type of curiosity. I explore with clients the negative problem patterns that seem to be inhibiting or intruding in their lives. I'm like a geographer in an unfamiliar territory, exploring the topography and coastline of Problem-land. I want to learn the details of the problem or symptom, *and* help the client find ways of escaping it. By isolating the problem, together clients and I can intervene in the patterns that make up the problem, or change the contexts around the problem so they no longer contain the problem or symptom (O'Hanlon, 1982, 1987; O'Hanlon & Wilk, 1987; O'Hanlon & Weiner-Davis, 1989).

Clients' descriptions of problems help me to understand what they mean by the words they use, so I don't impose so much of my own interpretations on those words. In addition, I am searching for any aspect of the problem that repeats, that indicates a pattern. Inspired in part by Erickson and the strategic/interactional therapists who followed him, I have found it helpful in ferreting out the patterns of the problem to explore how often the problem typically happens, when it typically happens (time of day, time of week, time of month, time of year), the duration of the problem (how long it typically lasts), where it typically happens, who is involved and what the person and others who are around usually do when the problem is happening. Once clients and I recognize a problematic pattern, we can begin to find ways of disrupting it or replacing it with a solution pattern.

Changing Problem Patterns

I typically suggest changes in the problem pattern after I have enough details about the pattern to get a sense of the possibilities for change. That is, what would be a noticeable change that is within the person's power to bring about? Usually this involves changing actions, which may include altering:

- Sequence
- Antecedents
- Consequences
- Invariant actions
- Repetitive interactions
- Body behavior
- Location or setting

Linda, who was depressed and isolated, agreed to go to a coffeehouse when she got very desperate. She did not have to talk to anyone, but just to sit there for at least two hours. She began to go to the coffeehouse nightly, as she was usually depressed. After a time, she became a familiar face and the staff of the coffeehouse began to engage her in conversation. She made a few friends and began to volunteer at the coffeehouse, helping to book the musical acts they had decided to add to the atmosphere.

One can also suggest changes in the timing (frequency, time of occurrence, duration) of the problem:

Martha spent a good portion of her evening picking at her fingernails until they bled. Martha tried to stop this behavior, but she found it so compelling that she couldn't avoid it. The therapist suggested that Martha try an experiment and schedule fifteen-minute picking sessions each night. Martha found that during the nonscheduled times, the compulsion was gone, because she knew she had her scheduled time to engage in the habit. Martha found herself doing more productive and interesting things with her evenings. Occasionally, she even forgot to pick her nails.

Another option is to suggest changes in the nonverbal behavior (voice tones, gestures, body movements, eye contact, and so on) that typically occur with the problem:

Jenny was having trouble with her eating disorder (bulimia) during social occasions when food was present. Normally a very sociable person, she had almost decided to stop attending any social gathering that might have food. She would become so focused on the food during these gatherings (avoiding it, fearing that everyone would know she was compulsively eating) that she would have a terrible time. She would slink about the party, head down, avoiding any contact or conversation with anyone. Sometimes she would binge and sometimes not, but the experience was unpleasant regardless. Together we devised a plan to change the pattern. The next party she attended, she agreed to go up to at least three people, look them in the eye, and introduce herself, before she began to focus on the food. When she carried out the plan, she found she became so absorbed in the conversations she was having that food became a nonissue.

INVITATION TO SOLUTION-LAND: IDENTIFYING, EVOKING, AND USING SOLUTION PATTERNS

In addition to (or instead of) changing problem patterns, possibility therapists also seek to elicit and evoke previous solution patterns, including abilities, competencies, and strengths. The idea is not to convince clients that they have solutions and competencies, but rather to ask questions and gather information in a way that highlights for them that they do. The emphasis is on evoking a sense of competence and an experience of being able to solve problems. Too often, when clients become caught up in their problematic patterns, they do not recall the wealth of experience they have available. I search in various areas to find and help restore this sense of competence, often by identifying previously successful strategies for dealing with or resolving the particular problems the client has brought to therapy. The following are some techniques I use to gather information about solutions and to evoke them:

• *Find out about previous solutions to the problem, including partial solutions and partial successes.* Ask clients to detail times when they haven't experienced their problems, including times when they expected the problem but it did not occur. For example, you might ask, "From what we understand, usually you would have just backed down in the face of intimidation like that, but you didn't that one time. What did you do that was different this time? How did you get yourself to do it?" Or "You didn't cut yourself as much last night. How did you keep yourself from doing what you have usually done? What did you do this time instead of continuing to cut?"

• *Find out what happens as the problem ends or starts to end.* What is the first sign the client has that the problem is going away or subsiding? How can the person's friends, family, coworkers, and so on tell when the problem has subsided or started to subside? What will the person be doing when the problem has ended or subsided? How do these problem-free activities differ from what the client does when the problem is happening or present? Is there anything the person or significant others have noticed that helps the problem subside more quickly? Some sample questions to ask to help elicit this information: "When you stop cutting, how do you know it's time to stop? What cues do you notice that tells you are winding down or are going to stop? Then, what do you start doing as you finish the cutting?" Or "When the sexual compulsion starts to diminish and you are not feeling so compelled to go out and have sex with strangers, what do you start focusing on and doing instead?"

• *Find out about any helpful changes that have happened before treatment began.* Sometimes we therapists don't give our clients enough credit. At times, clients may have already begun solving the problem before they seek help. Just focusing on the problem enough to seek therapy can help the client make changes. It may be that the sense that they will get some help gives them enough hope and energy that they begin to make changes. The prospect of therapy can have a kind of flossing effect—the client begins to direct more attention and effort to the problem, in much the way we floss more vigorously or often in preparation of a visit to the dentist. Asking about positive pretreatment changes of this sort can yield important information about how people solve their problems or make changes (O'Hanlon & Weiner-Davis, 1989; Weiner-Davis, de Shazer, & Gingrich, 1987).

- *Search for contexts in which the person feels competent and has good problem-solving or creative skills.* These contexts may include hobbies or job skills. You might also identify situations in which the problem does not occur (e.g., work, in a restaurant, or whatever). Find out about times when the person or someone he or she knows has faced a similar problem and resolved it in a way that he or she liked—"vicarious situations" can be modeled or borrowed.

- *Ask why the problem isn't worse.* Have clients explain, in comparison to the worst possible state a person could be in, why their problem isn't that severe. This normalizes and helps put things in perspective and can give information about how clients restrain themselves from getting into worse trouble. Another way to do this is to ask the client to compare any incident of the problem to its worst manifestation and explain what is different about the times the problem is less severe.

METHODS OF ACKNOWLEDGING
WHILE OPENING POSSIBILITIES

It is important to acknowledge and validate clients' present painful problems without closing down for them the possibilities for change. Too much emphasis on change and possibility can give clients the message that the therapist does not understand or care about their suffering or dilemmas. Too much emphasis on the acknowledgment side can give the message that the client cannot change or encourages wallowing in the pain and hopelessness. The following methods are designed to combine both acknowledgment and invitations to change and possibility. Remember that these are suggested guidelines—if they start to become formulaic, they can be used disrespectfully or superficially. They are designed to be respectful and to deeply empathize with clients' suffering and possibilities.

Carl Rogers with a Twist: Introducing Possibilities into Past and Present Problem Reports

- Reflect back clients' problem reports with the problem restated into the past tense.

  CLIENT: I'm depressed.

  THERAPIST: So you've been depressed.

- When clients give generalities about their problems, introduce the possibility that the problem is not so general. Reflect clients' problem reports with qualifiers, usually of time (e.g., recently, in the last little while, in the past month or so, most of the time, much of the time), intensity (e.g., a bit less, somewhat more) or portion (e.g., a lot, some, most, many). Partialize totalizing statements.

CLIENT: I've been really depressed.

THERAPIST: You've been depressed most of the time lately.

- Translate clients' statements of the truth into statements of clients' perceptions or subjective realities.

CLIENT: From the things she has said and done, it is obvious she doesn't care for me or our marriage.

THERAPIST: Some of the things she's done have given you the sense she doesn't care.

The Moving Walkway: Introducing a Future with Possibilities

- Recast a problem statement into a statement about the preferred future or goal. Clarify what positive behavior or outcome is sought (e.g., "sleeping OK" rather than "stopping insomnia").

CLIENT: I think I'm just too shy to find a relationship. I'm afraid of women and being rejected.

THERAPIST: So you'd like to be able to get into a relationship?

- Use present or future tenses to bring reports of past helpful attention, action, and viewpoints into the client's current grasp or future expectations.

CLIENT: I stopped myself from bingeing by calling a friend.

THERAPIST: So one of the things you do to stop bingeing is call friends.

- Presuppose positive changes and progress toward goals by using words like *yet, so far, when,* and *will.*

CLIENT: I broke up with my girlfriend and can't seem to find another relationship.

THERAPIST: So you haven't gotten into a relationship yet. When you get into a relationship, we'll know we've done something useful here.

Specific Strategies

Here are some possibility therapy procedures used in therapeutic conversations. As noted, they must be used with real empathy, not as mechanical ploys.

• *Summarize, validate, and soften.* This strategy ensures that the therapist is listening adequately, as well as validating each person without taking sides. In addition, through slight word changes, the therapist can soften what might be a blaming or discouraging communication from one partner to another. In individual work, this can help to keep the possibilities for change open and help the person be less blaming or discouraged.

• *Use self-disclosure and storytelling.* This strategy has several functions. One is to join and equalize the relationship (we all have issues and struggles in life, not just clients). Another is to normalize by helping people realize that others may have the same kinds of issues, points of view, or feelings. Another purpose of this strategy is to suggest new possibilities for actions or points of view.

• *Identify and track specific problem patterns.* This helps the therapist understand what the clients are concerned about and how they experience the problematic situation. In addition to getting an idea of the identified problem, the therapist is searching for typical patterns in the problematic interactions or situations. This often involves the use of videotalk.

• *Identify and track solution patterns.* This strategy, often combined with getting specific, is used to evoke and highlight more helpful actions and points of view related to the problem based on the client's past experience.

• *Suggest possibilities.* This strategy offers ideas from the therapist's experience that might be helpful in the future, either based on what the person, couple, or family has said so far (usually derived from the solution patterns) or based on some ideas the therapist has. It is important to give these suggestions in a tentative manner, not to impose them on people. But it is just as important not to leave the therapist's ideas out of the conversation in the name of "neutrality" or a "nonexpert" position.

• *Name classes of solution or problems and initiate searches.* This strategy involves using vague, general words (*communication, frustration, love*) or inquiries ("It seems to me that all these situations have to do with either thinking or not thinking before you act.") to facilitate the evocation and organization of problem or solution categories or specific incidents that could be examples of those categories.

Inner Work in Possibility Therapy

Another method for doing possibility therapy involves *inner work*. It is based on the idea that people dissociate and devalue aspects of their experience as a result of their traumas and that these aspects begin to "have a life of their own," which can lead to inner or outer disturbances. As Carl Jung said, "Every part of us that we do not love will regress and become more primitive." I am suggesting that the things that people bring as symptoms or problems to therapy are hints about what parts of them that they haven't loved and that have regressed and become more primitive (see O'Hanlon, in Hoyt, 1996a). Let me explain how I came to this awareness:

> I saw a man, Jim, who had a severe case of obsessive compulsive disorder. Jim told me about the many intrusive obsessions he had. Jim's job was related to communication and teaching about communication. He would get so obsessed with thinking about how human beings communicate that he couldn't put

words and meanings together. Jim also suffered from other obsessions. When he was talking to someone, he would have this very vivid image of their rectum right in front of his face. As you might imagine, this was disruptive to his conversations. He would also develop this tension in his jaw and his neck and become terrified that he would have what he called "the Big Stutter," which was Jim's name for his fear that he would freeze up and not be able to communicate at all. This was his idea of Hell, since he lived to communicate. Jim also had a number of other obsessions, which I won't detail here. If one went away, another would immediately take its place. He was essentially symptomatic from the moment he woke up until the moment he went to sleep.

Jim didn't believe in hypnosis, but since the other forms of treatment he had tried (years of psychoanalysis, behavior therapy, marital therapy, and so on) were unsuccessful, I asked him to give it a try. We did a bit of hypnosis (see O'Hanlon & Martin, 1992) in the first session, but Jim looked very uncomfortable, moving around and tensing his facial muscles throughout the process. He wasn't impressed with the results but was willing to give it another try.

During the next appointment, I did a forty-minute hypnosis session with Jim. For about fifteen minutes during that trance, Jim was obsession-free—and continued to be for about two hours afterward. Even though Jim still wasn't convinced about hypnosis and didn't entirely believe he had been in trance, something seemed to have helped.

At the next session, Jim told me what had happened for him during the previous trances (or pseudotrances, since he didn't believe he'd been in one). Jim said he would have his obsessions, get tense, lose the meanings of words and begin to dwell on the idea that there would not be enough time for him to go into trance. So I began the next induction being extra careful to use the hypnotherapy language of inclusion and permission: "OK, for this trance you can keep your eyes open or you can close your eyes." Jim closed his eyes, as he usually did, and I said, "And as you're sitting there, I already know that you may be thinking you are not going to be able to go into trance, because we have talked too long and we don't have enough time now to do it. So you can think that, that's OK. You may be thinking that this trance stuff is a bunch of junk. And you can think that, that's OK. You may be distracted by one of your symptoms, maybe by the tension in your jaw and your neck. You may think you're too tense to go into trance and that's OK. You can be tense and you can still go into trance or you could relax. But you don't have to relax to go into trance. You can be thinking, wondering, how I'm coming up with the words that I'm coming up with and analyzing the words and sentences that I'm saying and that's OK. You might be worried about the Big Stutter and that's OK. You can just let yourself feel what you feel, think what you think, experience what you're experiencing—and not think what you don't think, not experience what you don't experience and not feel what you don't feel and you can continue to go into trance."

At that point Jim popped his eyes open. He said, "That's why I come here."

"So, you believe in trance now?"

Jim replied, "No, no. I still think that hypnosis is a bunch of shit. I come here to hear those words you just said. That's what helps me."

I said, "What do you mean?"

Jim said, "In some way, somehow, during the first couple of minutes of this thing that you call hypnosis, for a brief period of time I can't do anything wrong. It's the only time in my life when I can't do anything wrong. So you can skip this hypnosis stuff, but keep doing the stuff you are doing at the beginning of the hypnosis, because that's what is helping me."

That crystallized for me what I had been doing with many people, especially those people who had been abused. Their inner experience was often one of feeling that something (or everything) they were doing was somehow wrong. Having *all* of their experience validated and included is a very powerful intervention.

My approach, then, is to revalue people's devalued experiences. This is not just an abstract concept. I have been developing simple yet powerful methods for doing this revaluing.

• *First, I examine the symptoms that people are experiencing.* Is the person hallucinating? Plagued by feelings of fear? Inclined to get enraged beyond what is called for in the situation? I begin to focus on the recurring problem that the client or his or her intimates are complaining about.

• *From there, I extract a statement that is in the form of a positive or negative injunction:* "You shouldn't-can't-won't" *or* "You have to-must-should." These are akin to what have been called *negative symptoms* and *positive symptoms* in the area of schizophrenia. Negative symptoms refer to things that are normally present in people's experience but are notably lacking in *this* person's experience, such as flattened affect or an absence of emotion. Positive symptoms are things that are intrusive and amplified compared with the usual experience. For example, many people hear voices in their heads at times, but in disturbing psychotic experiences, the voices are much louder, intrusive, compelling, and congruent with my view of symptoms reflecting the devalued aspect of experience, usually unremittingly berating.

I construe these experiences as being driven by injunctions—statements about what the person must experience or is prohibited from experiencing. If the person is intruded upon by visual hallucinations, the injunction might be *You must see and attend to these images.* If the person feels fear most of the time, the injunction could be *You have to be afraid.* If the client has frequent rages, the injunction might be *You must be angry.*

• *Once I find the form of the injunction, I give permission and valuing messages to counteract this injunction.* For example, I might tell a person who has been hearing disturbing voices, *"You don't have to hear voices."* Or *"You can ignore the voices."* If the person is dominated by fear, the permission message might be *"You don't have to be afraid."* If the person is not experiencing any feelings at all, the permission message might be *"It's OK to feel."*

Permission can also be given in a way that includes both sides at once. *"You can be hallucinating and in touch with reality at the same time."* Or *"You can be frightened and calm at the same moment."*

It is vitally important not to give permission for destructive actions. I might say to someone, "You can feel like you want to scream and not scream." I would never suggest, "It's OK to scream at people." The permission, "You may feel so numb you feel like hurting yourself," is very different from giving someone the green light to self-destruct. I am only dealing with experience here. In my view, there are no inherently bad experiences, only those that have come to disturb the person because he, she, or someone else has considered that experience is wrong or sick and has decided that it must go.

POSSIBILITY THERAPY SUMMARY

- Acknowledge each person's feelings and points of view without closing down the possibilities for change.
- Search for exceptions to the problem.

  Gently steer the focus to what has happened when the problem hasn't occurred or has been less severe than usual.

  Don't try to convince clients of exceptions, let them convince you.

- Translate labels and vague words into action or process descriptions.

  Find video descriptions for labels. ("What does codependency, schizophrenia, or whatever look like?")

  Get specific about vague words and phrases. ("Something's bothering you? What specifically?" or "Everything?")

  Find action correlates for feelings and qualities. ("Tell me what kinds of things you do when you are depressed." "What would I see him doing when he is being narcissistic?" "How would I do a good depression if I learned your way of doing depression?")

- Focus on achievable goals and outcomes.

  Obtain a video description of actions or results that are under the person's or family's control that will be happening when the problem is solved. ("What would I see when he is being more considerate and loving?" or "How will someone know when she is being open?")

- Search for evidence of change and internal or external resources.

  When clients relate some positive change from the distant or recent past, find out in detail how they got the change to happen or influenced it.

Who or what has been helpful when they have been stuck or having difficulties previously.

- Suggest new ways of thinking about things or doing things.

Suggest different interpretations and actions involving the problem.

- Do inner work with problems that can be construed to be reflections of devalued aspects of people's experience (usually complaints about involuntary or automatic experiences).

Give permission and inclusion for the devalued aspects.

- Create a collaborative climate.

Equalize the power differential by including clients' views, reactions, and expertise whenever possible.

Give suggestions in a tentative way and acknowledge when your theories or biases are influencing you or steering the interview or interventions in a particular direction.

Endnote

1. *Editor's note:* Later in the same interview (Hoyt, 1994), Steve de Shazer elaborated: "To me . . . the danger of reading between the lines is that there might be nothing there. So you've just got to listen to what the client says. So just stick on the lines of things. The client says that getting out of bed on the south side makes for a better day than getting out of bed on the north side. Well then, goddammit, tell him to get out of bed on the south side. As crazy as it sounds." (p. 28). He also said, "A client tells you they've got a problem, then they've got a problem, and you better take it seriously. You also better take it seriously if they tell you they ain't got a problem. That's the other part of it. He comes in and somebody sent him because he drinks too much. He says he doesn't drink too much and it's not a problem. Leave it alone. Take it seriously" (pp. 29–30). De Shazer also made clear, "Don't let the theory get in the way. Theories will blind you" (p. 37). He went on to say, "I know what I don't want, and that's for anybody to develop some sort of rigid orthodoxies. I'm afraid of that. I'm always afraid of that. For me, it's a big point of concern. That there's a right way to do this and that. And to see my descriptions—and they've done this to me; I've probably done this to myself—to see my descriptions as prescriptions" (p. 39).

References

de Shazer, S. (1982). *Patterns of brief family therapy.* New York: Guilford Press.

de Shazer, S. (1985). *Keys to solution in brief therapy.* New York: Norton.

de Shazer, S. (1988). *Clues: Investigating solutions in brief therapy.* New York: Norton.

Hoyt, M. F. (1994). On the importance of keeping it simple and taking the patient seriously: A conversation with Steve de Shazer and John Weakland. In M. F. Hoyt (Ed.), *Constructive therapies* (pp. 11–40). New York: Guilford Press.

Hoyt, M. F. (1996a). Welcome to PossibilityLand: A conversation with Bill O'Hanlon. In M. F. Hoyt (Ed.), *Constructive therapies* (Vol. 2, pp. 87–123). New York: Guilford Press.

Hoyt, M. F. (1996b). A golfer's guide to brief therapy (with footnotes for baseball fans). In M. F. Hoyt (Ed.), *Constructive therapies* (Vol. 2, pp. 306–318). New York: Guilford Press.

Lipchik, E. (1994). The rush to be brief. *Family Therapy Networker, 18*(2), 34–39.

Nylund, D., & Corsiglia, V. (1994). Becoming solution-focused forced in brief therapy: Remembering something important we already knew. *Journal of Systemic Therapies, 13*(1), 5–12.

O'Hanlon, B. (1982). Strategic pattern intervention: An integration of individual and family systems therapies based on the work of Milton H. Erickson, M.D. *Journal of Strategic and Systemic Therapies, 1*(4), 26–33.

O'Hanlon, W. H. (1987). *Taproots: Underlying principles of Milton Erickson's therapy and hypnosis.* New York: Norton.

O'Hanlon, W. H. (1988). Solution-oriented therapy: A megatrend in psychotherapy. In J. K. Zeig & S. Lankton (Eds.), *Developing Ericksonian psychotherapy* (pp. 93–111). New York: Brunner/Mazel.

O'Hanlon, W. H. (1993a). Frozen in time: Possibility therapy with adults who were sexually abused as children. In L. VandeCreek, S. Knapp, & T. Jackson (Eds.), *Innovations in clinical practice: A sourcebook* (Vol. 12). Sarasota, FL: Professional Resource Press.

O'Hanlon, W. H. (1993b). Possibility therapy: From iatrogenic injury to iatrogenic healing. In S. G. Gilligan & R. Price (Eds.), *Therapeutic conversations* (pp. 3–17; with commentary by J. H. Weakland, pp. 18–21). New York: Norton.

O'Hanlon, B., & Beadle, S. (1994). *A field guide to PossibilityLand: Possibility therapy methods.* Omaha, NE: Possibilities Press.

O'Hanlon, W. H., & Martin, M. (1992). *Solution-oriented hypnosis: An Ericksonian approach.* New York: Norton.

O'Hanlon, W. H., & Weiner-Davis, M. (1989). *In search of solutions: A new direction in psychotherapy.* New York: Norton.

O'Hanlon, W. H., & Wilk, J. (1987). *Shifting contexts: The generation of effective psychotherapy.* New York: Guilford Press.

Walter, J., & Peller, J. (1992). *Becoming solution-focused in brief therapy.* New York: Brunner/Mazel.

Weiner-Davis, M., de Shazer, S., & Gingrich, W. J. (1987). Building on pretreatment change to construct the therapeutic solution: An exploratory study. *Journal of Marital and Family Therapy, 13*, 359–363.

CHAPTER EIGHT

Strange Attractors and the Transformation of Narratives in Family Therapy

Carlos E. Sluzki

The field of family therapy was born in the cauldron of interdisciplinary study. These origins provided us with a therapeutic approach for the relief of human suffering that was totally original and forced us to speak a language that was both novel and difficult: *information, feedback, metacommunication, circular causality, deviation-amplification* and *deviation-counteracting, self-fulfilling prophecies*—a language that today is familiar to us, and even sometimes old-fashioned.

Our interdisciplinary origins appear to have branded us in an indelible way, defining us as permanent inhabitants of an ever-changing frontier, destined to constantly explore new possibilities, challenging us with new languages that generate new horizons—that generate new languages. What was extraordinary yesterday is commonplace today, and what is extraordinary today may tomorrow become our guideline of choice for helping us think.

I embark on these introductory musings because I realize that what was difficult for me to grasp yesterday, the postmodern world of constructionism, is my orientation of choice today and, consequently, what was a foreign tongue for me yesterday, that of *narratives*, is now my customary language. However, instead of simply enjoying this familiarity, instead of harvesting the already

---

Note: A version of this chapter was given as a plenary address at the Congress of the Asociacion Sistemica de Buenos Aires, ASIBA, Buenos Aires, May 1997.

plowed and sown land, I find myself once again exploring new concepts, new languages.

In what follows I will present some ideas regarding clinical practices for narrative transformation (Sluzki, 1992a), framed in the languages of both social constructionism and Chaos Theory. An extended example from a consultation interview will illustrate the conceptual discourse.

CLINICAL PRACTICES:
FOCUSING ON NARRATIVE TRANSFORMATIONS

Seen through a postmodern lens, our activity as therapists consists of facilitating conversations that favor qualitative transformation in certain stories, namely, those that contain and maintain the problems or dilemmas or symptomatic behaviors that trigger our patients' or their families' consultation, stories that restrain them from the possibility of evolution or resolution or dissolution of those problems (e.g., see Anderson & Goolishian, 1988; Hoffman, 1989; Hoyt, 1994, 1996; McNamee & Gergen, 1992).

The therapeutic interview, if not the whole therapeutic process, consists of a set of activities occurring sequentially as well as simultaneously:

We specify and negotiate, sometimes explicitly and always implicitly, the politics of the encounter, aiming at establishing a modicum of agreement about the scope and boundaries of the therapeutic contract. This entails a negotiation about power, collective and individual responsibility, what will be defined as a problem, who has authorship and who has a voice, which values will guide us and will be respected, which are the thematic and ethical parameters that will be recognized as acceptable for the therapist and for each of the participants, and who will be in charge of monitoring the process. This agreement is a necessary precondition to enable us to become legitimate members of the conversational system.

Through our active exploration, we facilitate the description and enactment of stories that are dominant in the consulting system, from the point of view of each of the participants, as it unfolds throughout the interview.[1] We explore in this way the motives for the consultation and the explanatory hypotheses of each of the participants (Cecchin, 1987), clarifying, among others, the location of the functions *patient* (the locus of the problem) and *client* (the one seeking a change) (Watzlawick, Weakland, & Fisch, 1974), and existing alternative descriptions of their conflictual issues.

• In the course of that exploration, we generate information that proposes new elements, angles, logic, and priorities in the displayed stories or in the relationship among stories.

- The methodology used to generate that information—including circular questions, reframing, positive connotation, naive comments—has as one of its important effects that of destabilizing the structure or logic of the dominant stories in the complex web of narratives that constitute the reality of that family, through a process that, far from disqualifying the participants, provides them with authorship.

- Through that process, and responding to keys offered by the participants in the course of the session, we facilitate the transformation of the problem-based and problem-perpetuating stories into "better formed stories" that do not contain the problem as it has been described, or contain solutions or constructive alternatives, or displace the centrality of the original story within the complex web of narratives.

- Finally, we anchor the new stories through metaphors or examples that stem from, or resonate with, other stories and anecdotes provided throughout the session by that family, or through other models of consensus building such as homework, rituals, or prescriptions.

The narratives provided by the family about the nature of their problem are relatively stable and coherent systems: "This is the problem and these are the causes, explanations, ethical and behavioral consequences, and interpersonal implications." The aforementioned activities allow us, first, to incorporate ourselves as legitimate members of the network that maintains the original story and—without disqualifying that network—respectfully explore the stories that are brought to us, and then to reduce progressively the coherence of the narrative, challenging its presumed consensuality. In sum, we destabilize the narrative while we highlight, favor, or "seed" (Zeig, 1990) alternatives. Once legitimized by the participants, those alternatives are consolidated in such a way that they can be recognized, reconstituted, or incorporated as the participants' dominant descriptions.

Allow me to further explain one of the steps of this process. With our help, problem-maintaining stories become destabilized, disorganized, pushed further and further toward their threshold of disequilibrium (or "point of bifurcation," in the language of Prigoyine and Stengers, 1984; see also Elkaim, 1980; Elkaim, Goldbeter, & Goldbeter, 1980); that is, toward the limit beyond which a qualitative reorganization of the complex system unavoidably takes place. And—as happens in any system that reaches a point of bifurcation—when people's stories destabilize, people crave clarity, they seek ways to reconfigure and stabilize, to organize themselves once again with coherence. And while the specific shape of this new configuration is, in each case, unpredictable, our expectation is that the reconfigured story will not contain whatever was defined as the problem, or that it will contain novel solutions for it, or that another story will become the dominant one and overshadow the previous story. In summary, those who consult us will end the interview taking with them an alternate reality, grounded in a story that has more advantageous properties, that is "better formed" than the one with which they came.

THE DIRECTION OF THE CHANGE: STRANGE ATTRACTORS

Beyond being guided with "systemic optimism" (Stierlin, 1988), can we predict the direction of the transformation of a story? One first response to that question is, no, we can't; the evolution of complex self-organizing systems is, as we already mentioned, unpredictable. We can even bring to our aid the famous "Butterfly Effect"—a theoretical model of three systems with interconnected feedback loops proposed by Edward Lorenz and made famous by the felicitous metaphor that the flapping of the wings of a butterfly in one country may become a hurricane at the other end of the globe, a description that evokes the enormous complexity of the world's atmospheric system and hence the impossibility of long-range meteorological forecasts. This model served, in fact, to launch Chaos Theory into the scientific arena (Gleick, 1987; Capra, 1996).

However, Chaos Theory offers, in addition to a description of the problem, the sketch of a solution: while in each specific case it is impossible to predict the outcome of an evolving dynamic system, it is possible to predict qualitative traits in the evolution of those systems, as the so-called chaotic behavior contains *steps,* that is, entails deterministic patterns. The key to these steps lies in what in the mathematical world of the theory of complex systems are called *attractors:*

- Systems in stable equilibrium are organized around *punctual attractors.* A simplified example would be a pendulum in motion, whose punctual attractor is the neutral point of gravity, to which it ends up yielding.

- Systems close to equilibrium with predictable oscillations contain *periodical attractors.* A simplified example would be the effect on the waves of the shifting gravitational pull of the moon.

- Systems that are further away from equilibrium contain *strange attractors.* A simplified example would be the overall design of the trajectory of a marble made to roll in a basin.

When a complex system is destabilized until it reaches a bifurcation point, the system effectively chooses between various states or possible changes and organizes itself around them following steps that are generically predictable while, in each case, idiosyncratic. In summary, given certain conditions, the system changes qualitatively in a predictable fashion.

Trying to translate these processes to our field, in the course of a therapeutic consultation, and with the help of our destabilizing participation (Sluzki, 1992a), the relatively stable narrative that contains and maintains the problem becomes unbalanced. Now, when we push the conversing system (which includes us) toward disequilibrium, toward those thresholds of bifurcation, is it possible to influence the direction of the change? The answer is, as I hinted earlier, quantitatively no but qualitatively yes. It so happens that, in the course of the session, by the way in which we manage the therapeutic dialogue, we generate in and with our clients (or at least we plant the seed along the way for) a series of possible options, a set of potential strange attractors, that contribute to the probability that the presenting stories will be reconfigured around those new organizing principles as stories that are distinctly and qualitatively different, that have a "better form."

These "better-formed stories" (Sluzki, 1992b) contain scripts that:

- Appeal to (resonate with, attract) those who consult us.
- Are richer in connections between individuals and contexts.
- Do not require the presence of stereotyping and self-perpetuating diagnostic labels.
- Contain assumptions about evolution and change, progress and hope.
- Define the participants as active, competent, responsible, and reflexive.
- Presuppose that the participants follow ethical and moral principles such as good intent, self-respect and respect for the other, avoidance of suffering, promotion of evolution and change, and sense of collective responsibility.

A CONSULTATION INTERVIEW: "WE ARE BORN WEARING A SCAPULAR"

To exemplify this series of concepts, I will present transcribed fragments of an interview, with interspersed comments, that I conducted last year in a Spanish-speaking country with a family of farmers from a small town and two family therapists involved in their care.

The family was composed of a couple, sixty-six and fifty-six years old, and their four children—two daughters, thirty and twenty years old, and two sons, twenty-eight and eighteen. The twenty-eight-year-old son, Virgilio, had been a client of the region's mental health and chemical dependency services for many years, with behaviors that, over the years, had been clearly deviant and disruptive. He was an insulin-dependent early-onset diabetic, about five feet tall, with borderline intellectual ability, a long history of alcohol abuse, and a track record of never having lived outside of the family house nor having developed steady skills or interests. In contrast, his three siblings were autonomous and self-motivated. His oldest sister, a high school teacher, lives in a neighboring city, his second sister studied philosophy at a university and also lived on her own, and his younger brother was finishing high school and had plans to leave home to continue his studies.

For the past year and a half Virgilio had participated in the programs of a day hospital, where he was also engaged in individual therapy sessions every two weeks and, very occasionally, in family interviews. In spite of the relentless enticement of the therapeutic team, he had failed to develop any initiative toward autonomy, maintaining instead passive, irresponsible behavior.

The current therapists had conducted two family interviews prior to this consultation. They described this family, and specifically the father, as difficult to reach and impervious to the therapeutic team. They requested this consultation to expand their options, since they experienced themselves as stalled in an impasse. More specifically, they wished to see Virgilio develop autonomous plans and leave home, rather than remain passive and overattached.

The following fragments are from our consultation interview. Ellipses in parentheses (. . .) indicate breaks in the transcription. Simple ellipses indicate pauses by the speakers.

CONSULTANT: Good afternoon. How are you all? In the first place, thank you very much for having come here today. As you know, I come as a consultant, at the request of the therapeutic team. Since I have experience working with families with problems, they asked me to join them, just for this time. They were just beginning to tell me some things about the work they have done with you—you are the patient, right?—and with you all. And by what they told me, my impression is that in recent time there have been a series of positive changes in your lives. Is that the case as you see it?

(. . .)

FATHER: I believe so, he is better, because now he is more entertained. The most important thing is to be busy and entertained, as I think that what he needs is to be more relaxed and more calm. Because we have already told him that if this young man worked, and earned even a few cents, well, he would be happy. But at least he comes *[to the day hospital]* and it is as if he would be working, because he is busy and . . . he is better.

CONSULTANT: OK, good. And what is your point of view, ma'am?

MOTHER: I think that he has improved a lot in comparison to before. He has improved, but he hasn't changed the situation much, because I think that his expectations . . . what I think he wants I don't think he has. He is better, but I don't think that he has what he wants. He has improved, because at home he was very desperate. If he is always at home he despairs. So he plans to be, I don't know if with other people or like that, I think that among us he is a little . . . he is pressured because . . . I don't know why.

(. . .)

CONSULTANT: But fundamentally, in your life, is that also the way you sense it?

VIRGILIO: Yes, I have improved, but, well, I continue to become desperate. I haven't finished taking off.

CONSULTANT: You haven't finished . . . ?

VIRGILIO: I haven't finished choosing a path. I continue to be where I was in the beginning, without making up my mind. I haven't finished choosing a path, and also when I get desperate it is because I think that I am never going to find my path.

CONSULTANT: So, is it in that sense that you are desperate?

VIRGILIO: One step backwards, one step forwards and six backwards, and I finish every time at the same spot. That is, I stop myself. Each time that I try to do something for myself right away I stop myself.

CONSULTANT: And what is it that stops you?

VIRGILIO: Well, I think the family in general.

CONSULTANT: The family stops you? In what way can the family . . . ?

VIRGILIO: With their commentaries. That is, they hold me as much as they can, most of all my parents, as much as they can. They seem to get something out of that. Since I am not very secure and I have little faith in myself, well, they say, "Don't move from here," perhaps.

The "official story" is being displayed, centered in Virgilio's inability to move away from home as well as implicating his parents as the ones to blame (a not too infrequent byproduct of individual therapy). I begin to destabilize the story through challenging those assumptions.

CONSULTANT: What benefit would they get from stopping you, from holding you down?

VIRGILIO: Like, since I was young I have had problems, they want to protect me so much and I, to a certain degree, I allow them to.

CONSULTANT: However, they *[the therapists]* say that some things have changed for the good, right?

VIRGILIO: Yes, the relationship with my parents is better.

CONSULTANT: What have you all done in order to be able to improve relations between you?

This question further challenges the blame-based logic of the story—in itself one of the strange attractors around which the story seems to be organized. This is immediately picked up by one of the alleged culprits.

FATHER: Well, talking. Before, for example, I wouldn't say anything to this one because the man would escape and I couldn't say anything to him. And what Virgilio has said about us holding him down, I don't see that. . . .

CONSULTANT: That is his opinion. My question is, how have you managed to improve the relationships between you all?

FATHER: I already told you before. A person that comes from my town—I live in a small town and I have seen it—goes to a city and wants to hide, as it were. Instead, if you come from the capital you are open and loose and you talk and nobody stops you. Is that the way it is or is it not?

CONSULTANT: Aha, yes, yes.

FATHER: And this one *[Virgilio],* since he started to go to X *[the capital city],* he is less inhibited, more relaxed.

CONSULTANT: What you are saying is that these are your son's achievements?

FATHER: I think he is better, he has gained a lot, I think he is better, a lot, sometimes he walks here, other times. . . .

CONSULTANT: Excuse me. Not only does your son deserve the credit because he has opened up, because he has grown with his experience in the capital, but *you* also deserve some credit. You were saying that it is as if he is less inhibited, less fearful. . . .

FATHER: I am delighted. These ones *[his other offspring and his wife]* can talk with him, but I have to be careful to talk to him about things; anything that I could tell him he takes it wrong. Now it seems that he doesn't take it so wrong. He is desperate with his life. And I tell him, "Look, you shouldn't become desperate with your life because you are fine. If you are a diabetic, well, you are a diabetic," I have told him many times. "There are others who are worse off than you, that have their legs cut off, for example, that is very serious, it is sad." He already goes to the capital by himself, and comes back, he goes biking, I think that is fine. I think, if he would be working it would be well, very well, but he has the misfortune that the current job market is so bad that no one can find a job. He becomes desperate because he thinks that no job is ever going to come to him, which is very sad, because we don't need to take him to an office. He could do another type of job.
(. . .)

A non-blaming, patient-centered variation is proposed—an alternative "official story," carried by the father and organized around two attractors: outside circumstances—the job market—and Virgilio's limitations. In the following fragment I begin to enrich it and add future orientation, while essentially not challenging it—for the time being.

CONSULTANT: So you say that you want to go and work at a supermarket. Your sister had a reasonable idea: If you want *[to work]* you can go *[to the work place]* to find out. I had another reasonable idea: if I have a friend who is working, I would ask that friend to take me with him. What do you think about it?

VIRGILIO: I won't move, for example, to go to the supermarket and tell them that I want to work, that is what I am lacking. I say that I could work in many places; but to move, impossible.

CONSULTANT: And in what way could your family help you to move in this regard? Because if you don't have any experience looking for a job, then that is going to become more difficult, that is, if in your life you haven't developed the experience to look for a job. . . .

VIRGILIO: I don't know, perhaps by telling me directly to do it. They don't tell me either.

CONSULTANT: What do you mean by "tell you"? Who would be the person who has to do that? Who has the strongest voice, so that you would do it without resenting it?

VIRGILIO: Well, my father.

CONSULTANT: Uh huh, so it is your father who would have to help you. Uh huh.
(. . .)

FATHER: No, I have told him that he has to try and get jobs that are a little special, because in construction it's hard, I don't want him to work in construction either, it would be too hard. But if he can go to the supermarket, perfect, that would be lighter, or something similar.

CONSULTANT: A supermarket job wouldn't necessarily be lighter, but you don't have any reason to have to do light work, you are not a weak person, right?

VIRGILIO: Yes, yes.

CONSULTANT: So it is like any other job. OK now, once you are working, for instance, in a supermarket, do you think that your folks are going to be worried about you, or that they are going to get used to having a son who works?

The father has raised issues that may restrain an expanded story of Virgilio's options. Note that I attribute the concerns to the father, not Virgilio. And the focus becomes "the worries" rather than Virgilio's limitations, potentially a very different story.

VIRGILIO: *[mumbles]* Still, or that I am more worried about them than about myself.

CONSULTANT: What, what?

VIRGILIO: That still I would be more worried.

FATHER: About us? And why?

CONSULTANT: You would be more worried?

VIRGILIO: Yes, just the same, yes.

FATHER: How are you going to be more worried about us!

VIRGILIO: That is what you think, but also I would not be happy working. I have already told Mom that many times.

Mother is invited by the son as a spokesperson and she obliges readily, providing in the process an extremely important piece of information.

MOTHER: What is going on is that Virgilio finds himself with a problem, namely, that by remaining at home—we work in agriculture—he becomes more inhibited, as we tell him. He should feel free, like his brother does. Sometimes we are born wearing a scapular,[2] I don't know how to say it: "This one is for the house." It seems like Virgilio has picked that up, too. That one *[the other son]* has said, "Me, I am going to study, the farming is not for me." I would say that all the kids have done the same, but this one *[Virgilio]* is a little stuck. But it is not that he completely dislikes agriculture either. Virgilio likes it, really, he finds pleasure at home, but he is not totally into it because agriculture is very hard and he doesn't see himself with the capacity to take it on alone. He doesn't manage the tractor. If he did, well, he would be set. But the cattle are the only thing that he understands.
(. . .)

I highlight the new information and begin to enhance a story around it to "capture" all the participants around this new "attractor."

CONSULTANT: *[to Virgilio]* Do you see it the way your mother does? Oh, that's a different perspective on the subject! *[to the mother]* What a good observation! So—of course, now I understand—you are at home, but it is not that you are home so that your folks can take care of you; what happens is that you become part of the farm team.

MOTHER: Yes, he feels more included, while the others, already since the beginning, they have, well. . . .

CONSULTANT: And what would be inconvenient with you being part of the farm team? Wow, was I following a wrong track! Why would you want to work at the supermarket if, in fact, you can be a part of the farm team at home?

MOTHER: Do you want me to answer? No, well, it would be better if he is the one who says it.

VIRGILIO: Because I haven't yet become a member of the team.

CONSULTANT: How would it be to become a member? How would it be for you to incorporate yourself more, feel that you have become a member?

VIRGILIO: By doing more things.

CONSULTANT: Such as, for example, which are the things that you don't do but could do?

VIRGILIO: For example, I could do everything with the animals.

CONSULTANT: The animals, uh huh. And what is it that made you decide to not do that?

VIRGILIO: Well, not now, at least. Broadly speaking, my father. As long as my father is there I think it is very complicated for me to get into it.

CONSULTANT: Uh huh. What is it that is complicated for you? In what way does it seem complicated to you?

VIRGILIO: He makes it complicated, my father isn't going to let me do things. As long as he is there, I am not going to do it.

CONSULTANT: And what, are you going to wait until your father is stricken by a lightning bolt during a storm?

FATHER: *[laughing]* This is really good!

MOTHER: *[laughing]* Oh, what a disaster! *[everyone laughs]*

CONSULTANT: That is a bad way to do it, the lightning bolt method, because you might have to wait thirty more years.

MOTHER: They can't do it, they have never done things together, I don't know why, but. . . .

CONSULTANT: *[to the father]* And you, do you take care of the animals?

FATHER: Well, everyone does it, she *[the mother]* does, too.

VIRGILIO: Me? *[implying "Me, never!"]*

FATHER: When I am there, well, I go with him, between the two of us we do it, we feed the cattle, and I have cows, and I milk them, because I think that—

MOTHER: That no one can milk them like he does.

FATHER: That someone could get kicked, they could get angry.

CONSULTANT: Kick someone? Who can kick whom? A cow would kick Virgilio, or Virgilio will kick the cow? *[general laughter]*

FATHER: Either one, it could be either one.

MOTHER: What happens is that—

FATHER: Virgilio still hasn't told me, "Let me milk the cows today, I am going to do the milking today." At home now we milk mechanically but before I milked by hand, and well, often my mother milked and I would tell her, "I am going to do the milking today." I would get less milk because I wasn't used to doing it, but this one has still never told me, "I am going to do the milking today."

VIRGILIO: Nor will I say it to him.

CONSULTANT: Why, aren't you interested in milking?

FATHER: For me it is a little bit difficult to say, "Go do the milking."

CONSULTANT: *[to Virgilio]* Why is it that you don't tell him? You must have a reason for not telling him that.

VIRGILIO: Because of the comments that he would make later.

CONSULTANT: For example, what?

VIRGILIO: *[to the father]* You know very well.

CONSULTANT: But *I* don't know, that is why I am asking. What comments do you believe your father would make to you?

VIRGILIO: That I did it wrong!

CONSULTANT: Ah!

FATHER: But I think it is just fine if you don't do it right the first time!

VIRGILIO: What I want is a chance to do it for the first time.

FATHER: What I want is for you to tell me, "I'll go for it!" and I would tell you, "Well, look, this is done this way." "All right," you would tell me, "*you* do it."

CONSULTANT: So you are very sensitive to criticism from your father.

This relabeling destabilizes the cohesion of the prior description. In fact, it proposes a drastic reorganization of the story: It locates the responsibility in Virgilio (the issue is no longer father's criticism but Virgilio's sensitivity) while the label does not entail a negative trait (it is just that being too sensitive is problematic). This description may also facilitate father's acceptance of the new story: "It is not that I am doing things wrong, but that he is very sensitive to my criticism."

VIRGILIO: Yes, and that is what stops me. That is, if I start to do something and he tells me, or I understand that he doesn't think I am doing it right, well, I won't do it.

CONSULTANT: So it is much more difficult for you to learn.

VIRGILIO: Learn, and do.

CONSULTANT: Of course it is much more difficult, because to do you have to learn, and to learn one must learn by making mistakes, right? One learns by the criticism of the others. But if you are very sensitive to the criticism of your father, it is a difficult situation.

VIRGILIO: Yes. For example, that same comment, coming from other people who aren't my father. . . .

CONSULTANT: . . . You would tolerate.

VIRGILIO: . . . I would tolerate it, I wouldn't take it wrong.
(. . .)

In the following fragment I attempt to expand and anchor the new story, organized around Virigilio's sensitivity, by exploring whatever resonances it may have with his father's story.

CONSULTANT: *[to the father]* My question is, in your life experience, when you were young or an adolescent, were you also easily hurt or sensitive, or were you a person who was like your other children, with a less sensitive skin?

FATHER: Like my other children?

CONSULTANT: You, how were you like when you were twenty or twenty-two years old?

FATHER: Well, I don't know what to tell you.

CONSULTANT: The question is if you were a person. . . .

FATHER: Sensitive? I think I was not sensitive.

CONSULTANT: No. *[to the mother]* How old was he when you met him?

MOTHER: How old was he? When he was thirty years old, something like that.

CONSULTANT: And you, how old were you when you met him?

MOTHER: Me, ten years younger.

CONSULTANT: So, he was thirty and you were twenty. How, of all of the people in the world, did the two of you meet each other and form a couple?[3]

MOTHER: *[exchange of glances between them, with a broad smile and a hint of shyness]* Very difficult.

FATHER: [also smiling shyly] Well, it is easy.

(. . .)

CONSULTANT: And the farm where you are living, is it your family's or are you the owner?

FATHER: The farm? I bought it, I bought it.

MOTHER: Well, it was passed down from his parents.

CONSULTANT: So part of the family history is in this farm also. What also makes it important is that there be a person from this generation working on the farm, right?

FATHER: Well, now, I don't know if you know about this, but a lot of people have abandoned farming, it isn't the same as it was before, when a person would stay home more than anything else, you know, then it was a good business. Today people have gotten bored.

MOTHER: Today, here, if young people find a job they don't stay in the countryside.

FATHER: Yes, if they found work, none would stay in town.

(. . .)

FATHER: [to Virgilio] I have already told you more than once: I would like for you to look for a job so that you can appreciate what work is. Because you can always come back home, as it has happened to many people. Like the people who have gone to the Americas and have stayed for two weeks, thinking that they were going to bring their wallets filled with money, and they came back in two weeks stripped clean. I can understand why they don't go over there so much anymore. You [to consultant] are from there and you would know that many people have gone—from my family many, and from her family, too—and some have come right back, saying that that is a swindle, that there is no business there. And he can do the same, to go to look for work in the city and wherever, and then, "I don't like that job."

(. . .)

I then endeavor to enhance the mother's connections as well, and make more explicit an alternative construction that may encompass both the son's possible wish to remain on the farm and his father's possible wish to protect him.

CONSULTANT: [to the mother] Your work, do you enjoy it, or no?

MOTHER: Well, I don't dislike it.

CONSULTANT: You, sir, your job, do you like it?

FATHER: Farming? Yes, I do like it.

CONSULTANT: . . . In spite of seeing little future in that activity?

MOTHER: I don't see a lot of future in it. Of course, it is hard and—

CONSULTANT: I am trying to know why are you protecting your son from choosing farming, as if it had more disadvantages than advantages.

FATHER: I like the job that I have, but I am lamenting not having gone to work in a factory when I could have, as I did have that kind of an offer. But by then a person was forced to stay home. I have told him *[Virgilio]* to do what he wants.

CONSULTANT: I didn't totally understand what you just said.

MOTHER: It's that when a person does. . . . We, parents, often influence our children from the time they are born, as well as before they are born. And we want them to do all the things that we were unable to do ourselves, generally.

CONSULTANT: *[to the mother]* Did his *[the father's]* brothers leave from. . . .

MOTHER: They were free, they didn't feel tied.

CONSULTANT: And he was the one who stayed and says. . . .

MOTHER: Yes, and he continuously complains: "They left me here." Well, you should have gone! But he only wishes that he had left. Do you understand, it is that now. . . .

CONSULTANT: *[to the therapists]* What I realize is that everything was the reverse from what I was thinking! In fact, he *[the father]* is trying to protect his son so he wouldn't repeat his own situation. So he tells him—

FATHER: I keep him free to go wherever he wants.

CONSULTANT: Exactly, you are protecting him.

FATHER: I am not going to force him to stay or to leave.

CONSULTANT: No, quite the contrary. Even more. . . .

FATHER: He should be free.

CONSULTANT: I find your attitude very noble.

FATHER: Look, my father has told me that many times, when I was twenty years old—I am the oldest of the brothers. . . . Since I was ten years old I have been in this world doing the work I do now, and I have been told this many times. . . . I would tell him, "What am I doing here? I don't like to be pushed and pulled because I am the oldest," and I would tell him, "I am going to leave and go work somewhere else." He would tell me, "If you go I will get rid of the farm." He would leave the business, and then I would tell myself, "If I leave this . . . it would be a shame if another would take advantage of it." If I would have gone to work—at home there were others, my parents that could work, my brothers, and I was twenty years old, I was old enough to make a decision—perhaps I would have crashed. He would tell me that *[that he would sell the farm]* over and over again. For me that would have been very unpleasant: it would make me feel guilty, that because of me he had left the business, that because of me he would have sold it and someone else would run it. I don't know what would have happened. So I have resisted, and because of that I realize that one can't do that to a son. Instead, if he goes to work, I won't tell him that I will leave the business; I will continue on the farm until I die, if I can.

This moving revelation begins to anchor the new story. The consultant underlines it to anchor it in the therapists, that is, to help them change their own story of the family's problem.

CONSULTANT: *[to the therapists]* The interesting thing is that the father is protecting the son from repeating his own fate. It is very moving. *[to the father]* He is telling you, "Maybe I want to stay on the farm." And you are telling him, "Son, don't repeat my mistake!" You are regretting your decision of many years ago, you are thinking, "I should have gone somewhere else, to work outside," and you want to protect him against repeating what for *you* may have been a mistake.

FATHER: Not a mistake. I think that a person has to be somewhere.

CONSULTANT: True, it is your philosophy of life.

FATHER: I don't know if it would have been better or worse if I would have gone, I don't know.

CONSULTANT: Of course. That is why. . . .

FATHER: And that is why I tell him that he should try and go somewhere to work. If he doesn't like it, I am going to say, "Hey, if you don't like it. . . ." He is free, he can decide. If he wants, I can go with him wherever.

The tenacity of the corollary of the father's own life experience attempts against the new version. I challenge him, counting on having already established with him an empathic connection.

CONSULTANT: You are telling him that he is free to go.

MOTHER: And to stay, too.

CONSULTANT: That I am not so sure. *[to the father]* You are telling your son that he is free to go. Now, is he free to stay?

FATHER: Also.

CONSULTANT: But you, as a responsible father, think that you don't want him to repeat your mistakes. So, each time he says, "I want to stay," you tell him, "Why don't you go away for a while?" I think it is very noble on your part.

FATHER: Noble?

CONSULTANT: Of course, you do it in order for him not to repeat what has been for you the heavy load of a doubt: "What would have happened in my life if I had gone away to work? Maybe everything would have been very different."

FATHER: Yes.

CONSULTANT: It is the drama of your life, right?

FATHER: Yes.

CONSULTANT: So, since it is the drama of your life, you want to protect your son so he wouldn't repeat your drama. You want to make sure that he doesn't suffer. So you keep on telling him, "Go away, go away, go away." Well, this is your way of protecting him.

FATHER: *[agreeing]* Or else I don't tell him anything.

CONSULTANT: Well, it is your way to protect him. *[to the son]* Now I understand what you were saying about not being able to decide to stay. Because your father's message is, "Man, if you stay you haven't looked into the possibilities." Now, if you would consider working away from home it would be in order to please him, not because you want to make a career away from home. What a trap, right? (. . .) "I want to leave because he wants me to leave to go explore the world so that I don't repeat his life's mistakes. If I want to stay and I do, I am repeating his drama, and I don't want to frustrate him." I think that the alliance between the two of you is extremely intense and strong and loving.
(. . .)

FATHER: And I can tell you more: the problem that I told you about was that my brothers were working in the capital city, while I, who was the oldest, didn't earn anything at home.

MOTHER: Well, the problem . . . your son has the same problem, he doesn't earn anything.

CONSULTANT: Even more parallels.

The interview closed with comments about the usefulness of continuing this conversation in subsequent sessions, and with expressions of appreciation and gratitude to and by the family.[4]

Discussion

As occurs with any interview, this text can be analyzed from many perspectives.[5] From among them I will choose to comment on two, namely, the *locus* of my effort and the *specific processes* that were fostered.

I am a consultant, so my clients are the therapists that bring the family to the consultation. In the presentation that therapists make of a family I take for granted (how could it be otherwise!) that their description contains their own prejudices and difficulties, and their request is, in a generic way, that I help them to see the family differently, that I broaden their repertoire of alternative plausible narratives and, as a result, I help them generate different corollaries. The therapists involved in this consultation had already treated this patient in an institutional setting for a long time with an individual focus and with one goal in mind, namely, his independence—which represented the father's proposal that his son should go away to work, and which unavoidably ascribed negativity to the alternative, namely, to stay at home. Given this description, what they were trying to do was very logical, namely, to help the patient achieve independence by means of enticing him to seek work in the city. And when the results didn't reward their efforts, they did what we all tend to do in such circumstances, namely, more of the same. A hypothesis derived from these brave efforts was that there was something in the family that was working against their goals. And when the family was interviewed, the therapeutic team found that the description they held of the problem tended to be confirmed, as the family "didn't cooperate"—it was a "rigid" family.

As mentioned before, my responsibility as a consultant is to help in the consensual development of alternate descriptions that could be different enough to generate, among other attributes, different therapeutic corollaries. The description that the therapists made entailed a polarized battle between a son who was trying to become independent and parents who were retaining him, sabotaging his efforts to become self-sufficient. This description derived from premises that probably guided the therapists even before the first family interview. In consonance with that first description, my own first view of the parents, especially of the father, was, I would say, two-dimensional, poor, without texture. My first contact with them, in fact, corroborated that description: the father appeared to be closed up, inexpressive, primitive, insensitive; the mother, on the contrary, with vivacious eyes, was connected, expressive, the willing spokesperson for both parents and for the son. Hence, a good part of my own action during the first part of the interview was guided by my interest in multidimensionalizing *within myself* the image of the father, enriching it, making it more attractive to my own eyes, while disengaging from the story that had colonized them and me, one in which the son wanted to leave home to work outside but couldn't (a plot that defined him as pathological) or wasn't allowed (a plot that defined the parents as pathological). In fact, to disengage myself meant to disengage *us*, in other words, my supposition was that my changes could only occur in conversation, through collectively generating change in the unfolding and enacted story about the nature of the problem.

As I hope became clear in the example, once the story was destabilized, once it passed a "point of bifurcation," it tended to reorganize itself quickly around new attractors loaded both with familiarity and novelty: familiarity because it emerged from material provided by the participants, and novelty because it was qualitatively different from the "official story" offered by the therapists and described and enacted by the family in the first part of the interview. The qualities of the novel story were sufficient to predict its survival: it contained dramatic contextualized elements of the family history and was therefore recognizable by the family; it contained ethical values that were consonant with those of the family; it defined central players as capable, responsible people with good intentions; it presupposed in the participants self-respect and respect for each other, the desire to favor the evolution and to avoid the suffering of the other; and it opened the possibilities for solutions that the previous story didn't contain.[6]

O

My daily clinical experience continues, after all these years, to leave me in awe: we converse *in a certain way* with the people who consult with us (and that "certain way" is, indeed, the subject of this and so many other books!), and desirable qualitative transformations take place in the dominant stories and behaviors of the participants—myself included. The complex system of which we become an active part during a consultation may evolve in idiosyncratic fashions, but the result of our participation is frequently a story with an elegant design, and with liberating and empowering effects for all the participants.

Endnotes

1. The boundary of the consulting system is, in fact, arbitrary. For practical purposes we may define a consultation as *individual-centered* (but with whom does this individual share his or her reality?), as a *couple session* (but in what other social and meaning-sharing systems are these two people involved?), as a *family interview* (but what about the teacher who suggested the consultation because of the behavior of a child and has already proposed a diagnostic label to the family or assigned responsibility to the parents?), or as another *social network consultation* (such as family plus therapists, like the consultation that will be discussed later in this chapter or any other meaningful network).

2. In Spanish, *Nacemos con un escapulario puesto*—meaning that we are born with a preordained fate or life pathway.

3. This paradigmatic question ("How, of all the millions of people in the world, did the two of you get together?") has been systematically used since 1957 by the Bateson team and by researchers and clinicians at the Mental Research Institute, Palo Alto (see Watzlawick, 1966). Each time I chose to pose it I rediscover its strong evocatory power.

4. Because of an artifact derived from the choice of fragments, Virgilio's three siblings appear only as silent participants in the interview. That was not the case, since they were actively included at several moments. All in all, however, the position of the three tended to be relatively marginal, offering few interesting opinions and indicating (explicitly and through their body language) their desire to be left out of the discussion.

5. It could be analyzed, for example, from the *structural* point of view, identifying three subsystems: intergenerational alliance (mother-Virgilio), the subsystem composed by the three autonomous siblings, and the father as an isolated individual although occasionally protected by the mother. Maintaining that view, it could be described that the centrality of the mother, such as it unfolds at the beginning of the interview, was progressively reduced through a valorization of the relationship father-Virgilio and the enhancement in the protagonist position of the father. It could also be analyzed from a *trigenerational* view, defining that the process that took place in the session was one of discovery and denunciation of a sequence of "destiny without alternatives" transmitted from generation to generation against which both father and son fought in vain, while they perpetuated it with their ambivalence. It could also be explained as a paradigmatic *double bind* situation, and assume that the paralysis of Virgilio is the effect of a double message-in-context—"Do what you want" but "Don't repeat my mistakes"; "You are free" but "Obey me"; "You are the oldest son, the chosen one, and this condemns you"—in which case the therapeutic exorcism would consist of challenging the rules that prohibit metacommunication. And so on.

6. *Editor's note:* Notice the possible connections between strange attractors and the "preferred views" that Thomas Lund and Joseph Eron describe in Chapter Eighteen and the "empathic narratives" that Haim Omer describes in Chapter Twenty-One; all of these concepts suggest happier, more optimistic and empowered perspectives that appeal because they fit both the "facts" and the participants' desires (see Watzlawick, Weakland, & Fisch, 1974, p. 95).

References

Anderson, H., & Goolishian, H. A. (1988). Human systems as linguistic systems: Evolving ideas about the implications of theory and practice. *Family Process, 27,* 371–393.

Capra, F. (1996). *The web of life.* New York: Anchor.

Cecchin, G. (1987). Hypothesizing, circularity, and neutrality revisited: An invitation to curiosity. *Family Process, 26,* 405–413.

Elkaim, M. (1980). From general laws to singularities. *Family Process, 24,* 151–154.

Elkaim, M., Goldbeter, A., & Goldbeter, E. (1980). Analyse des transitions de comportement dans un systeme familial en termes de bifurcations [Analysis of behavioral transitions in a family system in terms of bifurcations]. *Cahiers Critiques de Therapie Familiale et de Pratiques de Réseaux, 3,* 18–34.

Gleick, J. (1987). *Chaos: Making of a new science.* New York: Penguin.

Hoffman, L. (1989). A constructivist position for family therapy. *Irish Journal of Family Therapy, 9,* 110–129.

Hoyt, M. F. (Ed.). (1994). *Constructive therapies.* New York: Guilford Press.

Hoyt, M. F. (Ed.). (1996). *Constructive therapies* (Vol. 2). New York: Guilford Press.

McNamee, S., & Gergen, K. J. (Eds.). (1992). *Therapy as social construction.* Newbury Park, CA: Sage.

Prigoyine, I., & Stengers, I. (1984). *Order out of chaos: Man's new dialogue with nature.* New York: Bantam, 1984.

Sluzki, C. E. (1992a). Transformations: A blueprint for narrative changes in therapy. *Family Process, 31*(3), 217–230.

Sluzki, C. E. (1992b). The "better-formed" story. In G. Cecchin & M. Mariotti (Eds.), *L'Adolescente e i suoi sistemi.* Rome: Kappa.

Stierlin, H. (1988). Systemic optimism—systemic pessimism: Two perspectives on change. *Family Process, 27,* 121–127.

Watzlawick, P. (1966). A structured family interview. *Family Process, 5,* 256–271

Watzlawick, P., Weakland, J. H., & Fisch, R. (1974). *Change: Principles of problem formation and problem resolution.* New York: Norton.

Zeig, J. K. (1990). Seeding. In J. K. Zeig & S. G. Gilligan (Eds.), *Brief therapy: Myths, methods, and metaphors* (pp. 221–246). New York: Brunner/Mazel.

PART TWO

CONVERSATIONS AND SONGS

CHAPTER NINE

Constructing Therapeutic Realities

A Conversation with Paul Watzlawick

Paul Watzlawick, Michael F. Hoyt

No one has done more to explicate the theory and practice of constructivist and interactional approaches in psychotherapy than Paul Watzlawick. Long affiliated with the Mental Research Institute in Palo Alto, California, during his distinguished career he has been the recipient of numerous awards for his many outstanding contributions. He has also been honored as a senior faculty member at each of the three Evolution of Psychotherapy conferences (held in 1985, 1990, and 1995). A prolific and extraordinarily erudite writer and editor, his eighteen books (of which there exist more than seventy foreign-language editions) include *Pragmatics of Human Communication* (Watzlawick, Beavin, & Jackson, 1967), *Change: Principles of Problem Formation and Problem Resolution* (Watzlawick, Weakland, & Fisch, 1974), *How Real Is Real?* (1976), *The Interactional View* (Watzlawick & Weakland, 1977), *The Language of Change* (1978), *The Situation Is Hopeless but Not Serious* (1983), *The Invented Reality* (1984b), and *Ultra-Solutions: How to Fail Most Successfully* (1988).

Despite numerous demands upon his schedule from various writing, speaking, and travel commitments, Dr. Watzlawick graciously responded to a series of written questions I put to him during the summer of 1997.

HOYT: At the Third Evolution of Psychotherapy Conference, you (1997a, p. 306) commented:

It is a great honor for me to make a commentary on Dr. [Thomas] Szasz's presentation. His *Myth of Mental Illness* (Szasz, 1961) was one of the most powerful single factors in my own professional development. It has helped me to do that 180-degree turn from being a Jungian analyst—a training analyst even— to a totally new perspective.

When I began to work as a Jungian analyst, I knew almost everything about Siberian creation myths, but I didn't know what to do with a person who chewed his finger-nails. That bothered me.

Above all, what Dr. Szasz's book helped me to understand was the fallacy of the belief that mentally normal people see the world as it "really" is, while so-called mental patients have a distorted view of it. This myth of a real reality has maintained itself almost exclusively in our field. But in a conversation with Heisenberg, back in 1926 in Copenhagen, Einstein already is supposed to have said, "It is wrong to assume that theories are based on observation. The opposite is the case. The theory determines what we can observe." And in philosophy since Kant and Schopenhauer, the same issues have been questioned.

> This leads me to ask: Why do you think the "myth of a real reality" has hung on so tenaciously in the psychotherapy field? What will therapists have to give up, and what will they gain, if they embrace the construction that we construct?

WATZLAWICK: They would have to give up the dogmatic belief in the "definitive truth" discovered by the schools of thought (and of therapy) they belong to. For—let us say—a physicist, this is much simpler, since it does not involve the "meaning of life."[1]

HOYT: In your own presentation at the Third Evolution Conference, "'Insight' May Cause Blindness" (1997b), you remarked: "One of the most important events in my evolution as a therapist was my discovery of a book by the philosopher Hans Vaihinger called *The Philosophy of 'As If'* (1924)." Please explain:

WATZLAWICK: According to Vaihinger, we always work with "fictions," and yet can arrive at practical results, after which the fiction "drops out." One of the countless examples contained in his book is the "fiction of liberty," which the judge uses only to arrive at a sentence: "The judge concludes that every man is free, and, therefore, if he has sinned against the law, he must be punished. . . . But the premise whether man is really free, is not examined by the judge. . . . Without the possibility of punishing men, of punishing the criminal, no government would be possible. The theoretical fiction of freedom has been invented for this practical purpose."

And later: "We have repeatedly insisted above that the boundary between truth and error is not a rigid one, and we were able ultimately to demonstrate that what we generally call truth, namely a conceptual world coinciding with the external world, *is merely the most expedient error.*"

HOYT: Was there a moment or incident that led you to see reality as *constructed?*

WATZLAWICK: No, there was not—it was the outcome of years of research and practice.

HOYT: What else led you to identify as a radical constructivist, and how is this related to your shift from an intrapsychic (monadic) to an interactional (systemic) way of conceptualizing problems?

WATZLAWICK: I was fascinated with the publications of the Bateson group; their insistence on a circular (rather than linear) causality of specific human behaviors, and their study of interactional (rather than individual) behavior patterns.

HOYT: At the "Unmuddying the Waters" conference we attended in Saratoga, California, during March 1995 (see Efron, 1995; Hoyt, 1997), some attention was given to the importance of acknowledging pioneers in the field. In addition to Szasz and Vaihinger, please comment on how each of the following has influenced you: *Gregory Bateson:*

WATZLAWICK: The famous anthropologist and one of the members of the outstanding Josiah Macy Conferences (which led to the development of cybernetics) opened my eyes to what nowadays is called the interactional view in our field. Unlike the analyst, the anthropologist does not ask, "*Why* does this person behave in this pathological manner?" but rather, "In what system of human interaction does this behavior make sense?"—whereby, of course, "make sense" does not necessarily mean that this behavior has to be "sane," "positive," "logical," or whatever in a rational sense.

HOYT: *Milton Erickson:*

WATZLAWICK: I met Erickson personally only twice, but our colleagues (the collaborators of Bateson) John Weakland and Jay Haley went to Phoenix numerous times and brought back fascinating information of Erickson's use of hypnotic principles also outside of trance states.[2] Of decisive importance for me (as a linguist by academic training) was Erickson's rule: "Learn and speak the client's language." As I would put it nowadays, this enables us to enter the client's "second-order reality," rather than (as I was taught in my training as analyst) to teach clients a new "language" (that of the analytic perspective), make them see the world in terms of this allegedly scientific language, and lead them to "insight."

HOYT: *Don Jackson:*

WATZLAWICK: The founder and first director of the Mental Research Institute, he had already abandoned the dogma of having to look for the causes in the past in order to bring about "insight" before he met Gregory Bateson. He was already practicing what later became known as "family therapy" (or to use the modern term, "systemic therapy"). He would see the clients (the "identified patients") together with their families and not rarely managed to make effective interventions during the first ten minutes of the first session.

HOYT: Who else?

WATZLAWICK: *Heinz von Foerster,* the famous bio-cybernetician.

HOYT: How would we act and see if we understood von Foerster's dictum (1981, 1984; see also Segal, 1986), "If you desire to see, learn how to act"?

WATZLAWICK: For me this is exactly the difference between the classical, dogmatic assumption that "insight" permits us to change our behavior, and the constructivist assumption that different, new behavior may (but need not) make us aware of possibilities that we were unaware of before.

HOYT: In an earlier discussion (1997, p. 307) you quoted Gregory Bateson as having precisely said that "An instinct is an explanatory principle." Is *insight* a parallel explanatory principle? In addition, is there something that produces change as it comes into awareness? Is *insight* an epiphenomenon that follows change?

WATZLAWICK: I would consider *insight* an explanatory principle in Bateson's sense, except that it is believed to have a magical effect—if applied in therapy.

In my view, the most frequent factor that brings about change in human lives is what Franz Alexander (Alexander & French, 1946) called a *corrective emotional experience,* that is, a chance event that suddenly opens my eyes for a different way out of my problem.

Insight may very well (and often does) *follow* change—which makes it into a consequence and not a cause.

HOYT: In *Change: Principles of Problem Formation and Problem Resolution* (Watzlawick et al., 1974, p. 26) you wrote:

It is generally held that change comes about through insight into the past causes which are responsible for the present trouble. But, as the nine-dot problem exemplifies, there is no cogent reason for this excursion into the past; the genesis of the self-defeating assumption which precludes the solution is quite irrelevant, the problem is solved in the here and now by stepping outside the "box." There is increasing awareness among clinicians that while insight may provide very sophisticated *explanations* of a symptom, it does little if anything to change it for the better. This empirical fact raises an important epistemological issue. All theories have limitations which follow logically from their premises. In the case of psychiatric theories, these limitations are more often than not attributed to human nature. For instance, within the psychoanalytic framework, symptom removal without the solution of the underlying conflict responsible for the symptom *must* lead to symptom substitution. This is not because this complication lies in the nature of the human *mind;* it lies in the nature of the *theory,* i.e., in the conclusions that logically follow from its premises. The behavior therapists, on the other hand, base themselves on learning and extinction theories and therefore need not worry about the dreaded consequences of symptom removal.

> And in a similar vein, in that paper at the Third Evolution of Psychotherapy conference, you (1997b, p. 310) seemed to dismiss totally the therapeutic utility of *insight:*

Different and often contradictory as the classical schools of therapy are among themselves, they have *one* assumption in common—that problems can be resolved only by the discovery of their causes. This dogma is based on the belief in a linear, unidirectional causality, running from the past to the present, which in turn generates the seemingly obvious need to gain insight into these causes before a change can take place. Permit me to make a somewhat heretical remark: Neither in my own life (in spite of three and a half years of training analysis), nor in my subsequent work as Jungian analyst, nor in the lives of my clients have I ever come across this magical effect of insight.

> Have you abandoned the idea of an *unconscious?* What is your response to those who, as you have put it (1997b, p. 317), assert that "the results of this treatment (if any) must be short-lived, superficial and cosmetic, because the deep, underlying causes have not been lifted into consciousness through insight"?

WATZLAWICK: I have not abandoned the *idea* of the *existence* of the unconscious, but I have totally abandoned the classical conclusion that only insight into the unconscious can bring about a change in the present. Once this conclusion is accepted as a scientific "fact," any approach *not* based on it must either be totally ineffective or—at best—be "short-lived" and so on.

HOYT: In your response to Dr. James Masterson's discussion of your presentation at the Third Evolution Conference, you commented (1997c, p. 320), "Let me briefly mention something that I found very useful in my approach to abandon totally; namely, diagnostic terms." Elsewhere you have argued that "therapy is what you say it is" (Watzlawick, 1990) and that "the construction of clinical 'realities' for the relief of suffering is the proper domain of therapy rather than the reification and imposition of putative and arbitrary concepts of 'normalcy'" (Watzlawick, 1992).

Please elaborate: What types of categories *do* you find useful for organizing your approach to patients?

WATZLAWICK: One of the basic principles of systems theory is that every system is its *own best* explanation.

I have stopped thinking: "This is a case F 39, therefore I have to do this and this. . . ." What matters to me (exclusively) is the patient's specific problem; and what he has done so far to solve it, that is, the *attempted solution,* which in our perspective is the main factor that maintains and exacerbates the problem.

Additionally, following one of Milton Erickson's most important rules, I "try to learn and speak the patient's language."

HOYT: In *Change,* you and your colleagues, following Ashby's (1956) cybernetic definition of the two kinds of change, wrote: "There are, then, two important conclusions to be drawn from the postulates of the Theory of Logical Types: (1) logical levels must be kept strictly apart to prevent paradox and confusion; and (2) going from one level to the next higher (i.e., from member to class) entails a shift, a jump, a discontinuity or transformation—in a word, a change—of the greatest theoretical and . . . practical importance, for it provides a way *out of* a system" (Watzlawick et al., 1974, pp. 9–10). Later in the book, noting that it is often the attempted solution that produces (or continues) the problem, you commented, "A system which may run through all its possible internal changes (no matter how many there are) without effecting a systemic change, i.e., second-order change, is said to be caught in a *Game Without End.* It cannot generate from within itself the conditions for its own change; it cannot produce the rules for the change of its own rules" (p. 22). You also provided four principles for the use of second-order change:

a. Second-order change is applied to what in the first-order change perspective appears to be a solution, because in the second-order change perspective this "solution" reveals itself as the keystone of the problem whose solution is attempted.

b. While first-order change always appears to be based on common sense (for instance, the "more of the same" recipe), second-order change usually appears weird, unexpected, and uncommonsensical; there is a puzzling, paradoxical element in the process of change.

c. Applying second-order change techniques to the "solution" means that the situation is dealt with in the here and now. These techniques deal with effects and not with their presumed causes; the crucial question is *what?* and not *why?*

d. The use of second-order change techniques lifts the situation out of the paradox-engendering trap created by the self-reflexiveness of the attempted solution and places it in a different frame (pp. 82–83).

So, my question: What are some of the modifications that have developed in your thinking about the MRI interactional approach since the basic principles were articulated in *Change* (Watzlawick et al., 1974) and *The Tactics of Change* (Fisch, Weakland, & Segal, 1982)? How has your understanding of *change* changed?

WATZLAWICK: It has not *changed* (in the sense of having become different), but I have constantly remained interested in the understanding of change, as it occurs normally and spontaneously in human lives, and its applicability to therapy.

HOYT: In the discussion after your presentation on "The Construction of Clinical 'Realities'" at the Second Evolution of Psychotherapy Conference, you commented (1992, p. 65):

The system imposes a certain world view, for example, on a child. But the child, being a person in his or her own right, reacts in a certain way. So you cannot just look at pieces of the system. It is wrong to believe that systems theory denies the dignity of the individual and the depth of his or her soul. Rather, mutual influences need to be taken into account: The way one behaves influences the system; the reactions of the system influence that person. That in no way denies one's dignity as an individual, although this accusation frequently is made.

While reminding us of the importance of systemic (circular, nonlinear) thinking, this statement would seem to acknowledge an external reality as part of the equation. Is there something outside our consciousness that therapists should be attentive to?

WATZLAWICK: Yes, everybody's second-order reality, which differs from mine, is an external reality of which I may be totally unaware (to avoid the term "unconscious").

HOYT: Some theorists have been critical of constructivism and social constructionism on primarily philosophical grounds. Barbara Held (1995), for example, has argued for what she calls a "modest realism," a recognition that there is a *there* there, an external referent by which interventionists gauge their work. She writes (p. 173):

Here I draw the reader's attention to what I consider to be a point of fundamental importance in understanding the confusion generated by the postmodern emphasis on the linguistic, and the postmodern linking of linguistic entities (including theories/propositions/stories/narratives/discourses) with antirealism.

It is this: *All theories are constructions* [emphasis in original]. . . . But then to say, as social constructionists/postmodernists say, that those constructed theories are the *only* reality we have—that is, that reality itself, or knowable reality itself, is *only* a "social construction" (because we supposedly have no direct, theoretically unmediated access or even an indirect, theoretically mediated access to any reality that is independent of the knower/knower's theory)—is to confuse two things: (a) the linguistic status of the theory itself with (b) the (extralinguistic or extratheoretic) reality that the theory is attempting to approximate indirectly.

How do you understand and respond to this line of criticism?

WATZLAWICK: As far as constructivism is concerned, only the *name* is modern. That our views of reality are *subjective* and by no means an objectively "true" view has been postulated by philosophers (e.g., Vico, Kant, Schopenhauer, Jaspers), by physicists (e.g., Einstein, Heisenberg, Schrödinger) and even by mathematicians.

Regarding the last two lines of the previous quotation from Held: Constructivism does not "confuse two things"—it makes a clear distinction between reality of the *first order* (as conveyed to us by our sensory organs in terms of perceptions), and reality of the *second order* (that is, the meaning, significance, and value that every one of us inevitably attributes to the first-order reality—which remain totally subjective, unprovable, and therefore the cause of human conflict and misunderstandings).

HOYT: Something about the (non)essence of the discussion about the two levels of "reality" seemed to be captured in a theater production of *Robin Hood* I saw the other night. Two characters were wandering in Sherwood Forest:

First Character: Where are we on the map?

Second Character: We're not on the map; we're in the forest!

This would seem to apply equally to the "co-constructivist" position that Speed (1984a, 1984b) advocated in response to your book *How Real Is Real,* as well as your reply to her that "adequacy" and "usefulness" in a particular situation do not (indeed, *cannot*) reveal a nonsubjective *truth* about reality (Watzlawick, 1984a). Do you agree?

WATZLAWICK: Yes, this is still my point of view.

HOYT: Other critics of constructivism (e.g., Pittman, 1992; Minuchin, 1992) have focused on the possibility of pernicious situations being dismissed as simply being "your opinion" or "the way you look at it." In a radical constructivist approach, what safeguards are there?

WATZLAWICK: I would never hold a client "responsible" for his reality construction. Since I am "speaking his language" (Erickson), my main questions may be, for instance, "How can we change things?" or "How can we get out of this unbearable situation?"

HOYT: How does that jibe with what you wrote in your Epilogue in *The Invented Reality* (1984b, p. 330):

("What reality is constructed by constructivism itself?") is a fundamentally wrong question. But we also see that this mistake had to be committed in order to reveal itself as a mistake. Constructivism does not create or explain any reality "out there"; it shows that there is no inside and no outside, no objective world facing the subjective, rather, it shows that the subject-object split, that source of myriads of "realities," does not exist, that the apparent separation of the world into pairs of opposites is constructed by the subject, and that paradox opens the way into *autonomy*.

Help! I may need a paradox: I realize that I may be slipping into just the kind of dualistic thinking that you were writing about, but how does one reconcile the notion of *responsibility* with the ideas of both *mutual (systemic) influence* and *personal autonomy*?

WATZLAWICK: Please, let me make it clear that—as I see it—even though we may not hold the client responsible for his reality constructions, he is—of course—responsible for (or a victim of) the practical consequences of these constructions.

HOYT: I've been puzzling over the relationship between *reframing* and what cognitive-behavioral therapists call *cognitive restructuring* or *schema change*. It seems that certain interactional patterns (and narratives) often persist, and that some kind of *working through* process (to use a term psychodynamicists favor) may be required for change to be maintained. What keeps clients from quickly and durably adopting different (and seemingly less painful or dysfunctional) constructions?

WATZLAWICK: The lessening or disappearance of their suffering.

HOYT: Are you saying that clients will often only change just enough to reduce their suffering to tolerable (from intolerable) levels? Sometimes a small change seems to get the ball rolling (leading to larger changes), but other times, not. Put in a different way, why resistance?

WATZLAWICK: At least in my experience, people who come into therapy demand, in essence, to have their problems solved, but not at the price of giving up what in their second-order reality is correct, right, necessary, and so on. So, in effect, they are demanding "change us, without changing us."

HOYT: This might be a good time to ask, why the term *brief therapy?* Was there something more intended than the simple temporal distinction with *long-term* approaches?

WATZLAWICK: No—simply its difference from the long-term classical approaches (which I myself practiced for years).

HOYT: What do you see as the major pragmatic distinctions (and similarities) between the MRI approach (Watzlawick et al., 1974; Fisch et al., 1982) and de Shazer's (1985, 1988) solution-focused method?

WATZLAWICK: Without claiming that I have fully understood these distinctions, I believe that my orientation is more interactional and system-oriented. My "patient" is the relationship.

HOYT: Weakland and Fisch (1992, p. 317; see also Shoham, Rohrbaugh, & Patterson, 1995) summarized the difference this way: "We focus primarily on attempted solutions that do not work and maintain the problem; de Shazer and his followers, in our view, have the inverse emphasis. The two are complementary." And in *Propagations: Thirty Years of Influence from the Mental Research Institute* (Weakland & Ray, 1995), de Shazer and Berg (1995, p. 252) affectionately opined:

(Is this a difference that makes a difference?) Of course, on a different level, deliberately replicating an exception—doing what works instead of what does not work—is a way of doing something different. But that particular something different is already part of the clients' repertoire and therefore promoting clients' cooperation (and task compliance) is greatly enhanced. Simply, a solution is developed by doing more of what is already working. Thus the flaw we see in the MRI version of Brief Therapy is that they actually take their philosophy seriously and, therefore, since their model ain't broke they do not try to fix it. Weakland, Watzlawick, and Fisch stubbornly continue to do more of the same since it works. We owe our development to this "flaw" and pushed beyond it; the ultimate tribute disciples can pay to their masters.

Comment?

WATZLAWICK: I am somewhat confused—surely, if something works, we all are likely to do more of the same. But our clients' attempted solutions rarely work—otherwise they would not ask for help—and in such a case, not only we humans typically do *more of the same.*

HOYT: In *Change* (Watzlawick et al., 1974, p. xvi) you wrote: "The problem, therefore, is not how influence and manipulation can be avoided, but how they can best be comprehended and used in the interest of the patient." You amplified this view in *The Language of Change* (1978, pp. 10–11):

All that heals can also be abused; just as, conversely, a poison can also cure. But especially today *any* form of influence, in particular anything that can be labeled as manipulation, is attacked and condemned as being unethical. These attacks are not merely directed at the abuses of manipulation—which, needless to say, are always possible—but to manipulation as such. . . . I shall merely summarize here: One cannot *not* influence. It is, therefore, absurd to ask how influence and manipulation can be avoided, and we are left with the inescapable responsibility of deciding for ourselves how this basic law of human communication may be obeyed in the most humane, ethical, and effective manner.

What guidelines can you suggest for strategic therapists to assure ethicality as well as effectiveness (or do the ends justify the means)?

WATZLAWICK: Whenever I am being accused of manipulation, I ask: "Can you describe to me *one* act of help that is not being manipulative? In saving a drowning man, you 'manipulate' him," and so on and on. Of course, everything that helps can also be abused—commercials and propaganda being prime examples. But what is new about that?

HOYT: I concur that influence is inevitable and that our job is to use it for the client's good. In the passage I quoted from *The Language of Change*, you mention having "the inescapable responsibility of *deciding for ourselves*" (emphasis added). When do we involve clients in this decision making? Many people use the term *manipulation* and object when they feel the client's wishes are not paramount; this may be especially important within the sometimes subtle, deliberately meaning-changing realm of constructive therapies. I think this is some of the concern behind recent discussions about the importance of "respecting client autonomy," "therapist transparency," and "ethical postures" (Freedman & Combs, 1996; Tomm, 1991; White, 1995). From your frame, how do think about *informed consent*?

WATZLAWICK: My "informed consent" is the question: "The next time you find yourself in the problem situation, would you be willing to carry out an experiment, namely to . . . ?"

HOYT: In an interview with John Weakland and Steve de Shazer that was published in *Constructive Therapies* (see Hoyt, 1994, p. 35), John was talking about European developments and remarked: "Usually, all I hear is what I hear from Paul [Watzlawick], and mainly what Paul will say is, 'A great deal is going on that you should know about.' . . . Then he says, 'But you don't read German.'" Pray tell?

WATZLAWICK: Our Institute is far better known overseas than in the United States. There exist about seventy foreign-language editions of my books, but what I consider more important is the fact that many approaches, similar but not necessarily identical to ours, are developed, taught, and applied, and by no means only in German-speaking countries.

John's remark about my alleged remark regarding "not reading German" must have been one of his little jokes.

HOYT: Why do you think reception has been better overseas? I've wondered if it has to do with the proximity of so many languages and cultures, which quickly brings home the idea that reality is constructed, not given or revealed. What might help further promote the systemic and interactional perspective in the United States?

WATZLAWICK: As you say, more exposure to other languages and cultures.

HOYT: What do you think (or hope) will be your enduring contribution to the psychotherapy field?

WATZLAWICK: I do not believe in any "enduring contribution" to any field of science. For me, the task of scientific research is the development of methods and techniques that are useful for a specific purpose, but will certainly be replaced by more effective approaches within a few years.

HOYT: Thank you.

Endnotes

1. Although scientists sometimes struggle, as Horgan (1995) nicely documents in *The End of Science,* with accepting the second-order idea of researching within paradigms rather than uncovering underlying fundamental truths about the universe.

2. See Watzlawick's (1982) paper, "Erickson's Contribution to the Interactional View of Psychotherapy," as well as Haley's (1985) three-volume *Conversations with Erickson.* Milton Erickson (1974) also wrote the Foreword to *Change,* in which he said (pp. ix–x): "Watzlawick, Weakland, and Fisch have, in this extremely important book, looked at this phenomenon [of change] and put it in a conceptual framework—illuminated by examples from a variety of areas—which opens up new pathways to the further understanding of how people become enmeshed in problems with each other, and new pathways to expediting the resolution of such human impasses. The relevance of this new framework extends far beyond the sphere of 'psychological' problems from which it grew. This work is fascinating. I think it is a noteworthy contribution—a damn good book—and a must for anyone seeking to understand the many aspects of group behavior."

References

Alexander, F., & French, T. M. (1946). *Psychoanalytic therapy: Principles and applications.* New York: Ronald Press.

Ashby, W. R. (1956). *An introduction to cybernetics.* London: Chapman & Hall.

de Shazer, S. (1985). *Keys to solution in brief therapy.* New York: Norton.

de Shazer, S. (1988). *Clues: Investigating solutions in brief therapy.* New York: Norton.

de Shazer, S., & Berg, I. K. (1995). The brief therapy tradition. In J. H. Weakland & W. A. Ray (Eds.), *Propagations: Thirty years of influence from the Mental Research Institute* (pp. 249–252). New York: Haworth Press.

Efron, D. (1995). Conference review. *Journal of Systemic Therapies, 14*(3), 1–3.

Erickson, M. H. (1974). Foreword. In P. Watzlawick, J. Weakland, & R. Fisch (Eds.), *Change: Principles of problem formation and problem resolution* (pp. ix–x). New York: Norton.

Fisch, R., Weakland, J. H., & Segal, L. (1982). *The tactics of change: Doing therapy briefly.* San Francisco: Jossey-Bass.

Freedman, J., & Combs, G. (1996). *Narrative therapy: The social construction of preferred realities.* New York: Norton.

Haley, J. (Ed.). (1985). *Conversations with Milton H. Erickson, M.D.* (Vols. 1–3). New York: Norton.

Held, B. S. (1995). *Back to reality: A critique of postmodern theory in psychotherapy.* New York: Norton.

Horgan, J. (1996). *The end of science: Facing the limits of knowledge in the twilight of the scientific age.* Reading, MA: Addison-Wesley.

Hoyt, M. F. (1994). On the importance of keeping it simple and taking the patient seriously: A conversation with Steve de Shazer and John Weakland. In M. F. Hoyt (Ed.), *Constructive therapies* (pp. 11–40). New York: Guilford Press.

Hoyt, M. F. (1997). Unmuddying the waters: A "common ground" conference. *Journal of Systemic Therapies, 16*(3), 195–200.

Minuchin, S. (1992). The restoried history of family therapy. In J. K. Zeig (Ed.), *The evolution of psychotherapy: The second conference* (pp. 3–12). New York: Brunner/Mazel.

Pittman, F. (1992). It's not my fault. *Family Therapy Networker, 16*(1), 56–63.

Segal, L. (1986). *The dream of reality: Heinz von Foerster's constructivism.* New York: Norton.

Shoham, V., Rohrbaugh, M., & Patterson, J. (1995). Problem- and solution-focused couple therapies: The MRI and Milwaukee models. In N. S. Jacobson & A. S. Gurman (Eds.), *Clinical handbook of couple therapy* (pp. 142–163). New York: Guilford Press.

Speed, B. (1984a). How really real is real? *Family Process, 23,* 511–517.

Speed, B. (1984b). Rejoinder: Mountainous seas are also wet. *Family Process, 23,* 518–520.

Szasz, T. (1961). *The myth of mental illness.* New York: Hoeber, 1974.

Tomm, K. (1991). The ethics of dual relationships. *Calgary Participator, 1*(Winter), 11–15.

Vaihinger, H. (1924). *The philosophy of "as if"* (C. K. Ogden, Trans.). Orlando: Harcourt Brace.

von Foerster, H. (1981). *Observing systems.* Seaside, CA: Intersystems Publications.

von Foerster, H. (1984). On constructing a reality. In P. Watzlawick (Ed.), *The invented reality* (pp. 41–62). New York: Norton.

Watzlawick, P. (1976). *How real is real? Communication, disinformation, confusion.* New York: Vintage.

Watzlawick, P. (1978). *The language of change: Elements of therapeutic communication.* New York: Norton.

Watzlawick, P. (1982). Erickson's contribution to the interactional view of psychotherapy. In J. K. Zeig (Ed.), *Ericksonian approaches to hypnosis and psychotherapy* (pp. 147–154). New York: Brunner/Mazel.

Watzlawick, P. (1983). *The situation is hopeless but not serious.* New York: Norton.

Watzlawick, P. (1984a). Commentary: But what about mountainous seas? *Family Process, 23,* 517–518.

Watzlawick, P. (Ed.). (1984b). *The invented reality: How do we know what we believe we know? (Contributions to constructivism).* New York: Norton.

Watzlawick, P. (1988). *Ultra-solutions: How to fail most successfully.* New York: Norton.

Watzlawick, P. (1990). Therapy is what you say it is. In J. K. Zeig & S. G. Gilligan (Eds.), *Brief therapy: Myths, methods, and metaphors* (pp. 55–61). New York: Brunner/Mazel.

Watzlawick, P. (1992). The construction of clinical "realities." In J. K. Zeig (Ed.), *The evolution of psychotherapy: The second conference* (pp. 55–62). New York: Brunner/Mazel.

Watzlawick, P. (1997a). Discussion. In J. K. Zeig (Ed.), *The evolution of psychotherapy: The third conference* (pp. 306–308). New York: Brunner/Mazel.

Watzlawick, P. (1997b). "Insight" may cause blindness. In J. K. Zeig (Ed.), *The evolution of psychotherapy: The third conference* (pp. 309–317). New York: Brunner/Mazel.

Watzlawick, P. (1997c). Response. In J. K. Zeig (Ed.), *The evolution of psychotherapy: The third conference* (pp. 320–321). New York: Brunner/Mazel.

Watzlawick, P., Beavin, J. B., & Jackson, D. D. (1967). *Pragmatics of human communication: A study of interactional patterns, pathologies, and paradoxes.* New York: Norton.

Watzlawick, P., & Weakland, J. H. (Eds.). (1977). *The interactional view: Studies at the Mental Research Institute, Palo Alto, 1965–74.* New York: Norton.

Watzlawick, P., Weakland, J. H., & Fisch, R. (1974). *Change: Principles of problem formation and problem resolution.* New York: Norton.

Weakland, J. H., & Fisch, R. (1992). Brief therapy—MRI style. In S. H. Budman, M. F. Hoyt, & S. Friedman (Eds.), *The first session in brief therapy* (pp. 306–323). New York: Guilford Press.

Weakland, J. H., & Ray, W. A. (Eds.). (1995). *Propagations: Thirty years of influence from the Mental Research Institute.* New York: Haworth Press.

White, M. (1995). *Re-authoring lives: Interviews and essays.* Adelaide, South Australia: Dulwich Centre Publications.

CHAPTER TEN

Honoring Our Internalized Others and the Ethics of Caring

A Conversation with Karl Tomm

Karl Tomm, Michael F. Hoyt, Stephen P. Madigan

> *Joy is the energy that allows a person to see with their own eyes.*
> *Consciousness moves from the level of imitation to imagination. . . .*
> *The joy of seeing oneself with new eyes after being released from*
> *unfocussed fear, anger, and sadness allows a spirit to sing.*
> —Winnie Tomm (1995, p. 31)

Karl Tomm has for many years been a professor of psychiatry and director of the Family Therapy Program at the University of Calgary Faculty of Medicine in Alberta, Canada. He is known both as an original thinker and as an integrator and explicator of key developments in the adjoining fields of family therapy and social constructionist theory. Through various publications (cited throughout the following pages) and worldwide workshops, he has shown special sensitivity to interactional processes in the roles of the family therapist, the ethics of therapeutic discourses and practices, and the social and systemic construction of the self.

We had planned to join together at the Therapeutic Conversations 3 conference in Denver, where we were all participating as faculty members, to do an interview focused on Karl's ideas and the development of his work. Stephen, the director of the Yaletown Family Therapy group in Vancouver, Canada, and the author of a number of valuable papers (e.g., Madigan, 1992, 1993, 1996a, 1996b, 1997; Madigan & Epston, 1995; see also Chapter Nineteen of this volume) had known Karl for many years. Michael had met Karl only once before. We got (re)acquainted over lunch a couple of days before the scheduled interview.

The actual conversation took place on Sunday morning, June 30, 1996. We were surprised when an audience of approximately two hundred people arrived for the 8:15 A.M. session. The room became extraordinarily still and focused almost as soon as we began; there was a kind of supportive attentiveness that contributed to what unfolded. As the following slightly condensed transcript—omissions indicated by (. . .)—may suggest, some of the qualities of Karl's work—thoughtfulness and intelligence, soul-searching and ethics, a focus on the systemic construction of the self—were in the air.

KARL: One of the things we decided we would like to do is have more of a discussion rather than just a one-way process of me being interviewed, because I'm interested in you guys as well. One thing I'm particularly interested in, that's relevant this morning, is your interest in me. I guess I'm interested in knowing more about the "distributed Karl" because I see myself as located not only within myself but also among others who know me, and in a sense, if I can get to know the distributed Karl in you, I can come home to myself in a new way.[1] So I'm curious about your interest in and experience of me.

MICHAEL: Well, I'd heard of Karl Tomm for a number of years and then I read the interventive interviewing papers *[Tomm, 1987a, 1987b, 1988]* and found them very well organized, very intelligent, very clear. I also read some earlier work *[Tomm, 1980; Tomm & Wright, 1979]* that was very organized and very clear, particularly in approaching the issues of being an executive or more directive therapist. In myself, I've been struggling with how to let go of that perspective and how to shift to more of an egalitarian position, how to allow more space and not be so in control; so I was interested to hear how you were making that evolution—so that, while maybe not walking in just the same path, I might be able to get some ideas.

KARL: See, I'm curious where that question is coming from, like why you're interested in that, why that particular aspect of my work appealed to you. What is it about you as a professional, as someone who is interested in this field, that led you to getting connected with me? There's some resonance here, right?

MICHAEL: Yes. Partly the clarity. I respond very well to organization, and when I've read things of yours I find them very organized and that attracted me. Then we also had that conversation on the bus at the last Therapeutic Conversations conference *[June 1994 in Reston, VA]*, and I thought "What a warm, wonderful person," and I wanted to make a further personal contact. I think that was some of it.

KARL: OK. What about you, Stephen?

STEPHEN: Well, in 1982 it was thirty below out at Woods Homes and I remember walking up a half-mile hill to your program where you were giving lunch-bag seminars at Foothills Hospital. My colleagues and I at that time were following whoever Karl was bringing to town. I was thinking of telling you the other day [at lunch] that when you brought the Milan team in that was fine *[see Tomm, 1984a, 1994b]* but when you brought [Humberto] Maturana in I had to form a support group in order to get a sense of Maturana! It was through you that I first met Michael White in October of 1986 *[see Madigan, 1992; Tomm, 1993a]*. So there's that stream—I feel that you've always had a really good nose for what's current and to embrace new ideas, so that's one way that I've come to be interested in you. It's more of an academic, theoretical, practice way.

KARL: You're bringing people in [for narrative therapy conferences] now, right?

STEPHEN: Yes.

KARL: To Vancouver. So, in a way, you and I are together in that.

STEPHEN: Yes.

KARL: Like you're younger and more energetic than I am now. *[laughter]*

STEPHEN: I don't know about energetic, but I think I'm younger.

KARL: You stayed up until two o'clock last night!

STEPHEN: That was my distributed self! *[pause]* I also wanted to speak to other places that I became very interested, and continue to be interested, in you. You appear to me to be a man to never duck the pain and never duck a fight. You stand up no matter what happens, no matter how many people are there that may disagree, you will voice your opinion. I think that you have taken some very difficult positions for a lot of us, but you always seem to be the front person out there, and I really respect that in you. And there was a time, and I'll say this publicly, when you began coming to Vancouver in the early nineties and I began to get to know you personally—and it is a very odd feeling for me sometimes to be around you, and you were the only person in the world that I would ever do this with, it was quite embarrassing—but I found that when I was around you, and I've spoken about this to you, I sort of have to move away because I tear up. I still have no idea why this is, but I think it comes from the enormous amounts of respect I have for you as a person. So there's you as a person in terms of your ethics and integrity, there's you as a rebel that will speak to very difficult issues, and there's you the man with the very good nose that seems to have brought a tremendous amount of theory and talent to North America. This is a long-winded answer. But that's part of the reason why I'm interested in you.

KARL: Thank you. I appreciate that. I haven't had a lot of respect for myself, in a way, and so if I can internalize some of the respect you have for me that could help in a way.

STEPHEN: Do you have a sense of the respect that you carry in this therapeutic world we travel in?

KARL: Well, I have a sense that I carry much more authority than I deserve, and it frightens me a bit . . . because sometimes when I say things, I realize afterward that I've affected a lot of people, sometimes in ways I didn't intend, you know, even offending people.

STEPHEN: Do you have a sense of the many ways that you affect people, at various levels across various ideas, not only to do with theory and practice but the way in which you affect, say, someone like me, that really respects your ability to wade through the pain and stay with the pain?

KARL: Well, I felt really connected to you because I felt your interest over the years and your enthusiasm for some of the things that I was also enthusiastic about. Like I felt we could come together in that enthusiasm, and seeing you doing some of the things you're doing now in Vancouver gives me a lot of excitement and pleasure. I guess it's because I see you doing what I used to do and I enjoy that, but I don't have to do the work anymore, I can just go and attend the meeting! *[laughter]*

STEPHEN: We have you doing a lot of work [at the upcoming Narrative Ideas conference] next year! *[smiles]* Do you see yourself as being influential in any way, or shaping what's going on in Vancouver? Do you have a sense of that?

KARL: Shaping Vancouver? *[asked jokingly]*

STEPHEN: As a city, yes. *[responding in kind]*

KARL: Well, I was born there, you know.

STEPHEN: Yes.

KARL: That's hard for me to imagine, actually.

MICHAEL: How does *our* internalized Karl Tomm fit with *your* internalized Karl Tomm? We're giving you this information, how you're "distributed," what you've meant to us in different ways (and I think we can speak for a lot of people), and yet I'm wondering if you're taking it in or if you're kind of saying, "Naaaah, that's what they think but they didn't really get me."

KARL: Well, my reaction is that you guys respect me too much. You don't know enough about me. I guess I feel like I've made a lot of mistakes in my life, in a lot of ways, and so I'm still learning from old mistakes. So I feel like, I don't want to be humiliated, that's not a good place to be, but I want to remain humble. So I'm cautious with respect to becoming too confident or too complacent with respect to what I've done and so forth. I'd like to be respected and feel some respect for myself.

MICHAEL: I experience this as frustrating. It doesn't feel like a healthy inter-personal process that we're doing.[2] It feels to me like—in a subtle way, you may not intend it—but you're discounting my feedback to you. I'm saying "You've meant a lot to me" and you're saying, "Well, if you really knew, you wouldn't think that."[3]

KARL: I appreciate you saying that, because I don't want to disqualify your appreciation of me. I want to be able to receive your gift. Maybe I could do that more easily if I could tell you about some of my mistakes. *[laughter]*

STEPHEN: I think so, that would make sense.

KARL: Yeah, because then if you hear them and still feel appreciative, that might be good.

MICHAEL: Pray tell.

KARL: First of all, I think I was raised to be extremely privileged: being male, being white, being socialized into a profession that had a lot of status, a psychiatrist. And I think that without realizing it I took advan-tage of these privileges, and I ended up inadvertently diminishing oth-ers, a lot of other people, crowding their space in various ways. I regret that very much. And also in terms of the whole gender dialogue and so forth, I realize that during my marriage I also closed space for my wife with respect to her emerging as a full person.

I like to think of Winnie and me as having between six and eight marriages. We began with a lot of passionate excitement and mutual discovery and so forth, which was great. Then when we started having children there was sort of a sudden increase in depth of commitment. I remember a critical moment of making a decision not to go on a third expedition I was planning. I used to climb: I was a mountaineer: I went to the Himalayas and the Andes. When we had our first daughter, I said, "This is crazy. I mean, why should I risk my life when I've got a child and a spouse to take care of and so forth?" So that was a shift into a different kind of marriage where I took my responsibility as a provider very, very seriously. But in the process, I drifted into taking Winnie for granted, and I remember at one moment, this happened many years later, I realized that toilets weren't self-cleaning! *[laughter]* I thought these things just remained clean automatically, and I had no idea what an incredible amount of work was going into sustaining me and maintaining my activities and my career. Of course, Winnie found that increasingly difficult to cope with and became rather depressed and rejecting of me—

not of me so much, but of the practices I engaged in of taking her for granted. So that led to a more difficult time in our lives where she began a protest and so forth and had to become a very strong feminist to cope with a guy like me who is pretty persuasive and powerful.[4]

STEPHEN: So what kept you open to that, to the six or eight marriages and to a different position on gender? What's kept you open to that?

KARL: I think it was my commitment to the relationship, partly for the wrong reasons, you could say, and you could say it was for the right reasons, in a different sense. Because my mother died when I was eight, I had this issue of loss all my life to cope with, so I didn't want to lose the relationship with Winnie. So I think I was hanging on to it more than I otherwise would have and we may well have parted company during those early years. It took me a long time to see what I needed to see in terms of the injustices that were going on. I remember a very critical moment when things started to shift for me and I became aware and started to make some of the changes you're referring to. I refer to this as "Winnie and I and the apple pie." We had this traditional arrangement where I'd bring home the bacon and she'd fry it. *[laughter]* I came home from work one day and we had a wonderful dinner. She had cooked this apple pie and we had the pie for dessert. It was just wonderful. I love apple pie, especially her apple pie. So I asked for a second piece and she said, "Well, help yourself." *[laughter]* I said, "No. I want you to serve me another piece." She said, "No." She just sat there, and I couldn't believe it. *[laughter]* How can this be? I felt totally powerless and I couldn't do anything about it. I started yelling and screaming; fortunately it didn't become physical, but I felt indignant. How could this be that I didn't have the power and authority to get her to submit? I remember what Maturana said about "Power is the effect, submission is the cause."[5] My power rules through her submission, and when she didn't submit I didn't have that power.[6] So for me, that was a very significant turning point in terms of realizing the injustices and imbalance of power I had just taken for granted at that point. Of course, she became very scholarly; she went to learn how to think by studying philosophy, getting her Ph.D., so she could maintain her position vis-à-vis me. We actually got to a point where I was intimidated by her knowledge. It was incredible! So I learned a lot from her.[7]

MICHAEL: What keeps you from accepting our feedback?[8]

KARL: Well, I wouldn't say I'm not accepting it. I'm just being cautious about it, I guess. What would you like me to accept that you feel I'm not?

MICHAEL: You said a few minutes ago—these are my words—"If you knew the other side you wouldn't be so generous toward me. And if you knew some of the negatives, I could be more accepting."

KARL: Yeah. Well, there's more to this, of course. I ended up being so invested in my career, which, in a sense, you've been the beneficiary of, right, in terms of what contributions I have made. But I didn't participate in raising our children to the extent that I could have. I left that all to Winnie. *[chokes up]* So I guess they paid a big part of the price for my so-called success.

MICHAEL: Is this self-imposed? I've recently gone through something myself. About ten weeks ago my older brother died. He'd been ill for some time. And when he died, while I miss him in some ways, I've experienced an enormous relief. He was quite emotionally abusive of me at times. And oftentimes when I would have a success, I wouldn't let myself fully experience the success because I'd hear his voice, so to speak—he's an internalized other. And he'd be critical: "Well, it's good, but not good enough," or "Well, that's good, but you didn't do this other thing," and so on. If I'd do something in error, make a mistake, I would really hear his voice. So I've struggled with this, too.[9] As I'm listening to you I've been kind of thinking, "How can *I* let myself feel good, how can I take my credits?" if you will. I oftentimes will say, "Yes, but. . . ." I recently published a book *[Hoyt, 1996a];* someone came up and congratulated me, and I told them the three typographical errors I've found in the book so far. *[laughter]* There's always a little flaw, it's not good enough, there's something wrong. I think as I'm hearing you, while I'm interested in your story, what resonates to me is that it's also bringing up for me my story of "Yeah, I do that, too." I think maybe that's sort of a deeper level of attraction.[10]

KARL: I guess maybe what I'd like is for you to . . . *[chokes up]* . . . to appreciate and respect my family for their support. *[weeps]*

STEPHEN: And what they've given us through you?

KARL: That's right. I suppose I should share with the group, some people will know, that Winnie died last November . . . *[chokes up]* . . . It's hard . . . I think this [interview] is turning out to be a little different than I anticipated. *[laughter]* . . . I think my family of origin, too, needs a lot of credit because they created conditions for me to be able to invest myself in my career instead of having to take a lot of responsibility in the family. *[chokes up]*

STEPHEN: It sounds like you stand on many people's shoulders to be with us. I just have a question: Do you have a sense of Winnie's respect of you now that you continue to be in the world?

KARL: I guess I should finish the sequence of marriages. . . . [Eventually Winnie] got into establishing herself and her career. She had to actually do so in another city because it was hard for her to do that in my shadow, as it were, so she got a position at the University of Alberta in Edmonton, which is three hours north of Calgary. So we lived apart during the week for six years. During that time, she really did come into her own, and that was really good for her and I supported that very strongly. Then we could really renegotiate as equals, which was a wonderful experience. It was a pleasure to be able to have that kind of egalitarian relationship. I felt really good about that and I think she did as well. Then the last part when she got ill and allowed me to take care of her, and I think she appreciated that a great deal[11] . . . *[chokes up]* . . . I don't want to stay on this too long *[laughter]* . . . I think there's a lot of other people I need to acknowledge in terms of my colleagues, my students, the client families I worked with. So, if you can appreciate and respect all of them, then it's easier for me to accept your respect for me.

MICHAEL: This may be presumptuous of me to say it this way, but I think you honor their memory by accepting our appreciation, with us knowing that we're honoring them as well. It's not just you, but it's all the people that have influenced you. I think it's a better way of honoring them, if you will, than saying, "Well, I really didn't do that much." I think you did it, with a lot of help.

KARL: Yeah, I agree.

MICHAEL: This isn't the interview I expected, either, but in another way, it is.

KARL: Ask me a good intellectual question. *[laughter]*

MICHAEL: "Well, in your 1988 formulation . . . " *[laughter]*

STEPHEN: *[pause]* What other areas are you beginning to get opened up to and why and what's influencing that?

KARL: Well, one of the other big areas for me is racism. I always thought of myself as nonracist or even antiracist. In Canada, we don't have a lot of minorities, or haven't until pretty recently. I didn't realize I was a racist until I realized that I had some discomfort with the thought of my daughters possibly marrying someone of a different race. I was curious about where that came from. When I looked at it, I could see that it was clearly a function of the way I think and feel about people of color or other ethnic backgrounds and origins. What's really interesting, my father and my whole family actually, but especially my father, was very opposed to Winnie and me getting married because my background is German and Winnie's background was English. The English and the Germans were at war, and there was no way I was going to marry someone who is part of the enemy, as it were. So that was quite a trauma for the family because prior to that my older brother and older sister married good German partners, and I was supposed to do the same. (. . .)

I always protested those kinds of demands or specifications, but when it came to my own views about myself and my privilege, I wasn't in touch with my white privilege at all until fairly recently, I guess. It wasn't until the last eight or nine years, I would say, that I really got in touch with this, and it was through that thought about my daughters, who they would marry. I remember actually at a workshop in London when this really came home to me. I had already done some thinking about it, but I was doing a demonstration interview in front of a group there and I was interviewing a white woman who had returned from Africa where she had lived for many years and she was now in England and she was being accused of being racist, and she just couldn't understand this. So I was asking her some questions, demonstrating reflexive questioning,[12] and there were some black social workers in the audience who were just jumping up and down in their chairs because of her blindness to her privilege of whiteness moving in front of her and she couldn't see that. I felt I had to do something about this because the process was so intense and the only way I could see myself doing anything about it was just to openly acknowledge *my* racism in front of that group, which is the first time I had ever done something like that. Then I started addressing the issue with them and particularly with one of the very militant black social workers that was involved. Of course, since then I've learned a lot through Kiwi [Tamesese, of the New Zealand "Just Therapy" group] and other colleagues, Ken Hardy, and so forth. I have taken up what I can in that cause. (. . .)

STEPHEN: How is opening up to culture and white privilege and gender shaping your practice at this time?

KARL: *[pause]* Well, those who know my work realize that I take the position of assuming that the mind is a social phenomenon first and foremost, and secondarily becomes psychological. So I see these dynamics of interaction that convey injustice as arising in interaction between persons and communities and so forth, which we then internalize. I see that I've internalized these things as someone who's been born into a culture that's been going for a long time already. It helps me, I think, to recognize possibilities for change because if one can re-externalize previously internalized dynamics, one can do something with them, work on them. These dynamics have an incredible history.[13]

Another area that I maybe should comment on is the fact of me being German and the Germans being involved in the Holocaust. Like I had an experience of existential guilt, if you like, when I was a kid, and I had no idea where this was coming from, but I felt this for years and it wasn't until I went to Yad Vashem, the museum in Israel, that I realized suddenly that I could have been an SS officer who sent people to their death. If I was born in a different time, in a different place I could very easily have done that and been part of that atrocity. When I realized that, I just trembled. I was just shaking inside because, of course, I don't want to. But I had to realize that it was a possibility for me. I didn't want to think that I could ever do something like that. I'd like to think that I would have the courage to say "No" and sacrifice my own life rather than doing that. But I had to be honest with myself and recognize that I'm so much a part of my culture that I could have ended up in that, given the anti-Semitism that was prevalent during that time. If I had been born fifteen or twenty years earlier, you know, and been born in Germany rather than being born in Vancouver, then I could have been there. And that was a very shaking experience for me.

One of the things that I guess I'm trying to do is my own personal process of becoming, as it were. Sometimes I think of myself as evolving from being a psychiatrist, to becoming a family therapist, to becoming just a therapist, then becoming a human being, but then that's— *[laughter]*

MICHAEL: *[interrupting]* That seems to be the usual progression! *[laughter]* (. . .)

KARL: [Thinking that you're a human being] can mean 'You've Arrived,' too—so I want to be a 'human becoming.' I want to keep on evolving as far as I'm able to until I do die. So I want to acknowledge in myself all of my possibilities or potentials, including those of being murderous, being suicidal, being psychotic, being delusional—and if I can get in touch with those possibilities myself I feel that I can work more effectively with whoever I'm working with. If I deny them and see that, "Oh, *you've* got that problem" . . .

STEPHEN: They become more aberrant and *Them versus Us.*

KARL: Right . . . they become more objectified. It's harder for me to honestly connect with them in creating this platform of *therapeutic loving,* which I see as so important.

MICHAEL: May I read you a quotation? This is something you said at the last Therapeutic Conversations conference, in 1994. Talking about preparing yourself to do therapeutic work, you said:

One of the things I do is I try to focus on my own emotional disposition to be in a relationship. I came to this through the work that I did on examining different ethical postures that we as therapists can adopt in relation to our clients.[14] I realized that probably the emotion of mutual caring and respect or *love,* I'd like maybe to use that term, is the most appropriate emotional dynamic to ground our therapeutic work in. I use the word *love* in the way that Maturana (Maturana & Varela, 1987) does, to talk about opening space for the existence of the other (Tomm, Dolan, & Furman, 1994).[15]

> When we were having lunch the other day, we were discussing some of the problems of the *DSM* [Diagnostic and Statistical Manual, *American Psychiatric Association, 1994]* and managed care and the objectification of people,[16] and I asked, "What do you think the solution is, or how are we going to move this in a healthy way?" I was really struck when you said, "We need more love." I wanted to ask you if you would reflect on that.

KARL: I know the term *love* is problematic in some respects because it means so many different things to different people. Yet at the same time, it is a term that captures people's interest because I think people can resonate with it. If we could find a way to open space for more loving to emerge in our culture generally, I think it would go a long way to countering some of the entrepreneurial values and the dollar-being-God ethos that is a part of our way of organizing ourselves in relation to each other. We give so much priority to "the bottom line," namely, the dollar. And I have a problem with this, too. This is something that's unresolved for me—I was raised in a context where I didn't have a lot of money.

(. . .)

Anyway, the money issue is such a big issue in our culture, and I think it's becoming a bigger issue; so how are we going to counter that? I think we need to find a way to open space for people to give priority to the richness of being in relationship.

I would like to introduce a slightly different sense of love. Rather than just opening space for the existence of the other, to say, opening space for the *enlivened* existence of the other. Just material existence is important, you know, but in American culture by and large we can handle that, but we need to enlarge that existence to add life to our lives and each other's lives. Certainly I get more excitement out of seeing other people being excited and responding, and it adds to my life. If people give me the gift of opening space for me to be a therapist, to have that joy of responding to them and opening space for them, that's fantastic. I get high on that.

MICHAEL: Stephen and I both have small children and we're very involved in nurturing and parenting. It's not enough to let them be there, to just say, "I'm going to open this space." Children thrive when they get welcoming and warming and nurturing, when we say "I'm going to open it and I'm going to enrich it, I'm going to take delight in your coming forward." Is that what you're referring to?

KARL: Yes. I think there's another dimension to this, though, in terms of the dangers of opening too much space. It's more than just being warm that I'm referring to. I think we need to sometimes look at the condition of the other and the situation the other is in and be prepared to do some work, some hard work—a labor of love—in terms of trying to do something that is going to, indeed, open possibilities. But even then, I think the possibilities sometimes need some structure to be optimal because if one opens too much space, one can give people the rope to hang themselves, and that can be risky. One can open the space for chaos or confusion.

I had an experience only a couple of years ago where I participated in creating the space for a woman to commit suicide. A young woman did take her life, and I feel partly responsible for that. . . . I don't know if you want me to tell you about this?

STEPHEN: Sure. Go ahead.

KARL: It was a young woman of about twenty-nine or thirty, who had been involved in various kinds of therapy activities for ten, twelve, fifteen years, something like that—since she was an adolescent. It's a long, complex story, but I got involved at a point where she was in a hospital and had been in the hospital for many months and a psychiatric colleague asked me to consult because they were having increasing difficulty with her in terms of escalating patterns of control and suicidality. For instance, she'd want to go out on a pass, and they'd say, "Well, you have to sign a statement not to hurt yourself or else we can't give you the pass," and she'd refuse; then she'd try to run out; then they'd take her clothes away and so on, put her in a hospital gown. It was just this kind of escalating thing. The family, of course, were trying hard to get her to not entertain suicide either. The more they imposed their wishes upon her, the more she felt compelled to assert her own independence or autonomy by wanting to kill herself. So, seeing this pattern, I began working with her and I recognized that she had a habit of disqualifying the good intentions of the hospital staff or the family or even me as a therapist. So I tried to externalize this disqualifying habit, but then I realized that she was experiencing my externalizing conversation as disqualifying her having this habit.

So I realized, "I can't do that, that's contributing to more difficulty here." So I thought, "Well, the only way to honestly get out of this is to give her the space to kill herself if she chooses to—with the hope that she might choose not to." I asked her whether she wanted me to do this with her. I had a separate meeting with her. I asked if she would want me to orient my work with the staff and the psychiatrist in charge in that direction. She said yes, that was what she would appreciate. So I embarked on that process with the staff and with her family. Her family could see the pattern because they had been in it for so many years, and so they recognized how they were caught in it, and they gradually accepted this. I invited them to meet with her individually to talk about the possibility of her death, to accept that as a possibility. But of course I opened space for them to feel entitled to have their preference for her staying alive and so forth; but I tried to help them stay at the level of preference rather than an imposition.

She started to improve, started getting better, going out, and being responsible. Then there was the issue of discharge, and we invited her to participate in that decision making and that eventually went well. So things gradually improved over a period of a few months, but there were some momentary slips. She used to be in conflict with the family, in struggles, and those dissipated and disappeared, but she had these inner conflicts that were still going on, which were harder to get at because she had internalized so many of these dynamics. There were lots of patriarchal issues going on with an older brother and the family business, and he was privileged in terms of the business. We tried to address all these issues insofar as we were able to.

Then there was a very trivial event that was a trigger that led to her suicide. Her father was looking at a book and the television was on. She came into the room—she was living at home at this time—and she picked up the channel changer and switched the channel. He looked around and said, "I was watching that," and she threw down the channel changer and ran off and they didn't know what this was all about. But his disqualification brought forth a whole series of prior life experiences with him, which she just couldn't cope with, as it were. She spent that night in the office on the computer writing letters to various people.

Fortunately, I had an appointment scheduled with her after this incident, and she mentioned it to me. So I was trying to help her recover from this and she was talking about leaving town and going to visit some friends in Vancouver. This seemed like a reasonable plan but I felt uncomfortable. It didn't seem right to me. So I asked her if we could have another family meeting before she left and she said to me, "Well, you promised me that you wouldn't force me to go back in the hospital." I said, "Yes, I did. I agree." And I said, "I realize that you don't want to have another meeting, but I would appreciate it if you would do it for my sake, because I'm having difficulty at this point." So she did— she called her family and, amazingly, later that day everybody showed up: both parents, all her siblings and their partners, and the psychiatrist from the hospital.

I managed to get my team together, a reflecting team,[17] and we had our last meeting with the family. She said, "No, I don't want to go back in the hospital. No, I don't want to try another medication. I've tried that many, many years, and this and that and everything, and so forth. I just want to go away and think and I want to have some time for myself." Then the whole family went out and had pizza together and she drove into the mountains, which she loved. And three days later, she in fact did kill herself.

It was, in a sense, fascinating. I mean, she wrote letters to everybody in the family that were very healing letters. They weren't negative, hostile letters. She sent me a card thanking me for giving her the choice and so forth. But I always felt that I should have done more. While I realize that may be an unfair position to take, I allow myself to take that position because it helps me to stretch myself, so I want to honor that. At the same time I want to accept her decision. What I found that was amazing is that the respect for her in the family took an incredible leap following her suicide. The respect she commanded for having the courage to do what she did, and especially in her father and her older brother, because up to that point, they tended to demean her and diminish her, not deliberately or consciously, but it was part of their way of being together. They had been socialized in these patterns. My feeling was, "If only we had more time." I don't know if time would have made a difference. It seemed to me it would have.

I made some other mistakes in my work with her, which I found very interesting. It makes me worry sometimes about the ethical posture of *empowerment,* the limits of that. One of the things she would say to me was, "It's too late. You know, I really appreciate what you're doing, but it's too late. If I had met you two years ago, maybe we could have done something." She would say, "I'm not entering into relationships with anybody," and then I would say, "But my experience is that you're opening up to me, that you're sharing a lot with me." That was a mistake because I was disqualifying her when she was saying she wasn't. After every interview she wouldn't commit to another interview. I'd offer another appointment and she'd say, "Well, I don't know whether

I'll be back or not." But she kept coming back so there was a relationship and it was evolving. But I had the idea that if I made it conscious that it would help her. Part of my idea in terms of ethical postures is inviting people to be consciously aware of their resources. In this case, that was a mistake because I think it invited her to experience being disqualified. So I think it would have been better to work with her more in the domain of *succorance*.

MICHAEL: May I interject a process comment? We've all sooner or later had a horrible case and we're not sure if we did the right thing. What comes across to me most in what you're describing now is your honesty, your clarity of thought, and your personal soul-searching. Instead of just dismissing it, what comes across most to me is how hard you've worked with yourself to stretch yourself. There's a lot of content in the case, but the degree of intelligence and integrity, of honesty with yourself, is remarkable to me.

STEPHEN: Yes.

MICHAEL: And especially to be willing to do that in a public forum.

STEPHEN: Which brings me to a question, then. Looking back on this hour-long interview, do you now get a taste of the love and the respect that we might have for you, *[laughter]* given who you are and how you are with us in this domain of therapy?

KARL: Of course, and I appreciate it. There's no question. Just this happening itself is a reflection of that, and your way of being with me has certainly conveyed that. So, thank you very much.

MICHAEL: When you take that in, how will that help you reauthor the internalized Karl Tomm?[18]

KARL: Well, I want to take it in as some self-respect and appreciation of self as I feel appreciated by you, but I guess I want to be a bit careful with it. I don't want to go too far and get arrogant. So I want to be careful about that.

STEPHEN: Should we commit to you now to keep on talking about that with you?[19]

KARL: Actually, if you could, I would really appreciate that. One of the things that I value the most from colleagues is offering feedback, constructive feedback, even if it seems negative or painful and hurts a bit. Like when it's offered in the spirit of honesty and integrity, that's where I learn the most. When people simply say, "That's great, that's great," that's nice and I appreciate that, too, and I should be more open to receive those gifts, but I find those less enabling because, I guess,

I'm afraid I have a propensity to arrogance or something. I need to keep countering that.

STEPHEN: That's interesting. Arrogance is something I see that isolates and I think in this domain what we're attempting to do is offer connection and not isolation.

MICHAEL: I want to thank you, Karl. I don't know what I was looking for in terms of the content of the interview, but I got it.

KARL: Thank you.

Endnotes

1. Tomm (1992; see also Epston, 1993; MacCormack & Tomm, 1998; Nylund & Corsiglia, 1993; and Chapter Twenty of this volume) has developed the idea that the "self" is made up of a person's internalized community of significant others. From this idea comes the useful therapeutic practice of "internalized other questioning," in which one can "step into" the experience of the other by being addressed as the other person and asked a series of questions. This can be used in various creative ways to both enhance one's sense of empathy as well as to achieve a greater awareness of how one may have taken into one's self another's views.

2. An allusion to Tomm's (1991a) "HIPs and PIPs" contrast of Healthy Interpersonal Patterns (virtuous cycles that open space and support growth and wellness) versus Pathologizing Interpersonal Patterns (vicious cycles that close down space and promote defensiveness and cut off healing and relatedness). Tomm (1996) had presented a conference workshop on "Bringing Forth Healthy Interpersonal Patterns to Replace Pathologizing Interpersonal Patterns" the afternoon before this conversation.

3. Karl's hesitance to wholeheartedly accept the admiration and respect being offered by Michael and Stephen appears to have been experienced by Michael as a form of rejection. A transient pathologizing interpersonal pattern (PIP) of disqualification coupled with protest emerges in the interview. Karl's effort to escape this PIP entails an initiative toward more self-disclosure, which was accepted. The resultant pattern of increased openness and vulnerability coupled with acceptance and appreciation led to a deepening of intimacy during the interview that surprised all of us.

4. Karl adds: It is inappropriate for me to take any credit for Winnie becoming a strong feminist. It would be more accurate to say that my sexist behavior gave Winnie plenty of reason to be angry with me and that she found support in feminist theory and knowledge to maintain a concerted protest of my domineering practices at the time.

5. In a related vein, Ritterman (1994) has observed that abuse requires three roles: the destructive process cannot continue if the *hater* stops perpetrating, the *victim* stops submitting, or the *witness* stops standing by passively.

6. Karl adds: I realize that placing responsibility for stopping any abuse on the victim or on bystanders (such as children) is inappropriate and dangerous. As pointed out by Phyllis Frank and others (Frank & Houghton, 1987; see also Chapter Twenty of this volume), the abuser must take full responsibility for his abuse. Women and children are sometimes killed when they try to stop the abuse. In this situation, Winnie took an enormous risk in defying my bullying. It is hard for me to respect myself in having resorted to such unfair intimidation practices. Indeed, I now support my internalized Winnie, who maintains a healthy protest within me. What I can respect in myself is my ability to acknowledge the sexist assumptions of male dominance and control I have enacted and my current efforts to escape those assumptions and practices. Needless to say, my growing awareness of these gender dynamics has profoundly influenced my patterns of clinical practice.

7. For a sample of her scholarly work, see *The Effects of Feminist Approaches on Research Methodologies* (W. Tomm, 1989), *Gender Biases in Scholarship: The Pervasive Prejudice* (W. Tomm & Hamilton, 1988), and *Bodied Mindfulness: Women's Spirits, Bodies and Places* (W. Tomm, 1995).

8. Michael still seems to be struggling with the pathologizing pattern of disqualification coupled with protest.

9. Michael adds: In fairness, he was also a beneficial influence, encouraging and teaching me a lot. On balance, the legacy is positive, but mixed. As I said in his eulogy, "I am sure Bill and I will be having more conversations before we're done."

10. Michael adds: As the interview unfolds, I join Karl with increasing self-disclosure. This continued afterward in a washroom conversation with him, as well, where I acknowledged my penchant for interviewing "famous" therapists as (in part) a way to obtain some of the appreciation and respect that I longed for from my older brother.

11. For an extraordinary report of her coping with her illness, see W. Tomm (1996).

12. Definition: "Reflexive questions are questions asked with the intent to facilitate self-healing in an individual or family by activating the reflexivity among meanings within pre-existing belief systems that enable family members to generate or generalize constructive patterns of cognition and behavior on their own" (Tomm, 1987b, p. 172; see also Tomm, 1987a, 1988; plus, for case reports, MacCormack & Tomm, 1998; Tomm, 1993b; Tomm, Cynthia, Andrew, & Vanessa, 1992). The many types of reflexive questions "seem to fall into natural groups: future-oriented questions, observer-perspective questions, unexpected context-change questions, embedded-suggestion questions, normative-comparison questions, distinction-clarifying questions, questions introducing hypotheses, and process-interruption questions" (Tomm, 1987b, p. 172).

13. The injustices of sexism, heterosexism, racism, ethnocentrism, classism, and so on are epidemic and deeply embedded in our dominant cultural patterns. They continue to produce widespread human pain and suffering and are continuously being reproduced unless we take a proactive stance to alter the pattern. We do not

arrive as *tabulae rasae,* but rather are prefigured by the situation in which we find ourselves. As Bill O'Hanlon (in Hoyt, 1996b, p. 106) has said in a conversation on related themes: "[Another] constraint is, I think, there are cultural traditions and explanations—what Heidegger [1962] calls the 'throwness.' You're not born as a blank slate. You're born into a culture that already shapes you by language and by practice, by interactions." James Hillman (1996, p. 55) elaborates some of the existential implications: "Heidegger or Camus, for instance, places the human being into the situation of 'throwness.' We are merely thrown into being here *(Dasein).* The German word for 'thrown' *(Wurf)* combines senses of the throw of the dice, a projection, and a litter of pups or piglets cast by a bitch or a sow. Life is your project; there is nothing to tell you what it's all about. . . . It's all up to you, each individual alone, since there is no cosmic guarantee that anything makes sense."

14. Tomm has described therapists' ethical postures in terms of how they combine the dimensions of *shared versus secret knowledge* and *increased versus decreased options,* with four possibilities resulting: the therapist can primarily engage in *succorance, empowerment, confrontation,* or *manipulation* (see Bernstein, 1990; Freedman & Combs, 1996, pp. 269–272; also Tomm, 1991b).

15. See also Michael White's discussion (in Hoyt & Combs, 1996, p. 34) of the importance of "reclaiming these sorts of terms in the interpretation of what we are doing—*love, passion, compassion, reverence, respect, commitment,* and so on. . . . What I am saying is that terms of description like *love* and *passion* are emblematic of discourses that can provide a point of entry to alternative modes of life, to specific ways of being and thinking—which will have different real effects on the shape of the therapeutic interaction, different real effects on the lives of the people who consult us, and different real effects on our lives as well."

16. Tomm (1990) has written passionately about the "spiritual psychosis" that results from the "DSM syndrome" of compulsively objectifying people. Tomm's (1991a, p. 28) "HIPs and PIPs" concepts are directly relevant: "The process of clinicians' assessing mental problems is, in itself, a culturally determined pattern of interaction which could have either pathologizing or healing effects. As already noted, when the process becomes one of sticking psychiatric labels on to persons, it can be pathologizing. Our alternative is for clinicians to distinguish, assess, diagnose, and label selected interpersonal patterns as pathological rather than the individuals involved in those patterns. This implies a fundamental shift from the personal to the interpersonal. . . . In other words, labeling PIPs pathologizes the pathology, not the person. A further effect of labeling an interaction pattern is that doing so leaves space for the persons involved to disassociate themselves from the pattern [that is, externalizes the problem but not the persons' autonomy—see Tomm, 1989] which could be the beginning of healing." For additional discussion of dilemmas of postmodern practice within the context of managed care, see also Hoyt and Friedman (in press).

17. See Andersen (1991), Friedman (1995), Madigan (1993), and Chapter Fourteen, this volume, for more on the uses of reflecting teams.

18. This question was inspired by a similar question asked of me (Michael) the day before by my colleague, David Nylund, as we reviewed the feedback from a workshop we had just presented (see Hoyt & Nylund, 1997). The workshop, interestingly, featured an application of Tomm's internalized other questioning technique to help therapists learn from their internalized clients. I can also detect a more distant echo from a supervisor-mentor, Robert Goulding, who emphasized the importance of not letting a discount or self-disempowerment pass as well as the value of deliberately connecting psychological work back to the person's initial goal (see Hoyt, 1995; Hoyt & Goulding, 1989).

19. See Madigan (1996a, 1996b; Madigan & Epston, 1995; and Chapter Nineteen of this volume) regarding the supportive value of "communities of concern."

References

American Psychiatric Association. (1994). *Diagnostic and statistical manual of mental disorders* (4th ed.). Washington, DC: Author.

Andersen, T. (Ed.). (1991). *The reflecting team: Dialogues and dialogues about the dialogues.* New York: Norton.

Bernstein, A. (1990). Ethical postures that orient one's clinical decision making. *AFTA Newsletter, 41,* 13–15.

Epston, D. (1993). Internalized other questioning with couples: The New Zealand version. In S. G. Gilligan & R. Price (Eds.), *Therapeutic conversations* (pp. 183–189; with commentary by M. White, pp. 190–196). New York: Norton.

Frank, P. B., & Houghton, B. D. (1987). *Confronting the batterer: A guide to creating the spouse abuse educational workshop.* New York: Volunteer Counseling Service.

Freedman, J., & Combs, G. (1996). *Narrative therapy: The social construction of preferred realities.* New York: Norton.

Friedman, S. (Ed.). (1995). *The reflecting team in action: Collaborative practice in family therapy.* New York: Guilford Press.

Heidegger, M. (1962). *Being and time.* New York: HarperCollins.

Hillman, J. (1996). *The soul's code: In search of character and calling.* New York: Random House.

Hoyt, M. F. (1995). Contact, contract, change, encore: A conversation with Bob Goulding. *Transactional Analysis Journal, 25*(4), 300–311.

Hoyt, M. F. (Ed.). (1996a). *Constructive therapies* (Vol. 2). New York: Guilford Press.

Hoyt, M. F. (1996b). Welcome to PossibilityLand: A conversation with Bill O'Hanlon. In M. F. Hoyt (Ed.), *Constructive therapies* (Vol. 2, pp. 87–123). New York: Guilford Press.

Hoyt, M. F., & Combs, G. (1996). On ethics and the spiritualities of the surface: A conversation with Michael White. In M. F. Hoyt (Ed.), *Constructive therapies* (Vol. 2, pp. 33–59). New York: Guilford Press.

Hoyt, M. F., & Friedman, S. (in press). Dilemmas of postmodern practice under managed care and some pragmatics for increasing the likelihood of treatment authorization. *Journal of Systemic Therapies.*

Hoyt, M. F., & Goulding, R. L. (1989). Resolution of a transference-countertransference impasse using Gestalt techniques in supervision. *Transactional Analysis Journal, 19,* 201–211. Reprinted in M. F. Hoyt, *Brief therapy and managed care: Readings for contemporary practice* (pp. 237–256). San Francisco: Jossey-Bass, 1995.

Hoyt, M. F., & Nylund, D. (1997). The joy of narrative: An exercise for learning from our internalized clients. *Journal of Systemic Therapies, 16*(4), 361–366.

MacCormack, T., & Tomm, K. (1998). Social constructionist/narrative couple therapy. In F. M. Dattilio (Ed.), *Case studies in couple and family therapy* (pp. 303–330). New York: Guilford Press.

Madigan, S. P. (1992). The application of Michel Foucault's philosophy in the problem externalizing discourse of Michael White. *Journal of Family Therapy, 14,* 265–279.

Madigan, S. P. (1993). Questions about questions: Situating the therapist's curiosity in front of the family. In S. G. Gilligan & R. Price (Eds.), *Therapeutic conversations* (pp. 219–230; with commentary by D. Epston, pp. 231–236). New York: Norton.

Madigan, S. P. (1996a). The politics of identity: Considering community discourse in the externalizing of internalized problem conversations. *Journal of Systemic Therapies, 15*(1), 47–62.

Madigan, S. P. (1996b). *Narrative therapy, eating disorders and the hospital ward.* Workshop, Therapeutic Conversations 3 Conference, Denver.

Madigan, S. P. (1997). Re-considering memory: Re-remembering lost identities back toward re-remembered selves. In C. Smith and D. Nylund (Eds.), *Narrative therapies with children and adolescents* (pp. 338–355; with commentary by L. Grieves). New York: Guilford Press.

Madigan, S. P., & Epston, D. (1995). From "spy-chiatric gaze" to communities of concern: From professional monologue to dialogue. In S. Friedman (Ed.), *The reflecting team in action: Collaborative practice in family therapy* (pp. 257–276). New York: Guilford Press.

Maturana, H. R., & Varela, F. J. (1987). *The tree of knowledge.* Boston: Shambala.

Nylund, D., & Corsiglia, V. (1993). Internalized other questioning with men who are violent. *Dulwich Centre Newsletter, 4,* 29–34.

Ritterman, M. K. (1994). A five-part poetic induction in favor of human decency (countering the hate movements). In J. K. Zeig (Ed.), *Ericksonian methods: The essence of the story* (pp. 465–481). New York: Brunner/Mazel.

Tomm, K. (1980). Towards a cybernetic systems approach to family therapy at the University of Calgary. In D. S. Freeman (Ed.), *Perspectives on family therapy* (pp. 3–18). Vancouver, BC, Canada: Butterworth.

Tomm, K. (1984a). One perspective on the Milan systemic approach: Part I. Overview of development, theory and practice. *Journal of Marital and Family Therapy, 10,* 113–125.

Tomm, K. (1984b). One perspective on the Milan systemic approach: Part II. Description of session format, interviewing style and interventions. *Journal of Marital and Family Therapy, 10,* 253–271.

Tomm, K. (1987a). Interventive interviewing: Part I. Strategizing as a fourth guideline for the therapist. *Family Process, 26*(1), 3–13.

Tomm, K. (1987b). Interventive interviewing: II. Reflexive questioning as a means to enable self-healing. *Family Process, 26*(2), 167–183.

Tomm, K. (1988). Interventive interviewing: Part III. Intending to ask lineal, circular, strategic, or reflexive questions? *Family Process, 27*(1), 1–15.

Tomm, K. (1989). Externalizing the problem and internalizing personal agency. *Journal of Strategic and Systemic Therapies, 8*(1), 54–59.

Tomm, K. (1990). A critique of the DSM. *Dulwich Centre Newsletter, 3,* 5–8.

Tomm, K. (1991a). Beginnings of a "HIPs and PIPs" approach to psychiatric assessment. *Calgary Participator, 1*(Spring), 25–28.

Tomm, K. (1991b). The ethics of dual relationships. *Calgary Participator, 1*(Winter), 11–15.

Tomm, K. (1992). *Interviewing the internalized other: Toward a systemic reconstruction of the self and other.* Workshop, California School of Professional Psychology, Alameda, CA.

Tomm, K. (1993a). The courage to protest: A commentary on Michael White's "Deconstruction and Therapy." In S. Gilligan & R. Price (Eds.), *Therapeutic conversations* (pp. 62–80). New York: Norton.

Tomm, K. (1993b). *Constructivist therapy.* Videotape, Distinguished Presenters Series. Denver, CO: International Association of Marriage and Family Counselors.

Tomm, K. (1996). *Bringing forth healthy interpersonal patterns (HIPs) to replace pathologizing interpersonal patterns (PIPs).* Workshop, Therapeutic Conversations 3 Conference, Denver.

Tomm, K., Cynthia, Andrew, & Vanessa. (1992). Therapeutic distinctions in an on-going therapy. In S. McNamee & K. J. Gergen (Eds.), *Therapy as social construction* (pp. 116–135). Newbury Park, CA: Sage.

Tomm, K., Dolan, Y., & Furman, B. (1994). *Sequencing questions to enable change.* Panel discussion, Therapeutic Conversations 2 Conference, Reston, VA.

Tomm, K., & Wright, L. M. (1979). Training in family therapy: Perceptual, conceptual and executive skills. *Family Process, 18,* 227–250.

Tomm, W. (Ed.). (1989). *The effects of feminist approaches on research methodologies.* Waterloo, ON, Canada: Wilfrid Laurier University Press.

Tomm, W. (1995). *Bodied mindfulness: Women's spirits, bodies and places.* Waterloo, ON, Canada: Wilfrid Laurier University Press.

Tomm, W. (1996). Case story: Experiences with complementary health workers. *Making the Rounds in Health, Faith, & Ethics, 9*(1), 1–4 (plus commentaries on pp. 5–8). Chicago, IL: Park Ridge Center.

Tomm, W., & Hamilton, G. (Eds.). (1988). *Gender bias in scholarship: The pervasive bias.* Waterloo, ON, Canada: Wilfrid Laurier University Press.

CHAPTER ELEVEN

Interviewing Fear and Love

Implications for Narrative Therapy

Robert E. Doan

Narrative therapy concerns itself with the deliverance of clients from the weight of oppressive and totalizing stories via liberating the client's voice and preferences (White & Epston, 1990; White, 1995; Epston & White, 1992; Parry & Doan, 1994; Freedman & Combs, 1996; Zimmerman & Dickerson, 1996). It seeks to identify the restraints that prohibit people from re-visioning the stories that are currently living them, and to deconstruct those restraints in a manner that provides room, space, and permission for clients to entertain alternate meanings and assumptions about themselves, others, and the world. It uses problem-externalizing dialogues in this process, and invites clients to compare a life lived under the dictates of the problem with one lived according to their own preferences and intentions. In this process, two distinct narratives are created for the client to compare and test for goodness of fit. Thoughts, language, feelings, and behaviors can be located in relationship to these accounts, and once this begins to occur, it is not uncommon to observe clients making steady progression in identifying themselves with their preferences and liberating themselves from the clutches of the problem. This being the case, it follows that if there were generic titles for these two accounts, titles that would fit the human experience regardless of race, culture, gender, religion, or whatever, the process of doing therapy and training therapists would be much easier.

It may seem a lofty and unlikely goal: to find common denominators of such breadth and magnitude. Nevertheless, this account will suggest and attempt to demonstrate that such generic distinctions do exist and can be used in the therapeutic setting. It is my strong suggestion here that Love and Fear represent such an archetypal dichotomy. Human beings, regardless of context, basically have the choice between a life informed by Fear or one guided by Love. Freedom to choose between these two options is unlimited. This is not to say that all people are created equal in this regard, or deny that some grow up in situations where Fear is far more dominant than others. Love is a much harder option for some than for others; however, it is an option. Indeed, it is an option that the vast majority (almost 100 percent) of clients in the author's experience have indicated they prefer.

Such a choice, from the narrative perspective, is far from trivial. The stories people tell themselves, or by default allow others to tell them, literally construct the self, the relations, and the world they inhabit. Stories authored by Fear are quite different from those penned by Love, and have very real effects on lives. This chapter illustrates this distinction threefold. First, transcripts are provided of imaginary interviews in which an investigative reporter probes the intentions and tactics of Fear and Love. Second, a case example demonstrates how the Fear-Love dichotomy can be applied in clinical practice. Finally, some of the implications and indications of Fear-based Therapy and Love-based Therapy are summarized to aid recognition of the fundamental choice between these two approaches.

INTERVIEWING FEAR AND LOVE

The following two interviews, drawn from the author's experience over the last twelve years, represent a composite based on client stories and feelings. An investigative reporter was hired to interview Fear and Love. (Several therapists were employed first, but none managed to interview Fear without trying to change or alter it in some manner—a therapeutic compulsion Roth and Epston [1996a, 1996b] have also noted. This resulted in Fear terminating the interview by leaving the room after being called "suspicious" and "resistant.") Here is what transpired.

Fear's Interview

REPORTER: Thanks for agreeing to see me. I appreciate your time.

FEAR: Before we start . . . are you a therapist?

REPORTER: No way! I'm a reporter for the local paper.

FEAR: Good. I've had it with those therapist types. They weren't interested in getting to know me at all. Just wanted to change me, tell me how bad I am.

REPORTER: Not to worry. My job is to write an article that represents you fairly. That's it.

FEAR: OK by me . . . if you think you're up to it. How long have you been writing?

REPORTER: Uh, for five years.

FEAR: That all? I had hoped for someone more experienced. Oh well, never mind, where do we start?

REPORTER: What would be most important for me to understand about you?

FEAR: I work by telling people I'll protect them . . . and I do.

REPORTER: How?

FEAR: By getting them to be aware of danger, to stay on guard, and to expect and prepare for the worst. I urge them to protect themselves, to build up defenses.

REPORTER: The world is a dangerous place and you remind people of this all the time. Is that your major job?

FEAR: Yeah, it's certainly one of them.

REPORTER: What are some others?

FEAR: To condense things, to limit options and responses.

REPORTER: Why is that important?

FEAR: Well, it keeps people and cultures contained. Keeps them from risking or learning too much.

REPORTER: Could you say more about limiting options and responses?

FEAR: Sure. My job is to narrow response options to two. Flight or fight. They're the only options that make sense in today's world.

REPORTER: And what if people don't listen to you?

FEAR: They'd have many potential choices.

REPORTER: How do you convince people this would be bad?

FEAR: It's easy. I get them to feel overwhelmed and incapable of choosing from so many possibilities. I make it easier by offering only two.

REPORTER: What else is important for you to teach people?

FEAR: That life isn't to be fun. It's too serious and scary to be enjoyed.

REPORTER: Life is to be lived like a deer during deer season.

FEAR: Absolutely! You've got it. There's all kinds of bad things that can happen to people out there. My job is to continuously remind them and get them focused.

REPORTER: So you tell people the world is a place of threat, of potential disaster.

FEAR: You're not going to disagree with me, are you? After all, that's how you reporter types make your living. Without me, what would you write about?

REPORTER: Are you saying you control the media?

FEAR: Let me ask . . . would you like to try and make a living reporting only good stuff? No disasters, murders, graft, or crime?

REPORTER: Uh . . . no, probably not.

FEAR: That's what I thought. I'm the best friend you've got. People like to read about me.

REPORTER: I have to admit, they certainly seem to. But let's move on. How do you want people to view themselves?

FEAR: As incapable of dealing with me head on. In fact, I convince them that if they feel me at all, there's something wrong with them . . . that they should do whatever is necessary to get rid of the feelings I give them.

REPORTER: And the way they get rid of you?

FEAR: Well, of course, they don't if I'm in charge. It's a trick. I use the flight-or-fight thing. I can get them to live a life of running and avoidance. Instead of facing me, they run and hide. In fact, I manage to convince people if they faced me they'd die. Actually, the opposite is true, but I don't let people know that.

REPORTER: Are you saying that if they faced you, they'd live?

FEAR: Yeah, but I get them to believe they'd live boring lives. I keep it interesting. Without me there wouldn't be the excitement and danger.

REPORTER: Is that where the fight part comes in?

FEAR: Sure. I get people to fight each other by using hurt and anger. That way they never deal with me. They rant, rave, and get violent instead.

REPORTER: So either way they go, fight or flight, you're still in charge?

FEAR: That's my job.

REPORTER: What are the main strategies you use?

FEAR: Abandonment, rejection, and not being good enough to be Loved.

REPORTER: I'm interviewing Love next . . . sounds like you use Love in some ways.

FEAR: That will be a dull interview, not much to write about. Love is such a patsy, it's easy to use. I make people desperate for it. Desperateness is one of my best friends.

REPORTER: I was looking forward to visiting with Love.

FEAR: Why? How are you going to sell *that* to the public?

REPORTER: Uh, well . . . I'll see how it goes, then decide. Now, back to what we were talking about . . . you use Love?

FEAR: Yeah, I get people to believe it's conditional . . . that they have to be nearly perfect to get it. I get them doubting they can ever get enough . . . or any, for that matter. I also get them to require that Love be shown in very narrow ways, to not recognize it in all its forms. In that way, they either conclude that they're not lovable, or that their significant others are not loving.

REPORTER: So you get people to believe it makes sense to protect themselves from the absence of Love in their lives.

FEAR: Sure. You know I'm right. Look at yourself.

REPORTER: What do you mean?

FEAR: Come on, you can't con an expert. You've been protecting yourself from being hurt again ever since your high school sweetheart ran off with your best friend. How else can you explain never marrying?

REPORTER: I don't think that's the reason.

FEAR: Whatever you say.

REPORTER: So you think you've controlled my Love life?

FEAR: Never mind, it's not important. What's important is that you feel comfortable and safe, right?

REPORTER: Yeah, right, er . . . what else do you control?

FEAR: I influence the entire planet in some major ways.

REPORTER: Can you give me some examples?

FEAR: I have most groups of people afraid and suspicious of most other groups. I use races, creeds, colors, and nationalities in this process . . . and genders, too. Paranoia, one of my most trusted workers, combines with Prejudice to pull this off. This allows me to be in charge of most political systems. I wrote the rule that all nations use as the basis for their foreign policy.

REPORTER: Which is?

FEAR: Survival of the country's political and geographic territory and culture. At the expense of all others if necessary. I get large groups of people to privilege and entitle their view of the world, and to protect that view against encroachment. I get them Fearful they could be culturally contaminated and diluted.

REPORTER: I'll bet you think you control economics, too.

FEAR: Of course. I've even been able to give the economy a bad case of depression.

REPORTER: You mean the Great Depression?

FEAR: See, you even made a proper noun out of it! I've been in charge ever since. All I had to do was introduce the notion of scarcity.

REPORTER: You're responsible for that?

FEAR: Yeah, isn't that something?

REPORTER: Have you infiltrated other areas?

FEAR: You bet. Marriage, for instance.

REPORTER: Could you say more?

FEAR: First, I get people to feel like failures if they don't marry. Second, I get them to expect so much of the institution that I'm able to convince them they're not getting what they need. I do this by getting people to believe that marriage will save them . . . or that having children will. I get both partners relying on each other for relief from me. I use their Love for each other to make them vulnerable. To get them to seek validation and purpose from the other. If they don't get it, in exactly the ways they need, I'm able to walk in and take over. It's pretty easy.

REPORTER: Sounds like you're having a field day.

FEAR: Yeah, things are going well.

REPORTER: I hesitate to ask what other parts of our culture you control.

FEAR: I wouldn't want to leave out the mental health profession. I'm really proud of that one!

REPORTER: Why is that such an important victory?

FEAR: Think about it. Of all the professions, maybe other than religion, the professional literature of this group concludes that unconditional positive regard, Love, is the essence of their work. They could be very dangerous to me.

REPORTER: But you managed to convert them?

FEAR: It wasn't hard. I used uneasiness of anyone that's different combined with the belief that the way you help people is by focusing on what's wrong with them. That diagnosing people from a deficit base is necessary to help them. I tricked them into focusing on me in their diagnostic model.

REPORTER: Can you be more specific?

FEAR: Sure. Take the *DSM-IV* as the major example. I'm at the bottom of every diagnostic category. They may as well just diagnose people as being afraid and showing it in a variety of ways. To diagnose someone according to the present schema, therapists have to focus on me in all my glory.

REPORTER: Are you saying that all the mental disorders in the *DSM* are actually just you in various disguises?

FEAR: Yeah. Isn't that slick?

REPORTER: I find that hard to believe.

FEAR: I'll be happy to prove it.

REPORTER: OK, I'm all ears.

FEAR: Well, the anxiety disorders are obvious. Right?

REPORTER: Yes, I suppose they are, but could you be more specific?

FEAR: Sure. Anxiety is Fear of the future . . . an ominous, worry-based expectation. I get people to believe that in order to be safe they have to fret about what might happen much of the time. I convince them that Worry is necessary and logical. I even get them to equate it with Love.

REPORTER: How do you do that?

FEAR: It's simple. I just convince them that Love and Worry are synonyms. But I don't need to tell you . . . you have firsthand experience in this area.

REPORTER: What?

FEAR: Yeah, right, like you're not aware of your obsessive-compulsive tendencies.

REPORTER: I don't think—

FEAR: What would happen for instance, if you didn't take your notes on a yellow legal pad and use a black felt-tip pen?

REPORTER: I could still—

FEAR: Then do it. Here, use this unlined paper and a pencil. Or even better, use this new laptop computer. I'll even give it to you!

REPORTER: Uh . . . no . . . uh, really, that's all right. I appreciate it, but I'll just stick with what I'm using.

FEAR: Of course you will. Otherwise you'd have a panic attack. Tell me when I get it wrong.

REPORTER: I just like to keep things neat. We'd best move on, our time is running out.

FEAR: Whatever you say. How about schizophrenia? You going to tell me those people aren't afraid?

REPORTER: Well, no, I can't.

FEAR: Of course not. And you know what they Fear? Other people! In fact, that's what I've got you humans most afraid of . . . each other!

REPORTER: OK, OK. What about the other categories?

FEAR: The mood disorders are Fear that things are never going to change, that the person can't do anything to alter their environment, or that they will never be lovable enough. Hopelessness and helplessness—a victim lifestyle—is just that . . . a Fear that they are powerless to do anything about the sorry state of their lives. In short, a Fear of helplessness.

REPORTER: Uhm . . . that makes sense.

FEAR: Next come the somatic disorders. Fear that something is wrong physically. Being supersensitive to the body's signals so that every little twitch is scary. How am I doing so far?

REPORTER: Too well as far as I'm concerned.

FEAR: Great! Let's keep going. The dissociative disorders are nothing more than a way of coping with extreme terror. These people had torturous childhoods. They have real reasons to be afraid.

REPORTER: I'll take your word for it.

FEAR: The same can be said of the personality disorders. All you have to do is look at their past. They are afraid of continued pain, disqualification, disregard, and even torture. Their world is defined by me.

REPORTER: How about the psychosexual categories?

FEAR: Do the words *performance anxiety* mean anything to you? Or if you enjoy sex you're dirty? How about Fear of pregnancy, or Fear of AIDS?

REPORTER: I get the picture. Do you want to say a few words about substance abuse?

FEAR: That's easy. I get people to self-medicate me away, to try and escape via drugs. There are several ways to flee, and substances are certainly among them. I get people to believe that if they are experiencing pain, there's something wrong with them. I persuade them to seek a pain-free existence . . . in any way they can. Once again, I don't need to tell you.

REPORTER: What do you mean?

FEAR: What's the first thing you do after a hard day of covering Fearful stories?

REPORTER: Uh . . . well . . . I relax.

FEAR: You bet you do! By tossing back stiff doses of scotch on the rocks.

REPORTER: So you're at the bottom of most of this stuff. You even get people to drink and use drugs.

FEAR: Absolutely. All the disorders in the *DSM* are, in one way or another, me influencing people to be afraid of life. Even the adolescent epithets of oppositional-defiant and conduct disorder are under my control. I get young people to be afraid that they are going to be totally consumed by the adult stories, or that they're never going to measure up and get the Love and acceptance they want. In these disorders, their responses are typical of the fight portion of the flight-or-fight option I give people.

REPORTER: So, to make the various diagnoses, people in the mental-health professions have to focus on the multiple forms you take in people's lives.

FEAR: Sure. And if you're around me a lot I have more chance to influence you, to get under your skin, so to speak. I have therapists watching for me constantly without even being aware they're falling under my spell. I work that way a lot. I get people to believe it makes sense to pay attention to me.

REPORTER: You made reference to religion, have you taken over there, too?

FEAR: For the most part. I've managed to turn God into a judgmental eye in the sky in most of them . . . not to mention what I've done with Satan and Hell. All I had to do to infiltrate religion was make God's Love conditional upon adherence to rules that most people are likely to break. Add the notion of eternal judgment . . . hot damn!

REPORTER: What are your goals for the planet?

FEAR: Like I said, everyone will be doing one of two things . . . fighting or fleeing. They'll do this at the individual, familial, cultural, and national levels if I hold sway. Please remember, however, that I only do this for your own good. Otherwise you'd be bunch of naive Goody Two-shoes innocents.

REPORTER: But fighting and running all the time . . . doesn't sound like much of a future to me.

FEAR: Oh, it's not so bad once you get used to it. Most people don't know how to live any other way.

REPORTER: And this includes mental health professionals?

FEAR: Absolutely. Their training hasn't rendered them immune, although if they paid closer attention, it might.

REPORTER: Anything you'd like to ask me?

FEAR: Are you sure you'll be able to write a fair article about me?

REPORTER: I don't know, I'm feeling anxious about it.

Note: The reporter was to have interviewed Love immediately after Fear, but this discussion was postponed due to doubts on the reporter's part that he could do an adequate job. The editor also had concerns regarding marketing the article if Love took part. It took him a couple of weeks to decide. Love waited patiently in the wings during the interim.

Love's Interview

REPORTER: Sorry about the delay. I haven't been feeling too good lately.

LOVE: No problem. I understand. Fear can be a harrowing experience.

REPORTER: Boy, that's for sure!

LOVE: I've encountered this before . . . and by the way, I like the fact that you take your notes by hand. Seems more personal that way.

REPORTER: Really? Uh, thanks! Let's get started. I'll ask you the same first question I asked Fear. What would be most important for me to know about you?

LOVE: Given what you've been through the last couple of weeks, I'd want you to know that I'm much stronger than Fear. Fear doesn't stand much of a chance in my presence.

REPORTER: Really? How so? Fear feels pretty strong.

LOVE: Fear uses self-doubt, uncertainty (especially of the unknown), and lack of faith to influence people. Just to name a few of its strategies. People who get in touch with me realize they are worthy of self-Love and the Love of others. I provide hope where Fear offers hopelessness, trust in lieu of distrust, positives instead of negatives . . . you get the idea.

REPORTER: How can you do this? Fear seems to think it has control of most people.

LOVE: Fear always was a braggart. It isn't as dominant as it pretends. Remember, in Fear's rule book there is nothing wrong with lying. But let me answer your question. Primarily I instruct people to listen to their own experience . . . to honor it. And, once having done so, to ask if they are experiencing joy, feeling connected and peaceful. If not, I suggest they are worthy of such feelings and to search themselves further. I suggest they go within so they won't go without. If people go within, they can find me. I've been there all along.

REPORTER: You seem to be saying that most people can connect with you if they really try. Is this correct?

LOVE: Yes. Not only do they have the ability, they have the desire. Most people prefer me above all else in life. They yearn for me. And I might say, rightly so: I'm worth the search.

REPORTER: So why do so many think you're hard to find?

LOVE: Fear manages to trick them into looking in the wrong places.

REPORTER: Where?

LOVE: Primarily they look without . . . outside themselves. Fear convinces them that the only way they can feel lovable is if others Love them.

REPORTER: But your message is different?

LOVE: Definitely. I'm right there, available all the time. Even beginners can find me if they use the right criteria.

REPORTER: Which are?

LOVE: When a person lets me guide them they experience joy, peace, and contentment. I expand while Fear constricts. I bring trust while Fear brings suspicion. I provide opportunity instead of obligation, hope instead of despair, gentleness in lieu of violence, compassion instead of prejudice and bias. I encourage people to be all that they are, to identify their highest choices and preferences, and to side with the notion they are in the process of becoming. *[see White, in Hoyt & Combs, 1996]*

REPORTER: Some might say this sounds too idealistic to be realistic.

LOVE: That's Fear talking. The Great Fear that stalks the land suggests that people do not have the capacity to be lovable, that protection and defensiveness characterize those that really understand. The Great Fear makes dire predictions about the state of the planet and prophesies a catastrophic end.

REPORTER: Certainly you don't think the planet is in good shape?

LOVE: I will admit that the fate of the planet hangs in the balance between me and Fear . . . and that Fear has made significant inroads. However, it is not too late. I am quite capable of turning things around. Never underestimate my power. People enjoy being around me, and can quickly be recruited if given even half a chance. I am inside people when they remember to look.

REPORTER: What an interesting way to put it. Are you saying that we have forgotten that we are loving beings?

LOVE: Not entirely, but to a significant extent. You still sing about Love, write stories about Love, base your religions on Love (at least theoretically), think about Love, yearn for Love, and so on. However, many have forgotten that I am available to be the informing basis of their daily, moment-to-moment lives. They hope for me, try to find me, yearn for me, and wish for me . . . instead of saying *I am Love*. So, quite obviously, they end up hoping, wishing, trying, and yearning rather than being. Of course, Fear uses this to convince them that they are hope-less. I, on the other hand, tell people to be hope-full . . . and to act on that hope in ways of being.

REPORTER: You make it sound easier than it is.

LOVE: I don't mean to imply that. Fear is a very worthy opponent. I find myself confused at times. Fear does not write happy endings. It brings tragedy, regret, and sorrow. I offer the opposite. People can either live their lives by *What would Fear do now?* or by *What would Love do now?* The differences between such existences are huge. Fear doesn't author happy endings. I do. In fact, I guarantee them.

REPORTER: Would you do away with Fear if you could?

LOVE: No. Without Fear I wouldn't exist. We are structurally coupled, like me and my shadow—we define each other. The issue is not whether Fear exists, but the extent to which it informs one's life and decisions. Fear is in charge when people choose it, create their world in relationship to it, or are constantly watching for it.

REPORTER: How would you respond to Fear's contention that it has taken over the arena of mental health, that the diagnostic system used is primarily under its direction?

LOVE: I'm sorry to have to agree. This is not to say that there aren't numerous individual clinicians that let me inform their work and view of others, but the dominant cultural view is based in pathology. It searches for what is wrong and dysfunctional and classifies people according to normative judgments that are socially constructed. Such diagnostic criteria act in the service of a medical heritage and are informed by the natural sciences and modernism. *[see Kirk & Kutchins, 1992; Gergen, Hoffman, & Anderson, in press]*

REPORTER: Could you say more about that?

LOVE: Diagnostic categories are socially constructed meanings put forth by the dominant professional culture. They can be viewed as a language agreement to make sense of certain behaviors in a certain way.

REPORTER: How is this process Fear-based?

LOVE: It is rooted in the scientific, reductionistic notion that if we can categorize, we can understand. And if we understand, we don't have to be afraid. Fear uses discomfort with the unknown and seemingly chaotic to recruit therapists into reifying invisible illnesses and actually writing stories about them in case notes and files.

REPORTER: And what would therapists do that are informed by you?

LOVE: They would ask themselves some very obvious questions.

REPORTER: Such as?

LOVE: The first would be, *What would Love do?* Followed closely by, *Do diagnostic categories actually help the client?* Who stands to gain most from such diagnostic criteria? Did the people being classified have any voice in the process? Is the basis for such labeling Compassion, Love, and Understanding, or Judgment, Fear, and Reductionism? I could go on, but you get the idea. The main point is that therapists would interview and interact with people as *people* rather than as problems that must be classified according to some professional domain of knowledge. Therapists would be interested in learning from the person the best way of helping him or her, and would be willing to let the client teach them this process. For instance, did you find it helpful when Fear labeled you as obsessive-compulsive?

REPORTER: No, it made me defensive.

LOVE: Yeah, it didn't point out that you have an intense desire to do your job well, that it's important to get it right.

REPORTER: It certainly didn't. Is that the way you see it?

LOVE: Look inside. Which rings more accurate to you, what I just said, or Fear's statement?

REPORTER: I like yours a lot better.

LOVE: Good.

REPORTER: Is there a model you recommend?

LOVE: I'm very encouraged by the emergence of the narrative, social construction, and language systems schools of thought. In the best senses of the term, they're *constructive therapies. [see Hoyt, 1994, 1996]*

REPORTER: How so?

LOVE: They are based in a collaborative partnership between clients and therapists that invites the clients' expert voice and perspective on their lived experiences. They bring me into the conversation via the notion that the client's knowledge is as valid as professional and formal bodies of thought.

REPORTER: Are there other ways Fear uses to tempt therapists out of loving stances?

LOVE: Perhaps the most obvious is the Fear of losing their jobs. Therapists are like everybody else. They have children, house and car payments, dreams for the future, and so on. Fear uses notions of scarcity and insecurity to get therapists to go along with a socially constructed system that supports identifying people by their deficits.

REPORTER: Even though they know better?

LOVE: Often. Most therapists have been exposed to the literature that supports the notion that the most important element in counseling is the successful establishment of the "core conditions" of a helping relationship. These are unconditional positive regard, empathy, and congruence. I was the originator of these notions, by the way.

REPORTER: Is there anything you'd like to say in closing?

LOVE: Yes. All people are in the process of deciding whether Fear or Love will inform their lives. It is the most important choice that any human has to make. The implications are extremely far-reaching. Whether you are client, therapist, mother, father, friend, or child . . . no matter what your station in life, the choice is there. Love or Fear? If you choose Fear you side with being cynical, distrustful, suspicious, hopeless, and believing in scarcity. Fear is judgmental and harsh, it gets you to react to hurt by striking back, convincing you the only safety lies in revenge. It supports being vexed and uncertain. Conversely, Love guides you to select faith, trust, hope, justice tempered with mercy, kindness that is discriminate, compassion, and understanding. You opt for self-dignity, superb self-respect, and a respect for others. Fear sponsors self-depreciation, while I promote self-appreciation. Fear speaks of obligation while opportunity is my favorite topic. This option between Love and Fear is really the only choice people have, but they have it every moment of every day as long as they live. If they say yes to me, I will say yes to them.

REPORTER: Thank you for your time.

LOVE: You're entirely welcome . . . and by the way, how are you feeling?

REPORTER: Much better. Thanks.

LOVE: That's OK. Hey, do you think that your readership will be interested in our little talk?

REPORTER: Yeah, as a matter of fact, I do.

LOVE: That's a very accurate way to put it. I am a fact, and I am available.

REPORTER: Thank you.

LOVE: Thanks for listening . . . I couldn't do it without you.

A CASE EXAMPLE

To illustrate how the Love-Fear dichotomy can be used in narrative therapy, a case example follows based upon a recent session with a thirty-five-year-old female. She is the single mother of a daughter, age fourteen, and is very concerned about the daughter's escalating tendency to use alcohol and drugs, stay out past curfew, and flunk classes at school. She has tried a number of approaches, most of them informed by the need to make more rules and establish more control over the daughter, and an increasing feeling that she is failing as a parent.

THERAPIST: I understand from our phone conversation that Fear has used the relationship between you and your daughter to introduce conflict into your family.

CLIENT: You can say that again!

THERAPIST: What would be most important for me to know about that?

CLIENT: I'm just so angry with her! I can't believe she's doing what she is. Two nights ago I found her drunk in her room. She'd downed half a bottle of whisky.

THERAPIST: That sounds pretty scary. Must have been awful for you to find her in that state.

CLIENT: God, yes! If she keeps going like this I don't know what will happen to her.

THERAPIST: Fear suggests that it won't be anything good, however?

CLIENT: Of course not. Nothing good can come from what she's doing.

THERAPIST: Let's see if I've got this so far. Fear has somehow infiltrated your daughter's life and has her drinking and drugging in an attempt to escape it. It also has managed to influence you by coaching you to predict the worst. It has you worried about the future and making catastrophic predictions about it. It probably uses hurt and pain on you as well.

CLIENT: I don't know if she's scared or not. I don't know what's going on with her. She won't talk to me, won't let me in. She says she hates me.

THERAPIST: Gosh, that has to hurt!

CLIENT: Yes, it does. *[tears form in her eyes]*

THERAPIST: So, how much of your life has Fear managed to take over in this way?

CLIENT: Most of it, I'm afraid.

THERAPIST: What an interesting way to put it.

CLIENT: What?

THERAPIST: You said you were afraid it had taken over.

CLIENT: I did, didn't I?

THERAPIST: Yeah, sounds like it's even using fear of Fear.

CLIENT: Yes, I guess it is.

THERAPIST: In this process of Fear taking over you life, what has happened to Love?

CLIENT: I still love her. Is that what you mean?

THERAPIST: Love is still around?

CLIENT: Of course.

THERAPIST: In spite of Fear's best efforts?

CLIENT: I still love her, she's my daughter. I don't think I'm showing it much, though.

THERAPIST: So Fear has been able to partially override the behaviors that Love promotes?

CLIENT: I can hardly stand to be in the same room with her . . . is that what you mean?

THERAPIST: So Fear is trying to steal Love away?

CLIENT: She won't let me love her.

THERAPIST: Fear is so strong, it has you convinced that she doesn't want your Love. That's really frustrating and hurtful. Do you find yourself wishing that Love was still in charge?

CLIENT: Yes, but she won't let me, she won't respond.

THERAPIST: That's got to be really difficult. Fear probably suggests you have to make her respond. Suppose she doesn't respond the way you'd wish, would you rather be informed by Love or Fear in your dealings with her? Which would result in your feeling better about yourself?

CLIENT: Probably Love, but I'm just so hurt.

THERAPIST: Yeah, I can tell that you are, it would be difficult to feel any other way under the circumstances.

CLIENT: Yeah, how can I?

THERAPIST: That's an interesting question. Is it OK if we pursue it?

CLIENT: Sure.

THERAPIST: What has Fear done to your Love for yourself?

CLIENT: What?

THERAPIST: Is it trying to convince you that you're not a very good person?

CLIENT: Not quite, more that I'm not a good parent.

THERAPIST: It's trying to steal your regard for yourself away in that area?

CLIENT: Yeah, big time!

THERAPIST: How is that affecting your life?

CLIENT: I think about it all the time. I haven't had any fun in weeks. I've stopped seeing the guy I'm dating. All I do is worry about her.

THERAPIST: So you're not doing any nice things for yourself?

CLIENT: No, now that I think about it, I'm not.

THERAPIST: And how about your Love for your daughter, is it trying to take that away, too?

CLIENT: Yes, it even has me hating her at times.

THERAPIST: So, why do you suppose Fear is doing this to you? What does it want?

CLIENT: I'm not sure. To make me miserable, I guess.

THERAPIST: Sounds like it's succeeding to some degree, even though this is not what you'd prefer.

CLIENT: It's certainly not what I'd prefer.

THERAPIST: Would what you'd prefer be more in line with Love?

CLIENT: Yes. I miss the closeness we used to have.

THERAPIST: I'm sure you do. You'd prefer closeness. What else?

CLIENT: Trust and respect . . . friendship, things like that.

THERAPIST: Does Fear offer you those?

CLIENT: No.

THERAPIST: What does it offer?

CLIENT: More and more worry. More pain.

THERAPIST: Does it try and convince you that Worry and Love are the same?

CLIENT: I'm not sure I understand.

THERAPIST: Does Fear tell you that if you love someone you have to worry about them, that if you don't worry then you don't love?

CLIENT: I'm not sure Fear tells me that. If you love you just naturally worry. It's just the way things are.

THERAPIST: So, Fear suggests that one of the highest forms of Love is worry . . . is that correct?

CLIENT: Yes.

THERAPIST: And what does Worry in the name of Love get you to do?

CLIENT: To protect her, to tell her what she's doing wrong, to somehow get her to understand that she's ruining her life. God, I just can't believe all this is happening!

THERAPIST: Let me see if I'm tracking with you. Fear has been able to convince you that the most loving thing you can do is worry. It has recruited you into parenting from a "What would Fear do now" stance.

CLIENT: But how could I not be afraid? Do you understand what she's doing?

THERAPIST: Let me be more clear. The issue is not whether to be afraid or not, it's whether to let Fear inform and dominate your parenting, to let it be in charge. If it was in charge, what would it tell you to do?

CLIENT: Take control, force her to change. Not let her out of my sight until she comes to her senses.

THERAPIST: How would it suggest you talk to her, what can it get you to say?

CLIENT: It gets me angry, raising my voice, telling her how screwed up she is. Things like that.

THERAPIST: Is this how you'd prefer to parent?

CLIENT: Not really, but I can't seem to help it.

THERAPIST: No, when Fear is in charge it won't let us do anything else. Love is another matter. What would Love tell you to do?

CLIENT: *[sits silent for a minute]* I really don't know. I'm so hurt and upset I can't think of a thing! Can you help me?

THERAPIST: Perhaps. Let's take her grades as an example. Let's say she comes home with all D's and F's.

CLIENT: She will. That's exactly what will happen.

THERAPIST: OK, let's say it does. What would Love do if she did? Before you answer, try and separate what Fear would tell you about Love. That might be hard.

CLIENT: God, I'm not sure I can. I'm going to be so upset, so angry with her. I still need you to help me with this.

THERAPIST: Which is more important, your daughter's grades or the relationship between the two of you?

CLIENT: Uh . . . gosh, I know the relationship should be.

THERAPIST: Is that what Love would say?

CLIENT: Yes.

THERAPIST: So, if Love were in charge, what would you do?

CLIENT: Maybe I'd tell her that.

THERAPIST: What?

CLIENT: That our relationship is more important than her grades to me.

THERAPIST: Would that shock her?

CLIENT: Oh, God, yes!

THERAPIST: Does she expect Fear to be in charge?

CLIENT: That and Anger.

THERAPIST: Can you remember a time when Love was dominant in your dealings with her even though Fear was trying to be?

CLIENT: Uh, I'm not sure I understand.

THERAPIST: Can you remember an instance when Fear could have taken over, but Love managed to prevail anyway?

CLIENT: I guess I used to do that a lot.

THERAPIST: Can you give me an example?

CLIENT: She made bad grades one semester when she was in elementary school.

THERAPIST: Did Fear try and use that?

CLIENT: Yes, but I realized that she was upset about something else and I talked to her about it.

THERAPIST: How did you realize that?

CLIENT: She told me. She was upset about being adopted, about why her mother hadn't wanted her.

THERAPIST: And what did you do?

CLIENT: I understood, told her it was normal to have such feelings.

THERAPIST: You understood that Fear was influencing her.

CLIENT: Yeah, I guess so.

THERAPIST: And what happened?

CLIENT: She seemed to appreciate it. She brought her grades up the next semester.

THERAPIST: Did Fear try and get you upset, angry, and worried?

CLIENT: Yeah, it tried.

THERAPIST: How did you stop it?

CLIENT: I don't know, I just understood. She was confused about the adoption thing.

THERAPIST: Is she confused now? Is Fear confusing her again?

CLIENT: Maybe.

THERAPIST: But this time it's more difficult for you to understand.

CLIENT: Yes, she's drinking and using drugs. I'm scared to death.

THERAPIST: Fear wouldn't want you to understand how frightened she is, would it?

CLIENT: No, probably not.

THERAPIST: Fear is telling you that you have no choice but to be scared. It wouldn't want you focusing on the relationship and how much you love her.

CLIENT: But we don't have much of a relationship left!

THERAPIST: I understand. When Fear is around relationships seldom stay good.

CLIENT: No, I suppose not.

THERAPIST: What would you predict will happen if Fear stays in charge? How will things turn out?

CLIENT: I'm certain they won't be good.

THERAPIST: Given that, how important would it be that you lessen Fear and increase Love in the midst of these troubled times?

CLIENT: Pretty important, I'm just not sure I can.

THERAPIST: But you'd prefer to?

CLIENT: Of course.

THERAPIST: Sounds like you're at a "Y" in the road. Down one fork Fear is waiting, while down the other is Love. Kind of a choice between "What would Love do now?" and "What would Fear do now?"

CLIENT: That pretty well sums it up.

THERAPIST: Love is asking what you would do if you held yourself, as well as your daughter, in high regard.

CLIENT: That's going to be hard to do.

THERAPIST: Fear will try and make sure it is.

CLIENT: I'm not sure I can hold either of us in high regard.

THERAPIST: It's really difficult to do in times of trouble, but it seems you think it's pretty important since you predict that Fear will lead to an unhappy ending.

CLIENT: Yes, it is important.

THERAPIST: How important?

CLIENT: Well, it's our lives we're talking about.

THERAPIST: Yes, it is. Which do you want in charge of your lives . . . Love or Fear? Do you really want to turn over the story to Fear?

CLIENT: When it's put like that . . . Love seems the only choice. Things would get better. Now I have to figure out how to keep it in charge, how to remember Love.

IMPLICATIONS FOR THERAPISTS

Therapists are not immune to the influence and ravages of Fear. Clinicians consistently encounter Fear-based stories and are intimately acquainted with the havoc Fear can produce in people's lives. Therapists are faced with the same choice that confronts their clients—the option between Love or Fear. Consider the implications of such a choice on the behavior of therapists:

Fear-based Therapy	*Love-based Therapy*
• Uses uncertainty to promote insecurity.	• Views not knowing as an asset.
• Adheres to deficit-based diagnosis.	• Regards compassion as more important than categories.
• Has a deep need to answer *Why?*	• Stresses *What?* and *How?* from client's frame.
• Provides therapists with built-in excuses like client "resistance" and "denial."	• Trusts clients and privileges their voice; lets clients define what is helpful.
• Worries more about agency policies and budgets than client needs or perspectives.	• Keeps client needs predominant while calmly solving the instrumental tasks of administration.
• Focuses on the deficits of the agency, system, insurance company, and so on.	• Does best it can within constraints of larger systems; doesn't tilt at windmills.
• Focuses on the failings of the therapist, gives them more import than successes.	• Defines success reasonably, and views becoming a good therapist as a process.
• Finds security in hierarchical therapy.	• Embraces collaborative therapy.
• Privileges academic and professional domains of knowledge to allay insecurity.	• Permits access to all knowledge areas that are pertinent to the situation.
• Is long on judgment and short on mercy.	• Is long on mercy and short on judgment.
• Rescues client so therapist can feel OK.	• Lets therapist validate self separate from client.

Fear has an ever-expanding array of contexts and cultural developments with which to influence therapists. Dealing with insurance companies, the medical establishment, licensing boards, HMOs, departments of mental health, and increasing amounts of paperwork and hours required on the job provide Fear with all the ammunition it needs. We are increasingly in the position of being able to empathize with our clients via our firsthand experience with Fear. If we cannot rise above its tyranny, how can we expect them to do so? As with our clients, Love stands ready to provide us with the self-appreciation we need for ourselves and enough compassion and mercy to serve our clients. Fear, however, invites us down a very different path. The choice is our own, each of us as an individual. I am confident that those attracted to the work of doing therapy will be more comfortable answering what may well be the only question that needs to be asked about any relationship:

What would Love do now?

References

Epston, D., & White, M. (1992). *Experience, contradiction, narrative, and imagination: Selected papers of David Epston and Michael White.* Adelaide, South Australia: Dulwich Centre Publications.

Freedman, J., & Combs, G. (1996). *Narrative therapy: The social construction of preferred realities.* New York: Norton.

Gergen, K., Hoffman, L., & Anderson, A. (in press). Is diagnosis a disaster? A constructionist trialogue. In F. Kaslow (Ed.), *Relational diagnosis.* New York: Wiley.

Hoyt, M. F. (Ed.). (1994). *Constructive therapies.* New York: Guilford Press.

Hoyt, M. F. (Ed.). (1996). *Constructive therapies* (Vol. 2). New York: Guilford Press.

Hoyt, M. F., & Combs, G. (1996). On ethics and the spiritualities of the surface: A conversation with Michael White. In M. F. Hoyt (Ed.), *Constructive therapies* (Vol. 2, pp. 33–59). New York: Guilford Press.

Kirk, S. A., & Kutchins, H. (1992). *The selling of DSM: The rhetoric of science in psychiatry.* Hawthorne, NY: Aldine de Gruyter.

Parry, A., & Doan, R. E. (1994). *Story re-visions: Narrative therapy in the postmodern world.* New York: Guilford Press.

Roth, S., & Epston, D. (1996a). Consulting the problem about the problematic relationship: An exercise for experiencing a relationship with an externalized problem. In M. F. Hoyt (Ed.), *Constructive therapies* (Vol. 2, pp. 148–162). New York: Guilford Press.

Roth, S., & Epston, D. (1996b). Developing externalizing conversations: An exercise. *Journal of Systemic Therapies, 15*(1), 5–12.

White, M. (1995). *Re-authoring lives: Interviews and essays.* Adelaide, South Australia: Dulwich Centre Publications.

White, M., & Epston, D. (1990). *Narrative means to therapeutic ends.* New York: Norton.

Zimmerman, J. L., & Dickerson, V. C. (1996). *If problems talked: Narrative therapy in action.* New York: Guilford Press.

CHAPTER TWELVE

"Master of Faster" and "The Problem Talks Back"

Joseph Goldfield

HOYT: How did you get into writing rap songs?

GOLDFIELD: I had been working with teenagers in a group home in Oakland, California. Some of them expressed themselves in rap a lot, so I started to rap back. Many of our therapy sessions were totally in rap.

HOYT: That reminds me of Milton Erickson [Haley, 1985, pp. 223–224] using "word salad" to communicate with his patient, George [see Goldfield, 1994]. How did this lead to you performing raps for therapy conferences?

GOLDFIELD: I once made a rap song about family therapy for a course I was teaching at the University of Illinois. I thought it would be a nice learning tool for the students in preparing for their final exam. One of my students went to BFTC [Brief Family Therapy Center] and Insoo [Berg] heard about it. Then she commissioned me to write and perform one in honor of John Weakland at the brief therapy conference in New Orleans [see Goldfield, 1993]. After that, she commissioned me to do the ones for the Steve de Shazer and Michael White presentation in Milwaukee [White & de Shazer, 1996]. So really, Insoo has been my patron.

HOYT: What process goes into your creating the rap songs?

GOLDFIELD: It's hard to say. I hold in mind the context of the presentation I am writing it for, and the model I am writing about. The beginning is usually more gangsta hip-hop style, but as I get into the philosophy, techniques, and vignettes, I use these components to structure it.

HOYT: I hope that readers will imagine you in tough-looking rap clothes and a big boom-box blasting your background rhythms, as in the actual performances you did at the two-day White and de Shazer conference in 1996.

GOLDFIELD: I hope so.

HOYT: Thanks for the interview and the following raps. By the way, how do you say "Good-bye" in hip-hop?

GOLDFIELD: Word up! Be chillin'. Peace out.

HOYT: Word!

References

Goldfield, J. (1993). Rapnotic induction no. 1. *Journal of Systemic Therapies, 12*(2), 89–91. Reprinted in M. F. Hoyt (Ed.), *Constructive therapies* (Vol. 2, pp. 370–371). New York: Guilford Press.

Goldfield, J. (1994, December). *A utilization approach for working with adolescents and their families.* Workshop held at the Sixth International Congress on Ericksonian Approaches to Hypnosis and Psychotherapy, Los Angeles.

Haley, J. (1985). *Conversations with Milton H. Erickson, M.D.: Vol. 1. Changing individuals.* New York: Norton.

White, M., & de Shazer, S. (1996, October). *Narrative Solutions/Solution Narratives.* Conference sponsored by Brief Family Therapy Center, Milwaukee, WI.

○ *Songs on following pages* ○

The Master of Faster

Suppose while you're sitting there a miracle happens,
You hear some funky syncopated lyrical rappin'.
What will you notice, what will the signs be,
That you're hanging with the Homeys of the B.F.T.C.?

We don't pack no guns 'cause we carry Occam's razor,
Word up to Insoo Berg and Steve de Shazer.
They are our captains, they are heavy and have fame,
Don't mess with us, termination is our frame!

We don't waste no time 'cause suffering is real,
When a client comes in, we don't ask them how they feel,
We don't bring the family in to see their hierarchy,
'Cause we ain't co-dependent on normative malarkey!

We used to be slandered, accused of the quick fix,
Long-term propaganda questioned our ethics,
But now with managed care our rivals are afraid,
They tremble and don't dare to say we're just a Band-Aid.
We've become the norm, so later for the cynics,
We're taking over all the agencies and clinics!

You wanna join us now, you are ready to bang,
You're gonna say "Wow" when you comprehend our slang:
Six useful questions, perseverance and persistence,
Deconstructs and disses on that bad boy, Resistance.
It ain't our business if a client is deranged,
We only want to know about their pre-session change.
We take exception to problem talk,
Scale that mutha up and down, until it takes a walk.
If there's been trauma, don't be a dope,
Your client's in crisis, find out how they cope.
To position your client for their miracle blastoff,
Validate and normalize and compliment your ass off!

A couple came in due to yelling, screaming fights,
In a given week they kept the neighbors up six nights.
"What was different about night number seven?"
They cried and made up, made love, it was heaven.
As we talked about getting this to happen more,
They got lovey-dovey, so I left and shut the door!

Busted drug dealer came straight from making bail,
It was therapy with me or a long term in jail.
At first he was a Visitor, and then a Complainant,
He became a Customer after his arraignment.
I kept his goals realistic when he tried to sell me crack,
We settled on keeping the judge off his back!
Charges were reduced due to cooperation,
Community service and two years probation.
He lectures in the high schools, "Don't become a felon,"
He's doing telemarketing, legitimate selling.

A single Mom called, her kids were driving her crazy,
Four had A.D.D. and the other three were lazy.
One week later I met with them all,
I asked what had occurred since Mom made the call.
They all agreed she hadn't had a single conniption,
So I asked for an instead-video-description:
Suzie put the toys away after they played,
When Mom came home from work, Richard's bed was made,
Thursday night John and Linda made dinner,
'Though they accidentally microwaved the salad in the spinner,
Matthew made a schedule of who gets T.V., video games,
    the telephone, the Walkman, and C.D.,
Francine helped Brian with his homework after school,
They all agreed the week has been totally cool.
I was impressed, told them they were really smoking,
Gave a "more-of-the-same" 'cause nothing was broken!

Psychotic hearing voices, living on the street,
"What will be happening when we don't need to meet?"
"I won't get abducted by the U.F.O."
"When it passes you by, how will you know?"
"The C.I.A. will turn off the static in my head."
"When there's no more interference, what will be there instead?"
"I'll find my prescription and take my meds,
Go back to the shelter and sleep in a bed,
Stop by my mother's for some chicken soup,
Return to job training and my support group."
He decided taking meds was the easiest to get started,
The E.T.s cursed him out, then they promptly departed!

I'm going to give you compliments that ain't glib or fake,
But first I'm gonna chill, take my consultation break. . . .

You've all freaked the funk, now you're word to the max,
Jammin' with your client's goals is the hip-hop task,
'Cause if you wanna be a master of faster like me,
I've given you some clues, but your clients hold the keys.

© 1996 Joseph Goldfield. Reprinted with permission.

The Problem Talks Back

Nobody move! I'm stopping this convention,
I'm gonna tell my story, you better pay attention!
Narrative means to therapeutic ends,
Is dissin' on my Homeys, messing with my friends!
Yo, Michael White, our paths finally cross,
I'm The Problems' leader, I am their Boss!
I'm the kind of problem you never want to see,
When The Problems have a problem, then they call me!

Ever since the human cortex evolved,
When there's been suffering, my gang's been involved.
We're sophisticated, we ain't ordinary hoods,
I invented "stigma," "shall nots," "shame," and "shoulds."
I use social norms to create potential victims,
I see who conforms, that is how I pick them,
Distribute propaganda to scare and subjugate them,
Then I send my gangs out to problem saturate them!
When people tried to save the masses from our curse,
Whatever they attempted, we always made things worse.
Shamans consulted the spirits of their dead,
So we dressed up like their ancestors and played with their head!
Religions offered solace to those we put in need,
We made a stronger offer: pleasure, sin, and greed!
Philosophers were always worthy adversaries,
Now their books gather dust in the libraries.
When science came along, we really got ecstatic,
Objectifying-thing-i-fying, helped us wreak new havoc!
Attempts at protection were doomed from the start,
My gang avoids detection, we're insidious and smart!

Until, Michael White, we ran into you,
And your boy Epston's been messing with us, too!
We had had our way, all through the millennia,
Until that fateful day you dissed my boy Schizophrenia.

He had a gang, The Voices, they whispered in Gail's ear,
Told her all kinds of things that only she could hear.
They spoke to her soothingly, using hypnosis,
And told her that she'd have to live with her psychosis.
The world outside was dangerous, they would sternly warn her,
The only safe place was in her little corner.
If she tried to get away they'd tell her that they hated her,
Or they'd yell and carry on until someone sedated her!
When she went to therapy they wouldn't say a word,
But later they would rephrase what she thought she heard.
When she called you, they laughed and said "We love it!"
But after her first session, she told them all to shove it!
They were dumbfounded, it was eerily quiet,
To prevent another session, The Voices staged a riot.
They tried to drag her back to the shadows of chronic,
By turning up the volume way past supersonic!
When you asked about the new story Gail was writing,
The Voices starting arguing, there was in-fighting.
They became demoralized, they were out of sorts,
Gail made them behave like ordinary thoughts.
She finally broke through their shackles and their fetters,
By reading out loud, your follow-up letters.
The Voices went down, out with laryngitis,
That's when I heard Michael White was someone who could fight us!

My Homeboy Sneaky Poo was as sly as a fox,
He had turned Nick's house into a big litter box!
Poo enjoyed his work, he was having a ball,
He taught Nick how to paint with his doodoo on the wall.
Nick's parents were freaking, 'cause Poo was in control,
Nick was going everywhere, except the toilet bowl!
His mother had self-doubts, she was at wits' ends,
His father stopped their visits to family and friends.
They were really stumped, they were in a total bind,
'Cause everywhere they looked, you know what they would find!
When they called you we assumed a home-visit,
Poo was planning something big, and we didn't want to miss it.
But they had a family meeting, held it in the loo,
And made it to your office without Sneaky Poo.
When they got home, Poo started fainting,
'Cause Nick was removing their most recent painting!
He got potty trained for Number Two and Number One,

His parents praised his first unique outcome!
They didn't let Poo come back in and play,
Nick told him that they weren't friends, he'd have to go away.
Poo's mood declined, he really hit the skids,
He didn't respond when I lined up other kids.
He lost his creativity, he's no longer inventive,
Now he sees a shrink 'cause he's anal-retentive!

The Eating Disorders were led by "Anorexia,"
She got young girls to starve themselves, believing they were sexier!
Distorted their perceptions of how much food they ate,
Had a billion dollar racket built around weight.
Other gang members were "Weakness" and "Anemia,"
"Obsession" and "Denial," "Bingeing" and "Bulimia."
They always cast their web by creating a mystique,
Being in vogue means an ultra-thin physique.
The gang created menus of ever-shrinking portions,
Manufactured mirrors that reflected back distortions.
They made their victims exercise, worked them into frenzies,
Imbalanced their electrolytes and robbed them of their menses.
They were ruthless, they were cold, they were vicious, they were mean,
But things started changing when you came on the scene.
You told her victims "Anorexia" was just a bully,
Their appetites returned, they started eating fully.
You asked them lots of questions, most of them leading,
They threw away their tubes and got off of forced feeding.
As they got stronger, and beat back "Fatigue,"
They formed the Anti-Anorexia League!
Lately "Anorexia's" been out of circulation,
She's got her hands full, due to pending litigation,
She's suing the League for defaming her with slander,
Disrupting her business with their propaganda.

Michael White, I came here to put you in your place,
I told all my Homeys I'd be up in your face!
But mapping your influence has made me realize,
You've been authoring my downfall and my gang's demise.
You've named us, you've defamed us, you've put us on the run,
Externalized and recognized, we ain't having fun.
Moriarty had Sherlock Holmes, Napoleon Waterloo,
The Problems were the problems, 'til we got stuck with you!
As I've been rappin' and checking out my text,

I've begun to wonder what I'll do next.
Business is shrinking, I'm working longer days,
Being The Problems' Boss no longer pays.
I've had my sparkling moments, my career's been a success,
My reputation's awesome, but I don't need the stress!
I came here to thwart you, that was my intention,
But I don't want to sweat it, I'm outta this convention!

PART THREE

SPECIFIC CLINICAL APPLICATIONS

CHAPTER THIRTEEN

Children's Stories, Children's Solutions

Social Constructionist Therapy for Children and Their Families

Jeff Chang

Social constructionism, nonstructuralism, collaboration, and pragmatism guide my work, rather than an allegiance to any particular model of therapy. Practices from solution-oriented and narrative therapy have provided most of the methods for operationalizing these guiding ideas. Although some have highlighted the differences between these approaches (de Shazer, 1993; Madigan, 1996; White, 1993), I could not help but see the similarities and the possibilities for crossover and blending of methods (Chang & Phillips, 1993; Durrant & Kowalski, 1990; Eron & Lund, 1996; Friedman, 1994; Selekman, 1993, 1997). What emerged was a pragmatic integration based on the commonalities on which I chose to focus. The following is a description of some of what I have learned from teachers of therapy, from my young clients (aged six to eleven), and from their parents. I will discuss some important ideas that guide my work, then describe some useful learnings from child development, and finally outline specifically how I apply these ideas in my work with children and their families.

SOCIAL CONSTRUCTIONISM AND NONSTRUCTURALISM

I understand social constructionism to operate at many different levels and often think of peeling away layers of an onion to make sense of this for myself.[1]

First, I perceive the "big ideas" or "discourses" that, over time and history, have been taken for granted by most people in Western culture. These include the primacy of capitalism and corporatism; the preference for knowing through modernist, scientific thought; the way women and men relate; the way races interact with one another and some dominate others; and the nature of childhood. Then I look to not-so-big ideas that influence children and families in more local ways. These rest on the big ideas. For instance, the not-so-big idea that a child should achieve "up to his potential" in school rests on the larger idea that the capitalist ladder is kinder to those who have more education. So too, the concept that children can be classified as "ADHD" or "learning disabled" rests on the primacy of scientific thinking. These I call *beliefs* or *worldviews* (see Wright, Watson, & Bell, 1996). Earlier, White (1986) called them "restraints of redundancy."

Social construction also occurs at a more micro level. Interactions within the family and between the family and the therapist can cocreate or erode meanings of events. Asking about exceptions or unique outcomes, externalizing the problem, or requesting that family members "pay attention to what Elizabeth does when she goes to school in spite of her fear," can erode fixed ideas. "Reality" is viewed as constituted through the language that is used to describe it (de Shazer, 1994; Freedman & Combs, 1996), and the interactional patterns in which it is embedded (Watzlawick, 1984). I call these *patterns*. Earlier, White (1986) referred to them as "restraints of feedback."

In clinical practice, I usually work from the micro to the macro, since families typically experience more respect and acknowledgment when they are talking about what matters to them directly. Working with both patterns and beliefs bears directly on the problems brought to therapy, and affects the family's experience more directly. Being aware of the discourses provides context to help me understand what I am doing, and keep me aware of the social constructions that support the patterns and worldviews.

Structuralism refers to the idea that problematic behavior is symptomatic of a "deeper" pathology (de Shazer, 1991). While the metaphor of "surface" and "depth" to describe psychosocial problems has become a truism in our culture (de Shazer, 1994), this distinction muddles clinical problems by inviting a search for etiology. With tongue only partly in cheek, White (1984) proposed that the search for etiology be dealt this way: "After carefully and painstakingly taking a history of the problem, [the therapist] announces that s/he is sure, beyond a shadow of a doubt, that the problem is caused by at least one out of seven identifiable chance events. The therapist can also state with conviction that these could be narrowed down to three or four possibilities with a further 10–15 years research into the history of the problem" (White, 1984, p. 153). In other words, "the problem is the problem" (White, 1986).

COLLABORATION

When we realize that the kinds of conversations we have with clients constitute the way they view themselves and the therapy process, we are naturally
led to a collaborative stance. Collaboration has been described as "minimizing
the hierarchy" (see Chapter Fourteen of this volume), "leading from one step
behind" (Berg & Anderson, 1994), or "not knowing" (Anderson & Goolishian,
1992). How does one operationalize this with children, who require adult guidance, structure, protection, and indeed hierarchy?

To state what should be obvious, I do my best to listen and to treat children's
time as valuable as mine. This means including them in the conversation, listening to what they say, and respecting their unique knowledge, which may lead
to unorthodox solutions. Unfortunately, it appears that we are not as good at
doing this as we aspire to be. For example, Cederborg (1997) found that many
family therapists, despite their belief that it is important to have children attend
family therapy, scarcely spoke with them, or worse yet, assumed that they knew
the children's needs without even speaking to them. Thus, the idea that children
should be seen and not heard (or not heard from) is alive and all too well among
therapists. Including children in the conversation means using modes of expression that children prefer, as opposed to trying to fit them into a Procrustean bed
of adult talk. I describe some ideas for doing this later in this chapter. In setting
the stage for therapy, I address directly with children their understanding of why
we are meeting and what will happen. Six-year-old Michael attended at my office
with his mother Kelly over concern about his outbursts of anger.[2] Like many parents, Kelly had told Michael that I was "like a doctor," not an image that typically engenders comfort or collaboration among children.

JEFF: Michael, what did your mom tell you about coming here today?

MICHAEL: I can't remember.

KELLY: We talked about it, remember, like a doctor?

MICHAEL: Oh, yeah. Mom said it was like going to the doctor,
but for your feelings.

JEFF: Really? Do you like going to the doctor? *[Michael shakes his head]*
Well, when you go to the doctor, like if you've ever had an operation,
do you do anything when you're getting an operation.

MICHAEL: *[thinking me a bit stupid]* No, you're asleep. My mom gots *[sic]*
her gall bladder out and she was asleep. *[Kelly looks chagrined]*

JEFF: Right, you cannot do much to help if you're asleep. You just go there,
the doctor cuts you open, and they pull your guts out . . . and sew you

up, and you don't do anything, just lie there asleep, right? *[Michael nods his head]* OK, well what I like to be called is like a coach. Were you ever in any sports?

MICHAEL: Tee-ball and soccer. My coach for tee-ball was Mr. Sykes, Caitlin's dad. Mom . . . *[conversation about who was the coach for soccer]*

JEFF: So what does a coach do?

MICHAEL: Teach us how to play the game, help us practice. . . .

JEFF: Right. What about if you lost really bad, 37 to 1, and you were really sad and wanted to give up?

MICHAEL: He would say, it's not so bad, cheer up, you can do it.

JEFF: Right. So if you have a really good coach, but the players don't try, will you win the game?

MICHAEL: No.

JEFF: And if you have players that try really hard, but don't get shown properly by the coach how to play the game, is that good? Will that be a good team? *[Michael shakes his head]* And sometimes the coach can see things you can't see from where you are.

MICHAEL: And sometimes I can see things the coach doesn't see!

JEFF: Right. So if we work together—I'll be the coach and you can be the player, we should be able to help you with your Temper. Deal?

MICHAEL: Deal! *[we shake hands, and I invite Kelly to shake on it, too]*

The coaching frame allows me to adopt a collaborative yet appropriately adult stance, and suggests to the child that his participation in solution-building is necessary.

PRAGMATISM

Amundson (1996) has argued that, rather than being held captive to specific models of therapy, we would do better to cultivate "pragmatic habits of thought" (p. 476). Our models of therapy must "earn their keep . . . a theory is asked to perform, to reveal itself in relation to its utility, in the light of the clinical moment" (p. 477). This means subjecting our practices to the ultimate test—the fit with the experience of the client. In other words, "If it works, keep doing it; if it doesn't work, do something different" (de Shazer, 1988).

CHILD DEVELOPMENT

While some postmodern colleagues have eschewed a normalizing discourse (e.g., Madigan, 1996; Madigan & Epston, 1995; Sanders, 1997), I have taken the position that such ideas—Erik Erikson's (1950) psychosocial development stages and Jean Piaget's (1973, 1977) cognitive development stages—can be useful if they are subordinated to the knowledge and experience of our clients (Chang, in press-a). Also, in the rush to disavow ourselves as postmodernists from normalizing, modernist ideas, the rich social constructionist literature on child development is often overlooked (e.g., Bruner, 1987; Bryant, 1979; Butterworth, 1987; Feldman, 1987; Lloyd, 1987; Smedslund, 1979). I have found the ideas discussed in the following paragraphs helpful for understanding and collaborating with children's constructions.

Experiencing Versus Expressing

Memory researchers and specialists in cognitive and language development generally assert that elementary-aged children have richer experiences of events in their lives than they can typically express verbally (Fivush, Kuebli, & Clubb, 1992; Price & Goodman, 1990; Nelson, 1986). In the context of conversations with adults, children are quite sensitive to their conversational partners, and begin to anticipate their listeners' needs when they converse. They engage in metacognition, that is, they evaluate what they are saying and check that it fits with criteria about the purpose and context of conversation.

Representation and Cognition

Children between the ages of six and eleven have typically developed the ability to de-center, that is, to construe events from others' points of view. They can create mental representations of a series of concrete actions, usually events that they have already experienced. It is much more difficult for children of this age to create mental representations of abstractions, so it is helpful if concrete objects or visual representations are used to aid the creation of representations. Inductive reasoning—the use of specific observations to arrive at a more general theory—is mastered by children of this age. Yet until the age of twelve or thirteen, young people have a very hard time reversing this process—that is, to begin with a theory or principle and hypothesize about what ought to be observed if the theory is correct (Bryant, 1979).

Storage and Retrieval

It is generally agreed that, before the age of ten or eleven, children do not store memories as sequential narratives. What is stored in memory tends to be very accurate, specific, and discrete, and can be organized into therapeutically useful experiences by repeated telling (Bull, 1995; Fivush & Shukat, 1995; Poole & White, 1995; Saywitz, 1995).

Psychosocial Tasks

Erik Erikson (1950) suggested that school-aged children have a need to exercise mastery over the world—what he termed the struggle of "industry versus inferiority." While stage theories of normal development have been criticized from a postmodern or narrative perspective (e.g., Sanders, 1997), experientially, Erikson's assertion rings true to me. Children between the ages of about six and eleven love to influence the world and they love to note their impact and mastery on it. My experience as a Cub leader, as well as a parent and therapist, has provided many examples of children taking delight in being able to have an impact upon the world with their efforts.

FIVE KEY TASKS OF THERAPY

My map for a social constructionist therapy (Chang, in press-b) includes five key tasks: developing and maintaining a cooperative relationship; understanding the clients' competencies and worldview; negotiating or constructing the problem so it is solvable; finding, eliciting, or creating meaningful experiences of change (in session and between sessions); and amplifying, anchoring, and maintaining these experiences of change. These do not necessarily need to be performed in any specific order, and you may find yourself doubling back to catch up with yourself.

Develop and Maintain a Cooperative Relationship

Imagine being at your graduate school office. You receive a phone call telling you to meet with your committee in two hours. When you ask the reason you are to meet, it is vague. Dutifully you go. The others, all senior to you, are already there. As you enter, you are informed that your comprehensive oral examination in research methods has been moved up, and in fact, the exam is . . . now. How would you react? Would you be anxious? Angry? Would cooperation come easily to you? This might correspond to the experience of a child entering therapy, and I would be tempted to ask, "Why would anyone cooperate with such a procedure?"

Inviting Customership from Children. Imagine for a moment another scenario. As a preteen, who was the person you always looked forward to seeing? Maybe it was an older sibling's boyfriend or girlfriend, an aunt or uncle, a grandparent, family friend, coach, Cub or Scout leader, or teacher. What was significant about that person? If you are anything like me, it wasn't very complicated: the person listened to you, was more fun and interesting than your parents, and seemed to really want to spend time with you. When my son Paul is around certain people (Grandpa, Uncle Matt, and our friend Scott are just three), I may as well not exist. Paul would do anything for them. In therapy we are responsible for initiating relationships that can support the child's desire to experiment with different behaviors. Solution-focused ideas about relationship (Berg, 1994; de Shazer,

1988; Miller, Duncan, & Hubble, 1997) suggest that we fit our recommendations for client action with their relationship to our services. In the context of a lack of familiarity, anxiety, and perhaps a feeling of "I am a bad kid," children generally do not come with a customer-style relationship. It's our responsibility to ensure that our invitations to relationship are really inviting. One has to be a good host to "host therapeutic conversations" (Furman & Ahola, 1992).

The easiest way to do this is to get the relationship off on the right foot. From the beginning, I work to place myself in the position of a "therapeutic uncle." If the child is in the waiting room with a parent, I make sure that I spend time on the floor, meeting the child there before inviting the family into my office. I engage in small talk about interests, schools (and getting out of school to see me), siblings, and the like. My own personality is to be a bit boisterous, and I typically use that to my advantage by acting playfully, all this before I ever get into my office.

Goaling with Children. The process of solution-focused therapy, put simply, is to find out what the client wants by forming a picture of hypothetical solutions, bridging from the hypothetical to real-life exceptions, and using these to negotiate the next small step. This process has been called "goaling" (Walter & Peller, 1996), since setting goals does not just happen in the first session, but is a fluid process all through therapy. Children from six to eleven have difficulty using the hypothetical big picture to generate proximal goals, but can move from specific instances to the big picture. Therefore, when children have a hard time imagining a hypothetical solution even with the aid of visual prompts, I tend to negotiate small, proximal goals with children. If the goals are simple and clear enough, it is not necessary to have them orient themselves to the larger hypothetical solutions.

Returning to six-year-old Michael, I learned he had a three-year-old sister, Marie. Like many older siblings, he found Marie to be more than a minor irritant at times. We had already had some externalizing conversations about "Temper." This conversation demonstrates forming a simple goal based on the child's life experience:

JEFF: So I bet your sister bugs you at times.

MICHAEL: Yeah! She hangs around when I'm playing with my friends. I don't like that very much . . . and she comes into my room and if I'm watching TV, she stands right in the way. . . . last week she poked me when I was watching TV.

JEFF: Wow, that's too bad. What do you do to get her to stop?

MICHAEL: Well, sometimes I hit her.

KELLY: And that's one of the reasons we're here and that's what I'm worried about.

JEFF: What about when you don't hit her? What else do you do?

MICHAEL: I don't know.

KELLY: Well, the other day he was really good, he just walked away.

JEFF: Really. How did you do that?

MICHAEL: I said to myself, "I better get out of here or else I will get in trouble for hitting her."

JEFF: What else do you do?

MICHAEL: Sometimes I ask her nice.

JEFF: Really, what do you say?

MICHAEL: I say, "Marie, please leave me alone."

JEFF: What if she doesn't listen?

MICHAEL: *[casting a glance at his mother]* Well, sometimes I tell her to buzz off.

KELLY: Yes, well, "buzz off" is OK, but sometimes it goes further, if you know what I mean.

JEFF: Mm hm. I'm sure I do. Michael, remember we were talking about Temper a few minutes ago, and how Temper is spoiling things for you.

MICHAEL: I hate Temper!

JEFF: Yeah, Temper is really bad to you, eh? . . . *[we discuss some things that Temper encourages Michael to do]* . . . All that stuff is pretty bad, eh?

MICHAEL: Yeah.

JEFF: I have an idea about how to stop Temper from spoiling your life.

MICHAEL: What is it?

JEFF: Well, you know how you ask your sister to leave you alone?

MICHAEL: Yeah.

JEFF: Well, I was wondering if you could tell Temper to leave you alone, just quietly, inside your head.

MICHAEL: Yeah, but what if it doesn't work?

JEFF: Well, what is the next step with Marie?

MICHAEL: I tell her to buzz off!

JEFF: Yeah, well, don't say anything any meaner to Temper, no swears, OK? And inside your head, just quiet, right? OK, let's practice. . . . *[we simulate a Temper onslaught and Michael practices telling Temper to go away and even to buzz off]*

As I have surveyed colleagues, students, and workshop audiences, there seems to be a consensus that at most 30 percent of those parents presenting for child therapy enter with a customer-type relationship, that is, wanting assistance to develop new solutions. The rest perceive that there is a problem and see it as residing in the child. Why? Adults naturally think they're right. Moreover, if they have experienced traditional therapy or school-based intervention, they may feel blamed for the child's problems. I keep this in mind as I ask for parents' help. A respectful, "not-knowing" listening style, founded on the belief that there are many possible ways to view reality, invites parents to participate as partners in therapy. I usually tell parents that it is my general practice to see the child and the parents he or she is living with in the first session to obtain the necessary information about the situation, without implying that parents are to blame for the problem.

In the initial session, I am also listening carefully about how the referral came about. The family physician or pediatrician, school, child protection worker, or grandparent may be motivated to do something. I am curious and listen carefully for whose idea it was to come, who has something to gain or lose, who might be distressed or bothered by the child's behavior, and who might be willing to take action toward solution development.

Understanding the Clients' Beliefs, Worldview, and Strengths

Typically, children experience problems as part of themselves, and may almost viscerally have adopted an identity of *badness*. Parents, on the other hand, often have well-developed accounts or causal beliefs about the problem. At times, they are well read and have developed sophisticated clinical hypotheses—often more sophisticated than mine, since I do not find structuralist explanations helpful. I do my best to listen carefully, uncritically, and respectfully, acknowledging that many different understandings of their stories are possible. I might simply listen, in what Freedman and Combs (1996) call a "deconstructive" manner, or I might ask questions that elicit beliefs (Wright, Watson, & Bell, 1996) about the problem such as these:

- What theories do you have about the cause for this behavior?
- Do you think that Ken can control the tantrums?
- Are you confident that the medication can help Troy with his "hyperness?"
- Who first diagnosed Ken with ADHD? How did he or she arrive at this conclusion?

Miller, Duncan, and Hubble (1997) note that one of the important features of a working therapeutic alliance is agreement between clients and therapist on tasks, goals, and method. Tasks must make sense to the clients given their worldview. The parents' worldview probably contains ideas about previously attempted solutions, so it is important to understand these as well.

The Child's Competencies. It's important to get to know what children are good at, and how they got that way. Special talents, interests, and skills can give the therapist clues about frames of competence that the child may already experience. For example, nine-year-old Ken had been enrolled in and enjoying tai kwon do for three years. When I heard this, I looked at him as if he was dangerous and asked him to come and stand in front of my chair.

JEFF: Tell me, Ken, if I was attacking you, and I did *this [directing a half-speed punch toward his abdomen]*, what—Whoa! *[as Ken intercepted my punch]*

KEN: *[looking proud]* That's what I'd do!

JEFF: Wow, how did you get so fast?

KEN: *[smiling]* I just did it over and over again.

JEFF: Oh, you're not so fast, what if I did this: *[directing a mock punch toward his face, which he deftly deflected]* Hey! *[Ken laughs]* OK, what about this: *[kicking my leg out toward him while still sitting in my chair; he easily blocks the kick]* Hey! Tell me how you got so good.

KEN: Well, I just practiced over and over.

JEFF: What do you mean, you practice?

KEN: We just do the same thing over and over.

JEFF: Isn't it boring? Doing the same thing over and over?

KEN: No, it's fun.

JEFF: How can it be fun? Doing the same thing over and over again.

KEN: You get better at it the more you do it.

JEFF: Oh, and it makes you feel good to get better at it. So practicing works to help you get better. I see.

KEN: *[a bit exasperated with me]* Now you get it!

JEFF: But OK, tell me this: is practicing kind of hard sometimes?

KEN: Yeah.

JEFF: So don't you feel like giving up?

KEN: Well, sometime I do, but I don't.

JEFF: Why not?

KEN: I think about how I got better and what I'm learning.

JEFF: What about at first, when you were still new and your learning was slow?

KEN: It was harder at first.

JEFF: . . . but you kept going. You stuck with it?

KEN: *[proudly]* I kept going!

JEFF: Do you know what "persistent" means?

KEN: No.

JEFF: Persistent is when you stick to something and stick with it and stick with it, and don't give up, even if it is hard. Do you think you are a persistent person?

KEN: *[proudly]* Yeah!

There are multiple views of this vignette. From an Ericksonian frame, Ken and I symbolically practiced his being in control while we had a metaphorical conversation about the nature of change. At a content level, we know that he has had at least one experience in his young life about practice and repetition leading to learning and change. From a social constructionist perspective, we might say that this conversation, in a small way, was constitutive of Ken's self-concept—he didn't previously think of himself as persistent, or competent in other ways, until this view was drawn forth, but now perhaps persistence is an emerging part of his emerging identity or self-concept. As it turns out, Ken was able to see persistence as an attribute when he was overcoming Temper.

Negotiate or Construct the Problem So It Is Solvable

A solution-focused approach would generally look to develop hypothetical solutions (Berg, 1994; De Jong & Berg, 1997), perhaps by posing the "Miracle Question" or a variety of other possibilities (Walter & Peller, 1992).[3] The client's response to the Miracle Question is typically used to bridge to real-life exceptions: "Is any small part of this happening already?" This process is much like the process of beginning with a theory or general principle and predicting what might happen in light of the theory. Especially with children, if this is only done with verbal as opposed to visual representation, the therapist will probably face a litany of "I-don't-knows." I have found it useful in these cases to use more experience-near representations of hypothetical solutions, such as drawing or acting out the scene. Consider Ben (aged eight), who was troubled by outbursts of aggression largely provoked by his younger brother, who taunted him by making faces and calling him names. I took the role of his brother. Ben chose to imagine a miracle of turning himself into a "mute" (although I think he meant "mime") and therefore not talking back to or threatening his brother when he was feeling provoked. As a "mute" he was able to experience himself as having mastery over his feelings of anger, as having fun, and being funny. Ben also practiced appropriate ways of telling his brother to stop bothering him, and controlling the welling feelings of anger that he often experienced. Ben was able to imagine and enact his parents' reactions to his helpful solution behavior.

Children can also be assisted to develop hypothetical solutions by drawing pictures of the miracle. The visual portrayal of hypothetical solutions helps children enrich their descriptions of what the solution will look like. With nine-year-old Zachary, the interactional component of the miracle drawing was particularly influential with his parents. He was "doing my homework, listening, and not swearing." He drew his mother spending time with him in the evening like she used to "before my temper got bad." He put his father in another corner of the drawing patiently helping Zachary with homework. The drawing prompted Zachary to identify more instances in which parts of the miracle picture had already happened. Previously discouraged and self-blaming, Zachary's parents, Jim and Rita, were affirmed when Zachary was able to identify helpful aspects of their behavior that were already happening. It was not difficult for them to keep doing more of what was working. Rather than me commenting on what they were doing wrong, and trying to correct them, their son commented on what they were doing right.

Although I use art material and play as media for expression, I do not consider what I do to be "play therapy" or "art therapy." I greatly respect those trained in these modalities. My goal is not to elicit material with the purpose of intervening in unconscious processes, nor to create a transference-type relationship to allow a corrective emotional experience. It is simply to allow room for alternative avenues of expression for my young clients.

Videotalk: Developing Clear Problem Descriptions. While a focus on solutions, exceptions, and competencies is to be preferred, at times it is necessary to seek a problem description. When the clients' (particularly the parents') experience and conversation is so dominated by the problem that interrupting them would be seen as disrespectful and dismissive (Nylund & Corsiglia, 1994), I ask them to carefully and specifically describe the problem pattern. O'Hanlon and Weiner-Davis (1989; see also Chapter Seven in this volume) call this "videotalk." In a social constructionist therapy, questions do not function merely to get information, but to give information and imply different or multiple ways of viewing things to the one questioned. So, by seeking a clear behavioral description, I try to get information that assists me to conceptualize the problem in terms of patterns, beliefs and worldview, and discourse. As long as the focus is on the problem, I find it more useful to invite conversations that imply agency, rather than those that see the problem as a fixed entity or essential quality of the person.

Problem labels often take over the way a young person thinks of himself. Ten-year-old Matthew reported to me in our initial meeting, "I have ADHD." I wanted to turn this totalizing label into a description. "ADHD," in this case, was a constraining label and closed down alternatives for him. By asking for a behavioral description, I sought to crystallize a more helpful view that would

open possibilities for change. To find out about the specific behaviors and interactional patterns involved, I asked questions like:

- When ADHD is bothering you, what kinds of things do you do?
- What else do you (or does he) do that you don't want to?
- What does that look like?
- When he does that, what do you do in response?
- What do you say to him?
- Then what happens?

Sequences of behavior and interaction may be experienced as automatic.
Matthew's experience was that the ADHD was overwhelming and came upon
him too fast to do much about it: "I don't know what gets into me." Asking
about the bodily and cognitive aspects of the problem can suggest points of
entry for pattern interruption (O'Hanlon & Weiner-Davis, 1989; Chapter Seven,
this volume). Also, it can imply agency, as aspects of the problem pattern that
go previously unnoticed can be clarified. When I asked Matthew, "What part of
your body does ADHD go into?" he replied, "I feel all jumpy inside . . . ," "My
hands get all tingly," and "My leg shakes when I sit in my desk at school."
I also asked Matthew, what ADHD said to him inside his head. He told me it
said, "I don't care," "I think that I don't want to do what the class is doing,"
"BORING!!!!" He added, "Afterwards [after feeling out of control and misbe-
having], I thought *stupid, stupid, stupid!*" In taking apart the problem pattern,
the problem can be cut down to size and the therapist can acknowledge the
family's felt experience.[4]

Normalizing Conversations. Normalizing conversations can further help in
cutting problems down to size. Although others have rightly criticized the discourses of *normality* and *abnormality* as pathologizing of those with unique or
unusual abilities or experiences (Madigan & Epston, 1995; Sanders, 1997), I
have maintained elsewhere, with apologies to Bruce Cockburn, that "the trouble
with normal is the way it gets used" (Chang, in press-a).[5] Parents may have
pathologized their children by coming to hold beliefs about the way children
"should" develop and behave. For instance, misbehaving boys are commonly
worried about by parents who are concerned that their children "show no
remorse" for their actions and appear to have "no conscience." This may lead
to interactional patterns in which the more the parents attempt to encourage
remorse (or guilt) by earnestly trying to convince boys of the error of their ways,
the more the boys are likely to clam up and disengage, engendering even more
earnest efforts to invite remorse, and so on. This interactional pattern might be
derailed by some conversation about gender socialization (C. Gilligan, 1982) or

moral development (Kohlberg, 1981). Metaphorical stories can also be told to normalize parents' experience. Rather than resorting to mystical ideas about "using your unconscious," it is probably sufficient to tell parents about another set of parents who faced a similar situation, and how they handled it—and of course, to observe and listen carefully to their response (O'Hanlon & Weiner-Davis, 1989). This enables the family to negotiate a more solvable problem definition based on changing a specific behavior rather than engendering remorse or figuring out why the young person is behaving in a so-called abnormal fashion. Thus the use of ideas about what is "normal" or "abnormal" should be judged by pragmatic effect (Amundson, 1996), not a predetermined position about what is appropriate. The critique of the terms *normal* and *abnormal* provides a useful caution, but should not operate as a prohibition.

Externalizing the Problem. My exchanges with Michael, Ken, and Matthew (quoted earlier in this chapter) all had elements of externalizing conversations. In such conversations, the person is addressed as separate from the problem, and therefore as having a relationship with the problem (Roth & Epston, 1996). This is not a technique but an attitude; it is founded on the belief that persons are not problems and that problems do not reside in the essential nature of persons (Zimmerman & Dickerson, 1996). Externalizing the problem decreases conflict over who is "to blame" for problems, reduces the sense of failure in families, unites family members against the problem, and opens family members to view the problem situation in different ways (White, 1988a, 1988b). This can provide the family with a mutually acceptable problem definition.

Deconstructive Questioning. Deconstructive questioning occurs as an outgrowth of deconstructive listening. This process "invites people to see their stories from different perspectives, to notice how they are constructed (or *that* they constructed), note their limits, and discover that there are other possible narratives" (Freedman & Combs, 1996, p. 57, emphasis in original). Curiosity and a "not-knowing" attitude inform a deconstructive stance,[6] and deconstruction should not be confused with "reframing" beliefs or labeling them as "irrational."[7] The following types of questions, used in the context of externalizing conversations, might be asked of parents:

- How did you come by the idea that Jason can't control his bed-wetting?
- How do you think your experience of childhood fears affects the way you treat Alyssa when she is fearful?
- What's the history of the idea that boys should not give in to fears?
- Does Temper have any helpers or partners? What seems to be giving Temper a boost?

- When you think you are failing Brian as a parent, how does this affect your response to him?

- What does Hyperness do to get between the two of you as parents?

Find, Elicit, or Create Meaningful Experiences of Difference: In Session

A social constructionist therapy seeks to constitute a reality more focused on solutions, competence, and abilities than on problems and pathology. Thus, the fourth critical task in such a therapy is to inculcate, in the experience of the child and family, "a difference that makes a difference" (Nunnally, de Shazer, Lipchik, & Berg, 1986; de Shazer, 1991). This is done both in the session through the interviewing process (Lipchik & de Shazer, 1986), and between sessions by asking the child and family to perform end-of-session tasks.

Eliciting Exceptions and Unique Outcomes. I am most curious about when the problem is not present or what the family is doing the decrease the presence of the problem in their lives. Many sources provide guidance as to how to ask such questions, which, from a narrative framework, can be seen to elicit "unique outcomes" or "sparkling moments" (Freedman & Combs, 1996; White, 1988b), and from a solution-focused framework can be seen to elicit "exceptions" (De Jong & Berg, 1997; de Shazer, 1985, 1988; Walter & Peller, 1992).[8] Since children recall and experience their lives more richly than they can say, nonverbal modes of expression are useful in generating the news of a difference.

Drawings of real-life exceptions and solutions reify the experience of mastery and enrich the verbal descriptions that children and their parents provide. Kayla (age eight) drew a picture of her being able to go to school without fear. The picture prompted her to recall that she has been reminding herself that she had specific friends at school, that she has reviewed with her mother that morning what to do if she had gotten "queasy" at school, and that when she did notice herself get "queasy" with "butterflies in my stomach," she took a deep breath. Kayla took copies of the drawing to school and her bedroom to serve as a reminder of what to do. For children at this age, a visual representation is useful to prompt recall of helpful associations, and to enrich and deepen the experience of mastery over the problem.

The Highlight Package. Since routine is important to children, I generally conduct sessions in fairly predictable ways. Boys especially, who make up most of my preteen caseload, usually know what the highlights are in a television sportscast. In Canada, where I practice, many boys are particularly cognizant of hockey and whether their favorite player scored or made a great save. Thus the *highlight package* has became a fixture in my sessions. The second and subsequent sessions typically begin with a revisitation of "great plays," "goals," and "fantastic saves" that the young person has made. The family is asked to prepare for the highlight package by selecting out the "plays of the week" to report to me in the next session. Thus, this interview procedure links to a between-session observation task as well. One enthusiastic father, a hockey fanatic, helped his son develop a play-by-play report of the highlights in the distinctive cadence and phraseology of the late great Canadian hockey announcer, Danny Gallivan. The highlight package forms a ritual to begin each session by discussing the solution behaviors since the last session. Family members often correct each other (children love to correct their parents with my playful support) to ensure that the highlight package is the first order of business.

Interactive Storytelling and Writing. The framework of a short story (see Durrant, 1990)—with a beginning, middle, and end stage, and with the child client as the central character—engages children and provides a familiar linguistic structure. I usually take the role of scribe and editor, although parents are often interested (or drafted by their children) into doing this. Typically, we use ten or fifteen minutes at the end of the session to commit the story to paper or computer. The beginning of the story is informed by the problem description. The middle part of the story is developed over several sessions, and is edited to focus on the highlights and solution patterns. The ending of the story points to a problem-free future in which the goals of therapy have been met. The narrative structure provides more coherence for children, since it is more likely that they will have the cognitive ability to project forward in time from a symbolically represented event, as opposed to projecting backward from a hypothetical solution. It should be noted, again, that the stories are not interpreted by the therapist. Here, the stories simply provide an alternative means of expression for children who are less fluent in typical therapy-type conversation styles, in contrast to other models (e.g., Gardner, 1971), which use the stories as material for intervening in unconscious process.

Scaling. Scaling questions (De Jong & Berg, 1997) are used in solution-focused therapy to track progress as experienced by the client and to negotiate incremental goals. With children, visual representations can be used to assist the child to communicate experience of the problem and to differentiate "what it will be like when it goes up a notch." Janet Roth and Christina Hayes of Australia have developed a scaling kit that contains a number of "interesting concrete items (usually, but not always, ten of each), which help to 'make the intangible become tangible'." Roth's favorite is a "face (royal blue and about ten inches across), with a big soft red fluffy nose, two large beaded eyes, and ten glass teardrops that are held in a small red satin drawstring bag." The children put the teardrops on the face to scale sadness (J. Roth, personal communication, 1997).

Enactment and Rehearsal. Solution behaviors can be playfully acted out instead of simply discussed. When clients are willing and interested, doing this can lead to rich experiences of difference. Recently, ten-year-old Jesse and his mother, Lorraine, demonstrated for me in session a number of solution patterns such as how Lorraine helped Jesse to calm down after an argument; how Jesse got ready for school and made his lunch without prompting in the morning; and how Jesse made a decision to come home right away after school instead of taking off with his friends, among others.

Find, Elicit, or Create Meaningful Experiences of Difference: Between Sessions

End-of-session interventions are used to increase the clients' noticing of solution patterns and increase the performance of solutions, "changing the viewing and doing of the problem" (O'Hanlon & Weiner-Davis, 1989). While relationship styles of "visitor," "complainant," and "customer,"[9] the presence or absence of exceptions, and whether the exceptions are random or deliberate (De Jong & Berg, 1997), are all typically used by solution-focused therapists, I tend to depend on the relationship pattern almost exclusively when working with children. This is because, with children, I find it more helpful to develop the experience of competence and mastery—"industry versus inferiority" (Erikson, 1950), as it were—rather than be concerned about whether the reported exception is a real-life one, or whether it is random or deliberate. Because children find it difficult to express all they're experiencing, I focus on enriching and deepening their experience. Also, as solution-focused therapists tell us (Berg, 1994; Berg & Miller, 1992; De Jong & Berg, 1997), relationship patterns are highly fluid and can depend a great deal on how the goal is negotiated. Therefore, I tend to develop simple and focused tasks for children. The frames of *practice* and *experiments* are particularly useful. For example, with Michael, I negotiated a simple task, namely, "telling Temper to go away, inside your head, and if Temper really starts to fight back to tell it to buzz off."[10]

On the other hand, with parents, I remind myself to be more conscious of their experience of exceptions—do exceptions seem random or intentional? As I noted earlier, it is my observation—confirmed by colleagues, students, and trainees in my workshops—that about 30 percent of the time, parents enter the first session of therapy concerning their children in a customer-style relationship. Most often, they are looking to the therapist to work some magic with the child. They have a felt experience of the child's problematic behavior, but may not feel that action on their part is involved in the solution. Therefore, in the first session, I usually ask parents to be on the lookout for small behavioral changes made by the child. In the next session, I attribute "positive blame" (De Jong & Berg, 1997) to them for the changes. I follow a fairly standard solution-focused manner of developing an end-of-session intervention, with compliments, a bridging statement, and a homework task (De Jong & Berg, 1997). For example, I gave the following message to Michael and Kelly:[11]

> I want to say a few things because I was so impressed with what I saw today. First of all, Kelly, I want to note how perceptive you are. You have given me a lot of information today about Michael's behavior, which is very valuable to me in thinking about what is going on. You're very good at noticing what he does. Also, your concern is very well placed and not overblown at all. I think that the timing of your contacting the EAP [Employee Assistance Program, the source of the referral] to come here was great, since we can nip this thing in the bud. Michael, you have some good ideas already about how to keep Temper from spoiling your life. And you did a great job practicing some new tricks to get Temper away. Michael, I would like to ask you to keep practicing the tricks we practiced today for how to keep Temper away. Kelly, because you are so good at observing, I would like to ask you to keep track of any small changes that occur in Michael's behavior, so that you can let me know what he did and how he did it, and also notice the changes that occur in your responses to him.

Retelling and Rereading. Child development and memory specialists tell us that when children retell accounts of their lives, it prompts recall. I would assert that retelling stories of competence enhances their robust experiences of competence. Seven-year-old Bradley and I wrote a story in which he was featured overcoming the "Squirmies" (his name for attentional problems). Reading this story aloud with one of his parents (sometimes he would read and sometimes his parent would read) was a regular habit (two to four times a week) for about six weeks. New developments in the story were added as the therapy progressed.

Ken, the tai kwon do aficionado, had regular "bragging meetings" with his mother most evenings. She was given a little instruction about how to ask about exceptions and unique outcomes, and Ken was asked to keep track of what he was doing to overcome Temper at school.

Amplify, Anchor, and Maintain New Experiences

In subsequent sessions, the emphasis is on amplifying change. Ideas about questioning to amplify change, from either a solution-focused or narrative perspective, can be found elsewhere (e.g., De Jong & Berg, 1997; Freedman & Combs, 1996; Walter & Peller, 1992; White, 1988b). I might be inclined to modify these guidelines by emphasizing "how" questions with adults (whose ability to recall and recount events may provide more useful information in this regard), whereas with children, I tend to deemphasize "how" questions and instead focus on the retelling of the problem-free situation or problem-defeating behaviors so as to inculcate these into the child's experience. The child's experience of competence is enhanced in the retelling.

Creating an Audience for Change. Many other practitioners have written about therapeutic letters, certificates, celebrations, and rituals in a more thorough manner than I could do justice to here. Letters that summarize and highlight competencies and strengths (Nylund & Thomas, 1994; White & Epston, 1990) serve to enrich and thicken the descriptions of solution knowledges. Clients have reported that letters are worth between 3.2 and 4.5 sessions of therapy (Freedman and Combs, 1996). Certificates (Freedman & Combs, 1996; Metcalf, 1995) are also useful in this regard. Nylund (1997) has used a "news release" format that is faxed or sent to relevant people in the child's social context. Recently, I've been experimenting with using a cyber consulting group in which colleagues in all parts of the world, and their clients, have corresponded with my clients and exchanged solution knowledges by e-mail. Children are particularly excited by getting a response from an age-mate in Sweden, New Zealand, or California, exchanging advice about how to deal with a vexing problem. Making knowledge public—with the client's consent, of course—by opening up meetings to teachers, residential staff, or social workers, circulating letters and certificates to others, and having celebratory meetings to highlight change—can give children a useful sense of mastery, share their success with others, and sensitize others to attend to solution behavior instead of problem patterns.

THE HEART OF THE MATTER

In this chapter, I have listed guiding ideas of social constructionism, nonstructuralism, pragmatism, and collaboration; relayed useful knowledge from developmental psychology; and described how I have operationalized these ideas in clinical practice. But nothing I've said so far touches the *heart and soul* of working with children. Stephen Gilligan (1996, 1997), discussing his Self-Relations Model of psychotherapy, assumes that we have "an indestructible tender soft spot" that "exists at the core of each person." As an example of connecting with the tender soft spot, he writes, "everyone has had the experience of being 'turned on' by the presence of a young life" (1997, p. 4). I noticed this as I began to listen seriously to children, not simply to see them as a hassle in conducting and managing sessions.[12] Please open yourself to the felt sense of your tender soft spot and the connection to that of your clients, young and old.

Endnotes

1. I realize that by using the term *level* I am using a structuralist metaphor.

2. Names of all clients have been changed so as to protect their confidentiality. All clients, young and old, consented to the use of their stories in this way.

3. The Miracle Question: "Tonight, while you were asleep, suppose a miracle happened, but you were not aware of it because you were asleep. What would be different the very next day that would tell you that a miracle had happened? What would be the first thing that you'd notice?" (de Shazer, 1985, 1988).

4. For further discussions of narrative approaches to ADHD, see Nylund & Corsiglia (1996) and Law (1997).

5. Bruce is a Canadian musician and social justice activist. I've appropriated the title to his song, "The Trouble with Normal" (Cockburn, 1983).

6. As de Shazer (1991, p. 50) notes, *deconstruction* is not the opposite of *construction,* whose opposite is *destruction.*

7. In fact, I was concerned about discussing the process of deconstruction in the section titled "Negotiate or Construct the Problem So It Is Solvable," as it might suggest more of an interventive stance that I would intend. In any event, I decided to place it here, because unpacking or unraveling the strands of influence that undergird the problem very often leads to a subtle shift of the problem definition or the perceived locus of the problem. In the course of developing their description, people tend to turn away from an explanation based on blame, from immovable labeling and the belief that the problem "lives inside" the child, toward a view that is more open to multiple ideas or new possibilities.

8. The interesting question of how "exceptions" and "unique outcomes" may differ is beyond the scope of this discussion (see Chang & Phillips, 1993; de Shazer, 1993; White, 1993; White & de Shazer, 1996). Clients prefer both.

9. It is important to note that these are descriptions of relationship patterns, not classifications of persons.

10. The idea of "telling Temper to go away" came from the client. This is different from a cognitive-behavioral restructuring approach, especially one aligned with the so-called rationalist school, which presumes that clients' ideas need to be changed and thus the therapist, from an expert position, identifies alleged distortions in the clients' thinking and then prescribes the needed "correct" view (see Chapter Four of this volume; Meichenbaum, cited in Hoyt, 1996; Hoyt & Berg, 1998). In contrast, my work is more client-driven; the effort is directed toward identifying client strengths and solutions, and helping the client identify those.

11. The end-of-session intervention message is based on the therapist carefully listening for the client's worldview, motivations, intentions, and competencies. Much of context of this particular message is not fully conveyed here because of the excerpted nature of the vignette. I would not want to give the impression that change in therapy is created largely or solely by brilliant and amazing end-of-

session intervention messages, as has been the impression generated by earlier incarnations of "brief therapy" (e.g., Haley, 1976; Madanes, 1984).

12. For a discussion of the importance of taking the client seriously, see de Shazer and Weakland, in Hoyt, 1994.

References

Amundson, J. K. (1996). Why pragmatics is probably enough for now. *Family Process, 35*, 473–486.

Anderson, H., & Goolishian, H. A. (1992). The client is the expert: A not-knowing approach to therapy. In S. McNamee & K. J. Gergen (Eds.), *Therapy as social construction* (pp. 25–39). Newbury Park, CA: Sage.

Berg, I. K. (1994). *Family-based services: A solution-focused approach.* New York: Norton.

Berg, I. K., & Anderson, H. (1994, July). *Supervision: Leading from one step behind.* Workshop at Therapeutic Conversations 2, Reston, VA.

Berg, I. K., & Miller, S. D. (1992). *Working with the problem drinker: A solution-focused approach.* New York: Norton.

Bruner, J. (1987). The transactional self. In J. Bruner & H. Haste (Eds.), *The child's construction of the world* (pp. 81–96). London: Methuen.

Bryant, P. (1979). Inferences. In A. Floyd (Ed.), *Cognitive development in the school years* (pp. 67–86). London: Croom Helm.

Bull, R. (1995). Innovative techniques for the questioning of child witnesses, especially those who are young and those with learning disability. In M. S. Zaragoza, J. R. Graham, G. C. N. Hall, R. Hirschman, & Y. S. Ben-Porath (Eds.), *Memory and testimony in the child witness* (pp. 179–194). London: Sage.

Butterworth, G. (1987). Some benefits of egocentrism. In J. Bruner & H. Haste (Eds.), *The child's construction of the world* (pp. 62–80). London: Methuen.

Cederberg, A. C. (1997). Young children's participation in family therapy talk. *American Journal of Family Therapy, 25*(1), 28–38.

Chang, J. (in press-a). The trouble with normal. *Journal of Systemic Therapies.*

Chang, J. (in press-b). Five things to do in social constructionist therapy. *Journal of Collaborative Therapies.*

Chang, J., & Phillips, M. (1993). Michael White and Steve de Shazer: New directions in family therapy. In S. G. Gilligan & R. Price (Eds.), *Therapeutic conversations* (pp. 93–111). New York: Norton.

Cockburn, B. (1983). The trouble with normal. In G. Martynec (Producer), *The trouble with normal* (musical recording). Toronto: High Romance Music.

De Jong, P., & Berg, I. K. (1997). *Interviewing for solutions.* Pacific Grove, CA: Brooks/Cole.

de Shazer, S. (1985). *Keys to solution in brief therapy.* New York: Norton.

de Shazer, S. (1988). *Clues: Investigating solutions in brief therapy.* New York: Norton.

de Shazer, S. (1991). *Putting difference to work.* New York: Norton.

de Shazer, S. (1993). Commentary: de Shazer and White—Vive la différence. In S. G. Gilligan & R. Price (Eds.), *Therapeutic conversations* (pp. 112–120). New York: Norton.

de Shazer, S. (1994). *Words were originally magic.* New York: Norton.

Durrant, M. (1990). Saying "boo" to Mr. Scarey: Writing a book provides a solution. *Family Therapy Case Studies, 5*(1), 39–44.

Durrant, M., & Kowlaski, K. (1990). Overcoming the effects of sexual abuse: Developing a self-perception of competence. In M. Durrant & C. White (Eds.), *Ideas for therapy with sexual abuse* (pp. 65–110). Adelaide, South Australia: Dulwich Centre Publications.

Erikson, E. H. (1950). *Childhood and society.* New York: Norton.

Eron, J. B., & Lund, T. W. (1996). *Narrative solutions in brief therapy.* New York: Guilford Press.

Feldman, C. F. (1987). Thought from language: The linguistic construction of cognitive representations. In J. Bruner & H. Haste (Eds.), *The child's construction of the world* (pp. 131–147). London: Methuen.

Fivush, R., Kuebli, J., & Clubb, P. A. (1992). The structure of events and event representations: A microdevelopmental analysis. *Child Development, 63*, 188–201.

Fivush, R., & Shukat, J. R. (1995). Content, consistency, and coherence in early autobiographical recall. In M. S. Zaragoza, J. R. Graham, G. C. N. Hall, R. Hirschman, & Y. S. Ben-Porath (Eds.), *Memory and testimony in the child witness* (pp. 5–23). London: Sage.

Freedman, J., & Combs, G. (1996). *Narrative therapy: The social construction of preferred realities.* New York: Norton.

Friedman, S. (1994). Staying simple, staying focused: Time effective consultations with children and their families. In M. F. Hoyt (Ed.), *Constructive therapies* (pp. 217–250). New York: Guilford Press.

Furman, B., & Ahola, T. (1992). *Solution talk: Hosting therapeutic conversations.* New York: Norton.

Gardner, R. A. (1971). *Therapeutic communication with children: The mutual storytelling technique.* New York: Science House.

Gilligan, C. (1982). *In a different voice: Psychological theory and women's development.* Cambridge, MA: Harvard University Press.

Gilligan, S. G. (1996). The relational self: The expanding of love beyond desire. In M. F. Hoyt (Ed.), *Constructive therapies* (Vol. 2, pp. 211–237). New York: Guilford Press.

Gilligan, S. G. (1997). *The courage to love: Principles and practices of self-relations psychotherapy.* New York: Norton.

Haley, J. (1977). *Problem-solving therapy.* San Francisco: Jossey-Bass.

Hoyt, M. F. (1994). On the importance of keeping it simple and taking the patient seriously: A conversation with Steve de Shazer and John Weakland. In M. F. Hoyt (Ed.), *Constructive therapies* (pp. 11–40). New York: Guilford Press.

Hoyt, M. F. (1996). Cognitive-behavioral treatment of posttraumatic stress disorder from a narrative constructivist perspective: A conversation with Donald Meichenbaum. In M. F. Hoyt (Ed.), *Constructive therapies* (Vol. 2, pp. 124–147). New York: Guilford Press.

Hoyt, M. F., & Berg, I. K. (1998). Solution-focused couples therapy: Helping clients construct self-fulfilling realties. In F. M. Dattilio (Ed.), *Case studies in couple and family therapy* (pp. 203–232). New York: Guilford Press.

Kohlberg, L. (1981). *The philosophy of moral development: Moral stages and the idea of justice.* New York: HarperCollins.

Law, I. (1997). Attention deficit disorder: Therapy with a shoddily built construct. In C. Smith & D. Nylund (Eds.), *Narrative therapies with children and adolescents* (pp. 282–306). New York: Guilford Press.

Lipchik, E., & de Shazer, S. (1986). The purposeful interview. *Journal of Strategic and Systemic Therapies, 5,* 88–99.

Lloyd, B. (1987). Social representations of gender. In J. Bruner & H. Haste (Eds.), *The child's construction of the world* (pp. 147–162). London: Methuen.

Madanes, C. (1984). *Behind the one-way mirror: Advances in the practice of strategic therapy.* San Francisco: Jossey-Bass.

Madigan, S. P. (1996). The politics of identity: Considering community discourse in the externalizing of internalized problem conversations. *Journal of Systemic Therapies, 15*(1), 47–62.

Madigan, S. P., & Epston, D. (1995). From "spy-chiatric gaze" to communities of concern: From professional monologue to dialogue. In S. Friedman (Ed.), *The reflecting team in action: Collaborative practice in family therapy* (pp. 257–276). New York: Guilford Press.

Metcalf, L. (1995). *Counseling toward solutions.* New York: Simon & Schuster.

Miller, S. D., Duncan, B., & Hubble, M. (1997). *Escape from Babel: Toward a unifying language for psychotherapy.* New York: Norton.

Nelson, K. (1986). *Event knowledge: Structure and function in development.* Hillsdale, NJ: Erlbaum.

Nunnally, E., de Shazer, S., Lipchik, E., & Berg, I. (1986). A study of change: Therapeutic theory in process. In D. Efron (Ed.), *Journeys: Expansion of the strategic-systemic therapies* (pp. 77–96). New York: Brunner/Mazel.

Nylund, D. (1997, May). *Narrative therapy with children: Using play and imagination.* Workshop sponsored by Solutions Consultation and Training, Calgary, AB, Canada.

Nylund, D., & Corsiglia, V. (1994). Becoming solution-~~focused~~ forced in brief therapy: Remembering something important we already knew. *Journal of Systemic Therapies, 13*(1), 1–8.

Nylund, D., & Corsiglia, V. (1996). From deficits to special abilities: Working narratively with children labeled "ADHD." In M. F. Hoyt (Ed.), *Constructive therapies* (Vol. 2, pp. 163–183). New York: Guilford Press.

Nylund, D., & Thomas, J. (1994). The economics of narrative. *Family Therapy Networker, 18*(6), 38–39.

Piaget, J. (1973). *The child and reality* (A. Rosin, Trans.). New York: Viking.

Piaget, J. (1977). *The development of thought* (A. Rosin, Trans.). New York: Viking.

Poole, D. A., & White, L. T. (1995). Tell me and tell me again: Stability and change in repeated testimonies of children and adults. In M. S. Zaragoza, J. R. Graham, G. C. N. Hall, R. Hirschman, & Y. S. Ben-Porath (Eds.), *Memory and testimony in the child witness* (pp. 24–43). London: Sage.

Price, D., & Goodman, G. (1990). Visiting the wizard: Children's memory for a recurring event. *Child Development, 61,* 664–680

Roth, S., & Epston, D. (1996). Consulting the problem about the problematic relationship: An exercise for experiencing a relationship with an externalized problem. In M. F. Hoyt (Ed.), *Constructive therapies* (Vol. 2, pp. 148–162). New York: Guilford Press.

Sanders, C. (1997). Reauthoring problem identities: Small victories with young persons captured by substance misuse. In C. Smith & D. Nylund (Eds.), *Narrative therapies with children and adolescents* (pp. 400–422). New York: Guilford Press.

Saywitz, K. J. (1995). Improving children's testimony: The question, the answer, and the environment. In M. S. Zaragoza, J. R. Graham, G. C. N. Hall, R. Hirschman, & Y. S. Ben-Porath (Eds.), *Memory and testimony in the child witness* (pp. 113–140). London: Sage

Selekman, M. D. (1993). *Pathways to change: Brief therapy solutions for difficult adolescents.* New York: Guilford Press.

Selekman, M. D. (1997). *Solution-focused therapy with children: Harnessing family strengths for systemic change.* New York: Guilford Press.

Smedslund, J. (1979). Piaget's psychology in practice. In A. Floyd (Ed.), *Cognitive development in the school years* (pp. 34–42). London: Croom Helm.

Walter, J. L., & Peller, J. E. (1992). *Becoming solution-focused in brief therapy.* New York: Brunner/Mazel.

Walter, J. L., & Peller, J. E. (1996). Rethinking our assumptions: Assuming anew in a postmodern world. In S. D. Miller, M. Hubble, & B. L. Duncan (Eds.), *Handbook of solution-focused brief therapy* (pp. 9–26). San Francisco: Jossey-Bass.

Watzlawick, P. (Ed.). (1984). *The invented reality: How do we know what we believe we know? (Contributions to constructivism).* New York: Norton.

White, M. (1984). Pseudo-encopresis: From avalanche to victory, from vicious to virtuous cycles. *Family Systems Medicine, 2*(2), 150–160.

White, M. (1986). Negative explanation, restraint, and double description: A template for family therapy. *Family Process, 25*(2), 169–183.

White, M. (1988a). The externalizing of the problem and the reauthoring of lives and relationships. *Dulwich Centre Newsletter,* Summer. Reprinted in M. White, *Selected papers* (pp. 5–28). Adelaide, South Australia: Dulwich Centre Publications, 1989.

White, M. (1988b). The process of questioning: A therapy of literary merit? *Dulwich Centre Newsletter,* Winter, pp. 8–14. Reprinted in M. White, *Selected papers* (pp. 37–46). Adelaide, South Australia: Dulwich Centre Publications, 1989.

White, M. (1993). Commentary: The histories of the present. In S. G. Gilligan & R. Price (Eds.), *Therapeutic conversations* (pp. 121–135). New York: Norton.

White, M., & Epston, D. (1990). *Narrative means to therapeutic ends.* New York: Norton.

White, M., & de Shazer, S. (1996, October). *Narrative solutions/solution narratives.* Conference sponsored by Brief Family Therapy Center, Milwaukee, WI.

Wright, L., Watson, W., & Bell, J. (1996). *Beliefs: The heart of healing in families and illness.* New York: HarperCollins.

Zimmerman, J. L., & Dickerson, V. C. (1996). *If problems talked: Narrative therapy in action.* New York: Guilford Press.

CHAPTER FOURTEEN

Minimizing Hierarchy in Therapeutic Relationships

A Reflecting Team Approach

S. Michele Cohen, Gene Combs, Bill DeLaurenti, Pat DeLaurenti, Jill Freedman, David Larimer, Dina Shulman

What we report here is a work in progress—our team's description of practices that served to minimize hierarchies in working together over the course of a particular therapy and of the effects these practices have had on us both personally and professionally. In what follows, we will introduce ourselves and describe our approach, share some personal reflections about our experience, and then offer some questions that we have found useful and important. Our intention (see Combs & Freedman, 1994) is to invite readers to reflect upon the impact of how hierarchy may be structured in their own therapeutic work and to suggest some ways—and reasons—we have found for socially constructing therapeutic relationships that minimize hierarchy. When the seven of us began working together, we didn't know that our labor would be so long, so challenging, or so rewarding.

THE TEAM

Our team came together in the course of a live supervision program in narrative therapy (Freedman & Combs, 1996; Monk, Winslade, Crocket, & Epston, 1997; White, 1991, 1995a; White & Epston, 1990; Zimmerman & Dickerson, 1996) using a reflecting team format (Andersen, 1987, 1991; Friedman, 1995; White, 1995b). Members included Pat and Bill DeLaurenti, a couple who came to consult about problems in their relationship; Michele Cohen, Dina Shulman, and David Larimer, who had signed on for supervision of their work; and Jill Freedman and Gene Combs, who had offered the supervision. Michele and Dina each served as therapists at different points in the process and reflecting team members at other times. David was a member of the reflecting team throughout. Gene and Jill at different times were either members of the reflecting team or supervisors.

When this team first met, Jill and Gene had been working for several years to set up structures and practices that might minimize hierarchy in their narrative therapy supervision program. Michele, Dina, and David were a group of supervisees who fully embraced the collaborative and egalitarian ways of working proposed. Pat and Bill learned of our program through David, who was seeing Pat individually. Both members of the couple had some initial reservations, but they agreed to come for three sessions.[1] After the agreed-upon sessions, Pat and Bill decided to continue. They found that participating in a process where their ideas and opinions were valued and where they had the opportunity to listen in on the thoughts of the therapists made the experience of therapy less blaming and demeaning than they had feared it might be. The entire team met every other week for a total of eleven sessions.[2]

We have been fortunate in this project to have been able to take the team process a bit further than any of us had before by continuing to meet as a team outside of the therapy. When the formal supervision program ended, we were all so pleased by the experience that we decided to offer a workshop together on minimizing hierarchy. Our proposal was accepted for the Narrative Ideas and Therapeutic Practice conference in Vancouver in 1997. Planning for that presentation gave us more experience in working together as a collaborative group, and the presentation in March was so well received that we decided to continue working together to write this paper.

The entire group met three times over a four-month period to discuss the form and content of this paper. We agreed that Pat, Bill, Michele, Dina, and David would each write several pages that gave a snapshot of what they found important and memorable about the work we did together. Jill and Gene would then put those pieces together with some thoughts of their own, and the whole paper would be circulated to all group members for comment and revision.

JILL AND GENE'S INTRODUCTION

As you will see throughout this chapter, we have minimized hierarchy in a number of ways, but we have not eliminated it altogether. As the people who set up this situation in the beginning, the two of us continue to have a somewhat bigger voice and to bear somewhat more of the responsibility for what happens. If you, as a reader of this paper, have ideas about how we might make our work more collaborative and egalitarian, we would love to hear from you. Before we talk about *why* we are interested in minimizing hierarchy, we would like to describe the structure our team followed as we worked together and some of the practices we used within that structure.

The Structure

We scheduled two hours for each meeting, and we divided that time into the following segments (see Exhibit 14.1):

A *presession meeting* between therapist and supervisor, with the couple and the team listening in from behind the mirror. The therapist typically used this time with the supervisor to develop the story of her own struggles and growth as a therapist. As a part of this conversation, she would identify things that she would like the team to reflect on as they observed her work on that particular evening. This presession meeting lasted about twenty minutes.

A *therapy session*, lasting about an hour, in which the therapist interviewed the couple. The team, including the supervisor, was behind the mirror.

About forty minutes into the therapy session, there was a break for a *reflecting team* (Freedman & Combs, 1996; White, 1995b). In the reflecting team format, first developed by Tom Andersen (1987, 1991), the team observing the therapy session switches places with the therapist and family (or client) and has a conversation that the therapist and family observe. Then, after switching places again, the family comments on the team's reflections. At this point in our structure, the couple and therapist joined the supervisor behind the mirror while the rest of the team members went in front of the mirror and reflected on what they noticed and what they were curious about in the therapy. Reflections usually focused on some alternative story that the couple was developing.

After the reflecting team had met for about ten minutes, the therapist and the couple resumed their places in front of the mirror for ten minutes or so to talk about what stood out for them from the reflecting team's comments.

Then there was a *post-therapy meeting* for about twenty minutes, which took different forms at different times at the discretion of the therapist. Sometimes the reflecting team would reflect on the therapist's work and the therapist would reflect on the team's reflections. At other times the supervisor would interview the therapist to develop her story of herself as a therapist. The couple and other team members observed from behind the mirror.

Each two-hour session ended with twenty minutes or so of *post-therapy deconstruction* (Madigan, 1993; White, 1995b), where everyone involved sat together in the same room. Anyone could ask questions of the therapist or reflecting team members about the thoughts and intentions that shaped what they did and didn't do in the session.

We believe that several things about this structure serve to minimize hierarchy. The presession conversation demystifies and de-deifies therapists. As peo-

Exhibit 14.1. Structure of Our Team Process

1. *Presession Meeting* (20 minutes)
   Therapist and supervisor talk in front of mirror, family and reflecting team listen behind mirror.
2. *First Part of Therapy Session* (about 40 minutes)
   Team and supervisor listen behind mirror while therapist and family talk in front.
3. *Reflecting Team* (about 10 minutes)
   Therapist, family, and supervisor listen behind mirror while team talks in front.
4. *Second Part of Therapy Session* (about 10 minutes)
   Team and supervisor listen behind mirror while therapist and family reflect on team's reflections in front.
5. *Post-Therapy Meeting* (about 20 minutes)
   Either:
   Reflecting team reflects on therapist's work, then therapist and supervisor reflect on their reflections.
   Or:
   Supervisor interviews therapist to bring forth story of his or her development as a therapist.
6. *Post-Therapy Deconstruction* (about 20 minutes)
   Everyone asks therapist and reflecting team members questions to deconstruct their intentions and motivations in the session. (Everyone is in front of mirror.)

Note: All times in this table are approximate. In practice, the times varied according to the desires of the participants.

ple who have come for help listen in on the therapist and supervisor, they can experience the therapist as a growing, developing practitioner who, like them, is striving to bring forth preferred ways of being in the world. The reflecting team assures that team members do their thinking, planning, and discussing out loud, in front of the people who have come for help, again demystifying the therapists' ideas. The post-therapy deconstruction gives space for everyone to evaluate each session, question any other member of the team about his or her motives and intentions, and examine the effects of what was or wasn't done.

The Practices

Perhaps the most important contribution therapists can make to minimizing hierarchies is an intangible one that has to with taking on particular presuppositions, both about the people we work with and about the therapist's role. We believe that the people we work with are knowledgeable about what is helpful and meaningful in their struggles. We assume that our role calls for some expertise in asking questions, but it does not imply that we are experts on other people's problems or on how they should think, act, or feel. Our way of being with people stems from and conveys these presuppositions. We hope that our manner, tone of voice, posture, and the like invite people to enter into collaborative therapeutic relationships with us.

Additionally, there are a number of things that we do intentionally to minimize hierarchies:

• *Not talking about people outside of their presence,* a practice built into the structure we have just described, is exceedingly helpful in maintaining the kind of respect that makes collaborative partnerships work. We find that over time this practice shapes not only what therapists do, but what they think.

• *Reflecting teams,* in which therapists respond to new developments in people's lives while those people observe, have transformed the way many therapeutic teams work. It was an important part of how our team worked in this project.

• *Asking questions* rather than making statements sets the whole tone of therapy and contributes to a context in which the voices of the people who have come to consult with us are honored. As Karl Tomm (1988) points out, asking questions defines the domain of "appropriate" answers, but the answerer draws on his or her own ideas, knowledge, and values in constructing answers. Asking questions from a position of genuine "curiosity" (Cecchin, 1987) or "not-knowing" (Anderson, 1990; Anderson & Goolishian, 1992) is essential if questions are to actually function to help minimize hierarchies.

• *Striving to not make assumptions* also helps minimize hierarchy. We try to notice things we are taking for granted, and to question them, so that we don't unwittingly construct the therapy on our own taken-for-granted worldview. We believe that this minimizes the tendency for us to impose our values and beliefs on people. We know that this simple-sounding practice is humanly impossible to achieve fully, but we believe that striving for it is worthwhile.

One way of inviting others to question our assumptions is through what Michael White (1991) has called *transparency.* In practicing transparency we let people in on the experiences that shape our thoughts and intentions rather than presenting them as expert knowledge. A benefit of working with a team is that team members can ask each other *situating questions.* These questions invite team members to identify and describe the experiences, intentions, and motivations that shape their contributions to the therapy, thus making them more transparent. We find that questioning each other and being questioned develops habits of self-reflection that carry over into those more typical contexts in which we work alone. It helps us to be more explicit, even when we aren't working with a team, about where our ideas come from, what our intentions are, and what our values and biases are.

• *Including the people who consult us in presession and postsession meetings* invites them to join the team in planning, deconstructing, and evaluating the therapy. They see therapists struggling with their own stories in a process similar to therapy. This invites them to perceive the therapists as people, rather than as experts. We have found it particularly useful to ask clients to evaluate therapy. Not only do we get invaluable guidance and direction from these evaluations, we can also look back at our work through different eyes and see "sparkling moments" we have not seen before.

PAT REFLECTS

When I walked in for our first session I wasn't sure what was going to happen, so I felt very uncomfortable. As the sessions continued, I felt more at ease and looked forward to the next one. It was different for me than most of my sessions with doctors or therapists over the years. At most of my previous sessions I felt like I was a very small person and the doctors and therapists were giants. I felt they were better and smarter than me. You see, I have always put them up on pedestals.

What was different for me in this new setting was that at every session I learned that you are not just a client and a therapist, you are a team working together for the same end result. The other team members are not better than me, they are human like me—even though Bill and I were the clients and they were the therapists, and one might usually be seen as outranking the other. As the sessions went on I felt that the gap between everyone got smaller and smaller. That's when we became a team or a family working together. I feel because of this the end result was achieved sooner.

Being present during the pre- and postsessions and the reflecting team discussions made therapy more comfortable. During the presession you got to see what to expect during the session, about how it might be done differently to improve the quality of the session for both client and therapist. When it was time to switch for the reflecting team it was even better. You could see how everybody sees things differently. We got instant feedback and input about our session. We were also included, if we wanted to be, in the postsession. We all sat in a circle and discussed how the session went. As clients we were able to give our opinions about how the session went and to comment on anything the therapist did well or could improve on.

Was there anything I could suggest to improve this process? I'd have to say no, because I have never been in that kind of situation before. I was glad to be a part of this process. Everyone benefitted from it. We all learned from this. Gene and Jill were learning how to better shorten the bridge between supervisor and therapist. The therapists also learned how to shorten the bridge between themselves and their clients. All to improve the quality of the outcome.

I was excited when I was asked if I would like to be included in the presentation of this process, but I wasn't sure how I wanted to be a part of it. I attended the planning meetings and gave input and feedback. The only way I felt comfortable to participate in the Vancouver conference was to write this in the form of a letter, which has now become my contribution to this paper. I am glad to have this opportunity to help others see how important it is to shorten the bridge or, as they say, "minimize the hierarchy."

BILL REFLECTS

I became a team player in a rather strange way. Pat's psychiatrist (a hierarchy person) told her that if she wanted to continue seeing her, Pat and I would have to go to counseling. I was planning on not doing this, but then her counselor (David, whom I had confidence in) suggested this group.

At first I was a little unsure of what was going to be done. After things got under way, I felt more comfortable. Even though you knew others were watching, you felt more relaxed than if you were just with one person. I really didn't know why this was at first, but as time went by, I realized that it was because we were becoming a team (also friends). We were all pretty much on the same platform.

Because of the presession, postsession, and reflecting team, there was a lot more input and feedback. Things seemed to move along smoothly, because of so many team players. Things were made clearer because we checked in with one another every so often. While watching the presession, you sometimes would learn what the student and supervisor thought of previous meetings and what they might want to try next. Every time the reflecting team talked, many more questions or comments were brought up. I believe because of the reflecting team, the conversation seemed more equal to us, the clients.

It felt good knowing that even while you were learning new and helpful things, you were also helping the students and the supervisors learn some new things. Even though supervisors have more knowledge of the process, you felt more like you had an equal voice. This was unlike some one-on-ones that I have experienced. It was also nice to hear how the team thought we were doing and where they saw us going. It was great to be able to get some suggestions on what we could try to possibly improve things rather than to be told what we have to do.

It seemed that after every meeting, on our way home, we would continue talking about what we had learned and what we could possibly do to improve our situation even more. I think this was because we felt more comfortable or positive with ourselves.

DINA REFLECTS

The process of doing what we call therapy can be rewarding or frustrating, empowering or oppressing, energizing or isolating. What determines this difference in experience? I have struggled to decipher what exactly "it" is—what influences people's experience of therapy. Not only what influences me, as a clinician, but what influences my clients. Is "it" the same for every person? I continue to struggle. However, during this supervision program and my work with Pat, Bill, Michele, David, Gene, and Jill, I began to develop some ideas of what "it" is for me.

The team and I had been working with Pat and Bill for about a month when—during my presession—Jill and I were discussing thoroughness in therapy. Jill wondered what might get in the way of my being thorough during the upcoming session. We found that excitement at times gets me to leap forward and move too fast, leaving the people I am working with confused and frustrated. We also discussed ways in the past that I might have stood up to the negative effects of excitement by checking in with my clients and clarifying with them what I was hearing. Michele, David, Gene, Pat, and Bill were witnesses to this discussion through a one-way mirror.

As foreseen, excitement showed up full force during the session. Pat and Bill were discussing the times when their communication together worked. I saw them making great strides and wanted them to realize the magnitude of what they were saying. At one point, I found myself sitting on the edge of my chair, leaning forward, asking question upon question to build on this new story I was hearing. I realized that I was not fully listening to their answers before asking another question. I somehow stopped myself and said, "Am I jumping ahead? I'm getting excited. . . . " Another time during the session I found my mind racing forward once again. I could not seem to formulate any question that made sense, so I just said, "Am I getting excited? Would you like me to rephrase the question?"

After each of these examples I was met with smiles (and maybe a little relief) from Pat and Bill. I heard some friendly laughter from the team through the mirror. Encouraged by those responses, I was able to slow down and start again unencumbered by overexcitement.

During my conversation with Jill in the post-therapy meeting, we reflected on this experience. The first thought that came to me was, "What a luxury!" Knowing that Pat and Bill had heard the conversation about excitement in the presession, knowing that they knew about my goals for the therapy session, was really helpful. Having support for saying out loud, "Oh, no, I think I'm getting excited" allowed me to be clear and unapologetic about what was happening and to involve Pat and Bill in the discussion about what to do instead of trying to do all this secretly in my head. I felt mildly embarrassed, but I did not feel incompetent.

The freedom to speak openly and honestly also seemed to help me focus. I was able to readjust and ask an appropriate question without losing contact by withdrawing into a private (and probably overly critical) conversation with myself. With everyone involved, I was filled and gratified with a sense of teamwork.

At first, the idea of having my clients witness discussions of my struggles and fears as a therapist was daunting. I wondered how these people would think that I could help them if they were to know my insecurities and struggles. I was anxious. I had to fight the grip of societal ideas about what a therapist should know and how a therapist should act.

It helped to remember times I have felt quite isolated, working alone in my office hour after hour. The idea of working with my clients as a team seemed like a natural antidote to isolation. As I confronted the anxiety and took some risks, I found myself working in a freeing, comfortable, and educational environment. I didn't just *think about* working as a team with the people who came to consult me, I actually did it. We all helped each other.

In the beginning of my work as a therapist I had felt that I had to play the expert therapist who knew all the answers to any problem. I had always felt uncomfortable in this role, but I thought that people would want that from me. From the moment I started learning about narrative therapy, I have tried to avoid the role of expert, but it was not until I experienced Pat and Bill observing my struggles as a therapist that I could know that I was really shedding this costume.

During the training program I was supported in working with a high degree of transparency, sharing my thoughts and struggles with my colleagues and clients. As this transparency grew, I was able to relax and do my work without worrying about acting like an "appropriate therapist." Pat and Bill told us that it made them feel better to know that their therapist was human and had problems of her own. They said that when they didn't have to relate to us as experts, when they could treat us as actual human beings who were learning from them as well as helping them, they felt more comfortable.

Most of the time, one does not have the luxury of working with a reflecting team and being supervised before and after a session. Since the training program ended, I have tried to incorporate these ideas when working on my own. I have continued to see Pat and Bill in counseling, and by constantly checking in with them, I feel that we have become a collaborative team. They let me know when I let excitement rush me. I consult with them to be sure we are still moving in the direction that they want. They seem to feel comfortable letting me know when something has been helpful and when something has not. I look forward to seeing Pat and Bill more than I used to look forward to sessions when I thought I was working alone. I find our sessions more productive. I know that when I see Pat and Bill we will struggle *together* to figure out how to make our therapy experience as helpful and comfortable as possible.

DAVID REFLECTS

To clearly illustrate how working with Pat, Bill, Dina, Michele, Jill, and Gene continues to shape me and my work with clients, it is important to provide some background information. For the past few years I had been working with Pat on an individual basis, occasionally seeing her with Bill. There were also occasions when I saw Pat and Bill along with their two children. As I had worked with Pat in that period, I believed that I had always treated her with respect and always thought we were working together in this process.

Approximately eight months prior to the time that Pat and Bill and I began working with the team, I had been hearing repeatedly from Pat that our work together was going in circles. At the time what I believed was that Pat wasn't listening to me or doing the things I thought she needed to do to move ahead. Consequently, I continued to hear Pat say during those eight months that we were going in circles.

Interestingly enough, about six months after we had completed our presentation in Vancouver, Pat made the statement that we were again going in circles. This time by the end of the session we were able to make some changes that appeared to have us moving in a different direction, not merely going in circles. Pat and I have since had several conversations about what was different this time from the first time.

We believe that as a result of working with the team I have been developing a much clearer understanding of how people can work collaboratively and of the power of genuine curiosity. This has had big effects on the way I listen to Pat. This time I wasn't trying to convince Pat to accept my version of what she wasn't doing or what she needed to do. Instead, I was influenced by a belief that it was important to listen with curiosity. As Pat talked about what she thought was inviting us to go around in circles and what she believed could help us get out of going around in circles, it appeared that we were developing more of a partnership. We were making therapy more useful and finding a direction that both she and I would prefer.

In our work with the team I have seen myself take some ideas of narrative therapy (such as collaboration, curiosity, and avoiding expert knowledge) and feel them come alive in my relationship with Pat and with other people.

There is a growing belief in collaboration that encourages Pat and me to have regular conversations about what is working, what we would prefer to work on, and how to go about doing that. This work continues to be transforming and challenging. It shapes the way I listen and what I listen to, adding complexity and subtlety to my understanding of the power of curiosity and of minimizing hierarchy in my relationships with others.

MICHELE REFLECTS

As a narrative therapist, I am interested in collaborating with people to minimize the influence of problems in their lives. One of the things that attracted me to the narrative approach was that it would support me in working as a team member, sharing my impressions, ideas, and agendas, and asking people's guidance in correcting my errors and misbeliefs. I like relating to the people who consult with me as a person who is in it with them rather than as an expert who evaluates their situation from a professional distance and then tells them the correct way to act, think, and feel.

In the session that I want to focus on, I experienced Pat as confronting Bill about a problem that plagued their relationship. She stated that she felt very upset that Bill constantly walked in front of her, not side-by-side. She compared this to the way a master and servant would walk. She said that one effect of this problem was to make her feel "not quite equal, like a little kid" and as if Bill "just doesn't care." She believed that this pattern had been going on for a long time. Pat seemed to be saying that she felt like she was one-down in a hierarchical relationship, and that this feeling brought on the further feeling that Bill didn't care for her. Even though Bill refuted the claim, stating that he was "just a fast walker," it seemed to me that Pat was glimpsing a preferred direction for her life with Bill. I was curious to hear more about this new direction and the possibilities Pat thought it might offer.

The situation that Pat described with Bill is just the sort of situation that our team is working to avoid in therapeutic relationships. We want the people who consult us to feel that they are our equals and that we care about them and their situations. At the time of this session, I was just beginning to notice and try to deconstruct the societal influences that might lead me to feel or act expert or "one-up" with people who were consulting me. Asking questions to explore what supported hierarchy and what its effects were in Pat and Bill's relationship gave me an opportunity to grapple with its supports and effects in my own life as a therapist.

In the first reflecting team (we had two in this particular therapy session) Jill wondered if Pat knew that other women shared her feeling of being like a servant or a little kid rather than like an equal partner in their marriages. This question invited me to think about the societal supports of hierarchy, and to use that mind-set in the rest of the session. Since that session, a concern with societal influences has become a more direct part of my work. I am more and more able to ask questions that help me break the grip of societal assumptions on my eyes and ears and in turn on the eyes and ears of those I work with.

After the first reflecting team, Pat was able to share that she was not aware of the notion that other women shared this experience. She was intrigued to hear that she was not alone. I wondered out loud about what possibilities this knowledge opened up for her. She wondered how other women handled it. In response to further questions from me, Pat talked about having a dream, "just a dream," that one day she would take the lead when she and Bill were shopping. She would know what she wanted to do, to see, and to buy. Bill would follow *her* for a change.

It was encouraging for me to hear these ideas from Pat. It raised interesting new questions in my mind. How might this dream help her to challenge hierarchy if it showed up in other contexts? Would this experience allow her to feel more equal in our work? Would she be able to let me know if I was "taking the lead" too much?

During the second reflecting team Dina voiced the concern that Bill might feel picked on by the way we had made space for Pat to express her feelings of inequality. By empowering Pat did we disempower Bill? By asking these questions, we invited Bill to let us know whether we were on a track that suited him. In reflecting on the team's reflections, he said that he didn't feel ganged up on. He assured us that he grew up with four sisters, and he was willing to hear anything we might be thinking regarding men's disrespectful treatment of women. He said he was just glad that Pat was talking: "She could say anything, I'm just glad to hear her talk."

In our work since this particular session, Pat, Bill, the team, and I have been able to have open-ended discussions about the broader social context that supports hierarchies and inequalities. We have been able to free up our environment enough to create an area where we could explore the problem of hierarchies in personal and professional relationships. We have developed a more complex understanding of how discourses in those larger realms create closed-off areas where people often fear to tread—an understanding of how labels, fear of not doing it right, and societal silence lead us to collude with the problem.

I believe that narrative therapy's emphasis on questions (instead of answers or so-called truths) is an important factor in our success. Focusing on asking questions rather than giving answers helps us stay grounded in the experience of the people who consult with us. Are our ideas tracking with their ideas? Do they feel comfortable with the direction of the work? Are we getting it right? Are we attending too much to our own agenda? Constantly raising questions such as these produces an environment that allows therapists and the people who consult with them to be mutual catalysts and witnesses of change—a place in which it feels safe for everyone (therapists, too) to try on new ideas, perceptions, and behaviors. We all become members of the same team, supporting each other in the process of change and benefiting from the effects of each other's changes.

WE ALL REFLECT

We would like to end by providing our thoughts about two questions that readers of this paper might be considering at this point: "Why should I try to minimize hierarchy in therapy?" and "Since I don't usually work with a team, how can I minimize hierarchy in my day-to-day work?"

Why Minimize Hierarchy?

- So that the people who consult therapists can feel larger.

  Remember how I (Pat) said that in most previous therapy I felt like a very small person consulting a giant on a pedestal? I feel like a healthier, more competent person when I feel that I am as big as my therapist.

  Both of us (Pat and Bill) believe that things went smoother and faster when we were all working together as a team or family.

- So that therapy will be more comfortable.

  All of us (Pat, Bill, Dina, Michele, David, Jill, and Gene) are much more comfortable in this team atmosphere where everyone's expertise is valued and no one is expected to have all the answers.

- So that lots of different viewpoints can be shared.

  We all agree that being able to view a difficult situation from more than one perceptual position makes it harder to be stuck. The more points of view, the more possible directions we might move. Minimizing hierarchy maximizes the value of each new viewpoint.

- So that everyone's opinion is valued in evaluating the work.

  Remember how I (David) kept going around in circles with Pat before we learned more about how to minimize hierarchy in our relationship?

- So that we can learn to recognize and challenge oppressive hierarchies in the larger culture.

  Through our struggles to work together more collaboratively, I (Michele) am more able to see some of the ways our larger culture supports and fosters undue hierarchy.

I (Gene) have been struck over and over again at how Pat's efforts to claim more of a voice for herself support and are supported by our efforts as a team to minimize the influence of cultural prescriptions for hierarchy in our teamwork.

- So that we don't reproduce in therapy some of the oppressive politics that may have contributed to people's problems in the first place.

  As White (in Hoyt & Combs, 1996) has noted, "accountability structures" serve to counter such recapitualizations. The structure we have described helped make us (Michele, Dina, David, Jill, and Gene) accountable to Pat and Bill by showing them our process and including them in evaluating it and questioning us.

- So that therapists can stay grounded in the experience of the people who consult with us.

  We (Michele, Dina, Jill, and Gene) all could tell stories similar to the one of how David and Pat stopped going in circles. The therapy process is much more creative when we act on the belief that the ideas of those we consult with are at least as meaningful as our own.

- So that therapists can learn and grow as they work with others.

  We all agree that when therapists think they have to be experts or that professionalism demands that they maintain a distanced authority, their opportunities for growth and learning are severely restrained. Minimizing hierarchy maximizes the space for development as a person.

- So that secrecy, shame, and blame are minimized.

  Remember how free and open I (Dina) could be with Pat and Bill once I knew they had heard me discuss "excitement" with Jill in the presession? When I thought I had to keep this sort of discussion secret, inside my head, it was embarrassing. It made me feel stiff, distant, and awkward. It feels much better to be transparent about such things.

  We (Pat and Bill) agree. The willingness of team members to talk about their personal struggles in the therapy process helped us to feel valued and respected. Feeling valued and respected helped us become more invested in the therapy process.

- So that neither therapists nor the people who consult them will feel isolated.

  I (Dina) mentioned this in my earlier reflections, and we all agree that maximizing equality and collaboration minimizes isolation.

How Can We Minimize Hierarchy in Our Day-to-Day Work?

All the therapists involved in this project agree that working as a team in the structure that has evolved in the Evanston Family Therapy Center training program has helped us to minimize hierarchy in our work without the team. Most of the structures and practices used in the supervision can inspire similar ways of working when there is no team present. We can think out loud at the beginning of a session about the things that might constrain us from being our best selves, thus alerting both ourselves and the people we are working with to these enemies of good therapy. If these constraints start to appear in the session, we have already paved the way for talking about them and dealing with them directly. We can pause at intervals to reflect on what we are hearing and seeing, becoming a one-person reflecting team. After our reflections we can ask the people we are working with to respond, letting us know if what seems remarkable to us is meaningful to them. As we end a particular session, we can ask people to evaluate and deconstruct the session in much the same way that it happens in the team supervision.

We can strive to stay grounded in the experience of those we work with. I (Michele) have found the following questions helpful: Are my ideas tracking with the other people's ideas? Do they feel comfortable with the direction of the work? Am I getting it right? Am I attending too much to my own agenda?

We (Pat and Bill) think that collaborative therapy asks clients to work hard. It may not be for everybody. We spent twice as much time in each therapy session as we were used to spending. Rather than focusing exclusively on our dilemmas, we listened to therapists talk about some of the difficulties they were experiencing as therapists. Personally, we are glad to have put in the extra time and effort—the payoff is well worth it.

SOME QUESTIONS WE'VE FOUND IT USEFUL TO ASK OURSELVES

In closing, we (Jill and Gene) would like to offer the following list of questions. We have found them helpful in our quest to deemphasize hierarchy in our work both with and without teams. We have included a few blank spaces so that you can collaborate with us in extending the list and personalizing it for yourself. If you would be willing to send us any questions you add, we would be very glad to receive them and to circulate them to other interested people.

- Am I feeling or acting like an expert?

- Are we collaboratively defining problems based on what is problematic in this person's experience?
- Am I making my work as transparent as possible (being forthright, open, and honest about what I'm bringing into the work)?
- Am I checking in about ideas instead of assuming them to be correct?
- Am I contributing to the creation of a context in which everyone involved has a voice in the relationship and the process?
- Am I inviting discussion of differences (not assuming that there is one right way of thinking about things)?
- Whose language is being privileged here? Am I trying to accept and understand this person's linguistic descriptions? If I am offering ideas in *my* language, why am I doing that? What are the effects of doing that?
- Am I evaluating this person, or am I inviting her or him to evaluate a wide range of things (such as how therapy is going, preferred directions in life, and so on)?

- _____
- _____
- _____

Endnotes

1. A psychiatrist Pat was consulting had said that she would no longer see Pat unless Pat and Bill were in marital therapy. Bill did not want to come, but agreed to try things out for three sessions. Pat did not like it that she had been prescribed couple therapy with an ultimatum by her psychiatrist.

2. When the year-long team supervision program ended, the couple continued meeting with Dina, and Pat continued her ongoing individual therapy relationship with David.

References

Andersen, T. (1987). The reflecting team: Dialogue and meta-dialogue in clinical work. *Family Process, 26,* 415–428.

Andersen, T. (Ed.). (1991). *The reflecting team: Dialogues and dialogues about the dialogues.* New York: Norton.

Anderson, H., & Goolishian, H. A. (1992). The client is the expert: A not-knowing approach to therapy. In S. McNamee & K. J. Gergen (Eds.), *Therapy as social construction* (pp. 25–39). Newbury Park, CA: Sage.

Cecchin, G. (1987). Hypothesizing, circularity, and neutrality revisited: An invitation to curiosity. *Family Process, 26,* 405–413.

Combs, G., & Freedman, J. (1994). Narrative intentions. In M. F. Hoyt (Ed.), *Constructive therapies* (pp. 67–91). New York: Guilford Press.

Freedman, J., & Combs, G. (1996). *Narrative therapy: The social construction of preferred realities.* New York: Norton.

Friedman, S. (Ed.). (1995). *The reflecting team in action: Collaborative practice in family therapy.* New York: Guilford Press.

Hoyt, M. F., & Combs, G. (1996). On ethics and the spiritualities of the surface: A conversation with Michael White. In M. F. Hoyt (Ed.), *Constructive therapies* (Vol. 2, pp. 33–59). New York: Guilford Press.

Madigan, S. P. (1993). Questions about questions: Situating the therapist's curiosity in front of the family. In S. G. Gilligan & R. Price (Eds.), *Therapeutic conversations* (pp. 219–230). New York: Norton.

Monk, G., Winslade, J., Crocket, K., & Epston, D. (Eds.). (1997). *Narrative therapy in practice: The archaeology of hope.* San Francisco: Jossey-Bass.

Tomm, K. (1988). Interventive interviewing: Part III. Intending to ask lineal, circular, strategic, or reflexive questions? *Family Process, 27*(1), 1–15.

White, M. (1991). Deconstruction and therapy. *Dulwich Centre Newsletter, 3,* 21–40. Reprinted in S. G. Gilligan & R. Price (Eds.), *Therapeutic conversations* (pp. 22–61). New York: Norton, 1993.

White, M. (1995a). *Re-authoring lives: Interviews and essays.* Adelaide, South Australia: Dulwich Centre Publications.

White, M. (1995b). Reflecting teamwork as definitional ceremony. In M. White, *Re-authoring lives: Interviews and essays* (pp. 172–198). Adelaide, South Australia: Dulwich Centre Publications.

White, M., & Epston, D. (1990). *Narrative means to therapeutic ends.* New York: Norton.

Zimmerman, J., & Dickerson, V. (1996). *If problems talked: Narrative therapy in action.* New York: Guilford Press.

CHAPTER FIFTEEN

Escaping the Lost World of Impossibility

Honoring Clients' Language, Motivation, and Theories of Change

Barry L. Duncan, Mark A. Hubble,
Scott D. Miller, Susanne T. Coleman

It is only theory that makes men completely incautious.
—Bertrand Russell

We have all experienced that sinking feeling when certain clients appear in our offices. Although we find explanations aplenty for these clients, nothing seems to help, and we become resigned to the idea of impossibility. To cope with impossibility, we spend thousands of dollars to learn fanciful, highly publicized methods of treatment. Unfortunately, we know that we can never perform the magic witnessed on videos or reported in edited transcripts. Beleaguered and growing in cynicism, we continue our search for designer models in the therapy boutique of techniques.

Intrigued by impossible cases, tired of reaching for the method of the month, and dissatisfied with blaming our clients or ourselves, we embarked on a project to explore impossibility (Duncan, Hubble, & Miller, 1997a). We welcomed those cases that strike fear into the hearts of therapists. We did not solicit these cases because we thought of ourselves as "impossibility-busters." Rather, we recruited these impossible cases because clients are the best teachers of therapy. This chapter presents our day in school with multiple treatment failure cases, and focuses on how clients' language, motivation, and theories of change provide vehicles for escaping impossibility.

Note: The authors wish to thank Jeff Blyth for invaluable library assistance.

EVERYTHING WE NEEDED TO KNOW ABOUT THERAPY WE LEARNED FROM A TEN-YEAR-OLD

While we pursue the unattainable we make impossible the realizable.
—Robert Ardrey

Molly, a delightful ten-year-old, was referred for treatment by her mother. Molly's parents were divorced. She was sleeping in mother's bed and having trouble adjusting to a new apartment, school, and friends. In an intake performed at their HMO clinic, Molly was identified as coming from a "dysfunctional family," and was described as being "triangulated" in parental conflict. Diagnosed as having "separation anxiety disorder," she was referred to a weekly children's social skills group.

After a few weeks, mother reported that Molly was experiencing nightmares. The group therapist started seeing Molly individually. The therapist pursued Molly's impressions of her parents and encouraged her to remove herself from their problems. Following six months of concurrent group and individual treatment, there was little improvement.

Molly's mother next requested a female therapist. Because Molly asked if her new therapist ever felt ugly, it was surmised that Molly had self-esteem issues. Individual therapy revolved around playing games to see what "themes came out." The therapist suspected sexual abuse.

Still concerned about her daughter's lack of progress, mother requested a therapist outside the clinic. Instead, a psychiatric evaluation was ordered. The evaluation noted that Molly still slept in mother's room and that the nightmares remained. Imipramine was prescribed to relieve Molly's separation anxiety. No change occurred.

Molly, in twice-weekly treatment for over a year and now on medication, had become, at the age of ten, an "impossible" case. Molly was a veteran of the mental health system—a casualty of our treatment technologies—not because her helpers were intentionally insensitive, but because of the obstacles that the process of helping *itself* often imposes. Looking back, we can reconstruct how customary practice unleashed the three horsemen of the therapeutic apocalypse: *attribution creep, more of the same,* and *inattention to motivation.*

What's in a Word?

A word carries far—very far—deals destruction through time as the bullets go flying through space.—Joseph Conrad

One rapid freeway to failure arises from what we call *attribution creep.* Whether the experience is borne in simple trait ascriptions or by establishing a formal diagnosis, once set in motion, the expectancy of hard going can be surprisingly resilient. If left unchecked, the expectation becomes the person and clinicians will unwittingly select or distort information to conform to their expectations (Furman & Ahola, 1988; Olson, Jackson, & Nelson, 1997).

In a classic study, Rosenhan (1973) trained a group of normal confederates to obtain psychiatric hospitalization. To gain admission, they falsified a single psychotic symptom (hearing voices). The pretend patients were admitted for stays ranging from seven to fifty-two days. During their hospitalizations, the pseudo patients showed no sign of psychosis, yet the original diagnosis not only remained in place, but also came to serve as a confirmatory bias. An examination of the records revealed that the staff distorted normal behavior of the confederate patients to conform to prevailing notions about schizophrenia.

Attribution creep erodes therapists' ability to confirm and affirm clients' strengths—especially those of therapy veterans—because they are often viewed as not having any. When therapy is ineffective, it adds to the veteran's burden by appearing to prove the problem's characterological origin. Diagnoses are even tendered as retaliatory explanations for treatments gone awry—"purple hearts" of failed therapy.

Consider Molly: The explanatory labels colored how her helpers regarded her. Molly became a psychiatric condition, a phenomenon observed in Rosenhan's research. For instance, when she asked her therapist about having ever felt ugly, Molly's question was assumed to be symptomatic of self-esteem issues. The possibility that her question reflected the normal concerns of a preadolescent was not or perhaps could not be entertained. Because the categories of "dysfunctional family," "triangulated," and "separation anxiety disorder" were established, her therapists were constrained to perceive her behavior through the perceptual filters created by the diagnoses and clinical descriptions. This is likely to produce what Hoyt (1994a/1995, p. 214) has aptly termed a *self-unfulfilling prophecy*.

Theory and tradition provide another avenue for the onslaught of attribution creep. Clients eventually take on the characteristics defined by the therapist's theoretical premises. Molly's first therapist, perhaps following a family therapy tradition, investigated the relationship between Molly's symptoms and her parents' conflict. The therapist followed this line of inquiry despite an unremitting problem. In addition, there was no evidence that Molly was a victim of sexual abuse. Throughout all her therapies, sexual victimization was never brought up by Molly or her mother, or confirmed. Yet because it was hypothesized by one of her therapists, it became central to Molly's treatment. The therapy then was sidetracked from directly resolving the presenting complaint toward satisfying the requirements of a theory. This was not an agenda shared with the client or her mother.

Doing More of the Same

The more things change, the more they remain the same.—French Proverb

Impossible cases also arise by persisting in approaches that are not working. One of the contributions of the Mental Research Institute (MRI) is their assertion that the unyielding nature of a problem arises in the very efforts to solve it (Watzlawick, Weakland, & Fisch, 1974). Over time, a vicious, downwardly spiraling cycle ensues with the original difficulty growing into an impasse, immense in size and importance. The attempted solution has become the problem.

Therapists are no strangers to this complaint/solution cycle. Intractability develops in clinical situations when therapists repeatedly apply the same or similar strategies. Doing more of the same was in full force with Molly. Each therapy persisted in a chosen approach (detriangulation, exploration for abuse, social skills training, and medication) in spite of direct evidence that the problem was not changing. Although on the face of it, the therapies looked different (group, individual, psychopharmacotherapy), they operated on the shared view that Molly suffered from a "disorder" and that something could be done *to* her by experts that would alleviate (read: fix) the problem.

The helpers met, assessed Molly, and assigned both the diagnoses and the interventions. She was left out of the decision making, but was expected to participate. This latter point bears on the third pathway to impossibility, inattention to the client's motivation.

What's the Motivation?

Beware lest you lose the substance by grasping at the shadow.—Aesop

There is no such individual as an unmotivated client. Clients may not share our motivations, but they certainly hold strong ones of their own. When their points of view are ignored, dismissed, or trampled by the therapist's theory, resistance is a predictable outcome. To the therapist, the client begins to look, feel, and act impossible. To the client, the therapist comes across as uncaring, uninterested, or patently wrong. At this stage, the therapy has changed from a helping relationship to a clash of cultures with no one the winner.

Research has now established that the critical process-outcome link in successful therapy is the quality of the client's participation (Orlinsky, Grawe, & Parks, 1994). Clients who collaborate in therapy, are engaged with the therapist, and involve themselves with a receptive mind will likely profit. Owing to the importance of clients' positive involvement for outcome, their motivation—not only just for being in therapy, but also for achieving their own goals—has to be understood, respected, and actively incorporated. To do less or to impose agendas motivated by theoretical prerogatives, personal bias, and perhaps some sense of what would be good for the client is to invite impossibility.

The goals and tasks selected for Molly's treatment did not reflect her input. The clinicians apparently omitted asking Molly for her ideas about her problem or possible solutions. What she thought or wanted wielded little influence in their deliberations. We later learned that Molly "resisted" her therapists' efforts to change her.

DINOSAURS, THEORIES, AND CONSTRUCTIVE IDEAS

Daring as it is to investigate the unknown, even more so it is to question the known.—Kaspar

In the summer of 1964, John Ostrom and Grant Meyer, Yale paleontologists, were walking along the slope of an eroded mound in South Central Montana. They came across the fossil remains of a creature from a genus that Ostrom would later call *Deinonychus* (Terrible Claw). While uncovering dinosaurs has recently become relatively commonplace, the finding of the deinonychus was a monumental event at the time. Indeed, its discovery shook the very foundation of paleontological thought and fueled the flames of a major revolution in the way dinosaurs were viewed. Whereas before, dinosaurs were seen as ponderous, cold-blooded, shuffling monsters, the deinonychus, by its skeletal anatomy, pointed to the undeniable existence of an agile, swift-footed, aggressive, larger-brained, and perhaps even warm-blooded hunter that was anything but slow, sprawling, and stupid.

As a result of the chance encounter with the deinonychus, the earlier orthodoxy, solidly in place in paleontology, was doomed, soon to be as extinct as the animals it presumed to explain (Wilford, 1986). In many ways, constructivism and social constructionism provide a similar shift within mental health disciplines. Constructive ideas transform Jurassic models of therapy into agile metaphorical representations serving only as sources of ideas, stories to swap in the search for possibilities. Further, a constructive perspective provides a strong rationale for respecting the preeminence of the client's worldview (Duncan, Solovey, & Rusk, 1992). It suggests that meeting clients within their idiosyncratic meaning systems and privileging *their* experiences, perceptions, and interpretations will best serve the therapeutic process.

MOLLY: MAKING THE IMPOSSIBLE SIMPLE

Keep your hands open, and all the sand of the desert can pass through them. Close them, and all you can feel is a bit of grit.—Taisen Deshimaru

There is an old story about two apprentice Zen monks who are discussing their respective masters (Duncan, Hubble, & Miller, 1997b). Proud to be the student of a famous monk, the first novice tells his companion about the many miracles that he has seen his master perform. "I have watched," the young novice says, "as my master has turned an entire village to the Buddha, has made rain fall from the sky, and has moved a mountain so that he could pass."

The other novice listens attentively and then, demonstrating his superior understanding of Zen, responds, "My master also does many miraculous things. When he is hungry he eats. When he is thirsty, he drinks. When he is tired, he sleeps."

Our clients taught us that, like the first monk, we had become too enamored of the "miracles" touted by the "masters," instead of the more simple but enduring acts of validating the client's resources, courting a positive client experience of therapy, and honoring the client's theory of change. These are the "eating, drinking, and sleeping" of escaping impossibility.

Validating the Client's Resources

> Until lions have their historians, tales of hunting will always glorify the hunter.—African proverb

Another potent rationale for the primacy of what the client brings paradoxically emanates from the opposite of a constructive perspective—namely, modernist empirical research about psychotherapy outcomes. Lambert (1992) concluded in his review of forty years of research that specific approaches and their techniques are responsible for no more than 15 percent of clients' improvement—roughly the same proportion attributable to hope and placebo. Far more significant to successful outcome are so-called *extratherapeutic factors*—the resources clients bring into the therapy room and what influences their lives outside it (Miller, Duncan, & Hubble, 1997).

These factors might include persistence, openness, faith, optimism, a supportive grandmother, or membership in a religious community: all factors operative in a client's life before he or she enters therapy. They also include serendipitous interactions between such inner strengths and happenstance, such as a new job or a crisis successfully negotiated. In his review of four decades of outcome research, Lambert (1992) ascribes 40 percent of improvement during psychotherapy to such client factors.

Additional support for our assertion that the client is the primary agent of change can be found in several areas of research (see Bohart & Tallman, in press, for a complete review): studies demonstrating that therapist's level of experience and training does not influence successful outcome (e.g., Christensen & Jacobson, 1994); comparisons between client self-help change efforts and psychotherapy yielding no differences in outcome (e.g., Jacobson, 1995); and the myriad of studies demonstrating the human capacity for change without the benefit of therapy (Prochaska, in press). These findings seem to point to the inevitable conclusion that it is the client who is the star of the drama called therapy.

Molly provides a strong endorsement to the importance of the client and what he or she already possesses.[1] In our first session with Molly, we asked her what she believed would be helpful for resolving the "nightmares and sleeping in her room" problem. To this, Molly expressed astonishment that someone finally wanted her opinion. She then suggested she could barricade herself in her bed with pillows and stuffed animals, thereby "warding off" her fears.

In session two, she reported her plan was working, and therapy ended shortly after. As Molly illustrates, escape from impossibility requires the therapist to allow the client's resources and ideas to take center stage because they are the most salient factors in achieving the desired outcome. We seek and nurture the "symptoms of solution" (Miller, 1992). The excerpts that follow come from session three. Molly told us:

> Psychiatrists just don't understand. . . . You also have the solutions, for yourself, but they say, "Let's try this and let's try that." You're like, "I don't really want to do that." *So, what I'm saying to all psychiatrists is we have the answers, we just need someone to help us bring them to the front of our head.* It's like they're locked in an attic or something. . . . I feel a lot better now that I came up with the solution to sleep in my own room and I did it and I'm proud of myself. And I couldn't be proud of myself if you told me, "How about if you barricade yourself in with pillows, maybe that'll work." I wouldn't feel like I've done it, so basically what I'm saying is, *you don't get as much joy out of doing something when somebody told you to do it. You want to be proud of it.*

When provided the opportunity, Molly revealed her inventiveness. As soon as her resources and ideas were allowed central consideration, when she was regarded as a competent partner, her sleep disturbance ended.

Clients like Molly taught us that neither we nor our carefully acquired theoretical orientations were the defining factor in our work. Clients are the main characters, the heroes and heroines of therapy. We are merely the supporting cast, at times only extras who bear witness to an unfolding story.[2] Therapists are just resources clients use in their self-change efforts (Bohart & Tallman, in press).

Courting a Favorable Impression of Therapy

> Some patients, though their condition is perilous, recover their health simply through their contentment with the goodness of the physician.—Hippocrates

Just as clients carrying certain diagnoses are rarely appreciated for their capabilities or ideas, clients considered impossible are rarely courted for a favorable impression of therapy. This is curious, given that client perceptions of relationship factors such as empathy, warmth, respect, and genuineness account for 30 percent of successful outcome (Asay & Lambert, in press; Miller et al., 1997). Furthermore, client positive ratings of the relationship in as early as the second session predict favorable outcome (Bachelor & Horvath, in press).

Blatt, Zuroff, Quinlan, and Pilkonis (1996) analyzed client perceptions of the relationship in the largest, most sophisticated outcome study ever done (the NIMH depression project). This study compared cognitive, interpersonal, and pharmacological treatment of depression. The more the clinician was perceived as empathic, caring, open, and sincere, the better the outcome at termination. Overall, improvement was minimally related to the type of treatment received (even drug treatment—see Greenberg, in press), but substantially determined by the client-rated quality of the relationship.

The relationship has also been conceptualized and studied as an *alliance,* a partnership between the therapist and client that emphasizes collaboration in achieving the goals of therapy (Marmar, Horowitz, Weiss, & Marziali, 1986). In a representative study, Bachelor (1991) found that client perceptions of the alliance yield stronger predictions of outcome than therapists', and that from the client's viewpoint, the most salient factors to success are therapist-provided warmth, help, caring, emotional involvement, and efforts to explore relevant (to the client) material.

Consider Molly's following statements in light of the significance of client perceptions of the alliance to outcome:

MOLLY: My other therapists never asked me what I wanted to work on. They asked me questions about the subjects that I don't really want to answer. Shouldn't I be telling you what I think about this?

THERAPIST: *[laughs]*

MOLLY: I mean you're not here to tell me my life or anything. I should come in and tell the person, "This is what's happening with this situation" and instead they're *[the therapists]* saying, "Your mom tells me you're doing such and such a thing" and like, *"When did I start having problems with that?" [therapist laughs]* . . . And it is like they think they are some almighty power or something! *[both laugh]* Like they are God. *[Molly sings as if in a choir]*

THERAPIST: Right. *[laughs]* Oh, that is music to my ears, Molly! You know, we think a lot alike.

MOLLY: It's like hang on, *I am also somebody.*

Molly makes it clear she felt discounted and ignored. What she perceived as important and what she valued were not solicited. Given the significance of the client's perceptions of the relationship and the quality of the client's participation in therapy, it is not difficult to see why Molly did not succeed in earlier "treatments." Experiences like working with Molly taught us to view the first session as a first date, where our motive was to woo the client's favorable impression of therapy and court his or her participation.

THE CLIENT'S THEORY OF CHANGE

People are generally better persuaded by the reasons which they have themselves discovered than by those which have come into the minds of others.—Blaise Pascal

Because all approaches are equivalent with respect to outcome (Duncan, Miller, & Hubble, in press; Elkin et al., 1989), and technique pales in comparison to client and relationship factors (Hubble, Duncan, & Miller, in press), we came to see impossibility as partly an epiphenomenon: an unwelcome result of leaving clients out of the process or diminishing the import of their participation. This prompted us to consider our clients' frame of reference, their worldview, as the determining "theory" for our work.

Our perspective builds on the MRI concept of *position*, or the client's beliefs, values, and attitudes that specifically influence the presenting problem and the client's participation in therapy (Fisch, Weakland, & Segal, 1982), and especially John Weakland's emphasis on taking the client seriously (Hoyt, 1994b; Miller, Duncan, & Hubble, in press). We have also been influenced by attribution theories and research that explain and demonstrate the importance of congruence between therapists' and clients' views of problem causality (see Worthington & Atkinson, 1996). We understand the client's theory of change to contain all the ingredients of any psychological theory. It covers etiology, treatment, and prognosis. It includes clients' thoughts, attitudes, and feelings about their problems, and how therapy may best address their goals. Within the client is a theory of change waiting for discovery, a framework for therapy to be unfolded and performed for a successful outcome. *Each client presents a new theory to learn and a new therapeutic course to pursue.*

Learning and Honoring the Client's Theory

The great enemy of clear language is insincerity.—George Orwell

Exploring the client's theory may be facilitated by viewing ourselves as aliens from another planet. We seek a pristine understanding of a close encounter with the client's unique interpretations and cultural experiences. To learn clients' theories, we must adopt their views in their terms with a very strong bias in their favor. We must suspend our "psycho-centrism."

We begin by listening closely to the client's language. Patton and Meara (1982) investigated the relationship between client satisfaction and the similarity and/or difference in the language spoken by the client and therapist. By measuring different stylistic aspects of spoken language, the researchers demonstrated what most therapists know: higher ratings of client satisfaction are significantly related to similarity in client-therapist linguistic style.

Beyond simply a joining tactic to enhance compliance, using clients' language privileges their idiosyncratic understandings, and conveys to clients the importance of their ideas and participation. It represents one more way for therapists to keep clients center stage, respect their contribution to change, and build on what clients already know (Miller et al., 1997). Speaking the client's language prevents the client from being trapped in and influenced by a particular theoretical view and increases the chances that any change will generalize outside therapy. Finally, speaking and working within the client's language provides the container for learning the client's theory.

Next we make direct inquiries about the client's goals for treatment and ideas about intervention. What the client wants from treatment may be the single most important piece of information that can be obtained. It provides a snapshot of the client's theory and a route to a successful conclusion. We acknowledge to the client that people often have a pretty good hunch not only about what is causing a problem but also what will resolve it, and we ask:

- What did you (hope/wish/think) would be different as a result of coming for treatment?
- What would have to be minimally different in your life for you to consider our work together a success?
- What ideas do you have about what needs to happen for improvement to occur?
- Do you have a theory of how change is going to happen here?
- In what ways do you see me and this process being helpful to attaining your goals?

We also simply listen for or inquire about the client's usual method of or experience with change, paying particular attention to:

- How does change usually happen in the client's life?
- What does the client (and others in the client's life) do to initiate change?

Finally, discussion of prior solutions also provides an excellent way for learning the client's theory of change and preferred modus operandi. Exploring solution attempts enables the therapist to hear the client's frank evaluation of previous attempts and their fit with what the client believes to be helpful.

- What have you tried to help the problem or situation so far? Did it help? How did it help? Why didn't it help?

Honoring the client's theory occurs when a given therapeutic procedure coincides with and is complementary to the client's preexisting beliefs about the problem(s) and the change process. We therefore simply listen and then amplify the stories, experiences, and interpretations that clients offer about their problems as well as their thoughts, feelings, and ideas about how those problems might best be addressed.

Consider a study (Hester, Miller, Delaney, & Meyers, 1990) comparing the efficacy of traditional alcohol treatment, which views problem drinking as a disease, with a learning-based approach, which views problem drinking as a bad habit. Predictably, both approaches were found to be initially equally effective. What was surprising was the difference that emerged six months later related to the beliefs the *clients* held about alcohol problems *prior to* treatment. Clients who believed that alcohol problems were caused by a disease were much more likely to be sober at six-month follow-up if they had received the traditional alcoholic treatment. Clients who believed that alcohol problems were a bad habit were more likely to be successful if they had participated in a therapy that had treated them as such. It was the *match* between client beliefs and therapeutic approach that proved crucial.

Along similar lines, Claiborn, Ward, and Strong (1981) placed clients in conditions that were discrepant and congruent with the therapist's beliefs about problem causality. Clients in the congruent condition showed greater expectations for change, achieved more change, and rated higher levels of satisfaction than those in the discrepant condition. Tracey (1988) investigated attributional congruence (agreement between therapist and client) about responsibility for the cause of the problem, and found that agreement was significantly related to client satisfaction and client change, and inversely related to premature termination. Finally, two studies (Atkinson, Worthington, Dana, & Good, 1991; Worthington & Atkinson, 1996) found that clients' perceptions about the similarity of causal beliefs with their therapists were related to ratings of therapist credibility, how well they felt understood by the therapist, and how satisfied they were with the therapist's approach and therapy in general.

These studies provide strong support for *really* taking the client's views seriously! Returning to Molly one final time, she explains how not securing her theory of change missed the mark. It is clear that Molly's and her former therapist's beliefs about how people change in therapy were not congruent:

THERAPIST: I knew you'd seen other therapists about not being able to sleep in your room, but yet—

MOLLY: It didn't help. I didn't want to do it. They weren't my ideas and they didn't seem right. Like my other therapist said, "Let's try this for five minutes, then go for ten minutes, then fifteen, then go for the whole night." I did it once and I decided, "This isn't helping!" So I basically ignored it.

Given the frequent hyping of the method-of-the-month, there's a temptation to turn Molly's case into one more invariant therapeutic prescription: ask what they'd like to do (or prescribe a ritual, or paradoxically restrain rapid change, or . . . whatever) and watch the miracles roll out the office door! This is not what we're saying. Not all cases will blossom from the first question about the client's theory. Constructive therapy is a process-determined synthesis of ideas that evolves from listening and engaging the client's participation. The pillow barricade was Molly's theory of what she needed for change. It is not a surefire cure for other so-called separation-anxiety cases. Other clients will unfold their own unique theories and possibilities.

We are also not saying that we never offer ideas or suggestions, or that we do not contribute to the construction of the client's theory of change. Exploration for and discovery of the client's theory is a coevolutionary process—a criss-crossing of ideas that generates a seamless connection of socially constructed meanings. The degree and intensity of our input varies and is driven by the client's expectations of our role. The client's theory of change is an "emergent reality" that unfolds from a conversation structured by the therapist's curiosity about the client's ideas, attitudes, and speculations about change.

CASE EXAMPLE: WORD GAMES

It is easier to discover a deficiency in individuals, in states, and in Providence, than to see their real import and value.—Hegel

The following case further illustrates how the nuances of language serve as a container for learning and honoring the client's theory of change. The sessions occurred at Family Therapy Associates, the training clinic of the Department of Family Therapy at Nova Southeastern University, Ft. Lauderdale, Florida. It is worthy to note that the physical appearance of the client (called Dan) gave rise to attribution creep. The therapist quickly made several judgments regarding Dan's character based on his greasy long hair and beard and his dirty, smelly clothes. The therapist noted these judgments and openly discussed them with the supervisor and team. Acceptance of the therapist's view into the team's conversation enabled her to articulate and examine her ideas, thereby preventing them from covertly and negatively influencing the session. The therapist ultimately witnessed her prejudices fade away as she helped unfold Dan's competence, individuality, and tenderness toward his wife and child.

Session One, Excerpt One: "A Very Bad Day"

PEG: I called on a very bad day, which there have been a lot of lately. And now I'm embarrassed.

THERAPIST: That makes sense to call on a very bad day because bad days are when we try to reach out to someone.

PEG: I feel that our marriage is going to end. I don't feel that we are going to be together if it continues.

THERAPIST: Do you know what she means by "if it continues"?

DAN: Yeah, I'm not working. I'm staying home with the baby. I drink during the day, sometimes too much. It's more practical for her to work and me to stay home. There just aren't any good day cares around us. She is going to college, and she's bettering herself, and I just seem to be in a rut. Everything's a Catch-22.

THERAPIST: When you say "if it continues," what exactly is the "it"?

PEG: I mean, like closeness, sex. Unless I start it, we don't have sex. I decided not to start it anymore.

From the first statements of the session, the therapist uses the clients' language. The therapist's response of "very bad day" matches Peg emotionally and seems to help her feel more comfortable. The use of "if it continues" enables the therapist to explore what the clients view as relevant, and encourages their meanings to come forth. Although the conversation has just started, Peg already indicates a possible goal in her statement, "we don't have sex."

Session One, Excerpt Two: "You Have to Be Sober"

THERAPIST: How do you think coming here can be helpful?

DAN: When we first got together I used to hug her and kiss her for no reason. I was much more affectionate. I haven't been doing it, like I used to. . . . I know it could be helpful because it's getting me to talk and maybe could get me to do what I used to do.

PEG: I don't think when you are watching a child you should be drunk.[3] You have to be sober. And he drinks around bums. And I don't want my daughter around that. I don't understand how he can even do that if he loves her. And the other day when I came home, he looked like a bum. He was still drunk from the day before. That was the day we ended up having the big fight.

THERAPIST: And that was the day you called here.

PEG: Yeah. When I made the call it was just because I was hoping somehow our marriage could be together. I don't know. I don't give it much hope. When we got married I trusted him and I respected him. I don't trust him any more and I don't respect him. When that's gone your marriage is gone.

The therapist directly inquires about the couple's ideas and expectations and they reveal their theories of change. Dan believes that being affectionate to his wife the way he used to will help the marital problems. For Peg, in addition to closeness and sex, a successful marriage requires trust and respect. For Peg to trust and respect Dan, she needs for Dan to be sober while watching their daughter. The goals *and* the means to achieve the goals have been identified. As we will see in the following excerpt, after a break with the team, the therapist strives to co-create possibilities to implement their theories of change.

Session One, Excerpt Three: "I Never Looked at That"

THERAPIST: The team and I were very taken by your ability to talk honestly about your marriage. You both want the same things. Dan, you want to be able to go up behind Peg and be affectionate by grabbing her waist or giving her a kiss on the cheek and *[to Peg]* that is what you are looking for.

PEG: Uh huh, more closeness.

THERAPIST: That is something he wants to give you. And like Dan said, he is in a Catch–22, trying to decide "I'd really like to go back to work, but is putting my child in this day care really the best thing for her?" That is a struggle of a good parent. And it shows, Peg, the responsibility that it takes to be a good father. *[to Dan]* What you are doing is putting your child before yourself.

PEG: I never looked at that.

The therapist compliments the couple and validates Dan's struggle regarding working and placing his daughter in an inadequate day care. Highlighting Dan's struggle as a "good parent" provides Peg with a different view of her husband, consistent with her hopes to regain trust and respect for him. The therapist honors Dan's theory of change regarding affection and Peg's desire for closeness and sex. The therapist uses the clients' language (e.g., affection, waist grabbing, kissing, Catch–22) to emphasize the clients' meanings. To further encourage a new view of Dan, and the possibility of noticing the changes the couple desired, the clients were asked to note the things they wanted to continue in the relationship (the first session formula task, de Shazer, 1985).

Session Two, Excerpt One: "He Hasn't Been Drunk"

PEG: He has been nicer.

THERAPIST: So, how has he been nicer?

PEG: He's more attentive. He's kissed me and more.[4]

THERAPIST: He's been more attentive, he's kissed you. Now give me an example, like how is he more attentive?

PEG: Well, like if we pass each other, like walking through the house, he'll stop and give me a kiss or a hug.

DAN: It's been missed for a long time, so I figured the best thing to start with is go back to what I used to do, when we were getting along real good.

THERAPIST: Like you used to do, huh? How else has he been nicer?

PEG: He hasn't been drunk.

THERAPIST: In two weeks? How have you managed not to get drunk in two weeks?

DAN: Just don't do it. It's no big deal.

THERAPIST: It just wasn't a big deal, huh?

DAN: It's not difficult. Just decided not to do it and didn't, that's all.

THERAPIST: Great!

PEG: He wants to save the marriage.

The therapist continues using the clients' language to keep their meanings central stage and to validate the clients' beliefs and values regarding their solutions. Dan repeats his theory of change by stating, "So I figured the best thing to start with is go back to what I used to do." Peg is beginning to respect Dan because he "Hasn't been drunk" and "He wants to save the marriage." Since going back to the way things were emerges as a potent solution, the therapist unfolds its meanings to the clients.

Session Two, Excerpt Two: "Word Game"

THERAPIST: What other things did you do when you first met?

DAN: We used to make each other laugh.

THERAPIST: When you were laughing more together, how did you used to get her to laugh?

DAN: I remember we were laughing, we just got into a word game that we used to play. You know, two words that sound the same, and don't mean the same.

PEG: We make fun of the English language.

DAN: *Sun* and *son*.

PEG: *Maid* and *made*.

The therapist explores the clients' experiences and discovers additional resources to empower the changes the couple has made. Laughter and word games characterize the rest of the session. After a discussion break with the consulting team, the therapist accommodates their word games in a final message to the clients.

Session Two, Excerpt Three: "Is That *Light* or *Light*?"

THERAPIST: The team really enjoyed the word game you guys played with each other. We decided a word game for what was going on in your relationship right now was "Light."

PEG: Is that *light* or *light*? *[laughs]*

THERAPIST: That's it, exactly. In both ways it's *light* and *light* in that as things have gotten lighter between the two of you, you're able to laugh together, you're hugging more, you're kissing more, and you're talking more. And as you're doing all these things, your relationship's getting lighter, he's being nicer, he's not drunk, you're trusting in him more, you're respecting him more.

PEG: Yeah.

THERAPIST: As your relationship continues to get light, the light of your fire is getting brighter. You've rekindled your relationship and it continues to get brighter as you give it attention. Yet things happen sometimes and you can't give a fire as much attention. Kids get sick, adults disagree, and it might look like the fire's gone out. Yet if you stoke it and give it a little bit of attention and start rekindling it and putting more wood on it, and doing the loving things you do, the fire will light again.

DAN: You need to pay attention to it.

PEG: Yeah.

The clients' words from both sessions (e.g., light, laughing, hugging, kissing, talking, nicer, trusting, respecting, not drunk, rekindle, attention) are interspersed throughout this segment. After the break, the therapist weaves all the threads together to form a tapestry of the client's language, meanings, and theories to highlight the noted exceptions, resources, and solutions. The clients' "word game" provides the framework for validating their ideas to improve their relationship.

Peg and Dan demonstrate how the nuances of the client's language can be accommodated by the therapist and serve as a container for learning and honoring the client's theory of change. Such an accommodation requires the placing of clients' subjective experience over theoretical preferences and pragmatically privileging the clients' voice as the source of wisdom and solution. It is worthy to note that Dan and Peg resolved the drinking problem without intervention by the team, further testament to their inherent resources.

INVENTIONS AND DINOSAURS

Despite the fortunes we spend on workshops selling the latest fashion, the competition among the more than 250 therapy schools amounts to little more than the competition among aspirin, Advil, and Tylenol. All of them relieve pain and work better than no treatment at all. None stands head and shoulders above the rest (Duncan et al., in press).

We are no longer enamored of theory and technique, but instead are entranced by the accomplishments of our clients. We are not "true believers" in constructivism or empiricism, but rather appreciate how each lens "corrects" our vision in favor of the client. Therapy models are merely potentially helpful "lenses" (Hoffman, 1990) to be shared as they fit the client's "frame" and "prescription." Technique provides nothing intrinsically therapeutic, but rather something akin to a magnifying glass: bringing together, focusing, and concentrating the forces of change to a point in place and time, helping them to ignite into action.

Because words are so important, we prefer to view *interventions* as *inventions*. According to *Webster's Collegiate Dictionary* (Mish, 1993), "to intervene" is to "come between by way of hindrance or modification." The word *intervention* does not capture the dependence of therapy on the client's resources and ideas or how technique is successful to the extent that it emerges from the client's positive evaluation of the relationship and honors the client's theory of change.

"To invent," the dictionary says, is to "find or discover, to produce for the first time through imagination or ingenious thinking and experiment." Every technique is used for the first time, invented by clients to fit their circumstance. Clients are the inventors; we are their assistants.

Just as the discovery of the deinonychus dramatically changed how dinosaurs were viewed, the discovery of the importance of the *client* is shifting the sands of how psychotherapy is conducted. We hope that the powerful support for privileging the client's experience provided by constructive and empirical rationales will continue to shift the field's view in three ways: (1) from clients as slow-witted plodders (or pathological monsters) to resourceful, motivated hunters of more satisfying lives; (2) from the therapist as the leading character in the drama of therapy to the client as the hero of the therapeutic encounter; and (3) from the primacy of the therapist's theory of therapy to the primacy of the client's theory of change.

Endnotes

1. The case of Molly has generated its share of controversy. Those who have viewed the videotape in workshops have overwhelmingly been charmed by Molly's spunk and insightfulness, and delighted at her incisive characterization of her previous therapies and what is helpful about therapy. However, some have strongly criticized it as unrepresentative, naive, and simplistic. Molly's simple solution to her problem was perhaps too much of a non sequitur to the presumed complexity of her case, leading some to discount the outcome. This is precisely our point regarding the inherent obstacles that the helping process itself some-times imposes on cases that do not respond to traditional intervention. When the three horsemen (attribution creep, more of the same, inattention to motivation) are avoided, sometimes the solution *is* simple. One prominent reviewer was offended by our "joining with the girl as if she were unquestionably telling the absolute truth," was "embarrassed" by our "complete induction into her view," and criticized us because we "fell in love with her." We are guilty as charged on all three counts—but we see these criticisms as major strengths in approaching impossible cases.

2. Using a golf metaphor, Hoyt (1996) has suggested that collaborative, competency-based therapists remember that we are the caddy, not the pro; that our job, essentially, is to hand clients their clubs.

3. We would, of course, consider possible child endangerment and, if necessary, involve child protective services. It is important, however, not to overreact, and to allow things to unfold. At this point in the session we are fostering the alliance and attempting to initially understand the clients' language, motivations, and theories of change.

4. Given the couple's giggles and nonverbal behavior, the team unanimously believed that the couple had been sexual as well. Peg was embarrassed and did not mention the sex, so the therapist chose not to inquire further and instead focused on Dan's attentiveness.

References

Asay, T., & Lambert, M. (in press). The empirical case for the common factors in therapy. In M. Hubble, B. Duncan, & S. Miller, (Eds.), *The heart and soul of change: The role of common factors across the helping professions.* Washington, DC: American Psychological Association Books.

Atkinson, D., Worthington, R., Dana, D., & Good, G. (1991). Etiology beliefs, preferences for counseling orientations, and counseling effectiveness. *Journal of Counseling Psychology, 38,* 258–264.

Bachelor, A. (1991). Comparison and relationship to outcome of diverse dimensions of the helping alliance as seen by client and therapist. *Psychotherapy, 28,* 534–549.

Bachelor, A., & Horvath, A. (in press). The therapeutic relationship. In M. Hubble, B. Duncan, & S. Miller, (Eds.), *The heart and soul of change: The role of common factors across the helping professions.* Washington, DC: American Psychological Association Books.

Blatt, S. J., Zuroff, D. C., Quinlan, D. M., & Pilkonis, P. (1996). Interpersonal factors in brief treatment of depression: Further analyses of the NIMH Treatment of Depression Collaborative Research Program. *Journal of Consulting and Clinical Psychology, 64,* 162–171.

Bohart, A., & Tallman, S. (in press). The client as a common factor: Clients as self-healers. In M. Hubble, B. Duncan, & S. Miller, (Eds.), *The heart and soul of change: The role of common factors across the helping professions.* Washington, DC: American Psychological Association Books.

Christensen, A., & Jacobson, N. (1994). Who (or what) can do psychotherapy: The status and challenge of nonprofessional therapies. *Psychological Science, 5,* 8–14.

Claiborn, C., Ward, S., & Strong, S. (1981). Effects of congruence between counselor interpretations and client beliefs. *Journal of Counseling Psychology, 28,* 101–109.

de Shazer, S. (1985). *Keys to solution in brief therapy.* New York: Norton.

Duncan, B., Hubble, M., & Miller, S. (1997a). *Psychotherapy with "impossible" cases: The efficient treatment of therapy veterans.* New York: Norton.

Duncan, B., Hubble, M., & Miller, S. (1997b, July/August). Stepping off the throne. *Family Therapy Networker,* pp. 22–33.

Duncan, B., Miller, S., & Hubble, M. (in press). Some therapies are more equal than others. In W. Matthews & J. Edgette (Eds.) *Advances in brief therapy.* New York: Brunner/Mazel.

Duncan, B., Solovey, A. & Rusk, G. (1992). *Changing the rules: A client-directed approach.* New York: Guilford Press.

Elkin, I., Shea, T., Watkins, J. T., Imber, S. D., Sotsky, S. M., Collins, J. F., Glass, D. R., Pilkonis, P. A., Leber, W. R., Docherty, J. P., Fiester, S. J., & Parloff, M. B. (1989). National Institute of Mental Health Treatment of Depression Collaborative Research Program: General effectiveness of treatments. *Archives of General Psychiatry, 46,* 971–982.

Fisch, R., Weakland, J. H., & Segal, L. (1982). *The tactics of change: Doing therapy briefly.* San Francisco: Jossey-Bass.

Furman, B., & Ahola, T. (1988). Seven illusions. *Family Therapy Networker, 12*(5), 30–31.

Greenberg, R. (in press). Common psychosocial factors in psychiatric drug therapy. In M. Hubble, B. Duncan, & S. Miller, (Eds.), *The heart and soul of change: The role of common factors across the helping professions.* Washington, DC: American Psychological Association Books.

Hester, R., Miller, W., Delaney, H., & Meyers, R. (1990, November). *Effectiveness of the community reinforcement approach.* Paper presented at the 24th annual meeting of the Association for the Advancement of Behavior Therapy. San Francisco.

Hoffman, L. (1990). Constructing realities: An art of lenses. *Family Process, 29,* 1–12.

Hoyt, M. F. (1994a). Is being "in recovery" self-limiting? *Transactional Analyses Journal, 24*(3), 222–223. Reprinted in M. F. Hoyt, *Brief therapy and managed care: Readings for contemporary practice* (pp. 213–214). San Francisco: Jossey-Bass, 1995.

Hoyt, M. F. (1994b). On the importance of keeping it simple and taking the patient seriously: A conversation with Steve de Shazer and John Weakland. In M. F. Hoyt (Ed.), *Constructive therapies* (pp. 11–40). New York: Guilford Press.

Hoyt, M. F. (1996). A golfer's guide to brief therapy (with footnotes for baseball fans). In M. F. Hoyt (Ed.), *Constructive therapies* (Vol. 2, pp. 306–318). New York: Guilford Press.

Hubble, M., Duncan, B., & Miller, S. (Eds.). (in press). *The heart and soul of change: The role of common factors across the helping professions.* Washington, DC: American Psychological Association Books.

Jacobson, N. (1995). The overselling of therapy. *Family Therapy Networker, 19,* 40–51.

Lambert, M. J. (1992). Implications of outcome research for psychotherapy integration. In J. C. Norcross & M. R. Goldfried (Eds.), *Handbook of psychotherapy integration* (pp. 94–129). New York: Basic Books.

Marmar, C., Horowitz, M., Weiss, D., & Marziali, E. (1986). The development of the Therapeutic Alliance Rating System. In L. Greenberg & W. Pinsof (Eds.), *The psychotherapeutic process: A research handbook* (pp. 367–390). New York: Guilford Press.

Miller, S. D. (1992). The symptoms of solution. *Journal of Strategic and Systemic Therapies, 11,* 1–11.

Miller, S., Duncan, B., & Hubble, M. (1997). *Escape from Babel: Toward a unifying language for psychotherapy practice.* New York: Norton.

Miller, S., Duncan, B., & Hubble, M. (in press). The revolutionary influence of John Weakland. In W. Ray & S. de Shazer (Eds.), *Evolving brief therapies: Essays in honor of John H. Weakland.* Galena, IL: Geist and Russel.

Mish, F. C. (Ed.). (1993). *Webster's Collegiate Dictionary* (10th ed.). New York: Merriam-Webster.

Olson, K. R., Jackson, T. T., & Nelson, J. (1997). Attributional biases in clinical practice. *Journal of Psychological Practice, 3*(1), 27–33.

Orlinsky, D. E., Grawe, K., & Parks, B. K. (1994). Process and outcome in psychotherapy—Noch Einmal. In A. E. Bergin & S. L. Garfield (Eds.), *Handbook of psychotherapy and behavior change* (4th ed., pp. 270–376). New York: Wiley.

Patton, M., & Meara, N. (1982). The analysis of language in psychological treatment. In R. Russell (Ed.), *Spoken interaction in psychotherapy* (pp. 101–131). New York: Irvington.

Prochaska, J. (in press). The stages of change as a common factor. In M. Hubble, B. Duncan, & S. Miller, (Eds.), *The heart and soul of change: The role of common factors across the helping professions.* Washington, DC: American Psychological Association Books.

Rosenhan, D. L. (1973). On being sane in insane places. *Science, 179,* 250–258.

Tracey, T. (1988). Relationship of responsibility attribution congruence to psycho-therapy outcome. *Journal of Social and Clinical Psychology, 7,* 131–146.

Watzlawick, P., Weakland, J. H., & Fisch, R. (1974). *Change: Principles of problem formation and problem resolution.* New York: Norton.

Wilford, J. (1986). *The riddle of the dinosaur.* New York: Knopf.

Worthington, R., & Atkinson, D. (1996). Effects of perceived etiology attribution similarity on client ratings of counselor credibility. *Journal of Counseling Psychology, 43,* 423–429.

CHAPTER SIXTEEN

Solution-Focused Couple Therapy

Helping Clients Construct Self-Fulfilling Realities

Michael F. Hoyt, Insoo Kim Berg

What we talk about and how we talk about it makes a difference
(to the client). Thus reframing a "marital problem" into an "individual problem"
or an "individual problem" into a "marital problem" makes a difference
both in how we talk about things and where we look for solutions.
—Steve de Shazer, *Words Were Originally Magic* (1994, p. 10)

Solution-focused therapy is an intervention approach that has been described and applied in a wide variety of situations (see de Shazer, 1982, 1985, 1988, 1991, 1995; Berg, 1994a; Berg & Miller, 1992; Berg & Reuss, 1997; De Jong & Berg, 1997; Dolan, 1991; Miller & Berg, 1995; Miller et al., 1996; Walter & Peller, 1992). Initially, the approach emerged in an inductive manner, that is, from studying what clients and therapists did that preceded their declaring problems "solved." It was noticed that problems were described as solved (or resolved, dissolved, or no longer problems) when clients began to engage in new and different perceptions and behaviors vis-à-vis the presenting difficulty. This recognition led to de Shazer's "basic rules" of solution-focused therapy (see Hoyt, 1996a):

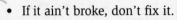

- If it ain't broke, don't fix it.
- Once you know what works, do more of it.
- If it doesn't work, don't do it again; do something different.

Following from these rules, some basic heuristic questions can be derived: What is the client doing that works? What does the client want? What can the client do toward what is wanted? What can help keep the client going in the desired direction? When should therapy end?

Note: A version of this chapter appeared in F. M. Dattilio (Ed.), *Case Studies in Couple and Family Therapy.* New York: Guilford Press, 1998. Used with permission.

FOCUS ON SOLUTIONS, NOT PROBLEMS

Solution-focused therapy can be understood as a constructivist, postmodern, poststructural approach (de Shazer & Berg, 1992), one that conceives therapy as a process whereby the client and therapist co-construct more desirable "realities." The basic guiding principle is that as therapists we are actively involved—whether we realize it or not—in helping clients construe a different way of looking at themselves, their partners, their situations and interactions. How we look influences what we see and what we see influences what we do—and around and around the process goes, recursively (Hoyt, 1994a, 1996b). All questions are leading questions, directing attention and consciousness here rather than there, there rather than here. Solution-focused therapy is just that: intervention that purposely directs attention and energy toward the expansion of desired outcomes. *Building solutions* is not simply the reciprocal or inverse of *having problems;* indeed, development of a solution often involves a reformulation or different construction such that the former position loses its relevance or simply "dis-solves."

A problem arises and a couple seeks therapy (intervention) when the partners view their situation in such a way that they do not have access to what is needed to achieve what they consider reasonable satisfaction. While support can be given and skills taught, the primary emphasis in solution-focused therapy is on assisting clients to better utilize their own existing strengths and competencies, with a recognition that how clients conceive their situation will either empower them or cut them off from existing resources. The solution-focused therapist thus interviews purposefully (Lipchik & de Shazer, 1986; Lipchik, 1987) to "influence the clients' view of the problem in a manner that leads to solution" (Berg & Miller, 1992, p. 70). As de Shazer (1991, p. 74) writes, "The therapeutic relationship is a negotiated, consensual, and cooperative endeavor in which the solution-focused therapist and client jointly produce various language games focused on (a) exceptions, (b) goals, and (c) solutions (de Shazer, 1985, 1988). All of these are negotiated and produced as therapists and clients misunderstand together, make sense of, and give meaning to otherwise ambiguous events, feelings, and relationships. In doing so, therapists and clients jointly assign meaning to aspects of clients' lives and justify actions intended to develop a solution."

ORIENTATION

A few general points about solution-focused therapy may be highlighted in preparation for the case to be described in this chapter.

• There is usually a "future focus," the therapist drawing attention toward what the clients will be doing differently when they have achieved a desired outcome or solution. The language presumes or presupposes change ("After the miracle . . ."). Questions are designed to evoke a self-fulfilling map of the future (Penn, 1985; Tomm, 1987). The purpose is therapy, not archeology; blame-talk and escalation of negative affect are avoided in favor of eliciting movement in helpful directions.

• The therapist assumes a posture of "not knowing" (Anderson & Goolishian, 1992), allowing the clients to be the "experts" rather than having the therapist tell the clients what is "really" wrong and how to fix it. This is not to say that the therapist abdicates his or her role as skillful facilitator, but does imply that the clients' language and ideas—their way of "storying" their lives—will be given full respect and seen as valid and real.

• Focusing on strengths, exceptions, solutions, and a more favorable future inspires clients (and therapists) and promotes empowerment. The therapist-client relationship is evolving and dynamic. Flexibly renegotiating goals, and appreciating and working with clients' sense of their situation, maintains therapist-client cooperation and vitiates the concept of *resistance* (Berg, 1989; de Shazer, 1984).[1]

• Well-formed goals have the following general characteristics: they are small rather than large; salient to clients; articulated in specific, concrete behavioral terms; achievable within the practical contexts of clients' lives; perceived by clients as involving their own hard work; seen as the "start of something" and not as the "end of something"; and treated as involving new behavior rather than the absence or cessation of existing behavior (de Shazer, 1991, p. 112).

• Questions are asked and responses are carefully punctuated to build or highlight a positive reality facilitative of clients' goals. As noted earlier, all questions are in effect leading questions, inviting clients to organize and focus their attention and understanding in one way rather than another (Tomm, 1988; Freedman & Combs, 1993). As Hoyt has written elsewhere (1996c), the therapist functions like a special kind of mirror that can become convex or concave and swivel this way or that. Rather than providing a "flat mirror" that simply "reflects and clarifies," the solution-focused therapist purposely and differentially expands and contracts the reflected image, so to speak—opening parts of the story and closing others, making "space" for (or "giving privilege" to) discourses that support the realization of clients' goals. The therapist endeavors to help the couple build a solution.

As the story about the three baseball umpires disputing their acumen (Hoyt, 1996d, p. 315) has it: The first umpire, who prides himself on ethics, says, "I call them as I see 'em." The second ump, who believes in objective accuracy, says, "Not bad, but I call 'em the way they are." Finally, the third ump speaks: "They ain't nothing until I call 'em!"

In the following transcript, we want to show the details of how a solution-focused therapist selects what to highlight, how the therapist and clients cocreate how they will "call 'em," and what results.[2]

The Case of Bill and Leslie

Leslie and Bill had been married for approximately seven years and had two children, aged five and three. Bill also had another child from a previous marriage, but he rarely saw this child even though he made child-support payments. Bill was an attorney working for a large law firm and Leslie was a consumer-services director for a large telephone company. Leslie initiated therapy; when she told Bill she was "unhappy" and wanted "marriage counseling," he agreed to attend. This was their first session, held at the Brief Family Therapy Center (BFTC) in Milwaukee. Insoo Kim Berg (IKB) was the therapist.

The session began with socializing and joining, in which the therapist and clients introduced themselves and started connecting. The couple quickly began to present their conflict, both in words and in action. Leslie complained that Bill worked a great deal entertaining women clients, while Leslie did her full-time job outside the home and also maintained the children and household; Bill countered that he was working seventy hours a week to make partnership in his law firm and thus to provide better for his wife and family. Tensions mounted.

IKB: How long have you been together?

BILL: Seven years.

LESLIE: Seven long years. *[rolling her eyes]*

IKB: And so it sounds like you both are feeling very frustrated about what's going on or what's not going on with the two of you.

BILL: Yeah, I mean she has zero understanding about what's going on.

IKB: Right.

BILL: It makes it very difficult. We used to communicate.

LESLIE: See, that's part of the problem.

BILL: But now—

LESLIE: See, it's always me. *I* have the zero understanding. *He* understands it all. That's the problem.

IKB: Uh huh.

LESLIE: He . . . I don't think he is frustrated. We wouldn't be here if it weren't for me making the appointment.

IKB: Right.

LESLIE: I think he's happy that it just goes on and on and I just work myself to a frazzle.

BILL: I'm frustrated, but I think it's *our* responsibility.

IKB: Mmm hmm.

BILL: You know. I mean we should be able, as two adults, to sit down and talk about our problems.

LESLIE: Well, as two adults we ought to be able to do a number of things.

BILL: When we do, it goes just like this. She just goes on and on and on and I don't have an opportunity. . . .

Orienting Toward Progress. Following Gergen and Gergen (1983, 1986) and de Shazer (1991), we think of three types of narratives: *progressive narratives* that justify the conclusion that progress is being made; *stabilizing narratives* that justify the conclusion that life is unchanging; and *digressive* (or *regressive*) *narratives* that justify the conclusion that life is moving away from goals. The story line Bill and Leslie were enacting did not seem to be taking them where they wanted to go, so at this juncture the therapist interrupted the escalating cycle of complaints and problem talk to elicit the clients' view of a desirable outcome of therapy. This redirected attention to progressive narrative by refocusing the interaction on constructing solution talk.

IKB: What do you suppose needs to happen as a result of your being here today, so you can look back—oh, let's say a few months from now, when you look back at this period in your life—so you can say to yourselves: "That was a good idea that we went and talked to Insoo, that was helpful." What needs to happen?

LESLIE: I would hope that Bill could come up with some kind of understanding of what are his responsibilities and that in these sessions he could really hear what I am saying—because at home he really doesn't listen and therefore he could change his behavior so that we could be as we were earlier in the marriage.

IKB: Really?

The therapist's question responded to an indication of a more satisfying life in the past. In the next exchange, Leslie lays out her complaints: when Bill understands his responsibility he will change his behavior and they will return to how they were earlier in the marriage. Notice how the therapist builds consensus between the couple.

LESLIE: You know. Listening to one another and communicating.

IKB: Right.

LESLIE: But he seems to have strayed from that.

BILL: That's what, that's what we need.

IKB: What? *[trying to refocus the conversation]*

BILL: Communication.

IKB: OK.

BILL: If we can come out of this with some ground-level communication, I will think that it has been successful.

IKB: OK.

LESLIE: You know, I appreciate him as a husband. I do love him.

IKB: You do? *[emphasizing this positive aspect of their relationship]*

LESLIE: And I know he does work hard.

IKB: You do love him. *[further highlighting positive]*

LESLIE: Yes, I do. I do.

IKB: OK. When he is more responsible what will he be doing that he's not doing right now that will let you know he's being more responsible? *[presupposing change with "when" rather than "if"]*

LESLIE: He will take more responsibility for our children. He will take more responsibility for his own son, whom I love very much, too.

IKB: OK.

LESLIE: He will take responsibility to include me—have respect for me. Include me in his activities and have respect for me.

Getting Specifics. Having identified a positive in general terms, the therapist now asks for a specific behavioral description.

IKB: What will Bill be doing exactly that will let you know that he is being responsible around the house with his children, with his son? *[establishing behavioral indicators that Bill is more "responsible"]*

LESLIE: Well, right now I'm always reading the bedtime stories because he's out doing whatever.

IKB: OK. So he will be doing some of those? *[refocusing on behavioral criteria]*

LESLIE: Yes. Especially on weekends when you don't have to carry the load that you carry during the week.

IKB: OK.

LESLIE: I would like some help around the house. He thinks that I'm the built-in maid, it feels like.

IKB: What would he be doing?

Leslie responded by complaining that she did all the washing, ironing, and cooking. Bill suggested hiring someone to do housework, Leslie replied that they couldn't afford it, and Bill rejoined the argument with a comment about Leslie not wanting anybody else taking care of the kids. At this point the therapist refocused on the thread of Leslie's small but specific behavioral goal that Bill help at bedtime. She tried to amplify the positive possibility rather than the complaint, to build a shared vision of their life.

IKB: So he will be reading bedtime stories?

LESLIE: Yes.

IKB: He will be doing what else?

LESLIE: He would be helping with the shopping. He would be helping with household duties, the cleanup.

IKB: Like what? You mean washing dishes?

LESLIE: Yes. He could help once in a while.

BILL: Hold it.

LESLIE: Once in a while you could help wash the dishes.

BILL: Wait a minute. I'm going to be frank. *[pointing out a different path to the shared vision]*

IKB: OK.

BILL: If I work seventy hours a week, I do not have time to wash dishes!

LESLIE: But I have time 'cause I work fifty-plus hours. I have all the responsibility of—

BILL: That doesn't even make sense.

LESLIE: —the children.

BILL: Look. That doesn't even make sense.

LESLIE: Well, we have a dishwasher. It's not that difficult. You could help.

The therapist persisted in attempting to refocus the conversation toward the desired outcome. It is common for couples to become distracted and embroiled in problem-talk when their trigger words are used. Therefore, it is particularly helpful for the therapist to focus on what the client wants and not on what may interest the therapist.

IKB: I need to know from both of you what needs to happen so that I am helpful to both of you. So let me come back to this. What would he be doing different? Let's say six months down the road?

LESLIE: I think even though it's important that he is building a partnership and I realize it takes time and I try to be supportive. . . .

IKB: Right. OK.

LESLIE: He also has to build a relationship at home. *[to Bill]* We have little ones that don't even know you.

IKB: So what would he be doing to build a relationship at home?

LESLIE: He would be communicating more with me.

IKB: OK.

LESLIE: He would be taking an active role with our children. Our children. He is just someone who comes in during the morning and leaves. I mean, they don't even have a concept of who you are. And I think that's a shame.

IKB: OK. Now. . . .

BILL: Uh—you—uh. *[Starting to argue back]*

IKB: Let me come back to you, Bill, on this. I'm assuming you want to have this relationship with Leslie also? *[returning to the shared vision and refocusing toward the goal]*

BILL: Yes, of course. I love her as well.

IKB: You *do.*

BILL: Yeah.

IKB: Does she know how much you love her?

LESLIE: Do I know?

BILL: She should. I mean, you know.

IKB: Yeah? What do you think? Does she know?

BILL: You know. We've been together for seven years. I love her and I haven't left her. I wouldn't leave her. This is my wife. I love her. I love my children as well.

LESLIE: Do you see this? *[holding up Bill's left hand, which is ringless]* He has a wedding ring. I wear mine. He doesn't wear his. He doesn't wear his.

IKB: Uh huh.

BILL: I figure that they're *[the children]* three and five years old, that if I put in these hours now, when they are older they'll be able to appreciate me more that I will then have more time to spend with them.

IKB: I see.

BILL: That's the principle that I'm operating on. Either I can stay at home and wash dishes or I can spend seventy hours a week trying to build up this practice so that as an eventuality you won't even have to work, and you don't seem to have any patience or understanding or cooperation.

LESLIE: I won't have to work?

IKB: Oh, wow. So you really are working for the future. *[building the shared vision once more]*

BILL: Yes. Absolutely. I'm trying to secure a future not just for myself but for all of us.

Using the Miracle Question. As the interview proceeded, the therapist then introduced the "Miracle Question" (de Shazer, 1988). Notice how as common goals began to emerge, the affect changed. Also notice how detailed and specific were the elicited behavioral descriptions of what would indicate the beginnings of a desired outcome.

IKB: OK. I'm going to ask both of you some very strange questions that will take some imagination on both of your parts. Let's say as a result of a miracle, the problem that brought you here today is gone. *[snaps her fingers]* Just like that.

LESLIE: That would be a miracle! *[laughs]*

BILL: *[laughs]*

IKB: That would be nice. Wouldn't it? But this miracle happens in the middle of the night when both of you are sleeping. Like tonight, for example. So you don't know that it has happened. *[both Leslie and Bill chuckle]* So when you wake up tomorrow morning, what will be the first small clue to you that: "Wow! Something must have happened during the night! The problem is gone!" How will you discover this?

BILL: I'll smile first thing in the morning, instead of avoidance.

IKB: You will smile at Leslie.

LESLIE: He would put his arm around me.

IKB: He'll put his arm around you. OK.

LESLIE: That would be a real sign of a miracle at this point.

IKB: OK. All right, so suppose he does. What will you do in response to that?

LESLIE: I won't turn my back to him. *[laughs]*

IKB: All right. OK. Is that right? Is that what she would do? Would that be a miracle for you?

BILL: Yeah. That definitely would.

IKB: That would be a miracle for you.

BILL: It would be very different.

IKB: It would be different. OK.

BILL: Yeah. It would be a miracle.

LESLIE: Mmm hmm.

IKB: OK. So when she turns her back toward you, I mean, so she's facing you. When you smile at her she'll face you instead of turning her back toward you. What will you do when you see her do that?

BILL: I don't know. I suppose I'll embrace her, probably.

IKB: Uh huh. So you will give her a hug.

BILL: Yeah.

IKB: What about you, Leslie? What will you do when he gives you a hug?

LESLIE: Well, if he hugs me I'll hug him back.

IKB: Uh huh. OK. OK. What will come after that?

LESLIE: Tomorrow's Saturday, you never can tell! *[said sexily; Bill and Leslie laugh]*

IKB: *[laughs]* OK.

BILL: A miracle!

Using an Exception Question. The therapist then posed an *exception question* to find recent problem-free times that the couple might have already achieved on their own. Once identified, such exceptions often can be built upon.

IKB: When was the most recent time when you had a morning like that? Maybe not all of it, but just pieces of that, part of that miracle picture?

BILL: It's been a while.

LESLIE: Probably right after Evelyn was born.

IKB: Is that right?

LESLIE: That's almost two years, almost three years ago.

IKB: Wow. That was a long time ago.

LESLIE: Yeah. I think so. Am I right? Can I be right sometimes?

BILL: Well, I don't know if it's quite that long; somewhere in that framework, but I wouldn't say it's been that long.

IKB: Well, not all of it, but just pieces of it? *[seeking a small positive exception rather than buying into bickering]*

LESLIE: It's been a couple of years.

BILL: It's been a while.

LESLIE: But we've been avoiding. He's out a lot. I take care of the kids. I bury myself in my job. But I don't—I'm not married to my job.

IKB: Right.

LESLIE: You know. I'm married to him. And my job is important. My children are precious to me. But I want the whole thing and I want to. . . .

IKB: You want this relationship back.

LESLIE: Right. I know it won't always be, you know, peaches and cream, but it's not supposed to be, you know. . . .

Not getting a more recent exception to build upon, the therapist returned to their positive response to the Miracle Question by using *relationship questions,* that is, each client's perception of others' perceptions of him or her.

IKB: So let me come back to this tomorrow morning. When the children see the two of you tomorrow morning, what would they see different about the two of you that would tell them: "Wow! Something happened to Mom and Dad."

BILL: Wow.

IKB: I mean, if they could talk. I realize they're very young and they may not be able to have the right words for it, but if they could talk.

LESLIE: Well, Carl knows something is going on, because he always asks me, "Why are you and Daddy always yelling at each other?" You know, I tell him not to yell at his little sister and—see, I haven't told you this—and then he says to me, "Well, you and Daddy are always yelling."

IKB: Yeah. So what would he notice different about the two of you tomorrow morning? *[persistently returning to image of desired positive outcome]*

BILL: Some warmth.

LESLIE: Yeah. I don't think our kids have seen us embrace lately. They probably won't even remember it.

IKB: So he may see the two of you embracing. What else? What else would he see?

LESLIE: We would go somewhere together. That would really be a miracle. You know, instead of me—

IKB: You mean the family of four. *[interrupting to maintain solution-building set]*

LESLIE: All four of us.

IKB: All four of you will go somewhere. Some place fun? *[focusing on solution, not problem]*

LESLIE: Yeah. Someplace fun where we're not just dropping them off on the way to work, you know.

IKB: OK.

BILL: Just all of us being in the same space would be a miracle.

LESLIE: Not getting ready to go to the babysitter's or day care and not getting ready to go to bed. It would really be different.

IKB: That would be different.

Building Interactional Bridges. The therapeutic task now was to bridge the emerging images of changes and possible solutions by highlighting the interactional aspect of this new and different vision. The partners' shared vision for how they want their lives to be—in concrete and behavioral, measurable detail—was examined from several points of view, including that of the children ("if they could talk").

IKB: I'm not sure if this is realistic or not, but suppose you do, how would Leslie be different with you? What would she do different?

BILL: Well, I suppose, she'd be warmer.

IKB: She'll be warmer with you?

BILL: We'd get along better. We would communicate.

IKB: OK. Say some more about this getting along. What would go on? What would go on between the two of you?

BILL: If we just try to get along we could get along, but if we have to get along at the cost of me suddenly, you know, not giving the time that I need to give to my job, as an eventuality it's going to affect us financially. I'm trying to look out for our future, and I think that we have to invest some time in that in order to make the whole thing work.

IKB: Got you.

LESLIE: There are some ways that we could be investing and doing our money differently—

BILL: I love our children and I love you, you know, but I'm trying to build something.

LESLIE: There's some ways we could be saving money and doing better financially that don't require you to be out of the house seventy hours a week and meeting with these female clients. "Clients" in quotes, OK?

BILL: Well, then, you tell me what it is then. *[angrily]*

LESLIE: Because if you were home every night—

BILL: You tell me what it is, then. *[angrily]*

IKB: Hang on a minute. What has to come first? In order to do whatever you'd like to see happen between the two of you, what might be the first small step to help you move toward that?

The therapist actively intervened to stop the negative escalation. She did not ignore the angry affect, but attended to Leslie's insistence that Bill become an active partner in raising the children and responding to her wishes. This was pursued by refocusing the discussion on what small steps would move them toward their vision of greater closeness and cooperation, rather than another round of accusations and rebuttals.

LESLIE: He could be honest.

IKB: What would it take, do you think, knowing Leslie as well as you do, what would it take for her to believe you that you are being honest? *[tracking Leslie's comment while highlighting progressive interaction and constructively using Bill's position as an expert on Leslie]*

BILL: I don't know. What would it take? I'm willing to try.

IKB: Oh, you are? *[highlighting husband's positive motivation with question]*

LESLIE: It would help if you would call. If you would let me know about what time you're going to come home. I don't need to know every client that you're going to meet, but I would like to be included in your life in a way that I think is respectful.

IKB: Ahh. That's what you really want, isn't it?

This was a good example of how partners often do not know initially what are the first small beginning steps toward better communication. The jump between the issue of "honesty" and Bill's calling to let Leslie know what time he will come home was not obvious.

IKB: You want to be part of Bill's life.

BILL: I'll call. I can do that. That's not unreasonable. And sometimes I get caught up in business and I don't call.

IKB: I see.

BILL: OK. But I can call. That I can do.

IKB: *[to Leslie]* What do you need so that you feel that Bill understands how hard you are working to make this marriage work? What do you need from Bill?

LESLIE: I need some support from Bill. I work more than eight hours a day also, and I come home. I mentioned that I needed him to take more responsibility with the child-care arrangements, everything. Doctor appointments, shoes, clothes. I do all that. He doesn't even ask me any questions about how was the day with the kids. You come in and say, "How are the kids?" And you know, sometimes you're not even listening. You walk right by.

IKB: So his asking?

LESLIE: I could say they had both been in a train wreck and you wouldn't even hear it.

IKB: So his asking and being concerned—sounds like that's what you want.

BILL: Well, I mean she's made an assumption that I don't hear. I mean, if I didn't want to know, I wouldn't ask.

LESLIE: I don't think so. When you come in the house it's common courtesy, you're going to ask how your kids are, but one day I think I'll try that. You know, "The kids have been in a train wreck." I'm going to see if you hear me.

BILL: That's not common courtesy. These are my children.

LESLIE: See, I'm female. I wouldn't come in the house without asking how are the kids. I mean, I guess you just expect that to happen, you know. *[possibly inviting the female therapist to join in a discussion against the husband; instead, the therapist attempts to refocus on what would be helpful]*

IKB: So what . . .

LESLIE: OK. I know he loves the kids. I'm not accusing you of that.

IKB: Oh, you do! Does Bill know how much you love him?

LESLIE: Well, earlier in the marriage—

BILL: No, not earlier. Let's talk about right now.

Using Scaling Questions. Leslie went on to complain that she felt her husband no longer found her attractive; that she wondered if he had other "romantic or sexual interests"; and that he might be staying because, like the saying goes, "It's cheaper to keep her." When the therapist said, "You really want to change that," Leslie responded, "It's going to have to change or else I'm going to be someplace else." The therapist then posed a series of scaling questions, each designed to "make numbers talk" (Berg & de Shazer, 1993)—that is, to help the partners articulate their conceptions of their relationship and what would be needed to help it progress in the directions they desired.

IKB: Let's say on a scale of one to ten, as things are right now—and you know what you've been through, the two of you know what you've been through, and you know what the issues have been and you know what the issues are better than I do right now—let's say ten stands for that you will do just about anything humanly possible to make this marriage work. That stands for ten. OK? And one stands for you're ready to throw in the towel and you're ready to walk away from this. Where would each of you say you're at on this scale of one to ten?

BILL: *[pauses, thinks]* Hmm.

LESLIE: Honestly?

BILL: Seven.

IKB: Seven. How about for you, Leslie?

LESLIE: Well, the past year or so I think I've been at a ten, quite frankly, but the way I'm feeling now I'm probably—well, let's put it this way—I've talked to a lawyer. I've talked to a lawyer, just to inquire about what my rights would be. I'm probably about a five.

IKB: About a five.

LESLIE: I'm in the middle somewhere.

IKB: Yeah.

LESLIE: I don't want it to go to the one but . . .

IKB: You don't want to be at one.

LESLIE: No, but I can't . . . I feel like I'm pulling it alone.

IKB: Right. Uh huh.

LESLIE: *[to Bill]* I'm surprised you're at a seven.

IKB: Now, I have another set of numbers questions here. Knowing how things are right now between the two of you, let's say ten stands for you have every confidence that this marriage is going to survive. OK? Ten stands for this marriage has every chance of making it. And one stands for the opposite—there's no chance this marriage is going to make it. Where would you say things are right now?

LESLIE: Well, if we worked at it, I could say it would be more than a five.

IKB: Really? So you see a lot of potential in this?

LESLIE: Well, we do love each other. I know it doesn't sound like it but I think we do.

IKB: You do.

LESLIE: I know I love him.

IKB: Does he know? Does Bill know how much you love him?

LESLIE: He ought to.

IKB: Bill, what would you say the chances are of this marriage making it?

BILL: Uhm. I would really say an eight.

IKB: Eight.

BILL: You know, I mean, I want this to work. I'm willing to try to make it. We have to find some kind of way to compromise, though. I mean, I didn't go through undergrad and law school, working in the mail—all that bullshit—just to now suddenly, chuck it all away. I mean, we can't—

LESLIE: I don't want you to chuck it all away.

IKB: What would it take, do you think, from your point of view, Leslie—what would it take for you to go from five to six, so you can say it's just a little bit better? It's not perfect yet, it's not all the way up to ten, but it's just a little bit better. What has to happen between the two of you so that you can say that to yourself?

LESLIE: Well, he could call like he said he would, and. . . .

IKB: That would help?

LESLIE: Yeah, if he could just make some effort with trying to share some of the responsibilities. I would recognize it. I know he has to work.

IKB: So calling would help you a little bit.

LESLIE: I mean, I don't know. Maybe if he could hug me sometimes.

IKB: He could what?

LESLIE: He could hug me sometimes. To make me feel like a wife.

IKB: OK. That would help also. Now what would that mean? What does that mean? How would that help? His hugging you and calling you and . . . I don't understand that. How would that be helpful for you? *[trying to understand Leslie's personal construction of what hugging and calling means in the context of their relationship]*

LESLIE: Because for me, first of all—he doesn't believe it—but I do worry about him. It can be dangerous out there. And two, I could, we could talk just about what his day has been like. I would know what time he was going to come home. Maybe I would sit up and we could have, you know, a late dinner together.

IKB: Uh huh.

LESLIE: Sometimes I sit up and I don't know what time . . . I just fall asleep and then he comes in and the next thing I know he's in the bed, but then he's asleep and . . .

IKB: . . . so some more personal and private time together.

LESLIE: Right. The kids still go to bed relatively early, and I'm just, you know, doing some paperwork or I end up watching TV alone. I don't know what time he's coming in.

IKB: OK. What about it will be helpful for you? Having those kind of private times between the two of you?

LESLIE: We used to have those private times.

IKB: You used to have those.

LESLIE: Before the kids were born, and it was something I looked forward to. You know, I mean, we—he was working long hours. But that was our special time and we talked. I mean, I knew people at his office before—not always personally—but because we talked about those things, and I talked about problems on my job.

IKB: So when you have this private time talking about what his day's been like, what his work is like, and he also asks you about what your day has been like and having this time without children . . . how would that be helpful?

LESLIE: It was close. Your husband is your main confidant. We would have the relationship, and then I remember the times we would even go to bed and make love and it would be nice. And it was beautiful.

IKB: Uh huh.

LESLIE: And that doesn't happen anymore, either.

IKB: Right. So that's what you're looking for. Some special moments with Bill that you feel close to him and you feel like he's your confidant.

LESLIE: *[to Bill]* Didn't you like those? I mean, I thought it was fun. I looked forward to it. I mean, no matter how bad the day was, I could look forward to it at some point, you know, over salad or whatever. Maybe even a glass of wine. We would talk. We would have good times.

IKB: *[to Bill]* Is there something that Leslie can do to make it easy for that to happen?

BILL: Yeah!

IKB: What? What can she do to make it easier for that to happen?

LESLIE: I'm listening. I'm all ears. What can I do? I'll do it . . . within reason.

BILL: Just be understanding.

IKB: What does that mean: "be understanding"?

BILL: I mean, don't pressure me.

IKB: OK.

BILL: And know that I love you and I love our children. You know, I'm really and truly trying, and it's difficult, and a lot of times I just don't have the time, you know, but that—

LESLIE: You're going to be able to make time? Is that what I'm hearing?

BILL: I'm going to try the best I can, you know? But I have a vision and you need to help me with this vision, and if the vision calls for you maybe to do a little more now, I guarantee you'll do a little less later.

Giving Feedback and Suggestions. At this point the therapist took a five- or ten-minute break, asking the clients to sit in the waiting room. This pause can be used to reflect upon what has occurred and to plan a message or feedback to present to the couple when the session is resumed. This time can also be used to consult with colleagues, including any team that may have observed the session.

The session presented here was difficult and not atypical. Both partners brought up important issues. For Bill, his way of caring about his family was to be a good provider and to be successful financially. He referred to his vision of the future, which was to be a good provider so that Leslie could even stay at home and not have to go to work—a view that in some ways was very traditional. At the same time, he recognized that there needed to be some balance. On the other hand, Leslie's issues had to do more with the here-and-now: the family relationship, time with the children, helping her out, doing things together, more intimate moments like they used to share earlier in their life together. What she wanted and what he wanted both had to do with the relationship; they were coming from very different angles, but were moving toward the same vision of their life. The therapist's task was to help them somehow figure out how they could see themselves working cooperatively together, incorporating both the vision of the future as well as what needed to happen in their current life. They would then be in a position to bring their skills and resources to bear in a more mutually satisfying way.

When a therapist invites a couple back into the room after taking a break, there are typically three components to what is said (de Shazer, 1985, 1988): an *acknowledgment and validation* of the clients' point of view; a *bridging statement* that leads to the suggestion or directive that is to be offered; and the *suggestion* or *directive,* a message designed to guide the couple toward perceptions and behaviors that are more consistent with their goals. In what follows we will see how the therapist complimented and positively framed Leslie and Bill's coming to therapy and their expressed concerns as the beginning step. She then offered suggestions for each person to notice what the other was doing to make the relationship better, but not to tell the other what had been noticed. This task was carefully constructed to shift attention from what was *wrong* to what was *right*—to help the partners watch each other from a different point of view, each noticing positives about the other. The suggestion not to tell the other what had been noticed was given for two reasons: to make the task interesting and capture the partners' attention and cooperation, and to permit each partner to give favorable credit to the other even for something that was inadvertent.[3] Consistent with the social constructionist idea that we all make meaning and build "reality" out of ambiguous circumstances—that how we look determines what we see and what we see determines how we act, and that this feeds back self-recursively—this observational task purposefully focuses the partners' attention toward constructing a more mutually self-fulfilling relationship.[4]

IKB: I really have to tell you that I think that your calling to set up this appointment was really good timing. It sounds like you both are very concerned about what's not happening between the two of you, and you want to do something about that. And I am very impressed, Bill, that you responded to Leslie's initiating this meeting and your willingness to take time from your very busy schedule, and obviously this relationship is very important to you.

BILL: Yes . . .

IKB: And that's why you are here, to do something about this. Both of you really care about this relationship a great deal. But both in a very different way. Let me explain to you about this. Bill, your way of caring about this relationship is to have this vision of the future—how you want things to be. That is, you're accustomed to sacrificing a lot for the future, and that's how you still see it, in order to have a better future, even to the point of maybe Leslie staying home one of these days.

BILL: Yeah.

IKB: That finally you could earn enough money so that she could stay home. And so you have this vision of the future, how you want things to be. And that's how you care about this relationship. On the other hand, Leslie, your way of caring about this relationship is to be paying attention to now, when the children are young.

LESLIE: Mmm hmm.

IKB: You want the two of you to do more things with the children. You want to share this experience of raising children together. You want to stay close and have more intimate moments and somehow try to make it—sort of like have it all, right? And that's how you care about this relationship. So there's no question in my mind that both of you care about each other in a very different way. And that gets misunderstood. And I think that both of you need both ways. Any relationship needs both—that is, to pay attention to here and now as well as the future. You need to do both. You need to—like Bill said, it's a matter of a balance. How to balance here and now, and also worrying about the future.

BILL: Mmm hmm.

IKB: And so I think that you two have a very good start because you're already thinking about right now as well as the future. So the next task for the two of you is to figure out how to fit your concerns together. *[the bridging statement]* I don't think it's either your way or your way. It's the blending of the two. In order to do that, both of you have to work together to strike this balance. And I really like the way that you want to get started on this. You have lots of ideas of how to get started on that—

like sort of stealing those few moments here and there without the children, that certainly would help. So what I would like to suggest to you between now and the next time we get together, is for each of you to keep track of what the other person is doing. For you [to Leslie] to keep track of what Bill does, and for you [to Bill] to keep track of what Leslie does to make things a little bit better for the marriage. And it's important for you not to discuss it, but just keep track of them. And when we come back together we will discuss this more, the details of them. But I want you to sort of observe, file it away, and then when we get together we'll talk about it. OK?

The couple agreed to perform the task, a subsequent appointment was scheduled, and the session was adjourned.

Follow-up. When Bill and Leslie returned for their appointment two weeks later, they were smiling and looked relaxed. Bill announced that he had taken time off from his busy schedule to go with Leslie and the kids to the zoo on Saturday morning. The therapist complimented them on this and explored with them how they had managed to accomplish it. Consistent with the thrust of the first session, and in keeping with the second basic rule of solution-focused therapy—*Once You Know What Works, Do More of It*—throughout the session efforts were made to elicit, reinforce, amplify, and extend favorable changes (see Adams, Piercy, & Jurich, 1991; Weiner-Davis, de Shazer, & Gingrich, 1987). This included getting details of positive movement and exploring the meanings each partner assigned to favorable developments, complimenting each partner's efforts and accomplishments, asking scaling questions about their hopefulness and what would strengthen it, refocusing on goals and finding out what each person did do and could do to further solutions, and developing future goals to help them stay on track.

Throughout this session—and the therapy—the therapist worked to help the couple avoid escalating past complaints (which usually trigger a cycle of blaming-accusing-defending–blaming the other and so on). Instead, she asked questions and otherwise directed the clients forward, escalating the future by helping them create a view consistent with how they would like to be. Their communication style was reframed as "passionate" rather than "conflictual" to help them remain engaged and moving in a positive direction rather than falling into the stalemating perceptions of "right and wrong," "black and white," and "husband versus wife." As a task to keep them on track, Bill was asked to notice what Leslie did, in her own way, to stay in communication with him; and Leslie was asked to notice what Bill did, in his own way, to keep her included, thus shifting their "noticing" from "noncommunication and exclusion" to "communication and inclusion."

Thinking About Practice: Some Questions and Possible Answers

The case we have reported here raises several issues:

• *There did not seem to be a lot of attention given to exploring underlying issues, including anger. Is this typical?* Throughout the therapeutic interaction, the emphasis was on doing what works. The therapist repeatedly focused on those aspects of the clients' presentation that suggested movement in the direction (outcome) they wanted to go. It may sometimes be useful to facilitate the expression of anger and other so-called negative affects, especially if this is part of what the clients require to feel that therapy can be useful, although experience suggests that an abreactive approach often simply leads to more animosity and further alienation. In the case presented here, reinforcing Leslie's "victim" position would not have been likely to move things forward. The therapist, by word and demeanor, acknowledged the couple's frustration and unhappiness. Patients need to know that their experience has been heard and appreciated as valid. It may be more therapeutically helpful in the long run, however, to look for positive intentions that have not yet worked out and to highlight them.[5] Each case is unique, so guidelines have to be general.

• *Was Bill having an affair? Why wasn't this important issue focused on?* It is important to be reminded of the "big picture" of what this couple wanted and how they imagined their lives could be different. Leslie—in her frustration and anger at being treated as if "It's cheaper to keep her" and feeling unappreciated for her own long hours of work—said many negative things such as that Bill was indifferent and unconcerned about her or his children. It is interesting to note that when viewing the videotape of this session (Berg, 1994b), many therapists immediately become focused on the issue of affair/no affair and not on other issues such as why Bill thought himself too busy to wash dishes or help with the shopping or child care as Leslie wanted him to do. We believe that therapists tend to hear selectively, according to their own constructions of what leads to marital conflict (and resolution). What proved to be therapeutic in this case was to address what would help the couple move in the direction of greater trust in the here-and-now. Once the present reality improves, it is easier for persons to let go of what may (or may not) have happened—to let it be past. We once heard John Weakland say to a client who was focused on a particular idea, "Would it be OK with you if we solve the problem and then come back to that if you're still interested?" This helped move the client into a present-to-future orientation and allowed therapy to occur. We also have to be careful, of course, that a client does not feel discounted. However, when we say that an issue is important, we need to ask, "Important to whom?" Sometimes it is the therapist more than the client who feels something has to be addressed or dealt with directly, and this may lead to the kind of either-or thinking that can produce a therapeutic impasse.

• *How does solution-focused therapy address issues of ethnicity and cultural diversity?* By working within the goals, ideas, values, and worldview that clients present, solution-focused therapy is sensitive to the cultures that clients bring to the consulting room. It should be *their* therapy, not the therapist's. The solution must fit their frame of reference, not that of the therapist. Moreover, the therapeutic alliance is foremost, and is based on a high regard and respect for what makes sense to the client, not to the therapist. This means that as therapists, we have to have skills to join and work with folks of varying ethnicities, and we also have to be clear about what our values (tacit as well as explicit) may be so that we do not impose them. In the case presented here, the couple was African American; the therapist was Korean American.

DOING WHAT WORKS

The solution-focused approach, because of its strong constructivist and anti-pathologizing slant, places emphasis on assisting clients to develop a new perspective that allows them to draw more effectively upon existing resources and competencies (e.g., finding exceptions to help build solutions). Solution-focused therapy eschews the imposition of concepts of deficit or pathology and may even say that there may not be any relationship between the problem and solutions (De Jong & Berg, 1997; de Shazer, 1991; Fish, 1995; Hoyt & Friedman, in press). The therapeutic task is to construct a detailed description of what *solutions* might be like and to build consensus around these solutions, not to tear down barriers.

Examination of various effective brief therapies suggests that they all share certain basic characteristics (Budman, Hoyt, & Friedman, 1992; Hoyt, 1995):

• Rapid and positive alliance

• Focus on specific, achievable goals

• Clear definition of client and therapist responsibilities and activities

• Emphasis on client strengths and competencies with an expectation of change

• Assistance for the client to move toward new perceptions and behaviors

• Here-and-now (and next) orientation

• Time sensitivity

Whatever one's particular theoretical orientation, as therapists it is incumbent upon us to join with our clients to notice and amplify what works for them in achieving their goals. Consistent with the solution-focused model, we are interested in what works and we recognize that there are multiple perspectives and paths for constructing self-fulfilling realities.[6]

Endnotes

1. As Shoham, Rohrbaugh, and Patterson explain: "Here the distinction between customer, complainant, and visitor-type relationships offers guidelines for therapeutic cooperation or 'fit' (de Shazer, 1988; Berg & Miller, 1992). If the relationship involves a *visitor* with whom the therapist cannot define a clear complaint or goal, cooperation requires nothing more than sympathy, politeness, and compliments for whatever the clients are successfully doing (with no tasks or requests for change). In a *complainant* relationship, where clients present a complaint but appear unwilling to take action or want someone else to change, the therapist cooperates by accepting their views, giving compliments, and sometimes prescribing observational tasks (e.g., to notice exceptions to the complaint pattern). Finally, with *customers* who want to do something about a complaint, the principle of fit allows the therapist to be more direct in guiding them toward solutions" (1995, p. 153, emphasis added).

2. The excerpts that follow are drawn from the first session of a reconstructed case presented on a professional training videotape by Berg (1994b). Particularly in the spirit of the postmodern perspective informing the work to be reported, it is important to realize that what follows is a construction about a construction, not "what happened." Therapy, as John Weakland (quoted in Hoyt, 1994b, p. 25) said about life, is made up of "one damn thing after another." Any report can only be a gloss, a few brush strokes that can suggest (or obscure). Still, some useful approximations (or misunderstandings or misreadings, since each person takes his or her own meaning—see de Shazer [1993] and de Shazer and Berg [1992]) may be receivable. For additional applications of solution-focused principles to couple therapy, see de Shazer and Berg (1985), Friedman (1996), Hudson and O'Hanlon (1991), O'Hanlon and Hudson (1994), Johnson and Goldman (1996), Lipchik and Kubicki (1996), Nunnally (1993), Quick (1996), and Weiner-Davis (1992).

3. This observation task, in which each member of the couple is to notice what the other person was doing to improve the relationship (but not reveal what had been noticed), is somewhat similar to the "jamming" tactic an MRI strategic therapist (Fisch, Weakland, & Segal, 1982, pp. 156–158; Shoham, Rohrbaugh, & Patterson, 1995, p. 149) might employ—that is, having one partner randomly perform a negative behavior and having the other try to guess (without telling) when the behavior is "real" or "fake." The intention of the MRI strategy is to disrupt a problematic interactional pattern by reducing the informational value of interpersonal communication, whereas the BFTC observation task (noticing the positive) is designed more to shape viewing in order to support a more favorable interaction.

4. A related example is provided by Furman and Ahola (1992, p. xix) in their book *Solution Talk: Hosting Therapeutic Conversations*. They tell of a woman who complained about the rudeness of a man she knew. A friend offered to intercede, and a few weeks later the woman reported that the man was completely changed. When she asked her friend if the man had been confronted, the friend replied, "Well, not really. I told him that you think he is a charming man." If we see

someone in a positive light, we are more likely to respond in kind; this may help produce a "virtuous" instead of a "vicious" cycle.

5. After watching portions of the videotape (Berg, 1994b) depicting the case presented here, then-seven-year-old Alexander Hoyt remarked, "Dad, that's good. Instead of letting them fight she's getting them to talk about ways they could be happier."

6. At a conference held in Saratoga, California, in March 1995 (see Hoyt, 1997), a number of leading brief therapists of varying theoretical persuasions discussed the importance of acknowledging connections and collaboration rather than promoting a divisive pitting of one approach against another. We applaud the both-and idea that everything is not "revolutionary" and "completely different."

References

Adams, J. F., Piercy, F. P., & Jurich, J. A. (1991). Effects of solution focused therapy's "formula first session task" on compliance and outcome in family therapy. *Journal of Marital and Family Therapy, 17,* 277–290.

Anderson, H., & Goolishian, H. A. (1992). The client is the expert: A not-knowing approach to therapy. In S. McNamee & K. J. Gergen (Eds.), *Therapy as social construction* (pp. 25–39). Newbury Park, CA: Sage.

Berg, I. K. (1989). Of visitors, complainants and customers. *Family Therapy Networker, 13*(1), 27.

Berg, I. K. (1994a). *Family-based services: A solution-focused approach.* New York: Norton.

Berg, I. K. (1994b). *Irreconcilable differences: A solution-focused approach to marital therapy.* Videotape. Available from Brief Family Therapy Center, Milwaukee, WI.

Berg, I. K., & de Shazer, S. (1993). Making numbers talk: Language in therapy. In S. Friedman (Ed.), *The new language of change: Constructive collaboration in psychotherapy* (pp. 5–24). New York: Guilford Press.

Berg, I. K., & Miller, S. D. (1992). *Working with the problem drinker: A solution-focused approach.* New York: Norton.

Berg, I. K., & Reuss, N. H. (1997). *Solutions step by step: A substance abuse treatment manual.* New York: Norton.

Budman, S. H., Hoyt, M. F., & Friedman, S. (Eds.). (1992). *The first session in brief therapy.* New York: Guilford Press.

De Jong, P., & Berg, I. K. (1997). *Interviewing for solutions.* Pacific Grove, CA: Brooks/Cole.

de Shazer, S. (1982). *Patterns of brief family therapy.* New York: Guilford Press.

de Shazer, S. (1984). The death of resistance. *Family Process, 23,* 79–93.

de Shazer, S. (1985). *Keys to solution in brief therapy.* New York: Norton.

de Shazer, S. (1988). *Clues: Investigating solutions in brief therapy.* New York: Norton.

de Shazer, S. (1991). *Putting difference to work.* New York: Norton.

de Shazer, S. (1993). Creative misunderstanding: There is no escape from language. In S. G. Gilligan & R. Price (Eds.), *Therapeutic conversations* (pp. 81–90). New York: Norton.

de Shazer, S. (1994). *Words were originally magic.* New York: Norton.

de Shazer, S., & Berg, I. K. (1985). A part is not apart: Working with only one of the partners present. In A. S. Gurman (Ed.), *Casebook of marital therapy* (pp. 97–110). New York: Guilford Press.

de Shazer, S., & Berg, I. K. (1992). Doing therapy: A post-structural re-vision. *Journal of Marital and Family Therapy, 18*(1), 71–81.

Dolan, Y. D. (1991). *Resolving sexual abuse.* New York: Norton.

Fisch, R., Weakland, J. H., & Segal, L. (1982). *The tactics of change: Doing therapy briefly.* San Francisco: Jossey-Bass.

Fish, J. M. (1995). Does problem behavior just happen? Does it matter? *Behavior and Social Issues, 5*(1), 3–12.

Freedman, J., & Combs, G. (1993). Invitations to new stories: Using questions to explore alternative possibilities. In S. G. Gilligan & R. Price (Eds.), *Therapeutic conversations* (pp. 291–303). New York: Norton.

Friedman, S. (1996). Couples therapy: Changing conversations. In H. Rosen & K. T. Kuehlwein (Eds.), *Constructing realities: Meaning-making perspectives for psychotherapists* (pp. 413–453). San Francisco: Jossey-Bass.

Furman, B., & Ahola, T. (1992). *Solution talk: Hosting therapeutic conversations.* New York: Norton.

Gergen, K. J., & Gergen, M. J. (1983). Narratives of the self. In T. R. Sabin & K. E. Scheibe (Eds.), *Studies in social identity.* New York: Praeger.

Gergen, K. J., & Gergen, M. M. (1986). Narrative form and the construction of psychological science. In T. R. Sabin (Ed.), *Narrative psychology: The storied nature of human conduct.* New York: Praeger.

Hoyt, M. F. (Ed.). (1994a). *Constructive therapies.* New York: Guilford Press.

Hoyt, M. F. (1994b). On the importance of keeping it simple and taking the patient seriously: A conversation with Steve de Shazer and John Weakland. In M. F. Hoyt (Ed.), *Constructive therapies* (pp. 11–40). New York: Guilford Press.

Hoyt, M. F. (1995). *Brief therapy and managed care: Readings for contemporary practice.* San Francisco: Jossey-Bass.

Hoyt, M. F. (1996a). Solution building and language games: A conversation with Steve de Shazer. In M. F. Hoyt (Ed.), *Constructive therapies* (Vol. 2, pp. 60–86). New York: Guilford Press.

Hoyt, M. F. (Ed.). (1996b). *Constructive therapies* (Vol. 2). New York: Guilford Press.

Hoyt, M. F. (1996c). Introduction: Some stories are better than others. In M. F. Hoyt (Ed.), *Constructive therapies* (Vol. 2, pp. 1–32).

Hoyt, M. F. (1996d). A golfer's guide to brief therapy (with footnotes for baseball fans). In M. F. Hoyt (Ed.), *Constructive therapies* (Vol. 2, pp. 306–318). New York: Guilford Press.

Hoyt, M. F. (1997). Unmuddying the waters: A "common ground" conference. *Journal of Systemic Therapies, 16*(3), 195–200.

Hoyt, M. F., & Friedman, S. (in press). Dilemmas of postmodern practice under managed care and some pragmatics for increasing the likelihood of treatment authorization. *Journal of Systemic Therapies.*

Hudson, P. O., & O'Hanlon, W. H. (1991). *Rewriting love stories: Brief marital therapy.* New York: Norton.

Johnson, C. E., & Goldman, J. (1996). Taking safety home: A solution-focused approach with domestic violence. In M. F. Hoyt (Ed.), *Constructive therapies* (Vol. 2, pp. 184–196). New York: Guilford Press.

Lipchik, E. (Ed.). (1987). *Interviewing.* Rockville, MD: Aspen.

Lipchik, E., & de Shazer, S. (1986). The purposeful interview. *Journal of Strategic and Systemic Therapies, 5,* 88–89.

Lipchik, E., & Kubicki, A. D. (1996). Solution-focused domestic violence views: Bridges toward a new reality in couples therapy. In S. D. Miller, M. Hubble, & B. L. Duncan (Eds.), *Handbook of solution-focused brief therapy* (pp. 65–98). San Francisco: Jossey-Bass.

Miller, S. D., & Berg, I. K. (1995). *The miracle method: A radically new approach to problem drinking.* New York: Norton.

Miller, S. D., Hubble, M., & Duncan, B. L. (Eds.). (1996). *Handbook of solution-focused brief therapy.* San Francisco: Jossey-Bass.

Nunnally, E. (1993). Solution-focused therapy. In R. A. Wells & V. J. Giannetti (Eds.), *Casebook of the brief psychotherapies* (pp. 271–286). New York: Plenum.

O'Hanlon, W. H., & Hudson, P. O. (1994). Coauthoring a love story: Solution-oriented marital therapy. In M. F. Hoyt (Ed.), *Constructive therapies* (pp. 160–188). New York: Guilford Press.

Penn, P. (1985). Feed-forward: Future questions, future maps. *Family Process, 24,* 289–310.

Quick, E. K. (1996). *Doing what works in brief therapy: A strategic solution-focused approach.* San Diego, CA: Academic Press.

Shoham, V., Rohrbaugh, M., & Patterson, J. (1995). Problem- and solution-focused couple therapies: The MRI and Milwaukee models. In N. S. Jacobson & A. S. Gurman (Eds.), *Clinical handbook of couple therapy* (pp. 142–163). New York: Guilford Press.

Tomm, K. (1987). Interventive interviewing: Part I. Strategizing as a fourth guideline for the therapist. *Family Process, 26,* 3–13.

Tomm, K. (1988). Interventive interviewing: Part III. Intending to ask lineal, circular, strategic or reflexive questions? *Family Process, 27*(1), 1–15.

Walter, J., & Peller, J. (1992). *Becoming solution-focused in brief therapy.* New York: Brunner/Mazel.

Weiner-Davis, M. (1992). *Divorce busting.* New York: Simon & Schuster.

Weiner-Davis, M., de Shazer, S., & Gingrich, W. J. (1987). Using pretreatment change to construct a therapeutic solution: An exploratory study. *Journal of Marital and Family Therapy, 13,* 359–363.

CHAPTER SEVENTEEN

Solution-Focused Ideas for Briefer Therapy with Longer-Term Clients

James W. Kreider

Ino longer shuffle my feet and avert my eyes when reporting that I, a "brief therapist" (and trainer), see some clients "long term." Those clients who have great difficulty forming goals, let alone developing relationships, have taught me that the terms *brief* and *long term* have as much to do with approach as they do with measures of time (see Hoyt, 1990/1995). Some clients do not change as rapidly as others, no matter how skillful their therapists or what therapy model they employ. This is not necessarily resistance or dependence: different people simply require different lengths of time in therapy (see O'Hanlon, 1990). Briefer therapy with longer-term clients no longer seems an oxymoron but a way to reduce the polarization between brief and long term (see Yapko, 1990).[1] We can still be guided by brief therapy principles while providing intermittent, outcome-oriented therapy for as long as clients have therapeutic goals.

Focusing on the past as a way to understand and help distressed clients runs the risk of further reifying their helpless past perceptions, further limiting what they might consider possible for their futures. It would, however, be no more helpful to deny someone's past in hopes that doing so would make therapy progress more rapidly. A troubled past is often less of a problem than the meanings attributed to that past, so my general approach is to engage clients in therapeutic conversations that help them integrate their abilities and challenges, their past experiences and future potential, and their pain and resilience in an emotional, interpersonal, and historical gestalt that opens the door to present and future possibilities.

My intention here is to articulate a variety of ideas that I have found useful in my work with longer-term clients who are the "therapy veterans" (Duncan, Hubble, & Miller, 1997)—people often labeled untreatable, resistant, chronic, characterological, or persistently mentally ill. While my underlying theoretical orientation is solution-focused therapy (de Shazer, 1985, 1988, 1991; Walter & Peller, 1992) with its emphasis on client competencies rather than pathologies, my hope is to offer a range of options for therapists of various orientations— including those whose native language is not constructivist postmodernese—to consider in their work with clients who change more slowly.

DEVELOPING GOALS WITH LONGER-TERM CLIENTS

Many longer-term clients seem to struggle with identifying achievable goals for therapy, often appearing to hope that therapy will somehow magically alleviate their great distress. They are often intensely focused on their pain and problems, and equally often feel unable to do anything about them.

If clients spend their therapy time focused on problem-talk rather than on making pragmatic life changes, they are likely to continue experiencing even more failures, feeling even more hopeless about their ability to bring about desired changes, and experiencing even more unhappiness. As their sense of helplessness grows, the hope that someone else can make their lives more livable seems to grow proportionally. Rather than feeling empowered to take action on their own behalf, they look more to partners, children, family members, therapists, or others in a codependent fashion for a sense of direction and security.

By focusing on vague or global goals—rather than positive developments that are small, specific, and within the client's control—both the client and therapist often become lost in generalizations, unable to initiate the practical steps that can increase one's sense of competence and mastery. In this regard, vague or global goals in therapy promote an ambiguous relationship, which in turn seems to be an invitation for projections and dependent fantasies. Many longer-term clients who present with amorphous goals find themselves hampered by limiting generalizations such as "I am not worthy," "I am not capable," "I am not lovable." These powerful core beliefs persistently filter life experiences in ways that reinforce the sense of vulnerability, hopelessness, and helplessness. Assisting individuals to learn where and how to start making changes in concrete and practical ways helps them deconstruct these generalizations through their lived experience, revealing possibilities where only limitations used to exist.

Many longer-term clients expend a good deal more energy on trying to stop something (feeling bad, someone treating them unfairly, and so on) than on trying to start a pattern that could be more rewarding (doing things that make them feel good, engaging in relationships that are rewarding, and so on). This often leaves longer-term clients struggling to achieve goals that are not within their control, thus reinforcing their experience of being unable to successfully manage life. In addition, it tends to distract them from proactively looking toward what they want in life, leaving them feeling like perpetual victims or reactants to life. Asking *"What do you imagine you'd be doing if you weren't so unhappy?"* begins to shift the focus from what clients don't want to what they do want, encouraging self-direction.

When longer-term clients have difficulty identifying therapeutic goals, it may be tempting for therapists to think they need to just listen or allow a relationship to develop. This often results in ignoring the purposes for which the relationship exists, which are clarified by actively exploring goals *with* clients. An additional challenge to goal development with many longer-term clients is that when therapists perceive clients as being vulnerable (or putting others at risk), they are less likely to allow them to set their own goals (Self, 1991).[2] When therapists forget to ask "What do *you* want?" they miss an important therapeutic opportunity for developing a progressive (empowering, mastery-enhancing) relationship rather than a regressive (dependent) relationship.

DEVELOPING A THERAPEUTIC RELATIONSHIP WITH LONGER-TERM CLIENTS

While traditional therapists often overly focus on the relationship, new brief therapists are more likely to overly focus on the techniques of brief therapy (including the solution-focused questions that are highlighted with italics throughout this chapter).[3] This may result in clients feeling "rushed" or "forced" (Lipchik, 1994; Nylund & Corsiglia, 1994). We *must* hear and acknowledge what clients want to share about their pain and problems in order to form an alliance. However, we must not let this distract us from also listening carefully for their hopes for a better future and for currently existing resources that may help them move toward that preferred future. These are the therapeutic gold nuggets embedded in the gravel of problem-saturated stories.

It may also be tempting to psychologically distance oneself by tuning out the demanding client. I became aware of my temptation with certain clients to drift into inattention. Rather than thinking of this as a countertransference problem (as I first thought), I have found it more useful to consider that certain types of interactions have a hypnotic effect on me. I noted feeling somewhat depersonalized in these interactions, which made it feel as if I couldn't connect with the client. This was intriguing since these same individuals often stated intense desire to be cared for, heard, understood, and accepted. I noticed that they tended not to make much eye contact (or had their eyes dilated) as they appeared to get lost in their stories about how painful and hard their lives were. In hypnotic terms, they were experiencing a *negative hallucination* (deleting information from awareness . . . me!) while *positively hallucinating* (absorbed in their own inner experience). They were not present with me, but engaged with their own constructs about the past and the future. When this happens, both therapist and client can easily become hypnotized by—and lost in the content of—clients' painful stories.

I gradually realized that if I kept myself out of trance by being an active participant in clarifying what the client wanted from our therapy relationship, I was interrupting the typical trance that was more focused on internal experience than on our present interaction. By actively engaging longer-term clients in focused, cooperative, mutual work (beginning with goal development), the possibility is created for developing a collaborative relationship where both of us are present as partners in cocreating change. This is very different from feeling like an observer to the dramatic ups and downs ("traumas") that longer-term clients often experience. Being an active partner in therapeutic change creates a powerfully positive and generative connection between client and therapist.

This idea can be quite challenging to operationalize with some clients. Many longer-term clients appear to have great difficulty with asking overtly for help. This may in part be due to dissociation, making it hard to know or trust what one feels or thinks. Sometimes the difficulty with asking for help may have to do with clients' having been depersonalized in their families, making it hard for them to believe that they deserve to want anything. Another compounding factor sometimes occurs when clients have been overtly or covertly exploited in primary relationships. Asking for something in therapy (e.g., acknowledging needs) may feel risky due to the potential for further exploitation.

It may be helpful to ask system-related questions with such clients. Questions about their views of others' views about therapy goals join their external locus of control while inviting them to consider personal choice. For example, one could ask: *"Since you don't know yet what you'd like from therapy, who might have ideas about what would be helpful for you to accomplish with me? What would they say would be useful for you to get from therapy? What difference would accomplishing [their goal] make for you? Is there part of [their goal] that is something you'd like me to help you achieve?"*

It is not uncommon for interpersonal problems to abound with longer-term clients. Boundary problems, intense triangles, codependence, love-hate relationships, control issues, and interpersonal distance or isolation are fairly common among longer-term clients. Individuals may also report intense fears about rejection, harm, or abandonment in their relationships. These same difficulties also sometimes emerge in the client-therapist relationship, where we can find ourselves overwhelmed (or hypnotized) by clients' complex interpersonal styles. But by patiently collaborating with longer-term clients in developing workable therapy goals that they view as important to their lives, we support a sense of personal agency and also help develop a relationship that can be profoundly therapeutic.

SOME SOLUTION-FOCUSED IDEAS ABOUT FOCUSING THE RELATIONSHIP

Solution-focused therapists try not to get distracted or hypnotized by longer-term clients' often extreme symptoms or histories. No matter how complex or chronic the person's problems or how devastating or bizarre the problem's effects, we approach clients as Milton Erickson did, as if dealing with the broad range of basic human experience (Erickson, Rossi, & Rossi, 1976). Solution-focused therapists seek to normalize rather than pathologize client symptoms (Berg & Miller, 1992). For example, responding to a client who says "I have suffered from depression since my breakdown" with "I think anyone would probably be down after such a depressing experience" acknowledges the client's view of his problem while placing it within normal life experience, and hence solvable, rather than as evidence of pathology. In addition to overtly suggesting that the client's experience is "normal," deconstructing the term *depression* makes it a simple descriptor of typical life experience rather the name of a disorder. In brief therapy we use common language, keep our assumptions simple, and avoid explanatory thinking or hypothesis generation (O'Hanlon & Wilk, 1987; de Shazer & Weakland, cited in Hoyt, 1994). We stay focused on helping clients achieve what they want.

Another solution-focused therapy idea that is useful when working with longer-term clients is to be conservative regarding therapy goals. Given the numerous difficulties that some clients experience, it is more useful to help them figure out how to take a small step toward progress with one of their concerns rather than seeking broad personality change or a so-called cure. Similarly, trying to solve every major dilemma that the client faces or may potentially face is likely to discourage both client and therapist. When clients feel overwhelmed by a number of problems, it is often useful to help them prioritize by asking *"Which of the problems that you are facing do you think will be easiest to start resolving?"* In addition, one can capitalize on clients' motivation with the related question, *"Which problem will make the biggest difference in your life when you figure out how to resolve it?"* The assumption underlying this question, that individuals were making useful changes before therapy began and will continue doing so after therapy ends, presupposes that change is likely to occur again.

Solution-focused therapy also assumes that small changes often lead to larger changes (de Shazer, 1985, 1988; Rosenbaum, Hoyt, & Talmon, 1990). Erickson (Gordon & Meyers-Anderson, 1981, pp. 16–17) illustrated this assumption in his statement: "You need to do something that promotes a change in the patient . . .

however small . . . and the change will develop in accordance with his own needs. It is much like rolling a snowball down a mountain side . . . as it rolls down it gets larger and larger . . . and it starts an avalanche that fits the shape of the mountain." One can often start the snowball rolling by simply asking *"What will be a small step toward your goal?"* Our task is to help increase individuals' hopefulness about change by helping them discover how to make useful, pragmatic changes in life.

It is often useful to find out when the client coped better in the past and then to explore ways to get back on track by again utilizing those coping skills and resources. Therapists might ask, *"How have you gotten back on track when things went downhill in the past?"* or alternatively, *"What will need to be different for you to feel confident that you are back on the right track again?"*

Brief therapies encourage us to plan for the ending of therapy at its very beginning and at every step along the way toward termination. This can be initiated by asking *"What do you want to be different in your life by the time you are ready to end therapy?"* A related question that partializes and concretizes therapy goals is, *"And what will you need to figure out today for you to be one step closer to feeling ready to end therapy?"*

These questions may be challenging for some longer-term clients—as well as for their therapists. They are valuable, however, in that they orient both client and therapist toward achieving the practical changes that will help the client prepare to successfully leave therapy at some point. By honestly yet gently addressing the idea that therapy is a purposeful, purchased, professional service that will eventually end, we can reduce the risk of inadvertently inviting a vulnerable client's fantasy that maintaining the therapy relationship is the means to a worthwhile future.

Some clients, however, have great difficulty responding to future-oriented, goal-directed questions such as the solution-focused "Miracle Question" (de Shazer, 1985, 1988), or even its simplified version: *"How would you like things to be different in the future?"* One very suicidal client responded to this question by stating, "My future is dark: there is nothing there." When asked the hypothetical question, "Suppose a miracle happened and you *could* see something different and better happening in your future, what would you see?" the client responded, "More of the same: more of all the bad things that have happened in the past, and that isn't worth living for." This way of punctuating time to create one's story line in life (bad things happened in the past and will repeat in the future) understandably increases the risk of suicide. It is still helpful to ask these clients future-oriented goal development questions but to shorten the time frame by asking *"What will need to happen in the next three months to make it worth continuing to struggle to make your life worth living?"* Alternatively, if the client is unable to answer this question, the therapist can facilitate a goal of maintaining by asking *"Even if you don't know how to make things better yet, what would be happening if you were able to just keep things from getting worse?"* (Note that the "yet" in the previous sentence suggests that something different may be possible in the future.)

An often-missed opportunity with longer-term clients occurs when we join them in focusing on their intense pain and problems but ignore joining them in their hopes, which they also bring to therapy. Asking the question, *"How were you hoping I might help you with your problem?"* can be very anxiety provoking for many longer-term clients, but it can facilitate the dialogue necessary to build a collaborative relationship. It is useful to open space in the dialogue to discuss what clients want from us and what we can and can't give them as early on as possible, even if it means facing both our client's and our own discomfort with self-definition. To begin addressing this, the therapist might ask, *"What will need to change in your life for you to know that our work together was beneficial?"* or *"How were you hoping I might help you with these difficulties that cause you such pain?"* When we help clients believe enough in their own competence to hope, try out new ideas, and do things differently in life, we have facilitated trust that is both intrapersonal (trusting one's self) and interpersonal (trusting another). To help clients do this, therapists must first trust that clients are capable of making a useful difference in their own lives.

PHASES OF BRIEFER THERAPY WITH LONGER-TERM CLIENTS

Briefer therapy with longer-term clients can be thought of as having four overlapping, interrelated phases that work together to focus the helping relationship on the achievement of therapeutic goals. The course of change is nonlinear, cyclical, and with significant variation between clients, hence it is important to take clients seriously about where they tell us they need to go in therapy rather than follow these four artificial phases.

Phase One: Developing a Strong Therapeutic Alliance

Many longer-term clients are acutely attuned to subtle cues and behaviors, which they may also misinterpret. By keeping what we say as simple and clear as possible, while mutually negotiating a very explicit therapy contract, we reduce the risks of miscommunicating and of inviting clients' projections. Also, systematically using client language and metaphors avoids challenging a longer-term client's fragile perceptions while indirectly validating subjective experience. This helps build rapport with clients. Perhaps more important, however, using clients' language requires therapists to listen carefully to each individual rather than being more involved with their theories than with their clients. Even paraphrasing what clients say must be done carefully lest we convey to them that we do not accept their words, views, or (ultimately) them.

It is generally not helpful to make statements such as, "It took a long time for you to get this way, so it will take time (*long* is implied) for things to get better." Such well-meaning statements, intended to normalize or offer support, often distract both client and therapist from clarifying what they will need to accomplish together in order "for things to get better." For the more dependent or vulnerable longer-term client, it is likely to be more useful to suggest, *"Many people find they can get a good start on solving their problems more quickly than they expected, and then feel ready to go it on their own for a while. Some find that the start is all they need, while others come back from time to time to figure out how to handle other things that come up later on."*

It is also useful to take every opportunity to identify client resources, no matter how small, as soon as possible. These include things such as ways the client makes him or herself feel better, calmer, or safer, by simply asking *"What helps keep you going even though things feel so bad?"* When clients respond by saying "I pray" or "I call the hot-line" or "I write letters," they often realize (as we do, too) that they have valuable coping resources as well as challenges.

Related to identifying client resources is accessing stories of competence. Listen for examples of competence embedded among the problem-saturated stories, and also access them directly by asking *"Can you tell me about any times in the past when you were able to overcome your difficulties [stand up to your problems], no matter how briefly?"* Continue to elaborate competence stories by asking *"How did you act [talk, see things] differently when that happened? How was that for you?"* Further elaborate on competence by asking *"What do others observe you doing differently at those times? How is it for you that they see you like that? What does this say about you?"* Telling and retelling stories of competence, no matter how small, helps integrate a self-view of being capable far more effectively than attempts to reassure clients (White and Epston, 1990). Doing so helps foster clients' belief in their own capacity for self-care, making it easier for them to consider ending therapy at some point.

Asking about exceptions to problems (when problems are less frequent or less intense) can help identify coping resources. For example, a man diagnosed with "paranoid delusions" was plagued by secret "backward meanings" in others' speech, the news, or his girlfriend's letters. This was so distressing that he couldn't face leaving his house for fear he might encounter more "backward meanings." Until asked, he considered it insignificant that he could function at work and not be tormented by these thoughts on the days when he "put up with the thoughts and told myself that 'whatever people say must be true' instead of looking for backward meanings." Recognition of this simple exception-to-the-problem sequence made a dramatic difference in both his psychological comfort and his ability to function in life.

If unable to find exceptions to specific problem sequences, it may be useful to ask for global exceptions, such as *"How have you been able to keep the spark alive with so much trauma in your life?"* The form of this question is intended to acknowledge both the ability to cope *and* the past trauma rather than one precluding the other. Additionally, such questions continually orient clients toward their own resources for coping with their challenging lives rather than toward us as the primary resource upon which they depend.

Some individuals are so pessimistic that even if they can identify an exception, they dismiss its significance. If clients do not see an exception as relevant, it is generally not useful to try to convince them that it is. It may be useful, however, to remain curious and ask questions about how things might be different in the future if somehow exceptions were to occur. Exception questions can be used in this way to plant the seeds of hope and possibilities.

It is also useful to ask repeatedly about supportive relationships in the client's life and to encourage expanding those relationships. One might ask, *"Who has been helpful in the past when things got tough?"* or *"If you were to call someone, who would be most likely to be helpful now?"* Questions such as these encourage a support network that can help maintain vulnerable clients. They also operationalize the assumptions that everyone has many untapped resources, and that therapy is about living life rather than a shelter from life.

Phase Two: Facilitating Symptom Relief Regarding Current Stressors

Symptom relief is particularly important for those whose past experiences dominate their present life story so powerfully as to preclude hopes for creating a better future. This phase is initiated with such clients by asking about their most immediate goals. By taking clients seriously about what they think is their most pressing need, concern is demonstrated for their sense of being in crisis or great pain, as well as for their hopes for symptom relief. We might ask, *"What do you want to be different in the next one or two months in order to feel a little bit better?"* or *"What will be a small sign that things are heading in a direction that will make you feel a bit more in control of your life?"*

Continually relating the ever-shifting content some clients bring to sessions to their goals helps to validate and encourage their efforts at self-direction, while facilitating a focus for therapy. This can be done by simply asking *"If things were better regarding [current concern], how would that affect [stated goal]?"* It may also be useful to ask, *"Which would you prefer to figure out today, something on this current concern or the goal you stated for therapy?"*

Between-session suggestions are often helpful to give clients something to focus on between visits (de Shazer, 1988). This can help them begin to discover their current resources and what is helpful, while also connecting and focusing sessions rather than reactively drifting with clients' intense and often shifting problem focus. We might ask, *"Which of those strengths that you used in the past [or imagine using in the future] will be most useful in helping you maintain until we meet again?"* or *"What is one thing you'd like to take from today's meeting to try out until we meet again?"* Metaphors, imagery rehearsal, and role-play are also useful in this phase to help clients begin accessing and integrating their resources to find relief from their current distress.

As progress begins, no matter how small, take every opportunity to help clients "punctuate" their experience in time. Asking *"When you* used *to have the problem, how* did *you respond?"* linguistically places the problem in the past. Asking *"How* are *things different* now *than when things* were *worse?"* highlights how the present is different from the past (hence progress). Stating *"I can appreciate your frustration about not having figured this out* yet" is empathic while also suggesting things may be different in the future. "When *you've discovered how to overcome your self-consciousness, who would you like to share that with?"* suggests that sooner or later change will occur. The question also helps identify an audience for change, which can help increase the motivation and hope that makes change more likely (White and Epston, 1990).

The previously mentioned suicidal man whose future looked "dark. . . . more of the same" provides an example of punctuating a narrative to highlight progress over time. He again became quite anxious and depressed as he faced the uncertainties of graduation from school and a bleak job search; he saw this as a "regression." I asked, *"How would this situation have affected you if it had occurred two years ago?"* He promptly responded, "Oh! I'd have lost it! . . . I guess I really am a lot better. . . . It's so easy to forget that." His smile of relief demonstrated the impact of becoming aware of his progress, making it easier to face upcoming uncertainties and the emotions they will likely evoke.

Medications may also be useful as one possible means toward increased client comfort and functioning. One severely depressed man who had repeated hospitalizations for both substance abuse and suicide attempts found that he could get out of bed and go to work (rather than cower in bed, overwhelmed as he thought of all that might go wrong and thus confirm his worst fears of being a "totally worthless human being") only with the help of medications. Prior to starting medication, whatever gains he made in one session seemed to evaporate before the next. Some people benefit from medication that reduces their distress enough to allow them to hope for things to be better and to begin taking experimental steps. As Hoyt (1996) has written, appropriate psychopharmacology can "restore restorying." It is important, however, that medications be offered as an option for the individual to consider, rather than used to make others feel better (including therapists).

Achieving short-term symptom-relief goals can validate clients' perception of their own needs while reducing the sense of crisis. Doing so often enhances the therapeutic alliance and increases clients' trust in us by demonstrating that we can help them get what *they* consider most relevant. This, in turn, may encourage them to risk allowing us to help them address additional and perhaps more challenging life goals, initiating the next phase.

Phase Three: Addressing More Major Life Goals and Desired Changes

Work at this phase is still focused on what clients define as therapeutic goals, but rather than being oriented to crisis and symptom relief as in the previous phase, goals here often reflect clients' recurring struggles at developmental mastery. The focus may be on intrapersonal skills such as anxiety management, problem solving, integrating rather than splitting, learning to stop and think rather than react impulsively, increasing self-direction and a sense of agency, or increasing self-esteem and self-confidence. The focus may also be on family-related issues such as accepting what can and can't be gotten from family, setting boundaries, finding positive connections with family, figuring out useful levels of distance and connection, making independent choices in the face of family expectations, or developing competence in new family roles (teenager, parent, spouse, and so on). Clients' more major life goals may also reflect the desire to increase competence in other social systems (work, friendship, and so on), such as learning to access support and companionship, finding self-esteem–building activities, developing sexual intimacy, or other experiences that facilitate multifaceted social support networks.

The previously listed options are some typical areas of potential progress that prepare longer-term clients for managing life without being in therapy, but each individual's goals—not our theories—will define what is most relevant for her or him to accomplish in therapy. Many clients benefit from asking the solution-focused Miracle Question (de Shazer, 1985) as early in therapy as possible; some do not. During this third phase, some longer-term clients who formerly rejected or had difficulty with the Miracle Question may find it more useful. As they experience progress, it is easier for them to hope for a different future and to invest in therapeutic conversations about that future.

Phase Four: Transitioning Out of Therapy

In this phase, one might ask, *"What will need to be different in your life for you to feel confident that you no longer need to see me [as often]?"* or *"How will you know when it's time to stop coming here for therapy?"*

Some longer-term clients become quite anxious about ending the therapy relationship. For those who do, it is often easier for them to consider taking steps toward reducing rather than ending therapy. It may also be easier for them to think about leaving therapy if there is the option of returning periodically without feeling that doing so is a sign of failure for either themselves or the therapist. It can be very reassuring for a therapist to tell clients that he or she will be available on an intermittent basis to help resolve concerns that arise over time. This commitment can make it easier for clients—and therapists—to consider that they don't need to be in therapy indefinitely just because they feel vulnerable or uncertain about their lives.

Scaling questions (de Shazer, 1985, 1988) can be especially helpful for focusing clients on their progress in therapy when they feel very anxious talking about the end of therapy and a relationship they aren't certain they can cope without. *"If a number ten were everything you wanted to accomplish in therapy, and a number one was where you were when you started therapy, where do you see yourself today?"* Or with someone who is very anxious about losing the support of therapy, one could ask: *"If one was when the problem was at its worst and ten is where you'll be when you feel confident handling it (at least most of the time), where are you at today?"* Continue by suggesting and asking, *"Since most things in life aren't perfect, how close would you have to get to a ten to feel like you have accomplished enough for this round of therapy?"* (Note that "this round" suggests the client can return.) Asking *"What will you be doing differently when you are one step closer to that number [having accomplished 'enough']?"* continues to focus the helping relationship on taking small, manageable steps toward the client's goals. Asking *"What would you like me to help you accomplish today so that in the future you will be more confident about handling things on your own?"* also focuses the relationship toward therapeutic goals while gently addressing therapy's eventual end.

It can be useful to spread sessions out as far as possible (see Hoyt, 1990/1995), while still demonstrating commitment to clients who need security and support over time. This can be initiated and negotiated by asking *"What is the longest period you can imagine handling things on your own at this time?"* Resources for independent coping can also be highlighted by asking *"What will you need to do to increase the odds that things will work out OK even if you weren't to come in for a while?"* A highly anxious man, with a long history of psychiatric care and hospitalizations, commented on the effects of spacing sessions: "This works well to meet every three or four weeks. It gives me time to deal with myself; time to answer some of my own questions." Earlier, while struggling to manage his significant waves of anxiety and suicidal feelings from one session to the next, we met weekly.

With longer-term clients who tend to construct their view of life through black-and-white perceptual filters, it is useful to normalize, predict, and plan for coping with life's ups and downs. If people can view setbacks as part of life, they are more likely to focus on how they can get back on track, whereas if they view setbacks as signs of illness, relapse, or incompetence, they are more likely to focus on therapy to "fix" them. We can offer a useful frame by asking *"Since life is full of ups and downs, how will you know when you are getting off track?"* followed by, *"And what will you need to do to get back on track?"*

We can keep the door open for therapy while planting the idea that the client is developing the capacity to also use other resources by asking, *"How will you decide if a little help from therapy is in order, or if you are best off figuring things out on your own this time?"* Also asking, *"If you got stuck and wanted some help, but decided to try something other than therapy, what would you do?"* gently encourages expanding the range of supportive resources. A related question is, *"Who could you turn to, if not to therapy, if things get difficult again?"*

Even when working briefly, some clients experience the therapist as a useful internal resource, as noted in a client's report that "Sometimes I think about what you would say when I'm stuck." This introjection can be encouraged by simply asking clients: *"If I had been there to help you through that problem, what do you imagine I might have said? What do you think you would have done then?"* We can also suggest, *"When a problem comes up again, you might imagine you could ask me whatever you want, then go ahead and try something out and see what happens."* This suggestion is extremely useful for clients who tend to depend heavily on others; it accepts and then transforms their dependence into independent action.

Questions with a shorter time frame are often useful with highly anxious or dependent clients who are easily overwhelmed by life's challenges. Therapists can support coping between sessions (that is, without therapy) by asking a version of the question, *"If you couldn't get in for therapy for a week or so, how will you know you handled things the best you could have on your own?"* To help increase clients' sense of agency, one can continue by asking *"What difference do you think it will make for you in the long run when you do figure out how to handle things more on your own?"* The preceding questions might well lead into discussing clients' feelings about ending therapy. This reflects the importance of balancing the focus on emotional, cognitive, and behavioral processes throughout the course of therapy, and also emphasizes the continual interplay between the therapeutic relationship and therapeutic goals.

SIGNS OF PROGRESS

The signs of progress that I use with all clients are particularly relevant with longer-term clients. One major sign of progress is when clients begin to develop more achievable goals. This often reflects not only a shift in *what* individuals focus on in therapy, but also a shift in *how* they focus themselves in their lives in general. Specifically, individuals who make this shift seem to become more clear about what they want from life and from others rather than feeling like passive recipients (victims) of whatever life dishes out.

Another sign of progress is when clients are more able to ask directly for help. This may indicate that they are allowing themselves to hope for something, and are also ready to risk allowing the therapist to help them pursue what it is they hope for. Progress in using the therapeutic relationship in this fashion often seems to also stimulate changes in how clients relate to others in their lives in useful ways (more assertive, demonstrating more self-worth, and so on).

Clients' beginning to think and talk about themselves as having both strengths and vulnerabilities reflects increasing integration, which is another sign of progress. For example, one longer-term client reported, "I know I'm overly sensitive to others' opinions, but I'm getting better at remembering I'm a worthwhile person no matter what others think." It appears that clients often become more self-accepting as they learn to live with their own (and life's) pain *and* potential rather than viewing life only through either-or lenses.

Shortly following these first three signs of progress, longer-term clients often also begin demonstrating a greater sense of personal agency, which often leads to another equally important sign: developing and using supports other than therapy. Believing that one can act on one's own behalf and having additional resources to help face challenges makes it easier for clients to consider life without therapy. This shift in view is noted in the comment of one longer-term client who stated early in therapy, "Therapy is the most important thing in my life." His previous therapist may have supported this view by encouraging him to come to therapy two or three times per week, especially when he felt more distressed. Later, when he felt that coming back in six weeks would be soon enough, he commented: "I can play guitar, hang out with friends, work, or go canoeing; I have a lot of things that get me through those desperate spells that used to panic me." His pride was unmistakable.

Essentially, each of these signs of progress has to do with the development of progressive narratives that include possibilities rather than a fixed "more of the same" view. This is illustrated in the comments of a man who met *DSM-IV* (American Psychiatric Association, 1994) criteria for both Anorexia and Borderline Personality Disorder: "I had the unusual thought that I am making progress, and that maybe I'm not the big freak I always imagined I was. I'm realizing that things can change with time and effort." As his sense of personal agency has increased, his feelings of depression and thoughts of suicide have dramatically decreased.

INITIATING BRIEFER THERAPY WITH CURRENT LONGER-TERM CLIENTS

Changing approaches midstream with longer-term clients can be difficult for both clients and therapists. I first realized this after returning from my initial solution-focused training at the Brief Family Therapy Center in Milwaukee and asked many of my clients, *"How will you know when you are ready to end therapy?"* The responses of some of my longer-term clients suggested that I should add Panic Disorder to their long lists of diagnoses, because panic is what the question elicited!

I have heard clients (and therapists) sometimes angrily use the terms *abandonment* or *betrayal* to describe their responses to therapists' attempts to make the therapy contract more explicit and goal directed after being in therapy for a protracted period of time without mutually negotiated therapy goals. Their feelings of being betrayed or abandoned probably had to do with the therapist's unilateral changing of a covert contract that implicitly promised that the therapist would "be there for you" indefinitely.

To begin the transition from a covert relationship focus to focusing the relationship on overt and mutually negotiated therapy goals, it is useful to gently orient the relationship toward what clients currently want from us. For example, with clients who tell stories about their problems without identifying any goals for change (asking for help), one can ask, *"Is there anything you'd like to ask me today, or wish I asked you, about this problem you have?"* Therapists can then gradually shift to focusing more on goals that will eventually make therapy a less essential part of the client's life by asking *"What will be a small sign that you are one step closer to being ready to come in less frequently?"* Be prepared to assure clients that you are not trying to get rid of them, but trying to make sure they get something useful from their time, money, and relationship with you. If timed carefully (e.g., after clients become aware of and "own" their progress), the conversation following this question is often perceived as a sign of success—a graduation rather than a rejection.

Continually, persistently, and gently focusing the relationship on therapy goals is often profoundly therapeutic, in that it helps longer-term clients discover and integrate their potential to learn and grow from life's challenges. Far more healing than simply learning to cope with challenging lives, such discovery and integration lead to an increased sense of competence, mastery, and personal agency.

TAKING THESE IDEAS TO WORK

The preceding solution-focused ideas often help make therapy briefer by developing a collaborative therapeutic relationship focused on facilitating progressive narratives that use both clients' competencies and their hopes for a different future. They will not, however, guarantee that therapeutic change will always occur in a brief amount of time. They simply help find a difference that makes a difference; this tends to make therapy more efficient by effectively using whatever time we have with any given individual.

Endnotes

1. I use the term *longer-term client* loosely, not as a definitive category with clearly defined criteria, but rather as a general grouping of people who tend to use therapy over extended periods of time. Such generalizations run the risk of treating ideas (specifically, the characteristics I discuss) as if they were truths rather than just constructs. In spite of this risk, it is assumed that we need concepts and metaphors to guide purposeful therapy (Combs & Freedman, 1994) and that readers will compare these ideas to their own direct experience to test their validity with any given client in any given situation.

2. While my emphasis here is on starting the positive and encouraging individual self-direction, ethical and legal mandates also require attempting to facilitate the ending of abusive or dangerous situations that we believe put clients or others at serious risk. Obviously, this requires clinical judgment.

3. Solution-focused questioning, like any technique, can be done skillfully or not. Done mechanically, without a purposeful sense of what to ask when, solution-focused questioning is most likely to be ineffective. Used skillfully, these questions are often like a light we offer clients to help them illuminate and integrate their own competence. Learning to use solution-focused questions in this fashion requires the same patience and practice that developing any complex skill requires.

References

American Psychiatric Association. (1994). *Diagnostic and statistical manual of mental disorders* (4th ed.). Washington, DC: Author.

Berg, I. K., & Miller, S. D. (1992). *Working with the problem drinker: A solution-focused approach.* New York: Norton.

Combs, G., & Freedman, J. (1994). Narrative intentions. In M. F. Hoyt (Ed.), *Constructive therapies* (pp. 67–91). New York: Guilford Press.

de Shazer, S. (1985). *Keys to solution in brief therapy.* New York: Norton.

de Shazer, S. (1988). *Clues: Investigating solutions in brief therapy.* New York: Norton.

de Shazer, S. (1991). *Putting difference to work.* New York: Norton.

Duncan, B., Hubble, M., & Miller, S. (1997). *Psychotherapy with "impossible" cases: The efficient treatment of therapy veterans.* New York: Norton.

Erickson, M. H., Rossi, E. L., & Rossi, S. I. (1976). *Hypnotic realities: The induction of clinical hypnosis and forms of indirect suggest.* New York: Irvington.

Gordon, D., & Meyers-Anderson, M. (1981). *Phoenix: Therapeutic patterns of Milton Erickson.* Cupertino, CA: Meta Publications.

Hoyt, M. F. (1990). On time in brief therapy. In R. A. Wells & V. J. Giannetti (Eds.), *Handbook of the brief psychotherapies.* New York: Plenum. Reprinted in M. F. Hoyt,

Brief therapy and managed care: Readings for contemporary practice (pp. 69–104). San Francisco: Jossey-Bass, 1995.

Hoyt, M. F. (1994). On the importance of keeping it simple and taking the patient seriously: A conversation with Steve de Shazer and John Weakland. In M. F. Hoyt (Ed.), *Constructive therapies* (pp. 11–40). New York: Guilford Press.

Hoyt, M. F. (1996). Introduction: Some stories are better than others. In M. F. Hoyt (Ed.), *Constructive therapies* (Vol. 2, pp. 1–32). New York: Guilford Press.

Lipchik, E. (1994). The rush to be brief. *Family Therapy Networker, 18*(2), 34–39.

Nylund, D., & Corsiglia, V. (1994). Becoming solution-~~focused~~ forced In brief therapy: Remembering something important we already knew. *Journal of Systemic Therapies, 13*(1), 5–12.

O'Hanlon, W. H. (1990). Debriefing myself: When a brief therapist does long-term work. *Family Therapy Networker,* March/April, pp. 48–50.

O'Hanlon, W. H., & Wilk, J. (1987). *Shifting contexts: The generation of effective psychotherapy.* New York: Guilford Press.

Rosenbaum, R., Hoyt, M. F., & Talmon, M. (1990). The challenge of single-session therapies: Creating pivotal moments. In R. A. Wells & V. J. Giannetti (Eds.), *Handbook of the brief psychotherapies* (pp. 165–189). New York: Plenum. Reprinted in M. F. Hoyt, *Brief therapy and managed care: Readings for contemporary practice* (pp. 105–139). San Francisco: Jossey-Bass, 1995.

Self, S. (1991). The other side of client possibilities. In *T. C. Times* (Newsletter of Therapeutic Conversations Conference, Tulsa, OK), *1*, 3.

Walter, J., & Peller, J. (1992). *Becoming solution-focused in brief therapy.* New York: Brunner/Mazel.

White, M., & Epston, D. (1990). *Narrative means to therapeutic ends.* New York: Norton.

Yapko, M. (1990). Brief therapy tactics in longer-term psychotherapies. In J. K. Zeig & S. G. Gilligan (Eds.), *Brief therapy: Myths, methods, and metaphors* (pp. 185–195). New York: Brunner/Mazel.

CHAPTER EIGHTEEN

The Narrative Solutions Approach for Retelling Children's Stories

Using Preferred Views to Construct Useful Conversations

Thomas W. Lund, Joseph B. Eron

A basic assumption of constructivism is that meaning and action are interwoven (Goolishian & Anderson, 1987).[1] How people view self and other is intimately connected to, in fact inseparable from, what they do about their life predicaments. *Narrative solutions* therapists are interested in how people have come to construct what they call "the problem" (Eron & Lund, 1993, 1996, 1998, in press). How is it that people become fixed on problematic views of self and other? How do these views shape what they do to maintain their difficulties? What key stories, past and present, inform current constructions of events and behavior? In this chapter, we'll focus on how problems develop for young children and families and how to conduct helpful conversations with them to resolve these problems.

Even card-carrying constructivists like ourselves, with years of experience talking with other people's children and families, can get caught in unhelpful conversations with our own children. Tom recently arrived at a large family gathering carrying his two-year-old daughter, Aimei. She proceeded to duck her head into his shoulder and refuse to talk to relatives who had not seen her for some time. Tom, for no discernible reason, explained to the relatives, "She's shy." This attribution did not go unnoticed by Aimei. When a very nice family member, self-appointed as an expert at warming up children, approached Aimei and attempted to get her to talk, she replied, "I shy." Thankfully, Tom was writing this chapter. He caught himself and did not use this term again.

We developed the narrative solutions approach over fifteen years at the Catskill Family Institute by studying helpful and unhelpful conversations (Eron & Lund, 1996, 1997a, 1997b). We looked closely at what worked and didn't work when we and our staff therapists talked with families in distress, and what worked and didn't work when family members conversed with each other. With young children experiencing dramatic symptoms, we noticed a pattern in how parents and other significant adults ascribed meaning to problematic behavior such that unhelpful conversations evolved. These conversations shaped the ways children and parents came to think of themselves and act, and this led to the persistence of problems. Let's look at the assumptions we make about problem construction and problem maintenance for young children and their families.

PREFERRED VIEW

• *Assumption:* People have strong preferences with regard to how they would like to behave, how they would like to see themselves, and how they would like to be seen by others. We refer to this constellation of ideas about self as a person's *preferred view.*

The concept of preferred view was implicit in the individual psychotherapy of Carl Rogers (1961), who proposed that people experience distress when there is a gap between their ideal self and self as perceived. Influenced by Milton Erickson, brief interactional therapists at the Mental Research Institute (MRI) in Palo Alto, California, stressed the therapeutic importance of understanding how people want to be seen by others (Weakland, Fisch, Watzlawick, & Bodin, 1974). More recently, narrative therapists have alluded to the idea of preferred view in their writings. For example, White and Epston (1990) assume that people experience problems when the stories of their lives do not sufficiently represent their lived experience. Therapy is geared toward helping people get in touch with preferred stories that fall outside of these dominant, "problem-saturated" accounts.

Parents generally have a preference to see themselves and to be seen by others as loving, competent, and caring for their children. Certainly their own childhoods and relationships with significant adults shape their preferences and the emotional valence of these preferences. For instance, a man who saw his father as distant and uninterested may have a strong preference to act and be seen as involved with his children. A woman who saw her mother as critical might have a strong preference to act and be viewed as loving and accepting, not critical of her own children.

Young children generally seem to have a preference to be seen as "good," worthy of being loved, and competent. Children often see themselves as "bad" when they think that significant adults see them in negative ways. Yet young children's preferences, hopes, and intentions are not well developed or articulated and often do not suffice to guide behavior. For example, it would be unwise to count on a two-year-old like Aimei to say "I not shy, Daddy" or "I like people" as a way to counter her father's attribution. Children look to the adults around them to provide love, guidance, and discipline. It is largely through the meaning parents give to children's behavior that children come to define who they are and wish to be.

THE PAIN OF DISJUNCTION

• *Assumption:* People experience negative and unsettling emotions such as sadness, frustration, and anxiety when they behave in ways that are discrepant with preferred views of self, when they see themselves in ways that are discrepant with preferred views of self, and when they imagine that others see them in ways that are discrepant with preferred views.

Additionally, parents of young children experience distress when their actual view of their children's behavior clashes with their preferred view of their children, or when they think that others view their children in nonpreferred ways.

While we were writing this chapter, Joe asked Tom what we call a *mystery question:* "How is it that an affable, entertaining person like yourself, with a daughter who sings your songs and giggles endlessly even at your worst jokes [preferred view], would worry about having a shy child?" Often such a question elicits past stories that inform us regarding how we talk with children. Tom recalled how he was shy around people he didn't know when *he* was a child. Tom's own preferences for Aimei included that she feel confident and able to assert herself in social situations. Tom also hoped that family members saw him as raising an assertive child. The *disjunction* (or gap) between his own preferences, his perception of Aimei's behavior, his construction of how family members viewed Aimei, and his sense of how they regarded him as a parent, all may have informed his unhelpful attribution about Aimei's behavior.

HOW PROBLEMS EVOLVE

• *Assumption:* When parents view children's behavior in ways that clash with their own preferences, hopes, and intentions, problematic interactions seem to emerge. This often occurs during times of family transition.

As children develop and families change, there are numerous occasions in which children and parents must give meaning to events. The sheer number of transitions and concomitant shifts in viewing and doing is daunting. Almost any new event requires parents and children to shift their thinking about self and other and decide how to respond. We all think of the usual life transitions such as the birth of a child, birth of a sibling, children walking, talking, toilet training, starting school, entering junior high school, adolescence, leaving home, and marriage. Families also weather unpredictable events such as illness or death of a family member, family moves, separation, and divorce. Almost any event can set off shifts in how parents view their children and how the parents respond—which then influences the child's view of self and behavior. For example, a child's first failing grade, the first call from a teacher with concern about a child, or the day a child comes home repeating an obscenity heard on the school bus all can cause parents to doubt themselves and change how they think of their children—with recursive implications for the child's self-image and subsequent behavior, and so on.

This assumption about problem evolution expands on a basic premise of the MRI brief therapy approach (Watzlawick, Weakland, & Fisch, 1974; Fisch, Weakland, & Segal, 1982), that problems develop from the mishandling of ordinary life difficulties. From this perspective, people slip into problem-maintaining patterns more by accident than by structural or systemic design. Bogdan (1986, p. 35) referred to this process as "accidentalism" to convey the random, not entirely predictable path to problems described in the MRI approach. De Shazer (1985, p. 18) touched on a similar theme in describing how complaints develop out of "damned bad luck." A seemingly trivial event can trigger the onset of a major problem by jostling the preexisting views of those affected by the event. Whether a life event turns into an enduring problem, however, hinges not only on how the event is construed but also on whether or not disjunctive views of self and other emerge in the wake of the event.

By their reactions, parents punctuate certain events with what they say and do. Aimei may not have noticed any significance to her putting her head into Tom's shoulder and not talking. Tom did. Thus Aimei chose her father's attribution, "shy," to explain her own behavior on a subsequent occasion. If this behavior continued to be noticed and this meaning made, Aimei might come to think of herself as a "shy person" and act in line with this limiting construction. In this way, parents shape children's preferences and the stories they develop and come to tell about their lives.

According to White and Epston (1990, p. 10), people arrange "their experiences of events in sequences across time in such a way as to arrive at a coherent account of themselves and the world around them. Specific experiences of events of the past and present, and those that are predicted to occur in the future, must be connected in a lineal sequence to develop this account. This account can be referred to as a story or self narrative."

Case One: How Parents Compose Children's Stories

We recall a seven-year-old boy named Matt who taught us about the power of children's stories. Matt helped us understand how children's actions do not always reflect their preferences and intentions, and how parents shape the stories children tell about who they are. Matt's pediatrician called Tom to see if he could see Matt immediately. He and Matt's parents, seated in his office, were very concerned. He reported that Matt was increasingly jealous of his three-year-old brother, Sam. He was hitting and pushing Sam to the floor daily. The day before their visit to the doctor's office Matt's mother went up to Matt's bedroom, where he and his brother were playing. Things were a bit quiet and she was concerned. Matt was in the process of tying Sam to a chair with a rope. When Tom spoke with the parents on the phone they asked questions like, "Does Matt have feelings? Does he care?"

After meeting with the family later that week, Tom met with Matt alone. The first fifteen minutes of the session largely consisted of Matt looking at Tom suspiciously and ignoring questions about what he liked to do. He finally looked at Tom and said, "When are we going to talk about *it?*"

TOM: Talk about what?

MATT: You know.

TOM: What do you think we are going to talk about, Matt?

MATT: Me, I'm bad.

TOM: You are?

MATT: *[looking surprised and a bit exasperated]* Yes.

TOM: You think you are bad?

MATT: I *am* bad.

TOM: How do you know that?

MATT: I do bad things to my brother.

TOM: I don't think that means you are bad.

MATT: *[looking more puzzled]* It doesn't?

TOM: No.

MATT: That isn't what Mom says.

TOM: What does your Mom say?

MATT: She says I used to be good but now I'm bad.

TOM: Do you like what you do to your brother?

MATT: No.

TOM: Why is that?

MATT: Because it's bad.

TOM: Oh, so you don't like doing things that might hurt your brother and you don't like Mom thinking that you are bad.

MATT: No, I don't.

Tom later spoke with Matt's parents, eager to share what he had learned from Matt about his actual intentions. When he mentioned that Matt seemed worried about being bad and that he didn't like what was going on, they almost fell out of their seats. When Tom asked the parents how they thought Matt's behavior could have evolved, they seemed stymied, although they did pinpoint a time of transition. The parents said that up until Sam was born, Matt was "a great kid." They then described their own worries about jealousy and how they went out of their way to include Matt in caring for Sam. This approach had its roots in repeated warnings from Matt's maternal grandmother and aunt that firstborn children get angry when they're not included in the new baby process. Matt helped change Sam's diapers and feed him. If he got rough with Sam, the parents were careful not to scold Matt for fear he would become more jealous. As Matt got more aggressive, the parents became upset and critical, questioning Matt's intentions toward his brother. Yet they still did not limit Matt's behavior. Matt managed his distress by attempting to get back at his brother, which caused the parents to further doubt his good intentions. They began to believe that Matt was a "bad boy."

As the conversation about problem evolution continued, the parents themselves got the idea that perhaps Matt wanted to be a good child and that he seemed unable to act in line with this preference on his own. They acknowledged that their own negative attributions were not helpful and they changed their tack. Rather than questioning Matt's values and intentions, insinuating to him that he was a bad boy, they told him they saw him as good. Still, they limited his unsupervised contact with Sam and sent him to his room when he acted aggressively toward Sam. In a sense, the parents teamed up to help Matt act in line with his preferred view of self. Over the course of seven sessions in a ten-week period, there was a dramatic improvement in Matt's behavior.

Case Two: Solving the Mystery of Problem Construction

Let's look at a case example that further illustrates how families construct problems and how to talk with them to deconstruct problems. Amanda Roth called Tom, concerned about her seven-year-old son, Frank. She said Frank was having terrible problems with anxiety. He'd tell her that his bedroom clothes dresser, which is white, changed colors. It appeared to him to be blue sometimes and red at other times. He'd come home from school with statements such as, "Mommy, it didn't feel like I was me today. My friends don't really feel like it's them." Frank had trouble going to sleep and spoke with his mother at length about these scary bedtime experiences. As one might expect, Frank's mother was very distressed by these dramatic symptoms, which had developed over a few months.

Ms. Roth spoke about a long talk she had with a close friend. Her friend read that anxiety symptoms were often inherited and encouraged Ms. Roth to delve into her own family history. Ms. Roth described how she had bouts of anxiety as a young adult and had used medication to help for a while. She worried whether Tom, a psychologist, could help Frank just by talking, or whether Frank should be referred to a psychiatrist who could prescribe medication for his symptoms. Tom offered to meet with family members for a session or two. With the parents' help, he said he'd like to piece together how these worrisome thoughts and feelings came into being, then to figure out what to do about them. Tom's hope was that the parents would become co-detectives in unraveling the mystery of how Frank's symptoms evolved. His intent was to respect their expertise in knowing their child. Ms. Roth asked that Tom meet with Frank alone to better understand what was happening from his point of view. Since we generally go along with people's preferences in arranging initial meetings, Tom agreed to this format.

The family that appeared in the waiting room included Frank, his thirteen-year-old sister (Lauren), mother (Amanda), and father (Edward). Frank easily left Mom and Dad to join Tom in his office. In their initial conversation, Frank talked about his worrisome experiences. His descriptions of symptoms included things changing, vanishing, and turning into other things. This account piqued Tom's curiosity about how transitional events might be affecting Frank and his family. However, when Tom asked about whether anything else had changed or was changing around him, Frank could think of nothing. Nor could he help pinpoint when his symptoms got worse. Finally he was able to place the onset somewhere between Thanksgiving and Christmas.

Ms. Roth's first concern was whether Frank had spoken openly with the therapist and she seemed relieved when Tom said he did. Tom remarked quizzically that all of Frank's symptoms involved things changing. Ms. Roth offered no explanation for these changes, but went on to say how worried she was that his symptoms were increasing. Mr. Roth, who had sat quietly, rolled his eyes and said that he felt that Ms. Roth was making more of these symptoms than she should be. He described Frank as a "happy guy" who played actively and enthusiastically with his father and expressed none of these concerns to him.

At this point the parents' competing perspectives became obvious. Turning toward her husband, Ms. Roth retorted, "You don't ask him. He doesn't see you as interested in this stuff. You're the fun guy." Then, looking to Tom, she said: "Ed thinks my talks with Frank at night make things worse. He thinks because

I reassure him by telling him that I had anxiety symptoms I make these things larger than they are." Mr. Roth said, "Amanda thinks I slough this off." Embedded in this conversation were clues regarding the parents' preferences for themselves as parents. As Tom asked more about Ms. Roth's interest in having Frank speak to her about his concerns, she described how her own mother did not have much regard for her feelings. As a parent, she wanted to be sure that her children would be comfortable speaking openly about their worries and concerns. Mr. Roth related how *his* father spent a lot of time with him building his confidence and how as a parent *he* hoped to do the same. Thus it became clear how past stories informed the parents' different constructions of present events, and their conflicting approaches.

The therapist persisted in being curious about Frank's statement about "things changing," and his comment that the problem got worse around Thanksgiving. "Had anything changed in the family or in school?" Tom asked. Ms. Roth responded: "Nothing *he [meaning Frank]* would know about." The parents went on to explain how they began talking about separating before the holidays. They were convinced that they had succeeded in concealing their conflict from their children, and that Frank had no inkling of this impending change.

Slowly, clues to the mystery of Frank's symptoms were emerging. As the conversation progressed, Ms. Roth began revising her perspective: "Maybe Frank did sense that something was going on. Maybe this stress brought out his inherited anxiety. We can't think about separating, how could we do that to him." Mr. Roth offered a different view: "Maybe we're not helping the kids by keeping things quiet." The parents agreed that it would be useful for Tom to explore some key questions with Frank in their next individual session. Did Frank have a vague sense that his parents might separate? Did his confusion make him anxious? If so, what might the parents do to be helpful?

When Tom met with Frank, the boy divulged that his sister had overheard the parents talking about separating and shared her secret with him. Frank then sought expert consultation on his own. He asked a friend in school, whose parents were divorced, what this was like. Frank's friend's story about separation was short but not so sweet: "Your father moves out and you don't get to see him anymore." Frank had little incentive to bring up the idea of separation to his parents. He didn't want to think about it and he didn't want to get his sister in trouble. He hoped that this bad dream would go away.

Apparently Frank's hearing about his parents talking about separation, a transitional event, kicked off his worry. Frank's experience of his dresser "changing colors" and the "different things" in his closet seemed a metaphor for the unspoken. As mentioned, young children cannot be counted on to articulate their preferences or their concerns. Although Frank showed curiosity about what happens when parents separate, and a desire to talk about this event, he wasn't about to be the initiator of a helpful conversation with his parents. Frank didn't say, "I heard from Lauren that you two might be separating" or "My friend told me that what happens is that I won't get to see Daddy anymore" or "I'm worried, please help me understand what's going on!" However, Frank's own account of how his worry evolved served to underline the importance of these missing conversations. We now had some clues to the ingredients of a helpful conversation that might resolve his dramatic symptoms.

To solve the mystery of problem evolution, we need to understand the meanings parents give to key transitional events. As mentioned, these meanings are informed by how parents prefer to view themselves and their children. When parents experience a clash between preferred views, how their children act, how they act, and how they see others seeing them and their children, negative attributions flow. In this case, Frank's mother was particularly sensitive to Frank's anxiety symptoms. She felt that there might be a genetic predisposition, implying that her son's anxiety was her fault.

Ms. Roth's actions were informed by her mind-set about being a good parent, a constellation of views and preferences shaped by history. She wanted to be different from her own mother. She wanted to be close to her son, to understand his feelings and talk with him about what bothered him. She acted in line with these preferences by speaking with Frank about his symptoms at bedtime. As Frank's symptoms worsened, the gap widened between preferences and effects. Although Ms. Roth wanted to see herself as a competent parent who could ease her son's symptoms through soothing conversation, their prolonged bedside chats failed to have the desired effects. She then considered, after a conversation with a friend, that her own defective genes might be the basis for her son's symptoms. As she felt that her husband and others saw her as unhelpful to her son, the defective parent theory began to solidify. These unsettling views about self and others fueled more-of-the-same problem-maintaining behavior. Ms. Roth persisted in talking with her son about symptoms, and avoided talking with her children about the pending separation.

Mr. Roth's actions were also informed by his construction of being a good parent. He preferred to see Frank as a well-adjusted boy and himself as a loving parent. His intention was to build his son's confidence to manage adversity, much as his own father had done with him. Mr. Roth also experienced a gap between preferences and effects. Despite his efforts to normalize things, Frank's symptoms were becoming more bizarre. Like his wife, Mr. Roth saw himself as a bad parent through his partner's eyes. He managed these troublesome gaps by retreating into silence, avoiding talk about symptoms and separation.

At the point the parents arrived for therapy, they were confused about the nature of their son's difficulties, unsure what to do, and blaming each other for the problem. Father was not talking about anxiety at all, while mother was coming to view anxiety as a real, fixed attribute of her son. The more Frank experienced anxiety, the more the parents persisted in these patterns of viewing and doing. Neither parent had an understanding of how the problem evolved, nor could they see that their own constructions shaped its course.

Moving Toward a Narrative Solution. Now that we have a sense of how the parents came to feel defeated, what might we say and do to help them feel empowered? How might we motivate them to rethink how the problem evolved in a way that harnesses their resources to find solutions?

Frank's account of talking with his sister about his parents' separation helped pin down the transitional event that kicked off the problem. Tom reassured Frank that the adults could help him with his concerns, then asked: "Would you like me to talk with Mom and Dad about these things that worry you or would you like me to be here while you tell them?" Interestingly, Frank chose the latter option.

In his parents' presence, Frank expressed *sadness* about his conversations with his sister and friend. Seeing that Frank was confused and worried about what was going on between them, the Roths were motivated to talk further with the therapist about what to do.

At the end of the second session, Tom met briefly with the parents. He began by noticing Frank's straightforward approach to talking about what bothered him. Turning to Ms. Roth, he said: "It seems like you've done what you set out to do. It's unusual to see a seven-year-old speak so openly with his parents, and show such confidence that they'll help him." Ms. Roth responded by revising her theory about Frank's symptoms: "Maybe he was confused about what was going on and didn't know how to tell us. I wonder if that's why he kept seeing things changing. It's funny, in a way Ed and I *have* been talking about changing his furniture."

Mr. Roth appeared relieved, confirmed in his preferred view that his son was a normal, happy boy responding to an upsetting circumstance. Ms. Roth then asked point-blank if Frank's confusion about the separation could be enough to account for such intense symptoms. Tom responded that in his experience, it could. He added that one way to tell would be for the adults to help Frank manage his worry about his parents' separation, then observe what happened to the symptoms.

Mr. and Ms. Roth arranged an appointment for the next day to discuss how they might approach a helpful conversation with Frank. In this session they filled in more of the blanks to understanding their son's anxiety. Apparently, Mr. Roth had rented an apartment and was already spending time away from the family. In an effort to maintain the appearance of normalcy, however, the parents told the children that their father was traveling on business, as he often did. As the parents talked, they began to question themselves whether their well-intentioned efforts to prevent anxiety had backfired. The therapist reassured them that reality—

as sad as it sometimes is—can be more reassuring than a seven-year-old's guesses about what the future might hold. The parents rapidly concluded that they were in a better position to reassure their son than his seven-year-old friend.

The session continued with the therapist imparting information about what was age appropriate and helpful to tell a seven-year-old about a parent moving out of the household. The parents left with clear guidelines for conducting a helpful conversation with Frank and his sister. They explained to the children that they would live with each parent on different days. They attempted to relieve Frank's worry about not seeing his father regularly, and assured him that both parents still loved him and his sister.

Six months later, Tom did a follow-up session with Frank and his parents. Frank's symptoms of anxiety and his experiences of furniture, closets, and himself and his friends changing had disappeared. He persisted in his wish that his family would stay together. Frank was sad, which the parents saw as appropriate to the situation and were handling as well as could be expected.

Shortly thereafter the parents contacted Joe for couple therapy. Although Frank's anxiety had dissolved and the Roths felt like capable parents again, sadness had afflicted the entire family. Mr. and Ms. Roth were now ready to explore what this enduring sadness meant. Did it mean they still loved each other? What had happened to alter their once-strong commitment? The conversation could now focus on their preferences as partners, and how their relationship had gotten off track. New mystery questions could be posed and answered.

Case Three: Solving the Mystery of Problem Construction II

Jan and Art Crews were thrilled at the birth of their second child, Jeremy, a brother to three-year-old Dennis. While Jan was in the hospital for ten days after a difficult delivery, Art's mother stepped in and cared for Dennis during the day and into the evening while Art worked. A large, close-knit family celebrated the mother and son's return home. Dennis was now seen as the big brother and a good candidate to fill the role as guide to Jeremy. When Jan Crews called to make the appointment, she seemed unsettled, embarrassed that they were seeing a child and family psychologist. She refused to give any information to the receptionist and through tears told the therapist that the family pediatrician recommended a psychologist. Ms. Crews was adamant about keeping Dennis out of the therapy and she and her husband arrived without children for the first session.

A first step in conducting a helpful conversation is to express interest in people's preferences, hopes, and intentions. The therapist strives to understand how the parents prefer to see themselves and joins with their positive intentions.

TOM: You told me on the phone that you were concerned that Dennis was not listening and that Dr. Martin suggested that you speak with me.

JAN: He was concerned.

TOM: How was that for you?

ART: It upset my wife.

TOM: Are you concerned?

JAN: I am concerned the doctor thinks we need a psychologist. We're just normal people.

TOM: Did Dr. Martin imply that you weren't?

JAN: No, but just to be here . . . a psychologist's office . . . we never expected. . . .

TOM: I see a lot of regular folks with regular kids. Kids can seem to be acting very strangely and they are regular kids with regular parents.

The parents wished to be seen as normal parents with a normal child. The therapist joined with this preferred view by letting the parents know he sees lots of regular folks with regular kids who may be acting in puzzling ways.

ART: Is it normal to be peeing all over the house and not caring about it?

TOM: All over the house?

ART: We spoke to Dr. Martin after we caught Dennis literally climbing on to our bed, taking his pants down, and peeing all over it. He looked dumbstruck when we saw him, but he wouldn't say why he was doing it and he really didn't seem upset that I was upset.

TOM: He's peed other places?

ART: All over the place.

JAN: And he's starting to say "No" all of the time. He seems kind of angry. Is this normal?

The parents described how Dennis would "sneak" around the house peeing, how he seemed to have "no conscience" about this behavior, how he defiantly retorted "No" when his parents made requests of him, and how he seemed more and more "whiny."

Keeping in mind the parents' preferences, the therapist explored how the problem was constructed. He investigated the pre-problem past. Was there a time when Dennis acted in ways that the parents preferred and when they regarded themselves as competent parents?

TOM: I take it from what you are saying that Dennis didn't always do this.

JAN: Dennis has always been a pretty easygoing child. I'm pretty relaxed usually, although you wouldn't know that today. He's a lot like me. He's changing, though.

TOM: He was easygoing until when?

ART: Well, we can pin that down to some time after Jeremy was born. He seemed pretty angry. We thought he'd be happy to have a little brother. He seemed pretty excited.

TOM: Before Jeremy was born where did he pee?

JAN: In his diaper.

TOM: Then he started taking his diaper off and peeing around the house at some point?

ART: No, my mother actually toilet-trained him while Jan was in the hospital.

TOM: How was that for you?

ART: My mother does a good job with kids. She has a special relationship with Jeremy.

TOM: How was that for you, Jan?

JAN: I felt bad missing out on that. But Art's mother does do a good job.

Mother described herself as easygoing, but acting out of character. She also described Dennis as easygoing and acting out of character. Two transitional events had taken place, the birth of Jeremy and Dennis's toilet-training. The therapist was interested in how these events affected shifts in meaning and action. When Dennis's behavior changed (he began peeing around the house) how did his parents construe this new behavior? Did their view of Dennis shift? Did they change how they regarded themselves as parents? What role did Dennis's grandmother play in the parents' construction of the problem?

TOM: I wonder what Dennis's view of all of this is? He's an easygoing guy. People were pleased with him?

ART: He's really the favorite grandchild and we always enjoyed the heck out of him.

TOM: Now people are not pleased with some of his behavior. You've actually caught him peeing on your bed. How did he react?

ART: He laughed.

TOM: What did you do?

ART: We didn't know what to do. I got pretty mad. I asked him if he wanted to be back in diapers.

TOM: Do you think he does?

ART: Dennis can use the potty and he seems proud when he does. My mother described how proud he was.

TOM: I wonder how she knew that?

JAN: Shirley and Dennis have a thing going where she makes a big deal out of his being the big brother. She says that he is very proud of this and that this was the motivation to use the potty in the first place.

TOM: Does she have some thoughts about how to handle things now?

JAN: Oh, yes. She thinks I baby him too much, that he should have been toilet-trained long before age three and that he regressed because I'm babying him again.

ART: She didn't exactly say that.

JAN: I think it's pretty obvious that she thinks it.

ART: My mother means well, but she pressures Jan, particularly.

TOM: Do you feel that you are babying Dennis?

JAN: Well, he's not toilet-trained anymore.

The therapist engaged the parents in a process we call *mystery questioning*, in which the problem is framed as a glitch or curiosity that fails to represent the truth of who people really are and commands an explanation. In this case a key mystery question was: "How did a normal, easygoing boy with normal, easygoing parents wind up engaging in such worrisome behavior and embroiling his parents in upsetting conversations?" Note how the parents offered clues to the evolution of the problem, and how the therapist and parents joined forces in rethinking its course.

TOM: You folks were pretty pleased with how things were going before this all started. Did you have concerns about babying Dennis?

ART: No.

JAN: No. . . . *[to Art]* Are you sure? I think you've sided with your mother on this.

ART: I know that it's been a bit of an issue with my mother. But come on, we've done pretty well up until now. It's really not been a problem.

TOM: Boy, leave it to a child having some trouble and we start wondering about what we've done to cause it. Do you believe Art?

JAN: I'm pretty sensitive to his mother and his sister. I do believe him.

TOM: Do you think this issue of babying has influenced how you treat Dennis now?

JAN: I try to treat him like he's older now. I guess I feel like talking to him about being the big brother has worked well for my mother-in-law so maybe I should do it.

TOM: What do you think, Art?

ART: I don't know, sometimes I talk to him about being a big brother
    and sometimes I worry that he needs more attention.

The parents both seemed to be questioning their parenting and were unclear
what to do with Dennis. They were looking at their present parenting in nonpreferred ways and were beginning to rethink the past. Jan was questioning her
former competence as a parent. She saw her mother-in-law as seeing her babying Dennis and perhaps to blame for his problem. She was wondering if Art felt
the same way.

TOM: Dennis has definitely found a way to get your attention. He sounds
    like he was up to this idea of being the big brother for a while, through
    the toilet-training and Mom's return from the hospital. That's a lot of
    changes for a little guy. Is that what makes you sometimes think he
    needs more attention?

ART: Maybe.

JAN: Do you think we've babied him? Should he have been toilet-trained
    sooner?

TOM: I'd have no reason to think that your judgment as parents was
    anything but great. You describe a happy little guy who was from all
    accounts, even grandma's, doing well. I've been very interested in how
    folks like yourselves and a good little guy like Dennis got into this,
    how you've come to doubt yourselves.

JAN: You said that this was a lot of changes for a little guy.

TOM: Yes.

JAN: I don't think I would have toilet-trained him in the first place.

TOM: Why?

JAN: I didn't think it was an issue. He was starting to show a lot of interest.
    I wouldn't have pushed it.

TOM: What do you think, Art?

ART: I never worried about it. I thought he was doing just fine.

The therapist focused the parents' attention on the many transitions that Dennis had weathered. He had experienced his mother being away for ten days for
the first time. He was toilet-trained by his grandmother. He had adjusted to having a baby brother and being a big brother. He went from being the apple of
everyone's eye to a source of controversy and confusion.

Seeing the problem in *transitional* terms is helpful to the parents. The problem is no longer a permanent property of the person, but a curiosity or mystery
that commands an explanation. Had the therapist focused on Dennis as
"enuretic" or "oppositional," the parents might now feel less empowered to

solve the problem and more inclined to look to experts to fix it. The problem might also continue to reflect negatively on who they were as parents, prompting them to ponder what they did wrong to cause enuresis or evoke opposition.

By exploring with the parents the mystery of how this problem evolved, an alternative explanation emerged that carries less blame and negativity. Jan repeated what the therapist said about Dennis going through "a lot of changes for a little guy." She realized that she wouldn't have toilet-trained Dennis in the first place had she trusted her own competence and downplayed her mother-in-law's know-how. Art supported Jan's reconstruction of the problem, confirming that Dennis and his parents were doing fine before the toilet-training was imposed. The parents were moving toward a "narrative solution." That is, solutions emerged as the parents reconsidered who their child was, who they were as parents, how the problem took shape, and what to do, within a more preferred narrative account.

As the session continued, the parents decided to put Dennis back in diapers. They agreed to tell him that he didn't have to worry about peeing in the potty for now. They also decided to spend more time with him and drop the big-brother lectures. Follow-up three months later indicated that Dennis was toilet-trained, largely by his own interest in it, and was no longer opposing his parents. The old Dennis had returned. So what happened to bring Dennis back? Or for that matter, what happened to get Dennis and his parents off-track in the first place?

Prior to Jeremy's birth, Jan saw herself as a competent parent and acted in line with this preferred view. Although she felt that her in-laws saw her as babying Dennis, this idea did not inspire self-doubt. When Jan returned from the hospital, she found that Dennis had been successfully toilet-trained by Art's mother and that he seemed to enjoy his big-brother role. However, when she and Art reclaimed their role as parents, Dennis began peeing all over the house and acting defiantly. At this point the mother-in-law's words of warning rang in her ears. When the therapist asked Jan if she thought that Art's mother was right about her babying Dennis, she retorted: "Well, he's not toilet-trained anymore!" Thus Jan began to feel that she had caused the problem by being overprotective. The gap widened between how she regarded her capabilities and how she saw others (her husband, mother-in-law, and sister-in-law) as viewing her. She compensated by trying harder to toilet-train Dennis, admonishing him for his babylike behavior and acting exasperated. What was once a "worry" had become a "problem."

Before Jeremy was born, Art also seemed comfortable with his parenting and his son's behavior and development. He, too, began to doubt his capabilities after Dennis was toilet-trained by Art's mother. Although Art seemed less affected by his mother's criticism, he appeared confused about what to do and did not assert his preferences. Once the problem was reconstructed along preferred-view lines,

Art supported Jan's idea about going back to diapers and taking the pressure off the big-brother mission.

The problem resolved as the gap narrowed between how Jan and Art preferred to view themselves as parents, how they acted, and how they imagined important others regarded them. The solution was not prescribed, but emerged through collaborative conversation about the "mystery" of problem evolution or construction.

The reader might ask: Why meander in this conversational approach to the problem? Why not cut to the quick and tell the parents that Dennis experienced too many transitions and suggest how to manage his behavior differently?

Although such a directive approach seems more efficient, the risk is that it would be less effective. The parents might take this as another person (in this case an expert) seeing them as unable to manage their son. If they viewed another significant person seeing them in nonpreferred ways, they would likely feel worse about themselves as parents. Disempowered parents are less likely to come up with suggestions on their own. Even if the parents did follow the therapist's advice and approach Dennis differently, they might do so from a position of weakness—requiring more cheerleading on the part of the expert to persist in this different approach. Another risk is that parents might not alter their story of who their child is. While they might manage the immediate behavior, their worry about their child might persist; for example, they might see Dennis as being at risk for Oppositional Defiant Disorder.

In the case reported here, solutions emerged from empowered and confident parents who, reminded of their past successes, figured out for themselves what to do differently. The shift in tone was striking when Jan said: "I don't think I would have toilet-trained him in the first place." In that statement, Jan is noticing her own capabilities, asserting her preferred vision of parenting, and trusting that she knows her son as well or better than anyone else.

SOME USEFUL QUESTIONS FOR ELICITING PREFERRED VIEWS

The following is a sampling of questions therapists ask about preferred views that guide helpful conversations with children and parents.

Gleaning Preferences About Seeking Help

- How did you [the caller] arrive at the decision to make an appointment?
- Does your [husband, wife, partner] have the same or different opinions about seeking help?
- What did you think of the [pediatrician's, teacher's, guidance counselor's] idea that you come for help?

- How did you wind up in a situation where [friends, relatives, parents, family court] urged you to come for therapy?
- How did you feel about this urging?

These questions are often asked over the telephone to arrange the initial appointment, and are continued in the first session. They are aimed at understanding the parents' preferences regarding help seeking, and assist the therapist in deciding with whom to meet and how to join with people once they arrive. For example, upon learning that Ms. Crews was sensitive about having her son see a psychologist, the therapist decided to meet with the parents without the children. In the first session, he reassured the parents that "normal kids can act in puzzling ways." Once parents see the therapist seeing them and their children in preferred ways, they become more open in talking about their circumstances and exploring solutions.

Preference and Effects Questions

- When you did [X behavior], how did you feel about it?
- Did you like the effects of what happened? On you? On others?
- Did others notice that you did [X behavior]?
- How did they think of you?
- Did you like how they thought of you?

These questions are designed to elicit preferences about the immediate events and behaviors that bring people to therapy. The responses allow therapists to determine whether people experience a gap between who they would like to be, how they act, and how they think important others regard them. When gaps are identified, the therapist highlights them in conversation with children and parents. For example, the therapist said to seven-year-old Matt, "Oh, so you *don't* like doing things that might hurt your brother and you *don't* like Mom thinking that you are bad." Matt responded, "No, I don't." The therapist then circulated this information to the parents, who began revising their view of Matt.

Preference and effects questions are also useful to ask once people are engaging in new behaviors that resolve the problem. For example, Matt might respond that he likes controlling his temper with his brother and feels better that his parents no longer see him as bad. Hearing Matt's response, the parents are not only more likely to persist in their new approach, but also may carry a more hopeful story of Matt into the future. Narrative solutions become solidified.

Once-Upon-a-Time Questions

- Was there a time when your child was not acting this way?
- How was that for you?

- How did your child think of himself [herself] at that time?
- How did others view you and your child at that time?
- Can you pinpoint when things changed?
- Why do you think things changed at that particular time?

These questions are aimed at understanding the pre-problem past. The therapist highlights times when people *were* acting in line with their preferences and elicits key stories about these events. Once-upon-a-time questions create a climate of mystery about how the problem became a problem. The therapist invites the parents to pinpoint the time of transition, and pursues *their* ideas about how and why things changed. Therapists and parents together begin to develop a more hopeful and helpful account of problem development.

Mystery Questions

- Why would a child who wants to be [good, competent, responsible] be acting otherwise?
- Why would parents who know their child and know what's best for their child [or other relevant preferred view] be doubting themselves as parents?
- Why would parents who have such a close relationship with their children [or other relevant preferred view] not be talking with their children about such an important event [as separation or whatever] and reassuring the children that they're still there for them?
- Why would easygoing parents with an easygoing child [or other relevant preferred view] be taking such a pressured approach to the problem?

Mystery questions invite parents to explain contradictions between preferred views and how children and parents have come to act. These questions are often asked after therapists are clear about preferred views and have investigated the pre-problem past. At this stage, the story of the child's problem—originally presented by the parents as fixed, certain, and known—has become fluid and somewhat murky. Mystery questions prompt the therapist and parents to develop a more useful explanation or problem construction, one that sparks solutions and perhaps alters what otherwise could become an unhappy life story.

SUMMARY AND CONCLUSIONS

In this chapter we've emphasized the innocence of problem evolution. We've focused on ordinary events at normal times of transition that bring about subtle shifts in how parents and other significant adults think, act, and interact around children. In so doing, we don't want to overlook the fact that many serious problems arise from terrible and traumatic events. Losses such as death of a parent or loved one and chronic illness have a profound impact on the meanings children make of their lives, regardless of how adults respond to these events. Irresponsible and destructive behavior on the part of adults also shapes how children come to think of themselves and how they act.

Still, even when children are physically or sexually abused or neglected by adults, the attributions adults make about these events greatly influence the stories children come to tell (or not tell) about who they are. When these adults take responsibility for their own behavior and its effects on their children (e.g., apologize or admit wrongdoing), children are more likely to acknowledge the event as bad and themselves as OK. A competent self-narrative may yet unfold. When adults deny responsibility for these devastating events, children are more likely to bear the burden of responsibility and come to think of themselves as deficient or defective.

The assumptions about problem construction presented in this chapter shed light on why parents often do not initiate helpful conversations with children about the parents' irresponsible acts. Parents who have regularly abused their children rarely state a preference for doing so or convey that they enjoy the effects on the children. These parents rarely have conversations with other adults who ask about their preferences or pose mystery questions that might highlight a gap between who they would like to be, how they behave, and the effects their actions have on others. To close the cavernous gap between their own preferences and actions, parents may deny their behavior, minimize its impact, or blame the victim—leaving children to make their own meanings of these events.

Problem construction has real impact on the lives people live. Should the unhelpful conversations that were occurring before our sessions with seven-year-old Frank and three-year-old Dennis have continued, one wonders who these children might have become. Would Frank have grown to be an anxious boy who needed medication; Dennis, oppositional and defiant?

In this chapter, we present the assumptions that narrative solutions therapists make about problem development in young children, and illustrate how therapists can talk with children and parents to help resolve problems. In helpful conversations, therapists "look for clues that reside in the tales people tell about their lives. They ask questions from a position of curiosity and respect, engaging help from people in putting together the puzzle of how their problem became a problem. The problem itself becomes a mystery that fails to represent the truth of who people are, and commands an explanation. The therapeutic conversation is designed to unravel the mystery of how the problem evolved, so that new solutions emerge" (Eron & Lund, 1996, p. 68). When empowered parents rethink how the problem was constructed in ways that confirm their preferred views of themselves and their children, they begin to conduct helpful conversations that bring out the best in their children.

Endnote

1. Paul Watzlawick (1984; see also Chapter Nine, this volume) is widely recognized for introducing constructivism to the field of family therapy. Social psychologist Kenneth Gergen (1985; see also Foreword, this volume) is generally regarded as the leader of social constructionist thinking, often embraced by narrative therapists. Although distinctions have been drawn between these schools of thought (see Efran & Clarfield, 1992), we do not emphasize these differences. Our *narrative solutions* approach is based on tracking how individual and social constructions, embedded in dialogue between people, are linked to problems; and how alternative constructions, embedded in conversation, are linked to solutions. We view the therapist as responsible for generating and managing helpful conversations inside and outside the treatment room.

References

Bogdan, J. (1986). Do families really need problems? Why I am not a functionalist. *Family Therapy Networker, 10*(4), 30–35, 67–69.

de Shazer, S. (1985). *Keys to solution in brief therapy.* New York: Norton.

Efran, J. S., & Clarfield, L. E. (1992). Constructivist therapy: Sense and nonsense. In S. McNamee & K. J. Gergen (Eds.), *Therapy as social construction* (pp. 200–217). London: Sage.

Eron, J. B., & Lund, T. W. (1993). How problems evolve and dissolve: Integrating narrative and strategic concepts. *Family Process, 32,* 291–309.

Eron, J. B., & Lund, T. W. (1996). *Narrative solutions in brief therapy.* New York: Guilford Press.

Eron, J. B., & Lund, T. W. (1998). Narrative solutions couple therapy. In F. M. Dattilio (Ed.), *Case studies in couple and family therapy.* New York: Guilford Press.

Eron, J. B., & Lund, T. W. (in press). Narrative solutions in brief couple therapy. In J. Donovan (Ed.), *Short-term couples therapy* (pp. 371–400). New York: Guilford Press.

Fisch, R., Weakland, J. H., & Segal, L. (1982). *The tactics of change: Doing therapy briefly.* San Francisco: Jossey-Bass.

Gergen, K. J. (1985). The social constructionist movement in modern psychology. *American Psychologist, 40,* 266–275.

Goolishian, H. A., & Anderson, H. (1987). Language systems and therapy: An evolving idea. *Psychotherapy, 24,* 529–538.

Rogers, C. R. (1961). *On becoming a person: A therapist's view of psychotherapy.* Boston: Houghton Mifflin.

Watzlawick, P. (Ed.). (1984). *The invented reality: How do we know what we believe we know? (Contributions to constructivism).* New York: Norton.

Watzlawick, P., Weakland, J. H., & Fisch, R. (1974). *Change: Principles of problem formation and problem resolution.* New York: Norton.

Weakland, J. H., Fisch, R., Watzlawick, P., & Bodin, A. M. (1974). Brief therapy: Focused problem resolution. *Family Process, 13,* 141–168.

White, M., & Epston, D. (1990). *Narrative means to therapeutic ends.* New York: Norton.

CHAPTER NINETEEN

A Narrative Approach to Anorexia

Discourse, Reflexivity, and Questions

Stephen P. Madigan, Elliot M. Goldner

Anorexia gains the upper hand over clients and therapists far too often. When this happens, it is frequently accompanied by despair, the possibility of further deterioration, and on occasion, death. The fear that a therapist experiences at this point can sometimes be overwhelming. Imagine what it might be like for clients, families, and loved ones.

> Carmen appeared at the door looking very close to death. There was a weak smile on her sunken face and, in an easygoing candor, she discussed her ongoing chest pains. Her tattered red shoes, bought only weeks ago, were showing signs that she had returned to her daily eight-hour walks. She was being eaten alive by anorexia; she had been leaning on death's door for a number of years; yet she was so casual. This is the perverse thing with anorexia—the process can be deceptively casual, yet devastating and sometimes lethal. It can keep you up at night.

Despite numerous theoretical and therapeutic approaches to the problem of anorexia, it remains slippery and difficult to locate. Anorexia has a way of desecrating prized theories and beliefs and it would be foolhardy to be inflexible. Over the years we have had to shift away from certain practice assumptions and have adopted others. If we don't maintain our flexibility, anorexia will certainly gain the upper hand.

We do not wish to add to the already long list of theories and practices that can be misused by therapists in competition for the "true" approach and correct understanding of the so-called underlying issues in anorexia nervosa. It is our view that our therapeutic professions have too often produced additional suffering for clients and families by insisting on the unearthing of controlling mothers, abusive fathers, enmeshed family boundaries, chemical imbalances, and so on.

We believe it is best for us to acknowledge that the particularities of the problem are complex, and that reductionistic assumptions will not adequately apply to each of the individuals who come to receive help from us. What we hope to relate in this chapter is not a catchall theory, but rather a set of ideas and approaches that appear to be helpful to most of the people we have worked with who are struggling against anorexia.

THE TEXTUAL IDENTITIES OF PERSONS

Through the *text analogy*, often referred to in terms of the *narrative metaphor* (Bruner, 1986), social scientists have come to realize that we cannot hold an essentialist knowledge of the world. Instead, they have proposed a less fixed and rigid idea that persons know life through their storying of lived experience (Epston, 1989). This story of lives through time is said to be performed within a set of language rules or games. It is a person's storied discourse, a discourse shaped and spoken through a sociopolitical and cultural context, that eventually determines the meaning given to an experience.

Gergen (1989, p. ix) writes that "the primary medium within which identities are created and have their currency is not just linguistic but textual: persons are largely ascribed identities according to the manner of their embedding discourse—in their own or in the discourse of others." The idea that a person's identity is textual runs counter to a more popular modernist definition that defines the individual as a sovereign and central object of identification. This idea that single, solitary minds are behind all words is the creative cornerstone of Western society's spirit of individualism. Foucault (1989) suggests that the coming into being of the notion of the "author" constitutes the privileged moment of individualization in the history of ideas, knowledge, literature, philosophy, and the sciences.

The Western myth of the individual is best placed in context by anthropologist Clifford Geertz (1973, p. 229) when he writes, "The Western conception of the person as a bounded, unique, more or less integrated motivational and cognitive universe, a dynamic center of awareness, emotion, judgment and action, organized into a distinctive whole and set contrastively against a social and natural background is, however incorrigible it may seem to us, a rather peculiar idea within the context of the world's cultures."

Therapists from every discipline have developed the compelling habit of describing persons as things. The "thingifying" of persons is supported and given a "truth status" (Foucault, 1989) through the technologies of science, government, and the popular press. The conventional culture of psychotherapy participates in the manufacturing of these solitary personhoods through totalizing techniques that place the problem inside the person's body, thereby decontextualizing the subject and the problem.

Our therapeutic approach abandons the idea of the self-as-object-of-knowledge, and the self as the identified problem in therapeutic practice. We suggest, in contradistinction, that a textual description for the identity of persons *rejects*

- Notions of the self as an inner wealth of deep resources in combat with primitive impulses.

- Ideas of a self alienated from a universe, an environment that it seeks to rejoin through rational comprehension of mysteries (scientific discovery) and through intense emotional attachments (romantic love).

- A sense of self as a consistent, knowable, enduring identity (humanism) that is nurtured or limited and can be known, measured, and directed.

- Therapies for the self that focus on discovering historical (psychoanalysis, family of origin) or environmental (behaviorism, cybernetics, systems) truths about the self and that arrogate to themselves the power to set the self in new directions.

A discursive approach (Law & Madigan, 1997) assists in the viewing of persons' lives as texts when problematic identities are considered within the constitutive nature of communities of discourse and power (Foucault, 1982; Madigan, 1996). The person and problem are viewed as mutually influenced within the particulars of a given discourse. Persons struggling with anorexia are imagined to be coping alongside powerful sets of dominant knowledge. Scientific psychology's position is to ignore the rhetorical and constructive context of how all versions of the world of persons and problems are produced—including its own. Ironically, this is one of the means by which anorexia survives.

By externalizing anorexia's internalized problem conversation, we create a linguistic separation of the problem and open space to consider the influences that promote the life of anorexia. Hence, anorexia is not viewed as "living inside" the person, nor is it seen as a manifestation of an act of control on the part of the person or a means of "getting attention." When anorexia is situated within a community's textual discourse, there is no need to pathologize the person's family. Anorexia is considered within a domain of language and viewed in terms of discursive body politics (Bordo, 1990).

EXTERNALIZING INTERNALIZED ANOREXIC CONVERSATIONS

From our experience of working on an eating disorder ward, in the community, and in independent practice, the way the problem of anorexia seems to work is to trap people into a set of intense fears and beliefs. It is tenacious and insidious.

> For Carmen, anorexia is there when she wakes in the night and feels alone. It is there around the clock: a "24/7"—twenty-four hours a day, seven days a week. Anorexia stands strong in every morsel of food, in the way it shows itself in negative comparison, in every mirror, in every clothing advertisement, in every way Carmen feels like she doesn't quite measure up. It demands perfection and criticizes her at every step. It is a slippery slope, a dominant discourse of contradiction and negation. It represents a confusing dialogic of fear that paralyses Carmen's hopes for progress and rediscovery.

It is critical for a person to be freed from anorexia's relentless discursive grip so as to rediscover his or her life. If the trap is still active, it is far too likely that anorexia will take hold again. This might be why treatments that focus primarily on weight gain rarely lead to prolonged recovery. It might also explain why forcing weight gain is so often ineffective in the long term. As long as the dominant fears and beliefs that constitute anorexia entrap the individual, the condition is highly likely to regain its ground.

Recognition of the importance of deconstructing debilitating beliefs and meanings is not unique to narrative approaches. Cognitive, motivational interviewing and other frameworks have stressed the centrality of core beliefs in providing an opportunity for change. In helping someone put anorexia behind them, there are other activities that may also be very important, including medical, nutritional, and emotional components (see Goldner & Birmingham, 1994). However, in almost all situations, a key area involves attention to the dominant narratives that emanate from the problem—and the institutional structures that support them. As these dominant narratives are deconstructed, the steel jaws of anorexia's trap can be released.

LOCATING THE PROBLEM

What is important in a narrative approach to problems is also the golden rule of real-estate buying: Location, Location, Location! If therapists can take the step to no longer locate problems entirely inside persons' bodies, then persons and problems begin to look very different. This is by no means a trivial step, as it paradigmatically shifts the therapist and client outside and beyond a hundred years of psychological science.

Carmen was of the belief that something terribly wrong was going on in her life. She didn't really hold the desire to get healthy but realized the anorexia was holding her life back in many ways. Carmen wondered if she was somehow a "marked person," destined for some unknown reason to lead an impoverished life. Carmen understood all her troubles as a result of her being a deficient person.

Madigan (1992, 1996) has described the therapeutic practice of *externalizing internalized problem discourse* as an elaboration of ideas advanced by White and Epston (1990; Roth & Epston, 1996).[1] This aspect of our work aims to discursively separate the person from the problem as a way to deconstruct taken-for-granted notions of anorexia and reconsider ideas of who constitutes the "self" who struggles against anorexia (Madigan & Epston, 1995).[2]

In the case of anorexia, the discursive scaffolding is complex. Systems that support anorexia have many discursive forms, and are manufactured through archives of dominant knowledge and carried out through powerful disciplinary practices (Law & Madigan, 1997; Madigan, 1997; Madigan & Epston, 1995). They may include specific cultural trainings around perfection, safety, and control; gender trainings of body surveillance and less-than-worthy identities; religious beliefs regarding body-purity, self-sacrifice, and guilt; the cultures of self-help that promote the politics of condemnation; and many more.

By affording ourselves the opportunity to reconsider what constitutes persons and problems from a poststructural position, a different set of therapeutic practices is instigated and the therapeutic relationship shifts.[3] Where we decide to discursively situate the problem and person locates the therapist's ideological practice beliefs.

The discourses of fear, perfection training, patriarchy, and guilt appear to be very common externalizations. Locating these internalized beliefs and their meanings within specific sets of dominant institutional, familial, cultural, and religious norms is extremely important.

We do not practice externalizing the problem as a therapeutic technique. Nor do we propose it as a strategy or trick. Externalizing internalized problem discourse is stationed within a landscape of specified political and philosophical thought. In brief, externalizing internalized problem discourse:

- Establishes a context where persons taken by anorexia experience their identity as separate from the problem.
- Proposes that the person's body, mind, and relationships to others are not the problem; the problem is the problem (an insight that counters the effect of labeling, pathologizing, and totalizing descriptions).
- Enables people to work together to defeat the effects of the problem.[4]
- Uses cultural practices of objectification to objectify anorexia itself, instead of objectifying the person as being anorexic.

- Challenges the individualizing techniques of scientific classification and looks at the broader context for a more complete problem description.

- Introduces questions that encourage the persons taken by anorexia to outline the devastating effects of the problem and locate the discourse of the problem within the trainings of a pro-anorexic community.

- Deconstructs the pathologizing thingification and objectification of women through challenging accepted and taken-for-granted social norms.

- Allows for the possibility of multiple re-remembered descriptions of the person, by bringing forth alternative versions of the past, present, and future (see Madigan, 1997).

- Counters the *dis-membering* effects of anorexia by encouraging persons toward *re-membering* themselves back toward membership groups, activities, and community (see Madigan, 1997).

REFLEXIVITY AND EARLY STRUGGLES

Working in close quarters with anorexia demands an enormous amount of internal reflection and questioning by everyone involved. We find that a regular practice of *reflexivity* (Lax, 1990; Madigan, 1993)—the practice of asking ourselves questions about our questions and therapeutic beliefs—enhances accountability to the client and allows the therapy to remain flexible. In considering how we might be helpful to Carmen, there are a number of reflexive questions we would consider asking ourselves and each other:

- In what ways might I get trapped into reproducing the most common misconceptions of anorexia in the session?

- In what ways can I avoid getting caught up in anorexia's trap of pitting Carmen against all those that wish to help?

- What are the untried and unique ways that I can show how much disrespect anorexia has for Carmen's life?

- How can I show a sincerity to help Carmen without scaring her off?

- What questions can I ask to allow Carmen to consider taking up her own personal protest against anorexia?

- In what ways can I be aware of my professional position, and my gender, to acknowledge and not misuse my power as a therapist?

When we first met Carmen, she told us that anorexia had been present in her life for a number of years. She remembered how a number of schoolmates had told her she was too thin and how a few spoke to the school counselor about her. Carmen told us that she felt that she had done something terribly wrong when her mother and father were called in to speak with the school counselor and nurse. When the family doctor told Carmen that she "was probably anorexic," she felt "confused." She knew she wanted to be "slimmer," but it seemed as though everyone was "exaggerating"—she had seen photos of girls with anorexia and they seemed so much thinner that Carmen felt fat by comparison. Over the ensuing months and years, Carmen felt progressively worse about the conversations that she had with people around her. They all seemed to focus on Carmen's inability to control her exercise and gain weight. A number of people, including her father and sister, seemed "constantly angry" with her. After a time, Carmen decided to withdraw.

Carmen told us that in the early days, she could not see herself as a person struggling with anorexia. The more her family members, counselor, and doctors insisted on anorexia as the problem, the more Carmen felt alone and misunderstood.

Had we met Carmen early in her struggle with anorexia, we would have considered inquiry into the following areas:[5]

- Carmen, why is it at this time that you have come to see someone like me?
- Do other people's descriptions of anorexia have any fit with your description of yourself?
- Why might this be a fitting description?
- What name might we come up with to describe the current situation?
- Has anorexia in any way taken things from your life that you value?
- In what ways has anorexia affected your relationship with yourself, your friends, your family, and so on?
- Are there ways in which anorexia has tricked your mind into thinking that an anorexic life is the best life possible?
- Do you think it tricks other young women's minds?
- If you could wager a prediction, what kind of a future does anorexia hold for you?

Carmen might have described her problem as an "everyone's on my case problem." Her naming of the problem would have allowed for a starting place to work together to find a solution. We might venture to ask, "Carmen, do you have any ideas on how best to get everyone off your case?" Or perhaps we might explore the feelings that surround the feelings of surveillance and being watched when everyone is on your case. We might begin to explore all the different places she feels watched by family, popular culture, friends, and counselors, and wonder about the effects these weight watchers were having on her life. We would begin to account for the varying arguments that surrounded the discourse, and locate this discourse in a life that Carmen preferred. We might ask "Whose watching of you is most in support of Carmen, and most against anorexia?" and "Whose watching of you most supports anorexia?" or "Are there aspects of you that are overlooked when people are only looking at anorexia's grip on you?" or "Do you have an outlook on yourself that you would like your life to look like?"

Instead, what happened to Carmen—who had been in treatment elsewhere—was her taking a stand against the methods the professional community was trying to use to help. The experience moved her relationship closer to anorexia and arguing against everyone who was trying to remedy the situation.

> As Carmen seemed to be dangerously ill, her counselor, family, and doctors saw no alternative but to force her against her will into hospital treatment. Carmen remembered being in a "full-blown battle" with the doctors, therapists, and others at the time. It was now a case of Carmen and anorexia against the world.

From our first meeting with Carmen we realized that the discourses supporting anorexia, and those that supported the view of a privatized anorexia within her, had driven a wedge between Carmen and the rest of the world. The discursive wedge brought forth a heightened symmetrical struggle, thereby disconnecting her from any hope of recovery. When a narrative approach was introduced to her relationship with the problem of anorexia, much of the symmetrical escalation was diffused for the first time. Our intent was to break the either/or, black/white position of anorexia and in so doing open discursive space for alternative possibilities.

CONSIDERING FAMILY

Carmen's family, like many others, often described their early experience with anorexia in terms of fear, shame, anger, frustration, and paralysis. Carmen's family felt they were totally to blame for the pain their child was experiencing, and this had a debilitating effect on the family's ability to cope. Their experience was constituted through a dominant discourse about anorexia, backed up by an archive of popular psychological, philosophical, and biological theories, that had held the family, and specifically the mother, responsible for their so-called anorexic child.

Despite the story of incompetence told about Carmen's family, they were able to take up multiple strategies with Carmen in an attempt to find a solution, and assist her in going free of the problem. The strategies they adopted sounded familiar to those many other families had taken up (see Epston, 1989). They included both a tactic of "tough love" and a more passive position they described as a "walking on eggshells" approach. Either way, the family felt the anorexia was taking over their entire lives.

Had we met Carmen's family early in their struggle with anorexia, these are some of the questions we would have considered asking:

- What have you been led to believe about the causes of anorexia?

- Why is it that professionals seem to blame parents as the cause of anorexia?

- What sorts of worry and worst-case scenarios do you get captured by when you consider your daughter's [sister's] struggle?

- What have you noticed that you do that helps your daughter's [sister's] health and undermines anorexia's grip?

- Can you think of any reasons why anorexia would not want this family to work together on this problem?

- Do you have any reason to believe that Carmen can someday go free of anorexia?

- What is it about this family that anorexia could never kill off?

A narrative approach to therapy helps to "unpack" dominant stories acting in support of the problem. These pro-anorexic tales include a biological basis of behavior as well as a strong element of parent blaming. The intent of our questions in the initial session is to bring forward hope through re-remembering experiences of courage, competence, appreciation, and change. Answers to our conversational inquiries often contradict how the family had been feeling "under the influence" of the professional community and their local culture.

Our questions act to open space for new descriptions, exceptions, and information previously restrained by the problem. The intent of the questioning is to include news of information and difference that weakens anorexia's version of the client and the family. Questions are grammatically designed to predict possible futures, moments of freedom, and victories over anorexia across the temporal plain. Throughout the session, therapist questions provide an alternative historical explanation for the onset of anorexia.

We sent Carmen's family an anti-anorexia survey (shown in Exhibit 19.1) and asked that each member of the family fill it out before the first session.

During the first session we take the opportunity to discuss the family's answers to the survey. Often we sit quietly in witness to the family's intimate knowledge of anorexia, and appreciate their hard-won ability in saying no to the possibility of surrender. In ensuing sessions we might pursue these questions with the family:

- How has anorexia made attempts to divide and conquer this entire family?

- As a parent, how has anorexia turned you against yourself? Has it tried to convince you that perfect parenting is possible?

Exhibit 19.1. Anti-Anorexia Survey

Thank you for participating in our anti-anorexia survey. We are currently surveying the wisdom of women and men who were at one time or another taken with anorexia, as well as a number of family members, partners, friends, and therapists. We will be using your replies to assist us in better serving your needs. Please take no more than thirty minutes to answer the following questions. Feel free to expand your reply beyond the space provided. Remember, there are no right or perfect answers.

1. How do you understand the problem of anorexia?
2. What are the ideas that you have come across about anorexia that have been helpful or not helpful to you in your life? Please explain by giving examples.
3. From your experience, in what ways have you found therapy helpful or not helpful?
4. Are there specific techniques through which anorexia recruits its victims?
5. Are there certain structures or beliefs of our society that may be viewed as supporting anorexia? If so, please describe these pro-anorexic structures.
6. In your experience what is anorexia's most effective weapon or strategy? Please explain.
7. In your experience are there any therapeutic practices that you have experienced that you would consider to be pro-anorexic? Please explain.
8. In your opinion why does anorexia recruit so many more women than men?
9. What effect does anorexia have on relationships—family, couples, friends?
10. What effect does anorexia have on relationships with professionals?
11. In what ways have you experienced other people standing against anorexia? Please explain.
12. Please name the three main pro-anorexic activities that you have ever experienced.
13. Please name the three main anti-anorexic activities that you have ever experienced.
14. What advice would you give to a person presently being recruited by anorexia?
15. What advice would you give to a professional presently working with people who are suffering the effects of anorexia or bulimia?
16. What advice would you give to a family member presently living with a person who is suffering the effects of anorexia or bulimia?
17. Where are the sites of anti-anorexic education most needed?
18. What are the most effective ways that anorexia finds to manipulate a person?
19. How many people do you think anorexia recruited in 1998 [1999, etc.]?
20. How many people do you think anorexia will recruit during the year 2000?
21. Are there any anti-anorexic activities that might be viewed as responsibilities of our community?
22. Do you think anorexia is genetic? Please explain.
23. Do you think anorexia will soon be exported to other countries? If yes, please specify how?
24. If you could had a few minutes face to face with anorexia what would you like to think you would say?
25. How would it feel to utter these words to anorexia or bulimia?
26. Final comments.

- Are there ever times when you are able to see or remember your daughter [sister] free from the grip of anorexia?

- What is it that you notice about your daughter [sister] during these times of freedom?

- What is it that you notice about yourself as a parent [sibling] during these times of freedom?

- What are your feelings now that we know that your daughter [sister] is not to blame for anorexia's hold on her?

- Who is it that sits behind the disciplines of anorexia? Have they ever tried to discipline you?

OUR WORK WITH CARMEN

Carmen wrestled with ideas of feeling less than worthy. She seemed to possess above-average intelligence and creativity, grew up in a loving dual-parent, middle-income home, was white and heterosexual, and had a university career. She had made an attempt at taking her own life, and was isolated from all persons who loved and supported her.

We first saw Carmen at a memorial for a young woman about her same age who had recently died an anorexic death. Carmen had not known this woman, yet she seemed shaken by the tragedy. Something terribly awful happens to everyone involved in the anti-anorexia community when anorexia takes a life. The execution seems to make everyone momentarily hopeless. Maybe this is why Carmen had turned the corner and asked for help; maybe this is why we all returned to work.

When Carmen called, she told us that she had been suffering from a "battle" with anorexia "for a few years." After this conversation we asked ourselves as therapists to consider the following reflexive questions (see Madigan, 1993):

- How can I bring out Carmen's hard-won knowledge about anorexia in a way that is Carmen supporting and anorexia defeating?

- In what ways can we draw out the marginalizing effects of anorexia in Carmen's life without her feeling ashamed and less than worthy?

- How can my enthusiasm for her not scare her away from help?

- How best can I take a position to "cheer lead" from behind?

- What can I do to honor her story of struggle that would not support anorexia growing bigger?

- How might I ask Carmen about the horrendous effects of anorexia without it humiliating and silencing her into despair?

- What is the best way to ask Carmen about her starved physical and emotional life?

- What is going to help me remain most hopeful about Carmen's life?

Deconstruction of Anorexic Recruitment Tactics

In the first few meetings with Carmen, we put forth the questions listed in this section. Our intent was to disrupt anorexia's story of who Carmen was as a person and to debilitate anorexia's relationship with her.

- In what ways has anorexia affected your relationship with yourself by telling you that you are not worthy? That you are its special protegé? That you are only an anorexic person?

- In snatching your concentration away from you, does anorexia push you further into its concentration camp?

- I wonder how it was that anorexia managed to wedge you away from your own thoughts and version of the world?

- Do you believe that you are only just the person anorexia tells you that you are?

- By what means did anorexia entice you into isolation and despair— would a good friend do this to you?

- How did anorexia trick you into thinking that hospitals and death were a better alternative to life in the free world?

- Do you think that the rule book of anorexia self-specialization specializes in torture and assassination?

- How is it that anorexia gets away with making people remember to forget their best qualities?

- How is it that anorexia tricks people with promises of safety while it silently takes them toward its ultimate aim—death?

Situating Anorexia in Alternative History

As therapists, we would also be concerned with taking up an historical account of Carmen's relationship with anorexia. Throughout the interview the questions would be a mix of general and specific inquiry. Questions that generalize assist clients to connect with others (breaking down the practices of isolation) and help them to reconsider and recollect alternative theories about anorexia (breaking down the practices of self-specialization). In "re-searching" Carmen's past relationship with anorexia, we might ask:

- What effect does being a slave to the idea of perfection have on anorexia overtaking a person?

- Were there factors in your life beyond your control that made anorexia look like an attractive option?

- What do you remember in your life that most helped anorexia along?

- When you think back to your first introduction to anorexia, were there promises made to you?

- Do you think anorexia makes these same promises to everyone? Or has it made you think that you are its special student?

- Did the abuse you suffered at the hands of [name] help along this feeling of being a less-than-person?

- Did the abuse you suffered at the hands of [name] somehow assist in anorexia's recruitment of you?

- Does the culture of "thinner is better" sway people's thoughts away from other unnoticed qualities in themselves?

Re-Remembering Counter Identities

That professionals are sometimes pejorative and blaming when working with persons taken by anorexia is well documented (Tinker & Ramer, 1983; Garner, 1985). The problem of anorexia engenders strong feelings of anger, hopelessness, frustration, and so on in some would-be *care*givers. Often, when working with someone like Carmen who has experienced blame and guilt and has been labeled "controlling" and "narcissistic" by professionals, we have had to work carefully at asking questions that would have the effect of contradicting these other professional discourses.

- Can you remember qualities of yourself prior to anorexia's onset that you would like to re-remember?

- Have there been stories told about you that help you to forget your finer qualities?

- Has there ever been a time during treatment that you have disagreed with the popular and professional version of you?

- How were you able to keep your own positive thoughts of yourself alive despite what others were saying?

- Can you name the quality in you that has kept you alive all these years despite anorexia's attempts to kill you?

- Can you remember qualities of yourself prior to anorexia taking you that you would like your therapists, family, and friends to re-remember?

- How have we professionals come to forget your best qualities?

Carmen appeared to respond to our questions by expanding the space in which she was able to maneuver. In separating the problem of anorexia from her self,

Carmen was more comfortable when discussing the losses that she had experienced. She seemed to find less shame in her own situation and she showed a strong interest in discussing the limits and boundaries of anorexia. In particular, her ability to talk to her family in different ways about the problem appeared to give her a renewed sense of her self. Carmen became more interested in connections with other women who were struggling with and recovering from anorexia and bulimia, and she experimented more vigorously with changes in her approach to eating and physical activity. Carmen was spending less time alone. She had arranged to spend time at the home of her sister and brother-in-law and would eat some meals with them. She walked less and visited more.

Experiencing and Appreciating Freedom

We highlight and support any and all anti-anorexic efforts clients make. Recognition of a person's counter-struggle while under anorexia's pressured regime is a magnificent experience for therapists and clients alike, and one worth truly appreciating. The following questions help outline, underline, and color in the picture of increasing freedom:

- At which time of the day are you most anorexic-free?

- How are you able to find this freedom?

- I have been wondering in what ways you have "stepped outside anorexia" this week, and I wonder what this stepping out steps you toward?

- I wonder who on the ward noticed these fantastic anorexic-free achievements?

- Was the time spent outside anorexia delicious?

- Do you ever catch yourself living outside anorexia's prison camp? What is it like? What color is your freedom?

- Do you ever find other people enjoying your mind instead of merely experiencing the mind that anorexia gives you?

- If you were to string together all of these victorious anti-anorexic moments, what effect would it have on anorexia?

- What rules of anorexia did you have to breach in order to attend this meeting today?

- Do you think that your anti-anorexic noticing of yourself has put anorexia on notice?

- Who in your life would be just barely amazed by your leaving anorexia behind?

- What advice do you have for my many colleagues who find themselves befuddled on how to best help people go free of anorexia?

- Have you ever plotted an escape from anorexia?

- I wonder what plans your own anorexic-free person has for you?

- I wonder which parts of your life you will retrieve and which good qualities will be re-remembered and come back to you once you go free of anorexia?

- I wonder how it will be for you when you are free to just have to measure up to yourself and not to the culture of anorexia's nagging torment?

- I wonder in which ways your comeback to your own life might be inspiring for other women?

Deconstruction of Culture Questions

As Carmen felt more freedom to explore the problem of anorexia and to demarcate its impact on her own life and the lives of others, she took on a certain vitality. She seemed to come out from underneath. Carmen joined in discussions with other women she had met who were struggling against anorexia. They were attending to anorexia's relationship to gender, culture, and society.

When we met with this group of women, we discussed the following questions:

- Why do you think anorexia attempts to devour some of the best women of our generation?

- Can you think of ways that anorexia "pushes its way" onto women?

- Can you identify anything in popular culture that feeds into a "not measuring up to" lifestyle?

- If a woman wanted to make a public protest over the destructive effects of anorexia, what would you suggest she do?

- Is the violence that anorexia perpetrates on your body similar to or different from male violence against women?

- What is it that our society promotes that leaves most women with a distorted sense of their own bodies?

- Can you figure out what and who most promotes perfection training?

Anti-Anorexia, Anti-Bulimia Leagues

Along with some of the other women that she had met, Carmen took part in the local Anti-anorexia, Anti-bulimia League meetings. The league was organized as a forum to sponsor alternative activities that would fight anorexic and bulimic recruitment in the lives of members and in others. A number of leagues have formed in various spots on the globe (see Grieves, 1997; Madigan & Epston, 1995) and constitute communities of caring and concern.

The Vancouver Anti-anorexia League was born out of anti-anorexic group work we were doing at St. Paul's Hospital in Vancouver, Canada. As highlighted in a *Newsweek* article (Cowley & Springen, 1995), the Vancouver league activities include international networking, community education programs, letter-writing campaigns, community organizing, protests against cultural misrepresentations of the body viewed to be pro-anorexic, teaching therapists alternative approaches to therapy, working alongside hospital staff assessing community needs, counseling high school students and teachers, running groups, and publishing the league's magazine, *RE-VIVE.*

Our Vancouver league has now been in operation for five years—and we are proud to be the longest-standing anti-anorexia league of this kind. We are indebted to our friend David Epston for introducing league ideas to us and to his ongoing creativity and support. The Vancouver group has assisted the formation of leagues and communities of concern in numerous cities across North America and the Western world. The anti-anorexia groups and subsequent research groups entertain discussions of the following questions:

- I wonder why anorexia is so bent on reducing the women of this group to second-class citizens? Does anorexia betray your human rights?

- Do you think it is right that anorexia forces the members of this group into lives of isolation, perfection, subordination, and suffering?

- During the group talk, were there ever times that you felt inspired enough to consider leaving anorexia behind?

- What was it like for you to sit among a group of anti-anorexic freedom fighters?

- I wonder if there are sometimes anti-anorexic qualities that you notice in one another that you may one day notice in yourselves?

FEAR AND LOATHING

Carmen did not find it easy to move away from anorexia's grip. She found that anorexia could be very convincing and she sometimes felt discouraged when fears loomed large. Carmen wished that she was able to gain freedom more easily. She was tired of being pushed around by the same old fears.

Fear is often involved in an ongoing negative recursion with anorexia. When we are questioning the effects that fear has had in a person's life, we will run the problem of fear through a discursive "filter" to situate the fear and expose the ways fear maintains its hold (Law & Madigan, 1997). We converse about fear's effects by exploring them through the discourses of gender training, educational training, "proper manners" training, friendship training, corporate and work training, class training, race training, religious training, homophobic training, body training, and so on. Each relevant discourse and effect can be carefully mapped out. Discourses are forever linking up with one another and it is within the therapeutic dialogic that we can begin to "connect the dots" and bring fear's claims into the open. Here are some issues and sample questions to consider when taking on the issue of fear-of-not-being-worthy in the person's life:

- *Regarding the scaffolding of presuppositions of what constitutes what is said to be "normal":* Could you give me an idea of what ideas or experiences support this idea of yourself as a less-than-worthy person?

- *Regarding the systems of knowledge supporting this view of what is said to be "normal":* Have there been persons in your life that have in some way helped this less-than-worthy view of yourself along? How strongly are these persons' past views of you influencing you in today's version of yourself?

- *Regarding the institutional structures supporting this view of what is normal (genealogy):* Do you think that there any larger institutional values (in our culture) that you have been influenced by that in some way encourage a less-than-worthy view of persons? What is your relationship to these values today?

- *Regarding the effects of this interpretation:* Are there ways that this view of yourself as a less-than-worthy person affect your relationships with other persons?

Discussion of how fear is produced (and reproduced) includes deconstructing the apparatus and disciplines of the self that help support problems, such as perfection training, an audience of surveillance, negative imagination, measured-down lifestyles, less-than-worthiness, and so on, and a reconstruction of preferred ways of being. Fear's production and discussion includes technologies of power that act upon the self, such as the discourses of professionalism, corporatism, sexism, racism, homophobia, and so on, and how these affect the life of the problems listed in this chapter. Fear employs all arguments simultaneously in a complete and negatively restrained recursion.

Other questions that involve the specific unraveling of anorexic fear tactics include the following:

- How were you able to push back the anorexic fear, when fear had you boxed into such a tight corner?

- What are some of the specific techniques you used to rid yourself of the panic that fear brought?

- What does it feel like to know that slowly but surely you are now controlling your fears?

- When you have those times that you are free of fear, how does your world look different?

- Do you think that there are times when you are free of fear and you don't recognize it? If so, do you think you are even more free of fear than you think?

- Do you think this fear is an imperfect fear?

Carmen continued to fight against anorexia and asked for the help of others. She elected to return to a hospital treatment program for a period of time in order to get past a weight ceiling that she was determined to rise above. Carmen's doctors noticed her movement away from anorexia and engaged in a productive relationship with her. Later, she returned to music school and experienced an enjoyment that she had forgotten for many years. Although Carmen continued to sense anorexia's potential to influence her, she kept a safe distance and actively maintained a protective network. She kept in contact with a number of her friends in the Anti-anorexia, Anti-bulimia League and sometimes sought the advice of therapists and doctors. Although not completely free, Carmen has made remarkable steps away from anorexia. We can't help but wonder whether she might have moved even further out of anorexia's reach had she found an open door earlier on.

RESEARCH ON NARRATIVE METHODS AND ANOREXIA

A number of researchers and theorists have turned their attention to methods that might ease the grip of anorexia (Vitousek, 1997; Garner, 1997). It has been too well recognized that anorexia is tenacious and resists many of the approaches that we professionals have attempted. Clients often pull back from treatment and fade away. Sadly, lasting recovery eludes a full half of those people who first come to hospital clinics in the grip of anorexia (Hsu, 1991).

We were led to put together a pilot research study. We hypothesized that a short-term narrative anti-anorexia group might be more effective than a control situation in facilitating recovery in women who were beginning treatment in a hospital program because of anorexia (Goldner & Madigan, 1997). Women were randomly assigned to the narrative group ($n = 10$) or the control situation ($n = 10$), which was a support group facilitated by an experienced counselor. Women in both groups received eight sessions of group intervention that included two sessions with family members. We found that women assigned to the narrative group were more likely to attend and remain connected to treatment. Furthermore, a few weeks after the end of the final session, women in the narrative group reported more hopefulness about recovery, defined themselves as more separate from the problem of anorexia, and reported less shame about the problem. Although this pilot study was too small to draw conclusions and has not yet followed the longer-term course of the participants, it suggests that a narrative approach holds some promise in providing an opening for people to move through in their escape from the hold of anorexia.

We hope that our narrative approach to anorexia may help free some of those who could not otherwise find a way out.

Endnotes

1. *Discourse* can be viewed as what can be said, who can say it, and with what authority.

2. For further readings on deconstruction, see Derrida (1976) and Parker and Shotter (1990).

3. Poststructuralism is critical of any universal claims about truth put forth by the modernists and studies how it is that certain ideas have survived through time and the structures that support these ideas and practices. For further reading on poststructuralism, see Hoagwood (1993) and Law and Madigan (1997).

4. See Madigan and Epston (1995) and their work with communities of concern and letter-writing campaigns.

5. Please keep in mind that these sets of questions are *not* formulaic, nor would we ask them of each client. Questions are informed by compassion, collaboration, and curiosity. The questions listed in this chapter represent a composite drawn from hundreds of interviews over many years.

References

Bordo, S. (1994). *Unbearable weight: Feminism, Western culture and the body.* Berkeley: University of California Press.

Bruner, J. (1986). *Actual minds, possible worlds.* Cambridge, MA: Harvard University Press.

Cowley, G., & Springen, K. (1995, April 17). Rewriting life stories. *Newsweek,* pp. 70–74.

Derrida, J. (1976). *Of grammatology* (G. C. Spivack, Trans.). Baltimore, MD: Johns Hopkins University Press. (Original work published 1967)

Epston, D. (1989). *Collected papers.* Adelaide, South Australia: Dulwich Centre Publications.

Foucault, M. (1982). The subject and power. In H. Dreyfus & P. Rabinow (Eds.), *Michael Foucault: Beyond.* Chicago: University of Chicago Press.

Foucault, M. (1989). *Foucault live: Collected interviews, 1961–1984* (S. Lotringer, Ed.). New York: Semiotext(e).

Garner, D. M. (1985). Iatrogenesis in anorexia nervosa and bulimia nervosa. *International Journal of Eating Disorders, 4,* 701–726.

Garner, D. M. (1997, April). Cognitive behavioural treatment of anorexia nervosa. *Proceedings of the 2nd London International Conference on Eating Disorders, London.*

Geertz, C. (1973). *The interpretation of cultures.* New York: Basic Books.

Gergen, K. J. (1989). Warranting voice and the elaboration of self. In J. Shotter & K. J. Gergen (Eds.), *Texts of identity.* Newbury Park, CA: Sage.

Goldner, E. M., & Birmingham, C. L. (1994). Anorexia nervosa: Methods of treatment. In L. Alexander-Mott & D. B. Lumsden (Eds.), *Understanding eating disorders: Anorexia nervosa, bulimia nervosa, and obesity* (pp. 135–157). Bristol, PA: Taylor & Francis.

Goldner, E. M., & Madigan, S. P. (1997, April). Narrative ideas in family therapy. *Proceedings of the 2nd London International Conference on Eating Disorders, London.*

Grieves, L. (1997). Beginning to start: The Vancouver Anti-anorexia, Anti-bulimia League. *GECKO: A Journal of Deconstruction and Narrative Therapy, 2,* 78–88.

Hoagwood, K. (1993). Poststructuralist historism and the psychological construction of anxiety disorders. *Journal of Psychology, 127*(1), 105–122.

Hsu, L. K. G. (1991). Outcome studies in patients with eating disorders. In S. M. Mirin, J. T. Gossett, & M. C. Grob (Eds.), *Psychiatric treatment advances in outcome research* (pp. 159–180). New York: American Psychiatric Press.

Law, I., & Madigan, S. (1997). Discourse, power and identity: A discursive approach. Unpublished manuscript.

Lax, W. (1991). The reflecting team and the initial consultation. In T. Andersen (Ed.), *The reflecting team: Dialogues and dialogues about the dialogues.* New York: Norton.

Madigan, S. P. (1992). The application of Michel Foucault's philosophy in the problem externalizing of Michael White. *Journal of Family Therapy, 14,* 265–279.

Madigan, S. P. (1993). Questions about questions: Situating the therapist's curiosity in front of the family. In S. G. Gilligan & R. Price (Eds.), *Therapeutic conversations* (pp. 219–236). New York: Norton.

Madigan, S. P. (1996). The politics of identity: Considering community discourse in the externalizing of internalized problem conversations. *Journal of Systemic Therapies, 15*(1), 47–62.

Madigan, S. P. (1997). Re-considering memory: Re-remembering lost identities back towards re-membered selves. In C. Smith & D. Nylund (Eds.), *Narrative therapy with children and adolescents* (pp. 127–142; with commentary by L. Grieves). New York: Guilford Press.

Madigan, S. P., & Epston, D. (1995). From "spy-chiatric gaze" to communities of concern: From professional monologue to dialogue. In S. Friedman (Ed.), *The reflecting team in action: Collaborative practice in family therapy* (pp. 257–276). New York: Guilford Press.

Parker, I., & Shotter, J. (1990). *Deconstructing social psychology.* New York: Routledge.

Roth, S., & Epston, D. (1996). Consulting the problem about the problematic relationship: An exercise for experiencing a relationship with an externalized problem. In M. F. Hoyt (Ed.), *Constructive therapies* (Vol. 2, pp. 148–162). New York: Guilford Press.

Tinker, D. E., & Ramer, J. C. (1983). Anorexia nervosa: Staff subversion of therapy. *Journal of Adolescent Health Care, 4,* 35–39.

Vitousek, K. (1997). *Motivation for change in anorexia nervosa.* Unpublished manuscript.

White, M., & Epston, D. (1990). *Narrative means to therapeutic ends.* New York: Norton.

CHAPTER TWENTY

Internalized Other Questioning with Men Who Are Violent

With Commentary by Alan Jenkins

David Nylund, Victor Corsiglia

In our work with adult male perpetrators of sexual abuse and violence, we have been influenced by the work of Alan Jenkins (1990). Rather than adopting causal theories of why men abuse, Jenkins finds it more helpful to view the abusive behavior from a theory of context and restraint (Bateson, 1972, 1979; White, 1989a). This approach promotes a therapy in which the perpetrator is invited to examine and challenge restraints that have stopped him from taking responsibility for the abuse. These restraints may include sociocultural traditions (e.g., men trained in patriarchal power tactics), interactional patterns (e.g., patterns of relationship imbalance between men and women in the context of marriage), and certain habits and beliefs (e.g., patterns of self-centered thinking). Once restraints are challenged, it becomes possible for the perpetrator to consider alternatives to abuse.

Jenkins utilizes a style of questioning that assists perpetrators to acknowledge the abuse, acknowledge culpability, and develop alternative ways of being and relating.[1] By engaging the abusive male through a therapeutic stance of curiosity and respect, a collaborative process can be achieved. This approach to therapy tends to promote the perpetrator's active participation in changing his behavior. This is in stark contrast to the traditional therapy approach, where

---

Note: A version of this chapter first appeared in 1993 in the *Dulwich Centre Newsletter, 2,* 29–36. Reprinted with permission.

the therapist is the "expert" and diagnoses the perpetrator, confronts his "denial," and gives directives and advice.

ENHANCING EMPATHY THROUGH "INTERNALIZED OTHER" QUESTIONING

A crucial phase of the therapy occurs when Jenkins invites the abusive man to grasp the potential impact of his abuse on others. Before the perpetrator can sincerely apologize to the victim and take full responsibility for his abuse, it is important that he understand the effects of his abuse by being "in the victim's shoes" (Jenkins, 1992). Jenkins aims to assist the abusive male in developing empathy by asking him a series of questions, such as: "What do you think it was like for your daughter to be forced into sex?" or "What do you imagine it was like for your wife to keep your abuse secret?"[2]

In facilitating the perpetrator's understanding of the impact of the abuse, we have asked questions similar to the type that Jenkins has described. However, we have found only partial success with these questions. The abusive men tended to guess what the victim endured. By guessing, we believed that some of these men were not adequately grounding themselves in the victim's experience. To address our concern, we have turned to Karl Tomm's (1992) ideas on "internalized other" questioning. His ideas have complemented and enhanced our interpretation and application of the Jenkins approach.

Tomm, known for his thoughtfulness and creativity with reflexive questions, discovered the practice of *internalized other* questioning from the work of David Epston (1993; see Tomm, 1987, Chapter Ten, this volume). Epston invented a practice referred to as *cross-referential questioning*.[3] These questions were designed to help couples who were dominated by a pattern of adversarial interaction. The questioning process begins with asking the couple if they want to depart from the conflictual patterns. If the couple agrees, Epston addresses one partner (for instance, Sam) as if he were the other partner (Sue) and asks him several questions. While addressing Sam, he may ask: "Sue, how has the conflict in your relationship affected you?" Sam is encouraged to respond from Sue's experience. Then Sue, who has been listening attentively, is asked to inform Sam to what degree he was able to comprehend and appreciate her experience. This process appears to deepen empathy and encourage new, healing patterns in relationships as each partner is invited to enter into an experience of the other's experience of him or her.

Tomm (1992) has expanded upon Epston's ideas by adopting a theoretical framework that supports the practice of "internalized other" questioning. Tomm has constructed a view of the self that is constituted by a constellation of internalized conversations. This view of the person enables a therapist to interview any significant other within a person. Since a person has internalized many conversations with others, he or she is able to access an "embodied" experience of another's experience (many times, quite easily and surprisingly). Such a theory and practice has enabled Tomm to utilize these questions in many other therapeutic contexts, including with abusive men. We also have found this practice of interviewing extremely valuable, and we utilize these questions in many therapeutic contexts.

Tomm argues that one's sense of self is generated in relation to others (1993a, 1993b). This emerging view of individuality, one that is constituted by relationship, association, and community, is at variance with the dominant Western view of individuality. The dominant practice of self tends to reinforce an account of individuality that is based on differentiation and individuation. White (1993) refers to these practices of self as "isolating individualities." These may contribute to a perpetrator's inability to "step into" the victim's experience due to being recruited into a practice of self that emphasizes separation and minimizes affiliation and connection. Such a version of individuality can be seen as a restraint that may hinder a man who has abused from relating respectfully and sensitively to a person he victimizes. We believe that "internalized other" questions not only open space for an abusive man to recognize the effects of his abuse on others, but may also create a relational space for the man that provides an avenue for him to challenge the narrowing and restraining influence of the isolating individualities. Confronting the "isolating individualities" may increase the likelihood for him to explore alternative individualities—ones that are associated with reciprocity, mutuality, and affiliation (White, 1993a, 1993b).

INTERVIEWING THE "INTERNALIZED OTHER"

We begin the process of therapy with a man who has abused by inquiring about his goals for therapy. We then invite him to address his abuse by focusing on the events leading up to the abuse, focusing on the abuse itself, and attending to his sense of desperation in saving the relationship (Jenkins, 1990).

If the perpetrator acknowledges the abuse with a certain degree of responsibility, we invite him to understand the impact of his abuse upon the victim. We stress that it is critical for him to "put himself in the victim's shoes" before he can establish nonabusive relationships. Next, we introduce the idea of the "internalized other." Since these questions can be quite painful and difficult, we challenge his readiness by commenting in such ways as: "I don't know if you can handle these questions." If he argues for his own readiness, we proceed by interviewing the person he victimized "within" the man.

The "internalized other" questioning process begins by addressing the man as the victim of the abuse (for instance, if a man had physically abused a woman named Jane, we would address him as Jane). We ask him several questions that may include the victim's experience of the actual abuse; the aftereffects of the abuse; and the effects of certain attitudes that justify abuse and practices of power that make abuse possible.[4] We end the interview by asking him to describe the experience of speaking from the voice of the victim in himself. We tend to notice a shift in the man's pattern of remorse (Jenkins, 1990, p. 165) after the interviewing process as he begins to experience a more genuine understanding of the impact of his abuse on the victim. This new awareness is based more on an emotional understanding of the abuse, rather than an intellectual understanding. The following two examples, with transcripts, will illustrate this interviewing process.

Case One: Steve

A twenty-seven-year-old man, Steve, came to our clinic voluntarily, in a state of crisis. He had physically assaulted his fiancee, Martha, three days prior to his first therapy appointment. In the first session, the therapist obtained details about the nature and extent of the abuse. Steve stated that he had never physically assaulted a woman before and was worried that his abuse would precipitate Martha's ending the relationship. He was particularly worried that Martha would leave him due to a previous experience of her being abused by an ex-partner. When they began their relationship, Martha had assertively stated to Steve that she would no longer "tolerate abuse from a man." In our session, Steve talked quite openly about his violence toward Martha and began to take responsibility. He was also clear with the therapist that he did want a violence-free relationship with Martha. In the second session, the therapist invited Steve to potentially understand the impact of his abuse. "Internalized other" questions were utilized at that point. The following dialogue is part of the transcript of the "internalized other" interview with Steve:

THERAPIST: [addressing Steve] Martha, what happened the day Steve abused you?

STEVE: [as his "internalized" Martha] It happened during an argument . . . I was supposed to go out with a friend and Steve became upset. He wanted me to stay home with him.

THERAPIST: What happened next? What did Steve do next?

STEVE: He started to accuse me of not caring about our relationship . . . that I cared more about my girlfriend.

THERAPIST: How did that feel . . . that he said you didn't care about your relationship, Martha?

STEVE: I was hurt and became angry.

THERAPIST: What did he do next?

STEVE: One thing led to another and we started arguing and I picked up the phone to call my girlfriend and then Steve grabbed me.

THERAPIST: Where did he grab you, Martha?

STEVE: On the neck.

THERAPIST: Was it a tight grip?

STEVE: *[pauses for a moment]* Yes.

THERAPIST: Martha, is Steve bigger than you? Does he have fairly big hands?

STEVE: Yes.

THERAPIST: So, when he forced himself on you like that . . . what was that like?

STEVE: It scared me . . . like he was out of control.

THERAPIST: What were you afraid was going to happen next, Martha?

STEVE: That he wasn't going to stop . . . I was choking.

THERAPIST: What did Steve's face look like?

STEVE: Mean.

THERAPIST: And then what happened next?

STEVE: He loosened the grip as I struggled to get away and he hit me in the face . . . on the cheek. I then ran to the bedroom and locked the door. Steve then left the house and took a drive.

THERAPIST: How were you feeling at that point?

STEVE: Scared and hurt *[Steve begins crying]* . . . I couldn't believe he would do this to me.

THERAPIST: When you saw Steve next, did he apologize and take responsibility? Or did he blame you?

STEVE: He did apologize . . . but he blamed me.

THERAPIST: How so?

STEVE: By saying that I shouldn't have reached for the phone . . . and I shouldn't have tried to get away . . . that I provoked him by doing so.

THERAPIST: Do you think it's right that Steve should blame you, Martha?

STEVE: No.

THERAPIST: How did this incident of Steve's abusing you affect your view of him as a person?

STEVE: It's making me think negative of him. I now have second thoughts of marrying him. This happened to me in a previous relationship. My ex-boyfriend hit me several times . . . he was very jealous.

THERAPIST: What was that like, Martha?

STEVE: He made me feel that it was my fault . . . and when Steve blamed me, he had me almost thinking I did something to provoke him. I now wonder if Steve is the jealous type, like my ex.

THERAPIST: So Steve attempted to trick you into self-blame like your ex?

STEVE: Yes.

THERAPIST: Why? . . . Are there some ideas in society that reinforce self-blame in women's lives? . . . That don't hold men accountable?

STEVE: Yes.

THERAPIST: Do you think you have been influenced by those ideas?

STEVE: Yes . . . but I was beginning to believe more in myself and trust in men until Steve did this.

THERAPIST: Do you see Steve as somebody who has been recruited by those traditional ideas? . . . Ideas that say "Hey, the woman deserves the abuse," and ideas that relegate women to second-class status in the relationship . . . and that they should have no life of their own? Or is Steve more interested in challenging those ideas and believing in ideas that support women having their own life and choosing their own friends?

STEVE: Well . . . I thought he was more modern . . . but I don't know now . . . I'm beginning to doubt him.

THERAPIST: So doubt and mistrust are affecting you? Do you think or have you seen Steve succumb to insensitivity and demand that you prematurely trust him . . . that he won't abuse you again? Or do you think he will be patient in earning your trust back?

STEVE: I'm not sure . . . good question!

THERAPIST: When he choked and hit you, Martha, did you almost begin to reexperience the previous abuse? Like it was happening all over again?

STEVE: Yes . . . I haven't been able to sleep well since then.

THERAPIST: So things have been painful for you. What could Steve do that you would experience as supportive? How could he best take responsibility for his abuse?

STEVE: He could give me some space. . . . *[moments later]* He could also take full responsibility for the abuse without blaming me. He could also be supportive of my having my own friends.

THERAPIST: Martha, do you think Steve understands and appreciates the courage and effort it took to escape the self-blame in your previous relationship? . . . That you have challenged some traditional ideas of women's ways of being?

STEVE: No, I don't think so.

THERAPIST: OK, let's stop there. *[after some moments of allowing Steve to collect and reorient himself]* How was that for you?

STEVE: *[as himself]* That was weird . . . I found myself wanting to answer from my point of view at first and found it difficult, at first, to really answer from her point of view . . . I think I understand her better.

Case Two: Ron

Ron, a thirty-nine-year-old married male, was referred to the clinic after his twelve-year-old daughter, Sharon, disclosed to her mother (Ron's wife) that she was sexually abused several times when she was eight years old. Ron had molested her by fondling her genitals and forcing her to orally copulate him. Ron did acknowledge responsibility for the sexual abuse, but only to a partial degree. He tended to minimize the extent of the abuse and the impact it had on Sharon and the family. He appeared to be more preoccupied with his own discomfort, since he was court-ordered to leave the family home (he was living with his parents at the time of his first therapy session with us). During the early stages of the therapy, Ron presented in a "helpless" state and attempted to invite his therapist to take responsibility for him by changing the subject or focusing on why he abused Sharon. The therapist declined those invitations and eventually was able to engage Ron in an inquiry into the details of the abuse. After several sessions, Ron appeared to be facing up to his abuse. This led to inviting Ron to grasp the impact of his abuse by interviewing his "internalized" Sharon. The following is an excerpt from that interview:

THERAPIST: *[addressing Ron]* Sharon, what was it like to be eight years old and be tricked into something you didn't understand, no less by your own father?

RON: *[as his "internalized" Sharon]* It was scary.

THERAPIST: Did you love and trust your father before he did this?

RON: Yes.

THERAPIST: So how did that feel? . . . To have him fondle you against your will? . . . To be forced into sex before you knew what sex was, Sharon?

RON: *[crying and visibly shaking]* It hurt . . . I was confused.

THERAPIST: What was it like to wonder if your Dad was going to molest you any particular night thinking, "When will my daddy do it again?"

RON: *[crying and shaking his head as if telling the therapist he couldn't answer]*

THERAPIST: You kept it secret for many years. What was that like, to keep it secret?

RON: I hated it . . . but I had to. I didn't think anybody would believe me.

THERAPIST: Did you feel something bad would happen? Such as, if you broke the secrecy, did you think that you would break your parents up, that they would split?

RON: Yes, I felt it would be my fault.

THERAPIST: So guilt began to take you over?

RON: Yes.

THERAPIST: I imagine that must have been an awful burden to keep it secret and feel responsible for your father's problem. Did he threaten or bribe you to keep it secret?

RON: No.

THERAPIST: Are you sure, Sharon?

RON: Well . . . maybe . . . when he would buy me things after he abused me . . . maybe he was doing that to bribe me and keep it secret.

THERAPIST: What did the abuse do . . . the self-blame, the guilt and the secrecy . . . how did it get you to feel about yourself?

RON: Awful.

Later in the interview:

THERAPIST: How is the abuse affecting you now, Sharon, as a twelve-year-old?

RON: Scared, embarrassed . . . I'm sort of shy around them.

THERAPIST: What message did your father give you about trusting men? I mean . . . he's your father, and he molested you.

RON: I don't trust men.

THERAPIST: Sharon, do you think your father is taking responsibility for the abuse?

RON: No . . . he's more concerned about having to leave the home . . . that he has no money and he has to go to therapy. He doesn't care how it's affected me and my mother.

THERAPIST: How do you feel about that?

RON: Angry.

THERAPIST: Do you think your father wants you to get in touch with your anger? Or would he prefer that you feel sorry for him?

RON: Feel sorry for him.

The interview continued with more questions about the impact of the abuse on Sharon. This interview was the turning point for Ron as he experienced more genuine remorse and began taking more responsibility and making amends to Sharon and his family.

DISCUSSION

"Internalized other" questioning, with its many possible benefits, is a practice that is not without its possible drawbacks. For instance, some men may experience the questions as somewhat confusing, complex, or unnatural. It is also possible that abusive men may answer in a contrived, superficial manner designed to please the therapist rather than ground themselves in the experience of the person they victimized. Lastly, some men may structure the experience of the victim's answers according to their own desires (Tomm, 1992). For example, in the first case reported in this chapter, Steve might have answered (as Martha) that he should blame Martha. If this occurred, the therapist might pursue a line of questioning about how Martha was trained to blame herself for others' behavior, or might simply ask Steve if that was how Martha would really feel, or alternatively, if he conned her into so answering. If Martha was present to observe the "internalized other" questioning, she could be asked for feedback on how Steve's responses matched or missed her actual experience (see Tomm, 1993b).

While noting the conceivable disadvantages, we find that interviewing the "internalized other" is considerably effective in opening spaces for men to recognize the effects of their abuse. These questions provide an experiential route (Tomm, 1993a, p. 77) for an abusive male to be grounded in the experience of the victim. This pattern of interviewing enables the man to experience more genuine remorse and prepares the man to make reparations to the victim.

"Internalized other" questions may also facilitate the offender's understanding of the effects of certain attitudes and techniques of power that make abuse possible. By rendering these effects more transparent, an abusive man can challenge these practices of power and experience a separation from them. Thus, "internalized other" questions can be utilized as an accountability practice for men trying to escape the dominant men's culture. We feel that when a male abuser experiences increasing alienation from these destructive attitudes of power and control, he is more likely to embrace alternative and preferred ways of being.

COMMENTARY

I very much enjoyed reading this chapter. David Nylund and Victor Corsiglia have outlined a valuable approach, "internalized other" questioning, to assist those who perpetrate abuse to examine, in an experiential manner, the potential impact of their abuse upon their victims.

After reading Nylund and Corsiglia, I decided to use and reflect on the process of "internalized other" questioning. I found the concept to be helpful and to facilitate rapidly the process of abusive males' learning to move beyond thinking about to feeling about the potential impact of their abusive behavior—that is, a shift from an intellectual to an emotional appreciation of their abusive actions.

I believe that this shift reflects one of the most critical aspects of change in men who abuse. The most significant indication of full acceptance of responsibility is a genuine interest in and willingness to try to experience the potential impact of the abuse upon the victim and others who have been affected.

The approach of "internalized other" questioning also raised several significant dilemmas which I think deserve consideration. I find it particularly important how such a concept is introduced to the client. An abuse perpetrator cannot actually "put himself in the victim's shoes." He can only try to imagine what harm he may have inflicted and what his victim might experience. In the absence of the victim's feedback, he can only guess what the victim has endured, and can only attempt to ground himself in a perception of the victim's experience. He is responding from his perceptions of the other person's experience. Consequently, it is important that he understands that he cannot know, or fully understand, the other person's experience. The critical shift that he can make is to direct his orientation from a focus on his own self-centered preoccupations and fantasies in which the world must revolve around his needs and feelings, to one in which he is genuinely interested in and trying to both think and feel about the other person's experience and the harm that he may have caused them.

This in itself does not result in a "more genuine understanding of the impact of his abuse upon the victim." Such empathy requires another step by which he may express his realizations about his abuse to the victim and significant others, and be open to unconditionally accepting their feedback on the validity and accuracy of his perceptions.

All too often, abusive men believe that they can and do know another person's experience or feelings. Their self-centered perceptions enable them to believe that they are experts in, and have ownership rights over, their partner's or children's knowledge and experience. For example:

"What you really need is—"

"What you really mean is—"

"I'm going to shake some sense into you—"

"You really like me touching you there, don't you?"

I find it helpful to invite men to try to think and feel about the potential impact of their abusive actions, but to understand that they can never know fully what this impact really is. The attitude and orientation toward genuinely wanting to understand the other person's experience is what appears to make a positive difference for the man himself and for those he has abused. Empathy begins with genuine attempts to try to appreciate and understand another person's experience, and it requires checking out, listening, and observing to assess the accuracy of these attempts.

A man may try to take an easier journey by attempting to get those he has abused to tell him about the impact of the abuse, before he has struggled to imagine it himself—to try to get others to do his work for him. This, of course, can be tantamount to perpetrating further abuses, as is checking out perceptions or making apologies before others are wanting this to happen. Those who abuse have already made demands they have no right to make, and taken things that are not theirs to take. They have no right to ask for anything more from those they have abused. Many are keen to pursue rapid forgiveness and forgetting, rather than genuine realization and understanding. There is much solo work, in thinking and feeling, to be done by these men before they attempt to express or check out their own realizations about their abusive actions. The process of "internalized other" questioning offers a valuable means of facilitating this work.

The notion of *potential impact* is a critical one in my work. Men who abuse often become preoccupied with the apparent impact on their victims and ignore the potential impact. For example, a child may not appear to be overtly distressed by her father's sexually abusive behavior. Consequently he may conclude, "It hasn't hurt her, she runs up to me," and so on. Victims of abuse sometimes indicate that they are unaffected by the abuse. They may be unready or developmentally unable to think or talk about their experience, they may hold themselves responsible, or they may experience a certain resilience that protects them from potential damage or distress. Nonetheless, they have been betrayed and abused by a trusted person. In this context, it is helpful to go beyond the notion of empathy and consider potential impact. The man should be invited to understand possible reasons why abuse victims sometimes behave as though unaffected by the abuse. If a man believes his daughter is unaffected by his sexual abuse of her, he may be invited to consider:

- Do you think that she is entitled to feel betrayed by her father?
- What do you think is stopping her from feeling betrayed?
- Do you think that she thinks your abuse of her is acceptable?
- What do you realize about your abuse that she may not?
- What would you like her to know about the truth of your abuse of her?
- Could you handle it if she let herself feel the betrayal you have acknowledged?

- If she let herself know that you treated her like a thing—something to masturbate on, that you just used her—rather than like your daughter who looked up to and trusted you, would you cope?
- Would it be healthier for her to feel hurt and betrayed by you or to try to justify your behavior?
- Would it be healthier for her to feel angry at you or ashamed of herself?
- What would be the healthiest way for you to think about it?

A man who has abused must learn to think and feel about the potential impact of his behavior if he is to cease abuse and relate respectfully and sensitively toward others, especially those he has betrayed and hurt. He must be prepared to label abusive behavior as such and understand the potential damage it can do, even if evidence of this damage is not evident or obvious in the behavior or experience of individuals he has abused.

"Internalized other" questioning offers an extremely valuable method to assist in this process, providing that abuse perpetrators understand that they cannot know the other person's experience and that they have a responsibility to examine the potentially damaging impact of their actions, regardless of the apparent impact demonstrated by the victim.

Endnotes

1. Jenkins has been influenced by the process of *relative influence* questioning that White (1989b, p. 37) describes: "Relative influence questioning invites family members to derive two different descriptions of their association with the problem that they present for therapy. The first is a description of the influences of the problem in the lives and relationships of family members; the second is a description of the influence of family members and their relationships in the life of the problem. Relative influence questioning also invites family members to participate in the construction of a new description of the problem itself—an externalized description." As we will discuss further, care has to be exercised, of course, so that men who abuse don't use externalization as a way to minimize their personal responsibility (see Tomm, 1989).

2. White (1991) refers to these types of questions as "experience of experience" questions. Tomm (1993a) refers to these same questions as "interpersonal perception" questions.

3. Epston has taken Tomm's designation of "internalized other" questioning to describe the process Epston initially referred to as "cross-referential" questioning (1993).

4. See White (1993a) and Jenkins (1990) for discussion on practices of power and attitudes that make men's violence possible.

References

Bateson, G. (1972). *Steps to an ecology of mind.* New York: Ballantine.

Bateson, G. (1979). *Mind and nature: A necessary unity.* New York: Dutton.

Epston, D. (1993). Internalized other questioning with couples: The New Zealand version. In S. G. Gilligan & R. Price (Eds.), *Therapeutic conversations* (pp. 183–189; with commentary by M. White, pp. 190–196). New York: Norton.

Jenkins, A. (1990). *Invitations to responsibility: The therapeutic engagement of men who are violent and abusive.* Adelaide, South Australia: Dulwich Centre Publications.

Jenkins, A. (1992). *The therapeutic engagement of men who abuse their partners.* Workshop, Bay Area Therapy Training Associates, Cupertino, CA.

Tomm, K. (1987). Interventive interviewing: Part II. Reflexive questioning as a means to enable self-healing. *Family Process, 26*(2), 167–183.

Tomm, K. (1989). Externalizing the problem and internalizing personal agency. *Journal of Strategic and Systemic Therapies, 8*(1), 54–59.

Tomm, K. (1992). *Interviewing the internalized other: Toward a systemic reconstruction of the self and other.* Workshop, California School of Professional Psychology, Alameda, CA.

Tomm, K. (1993a). The courage to protest: A commentary on Michael White's work. In S. G. Gilligan & R. Price (Eds.), *Therapeutic conversations* (pp. 62–80). New York: Norton.

Tomm, K. (1993b). *Constructivist therapy.* Videotape, Distinguished Presenters Series. Denver, CO: International Association of Marriage and Family Counselors.

White, M. (1989a). Negative explanation, restraint and double description: A template for family therapy. In M. White, *Selected papers* (pp. 85–99). Adelaide, Australia: Dulwich Centre Publications. (Original work published 1986)

White, M. (1989b). The process of questioning: A therapy of literary merit? In M. White, *Selected papers* (pp. 37–46). Adelaide, South Australia: Dulwich Centre Publications. (Original work published 1988)

White, M. (1993a). Deconstruction and therapy. In S. G. Gilligan & R. Price (Eds.), *Therapeutic conversations* (pp. 22–61). New York: Norton. (Original work published 1991)

White, M. (1993b). Commentary: Systems of understanding, practices of relationship, and practices of self. In S. G. Gilligan & R. Price (Eds.), *Therapeutic conversations* (pp. 190–196). New York: Norton.

CHAPTER TWENTY-ONE

Using Therapeutic Splits to Construct Empathic Narratives

Haim Omer

A recurrent issue in modern therapeutic debate is whether treatment should focus on the negative or the positive, on problems or solutions, on the pain or on the prize. The therapeutic narratives that characterize the leading therapeutic approaches could be easily placed in their relation to these two poles. Thus, on the "bright" pole we would find behavior therapy and the solution-oriented approaches; on the "dark" one, psychoanalysis and the starker varieties of existential therapy. Schafer (1976) characterized one side as prominently *comic* and the other as *tragic*. In this chapter I shall advocate a synthesis of the extremes: the richer therapeutic narrative is the one that embraces both the positive and the negative, allowing each its due salience and proper role. This should not, however, be a lukewarm compromise but a real synthesis that gives full expression to both sides.

DEFINING THE THERAPEUTIC SPLIT

Therapists of most persuasions agree that clients often pay a heavy price for their one-sided attitudes. They regard themselves or others as wholly good or bad; they view a piece of behavior as absolutely laudable or objectionable; they look at their past or future as black or white—and these totalist positions often spell trouble. The *therapeutic split* (Omer & Alon, 1997) is an attempt to counter these univalent constructions through a therapeutic message that enables the client to keep in mind, together, both the negative and the positive sides of the issue. The therapist proceeds by splitting the one-sided attitude into two contrasting aspects, but in such manner that the negative side is seen as implying the positive, and vice versa. The aim of the intervention is thus to make room for a more complex narrative and for options that would have been banned out of existence by the more simplistic frame of mind.

Therapeutic splitting is the mirror image of pathological splitting. In pathological splitting, the subject, unable to relate to an affective object as both good and bad, breaks it apart into two opposite ones. Thus, the mother is split into two mutually exclusive figures, one wholly good and the other wholly bad; the therapist is sometimes viewed as the epitome of all virtues, at other times, as the sum of all vices; and the self is now beauteous, strong, and true, and now ugly, base, and false. Often, one side of the split object all but disappears: thus, one may meet only with the bad mother, the evil therapist, and the negative self (their positive counterparts being relegated to the realm of fantasy). The therapeutic split works in the opposite way: faced with a one-sided attitude, the therapist offers a double description, but in such manner that one perspective calls to mind its counterpart. How can this be achieved?

The key lies in so constructing the split that both the positive and the negative aspects are viewed as such from the perspective of the client's own feelings, goals, and values. Pointing to the merits or demerits, or to the gains and losses inherent in a given pattern of behavior in ways that do not fit with the client's own views will never make for an effective message. Thus it hardly ever helps to tell a bulimic girl that her eating patterns jeopardize her chances of getting pregnant, or to encourage a perfectionistic and self-critical client by pointing to his positive achievements. In these clients' eyes, both the eventual infertility and the putative achievements do not count for much. The split can only be therapeutic if the client says "That's right!" to both its positive and negative sides. The whole message may then arouse the full-blooded response: "That's me!" This is the criterion of what I have termed elsewhere (Omer, 1997; Omer & Alon, 1997) an *empathic narrative*. When the therapeutic split is built as an empathic narrative, rejecting either of the two sides would almost imply the rejection of the other.[1]

A therapeutic split is called for whenever the therapist faces a monolithic attitude that seems to block progress. On such occasions, the therapist often feels tempted to react by offering the client the counterpart of his or her single-minded attitude. For instance, a self-rejecting client may be met by a supportive therapist; a self-complacent client, by a confrontative therapist. Experience shows that these well-intentioned positions often miss the mark. They contradict the rule of participation by jarring too glaringly with the client's experience.

Actually, they confront the client's one-sided attitude with a no less one-sided one. Evolving an appropriate therapeutic split may thus be a corrective not only to the client but to the therapist as well. Indeed, the split obviates the need for a one-sided therapeutic stance, be it supportive or challenging. The client, likewise, will tend less to discount the therapist's positive appreciation on the grounds that the therapist "sees only what is good" or to water down the painful side of the message on the grounds that the therapist "sees only what is bad."

Case One: Perfection

Susan wanted a partner who would give her heavenly sex. She had once had such an experience for a week. Usually, however, the vaginal orgasm of which she had such a glowing memory remained out of reach. Driven by her inner image, she would try with all her might, but the only result would be vaginal pains. Still, she believed, with the right partner the problem would vanish.

She had additional demands for any candidate: he should be handsome, well-dressed, sociable, intelligent, have a superior sense of humor, and not smoke.

In therapy, Susan would raise these issues again and again, all but forbidding the therapist to look in other directions. It was only very unwillingly that she filled the therapist in on her background. Whenever the therapist tried to guide the conversation or further explore an issue, Susan would say that that was not what she wanted to talk about. The therapist felt frustrated and began to develop a critical and challenging attitude toward Susan.

Susan had been married from the age of nineteen to twenty-three. From the beginning, she had felt there was something strange about her husband. He invariably implied, without telling why, that she disappointed him sexually. She ended by discovering that he was a transvestite. Even then, however, it took her almost two years to get the courage to divorce. She viewed her married years as a torture: being continuously put to the test and found wanting, never knowing for what and on what grounds. It was Kafka's *Trial* in real life.

Besides the orgasmic problem, she had other troubles. For instance, she felt a compulsive need to pick on hairs or black spots on her skin: she would do so until the skin was turned into an ulcerous sore. Small things disturbed her no end: for instance, if a boyfriend as much as touched the floor with his bare feet, he would not be allowed to reenter the bed without thoroughly washing himself. If any object disturbed the looks of her room or her office, she would have no calm until it was removed.

She wanted everything, her wayward feelings included, to obey her standards and her ideal blueprint: her process of choosing a partner, her orgasmic functioning, her therapy sessions. She knew that her demands were unusually high and she was proud of that.

The therapist had tried, unavailingly, to point out to Susan the irrational nature of her demands from herself and from others. He pointed out how Susan tried to control the therapeutic sessions just as she did her dates. This confrontative stance, however, was completely unhelpful. Susan almost left the therapy. Feeling that the treatment was at an impasse, the therapist decided to bring the case to a consultation group under my direction.

The therapist was keenly aware of the problem in the therapeutic interaction: the more he tried to help Susan toward leniency and flexibility, the more critical and perfection driven she became. This kind of stalemate is often indicative of an unempathic narrative: Susan was unable to recognize herself in the therapist's construction, in particular because the values underlying the therapist's narrative (in which "perfectionism" was viewed as a strictly negative quality) were too different from hers. The therapist, however, was concerned whether a merely supportive attitude would suffice: Susan was sacrificing her life to her purist and absolute standards. It would be unprofessional, if not downright dishonest, to leave Susan's one-sided patterns unchallenged. This is the kind of situation that calls for the formulation of a therapeutic split. The split would have to display both the merit and the price of Susan's perfectionism in terms that she could fully accept. The following message was developed and delivered to Susan in the following session:

> I was dissatisfied with the way I was conducting the therapy. This feeling led me to undertake a professional consultation, which changed my views and my attitude. I learned to understand better what your wish for perfection means to you and how it affects your life. Your striving begins with a feeling or an image of how you would like things to be. These images are extremely clear and detailed, probably more so than the inner images of other people. These feelings and images are exceptionally dear to you: they are your ideals of rightness, harmony, beauty, and sensuality. You feel, rightly, that you should not give up these pictures of perfection, for they are what is best and most valuable within you. Giving them up would be a gross self-betrayal. You would feel worse, not better, in doing so. I believe I went wrong in failing to understand this.
>
> Still, it is also true that you pay an awful price for the way your ideals impinge upon your life. They make you fight endlessly with yourself and with the world, for something always spoils the picture: there is always a hair in the wrong place or a black spot on the skin. The world keeps disappointing. This clash plunges your life in a turmoil of frustration and pain. You fight the black spot, scratch it and pick on it. The refractory skin, on its side, fights back and refuses to give in to the ideal. You become a bleeding sore. The same happens with sex. You have your own ultimative image, your cherished memory of an ecstatic week. In its name, you fight your own sexuality, demanding from it that it conform to your vision. Your body fights back and sex grows sour.

The tragic irony of it all is that you know full well how it feels to be picked upon, to be put under test, to be blamed for a failure again and again. This was precisely your experience with your husband. It is almost as if the badness of that experience had somehow infiltrated your very skin, continuing to persecute you in a different way: as you were once deemed disappointing, your life now disappoints you. I cannot believe that you must remain caught in this bind. There must be a way for you to be yourself, in full ownership of your values and ideals, without perpetuating in your own individual life the torture chamber from which you escaped with so much effort.

We must learn to keep both sides of the equation constantly before our eyes: the perfect inner images and the disappointing reality. We must have a place for both. Your images and dreams are valuable and vital not necessarily because they are realizable. Their value is in the inspiration they arouse, the sense of worth they give you, the way they fill your lungs with air and make your blood run in your veins. When the ideal turns into the drill of a sergeant major, it has become degraded.

Let us no longer split our conversation into two monologues: if you keep an eye only on the ideal and I on the sore on your skin, we will be talking at cross-purposes. We must enrich our sessions by keeping both sides in mind. I can only help you if I stop fighting you. Otherwise I will also be relating to you as a hair or a spot on the skin.

Susan reacted with a clear "That's me!" to the message. The therapeutic dialogue changed. Both partners were now able to entertain more complex and flexible positions. Susan would no longer interrupt the therapist when he tried to guide the session into new directions and the therapist learned to search for the value underlying her seemingly irrational behaviors. This increased tolerance also made itself felt in Susan's life. She learned not to subject her potential partners, her body, or her mind to the agony of unpassable tests. She engaged in a second divorce, from her inner tyrannous judge, but in a way that preserved the inspiring value of her harmonious images.

Case Two: In the Mire

Ron was the sensitive and talented adopted son of a school principal and a well-known surgeon. Although only eighteen, he had already composed music for various pop singers and groups. He had an amazing talent for organizing social events. He also looked like an angel. In spite of these assets, Ron had already attempted three times to commit suicide, tried almost every drug in the market, participated in burglaries, and worked for a few months as a male prostitute (servicing homosexuals). He seemed to be particularly at risk for dangerous developments immediately in the wake of an especially successful event. For instance, right after one of his songs was recorded and met with an excellent reaction, he joined a gang that broke into computer stores. Fortunately, up to now Ron had succeeded in extricating himself from each of his sallies into the underworld. He had stopped using crack and cocaine (after bouts of a few months each), had parted company with the gang, and had stopped prostituting himself. However, the periods in which something very bad was not happening were usually short.

He had first come to the attention of his school psychologist at the age of fifteen because of learning disabilities. In spite of his high intelligence, his marks were almost invariably mediocre or worse. The few scholastic successes he had had were soon followed by disappointment. The psychologist concentrated on his handicaps in reading and writing and, after about ten months of dedicated work, achieved a breakthrough. Ron became a voracious reader. In math and English, however (Ron was a Hebrew speaker), he still remained badly disadvantaged.

Ron developed an excellent relationship with the psychologist, but their joint work remained, for long, circumscribed to scholastic issues. She knew a bit about Ron's other problems from his parents. With her encouragement, Ron started to see a therapist. However, like many other experiments in his life, a good start with the therapist was followed by disappointment: when the therapist found out that Ron was using drugs, he made the continuation of the therapy conditional on an immediate withdrawal. Ron dropped out of the therapy.

Ron started to confide more and more in the school psychologist. He believed that he suffered from a self-destructive need. His attraction to drugs, thievery, lying, and prostitution felt truer to him than his positive achievements. The glitter of social success was merely external; the dark shadow was the true Ron. The counselor and Ron speculated on the possible link between Ron's attraction to the underworld and his being an adopted child. His self-degradation might then express his underlying feeling that he was basically worthless and actually belonged in the gutter from where he stemmed. The counseling relationship became a battleground between the dark and the bright sides of Ron. The counselor tried to rescue Ron by bolstering his self-esteem. This policy, however, stalemated the interaction: the counselor argued for all that was good—and Ron, for all that was bad. Ron said she was professionally committed to the positive. She retorted that Ron saw only the negative. This is precisely the situation that may call for a therapeutic split. The following message was therefore elaborated in a supervisory session and relayed to Ron piecemeal in the course of the coming sessions:

> I think we were wrong in thinking that you act out of self-destructiveness. Maybe the opposite is true: that you act out of self-defense. Whenever something good happens, you know that disappointment must follow. For you, disappointment is and always was an inevitable consequence of all positive expectation. You are terrorized by this certainty: that every rise must end in an awful crash. Against this haunting fear, you have only one protection: to keep one foot in hell, in the feeling that you belong in the mire. Then you can bear the fear. You can say to yourself, "Now I am not in danger of falling, for I am

already at the bottom." If you happen to take leave of hell for a while, as you did when you organized the Purim party or when your song met with acclaim, then you must quickly dip in the mire and renew your layer of mud. This is your defense: "I am there already! I have never given you or myself any reason to expect anything else." You may play around with good things, dabble with success, but not in earnest. Hope is your greatest enemy. You are like the hero of a story by Oscar Wilde: when the demons came to fetch him to hell he answered: "But I can't be taken to hell! I have always been there!"

Is there no way of living without this curse? I believe there is, but only by learning to disappoint. You pay the heaviest of prices because you don't know how to do it. Disappointing is a process, an ongoing interaction, a mutual grinding of teeth. To avoid this process you shatter the game, like a child who overturns a checkerboard. The price you pay is not only in terms of drugs and delinquency. It is also in your becoming dependent on outer, rather than on inner solutions, in your becoming enslaved to the external and the demonstrative. What you must develop instead is a deeper, inner darkness.

You must learn to be and to feel a disappointer, and know that you can bear it. Whenever something good happens, you must nurse within you the shadow of failure. You must keep its echo constantly in your inner ear as a background to each success. You must carry a black hole within your heart. This will be your insurance. An inner mire to protect you from hope. It is like with people who have lost their mothers in childhood: they often go through life with a protective pessimism that does not allow them to feel the danger of positive expectations. Having learned the smashing weight of loss, they will not hold anything for sure again. So, you must live always with a black inner prayer: "I am a disappointer, I know that the crash is around the corner. But I can disappoint because I do not give in to soaring hope. I can stand it because I am closer to it than to anything else."

Perhaps, before learning this prayer, you may still have to rise and fall a few times. The purpose, however, may now be to learn from each swing. Each new fall may then not be in vain but help to build this inner protection. Am I being overoptimistic? Maybe, but to say the truth, the external mire in which you usually sink yourself is, in a sense, smaller and less true than the internal one. For instance, you took drugs. But you also found out that you can get clean again. You prostituted yourself. But you also put a stop to it. The external mire is washable. Today you have it, tomorrow you don't. The inner one, however, is like an unremovable stain. You will go on saying: "I have this stain, because of my homosexual leanings, because my brain is warped, because I have such origins." The stain never leaves you. You cannot wash it away. You thought that your inner truth was drugs, thievery, and prostitution. These, however, were but external accidents. The shadow, the black hole and the dark prayer, are deeper and truer than these. The inner shadow may afford you a double protection: from success, because then you will feel the failure within the success, you will be saying kaddish [the Jewish ritual prayer for the dead] in the middle of the party; and from external accident, because, carrying the blackness within you,

you won't need them anymore. This is to be your constructive achievement in the way of blackness.

The counselor thus offered herself as a coach and partner in constructive pessimism. The ideas touched Ron deeply and he took up the challenge. The counselor no longer stood for all that was bright nor Ron for all that was dark. She became the reminder of the worm within the bud. The therapeutic split thus released the interactants from their one-sided and mutually exclusive positions. The counseling is still on and for the last six months Ron has had no "external accidents." He has disappointed his parents, his teachers, and himself in some exams and survived his success in a few others.

Case Three: The Wall and the Battering Ram

The therapeutic split can be very useful in marital therapy, for it helps to balance messages of support and confrontation to both spouses. In addition, if the message is symmetrical (each spouse receiving a communication involving a therapeutic split) the therapist is no longer suspected of favoring one side to the detriment of the other.

After seven years of marriage, Richard complained that Nira was uninterested in sex, sometimes avoiding him for months on end. He needed the bodily warmth, the contact, the feeling of a close togetherness. Nira complained that Richard did not help in the home and was emotionally demanding and explosive. She was extremely afraid of his anger: he would often scream at her viciously and had once slapped her in the face. Her response to his demands and attacks was to shut herself up ever more tightly.

Nira's mother had been thrown out of the parental home because she became pregnant (with Nira) by a student who disappeared after promising to marry her. The mother worked long hours to support herself, and Nira was sent to an institution in which the mother would visit her once a week. The mother married when Nira was four and a few years of family life, which registered most positively in Nira's memory, ensued. Nira had warm memories of her stepfather. With the years, however, he became violent toward Nira's mother and a bitter separation ended the family experiment. The mother remained deeply depressed for years and Nira grew up, from the age of ten, very much on her own. At the age of fifteen, Nira had her first sexual experience with a pop singer who took advantage of her neediness. He was coarse and offensive and, after three weeks, disappeared from Nira's life. Until she met Richard she had had no more intimate relations with men.

Richard's childhood and family of origin remained quite a blank throughout the therapy. He talked of his family in very general terms as "normal" or "run-of-the-mill." When the therapist told him she could get no clear picture of the family, Richard said that he saw his family distantly because the family relations had always been distant. He remembered envying other children for the close atmosphere of their homes.

In a few months of marital therapy, Richard became more involved with the home and the children. Sex improved in quality, but the frequency was still too low for Richard's taste: they were making love once a week and he felt he needed at least three or four times. In an individual session, Nira made it clear to the therapist that she felt she would never be able to satisfy Richard's sexual needs: she simply had to retreat into privacy, as if to refill her batteries, after each bout of openness. In spite of this problem, however, both the couple and the therapist sensed that things were going in the right direction, so they decided there was no immediate need for further sessions. The couple returned after four months: there had been no sex for two months and Richard had become explosive again. Only his new positive involvement with the children had remained in place. When the situation calmed down after two sessions, the therapist brought the case for a consultation. She felt they were in the same place as when they had stopped the therapy the previous time. Richard wanted more sex and Nira more consideration. The therapist felt that the two had become entrenched in their positions and that every attempt to make them budge was leading only to additional allegations and demands. Stopping the sessions at this point would probably repeat the fiasco of the first interruption. The following symmetrical split was therefore constructed in an attempt either to get the therapy moving or to end it in a different key.

> I was feeling that my work with you had reached an impasse. We seemed to be back to square one, and to tell the truth, I did not know where to go from there. So I decided to ask for a professional consultation and I want to share with you my new understanding of your marital and personal situation. I reached the conclusion that your problem is highly symmetrical. Both of you have highly acceptable and legitimate needs. However, in the very attempt to express and fulfill these needs you end up achieving the very opposite of what you intended.
>
> To begin with you, Nira, what is your chief personal need in your personal life and in the marriage? It is to find yourself a secure place, a protective enclosure where you may feel safe from attack, even if at the price of a certain loneliness. I think that this need is almost an inevitable result of the way you grew up. You were born to a mother whose whole existence was shattered by the rupture of her own protective enclosure. She was seduced and abandoned in the commonest and cruelest way. The result was that she and you were sent out into the wide world to pay for her innocent trust. This was your first lesson in the value of a protective enclosure and on the dangers of having it breached. Later on, your mother married and for a few years you had a real home. Even then, however, the security proved temporary: the home was destroyed and your mother remained devastated for years. Again, life was giving you the message: "Be wary of trust! Protect yourself! Don't let others in!" Also in your individual

life you were soon to pay the price of openness: your first intimate contact turned out to be your first lesson in abusive exploitation. You could almost say to yourself: "You fool! Haven't you learned the lesson? To let a man in so easily!"

You thus began your adult years with an instinctive reaction of shutting yourself tightly closed whenever you detected the most fleeting shadow of a possible invasion. Your body should be kept in total safety, at the very center of your citadel, encircled by layer upon layer of protective walls. This hope and need is not only legitimate: it was your great lesson in survival. It allowed you to grow without being devastated like your mother. Also with Richard you feel at times badly exposed to his escalating demands, criticisms, and attacks. Then you feel that you absolutely must shut yourself in. Ironically, however, it is the very intensity and absoluteness of this self-protection that may deprive you of your dream of security. And this, for two reasons. First, wherever there is a citadel there is an invader. If you build a wall, a battering ram will be swung on the other side. This is almost a law of nature: the stronger the defense, the more powerful the attack. The second reason that your dream of perfect security may prove its own undoing is that the more you burrow within the ground, the more the earth trembles. Your very self-entrenchment shakes the marriage and makes you ever more the prey to anxiety. Your hope thus ends up as your curse. You are left with lots of thick walls, a decided invader, a trembling burrow, and endless anxious expectancy. The real task is then to work toward another kind of security: one that is built out of togetherness rather than of self-isolation.

What about you, Richard? Your major wish in the marriage is the wish for closeness. That there be no barriers to intimacy, no distancing and no mutual exclusion. You want to feel loved and loving, touching and touched. I think it was in the name of this ideal that you decided to invest so much in the family and in the children, this last year. I believe that this wish ripened in childhood, when you looked with admiration and yearning at families that seemed close and warm. It was your natural reaction to your distant family. So, how can this hope prove self-defeating? I think you defeat yourself because you will not be contented with the intimacy and closeness of which your partner is spontaneously capable, but have very specific demands on how the closeness and intimacy should manifest themselves. For instance, you know that Nira can express closeness in sex, once in a while. This happened already and has recently become almost a weekly event. Her openness warmed your heart and excited your hopes. You said, "A good beginning! Now we only need to have it happen three or four times a week and all will be well!" What your hope actually says is that all you need is just another 400 percent improvement! Nira, however, does not believe that she can satisfy you there. She knows what it is for her to get her body out of the burrow so as to meet with you in full intimate openness. She also knows that when she succeeds, she is only proving to you that she is capable. Each success thus raises the expectation: Why not four times a week? Her achievement then becomes only a promise for more, only a first installment. At the very moment of satisfaction she feels she is disappointing you, for she cannot open herself four times a week. You may ask, why not?

Why can't she have me four times a week? Because she is very different from you in this respect. She has a different cycle of giving and recovering herself. She must come back to herself for a refill after a bout of intimacy. That's how she is built. Perhaps what we need to build, then, is a different kind of closeness: one that accepts the other's personal limitations as the very condition of togetherness."

Unfortunately, the message did not come up to our (the therapist's and consultant's) expectation. Nira was willing to work in that direction. Richard, however, felt betrayed. He stopped coming to the therapy, feeling that only he had been asked for a real sacrifice. The symmetry was not symmetrical after all! The therapist and the consultant (myself) are now trying to develop a new message that, while confirming Richard's right to stop the therapy, may also repair the damage of the negative ending.[2]

DISCUSSION

Many therapists who identify themselves with narrative perspectives in psychotherapy will probably find themselves nonplussed by the one-sided formulation and delivery of such lengthy therapeutic messages. Indeed, the term *narrative* has usually been associated with a tendency on the therapist's part rather to follow than to guide, to listen than to affirm, and to learn than to teach. If anything, the present therapeutic speeches evoke precisely the omniscient pontifical attitude that narrative therapists set out to eradicate. Let us consider this possible criticism in some detail.

The concept of *narrative* has had a meteoric career in the psychotherapeutic literature: it has been embraced by psychoanalysts (Spence, 1982; Schafer, 1983), family therapists (Boscolo, Cecchin, Hoffman, & Penn, 1987; White & Epston, 1990), cognitive therapists (Meichenbaum, in Hoyt, 1996; Russell & Van den Broek, 1992), followers of integrative and eclectic approaches (Omer & Strenger, 1992), as well as by theoreticians unidentified with any particular orientation (Bruner, 1986; Gergen & Gergen, 1986; Sarbin, 1986). This wide appeal stems from a variety of sources, including the demise of the assumption that therapy uncovers the unique hidden truth of past events; the growing belief, in all fields of psychology, that the mind constructs the perceived world; and the rise of hermeneutics and of the philosophy of language as general perspectives on knowledge and culture (see Omer & Alon, 1997, for a review). Behind all these, however, may well lie the high regard of psychotherapists for the well-wrought case story. Great therapists are great storytellers: good therapy might turn out to be good storying. What is common to all these approaches is not, as is sometimes supposed, the belief that the client must be the sole author of his or her life story but the understanding that the personal stories people come to believe and enact play a crucial role in the way they live. Stories may be saving or damning, be they initiated by the self or by others. The therapeutic messages illustrated in this chapter are grounded on this narrative perspective: they follow from the understanding that the one-sided narratives that had been current in the client's life or in the therapy had led to a dead end; they had, therefore, to be transformed into others, more open and rich.

The above examples of therapeutic splits were developed in the course of an extra-therapeutic discussion with a group of peers or with a supervisor. This is not necessarily so. The therapeutic split may develop gradually and organically out of the therapeutic conversation. Therapist and client may be jointly active in searching for the inextricable unity of positive and negative. For expository purposes, however, the clearest cases illustrating the need for and the pattern of a therapeutic split are those in which the therapy had reached an impasse on account of the one-sided constructions espoused by each side and the split was delivered in one piece.[3] Even when impasse develops, therapists do often succeed in overcoming it by a careful joint examination with the client, without any need for a one-sided intervention (Safran, 1993). Still, there are times when the impasse may preclude or vitiate such a joint examination, so long as the therapist does not take the lead in acknowledging and making good his or her contribution to the stalemate. The therapeutic splits illustrated in this chapter are such interventions: focused attempts initiated by the therapist to retrieve the treatment from a stalemate into which both sides had frozen. Elsewhere, I have termed these attempts *critical interventions* (Omer, 1994).

Am I apologizing? Am I trying to justify, by the special needs of impasse situations, the right of therapists to build a story of their own, to construct a therapeutic picture that fits their style, and to dictate their narratives to clients? As with the two sides of the therapeutic split, I will try to have it both ways, letting the apology stand where it is and appending to it what is perhaps a more challenging therapeutic creed: we have no alternative but to build actively, with the client's help, new portrayals to vie against the previous bleak ones, new plots to transform the self-defeating ones, new themes to open up options, and new meanings to infuse blood into a desiccated narrative (Omer & Alon, 1997). In all of these we will be irremediably active and our attitudes will transpire through our every word and every silence (Omer, 1996). But then, do we need no restraints to our narration? Yes, we must pass, as a minimum, the test of the client's full-blooded self-recognition. Our narratives are only therapeutic when they snugly fit the client's contours and are closely molded to the client's needs. Always, the client's refusal or lack of resonance will display the hollowness and the arbitrariness of our attempts. This is so whether we offer our narratives in the form of questions or of assertions, of short phrases or of lengthy disquisitions, in therapeutic letters or by word of mouth. The therapeutic split surely reflects my style: my tendency toward symmetry, double-description, a mix of support and challenge and—all right—verbosity. But still, the split will fail roundly unless it succeeds in sounding the client's own feelings, mobilizing the client's own values, and appealing to the client's own needs.

Endnotes

1. A similar parallelism may exist between a *pathological double-bind* (Bateson, Jackson, Haley, & Weakland, 1956) in which any response is experienced negatively, versus a *therapeutic double-bind* (Erickson & Rossi, 1975) in which any response is experienced as potentially positive.

2. See Omer (1991) on the reparation of a badly ended therapy by means of a letter proposing a new narrative about the therapeutic interaction.

3. There is a price, however: a message that is delivered in one shot may also crumble in one shot. We saw this happen in the third example. It is not usually true, however, that the therapy ends there. In my book *Critical Interventions in Psychotherapy* (1994) I have presented quite a few examples in which the therapy goes on and can even be enriched after the failure of a critical message.

References

Bateson, G., Jackson, D. D., Haley, J., & Weakland, J. H. (1956). Toward a theory of schizophrenia. *Behavioral Science, 1,* 251–264.

Boscolo, L., Cecchin, G., Hoffman, L., & Penn, P. (1987). *Milan systemic family therapy.* New York: Basic Books.

Bruner, J. (1986). *Actual minds, possible worlds.* Cambridge, MA: Harvard University Press.

Erickson, M. H., & Rossi, E. L. (1975). Varieties of double bind. *American Journal of Clinical Hypnosis, 17,* 144–157.

Gergen, K. J., & Gergen, M. M. (1986). Narrative form and the construction of psychological science. In T. R. Sarbin (Ed.), *Narrative psychology: The storied nature of human conduct.* New York: Praeger.

Hoyt, M. F. (1996). Cognitive-behavioral treatment of posttraumatic stress disorder from a narrative constructivist perspective: A conversation with Donald Meichenbaum. In M. F. Hoyt (Ed.), *Constructive therapies* (Vol. 2, pp. 124–147). New York: Guilford Press.

Omer, H. (1991). Writing a post-scriptum to a badly ended therapy. *Psychotherapy, 28,* 484–492.

Omer, H. (1994). *Critical interventions in psychotherapy: From impasse to turning point.* New York: Norton.

Omer, H. (1996). Three styles of constructive therapy. In M. F. Hoyt (Ed.), *Constructive therapies* (Vol. 2, pp. 319–333), New York: Guilford Press.

Omer, H. (1997). Narrative empathy. *Psychotherapy, 34,* 19–27.

Omer, H., & Alon, N. (1997). *Constructing therapeutic narratives.* Northvale, NJ: Aronson.

Omer, H., & Strenger, C. (1992). From the one true meaning to an infinity of constructed ones. *Psychotherapy, 29,* 253–261.

Russell, R. L., & Van den Broek, P. (1992). Changing narrative schemas in psychotherapy. *Psychotherapy, 29,* 344–354.

Safran, J. D. (1993). Breaches in the therapeutic alliance: An arena for negotiating authentic relatedness. *Psychotherapy, 20,* 11–24.

Sarbin, T. R. (Ed.). (1986). *Narrative psychology: The storied nature of human conduct.* New York: Praeger.

Schafer, R. (1976). *A new language for psychoanalysis.* New Haven, CT: Yale University Press.

Schafer, R. (1983). *The analytic attitude.* New York: Basic Books.

Spence, D. P. (1982). *Narrative truth and historical truth: Meaning and interpretation in psychoanalysis.* New York: Norton.

White, M., & Epston, D. (1990). *Narrative means to therapeutic ends.* New York: Norton.

CHAPTER TWENTY-TWO

From "Either-Or" to "Both-And"

Treating Dissociative Disorders Collaboratively

Robert A. Schwarz

There is a spectrum of phenomena of dissociation. At one end of the continuum are positive and healthy aspects; at the other end are the disorders of dissociation. For the sake of clarity, I will mostly be describing issues of therapeutic work with persons who fit the diagnosis of dissociative identity disorder (DID), formerly known as multiple personality disorder (MPD), which is at the extreme of the spectrum. Virtually all dissociative disorders are reactions to severe and repeated trauma in childhood. In MPD/DID, the usual experience of having one identity is either lost or never created. Instead, the person grows up with multiple identities and multiple versions of reality.

This chapter will first address the importance of therapists' embracing the tensions that exist between different theoretical perspectives, and will then discuss three conundrums raised by trauma and dissociation that can both clarify and challenge a postmodern worldview. Finally, it will address certain clinical issues, especially involving the therapeutic relationship, that become particularly relevant when treating highly dissociative clients.

THE IMPORTANCE OF INTEGRATION: PARALLELS BETWEEN THERAPISTS AND CLIENTS

The hallmark of trauma-based thinking is the reliance on "either-or" distinctions. This thinking pattern reaches its height in the splitting of a personality into separate and different parts (MPD/DID). The therapy of trauma involves helping clients move from an "either-or" perspective to a "both-and" perspective. "Both-and" thinking reaches its therapeutic and creative height when an individual can hold *seemingly* contradictory ideas together. The ideas I wish to present regarding a collaborative approach to treating dissociative disorders are an integration (perhaps collaboration) of constructivist and cooperative schools of thought—namely, Ericksonian (Calof, 1995; Erickson, 1980; Grove, 1993; Lankton, 1985; Lankton & Lankton, 1983; Schwarz, in press), solution-focused (de Shazer, 1985, 1988; Dolan, 1991, 1998) and narrative approaches (Epston & White, 1992; White & Epston, 1990; Wade, 1996)—with the more essentialist ideas found in the standard trauma-based therapy approaches (Briere, 1992; Herman, 1992; Horowitz, 1986; Meichenbaum, 1994; Peterson, Prout, & Schwarz, 1991; Schwarz & Prout, 1991; Terr, 1994; van der Kolk, 1988) as well as the dissociative disorders field (Kluft, 1991; Ross, 1989; Putnam, 1989). It is especially important to attend to the tension between the seemingly conflicting aspects of these approaches. It is crucial in treating this population that therapists actively embrace the tension that exists between conflicting ideas. If we are to ask our clients to integrate seemingly separate and supposedly opposing distinctions (of self), we must be able to do the same. Therapists need expert knowledge and maps about the territory of dissociative experience *and* must also allow the client to be an expert. Therapists must understand that reality is constructed *and* there is an essential fact of being brutally raped. An emphasis of this chapter will be on therapist-client relationships as the means to move from "either-or" to "both-and."

THREE CONUNDRUMS

With these tensions in mind, let us consider three theoretical conundrums that are evoked when considering trauma, MPD/DID, and cooperative and postmodern approaches.

Conundrum One: If a Tree Falls in the Forest and No One Is There to Describe It, Did It Fall? To what extent is MPD/DID a construct created by therapists or the therapeutic community via languaging? According to the *DSM-IV* (American Psychiatric Association, 1994, p. 487), the criteria for diagnosing MPD/DID are as follows:

- The individual presents with two or more distinct identities or personality states, each with its own relatively enduring patterns of perceiving, relating to, and thinking about the environment and self. (These personalities are often referred to as *alters*.)

- At least two of these identities or personality states recurrently take control of the individual's behavior.

- The individual is unable to recall important personal information that is too extensive to be explained by ordinary forgetfulness.

- The disturbance is not due to the direct physiological effects of a substance or a general medical condition.

Many people do not accept the existence of MPD/DID at all. The skeptical view is that multiplicity is something the client does in response to treatment. From this perspective, it is the way therapists talk with clients that constructs the world of dissociation. (See Spiegel & McHugh, 1995, for a good pro-and-con summary.) In essence, skeptics ask, "Where is the parsimony one wants to see in a scientific description?" Russian novels do not have so many characters! The degree of multiplicity sometimes appears to be a kind of status symbol, a contest of who has more parts. The doubting position is that the diagnosis appears to be a fad. If MPD/DID is as prevalent as the dissociative disorders community says it is, why don't more therapists see patients with the condition? How does one account for the explosion of cases over the last twenty years?

The countervailing argument is that MPD/DID is not a construct of therapists. It existed before and independent of therapist observation and subsequent commentary and clinical discourse. The disorder is seen as a creative response of the individual to extreme and prolonged abuse and trauma. Therapeutic constructs act like lenses and filters that allow the observer to observe what had been invisible. The explosion of MPD/DID diagnoses and discourse over twenty years is no different than, and is in fact related to, the explosion of reported rape and childhood sexual abuse cases. The recognition of the existence and the effects of childhood and adult trauma are finally gaining a level of privilege in our culture and the therapeutic community. The phenomenon of multiplicity is experientially real for clients, *independent of observation*. It is highly localized knowledge—perhaps the most localized knowledge of all narratives, in that it has only one person that knows the story and that person is broken into a community that is separated.

From this perspective, therapists working with dissociative disorders have simply been willing over the years to listen to the stories of these marginalized people. These therapists have been willing to break from the dominant therapeutic culture (of the time) and work with people in a different way. Historically, these therapists were marginalized, then gained a brief period of acceptance, and now once again are being marginalized.

Conundrum Two: What Is the Sound of One Hand Clapping? Unity Versus Multiplicity as the Dominant Story of Western Civilization. What is it about our culture that makes it so hard to accept multiplicity? Ross (1992) has suggested an intriguing parallel between Western patriarchal culture and a singular order: There is one God "up" in heaven; there is one Self "up" in the head. Both exert dominion of what is "down below." This is far different from the worlds of the Greek or Hindu gods or the multiple spirits of the Native Americans, and far different from the ideas of multiple points of view and the need for cooperation that is an inherent part of treating MPD/DID.

There is also a parallel between the individual person with MPD/DID and the larger global context. I would like to suggest that the rise of MPD/DID as a diagnosis in the postmodern era is not an accident. What can be more postmodern than having more than one reality inside oneself? (See the discussion in Gergen, 1991, and in Gergen, in Hoyt, 1996b, of the "saturated self" and "multiphrenia.") MPD/DID also points out the dark side of postmodernism, namely, the risks of fragmentation and the loss of meaning and focus. MPD/DID in individuals can be seen as a metaphor for the global dissociative (noncollaborative) multiplicity that is reaching a critical level of dysfunctionality. How much difference is there between one person splitting his or her personality into disowned parts that often attack each other and the human species breaking off into different nation states, tribes, and classes and attacking and killing each other? Is there really any difference between a dissociative client cutting herself because in the short term it relieves tension while in the long term it does harm, and corporations and governments allowing the poisoning of the ecosystem for near-term profits or fear of being voted out of office? The mistaken belief is that one part can have dominion over another part without hurting the entire whole.

Conundrum Three: If a Rose Is a Rose Regardless of the Name, What About Pain? That is, what is essential and what is constructed? In parts of the world there is a socially sanctioned practice of female genital mutilation (FGM), sometimes euphemistically and erroneously referred to, in quasi-medical terms, as female circumcision. FGM usually takes place between the ages of six and twelve. It involves the removal of part or all of the clitoris without anesthesia and without the use of a surgical blade. It is usually done by a woman with the consent of the mother. The child is usually taken out of the home with little ritual preparation and is usually terrified and screaming. It occurs at rates of up to 90 percent of the women in certain classes in certain countries (deMause, 1991).

The postmodern question has been raised by some that since this is a culturally sanctioned practice, it is quite possible that the event is not traumatic; it is a Western social construction to consider FGM to be traumatic. The idea being suggested—that a cultural norm can construct reality in such a way that it would prevent the perception of an individual's pain—is highly problematic. In fact, it is just this type of argument that exposes some of the flaws in the postmodern fervor against essentialism. This is the slippery slope into total relativism. To my mind, it is far more reasonable to argue that there are some essential aspects of experience. Although cultural norms and social factors can influence the meaning and the expression of pain and trauma, are we to believe these events did not hurt before we started studying them, and that it has only been since we have been languaging them in the West that they have caused people to suffer? And even if people were not consciously aware of their suffering due to the hypnotically restraining effect of culture, did sexual abuse constrain and restrain these people from living a better life from an unconscious level? Can we not define the unconscious as anything that has no access to a language matrix? These questions are at the heart of the etiology of dissociative disorders and the presentation of the disorder within the therapist's office and the culture at large.

The recognition that psychopathology is a reaction to real trauma as opposed to inner conflicts has been referred to as a paradigm shift (Bloom, 1997). People who present with MPD/DID and other dissociative disorders have had repeated overwhelming trauma in childhood (Glass, 1993; Putnam, 1989; Ross, 1989; Schwarz & Gilligan, 1995). As children, they begin to discover that autohypnosis and dissociation reduce the pain and suffering they experience. As they use these skills more, the skills develop. In addition, the child cannot rely on external comforts or external narratives, because for the most part they are not there. To make matters worse, the child can also tell that other children do not seem to share the same reality. So the child begins to turn inward. The normal mechanism of the imaginary friend can be taken to new heights. The child's personality begins to divide into parts or *alters*. The alters have their own character, their own dominant feeling and dominant story. The child can have different alters be "out" for different parts of the abuse. The motto of the child is "divide thyself and conquer." The child writes an internal book or play. The characters have specific relationships to each other to make the play work. There are rules. All the different alters are cooperating to further the play. They are cooperating even if they are fighting or hurting each other. The fight is at the level of the plot; the cooperation is at the level of the process.

The commonality between the types of alters and their relationships that one sees in MPD/DID is not based on cultural contamination by all these people reading popular books on MPD such as *Michelle Remembers* (Smith, 1989), *Sybil* (Schreiber, 1973), or *The Three Faces of Eve* (Thigpen & Cleckley, 1957), or from watching sensationalistic television shows. The commonality is due to the fact that there are not that many different ways to construct characters that can also make artistic sense of all the trauma and abuse. For that matter, there are not that many ways that the abusers can abuse. The narratives and fantasies of abusers are fairly consistent across the population (Salter, 1995), so the type of characters and stories to which the child must react are fairly limited.

COLLABORATIVE TREATMENT OF MPD/DID
AND OTHER DISSOCIATIVE DISORDERS

While not explicitly postmodern or narrative, the practice of most trauma therapists has been to allow a nonprivileged story to be told. This permits people who have only the implicit memory for traumatic events—with flashbacks but few words and images—to create a coherent narrative story of what happened to them, tracing its meaning and effects in their lives. Typically the therapist-defined central goals of treating all trauma-based problems (including MPD/DID) are the following: (1) To allow the client to create a *personal* narrative that will be relatively consistent with reality, yet will allow the client to derive meaning about what happened relatively free of the constraints of abusers and other dysfunctional family members and in a form that allows the creation of a relatively *positive* life; (2) to help the client manage the dysphoric affect that becomes conscious as part of the healing process; and (3) to help the client think and feel and behave in the here and now in ways that increase functionality (e.g., work, love, and play). To succeed at these goals with the minimum amount of pain and disruption to the client, the therapist must balance these long-range "expert" goals with the usually more immediate goals of the client, which can vary from getting rid of flashbacks to being less suicidal to improving child rearing or keeping a job. There will be tension between these goals, and their interplay will change over time.

No matter what scheme or theory is being applied, when working with dissociative disorders and survivors of childhood sexual abuse, it is of paramount importance to be respectful, caring, and patient. You must filter your theories and interventions through yourself as a creative and loving person who is being fully present and listening to an extremely hurt and wounded person. The therapist needs to detect and elaborate whatever resources that keep him or her being fully present and resourceful as well as detect and reduce anything that blocks or inhibits him or her from being fully present in a loving and creative manner.

FOCUSING ON THE THERAPIST-CLIENT DYAD

Perhaps the most important clinical contribution that solution-focused and other collaborative therapies has to offer for the field of dissociative disorders is the significance of focusing on the *therapist-client interaction* as the *unit of observation* for interventions. This requires specific attention to the experience and behaviors of the therapist in relation to the client's experience. The therapist must attend to what works and what does not work and make corrections in the treatment based on this analysis. Problems in treatment should be considered as feedback regarding problems in the therapeutic endeavor *between* the participants.

The experiential world of MPD/DID clients is highly imaginative and creative as well as idiosyncratic and often at variance with consensual reality. When therapists are insufficiently creative and flexible to meet clients within their world, a variety of problems arise out of the interaction. For instance, not many years ago some hospitals had a practice of interviewing "out of control" and "sadistic" alters in restraints! A client would be put into four-point restraints and then the out-of-control alter would be elicited and interviewed. One of the rationales for this approach would be that clients would feel safer knowing that they could not harm themselves. Not surprisingly, the alters would be out of control—thus appearing to justify the restraints that were used. Space does not allow a full analysis of the iatrogenic problems that this approach creates, but the approach clearly communicates that these alters are really so bad and out of control that they must be restrained. Imagine being an alter full of dissociated anger and rage, believing yourself to be irredeemable, and "waking up" to a bunch of doctors who have you restrained! One likely immediate response would be, "I must really be that bad and scary if they must resort to this just to talk to me," a reaction that promotes a spiral of increasing violence. The situation also immediately turns into a trauma reenactment if the person was ever tied down as a child.

Listening to the types of horrific trauma that are necessary to create dissociative disorders as well as dealing with the behavioral reactions to such trauma such as self-harm and suicidality (they are not the same) inevitably evokes reactions in therapists. The emotional reactions of therapists to these events will often lead to distressed states of mind, resulting in less-than-optimal therapeutic interventions. Minimal cues are sent from the therapist to the client because of the emotional reactivity of the therapist. A common question that therapists are often asked by sexually abused clients is whether or not the therapist believes them. Generally the best response is to wonder with the client whether or not this question reflects some of their own conflict (Calof & Schwarz, 1994). How the therapist is feeling will color how the therapist says what he or she says. For instance, a client once asked me whether I believed her stories of abuse in the midst of an emotionally laden conversation that was bothering me a great deal. My response at the time was, "Since I was not there, how could I know for sure?" This caused a large negative reaction. While my statement was true, and the client's reaction was more than required, it accurately reflected that I had moved away from being fully present in a loving and creative manner.

Working with people with dissociative disorders is usually longer-term treatment. Generally, it will involve significant problems along the way, including difficulties that the therapist has in either dealing with the client's behavior in session (e.g., aggressive alters telling the therapist that they are going to kill the client) or the inability to help clients control symptomatic behavior outside the session that is highly disruptive to the client's functioning (e.g., out-of-control dissociative states that jeopardize a job). How big such problems are and how often they emerge is highly variable from client to client and therapist to therapist for any number of reasons. These types of problems can be *technically* difficult, referring to the specific what-to-do actions needed to solve the problem. More important, they are difficult because they are a major source of *emotionally* charged reactivity for the therapist. Therapists need to take this state of affairs as a given that comes with the territory. Therefore, therapists must frequently take self-corrective measures to deal with these eventualities. The self-corrective measure that is the easiest to create is a consultation with oneself as if one were behind the mirror. In other words, the therapist needs to reflect on his or her interactions with the client as the unit of observation. The therapist needs to be a "customer" (de Shazer, 1985) for changing some aspect of his or her interaction with the client in order to effect an improvement in the therapy. The consultation with oneself (or a colleague, for that matter) should follow the rules of the central map of solution-focused therapy (de Shazer, 1985, 1988), which form the headings of the next three sections.

"If Something Is Not Broken, Do Not Fix It"

One of the first issues to assess is whether or not there is agreement on what is "broken," as well as on the desired goal. The operative question throughout treatment then is, "Broken according to whom?"

Disagreement about problems and goals can come from several sources. Misunderstandings about the meanings of words are one of the most frequent sources of disagreement. For instance, the concept of *integration* usually has very different meaning to the dissociative client than it does to the therapist. Integration is frequently interpreted as *death* by alters. Additionally, alters often take the word to mean instant integration. Furthermore, the client can read into the word the implication that there is something bad and wrong with multiplicity. It is not hard to understand why these ideas are resisted. A collaborative approach is not so driven by integration, although that is a long-term option. The focus is on accepting the fact that the client has different parts; and helping the different parts learn to communicate with each other, collaborate with each other to further functional living, and to learn from and respect and value each other. By the time these goals are accomplished, integration may not be a big deal. As Grove and Haley (1993, p. 183) report, "In [Milton] Erickson's approach, the goal was not to try and merge the personalities or to search for additional personalities. The goal was to persuade the personalities to communicate directly with each other and to . . . collaborate and make a positive contribution to the life of the total person." Grove (1993, pp. 16–17) elaborates: "There are several advantages to this orientation. By approaching secondary personalities as real individuals with their own independent needs and motivations, the therapist can more easily win the trust and cooperation of the secondary personalities. . . . Because the client's presentation of having multiple personalities is not viewed as a psychopathology, the therapist can approach all personalities with a more positive view."

Another major source of disagreement is the misunderstanding on the part of the therapist that a clear understanding and agreement has been reached throughout the system of alters, when in fact it has not. Certain alters may well have specific objections and concerns about the problem or goal. Self-harming behavior (e.g., cutting, vomiting, and so on) is a good example of problems related to opposition by specific alters. Sometimes clients will state that they have made a commitment to not harm themselves, but this has not included several key alters. Additionally, some alters (and even the whole client) may not even see self-harming behavior as much of a problem. They may at least perceive it as a better solution than the alternatives to not harming.

The usual emphasis of solution-focused therapy is on exceptions and solutions and the future, sometimes referred to as "solution talk" (Furman & Ahola, 1992). However, clients who have been sexually and physically abused often want and need to talk about the past and what has happened to them. They see "problem talk" as part of the solution. The fact is that they have not had anyone in their lives to listen to their story and they first need acknowledgment and validation (see Dolan, 1991; O'Hanlon, in Hoyt, 1996a). Then they need help to process its meaning for them. So it is important to cooperate with this need when it exists. When a therapist rushes past this important need it is often interpreted by the client that the therapist is yet one more person who does not want to hear what happened. The therapist becomes part of the old problem.

For many people who fit a MPD/DID diagnosis, dissociative behavior is a way of living. They often do not see certain behavior patterns as important factors in their problem. Even if such behaviors can easily be seen by the therapist as dysfunctional, the premature targeting of those behaviors as something to fix will usually create a resistant attitude or another negative reaction from the client. For instance, Mary habitually presented with a very gruff, "who needs you" attitude. Several previous therapists had labeled her "resistant" because she "dissociated her feelings." She acted out sexually and drank excessively. When she presented for treatment she challenged me in a variety of ways, including saying something to the effect of, "Who do you think you are trying to tell me to focus on my feelings?" I asked her what made her think that I would do such a terrible thing. Mary replied that it was really other therapists who kept forcing her to do this. Following Erickson's utilization approach, I commented, "It was absolutely rude of those therapists to try and force you to do a kind of therapy against your will." The effect was immediate. Mary looked very puzzled. Her body relaxed and became more open. I asked her what she wanted to work on. Mary replied that she was having problems raising her child. So we worked on this with both immediate practical value and as a prologue and relationship builder for later work. It is crucial to collaborate with clients' wishes about therapy. After all, the reason they became dissociative is that other people forced them to do things that they did not want to do.

Related to this issue is coming and going from therapy. Many dissociative clients often want to leave therapy even though they have many obvious problems. With some clients a collaborative decision can be reached that they will stay in treatment. Other clients need to be allowed to leave. Mary has been in and out of treatment half a dozen times in the past four years. Each time she has been in she worked well. She has even dealt with her feelings at times. Her functioning has improved in many areas, including her job and raising her child. She does not act out sexually or use drugs. She is beginning to think about going to college.

I have already implied the importance of working with alters, traumatic material, and dissociative defenses. However, it is no small matter to diagnose a client with MPD/DID or to start the therapeutic process of communicating with alters and dealing with traumatic material. The question of timing becomes important. In the case of undiagnosed clients, I am assuming at this point questions have been raised either by the spontaneously reported symptoms of the client or through some other diagnostic screening such as the Dissociative Experience Scale (Bernstein & Putnam, 1986). If dissociative symptoms are not reported as central issues and the client has identified other goals for the therapy, then the therapist should not raise the issue of dissociative disorder. One of two things will happen: the client will achieve the goals, or the client will not achieve the goals. In the latter case, dissociative symptoms will often be one of the blocks to completing the goal and can then be legitimately raised. In the former case, the client may spontaneously bring up some new concerns about dissociative problems now that the therapist has been helpful. In these cases questions and comments need to stay near the experiential data. The goal of the questioning is to assess client motivation as well as to try to increase the possibility of a customer relationship around the dissociative problems. The therapist might use the following line of questions:

- Does the experience of losing track of several hours or a day [or another symptom—for example, voices in your head] trouble you?
- What problems does it cause for you?
- Do you ever wonder what is going on, why is this happening?
- What theories do you have about it?
- What have other therapists said about this to you?

- What was that like for you?
- On a scale of 0 to 10, how much do these things disrupt your life?
- On a scale of 0 to 10, how motivated are you to understand and solve this problem?

A therapist might get a new client who has already been diagnosed with MPD/DID who does or does not accept the diagnosis. The client may accept the diagnosis, but might not want to work on trauma issues or work with the alters. In either of these cases, the therapist should work to help the client achieve his or her goals. A guiding solution-oriented question is, "To what extent is the client a customer for these interventions?" It would be an unusual client who was a 100 percent customer. So a modification might be to scale this question from 0 to 10. Anything less than a 7 would probably indicate that it is better not to proceed. The issues of parts or multiplicity should only be raised if the client sees their relevance in achieving better functioning, as defined by the client. The therapist could say:

- I am very interested in working in a way that would be most helpful to you. What has been helpful in previous treatment and what has not been helpful?
- How important (on a scale of 0 to 10) do you feel [or think] it would be to work with your alters [or deal with the trauma] in order to achieve your goals?

"If Something Works, Do More of It"

One of the first jobs of therapists in working with any type of seriously traumatized client is the identification of *resources*. Resources are defined here as states of mind and specific practices that help people effectively respond to problems (Schwarz, in press). In addition, resources can refer to specific people who support positive developments in the client. When problems are happening in treatment, one of the first places to look is to what extent has the therapist been inviting the client to build up resourcefulness. Beyond specific questioning techniques, therapists need to communicate to clients the importance of building resources to help them be part of the therapeutic team. I usually educate clients and therapists about this with the following metaphor: "Let us look at a hypothetical situation. Let us assume that your problems and traumas are represented in the denominator of a fraction and your resources are in the numerator. In this hypothetical situation the fraction is 1/100. We can either increase the numerator by one or decrease the denominator by one. Which would be the better use of our energy?"

Dissociative clients and others who have been seriously abused are expert in noticing what is wrong. They have had lifetimes of people pointing out the negative. Rarely have they been encouraged to appreciate a partially successful response and been encouraged to keep at it or do more of it. Therapists should be like one-minute managers (Blanchard & Johnson, 1982) and catch clients doing something right, especially partial responses. Interviewing clients about the activities and situations that make them happier, feel more complete or productive, decrease their symptoms, and so on are useful in themselves. But more important, spending time exploring these experiences affects the therapist-client dyad. It lets the client know that the therapist wants to hear about exceptions and strengths. It gives the therapist-client dyad positive targets to move toward, and communicates to all concerned that there is more to the client than the traumatized self.

Nevertheless, there will be other problems. Just as a solution-oriented therapist would look for exceptions in a client system, he or she needs to look for what has worked in the therapist-client system. Here are several avenues to explore:

- When has the therapist felt more resourceful in a similar context with the client? What is different about those times? This question implies that the therapist has already assessed how he or she is thinking and feeling as well as delineated the context.

- When has the client seemed to be more resourceful in a similar context? What was different about those times in terms of therapist actions or client actions?

- What does the client think would make things better, particularly in terms of what the therapist needs to do more of?

- When have things gone better in general, what was different about those times as opposed to the current situation?

Therapists need to reflect on what they do to cultivate positive and resourceful experiences in themselves both in and out of the therapy room (Schwarz, in press). Do they need to do more of some or all of those things?

"If It Does Not Work, Do Something Different"

It is the therapist who is the paid professional; blaming the client is of little use. A difficulty in treatment should be construed by the therapist as feedback that something is amiss in the interaction. The client is attempting to cooperate by giving the feedback. The therapist must assess what is the ongoing pattern of behavior, feeling, thinking, or theorizing in which he or she is engaging, as well as the client's reactions, that is not working. The problem may involve errors of omission or commission, or both. What needs to be different may be a behavior, a consistent feeling state, or a pattern of thinking.

There are a number of common problems to look for:

- *Not* thinking that the therapist is a substantial part of the problem.

- Not acknowledging and apologizing for mistakes. MPD/DID clients have had very little experience with people in positions of authority acknowledging and apologizing for their mistakes. When a therapist is able to apologize it enhances trust and role-models nondefensiveness.

- Attributing negative motivations to clients. One of the creative challenges for therapists is to help elicit positive motivations underlying what may appear to be very negative behavior. A common example is the construction of "self-sabotage."

Barbara was hospitalized and improving at a good rate. Then all of a sudden, she started to have problems and backslide. The therapist talked with Barbara about her self-sabotaging behavior. Barbara became upset and began to rapidly decompensate. A careful analysis of Barbara's pattern revealed that she was doing much better. Her expectations of herself increased beyond her ability to consistently meet them. Dissociative clients, like most other survivors of abuse, tend to be highly perfectionistic. She began to see herself as failing. She began to try harder, which only decreased her performance. The label of *self-sabotage* had a number of meanings to Barbara. One of them was an implied command, "Try harder!" When it was suggested to Barbara that she was trying too hard and doing too much, she began to improve again.

Highly idiosyncratic to each therapist and each therapist-client dyad are "person of the therapist" or *countertransference* issues. These terms are not usually used in postmodern discourses. No matter what you call them, however, these reactions exist and have a profound effect on the therapeutic relationship. As stated earlier, the goal is the detection and reduction of anything that blocks or inhibits the therapist from being fully present in a loving and creative manner. To achieve this goal with our clients we must also achieve it with ourselves. Table 22.1 provides a solution-oriented survey for therapists to help identify areas of relative strength and needed growth.

THAT WHICH IS MARGINALIZED EVENTUALLY GETS ANGRY

One of the important contributions of narrative therapy has been the delineation of the relationship between the dominant culture and story and marginalized cultures and stories. In the political world, that which is marginalized eventually gets angry. The same holds true for the interpersonal world of family culture as well as the intrapersonal world of ego-states and alters. In the therapeutic world, it becomes important to invite into the therapy that which has been denied. Dissociative clients often present highly distorted cognitions and beliefs. One of the most prevalent ones is that they are to blame for what happened to them. Related to this is the belief that they are bad or evil. This latter belief is most dramatically seen in people who describe sadistic or satanic

Table 22.1. Solution-Oriented Checklist for Therapist Development

1 Notices small positive changes even though no large ones have appeared	17 Feels comfortable while feeling angry with client
2 Fears (on an emotional level) that client may hurt self	18 Feels comfortable while feeling angry at abusers
3 Helps client focus on angry feelings	19 Feels comfortable while being asked to solve ambiguity
4 Helps client focus on sad feelings	20 Reflects ambiguity back toward client
5 Helps client focus on fearful feelings	21 Feels comfortable dealing with angry and hurtful aspects of client
6 Helps client focus on spiritual feelings	22 Feels comfortable dealing with childlike aspects of client
7 Helps client focus on joyful feelings	
8 Recognizes negative interactional patterns	23 Tolerates constructive criticism from client well
9 Does something different to change a negative interactional pattern	24 Talks with client about the consequences of dysfunctional coping skills without labeling
10 Shows sense of humor when appropriate	
11 Feels OK even when client is doing poorly	25 Accepts praise from client well
	26 Believes that the client can live a "good enough" life
12 Gives client praise for taking small steps	
13 Acknowledges own mistakes, using "I"	27 Looks for strengths and resources of client
14 Apologizes to the client for own mistakes	28 Acknowledges pain and weaknesses of client
15 Remains centered and present while listening to details of abuse	29 Other: _____
16 Feels comfortable while feeling sad or crying with client	30 Other: _____

Note: This table presents twenty-eight behavior patterns that as a therapist you may or may not do when treating clients who are recovering from trauma. Please rate the occurrence of each item according to this 0 to 10 scale: 10 = 100 percent of the time when it is appropriate, 5 = 50 percent of the time when appropriate, 0 = not at all. If you are not sure, just put what feels accurate at this point in time. There are two "other" lines for your use.

abuse. These individuals often have a subsystem of alters who are the designated bad or evil ones. It can be very difficult to sit with people who feel so unhappy about themselves. There is a tremendous temptation to attempt to correct these beliefs or at least to say quickly to the client, "You are not bad or evil." A useful solution-oriented question might be, "What would need to happen that would let you know that you are not bad?" An alternative intervention would be to scale the sense of badness by asking, "On a scale of 0 to 10, where 0 is good and 10 is bad or evil, where are you?" This could be followed by asking, "What would it look like for you to move up one point toward goodness?"

This type of intervention may be worth a try. If it works, the therapist should do more of it. But it may not work. Furthermore, the motivation in asking such a question may have more to do with the therapist's wishes than with the immediate needs of the client. Some clients experience this attempt to fix or change their alleged distortions as a dis-invitation. Such clients *know* that they are bad (and it makes no difference to them that the therapist or anyone else disagrees). They have done bad things. The fact that they were forced to do these acts may not seem relevant. What these clients deeply wish is for someone to listen to them talk about their badness. If the therapist appears unwilling to enter this world, it demonstrates to the clients that this aspect of themselves is truly ir004retrievable.

> Sharon was such a client. Once I stopped trying to talk her out of cognitive distortions and offered to listen and accept her "evilness," she would become more calm and would begin to talk about a range of things that had not yet been discussed. Nevertheless, it can be very difficult for a therapist to accept the client's evilness, because the client will talk as if the evilness is inside her. I have found that externalizing conversations around the client's "relationship with evil" begins to open up some room.

When engaging clients on the topic of evilness, the rule "If it works, do more of it" must be tempered with the idea "Just because a little of something is good, it does not mean more of it is necessarily better." In other words, therapists and clients must collaborate on how much is enough. Too much talk about a client's experiences with sadism and evil can overwhelm both client and therapist. It is usually a good idea to leave the last part of the session for sealing over and recomposing if one is going into this highly charged territory.

The treatment of self-harm is another example of how that which is denied gets angry as well as of the role of the personal reactions of the therapist. This is a common yet difficult problem in the treatment of dissociative disorders. It is a particularly good example of a behavior that requires a cooperative approach, yet is likely to stimulate strong emotional reactions from therapists that may undermine the goal of being cooperative. A common and often counterproductive intervention is for the therapist to insist that the client not engage in self-harm, without also attending to the underlying motivations behind the self-harming (Calof, 1995). This intervention has the effect of dis-inviting these aspects of self from the therapy. Briere (1992) has described the tension-reducing function of these behaviors. If the therapist summarily attempts to block these behaviors, one of two outcomes can occur. The first is that the client can become increasingly suicidal, because the previous coping skills were disallowed. The second outcome is that the client simply hides the self-harming behavior. In either case, the usual resistance to change is created by the therapist-client interaction. A more cooperative approach would involve an ongoing dialogue with the client about all of the different aspects of this behavior in relation to the client's life. The particular focus of the discussion might vary according to the style of therapy as well as to the needs of the particular client at a particular time for a particular alter. Topics can include focusing on:

- What motivates the self-harm?
- What are the costs and benefits of using those particular coping strategies?
- How did the client come to learn to use these strategies?
- How might the use or nonuse of these strategies change the client's view of herself?
- What is the client's relationship with these self-harming strategies?
- How do the strategies seduce or trick the client into using them?
- What does the client do to resist using the strategies?

SUMMARY AND CONCLUSIONS

The following are general guidelines that usually work with MPD/DID clients.

- *Therapy should do nothing to undermine a client's functioning.* Well-functioning clients should not be invited to deal with issues in the past if that is going to overwhelm them and precipitate a crisis that may lead to the loss of a job or to a hospitalization. It is generally far more productive to work on current problem-solving skills than to deal with issues of the past. With clients who are not functioning well, the primary job of treatment is to get them to function better rather than focus on their trauma. It may include specific strategies to deal with dissociative problems that impede functioning.

> Joan was diabetic. She was having trouble giving herself a blood test because it reminded one of her alters about some ritual abuse. We worked to teach her some grounding skills, we worked with one alter and clarified the distinction between the present and the past. Virtually no effort was made at the time to process the trauma of the past. She was able to give herself blood tests, which helped to stabilize her medical problem.

- *Communicate with all the different parts.* If a person has different aspects of self with different names, collaborate with their worldviews.
- *Treat each part with respect.* On a clinical level, the therapist must respect the needs of the part in its attempt to cope with the trauma and the world. On a personal level, be fully present. For instance, one client had a part that understood things backwards. So if I told her to relax, she would get more tense. I did not know this at first. A different part told me about this problem. If I was asking her questions, I would have to reinterpret what she was saying as the opposite of what she said. So from then on, I would initially communicate with this client in reverse. I would use an interspersal approach (Erickson, 1980) and say for example, "Do not *relax*. Do not *take a deep breath. . . .* " She would respond very well. After a while I could speak normally.

- *Treat each part as having highly localized knowledge that is useful.* Each part can have important information that can be useful in treating other alters in the system.
- *Parts that have been marginalized by the client need to be invited into the therapy.* The therapist needs to help demarginalize these parts over time. The angrier and nastier the part, the more it will have been marginalized, and the more important it is to make friends with it.
- *Help the client work toward collaboration among the parts.* Integration is only one form of collaboration. Remember the parts are in a system. Even the most dysfunctional behavior has collaboration in it. The system has a great deal of wisdom. However, the reason the client comes to treatment is that the wisdom is out of date and out of step with current needs. The system needs to update its operational procedures to collaborate differently.
- *Slower and safer is (almost) always better.* Working too fast or too intensely is one of the most likely ways to help a client decompensate. Herman (1992) has described the three phases of treatment for recovery of trauma: building safety, remembering and grieving, rebuilding connections with others. I see these as three paramount issues that occur throughout treatment. Instead of describing them as necessarily occurring in a linear fashion, I see them as recursive and reappearing throughout treatment. Establishing safety and concomitant motivation for change should usually be first in the sequence of therapy, but it also reappears as the primary issue at different points.
- *Get guidance from the client's system.* For example, cocreate "team meetings" in the client's head. Put questions to the "team." Make sure there is consensus. Check for problems. Do this as you would with a family or an organization.
- *Always look for positive motivation.* For example, even the most seemingly malevolent parts can be viewed as originally being volunteers to become like one of the abusers so as to learn how the abuser thinks and thus better predict that person's behavior, protect the rest of the system from having to engage in sadistic acts, and to try to get love from the abuser.
- *Help the client recognize that acting out is driven from the influence of outside sources.* The narrative technique of *externalization* (White & Epston, 1990) can be very useful for helping clients see those sources as separate from themselves.
- *In cases of parts acting out, support the client to find the positive intention of the acting-out behavior.* It may be helpful to ask, "Who is not listening to what the upset parts have to say?" Look for exceptions to acting-out behavior. Interview other parts about the good ideas of the acting-out part.
- *Learn hypnosis.* It helps to speak the language. For example, sometimes alters were created within contexts that were so horrible and poor in resources, and usually with so little preparation (at least in the client's narrative), that the

part is completely restrained from cooperating with treatment. In these situations, hypnosis can be used to go back in time and alter the conditions under which the parts were created so that there is more flexibility in their character. After all, clients with MPD/DID created their systems with auto-hypnosis. In the original context, and again in treatment, hypnosis is used as a means to write or rewrite the story. The therapeutic goal is not to change what happened to the client (which would be a serious mistake). The goal is to help the client change how he or she formed the alter in response to what happened. This is done in collaboration with all the relevant alters—the ones who did the creating in the first place. The client's alters are interviewed about what would need to be different so that the problematic alter would have more flexibility, and so on. Although therapists can offer some advice, such as preparing the part for the trauma that is about to happen (D. Calof, personal communication, March 1994), they must be careful not to force their own ideas regarding what would be best. When hypnosis is used properly, the results can be instantaneous, dramatic, and permanent for the better.

• *Focus at least as much attention on building the positive as on processing the negative.* One application of this idea when working with angry or "dark" parts is to spend some time asking them if they have had any good experiences, such as ever seeing a flower or a sunset. (The answer is usually negative.) Arrange for them to have some positive experiences, instead of exclusively dealing with the trauma that has made them so angry. (For other ideas, see Dolan, 1998; Schwarz, in press.)

• *Be prepared to tolerate ambiguity and conflict and intense emotion* (Calof & Schwarz, 1994). Therapists can anticipate and will need to tolerate the stress of hearing clients' horrific experiences.

• *Where "either-or" thinking was, "both-and" thinking shall be.* This applies to both therapist and client alike.

• *When there is an impasse, break the problem into smaller parts.* The pasts of MPD/DID clients are usually so dysfunctional that one cannot assume that they have learned specific skills, or have specific reference points, that may seem very ordinary to the dominant culture. For example, when clients fail to care for themselves adequately, therapists need to discern whether it is an issue of motivation or whether it is an issue of the task being too large. It is often very hard for MPD/DID clients to take care of themselves because they have had little experience in focusing their attention on knowing what they themselves like. They have childhoods replete with injunctions against their right to know and choose what they like. Even more basic than this, many clients literally do not attend to bodily sensations, nor do they discriminate between the different sensations they feel. It may be necessary to help clients learn in small steps how to discover which foods they like. For example, the client can buy eight different fruits and describe their taste and texture and the reactions they evoke, including which fruits taste most and least pleasing. Unfortunately, noncooperation approaches usually focus on issues of resistance and motivation, when from the client's point of view the problem is one of lack of skill or knowledge. The possibility that the client does not know certain key steps in a process that is taken for granted is often never considered. The result is that clients often feel increased shame and humiliation as well as increased anger. Not surprisingly, their resistance grows.

○

The hallmark of trauma-based and dissociative thinking is a rigid adherence to "either-or" dichotomies. This chapter has emphasized the importance of working collaboratively to dissolve dichotomies into "both-and" descriptions. In many ways it is a privilege to work with people who have had to overcome such abuse and violence that the only way that they could effectively resist the impact of the atrocities (Wade, 1996) was by splitting themselves into parts. It can also be a very difficult task that can stimulate many personal reactions from the therapist. It is the job of the therapist to help the client learn a more collaborative and integrative narrative between the parts so that the individual can be fully present in a loving and creative manner. In parallel fashion, I have attempted to weave a collaborative and integrative description of several schools of thought that can support a clinician to be fully present in a loving and creative manner.

References

American Psychiatric Association. (1994). *Diagnostic and statistical manual of mental disorders* (4th ed.) Washington, DC: Author.

Bernstein, E. M., & Putnam F. W. (1986). Development reliability and validity of a dissociation scale. *Journal of Nervous and Mental Disease, 174,* 727–735.

Blanchard, K., & Johnson, S. (1982). *The one minute manager.* New York: Morrow.

Bloom, S. (1997). *Creating sanctuary: Toward the evolution of a sane society.* London: Routledge.

Briere, J. N. (1992). *Child abuse trauma: Theory and treatment of the lasting effects.* Newbury Park, CA: Sage.

Calof, D. F. (1995). Chronic self-injury in adult survivors of abuse: Sources, motivations and functions of self injury (Part 1). *Treating Abuse Today, 5*(3), 11–17.

Calof, D. L., & Schwarz, R. A (1994, March 10). *Indirect suggestion, unwitting therapist influence and other iatrogenic issues in trauma work.* Paper presented at Advances in Treating Survivors of Sexual Abuse: Empowering the Healing Process II. San Diego. (Audiotape Available from Info-medix 1–800–367–9286.)

deMause, L. (1991). The universality of incest. *Journal of Psychohistory, 19*(2), 1–21.

de Shazer, S. (1985). *Keys to solution in brief therapy.* New York: Norton.

de Shazer, S. (1988). *Clues: Investigating solutions in brief therapy.* New York: Norton.

Dolan, Y. M. (1991). *Resolving sexual abuse: Solution-focused therapy and Ericksonian hypnosis for adult survivors.* New York: Norton.

Dolan, Y. M. (1998). *One small step: Moving beyond survivorship to a life of joy.* San Francisco: Papier-Mache.

Epston, D., & White, M. (1992). *Experience, contradiction, narrative, and imagination: Selected papers of David Epston and Michael White.* Adelaide, South Australia: Dulwich Centre Publications.

Erickson, M. H. (1980). *The collected papers of Milton H. Erickson on hypnosis* (E. L. Rossi, Ed.) New York: Irvington.

Furman, B., & Ahola, T. (1992). *Solution talk: Hosting therapeutic conversations.* New York: Norton.

Gergen, K. J. (1991). *The saturated self: Dilemmas of identity in contemporary life.* New York: Basic Books.

Glass, J. M. (1993). *Shattered selves: Multiple personality in a postmodern world.* Ithaca, NY: Cornell University Press.

Grove, D. R. (1993). Ericksonian therapy with multiple personality clients. *Journal of Family Psychotherapy, 4*(2), 13–18.

Grove, D. R., & Haley, J. (1993). *Conversations on therapy: Popular problems and uncommon solutions.* New York: Norton.

Herman, J. L. (1992). *Trauma and recovery: The aftermath of violence—from domestic abuse to political terror.* New York: Basic Books.

Horowitz, M. J. (1986). *Stress response syndromes* (2nd ed.). New York: Aronson.

Hoyt, M. F. (1996a). Welcome to PossibilityLand: A conversation with Bill O'Hanlon. In M. F. Hoyt (Ed.), *Constructive therapies* (Vol. 2, pp. 87–123). New York: Guilford Press.

Hoyt, M. F. (1996b). Postmodernism, the relational self, constructive therapies, and beyond: A conversation with Kenneth Gergen. In M. F. Hoyt (Ed.), *Constructive therapies* (Vol. 2, pp. 347–368). New York: Guilford Press.

Kluft, R. P. (1991). Clinical presentation of multiple personality disorder. *Psychiatric Clinics of North America—Multiple Personality Disorder, 14*(3), 605–630.

Lankton, S. R. (1985). A state of consciousness model of Ericksonian hypnosis. In *Ericksonian monographs: Vol. 1. Elements and dimensions of an Ericksonian approach,* pp. 26–41.

Lankton, S. R., & Lankton, C. (1983). *The answer within: A clinical framework of Ericksonian hypnotherapy.* New York: Brunner/Mazel.

Meichenbaum, D. (1994). *A clinical handbook/practical therapist manual for treating PTSD.* Waterloo, Ontario, Canada: Institute Press, University of Waterloo.

Peterson, C., Prout, M., & Schwarz, R. (1991). *Post-traumatic stress disorder: A clinician's guidebook.* New York: Plenum Press.

Putnam, F. W. (1989). *Diagnosis and treatment of multiple personality disorder.* New York: Guilford Press.

Ross, C. A. (1989). *Multiple personality disorder: Diagnosis, clinical features and treatment.* New York: Wiley.

Ross, C. A. (1992). Keynote address. Presented at the Third Eastern Regional Conference on Abuse and Multiple Personality, Alexandria, VA.

Salter, A. C. (1995). *Transforming trauma.* Newbury Park, CA: Sage.

Schreiber, F. R. (1973). *Sybil.* New York: Warner.

Schwarz, R. A. (in press). *Tools for transforming trauma.* New York: Brunner/Mazel.

Schwarz, R., & Gilligan, S. (1995). Book review *[The devil is in the details: Fact and fiction in the recovered memory debate].* Family Therapy Networker, 19(2), 21–23.

Schwarz, R. A., & Prout, M. F. (1991). Integrative approaches in the treatment of post-traumatic stress disorder. *Psychotherapy, 28,* 364–372.

Smith, M. (1989). *Michelle remembers.* New York: Pocket Books.

Spiegel, D., & McHugh, P. (1995). The pros and cons of dissociative identity (multiple personality) disorder. *Journal of Practical Psychiatry and Behavioral Health, 1*(13), 158–166.

Terr, L. (1994). *Unchained memories: True stories of traumatic memories lost and found.* New York: Basic Books.

Thigpen, C. H., & Cleckley, H. M. (1957). *The three faces of Eve.* London: Secker & Worberg.

van der Kolk, B. A. (1988). *Psychological trauma.* Washington: APA Press.

Wade, A. (1996, June 30). *Small acts of living: Resistance to violence and other forms of oppression.* Paper presented at Therapeutic Conversations 3 conference, Denver, CO, 1996. (Audiotape available from Info-medix 1–800–367–9286.)

White, M., & Epston, D. (1990). *Narrative means to therapeutic ends.* New York: Norton.

THE AUTHORS

MICHAEL F. HOYT, Ph.D. (Yale '76) is senior staff psychologist and former director of adult psychiatric services at the Kaiser Permanente Medical Center in Hayward, California. He is also a clinical faculty member at the University of California School of Medicine, San Francisco. He is the author of *Brief Therapy and Managed Care: Readings for Contemporary Practice* (1995), editor of *Constructive Therapies* (1994) and *Constructive Therapies, Volume 2* (1996), and coeditor of *The First Session in Brief Therapy* (1992, with Simon Budman and Steven Friedman). Hoyt is an internationally respected lecturer and workshop leader, known for his highly engaging and informative presentations. He has taught in Austria, Canada, England, Hungary, Japan, and Mexico. His audiences in the United States have included the Cape Cod Summer Symposia, the Institute for Behavioral Healthcare, Ericksonian Congresses on Hypnosis and Psychotherapy, Therapeutic Conversations conferences, and numerous universities, professional associations, managed care organizations, and community mental health centers. Hoyt has been honored as a Continuing Education Distinguished Speaker by the American Psychological Association and as a Distinguished Presenter by the International Association of Marriage and Family Counselors. With his wife and son, he resides in Mill Valley, California.

BARBARA A. ALLEN, A.C.S.W., M.P.H., Ph.D., is a psychotherapist, human ecologist, and mental-health planner. A long-time trainee of Fritz Perls and Virginia Satir, she was, with her husband (Jim Allen) and Erv and Miriam Polster, a founding and training member of the Gestalt Therapy Institute of Dallas. Over the years, she has established a suicide prevention center, three community mental health centers, and a freestanding crisis stabilization center. Formerly a clinical associate professor at the Tulsa Medical College and a trustee of the Fielding Institute, she has a consulting and supervising practice in Tulsa and Oklahoma City.

JAMES R. ALLEN, M.D., Dip. Psy., FRCP(c), M.P.H., is currently professor of psychiatry and behavioral sciences and professor of child-adolescent psychiatry at the University of Oklahoma Health Sciences Center, Oklahoma City, where he has a consulting and supervisory practice and is director of the Child Psychiatric Center and the Child-Adolescent Fellowship Program. He is a teaching and supervising member of the International Transactional Analysis Association, and a Gestalt and family therapist. He established the Department of Psychiatry at the Tulsa Medical College, where he was the first chair, and has been medical director of a community mental health center and a children's medical center.

HARLENE ANDERSON, Ph.D., is a founding member of the Houston Galveston Institute and the Taos Institute. She has authored and coauthored numerous professional papers and is the author of *Conversation, Language and Possibilities: A Postmodern Approach to Therapy*. She chairs the Commission for Accreditation for Marriage and Family Therapy Education, and is on the editorial review boards for several journals.

INSOO KIM BERG, M.S.W., is the codeveloper of the solution-focused therapy model and the director of the Brief Family Therapy Center in Milwaukee, Wisconsin. Her books and papers have been translated into several languages. The most recent ones include *Interviewing for Solutions* (1997, with Peter De Jong) and *Solutions Step-by-Step* (1997, with Norman Reuss). She serves on the editorial board of several journals, including the *Journal of Marital and Family Therapy*, and lectures extensively around the world.

JON CARLSON, Psy.D., Ed.D., is distinguished professor at Governors State University, University Park, Illinois, and director and psychologist at the Wellness Clinic in Lake Geneva, Wisconsin. He has authored twenty-five books and over a hundred journal articles. The books include *Family Therapy: Ensuring Treatment Efficacy, The Disordered Couple, The Intimate Couple*, and *Psychopathology and Psychotherapy*. Carlson has served as the editor of *Individual Psychology: The Journal of Adlerian Theory, Research, and Practice* for eighteen years, as well as currently serving as the founding editor of *The Family Journal*. He is a fellow of the American Psychological Association, diplomate of the American Board of Family Psychology, and has received distinguished service awards from the American Counseling Association, the American Psychological Association, North American Society of Adlerian Psychology, International Association of Marriage and Family Counselors, and the American Board of Professional Psychology. He and his wife of thirty years, Laura, are the parents of five children and have one grandchild.

JEFF CHANG, M.A., is a chartered psychologist (Province of Alberta) and a clinical member and approved supervisor of the American Association for Marriage and Family Therapy. Chang gained his sixteen years of clinical experience in youth and family agencies and employee assistance programs, and is now in full-time private practice. He is on the editorial board of the *Journal of Collaborative Therapies.* He has published several chapters and articles on brief therapy, narrative therapy, and residential treatment; is a sessional instructor at both Loma Linda University (a Canadian off-campus program) and the University of Calgary; and teaches workshops throughout the United States and Canada.

S. MICHELE COHEN, M.A., L.C.P.C., is a licensed professional clinical counselor. She is currently the clinical coordinator of a children's residential treatment center in Illinois. She has been practicing for nine years in the area of child, adolescent, and family psychotherapy. She completed her two-year post-master's training in narrative therapy at the Evanston Family Therapy Center with Jill Freedman and Gene Combs. While she was in the course of completing this chapter, her father suddenly passed away, and she would like to dedicate her work in his memory.

SUSANNE T. COLEMAN is a Ph.D. candidate in the Department of Family Therapy at Nova Southeastern University, Fort Lauderdale, Florida. Her research interests include the therapeutic relationship and pragmatic ways to utilize the client's language and perceptions to promote successful outcomes. She aspires to an academic position.

GENE COMBS, M.D., is codirector of the Evanston Family Therapy Center and a faculty member of the Chicago Center for Family Health. With Jill Freedman, he has coauthored numerous articles and two books: *Symbol, Story, and Ceremony: Using Metaphor in Individual and Family Therapy* (1990) and *Narrative Therapy: The Social Construction of Preferred Realities* (1996). He has a private practice in Chicago and in Evanston, Illinois, and consults to the Family Practice program at Cook County Hospital, Chicago.

VICTOR CORSIGLIA, Ph.D., is a psychologist who practices for Kaiser Permanente in the San Francisco East Bay area, where he remains dedicated to postmodern and narrative ideas and practice—a challenging undertaking in a large health-maintenance organization. He and David Nylund have collaborated on two other articles, one regarding solution-"forced" therapy and the other on working narratively with children labeled A.D.H.D. Corsiglia lives in the South Bay area with his wife and two children.

PAT DELAURENTI is a full-time housewife and mother.

BILL J. DELAURENTI has been a technical engineer at Lucent Technologies for the past twenty-seven years. He started out as a frame tester. From there he went into software programming and computer administration. He is now doing software programming, computer administration, cable designing, and CAD work.

ROBERT E. DOAN, Ph.D., is a full professor at the University of Central Oklahoma (Edmond), where he has been a faculty member in the Department of Psychology for the last ten years. During this time, he has also been actively engaged in private practice using the narrative approach. He is also an adjunct professor at the University of Oklahoma and a clinical consultant for various mental-health agencies in the Oklahoma City metropolitan area. In partnership with Alan Parry, he is the author of *Story Re-Visions: Narrative Therapy in a Postmodern World* (1994).

BARRY L. DUNCAN, Psy.D., is an educator, trainer, and therapist with over fourteen thousand hours of clinical experience. He is an associate professor in the Department of Family Therapy at Nova Southeastern University in Fort Lauderdale, Florida. Duncan, an approved supervisor of the American Association of Marriage and Family Therapy, has appeared on *Oprah* and has been featured in the *Family Therapy Networker, Psychology Today, USA Today,* and *Glamour.* With his colleagues Scott Miller and Mark Hubble, he cofounded the Institute for the Study of Therapeutic Change, which has culminated in four books: *The Handbook of Solution-Focused Brief Therapy* (1996), *Escape from Babel* (1997), *Psychotherapy with Impossible Cases* (1997), and the forthcoming *The Heart and Soul of Change.*

ALBERT ELLIS, Ph.D., is president of the Albert Ellis Institute for Rational Emotive Behavior Therapy in New York. He has practiced psychotherapy, marriage and family therapy, and sex therapy since 1943. He founded rational emotive behavior therapy, the first of the modern cognitive behavior therapies, in 1955. He has given hundreds of talks and workshops throughout the world, published over 700 articles, more than 60 books, and over 150 audio cassettes on psychology and psychotherapy. He has received top professional and scientific awards from the American Psychological Association, the American Counseling Association, the Association for the Advancement of Behavior Therapy, the

American Psychopathological Association, the Society for the Scientific Study of Sexuality, and other leading professional societies.

JOSEPH B. ERON, Psy.D., is the founder and codirector of the Catskill Family Institute. A clinical psychologist with twenty years' experience, he has contributed several chapters on brief family therapy, coauthored *Narrative Solutions in Brief Therapy* (1996, with Thomas Lund) and numerous articles and chapters on CFI's unique narrative solutions approach, and has presented and trained internationally.

JILL FREEDMAN, M.S.W., is codirector of the Evanston Family Therapy Center and a faculty member of the Chicago Center for Family Health. With Gene Combs, she has coauthored numerous articles and two books: *Symbol, Story, and Ceremony: Using Metaphor in Individual and Family Therapy* (1990) and *Narrative Therapy: The Social Construction of Preferred Realities* (1996). She is associate editor of the *American Family Therapy Academy Newsletter,* play and movie review editor for the *Journal of Feminist Family Therapy,* and reviews editor for the *Journal of Marital and Family Therapy.* She teaches internationally, and has a private practice in Evanston, Illinois.

KENNETH J. GERGEN, Ph.D., is Mustin Professor of Psychology at Swarthmore College, Swarthmore, Pennsylvania. He is joint editor of the Sage series *Inquiry in Social Construction* and associate editor of *Theory and Psychology* and *The American Psychologist.* Gergen is cofounder of The Taos Institute, a nonprofit organization dedicated to the cross-fertilization of social constructionist theory and societal practice. His edited works include *Texts of Identity* (1989, with John Shotter) and *Therapy as Social Construction* (1992, with Sheila McNamee). He is also author of *The Saturated Self* (1991), *Toward Transformation in Social Knowledge* (1993), and *Realities and Relationships* (1994).

JOSEPH GOLDFIELD, CSW-R, received his M.S.W. degree from the University of California, Berkeley. He is currently based in New York City. In addition to his private practice and agency work as a clinical social worker, he has presented numerous workshops on brief therapy as well as on Ericksonian utilization.

ELLIOT M. GOLDNER, M.D., is an assistant professor in the Department of Psychiatry at the University of British Columbia, Vancouver, Canada. His work is devoted to better understanding and treatment of the eating disorders.

LYNN HOFFMAN, A.C.S.W., is an internationally known lecturer on family therapy and author of *Techniques of Family Therapy* (1969, with Jay Haley), *Foundations of Family Therapy* (1981), *Milan Systemic Family Therapy* (1987, with

Luigi Boscolo, Gianfranco Cecchin, and Peggy Penn), and *Exchanging Voices* (1993). Hoffman is an adjunct lecturer at the continuing education program at the Smith School of Social Work in Northampton, Massachusetts, and the family therapy program at St. Joseph's College in West Hartford, Connecticut. She was awarded the Life Achievement Award for Distinguished Contribution to the Field of Family Therapy by the American Association of Marital and Family Therapy in 1988, and in 1994 was given an award for Distinguished Contribution to the Field of Family Therapy by the Massachusetts chapter. In 1995, she was a "State of the Art" speaker at the Milton H. Erickson Foundation's Evolution of Psychotherapy conference in Las Vegas. She is an advisory editor of *Family Process* and the *Journal of Marital and Family Therapy.*

MARK A. HUBBLE, Ph.D., is a graduate of the Menninger postdoctoral fellowship in clinical psychology in Topeka, Kansas, and is a member of the editorial advisory board of the *Journal of Systemic Therapies.* He founded and directed the Brief Therapy Clinic of the Counseling and Testing Center at the University of Missouri–Kansas City, served as a contributing editor for the *Family Therapy Networker* (winner of the 1993 National Magazine Award in the Public Interest category), and as a member of the faculty of the Dayton Institute for Family Therapy in Centerville, Ohio. Currently, he is a member of the senior faculty for the Family Therapy Institute of Columbus, Ohio. He is also one of the founders of the Institute for the Study of Therapeutic Change, a think tank based in Chicago. With Scott Miller and Barry Duncan, he is coauthor of *Psychotherapy with Impossible Cases* (1997) and *Escape from Babel* (1997), an examination of the defining influence of common factors in therapy. He is also coeditor, with Miller and Duncan, of *The Handbook of Solution-Focused Brief Therapy* (1996). The writing team is now preparing their fourth book, an edited work titled *The Heart and Soul of Change.*

ALAN JENKINS, M. Psych., is a clinical psychologist with Nada Consultants in Stirling, South Australia. He has eighteen years' experience working in the area of violence and abuse within families. He has developed models for therapeutic intervention that assist men and boys to find motivation to address and accept responsibility for their abusive behavior, so they can cease abuse and develop respectful ways of relating. These approaches have been adopted by domestic violence and sexual abuse treatment and prevention services in many parts of Australia, the United States, Canada, the United Kingdom, and New Zealand, and are detailed in several publications including his 1990 book, *Invitations to Responsibility: The Therapeutic Engagement of Men Who Are Violent and Abusive.* He consults within both government-funded programs and independent practice, and regularly presents trainings and conducts workshops in Australia and internationally.

JAMES W. KREIDER, L.S.C.S.W., B.C.D., N.B.C.C.H., is director of Kreider Consulting and Training Solutions, Lawrence, Kansas. He is also on the faculty of the Graduate School of Social Welfare at the University of Kansas, Lawrence, where he is also affiliated with the Counseling and Psychological Services.

CAROL LANKTON, M.A., is coauthor (with her husband, Stephen Lankton) of *The Answer Within, Enchantment and Intervention in Family Therapy,* and *Tales of Enchantment,* plus numerous chapters in the areas of family therapy and clinical hypnosis. She is a licensed marriage and family therapist, an approved consultant of the American Society of Clinical Hypnosis, and a clinical member of the American Association of Marriage and Family Therapy. She also serves as an advisory editor on the editorial board of the *Ericksonian Monographs.*

STEPHEN LANKTON, M.S.W., is the author of *Practical Magic* and *The Blammo Surprise Book,* and coauthor (with his wife, Carol Lankton) of *The Answer Within, Enchantment and Intervention in Family Therapy, Tales of Enchantment,* plus numerous chapters in the areas of family therapy and clinical hypnosis. He is a licensed marriage and family therapist, a diplomate in clinical hypnosis certified by the American Hypnosis Board for Clinical Social Work, an approved consultant of the American Society of Clinical Hypnosis, an approved supervisor and fellow of the American Association of Marriage and Family Therapy, a diplomate in clinical social work, and a fellow of the American Academy of Pain Management. He was the founding editor (1983–1994) of the *Ericksonian Monographs,* and in 1994 received from the Milton H. Erickson Foundation a Lifetime Achievement Award for Outstanding Contributions to the Field of Psychotherapy.

DAVID LARIMER, C.A.D.C., L.C.P.C., has been practicing for the last twelve years. Currently, he manages the addictions department for a five-county behavioral health center in the Illinois Valley. He also has been in private practice the last four years in Naperville, Illinois.

SUSAN B. LEVIN, Ph.D., is a faculty member and the executive director of the Houston Galveston Institute, Houston, Texas. Her clinical and academic work reflects a postmodern, collaborative approach to research and therapy. Sue has presented and published on topics including qualitative research, the effects of war and danger, women who have been battered, and working with children.

THOMAS W. LUND, Psy.D., a school and child psychologist with twenty-three years' experience, is codirector of Catskill Family Institute. He has published *Narrative Solutions in Brief Therapy* (1996, with Joseph Eron) and several articles and chapters on their narrative solutions approach, and has presented at conferences and workshops internationally. In addition to training psychotherapists, he teaches the art of conducting helpful conversations to clergy, teachers, case-workers in children's services, and others.

STEPHEN P. MADIGAN, M.S.W., Ph.D., has had his work in the area of anorexia, bulimia, and narrative therapy highlighted in *Newsweek,* the *Family Therapy Networker,* numerous international newspapers, and live interviews with the Canadian Broadcasting Corporation and National Public Radio. Madigan is director of training at Yaletown Family Therapy in Vancouver, B.C., Canada, a consultant with the Vancouver Association for Survivors of Torture, and a found-ing member of the Anti-Anorexia League. He is an American Association for Marriage and Family Therapy–approved supervisor and a member of the Amer-ican Family Therapy Academy. He and his colleagues at Yaletown Family Ther-apy host the annual international conference on narrative practice. In May 1998 he is organizing and producing the international Therapeutic Conversations con-ference in Toronto. He has published numerous journal articles and book chap-ters in the area of family therapy theory and practice.

SCOTT D. MILLER, Ph.D., is a therapist and acclaimed international trainer known for his engaging presentation style. He has presented to the American Psychological Association, the International Congress on Ericksonian Ap-proaches to Hypnosis and Psychotherapy, the International Society for the Study of Multiple Personality and Dissociation, and the National Association of Social Workers, among many others. He is also a member of the editorial board of the *Journal of Systemic Therapies.* With his colleagues Barry Duncan and Mark Hub-ble, he cofounded the Institute for the Study of Therapeutic Change, which has culminated in four books: *Handbook of Solution-Focused Brief Therapy* (1996), *Escape from Babel* (1997), *Psychotherapy with Impossible Cases* (1997), and the forthcoming *The Heart and Soul of Change.*

DAVID NYLUND, L.C.S.W., is director of training at Kaiser Permanente Medical Center, Department of Mental Health, in Stockton, California. He is also a lec-turer at the Professional School of Psychology in Sacramento, California, and a consultant to Midtown Family Therapy in Sacramento. He has published sev-eral articles and chapters on narrative practice and is coeditor of *Narrative Ther-apies with Children and Adolescents* (1997, with Craig Smith). He enjoys golf, hiking, reading fiction, drinking microbrews, and playing with his son, Drake.

WILLIAM (BILL) O'HANLON, M.S., has authored or coauthored thirteen books: *Taproots, Solution-Oriented Hypnosis, An Uncommon Casebook, Shifting Con-texts, Rewriting Love Stories, In Search of Solutions, A Brief Guide to Brief Ther-apy, A Field Guide to PossibilityLand, The Handout Book, Evolving Possibilities, Love Is a Verb (Stop Blaming, Start Loving), Seeds of Hope,* and *Frozen in Time.*

He has published twenty-seven articles and book chapters, and produced or coproduced six audiotapes, two computer programs, and several videotapes about therapy. His books have been translated into French, Spanish, Portuguese, Swedish, Finnish, German, Chinese, and Japanese. Since 1977, O'Hanlon has taught over six hundred therapy seminars around the world. He has been a top-rated presenter at several national conferences, including the Family Therapy Networker Symposium, the American Association for Marriage and Family Therapy, two major Ericksonian congresses, and the annual Cape Cod Summer Symposia. He was a developer of brief solution-oriented therapy and a contributor to Ericksonian therapy and collaborative-constructivist approaches. O'Hanlon is on the advisory board of the *Journal of Collaborative Therapies* and the International Association of Marriage and Family Counselors. He is a licensed mental health professional, certified professional counselor, and licensed marriage and family therapist. He lives in Santa Fe, New Mexico.

HAIM OMER, Ph.D., was born and grew up in Brazil. He emigrated to Israel at the age of eighteen. He studied at the Hebrew University of Jerusalem. He has five children. He is the author of *Critical Interventions in Psychotherapy* (1994) and *Constructing Therapeutic Narratives* (1997, with Nahi Alon). He teaches at Tel-Aviv University.

ROBERT A. SCHWARZ, Psy.D., is a licensed psychologist, an approved supervisor for the American Association of Marriage and Family Therapists, and adjunct clinical professor at Widener University. He is president of the Institute for Advanced Clinical Training. He was the organizer of the Therapeutic Conversations 2 and 3 conferences, as well as eight national conferences on treating survivors of trauma and abuse and four regional conferences on Ericksonian approaches to hypnosis and psychotherapy—providing training to over ten thousand therapists. Schwarz is coauthor of the book *Post-Traumatic Stress Disorder: A Clinician's Guide* (1991, with C. Peterson and M. Prout), and is currently working on a new book, *Tools for Transforming Trauma.* He has also published a variety of professional articles and two self-help audiotapes for survivors of trauma, and presents workshops nationally on Ericksonian and solution-oriented approaches to therapy and treating trauma. He maintains a private practice in Haverford, Pennsylvania, and is also a founding board member of Access Behavioral Care, Inc., a provider-owned and operated behavioral health network. Among his current interests is the application of improvisational comedy to improve creativity and performance in teams and organizations.

DINA SHULMAN, L.C.S.W., has a private practice in Evanston, Illinois. She has completed a two-year postgraduate program in narrative therapy taught by Jill Freedman and Gene Combs. She also contributed to the Foreword in *Narrative Therapy:*

The Social Construction of Preferred Realities by Freedman and Combs (1996). She conducts professional training on narrative therapy in the Chicago area.

CARLOS E. SLUZKI, M.D., is director of psychiatric services at Santa Barbara Cottage Hospital in Santa Barbara, California, and clinical professor of psychiatry at the University of California, Los Angeles. He has been professor of psychiatry at the University of Massachusetts Medical School (1984–1993) and at the University of California School of Medicine, San Francisco (1975–1983), director of the Mental Research Institute in Palo Alto, California (1980–1983), and editor-in-chief of the journal *Family Process* (1980–1988). A prolific writer, Sluzki has contributed over 170 books, chapters, and articles to the field, and is a highly reputed presenter at national and international professional meetings.

LEN SPERRY, M.D., Ph.D., is professor in the departments of Psychiatry and Preventive Medicine at the Medical College of Wisconsin, Milwaukee. He is board certified in psychiatry, preventive medicine, and clinical psychology (A.B.P.P.); is on ten editorial boards; and has published twenty-eight books and over two hundred papers and book chapters. He is listed in *Best Doctors in America, 1996–1997*, and is a fellow of both the American Psychiatric Association and the American Psychological Association.

KARL TOMM, M.D., is professor of psychiatry and director of the Family Therapy Program at the University of Calgary Faculty of Medicine, Alberta, Canada. He has a strong interest in postmodern theoretical developments, and has published on aspects of interventive interviewing, the ethics of therapeutic discourses and practices, and the systemic-social construction of the self.

PAUL WATZLAWICK, Ph.D. (University of Venice, '49) is senior research fellow at the Mental Research Institute in Palo Alto, California, and clinical professor emeritus in the Department of Psychiatry and Behavioral Sciences at Stanford University. He has previously held positions at the C.G. Jung Institute (in Zurich), the University of El Salvador, Temple University (Philadelphia), and the Centro Universitario Ticinese (Lugano, Switzerland). Watzlawick has received the Distinguished Achievement Award from the American Family Therapy Association, the Distinguished Professional Contribution to Family Therapy Award from the American Association for Marriage and Family Therapy, and the Lifetime Achievement Award from the Milton H. Erickson Foundation. He has also received honorary doctorates from the University of Liège (Belgium), the University of Bordeaux (France), and the University of Buenos Aires (Argentina). He is the author or editor (sometimes in collaboration) of eighteen books (which appear in more than seventy foreign-language editions), including *Pragmatics of Human Communication, Change: Principles of Problem Formation and Problem Resolution, How Real Is Real?, The Interactional View, The Language of Change, The Situation Is Hopeless but Not Serious, The Invented Reality,* and *Ultra-Solutions: How to Fail Most Successfully.*

NAME INDEX

461

SUBJECT INDEX

ACQ 8891